WORLD POLITICS IN THE TWENTIETH CENTURY

Peter R. Beckman

Hobart and William Smith Colleges

PRENTICE-HALL, INC.   Englewood Cliffs, New Jersey 07632

Library of Congress Cataloging in Publication Data

BECKMAN, PETER R.
    World politics in the twentieth century.

    Includes index.
    1. World politics—20th century. I. Title.
II. Title: World politics in the 20th century.
D443.B38 1984   327'.09'04   83-13654
ISBN 0-13-968768-8

Editorial/production supervision: Marion Osterberg
Cover design: Wanda Lubelska
Manufacturing buyer: Ron Chapman

Printed in the United States of America

10 9 8 7 6 5 4 3 2 1

ISBN 0-13-968768-8

Prentice-Hall International, Inc., *London*
Prentice-Hall of Australia Pty. Limited, *Sydney*
Editora Prentice-Hall do Brasil, Ltda., *Rio de Janeiro*
Prentice-Hall Canada Inc., *Toronto*
Prentice-Hall of India Private Limited, *New Delhi*
Prentice-Hall of Japan, Inc., *Tokyo*
Prentice-Hall of Southeast Asia Pte. Ltd., *Singapore*
Whitehall Books Limited, *Wellington, New Zealand*

For Fred, Eddie, Toby, Abigail, and Derek

Contents

Preface ix

CHAPTER ONE
Introduction 1

Understanding World Politics   1
Historical and Scientific Approaches to the Study of World Politics   3
World Politics and Conflict   5
Four Scientific Approaches to World Politics   10

Conclusion   29

CHAPTER TWO
1900–1909
The first and last decade of progress? 33

Part I: Diplomatic History   33
Prologue to the Twentieth Century   34
World Politics: 1900–1909   37

Part II: Scientific Approaches to World Politics   53
Systems Approach   53
Policy-Making Approach: The Russo-Japanese War of 1904–1905   60

CHAPTER THREE
1910–1919
Europe wanders into hell   66

Part I: Diplomatic and Military History   66
Pre-War Diplomacy   66
The Great War   73

Part II: Scientific Approaches to World Politics   88
Systems Approach   88
Policy-Maker Approach: The Kaiser and the 1914 Crisis   92
Interaction Approach: Game Theory and Ending the War   98

CHAPTER FOUR
1920–1929
A hopeful peace?   104

Part I: Diplomatic History   104
The Security Issue   104
The German Problem   108
The New Imperialists   118
A Small Cloud on the Horizon   120

Part II: Scientific Approaches to World Politics   121
Domestic and Environmental Factor Approach:
    The Impact of Marxism on Russian Foreign Policy   121
International Systems Approach   130

CHAPTER FIVE
1930–1939
Night and fog   137

Part I: Diplomatic History   137
Economic Collapse   137
Collective Security Falters   140
Hitler Completes the Destruction of the Versailles Treaty   142

Part II: Scientific Approaches to World Politics   155
Interaction Approach: The Bargaining Model and Hitler's Foreign Policy   155
Policy-Maker Approach: The Lessons Adolf Hitler Taught   163
Systems Approach: Collective Security, Appeasement, and War   166

CHAPTER SIX
1940–1949
Hell again and a peace called war   173

Part I: Diplomatic and Military History   173
The Second Great War   173
The Slide into the Cold War   186

Part II: Scientific Approaches to World Politics   192
Domestic and Environmental Factor Approach:
    Weapons and the Japanese Decision for War in 1941   192
Policy-Making Approach: The State Department and the Response
    to Vietnamese Nationalism in the 1940s   196
Interaction Approach: A Pattern Analysis of the Soviet-American Cold War   201
Systems Approach: A New World   207

CHAPTER SEVEN
1950–1959
An uncertain coexistence at midcentury   210

Part I: Diplomatic History   210
Korea and the American Response   210
The Soviets Look for Peaceful Coexistence   218
Decolonization and the Third World   228
The Impending Crisis   233

Part II: Scientific Approaches to World Politics   235
Systems Approach: Cold War in an American-Dominated World?   235
Interaction Approach: Pattern Analysis Revisited—
    The Cold War Gets Older, But Does It Get Colder?   241
Domestic and Environmental Factor Approach:
    Public Opinion and the Korean Intervention   244

CHAPTER EIGHT
1960–1969
Détente for some, war for others   251

Part I: Diplomatic History   251
The Cold War Bears Fruit   251
Vietnam   261
The World Beyond Soviet-American Relations   266

Part II: Scientific Approaches to World Politics   270

Multiple Approaches:
   The Third World, Capitalist States, and Political Economy   270
   Systems Approach: The International System and Regional Subsystems   282

CHAPTER NINE
1970–1979
Détente and doubts   **290**

Part I: Diplomatic History   290

Five Fundamental Changes   290
Détente Under Pressure   303
The Third World Achieves Some Autonomy   307

Part II: Scientific Approaches to World Politics   314

Prologue: Putting Things Together   314
Policy Makers and Policy Making: The American Invasion of Cambodia, 1970   317
Systems Approach: A Bipolar World   325

CHAPTER TEN
1980–2000
The future(s)   **330**

Prediction As a Goal   330

Domestic and Environmental Factor Approach   332
Policy-Makers and Policy-Making Approach   332
Interaction Approach   333
Systems Approach   334

Types of Prediction   335

Analytical Methods   336
Extrapolation Methods   336
Intuitive Methods   338
Goal-Inspired Methods   341

Predicted Futures for the Remainder of the Century:
The Fruits of the Scientific Approaches   343

System Predictions   343
Interaction Predictions   345
Policy-Makers and Policy-Making Predictions   347
Domestic and Environmental Factor Predictions   351

World Politics in the Future   355

What Is To Be Done?   356

Index   **360**

Preface _____

World politics is captivating. It has drama, terror, hope, and, from time to time, a touch of comedy. It reflects the best and the worst in the human condition. And it is ever present.

Consider these reports from a less-developed nation. Armed militants roamed the countryside, attacking foreigners and their own countrymen who had adopted foreign ways. Rejecting modernity, the militants demanded adherence to traditional religious beliefs and strict moral behavior. The government of this nation found itself in an awkward position. The militants helped awaken patriotism among the masses, which increased support for the regime and for its struggle to rid the nation of foreign imperialism. Yet they also were a potential revolutionary force. The government reacted by suppressing those militants who were too independent or hostile to the regime, while aiding those who accepted the regime's legitimacy or were politically neutral.

Given the collusion between government and militants, it was only a matter of time before foreign embassies, including the American embassy, came under siege by the militants. The government never quite decided how to deal with the besieged embassy personnel. It offered to negotiate for their release, but also attempted to have them killed. Some government officials openly took up the militants' slogan of "Destroy the foreigner." Others sought to curb the militants' action.

Such reports should have a familiar ring to them, even if the outcome does not: a multinational military force marched on the capital, raised the siege, pillaged the city, and forced the less-developed nation to pay reparations. The time was the turn of the century, the nation was China, and the uprising became known in the West as the Boxer Rebellion. Political turmoil, attacks on embassies, and "rescue missions" are not unique to our times. Nor are arms races and oil embargoes, power politics and dreams of peace. What may be unique to our times, however, is a belief that what happens just happens, and only to this nation or that generation.

This book is, I hope, an antidote to feelings of being isolated from the experience of others and of being powerless in the face of our coming future. It argues that knowing the history of world politics in this century offers us much—an opportunity to see how we are the products of the past (and therefore capable of molding our future), to see how others have confronted similar problems *and* radically different ones (and thereby prevent a numbing sense of bewilderment), and to see, on the other hand, that we cannot always do as we wish.

History, this book also argues, is not enough. The relatively recent application of social science to the study of world politics provides different perspectives on the world of the past, present, and future. Social science claims to provide a set of intellectual tools so that we may understand with greater insight, compassion, and profit how and why humans and their states behaved as they did. In the chapters that follow, I have combined a narrative of world politics from the Boxer Rebellion in 1900 to the present with various frameworks for analysis that current social science has given the study of world politics. The last chapter then looks ahead to the twenty-first century.

This particular approach to the study of world politics has two main sources: my teachers, who demonstrated that history and social science were linked together, and students in my classes who wanted to know more about "what happened" and "why." In the pursuit of the what and the why, I have been fortunate to have colleagues in the political science department at Hobart and William Smith Colleges who took the time to wrestle with my ideas. Gary Thompson, of the Warren Hunting Smith Library, helped with the index, and P. W. Crumlish, the librarian, debated a whole host of issues with me. I also appreciate the constructive comments of the following reviewers: Robert Art, Brandeis University; John P. Vloyantes, Colorado State University; Neil Richardson, University of Wisconsin; Curtis H. Martin, Merrimack College; Norman A. Graebner, University of Virginia; James N. Murray, University of Iowa; Stephen A. Snyder, University of Wisconsin; and Van Coufoudakis, Indiana University. Hobart and William Smith Colleges were kind enough to furnish financial support, and Debbi McLaughlin and Cindy Bulman transformed scrawl into typed copy. Stan Wakefield, Lisa Femmel, and Marion Osterberg of Prentice-Hall encouraged and prodded. For such support I am grateful. The pleasure of the project has been mine; the errors which remain, alas, are mine as well.

CHAPTER ONE

Introduction_____

UNDERSTANDING WORLD POLITICS

World politics often seems to be the drama of the unexpected. In 1965, Lin Piao, Defense Minister of the People's Republic of China, declared that "it has become an urgent necessity for the people in many countries to master and use people's war as a weapon against US imperialism and its lackeys. In every conceivable way US imperialism and its lackeys are trying to extinguish the revolutionary flames of people's war."[1] In 1972, with Lin dead, the People's Republic of China officially received the head of the imperialist camp, Richard Nixon—a man who had started *his* career by denouncing the evils of communism. And a year earlier, the People's Republic of China itself had entered the business of helping to extinguish the flames of people's war. It granted aid to the government of Sri Lanka (Ceylon) to help it crush a Marxist insurrection, and, along with the United States, it supported the right-wing Pakistani government's attempts to crush a people's war in Bangladesh.

The history of the twentieth century is replete with such examples of major changes in the behavior of states. Why have such changes occurred? Is there no constancy in the actions of states? How is the student of world politics ever to "get a handle" on such events and deal with such questions?

Alas, there are no single best handles or answers. The state of our knowledge about world politics is such that we can only offer a *variety of viewpoints* and encourage any student to adopt the ones that seem most satisfying, given his or her particular interests.[2] The variety of viewpoints available is legion, and any

---

[1]Lin Piao, "Long Live the Victory of People's War!" in *Readings in World Politics*, rev. ed., ed. Robert Goldwin and Tony Pearce (New York: Oxford University Press, 1970), p. 309.

[2]For an engaging discussion of the great debate on how to study world politics, see Klaus Knorr and James Rosenau, eds., *Contending Approaches to International Politics* (Princeton: Princeton University Press, 1969).

text on world politics must make some choice about what is included and what is excluded.[3] This text has selected five approaches as the most promising for an introduction to world politics. Those five can be divided into two groups, the "historical" approach and the "scientific" approaches.

You might ask, Why should anyone have to read about five different viewpoints? Would not *one* do just as well? To select just one would imply that it is the most useful of all. As you will see, each of the viewpoints discussed in this book deals with somewhat different aspects of world politics; none is complete in and of itself. A viewpoint's usefulness will therefore depend upon the type of questions we wish to ask about world politics. One model may be helpful in trying to answer the question, Why did the Soviet Union invade Afghanistan in 1979? That same model may be of less help in trying to answer the question, Under what conditions does rigidity in defensive alliances cause war?

Each approach will help us see a question or issue about world politics in a particular light. We need to be aware of the types of assumptions and biases each (and every) viewpoint has, because our view of world politics will be colored by those assumptions and biases. Your ability to uncover assumptions and biases in a viewpoint depends upon your familiarity with other viewpoints and their strengths and weaknesses. Your ability to refine and expand upon the existing viewpoints, including your own, also depends upon such familiarity.

As I have been pressing all these points on you, you may have found yourself muttering, But who needs viewpoints, anyway? The answer seems to be this: We all use viewpoints or models of the world when we think. Many models you have been taught or you have developed through experience. To give you some examples, consider the following:

> You have twenty pieces of pizza for a party of five people. How will you allocate the pizza? If you said, "Give each person four pieces," reflect on your allocation model. Was it a mechanical one that stressed equality? That is, did you divide the number of pieces by the number in the group? There are other allocation models. You might, for instance, allocate the pieces on the basis of the status or power of each of the people at the party. Or you might have used a self-allocating model—the hungriest (or quickest) will get the most. Many of our decisions in daily life are products of models and we are not conscious of it.

> Someone asks why you support a particular candidate in the Presidential primary or the November election. You quickly rattle off your reasons. If you examine those reasons, you should be able to identify your preference model. Does it emphasize such purportedly desirable characteristics as "leadership ability" or "ability to deal with the Russians"? Alternatively, is it based on your own identification with a particular party (Republican or Democrat) or orientation (liberal or conservative)? Even in the political realm, we are "prisoners" of models or viewpoints but often not conscious of our prisoner status.

---

[3]Although the approaches developed here are quite broad, such specific emphases as international law and organizations, regionalism, and integration receive little attention. The reader may want to consult the following as a good beginning to fill in these gaps: Inis Claude, *Swords Into Plowshares: The Problems and Progress of International Organization*, 4th ed. (New York: Random House, 1971); Joseph S. Nye, Jr., ed., *International Regionalism* (Boston: Little, Brown, 1968); Karl Deutsch, *Tides Among Nations* (New York: Free Press, 1979).

If, then, we habitually use models or viewpoints, we should take care to examine them. How do they provide intellectual order to what we see? Are there better alternatives?

Now that you are reasonably convinced that we need to talk about viewpoints or models, and that each is likely to be incomplete, you are bound to ask, Why not combine the viewpoints into one big viewpoint? My initial answer would be something like this: It is easier to understand the parts first and then turn to some synthesis. Furthermore, there is no guarantee that any larger model can be constructed. And finally, I hope you will be challenged enough to try your own hand at fitting the parts together.

Historical and Scientific Approaches
to the Study of World Politics

The *historical approach* has been the traditional method of dealing with world politics. In the early 1960s, this approach came under strenuous attack from scholars who advocated a more "scientific" inquiry into world politics. The historical approach has survived the attack, but it has not prospered.[4] Diplomatic histories have suffered a similar fate. The durability of the historical approach owes much to the insights it offers the student of world politics as well as to the inadequacies of the more scientific approaches that were meant to replace it.

Unfortunately, what challenge failed to do, apathy might. An interest in history has not been characteristic of our times. Few people have a lively sense of history or much historical knowledge. The inclusion of the historical approach in this text is a response to these concerns. It attempts to provide an historical account of world politics since 1900, so that we might develop a common, detailed base of reference. The historical approach also offers a particular explanatory model that is useful for students of world politics.[5]

The historian of world politics arrives at an explanation for why specific events happened as they did by a process of applying reasoned judgment to the materials at hand, such as documents, memoirs, and interviews. The intellectual process of the historian involves the identification of aspects thought to be important (such as wars, the creation of alliances, and revolutionary upheavals), the gathering of relevant information, and the assembly of it "into an account which provides a reasoned description or rationale based on fact and surmise for what happened."[6] In doing so, the historian often makes several assumptions that set

---

[4]Raymond Aron and Stanley Hoffmann have tried to keep the historical approach alive within political science. Aron's *Peace and War* (New York: Praeger, 1968) and Hoffmann's *Gulliver's Troubles or the Setting of American Foreign Policy* (New York: McGraw-Hill, 1968) and *Primacy or World Order* (New York: McGraw-Hill, 1978) are illustrative. Other works include Robert Osgood, *Ideals and Self-Interest in America's Foreign Relations* (Chicago: University of Chicago Press, 1953); Frederick L. Schuman, *International Politics* (New York: McGraw-Hill, various editions); and F. S. Northedge and M. J. Grieve, *A Hundred Years of International Relations* (New York: Praeger, 1971).

[5]It should be understood that I am not a historian, and that one function of the historian—a critical use of original source material—is not the function of this book. The historical sections draw on secondary sources, which are reports by historians of their conclusions regarding events drawn from the evidence they have examined.

[6]Davis Bobrow, *International Relations: New Approaches* (New York: Free Press, 1972), p. 20.

the historical approach off from the scientific approaches.[7] The historian tends to assume that events and explanations of them are unique. World War I, for instance, is an event different from any other (though sharing some similarities with others), brought on by causes that were particular to that war. The war in Vietnam had other characteristics and its own genesis. The historian tends to assume that events occur in a particular context, a context that gives meaning to the events. The communications revolution, for instance, allowed President Ford to communicate almost instantaneously with an Air Force pilot about to attack a Cambodian ship. Only three and a half decades earlier, intelligence that Germany would attack the Soviet Union that morning gave Stalin no advantage, because warnings could not be passed quickly enough to the Red Army field commanders. To remove the event from its context, argues the historian, is to misunderstand the event. The historian also assumes that tracing change over time is critical for description and explanation. To understand how the German government overturned the punitive features of the Versailles Treaty, one must follow the shifts in German policy and in its context (such as changing British public opinion and international economics).

The "scientific" approaches to world politics have developed in part as a reaction to the historical approach. Where the historical emphasizes the unique, the "scientific" assumes there are *patterns* to be found in world politics. Those patterns can be identified and described as *general classes of events*. World War I, for instance, is a member of a class of events called interstate wars. NATO is a type of alliance, as are the Triple Alliance and the Anglo-Japanese alliance. The Chinese, Russian, Cuban, and Portuguese revolutions comprise a common class of events. If we assume that there may be patterns in events, we may also assume— as the scientific approach does—that there may also be *similar explanations* that apply to a number of seemingly diverse events. The pressure to launch a military attack in an escalatory situation may be quite similar for the German government of 1914 and for the Israeli government of 1967. Ultimately, therefore, the "scientific" approach seeks to make accurate *generalizations* that apply to more than a single historical case or event. To do so, the scientific approach is more willing to remove events from their specific contexts and from the chain of time-related events the historian creates.

The second feature of the "scientific" approach that sets it off from the historical is its method of making those accurate generalizations about world politics. Of course, the historical approach strives to make accurate statements (and historians who fail to do so pay a heavy price). The scientific approach, however, stresses a consciousness of how the scholar arrives at a generalization. Definitions, measurement, the testing of hypotheses, and a relentless attempt to build theories are symptomatic of the scientific approach. Broadly put, the practitioner

[7]Historians disagree about what history is or should be, how it should be done, and how it differs from the scientific approaches. For a sample, see Georg Iggers and Harold Parker, eds., *International Handbook of Historical Studies* (Westport, Conn.: Greenwood Press, 1979); Paul Lauren, ed., *Diplomacy: New Approaches in History, Theory, and Policy* (New York: Free Press, 1979); Hugh Trevor-Roper, "What is Historical Knowledge for Us Today?" *Survey*, 17 (Summer 1971), 2–12; Paul Schroeder, "Quantitative Studies in the Balance of Power: A Historian's Reaction," *Journal of Conflict Resolution*, 21 (March 1977), 3–22; John Higham, "Comment 6," in *Public Opinion and Historians*, ed. Melvin Small (Detroit: Wayne State University Press, 1970), pp. 175–79.

of the "scientific" approach tries to specify the intellectual process by which he or she reached the conclusions so that you or I might see the flaws, as well as every creative application of intelligence. In doing so, the scientific analyst tries to minimize (or at least make obvious) the biases and preconceptions he or she brings to the study of world politics. The practitioner of the historical approach, on the other hand, essentially shows us the results of the study. He or she usually does not specify *how* those particular conclusions were drawn, rather than some others. Indeed, the historian may not be able to say how he or she reached those conclusions. He or she may see the work of the historian as a craft, much akin to that of a painter. *How* da Vinci painted the Mona Lisa can, of course, be answered in terms of technical detail—this kind of paint, these colors, those kinds of brushstrokes. *How* da Vinci chose to translate the "facts" before him (a human figure) into a description of that figure cannot be determined. The enigma of the smile of the Mona Lisa is symptomatic of our inability to describe the "how." After all, the subject may have "in reality" been quite homely, or of a sour disposition, or in manner everything opposite to what the portrait suggests. The descriptions and explanations a historian produces have a similar quality. We can describe the technical detail, such as the documents and memoirs used by the historian. That much of the *how* is usually clear. What we often cannot know is how those technical details were combined, judged, and refined to produce the "history." History may be great art, say the adherents to the "scientific" approach, but how do we know that it accurately reflects reality? Out of such a concern, the "scientific" approach derives part of its dynamism. And it, too, would like to produce great art.

Having drawn this initial distinction, I must apologetically add that so far, the "scientific" approach has generated more questions and hypotheses about patterns than tested generalizations or theory. The four broad "scientific" approaches used here are essentially of this nature. They are conceptual frameworks or models; that is, they are a rather coherent way of asking questions and generating hypotheses about world politics. The "explanations" each provides are different from the others but—and here is the rub—not rigorously tested. At best, then, these frameworks suggest what an explanation of world politics might look like. The four approaches can be categorized as (1) the domestic and environmental factor approach, (2) the policy-maker and policy-making approach, (3) the interaction approach, and (4) the systems approach.

World Politics and Conflict

Before we can discuss the four scientific approaches, we must begin with a number of definitions—and thus remain true to the assertion that these are "scientific" approaches. Indeed, even to speak of "world politics" implies that we can define and identify patterns of political behavior. Borrowing a phrase from Lenin, I shall define world politics as essentially a question of who does what to whom. World politics thus is a reflection of competing interests that are expressed through the organized efforts of political entities. The most prevalent political entity of the twentieth century has been the nation-state. But there have been other entities, such as international organizations (the League of Nations), regional organizations (the Warsaw Treaty Organization), and nonstate political entities (the Palestine Liberation Organization, the colonial empires). In addition, some non-governmental actors, such as the Nobel Peace Prize Committee and various multinational corporations like General Motors, have acted as if they were political entities.

If such nongovernmental entities as General Motors are said to act as if they were political entities, how can we distinguish the "political" in world politics from, say, economic or social behavior? For our purposes, *political* refers to the ability to make binding decisions that commit an entire entity to risk its very survival. If an entity has this capability, we will call it political and assume that it forms part of world politics. Under certain specified conditions, normally non-political entities may become political by this definition.

A word of caution here. The *political* I speak of here is not the same as the political of domestic politics. The political in the international realm differs from that of the domestic in two important respects. In the international, there is no institution or power or government with the ability to make binding decisions for all the states. In the domestic realm, the national government usually has that capability and exercises it. Most of us pay taxes, get insurance for our automobiles, and send our children to school. Even if we do not wish to, the government usually has the power to compel our agreement or acquiescence in its decisions.

The second, and related difference, is that in dealing with our fellow citizens, we have the ability to mobilize the organs and powers of government on behalf of our own particular interests. Such an ability is obviously not spread equally among the citizens of any state; there are always disenfranchised minorities and majorities. The point is, however, that some citizens can appeal to a higher agency to promote their interests or to thwart those of others. Such a higher agency does not exist in world politics. Therefore, if a state is to secure its interests or thwart those of other states, it essentially must rely on its own ability to persuade or coerce other states into behaving as it sees fit.

You may have noticed throughout this introduction that my discussion has implied that world politics is essentially a conflictual matter. The wars that have disfigured and transformed the twentieth century and the present balance of nuclear terror serve as reminders that terrifying levels of potential and actual violence underpin much of what states do. But is world politics synonymous with conflict? Does world politics not have strong elements of cooperation as well? There are three important observations to make at this point:

(1) K.J. Holsti has argued that *most* of the interactions that take place between states are cooperative, not conflictual.[8] Two studies of very different time periods indicate that conflictual actions may account for 25 to 30 percent of all state behaviors.[9] Thus it is important to recognize that, overall, cooperation is a dominant motif in world politics. We see it clearly in states establishing diplomatic relations and working to ensure harmony in those relations; in states hon-

---

[8]K.J., Holsti, *International Politics: A Framework for Analysis*, 2nd ed. (Englewood Cliffs, N.J.: Prentice-Hall, 1972), p. 493.

[9]For the 1870–90 period, see Alan Alexandroff, *The Logic of Diplomacy* (Beverly Hills, Cal.: Sage, 1981), p.65; for 1966, Charles McClelland and Gary Hoggard, "Conflict Patterns in the Interactions among Nations," in *International Politics and Foreign Policy*, rev. ed., ed. James Rosenau (New York: Free Press, 1969), p. 715

oring alliance commitments and granting what has come to be called foreign aid; in cooperating to make the use of poison gas illegal and to promote the mutual development of the Antarctic; and in reaching agreements to stop the expansion of navies or to terminate a conflict. Indeed, most of the business that emanates from the foreign ministries of states is probably designed to further harmonious relations, if for no other reason than to keep things running smoothly in the bureaucracies of these foreign ministries.

(2) In every set of conflictual actions, there is some element of cooperation. In the Cuban missile crisis of 1962—the most intense of the direct confrontations between the United States and the Soviet Union—the leaders of both states strove to avoid a nuclear holocaust and still "win" the contest. To avoid devastation, they had to reach an overall settlement based on compromise and had to take specific actions that would, as President Kennedy argued, show that the United States means what it says but would not force the other side into a corner where surrender or war were the only options.

We would also expect the converse to hold as well—that in every cooperative situation, there are elements of conflict. In the early decades of the twentieth century, the major powers cooperated in exploiting China. They did so because they feared the results of an attempt by any one state to take portions of China for itself. Moreover, each state sought opportunities to enhance its own privileges in China at the expense of the others, but to do so under the guise of cooperation. In more recent times we have seen the political conflicts that have emerged in the de facto alliance between the United States and Israel. While both have cooperated to secure the survival of the state of Israel, each has disagreed with the other over the best means to achieve peace in the Middle East.

In fact, the examination of conflict necessarily forces one to raise questions about cooperation as well. The two are inseparable in world politics. The real question is one of emphasis; this book emphasizes conflict. It does so for a number of reasons. Conflict has the potential to reduce the human condition; if we can do nothing more than prevent such a result, it may be well worth it. On the other hand, conflict may be necessary in world politics. Conflict may be the only means by which injustice can be dealt with. Conflict may be the only way in which small issues in contention can be resolved before they become larger issues, which would necessitate far greater conflict to effect a solution. Whatever our particular interest in conflict, to deal with it necessitates having an understanding of it. My interest in world politics might be best described as the development of an understanding of the causes, dynamics, and consequences of conflict. It is essentially up to you to decide how you feel about conflict in the international arena.

(3) While the emphasis is on conflict, *conflict* is a general, umbrella term that encompasses a whole range of actions and interactions between states. It does not exclusively mean war. Conflict can be thought of on two different levels.[10] Conflict can be a *perception* that the objectives, goals, or interests of one state are incompatible with another. For instance, George Kennan, an American diplomat, wrote an analysis of the Soviet Union that became the intellectual under-

---

[10]The following discussion draws on K.J. Holsti, *International Politics*, 1st ed. (Englewood Cliffs, N.J.: Prentice-Hall, 1967), p. 149.

pinning of much of the foreign policy of the United States in the post World War II period. Kennan argued that one of the ideas that motivated the Soviet government "is that of the innate antagonism between capitalism and Socialism. . . . [This] means that there can never be on Moscow's side any sincere assumption of a community of aims between the Soviet Union and powers which are regarded as capitalist. It must invariably be assumed in Moscow that the aims of the capitalist world are antagonistic to the Soviet regime and therefore to the interests of the peoples it controls."[11] To see the Soviet Union in this light meant to assume a deep and continuing conflict between the Soviet Union and the United States. It is likely that Kennan's Soviet counterpart was writing a similar analysis in 1947 about Washington's view of the world.

Conflict can also be seen as the *action* that one state undertakes against the interests or goals of another state, or that one state takes to protect itself against the demands and behavior of another. Conflict here refers to the behavior of one of several states in a particular relationship. Conflict still depends upon the perception by at least one party in a relationship that there is a threat to its interests. If state A demands that B surrender some of B's territory, we would call the situation one of conflict, because A knows that it threatens B's interests, and B sees itself threatened by A's demand. On other occasions, conflict may be less obvious but nonetheless real. State A may propose to B (as the United States did to Egypt in the 1950s) that B join A in a defensive alliance. State A's leaders assume that A's and B's interests are similar and that an alliance would be mutually beneficial. State B's leader, on the other hand, sees the offer as A's attempt to gain control over B. The perception and the response are conflictual.

Table 1–1 suggests a scheme for classifying conflictual actions and perceptions. The Japanese attack on the United States at Pearl Harbor in 1941, for instance, clearly falls at the right end of the scale. The Japanese government *perceived* the United States as an implacable foe; American embargoes on oil and iron were felt to constitute an economic declaration of war against Japan. The Japanese and American goals in the Pacific were mutually hostile. The Japanese believed that an expulsion of American power from the western Pacific was necessary. The American government felt that the Japanese had to be confined to northern Asia. And the daring Japanese carrier attack on the American fleet in Hawaii captures the essence of the use of force.

In the middle range of the conflict spectrum, we might find the American-Soviet conflict over Soviet intervention in Afghanistan in December, 1979. The American goal of protecting its (and its allies') influence and oil security in the Persian Gulf area and the Soviets' goals of protecting their relationship with a friendly Marxist regime in Afghanistan and curbing the growth of Islamic nationalism are not directed against each other. Nonetheless, the achievement of one imposes some costs on the other: Soviet domination of Afghanistan moves the Soviets closer to American security areas. American attempts to force the withdrawal of Soviets from Afghanistan threatens the Soviets with a loss of prestige and the possibility of a victorious rebellion by Muslim nationalists that might

---

[11]"X" [George Kennan], "The Sources of Soviet Conduct," *Foreign Affairs*, 25 (July 1947), 572, Excerpted by permission of *Foreign Affairs*, July 1947. Copyright 1947 by the Council on Foreign Relations, Inc.

TABLE 1-1 Types of Conflict and Intensity of Conflict

	INTENSITY OF CONFLICT			
	LOW	MODERATE	HEAVY	INTENSE
PERCEPTION OF GOALS	Complementary goals (parallel interests but pursued for different reasons)	Divergent goals (but not imposing major costs on the other if achieved)	Incompatible goals (such that their achievement will be costly to the other state)	Hostile goals (goals of a destructive nature are directed specifically against the other state)
PERCEPTION OF STATE	Other state is neutral	Other state is aggressive	Other state is hostile	Other state is an implacable foe
BEHAVIOR	Deny	Accuse		
		Protest		
		Disrupt relations		
		Expel diplomats		
			Reject	
			Aid opponent's opponents	
			Warn	
				Demonstrate (show of force)
				Subvert
				Threaten
				Use force

Source: Adapted in part from Maurice East, "Size and Foreign Policy Behavior: A Test of Two Models," *World Politics*, Vol. 25, no. 4 (July 1973), p. 569, copyright © 1973 by Princeton University Press; and Edward Azar and Thomas Sloan, *Dimensions of Interaction* (Pittsburgh: International Studies Association, 1975), p. xxi.

spill over to affect the Islamic peoples in the Soviet Union. American behavior in this instance was to warn (President Carter warned that the United States would resist if the Soviets threatened American or Allied oil supplies), and involved the disruption of relations (such as a grain embargo and the boycott of the Moscow Olympics).

On the other hand, toward the lower end of the conflict intensity scale, we find such events as the American-French tension in the mid-1960s. Both states had divergent goals regarding nuclear weapons. The United States wanted to avoid the proliferation of nuclear weapons; it offered to protect France under the American "nuclear umbrella." France, on the other hand, wanted its own nuclear weapons because of the status it gave France and because France did not believe that the United States would really risk its own nuclear destruction to save Europe from a Soviet invasion. Neither goal directly threatened the other, but both made relations more difficult.

Four Scientific Approaches to World Politics

The Domestic and Environmental Factor Approach   This broad approach tries to identify factors intrinsic to the state or in the environment in which a state exists. *Domestic factors* are essentially those characteristic of the people and their society. Such characteristics might include the political culture (how do people view themselves as political actors and the political system they are in?); the nature of domestic politics (it is stable? based on political parties? electoral?); the predominant form of economic organization (is it socialist? primarily agricultural?); or the current attitudes of the citizenry (are they xenophobic? tolerant of the use of force in world affairs? insistent that leaders prove themselves to be leaders?). *Environmental factors* are essentially the nonhuman characteristics of a society. Geography and geographic location are two such factors. Is the nation a continental state bordering on many nations (the Soviet Union), or few (the United States)? Is it essentially flat, with no natural defensive positions (Poland), or comprised of mountainous terrain (Switzerland)? A related factor is the natural resources available to the state within its borders. We would also consider human-made environmental features, such as the level of technology existing in a society and its presence in certain forms, most notably military weapons.

The argument of this particular approach is that the perceptions created by these domestic and environmental factors and the demands and interests imbedded in them lead to powerful expressions in world politics. Thus, for instance, a Marxist view of world politics would identify the class characteristics of the society as the central factor that accounts for the behavior of states. According to Lenin, a capitalist state seeks to subjugate other peoples (imperialism) and to vanquish other capitalist states.[12] It does so because the state is the captive of the ruling class; in this case, the capitalist entrepreneurs. That ruling class continually seeks to increase its own profits and historically has done so by degrading the life of the workers (the proletariat). However, in the nineteenth and twentieth centuries, it sought to still the discontent of the proletariat by extracting profits

---

[12]V.I. Lenin, *Imperialism: The Highest Stage of Capitalism* (New York: International Publishers, 1933).

from colonized people rather than from its own proletariat. The competition for colonial empire brought capitalist states into confrontations, which, Lenin said, inevitably led to World War I.

In a similar explanatory vein, others have pointed to the political culture of a society, or broader yet, the national character of a people, as a factor that shapes the politics of nations. Ruth Benedict, for instance, analyzed the Japanese national character and concluded that the Japanese from birth were taught to seek order, accept hierarchy, and "take one's proper station in life." This domestic ethos, she argued, applied to the international arena. The Japanese saw the proper nature of things as a hierarchical order of states in Asia with Japan at the top. Non-Asian nations had to be forced to retire from the scene, by war if necessary, to secure this order, which the Japanese assumed would prove beneficial to all Asiatics. When war failed—the Americans made the point forcefully—the Japanese abandoned the attempt to impose order, because they had a high sense of "situational realism."[13]

Various environmental factors have received considerable attention. Geographic location has in time past been an oft-discussed factor. Starting with Alfred Mahan and H.J. Mackinder, spatial locations of states and access to the seas have been hypothesized as shaping the behavior of states. Mackinder, for instance, suggested that humans are influenced by the physical reality of geography and how they interpret that reality.[14] In his view, one area of the world, because of its size, resources, and population, is the key to world politics. This "world island," as Mackinder called it, comprised Europe, Asia, and Africa, and could be divided into sections, of which Eastern Europe and the Heartland were most important. The Heartland (bounded roughly by the Baltic and Black Seas in the west, and Tibet, Mongolia, and Eastern Siberia in the east) was the pivot of world power. Access to the Heartland, however, was through Eastern Europe. On this basis, Mackinder formulated his famous dicta:

> Who rules East Europe commands the Heartland.
> Who rules the Heartland commands the World-Island.
> Who rules the World-Island commands the World.

Geography would encourage states in Eastern Europe (Germany and Russia) to struggle for the mastery of Eastern Europe, which in turn would lead to command of the world. Geography would also encourage other states to act to ensure that no one power came to dominate Eastern Europe—as Mackinder put it, to maintain a balance between Germans and Slavs.

Geography in its broadest sense also concerns the spatial distributions of animate and inanimate resources. Those resources, it has been argued, form the

---

[13]Ruth Benedict, *The Chrysanthemum and the Sword* (Boston: Houghton Mifflin, 1946). For a follow-up study of the results of the occupation of Japan, see Jean Stoetzel, *Without the Chyrsanthemum or the Sword* (New York: Columbia University Press, 1955).

[14]H.J. Mackinder, *Democratic Ideals and Reality* (New York: Holt, Rinehart and Winston, 1919). See also N.J. Spykman, *America's Strategy in World Politics* (New York: Harcourt Brace Jovanovich, 1942); Alfred Mahan, *The Influence of Sea Power Upon History* (Boston: Little, Brown, 1890); and Harold and Margaret Sprout, "Environmental Factors in the Study of International Politics," *Journal of Conflict Resolution*, 1 (No. 4, 1957), 309–28.

basis of a state's power or lack of it. Coal and iron made Germany and England the two powers to be reckoned with at the turn of the century, as oil makes historically minor states, such as Iran and Saudi Arabia, states to be reckoned with today.

As the twentieth century is the technological century, we would expect that technology would play an important role in world politics, and indeed that seems to be the case. Weapons technology is the most vivid example, with major revolutions in the ways of waging war coming every decade. A listing of some of those revolutions and their connections with various aspects of world politics appears in Table 1–2. Weapon systems and their evolution have always had a connection with world politics. Their employment in warfare and their role in supplying credibility for threats can be easily imagined. They have also encouraged states to engage in arms races, both to balance the level of armament achieved by a competitor (as in the celebrated nuclear arms race between the US and the USSR), and to find an effective counter to a weapons system developed by an opponent (as in the belated British development of the convoy system to counter German submarines in World War I). The potential that a new weapons system appears to offer has time and again pushed states to mobilize their resources and apply technology to achieve a breakthrough that gives them predominance. States without such resources or technological base appear to be condemned to an inferior power status. Such an appearance can be quite misleading, however. The Democratic Republic of Vietnam (North Vietnam) demonstrated that political mobilization and utilization of technology supplied by others could stalemate one of the most technologically advanced states, the United States.

Out of this concern for weapons, resources such as oil, and the ability to mobilize the citizenry, has emerged an emphasis on *power* as a key explanatory factor in world politics. One of the principal assumptions of the *power approach* is that states continuously seek to enhance their power. Thus world politics becomes essentially the struggle to acquire power and use it to dominate other

TABLE 1–2   Weapons and World Politics

WEAPON	RELATIONSHIP TO WORLD POLITICS
Machine gun	Stalemate on the Western front in World War I
Submarine	A threat to all seaborne commerce and the surface fleet; a cause of American entry into World War I; currently the only relatively invulnerable nuclear missile launching platform
Tank	The restoration of mobility on the battlefield
Airplane (bomber and fighter)	The restoration of mobility on the battlefield; the ability to destroy civilian targets before the defending army is destroyed; an offensive arm of total war
Nuclear weapons	Enormous destructive potential in a quick-strike weapon; the basis of a balance of terror between nuclear armed states; and a source of puzzlement as to how they are used diplomatically
Intercontinental ballistic missiles	The delivery system that allows nuclear weapons to achieve the balance of terror

states.[15] In such a world one would find two general types of states—the status quo state and the revisionist state. The status quo state, satisfied with the current distribution of power and the patterns of domination and subordination, seeks to preserve the international society as it exists. The unsatisfied revisionist state seeks to overthrow the existing order. World politics then is the continuous clash of power, of challenges and responses to the existing distribution of power.

Power is one of the key words in the vocabulary of political scientists. It is also one of the most difficult to define.[16] There are two broad distinctions we need to make about the term. First, *power* can be thought of as a *capability*, a capacity to do something under certain circumstances. The second way of defining power is to see it as *action*. *Power* then becomes getting another state to do something it would not otherwise have done (often called *influence*) or compelling another state to do something (often called *force*). Throughout this book when I speak of power in terms of actions, I will use the terms "influence" or "force." "Power" will refer to capability.

You might well ask why anyone should become so fussy about the choice of words and definitions. I suggested earlier that one of the hallmarks of the "scientific approach" is a concern for the meaning of concepts and ensuring that writer and reader are on the same wavelength when it comes to particular words. Part of my pickiness stems from this habitual caution that the approach encourages. There are more important reasons than habit, however. There is a crucial distinction between capability and action. In your own life, you have found that having the capability to do something does not necessarily mean that it will be done. How often have you heard the remark, "She has the capability to do the work but she just doesn't make the effort"? Or, "Everyone should be able to pass this course" (that is, they have the capability), but we have the well-grounded feeling that not everyone will. Because capability does not always translate into action, or successful action, we need to be able to distinguish between the two. The domestic and environmental factor approach stresses capability; it hypothesizes that having particular capabilities will produce certain kinds of state behavior.

Power has three different components that we need to keep in mind. Power is the capability to hurt, to hinder, and to help. By "hurt," I mean the capacity to deprive another of something that is valued. The classic example of the capacity to hurt resides in the military establishments of various states, which can deprive other states of lives, property, and contentment. By "hinder," I mean the capacity to block the acquisition of something valued. And by "help," I mean the capability to promote the acquisition of some value or resource by other states. Having markets that would provide economic rewards to another state, or having military resources that would make a defense agreement desirable are two areas in which we can say that a state has the capacity to "help" another.

[15]The most articulate exponent of this viewpoint is Hans Morgenthau, *Politics Among Nations* (New York: Knopf, various editions).

[16]For a sampling of various views, see *ibid.*; Klaus Knorr, *Power and Wealth* (New York: Basic Books, 1973); Inis Claude, *Power and International Relations* (New York: Random House, 1962); Wayne Ferris, *The Power Capabilities of Nation-States* (Lexington, Mass.: Lexington Books, 1973); and Annette Baker Fox, *The Power of Small States* (Chicago: University of Chicago Press, 1959).

No matter the particular factor employed, be it as specific as "public opinion" or as general as "power," those who argue that domestic or environmental factors cause world politics generally depict a rather straightforward relationship. We might represent such an argument as follows:

Domestic or environmental factor X ──────────→ World politics

(For example, the anticommunist orientation   (For example, the attempt to contain
of American public opinion after 1945)   the Soviet Union to its war time gains)

The Policy-Maker and Policy-Making Approach   The policy-maker and policy-making approach stresses the examination of world politics in terms of how policy is made and by whom.[17] Usually, but not always, the *end* result of such an analysis is to explain the actions of one state (its foreign policy), rather than the more inclusive subject of world politics. Thus,

Policy makers and policy making ──────────────→ Foreign policy

We might argue that policy making itself takes on particular characteristics because of the impact of various domestic or environmental factors. An anti-communist American public may force American foreign policy makers to be belligerent toward the USSR, regardless of their goals. This approach, however, suggests that there may not be any direct connection between environment and policy making. Indeed, we assume that there need not be. This will become clear as I delineate some of the more specific subapproaches found under this general approach.

Those who have adopted this particular approach have found it necessary to distinguish between two components of policy making: the policy makers and the policy process. The policy makers (often called decision makers) are those individuals who occupy positions accorded the right to make decisions that may, as the phrase goes, risk lives, fortune, and sacred honor. An approach oriented toward policy makers can be thought of as asking two general questions: (1) what images and goals do the policy makers have? and (2) what style and influence do they have? The general argument is that each of those components will affect policy.

The *image* a policy maker has of the world helps make sense out of the multitude of events that happen around the policy maker. Josef Stalin, for instance, had a strongly rooted image that the British and American governments wanted him to become involved in a war with his ally, Nazi Germany. Stalin was certain that Germany would attack the Soviet Union, but at some time in the future. The Soviet Union needed the time to prepare itself for the Nazi onslaught; Stalin was convinced that if he did nothing provocative toward the Germans, he would have his respite. Moreover, he was convinced that a German attack would be preceded by a series of escalating ultimatums like those Hitler had employed against the Austrians, Czechs, and Poles. Thus Stalin rejected British and American warnings of the German attack and warnings from his own agents within German dip-

[17]The classic work in this area is Richard Snyder, W.H. Bruck, and Burton Sapin, *Foreign Policy Decision-Making* (New York: Free Press, 1962).

lomatic and military organizations.[18] The initial German attack tore the Red Army apart. Stalin may have misperceived reality, but this approach suggests why the Red Army was not prepared to resist.

Policy makers develop their own *goals*. Most policy makers are committed to promoting the security and national interests of their own country. However, it is often the case that leaders and subordinates have different specific goals. As Graham Allison has suggested, where one stands on a particular policy issue often depends on where one sits.[19] The head of the nation's military establishment is likely to have different goals (as well as different images) than the head of the foreign ministry. While some of those goals are couched in terms of how the state should protect and promote its interests, the goals also reflect the policy maker's estimate of how certain goals better serve the interests of the particular organization he or she serves in. Robert Gallucci has pointed out how the United States Army advocated massive search and destroy operations in Vietnam because such an approach reflected the preparations the Army had made, ensured that the Army would remain in control of the ground war, and meant healthy budgetary appropriations. Various civilian policy makers, on the other hand, had argued for a strategy of creating defensive enclaves, especially in the coastal areas. Such an approach fit their conception that the war was a political rather than a military struggle. Civilians had pioneered in the development of "counter-insurgency" strategies for dealing with situations such as Vietnam. Moreover, many civilians thought that the enclave approach would permit a negotiated solution to the conflict if the opportunity arose.[20] Clearly, where one sat organizationally affected the images and goals of the particular policy makers.

In addition to the images and goals, we can say that policy makers have two other important attributes: *style* and *individual influence*. By *style*, I mean the experience that individual policy makers have in dealing with events, with others in their government, and with themselves. Czar Nicholas II, for example, believed that, as God had granted him the authority to rule all Russia, he as Czar must maintain the grant of absolute power. However, as an individual, Nicholas was both weak and dull-witted. Consequently, his decisions proceeded from irresolution to blind commitment to a particular goal or policy, no matter how unrewarding. Harry Truman, on the other hand, was self-confident (perhaps too much so), but woefully inexperienced in foreign policy. What he knew of Franklin Roosevelt's foreign policy was what he had read in the newspapers. Truman was initially a captive of the images and goals of his immediate advisors. He did learn with experience, but the years of isolation from foreign policy had taken their toll.

By *individual influence*, I mean the clout that individual policy makers have in the councils of government. Some decision makers have great power, as Hitler and Stalin demonstrated, but even their power may be circumscribed to some extent, or they may feel compelled not to challenge other power holders directly and

---

[18]Barton Whaley, *Codeword Barbarossa* (Cambridge, Mass.: M.I.T. Press, 1973).

[19]G. Allison, *Essence of Decision* (Boston: Little, Brown, 1971), and G. Allison, "Conceptual Models and the Cuban Missile Crisis," *American Political Science Review*, 63 (September 1969), 689–718.

[20]Robert Gallucci, *Neither Peace Nor Honor* (Baltimore: Johns Hopkins University Press, 1975), Chapter 5.

immediately. Other policy makers, such as the premiers and foreign ministers of France in the 1930s, are forced to share power with other ministers and nonpolitical leaders. As a consequence, they may never be able to direct effectively the affairs of state. From time to time, particular individuals such as military men (Tojo in Japan), religious notables (the Ayatollah Khomeini in Iran), and academics (Kissinger in the United States) have exercised great influence over the foreign policy of their states. That others have suffered decreases in influence has also affected policy.

As we have seen, one half of the policy-making approach concentrates on policy makers themselves. The other half of the approach is to look at the *process* by which policy makers create policy. In the analysis of world politics, there are two general frameworks that citizens and scholars employ—the rational framework and the political framework.[21]

The rational framework assumes that policy makers make decisions rationally. Ideally, decisions are made rationally when the following process occurs: individuals identify a problem and establish a goal to resolve the problem. They then identify and evaluate options in terms of their cost and effectiveness in accomplishing the goal. They select the best option and implement it. The implementation of the option becomes a state's foreign policy. As an illustration, we might consider the situation Anwar al-Sadat found himself in in the fall of 1977. The *problem* confronting Sadat was that the momentum Egypt and Syria had gained by the 1973 war had run out. The step-by-step diplomacy undertaken by the American Secretary of State Kissinger had now run into Israeli resistance to any further concessions. In Egypt there were growing questions about Sadat's political future. The Egyptian government decided to pursue the goal of forcing the United States and Israel to accept a lasting peace in the region. Sadat's options at the time appear to have been as follows:

1. He could end his hostility to the Soviet Union and reestablish a strong working relationship with the Soviet Communist party. In that way he could mobilize Soviet support for his goal.
2. He could build up his military establishment and launch another attack on Israeli-held territory.
3. He could offer major concessions to the Israelis and demand a suitable quid pro quo from them in return.
4. He could wait until his own position in Egypt became precarious enough to prompt Washington and Jerusalem to make the effort for peace in order to keep a more militant leader from coming to power in Egypt.

Sadat chose the third option as the least costly, most effective means of reaching his goal. He flew to Jerusalem and in word and symbol recognized the right of Israel to exist and live in peace (the concession on his part), in return for which he expected Israel to withdraw from the territories it had occupied in the 1967 war and to begin the process of the creation of a Palestinian state.

From the perspective of the rational framework, the goal chosen by the leaders explains the policy or behavior of the state, for the policy is the rational

---

[21]See Allison, *Essence*, or Allison, "Conceptual Models" for a general discussion; see also John Steinbrunner, *The Cybernetic Theory of Decision* (Princeton: Princeton University Press, 1974).

means to accomplish the goal. It may be that policy makers must operate with incomplete information and therefore make wrong estimates of options. It may also be that the goals that policy makers pursue are intensely idiosyncratic (How do I remain in power?) rather than reflective of a broader conception of the national interest (What benefits most Egyptians?). Nonetheless, this framework assumes a rational identification, analysis, and choice of behaviors in response to some rationally derived goal.

The political framework was explicitly developed as a counterbalance to the rational framework.[22] It suggests that, instead of looking at decisions as being made in an ordered, logical process, we would do well to think of decisions as political products. They are shaped by bargaining and compromise and are likely to take place in a disorderly, incremental fashion. Decisions will reflect the influence of various policy makers, their styles and images, and a whole host of unforeseen incidents and accidents.

This framework argues that *politics* is more the name of the game than rationality, because most issues appear to policy makers in different guises. In the Cuban missile crisis of 1962, for instance, the American Secretary of Defense initially argued that there was no military crisis because the strategic balance of power was unchanged, and no quick military response was needed. One of his subordinates argued just the reverse on both counts. The President felt the issue was a supreme *political* challenge—an international challenge by the Soviets and a challenge to his capacity as a leader. His initial reaction was to move quickly and unilaterally to deal with the missiles. The American Ambassador to the United Nations, on the other hand, saw the issue as diplomatic, to be treated diplomatically. Policy making is thus a *struggle* to define the problem, to establish goals, and to persuade others that one's preferred option is the one that should be adopted.

Because of the political process, we would expect the policy that emerges to be in the form of a *compromise*. That is, it would be a collection of pieces, which often reflects "something for everybody." It may be self-contradictory, ineffective, perhaps not even what anyone really wanted. It is certainly not the tidy product that the rational framework sees when it examines policy. The political framework would say that in the Cuban missile crisis, the policy choice was a maritime blockade of Cuba, which gave something to most of the decision makers, but with the caveat that if the blockade failed, something more drastic would be employed. As we shall see, the blockade *did* fail, because in many ways it was an untidy, contradictory compromise.

The introduction of these two alternative frameworks for the analysis of foreign policy making makes explicit one of the dilemmas inherent in this text. Which approach or model or framework is best? Which model should I use in the

---

[22]Methodological considerations helped spur a critical examination of the rational framework. When doing research using the rational framework, it often proves difficult to identify the actual goals policy makers pursue. To get around this problem, the researcher examines the foreign policy behavior of the state (which is more visible). The researcher then *assumes* that the behavior was rationally designed to accomplish some goal. He or she then *infers* that goal *from* the behavior and then argues in a circular fashion that the inferred goal accounts for the behavior. The discussion of Sadat's decision was constructed in this fashion. The rational framework is not unique to the study of world politics. Indeed, it is probably the framework we use to account for events and behavior of others in our own lives.

description of foreign policy? Does a rational framework seem more appropriate than the political framework? Or better said, *under what conditions* will one model give us greater insight and understanding of how and why particular states behave as they do? While I discuss this issue in the succeeding chapters, you should be prepared to try to draw your own conclusions. To aid you, let me report two hypotheses suggested by the work of Charles Hermann:[23]

> The political framework will approximate reality more closely when decisions are made by a group of policy makers who represent various sectors or organizations and whose consent or acquiescence is needed to make policy.
>
> The rational framework will approximate reality more closely when decisions are made by a dominant leader who actively consults others who offer relatively independent advice.

Undoubtedly, other factors will affect the type of policy process; the following chapters demonstrate a wide range of possibilities. Ultimately, we will want to draw some conclusions about which framework is best, not only in this instance, but for all the different approaches that this book explores as well.

The Interaction Approach   The policy-maker and policy-making approach essentially examines how and why *one* state produces a particular set of foreign policy actions. Of course, we might *compare* different states and their foreign policy outputs.[24] The focus, however, remains on the state. The *interaction* approach, on the other hand, picks up where the policy approach leaves off. It concentrates on the interplay between two states.

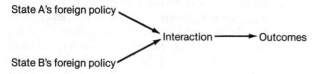

In this approach, the kinds of questions we are likely to ask are, (1) how do states interact and what patterns of interaction emerge? (2) why do they manifest those particular patterns of interactions? and, (3) what consequences (outcomes) are there of those interactions? In a basic way, this approach most clearly approximates what people have meant when they refer to "world politics." This approach, with its concern for war, alliance formation, diplomatic bargaining, and arms races, stands at the center of many discussions of world politics.[25]

---

[23]Charles F. Hermann, "Decision Structures and Process Influences on Foreign Policy," in *Why Nations Act*, ed. Maurice East, Stephen Salmore, and Charles Hermann (Beverly Hills, Cal.: Sage, 1978), pp. 80–82.

[24]The field of comparative foreign policy is a growing one. See among others, Roy Macridis, ed., *Foreign Policy in World Politics*, 5th ed. (Englewood Cliffs, N.J.: Prentice-Hall, 1976); Patrick McGowan and Howard Shapiro, *The Comparative Study of Foreign Policy* (Beverly Hills, Cal.: Sage, 1973); and James Rosenau, ed., *Comparing Foreign Policies* (New York: John Wiley/Halstead, 1974).

[25]For a summary of many of the empirically based findings about patterns of interaction, see Susan Jones and J. David Singer, eds., *Beyond Conjecture in International Politics* (Itasca, Ill.: Peacock, 1972) and Michael Sullivan, *International Relations: Theories and Evidence* (Englewood Cliffs, N.J.: Prentice-Hall, 1976).

Yet even here, the particular interaction approach one adopts will affect in a large degree what one sees. I have selected three such variants found in the interaction approach: *game theory, bargaining theory,* and *pattern analysis.* Each of these offers a particular way of viewing world politics, of describing what one sees, and of generating explanations of particular patterns of interactions.

Game theory. Unlike the other frameworks we have discussed, game theory is a nonempirical method of analysis. That is, it is a logical and mathematical model of how game players should behave under certain conditions. We can identify some of the principal conditions. First, players are assumed to be rational; they will play to increase their winnings, or, alternatively, to minimize their losses. Second, the choices the player can make are limited and identifiable. Third, how well or poorly a player does depends on his or her choice *and* on the choice of other players (hence, interaction is necessary). Finally, a player's choice of behaviors is conditioned by the values attached to certain outcomes.[26]

To illustrate, suppose that two states, A and B, find themselves embroiled in a dispute over territory that both would like to seize as a colonial possession. Let us also suppose that each government has the choice of either backing away from its claims of complete sovereignty over the territory, or pushing its claims. Such a situation might appear as:

STATE A

	Back away	Push
Back away	Cell 1	Cell 2
Push	Cell 3	Cell 4

STATE B

Each one of the boxes (called "cells") represents the *interaction* of the particular behavior of State A and the particular behavior of State B. It also represents the *outcome* of those interactions. For instance, if both back away (cell 1), peace will prevail between A and B, and both may be more receptive to cautious proposals to negotiate a mutually agreeable solution to the issue. On the other hand, if both push (cell 4), the relationship will be quite conflictual. War scares or the actual use of force may occur.

Cells 2 and 3 have different kinds of results. In cell 2, for instance, A pushed the issue while B backed away. It is likely that A would secure the territory sought. B is left without the territory (presumably a loss) but with peaceful relations (presumably something positive). In cell 3 the situation is reversed; B "wins" and A "loses" something. These notions of winning and losing are critical to game theory. They give the approach its dynamic quality. They are also the weakest part of the approach when it comes to the application of this logical, mathematical model to the real world, for *we as students* of world politics must assign values to the various outcomes. That is, we must decide what each outcome (or cell) is worth to each player.

[26]For an introduction to game theory, see Steven J. Brams, *Game Theory and Politics* (New York: Free Press, 1975); Martin Shubik, *The Uses and Methods of Gaming* (New York: Elsevier, 1975); and Anatol Rapoport, *Fights, Games, and Debates* (Ann Arbor: University of Michigan Press, 1961).

In the next illustration, I have assigned values to each cell. By common agreement, the value in the upper right corner of each cell is the value of the cell to the "top" player (in this case, State A). The value in the lower left of each cell is the value to the player "on the side" (State B). In this case, an outcome of both sides' backing away (cell 1) is worth +15 to State A and −5 to State B.

What the values actually mean is up to the analyst; they might be money, prestige, or resources won or lost. Their *relative amounts* are what is important for game theory. To reiterate, those values are values that I assigned.

Once the values are assigned, the framework is complete, and we can now identify what choice the rational player will make and what the outcome is likely to be. You take the part of State A; I will take the part of State B. What choice did you make? As B, I chose to "push," not because I am an aggressive person or because I have desires to injure your interests, but because it is the rational choice for me. The payoff values in the cells indicate that if I choose "push," the outcome will be +20 or +5 for me, depending on what you do. If I had chosen to "back away," I would have lost −5 or −25 depending on what you chose to do. Obviously, I want to minimize my losses where I can and maximize the gains. "Pushing" the issue is the rational choice for State B.

If you were a rational player, you would have elected to "back away." Your choices were to "back away," which might give you +15 or −10, or to "push," which might give you +10 or −20. Your choice is not as clear cut as State B's, but inspection suggests that if you want to minimize your loss (if you must take one) and maximize your gain (if you can get one), you should "back away."[27] Thus the outcome of our interaction would be cell 3, with a value of +20 for me and a −10 for you. If these values remain the same, and we both remain rational, we would expect to find the same outcome each time we played the game.

As I indicated, "game theory" is derived from abstract concepts and arguments. It is therefore artificial and has only a minimal connection to empirical events. Its use, however, lies in its ability to provide us with new questions about how and why states behave as they do and what might have to be done to change the policy choices and outcomes available to the players.

---

[27]Notice that the rational choice is determined by how well or poorly you might do relative to your own resources. Losing 20 is worse than losing 10. However, *if* you kept score in terms of how well or poorly you were doing vis-à-vis *your opponent*, you might make a different choice. In this illustration, if you know your opponent's payoff values, your *relative* position vis-à-vis your opponent would be in cell 1, +20; cell 2, +35; cell 3, −30, and cell 4, −25. In this case you might decide to "push." However, our use of the "game theory" approach will be based on the assumption that a player calculates costs and benefits relative to his or her own resources.

Bargaining theory. An alternative to game theory, but still part of the interactive approach, is bargaining theory. As I. William Zartman suggests, bargaining theory has the following general characteristics:[28] It involves interaction between states (or other entities) which are in conflict over some particular valuable, such as territory, trade, or alliance commitments. They recognize that there may be a mutually acceptable (though possibly inequitable) solution to the issue. "One party is presented with a choice between accepting the other party's proposal (offer, demand) or rejecting it and holding out in the hope of getting something better at the risk of getting something worse."[29] A solution emerges when one state makes changes in its demands or interests, or persuades the other state to make changes in its demands or interests. Bargaining is therefore a process by which two or more states reach some agreement through the mutual manipulation of each other's perceptions and expectations.

This particular approach assumes that interactions take place because a state cannot *by itself* satisfy its desires or goals at a price it is willing to pay. The United States negotiates with the members of Organization of Petroleum Exporting Countries (OPEC) because it does not have sufficient petroleum supplies within its territory and chooses not to pay the price to end its dependence on foreign oil (economic dislocation, political unrest, and major degradation of ecological standards in the United States). It is also unwilling to seize foreign oil-producing states and exploit them for its own purposes. And it does not have access to a world political system that might compel the delivery of oil.

Thus, bargaining will occur if nations have needs that cannot be unilaterally met, cannot be resolved by force, or cannot be resolved through a legislative or judicial process. In order to bargain, states must *communicate* their desires to each other and demonstrate a *commitment* to those desires. Bargaining theory assumes that *communication* is a central element. Indeed, the interaction that makes up world politics is essentially that of communicating offers, demands, threats, and promises.

From this perspective, every action of a state, verbal or otherwise, forms a communication to others. A state has an incentive to have its communications clearly understood. As it often happens, however, they may be ambiguous. Consider the case of two nuclear-armed states. State A begins to evacuate people from its population centers. From A's perspective, this is a purely defensive move, for it is only protecting its population from a possible attack by B. Therefore, it should not raise tensions between the two states. From B's perspective, however, the move is highly provocative and tension-producing, for it appears that A is "clearing the decks" for a sudden attack on B. After all, B's leaders *know* that *they* plan no attack on A, and hence the removal of the population *must* be a prelude to A's attack on B.

In order to make one's actions clear, words may be necessary in order to indicate the appropriate interpretation to be put on an event. Besides, words are of-

    [28]I. William Zartman, "Introduction," in *The 50% Solution*, ed. I.W. Zartman (Garden City, N.Y.: Anchor, 1976), pp. 7–18.
    [29]Glenn Snyder and Paul Diesing, *Conflict Among Nations: Bargaining, Decision Making, and System Structure in International Crises.* Copyright © 1977 by Princeton University Press, 1977. Excerpt, p. 23.

ten a cheaper resource to rely on in the short run than actions. Words, however, do have an important drawback. Words in and of themselves are not credible. Our belief or disbelief of someone's words rests on some characteristic of the person who has spoken the words ("she is a reputable person," "that government lives up to its word"), or the fact that the words represent a plausible interpretation of some action ("the quarantine of Cuba that we have instituted will continue until all Soviet missiles are removed").

Clarity alone is not enough. The other side must believe that we really want what we say we want and that we will do what we say we will do. Without either, a state's chances of reaching its goals are quite reduced. In most complex situations (which means world politics), there is usually no such thing as a 50-50 agreement. Any bargained solution is likely to be more advantageous to one state than to the other(s). Therefore, we would expect states to be insistent on "getting things their way." This approach suggests that a state will emphasize a commitment to its position in a dispute rather than emphasize flexibility. A show of flexibility may encourage the other side to remain firm in its demands rather than make concessions. Yet "flexibility" cannot be dispensed with, for if *both* sides lack it, an agreement is unlikely.

As you can see, bargaining theory suggests that a great deal of tension and ambiguity will exist in the interaction between states. This is reflected by the in-

INSTRUCTIONS[30]	MY COMMENT
"You are authorized to adopt, for negotiating purposes, initial positions more favorable to us than the minimum conditions set forth in these instructions.	Most initial positions are inflated a bit so that a few concessions can be offered (i.e., to show flexibility) without endangering the core objectives or damaging the credibility of one's claim to be committed to a particular position.
However, great care should be used, in putting forward a negotiating position, not to allow [the] talks to break down except in case of failure to accept our minimum terms;	Don't inflate the initial position so much that the other side assumes we do not really want a negotiated settlement and therefore cancels the talks.
not to appear to overreach to an extent to cause world opinion to question our good faith;	Bargaining in world politics takes place before a large audience that may have an important impact on how some solution is reached.
and not so to engage U.S. prestige in a negotiating position as to make retreat to our minimum terms impossible.	A negotiator needs to put some credibility into the inflated position; otherwise the other side will treat retreat as "fluff" and not a real concession. Yet to make it very credible means that to back away might lead the other side to assume that the negotiator will back away from everything in the bargaining position.
Our minimum position is essential to us but we must recognize that it will not be easy for [our] opponents to accept; the difficulty of your negotiations is fully appreciated here."	Cold comfort!

[30]Joint Chiefs of Staff to General Ridgway, June 1951, quoted in Harry Truman, *Memoirs, Volume II: Years of Trial and Hope* (Garden City, N.Y.: Doubleday, 1956), p. 459.

structions sent to the American commander in Korea, General Ridgway, who was authorized in 1951 to negotiate an armistice between the United States and United Nations forces on one side and the People's Republic of China and the Democratic People's Republic of Korea on the other. Next to those instructions I have provided an elaboration of the kinds of tensions and ambiguities inherent in a bargaining situation.

It took two years to negotiate an armistice agreeable to both sides in the Korean conflict. Bargaining theory helps us account for the time and difficulty in doing so. Bargaining theory is not the only type of theory that we might have employed using the interaction framework for analysis, however. A third (and the last type of interaction approach to be discussed) is what might be called "pattern analysis."

Pattern analysis. Pattern analysis looks for recurring patterns in the interactions among states and attempts to make general statements about those patterns. While such an approach may attempt to identify causes of such patterns, it often assumes that the *nature of the pattern* itself is its own cause. This approach is often called "stimulus-response." A classic example comes from the study of arms races between two states. Lewis Richardson in the 1930s, for instance, developed such a model of an arms race. Suppose, he argued, that two states have fundamentally peaceful intentions toward each other but each suspects that the other may have hostile intentions. Both states maintain military establishments to protect themselves from any aggression by the other. In the eyes of each, its own military establishment and weapons systems are purely defensive. The same cannot be said for the other's military establishment. It exists only for aggressive purposes.[31]

In this particular situation, the activity of the military establishment of one state will be keyed to the activity of the other. If one increases the size of its armed forces, the other will respond, which will produce a counter-response, and a corresponding counter-counter-response, and so on. Such an interaction pattern may continue until some equilibrium is reached (where the response pattern terminates) or until the interaction takes on a different character altogether (as in the outbreak of war).

Our interest in this approach is based on the feeling that we can understand certain important events in world politics without referring to such concepts as domestic factors, or the history of the relations between the two states, or who makes policy and how. Rather, the key—or so this approach argues—is in the dynamics of the interaction. To illustrate (and to introduce a bit of complexity), consider the Middle East in the early summer of 1967.

In 1967, there were two distinct but interrelated patterns of interaction. The first involved the rivalry between Egypt and Syria for the leadership of the Arab world.[32] From the perspective of pattern analysis, we would expect a continuing series of behaviors designed to establish the image of one state as the leader or to undermine the claim to leadership by the other. The second pattern is the more familiar one of Arab-Israeli hostility; in this particular example I will fo-

---

[31]Lewis Richardson, *Arms and Insecurity: A Mathematical Study of the Causes and Origins of War*, ed. Nicolas Rashevsky and Ernesto Trucco (Pacific Grove, Cal.: Boxwood Press, 1960).

[32]Malcolm Kerr, *The Arab Cold War*, 3rd ed. (London: Oxford University Press, 1971).

cus especially on Egyptian-Israeli interactions, although as we will see, Syrian-Is-
raeli interactions play a crucial role.

To see the patterns and their interplay, you should first consult Figure 1–1.
This illustration begins with a Palestinian raid on Israel from Syrian bases, initiating a common pattern of raid and Israeli reprisal. As tension mounted between
Syria and Israel, Syria began to use the issue in its rivalry with Egypt. Egypt responded with a military mobilization against Israel and initiated the action-reaction pattern of hostility with Israel. To each Israeli action, Egypt increased the
pressure, such as closing the Straits of Tiran, which connect the Israeli port of
Elath with the Red Sea. Each action-reaction gave both sides fewer options and
the feeling that a little more pressure would force the other side to desist or crumble. The Israeli air strike against Egypt on June 5, 1967, changed the pattern to

FIGURE 1–1   Patterns in the Middle East Crisis, 1967

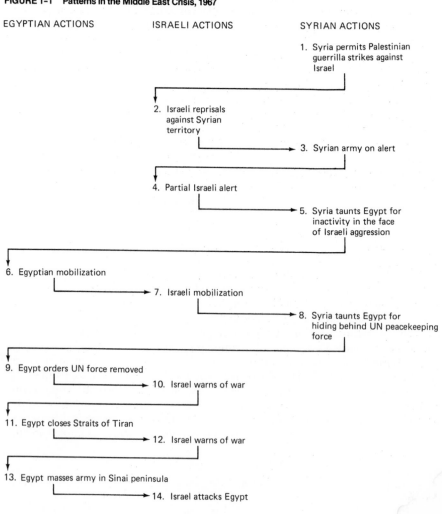

EGYPTIAN ACTIONS   ISRAELI ACTIONS   SYRIAN ACTIONS

1. Syria permits Palestinian guerrilla strikes against Israel

2. Israeli reprisals against Syrian territory

3. Syrian army on alert

4. Partial Israeli alert

5. Syria taunts Egypt for inactivity in the face of Israeli aggression

6. Egyptian mobilization

7. Israeli mobilization

8. Syria taunts Egypt for hiding behind UN peacekeeping force

9. Egypt orders UN force removed

10. Israel warns of war

11. Egypt closes Straits of Tiran

12. Israel warns of war

13. Egypt masses army in Sinai peninsula

14. Israel attacks Egypt

one of warfare, but this change can be seen as a logical step in this particular pattern of interaction.

World politics can be described and explained through this particular model of challenge and response. One of the goals of research in this area would be to identify particular pervasive patterns and to classify various' historical events according to the patterned characteristics they display. Some of the most important patterns that political scientists have discussed are listed in Figure 1–2. This discussion of pattern analysis concludes this brief orientation to the interaction approach. I turn now to the last scientific approach employed in this book.

The Systems Approach   In its basic form, the systems approach deals with the distribution of power among the states of the world and the consequences of that distribution of power for how states will act and interact.[33] The general argument of the systems approach is that particular distributions of power encourage states to adopt particular general patterns of behavior. Those particular patterns are quite pervasive and thus form relatively stable characteristics of world politics at a given point in time.

FIGURE 1–2   Examples of Interaction Patterns Found in World Politics

PREDOMINANTLY CONFLICTUAL PATTERNS

War: a patterned use of military force between states
Imperialism/liberation: a patterned subjugation/revolt of a people by/against a foreign state
Crisis/"escalation": a patterned exchange of threats
Arms races: a patterned competition in the production and deployment of weapons systems
Penetration: a patterned indirect entry of one state into the culture, society, and politics of another
Deterrence: a patterned set of perceptions about the ability of another state to damage one's own state even after suffering a first strike by one's own state
Alliance competition: a patterned mobilization of members of an alliance and the alliance's patterned responses to another alliance
Diplomacy: a patterned communication of states' interests and intentions
Patron-client manipulation: a patterned display of mutual influence between purportedly dominant and subordinate states
Collective problem solving: a patterned search for responses to immediate problems
Alliance formation: a patterned creation of agreements and occasionally institutions to promote long-term common interests (usually security)
Integration: a patterned dissolution of national identities and institutions in favor of supra-national identities and institutions.

MIXED PATTERNS

PREDOMINANTLY COOPERATIVE PATTERNS

---

[33]The classic work is Morton Kaplan, *System and Process in International Politics* (New York: John Wiley, 1957). For a survey and critique, see Kenneth Waltz, *Theory of International Politics* (Reading, Mass.: Addison-Wesley, 1979). My view of the systems approach is taken from Holsti, *International Politics*, 2nd ed., Chapter 2.

"Power" in this approach refers to capability. Unlike the role of "power" in the domestic and environmental factor approach, however, the systems approach tends to assume that the driving motivation in world politics is to *control* the power of others—to protect one's state from those with the power to hurt, to neutralize those with the power to hinder, and to gain the support of those with the power to help. In the absence of world government, the prudent policy maker must be most concerned with the question of which states have the power to hurt. That is, the *national security* issue is the predominant one in the view of all political leaders. This concern for power and security does not mean that military issues and military capability are the only concerns. Today we may have some difficulty understanding Imperial Germany's concern for its "standing" among the major powers, but we can sense that, *if* the German policy makers defined the issue in those terms, their first concern would be with those who had the power to deprive them of such values.

With this approach, we can envision policy makers anxiously scanning the horizon to identify those states that can threaten their security. *How* they will respond will be heavily influenced by the nature of the threats they face. Similar states will face similar threats, and therefore be likely to behave similarly. In this way, particular patterns of behavior and interactions will emerge. We would further expect that the patterns that do emerge will be those which stand the best chance of ensuring the security of the state. They will best protect the state from those with the capacity to hurt. As long as such patterns provide such benefits, we would expect policy makers to keep their policies in line with those patterns. We might go as far to say, as Morton Kaplan does, that such patterns become "rules" for continued protection of the state.[34]

We need to say a bit more about "the nature of the threat," for it is in the different types of threat that we expect to find different patterns of behavior. Political scientists have tried to deal with the myriad types of threats that may exist by speaking in general terms of the *structure of the international system*. The "international system" refers essentially to those states that interact with each other with some regularity. In practice, the system includes all powerful states and many of the lesser states. "Structure" means the distribution of power in the international system. Our answer to the distribution-of-power question generally takes two forms. First, how many states have most of the world's power resources? Structure is in part a question of *numbers*. Second, among the powerful, how is power allocated? Is it generally spread out equally, or do some states have far more than others? Structure is in part a question of *relative capability* and the *hierarchy of power*.

We are long overdue for an illustration of many of these points, and I will provide one that should be quite familiar to you. But at the same time that I provide the example, I would like you to be thinking ahead to the next question we need to deal with: Given this particular *structure*, what patterns of behavior are likely to emerge?

Any set of units that interact can be defined as a system. Consider your classroom as the system. How is power distributed? Figure 1–3 might be representative. The size of the circles is meant to reflect the relative capabilities of the

---

[34]Kaplan, *System and Process*, p. 23.

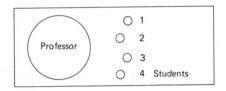

FIGURE 1-3   Structure of the Classroom System of Thirty Students and One Professor

various "actors." The number of the circles represents the number of major power holders in the system (the classroom). One actor, the professor, has the capacity to hurt (assignments, grades), while only a few student actors may have the capacity to hurt. Their modest capability might rest on an ability to shape student opinion or to distract the class. Note that most students in the classroom are unlikely to have any appreciable power (they do not appear in the figure at all). Thus, while the class might be made up of thirty students, only a handful will be powerful, but grossly inferior to the power of the professor.

You will notice that I have kept the question of power confined to the classroom. The four walls of the classroom separate it from the rest of the college or university. To put it in terms that we will use, there is a *boundary* separating the *system* (the classroom) from the *environment* (the rest of the institution). That boundary may be quite firm, in which case external factors or power cannot enter the system and change the distribution of power in the classroom or its patterns of interaction. In other cases, the boundary between the classroom and the environment may be less firm; in the late 1960s, "outsiders" often appeared in various classes and did shift power (in part because they could hinder the professor and were beyond the reach of his or her capability to hurt through grades).

Assume for the moment that the boundary between system and environment is relatively firm. The distribution of power in the classroom is as pictured in Figure 1-3. Given this particular distribution of power, are there particular patterns of behavior likely to emerge that will provide for the security of the actors in this system? This is the key question of systems analysis. If there are such patterns, we should be able to find them whenever we find a particular distribution of power, and we should be able to account for such patterns by referring to the particular distribution of power. If this approach works, we have a very powerful tool for the analysis of world politics.

What kinds of patterns of behavior does one find in the classroom? Students raise hands to be recognized in order to talk, and take their places in seats (often toward the back!) while the professor stands or sits up front, alone. Students ask, "Just what is it you want on this paper or exam?" Presumably these patterns have emerged to allow the student actors to cope with the enormous disparity in power. They are perpetuated because they seem to work—they seem to provide security. Of course, over time, they become habitual responses, so deeply engrained that the actors may no longer be aware of their function. Every once in a while there will be reminders. What happens to the student who "can't hold his tongue," to the creative student who writes an "off-the-wall" paper, to the students who talk to each other during class?

We would also expect that the distribution of power in the classroom would affect the professor's behavior in patterned ways. She speaks generally at will and often dictates the direction, tempo, and substance of the discussion. She establishes standards to be met and incentives and punishments for student performance. In many respects, however, it would appear that the behavior of the professor is remarkably restrained, especially in light of the power held. One explanation may be that great power in the face of smaller (but not absent) power has some built-in inhibitions. This argument will be developed later in some detail.

Perhaps you might be saying to yourself that there is another explanation of why professors' behaviors are restrained, other than the restraint inherent in the structure of the system itself. Behavior may be restrained because professors with bad reputations may not be retained, or may suffer precipitous drops in enrollment, or may find administrators beginning to ask questions about what is going on in the classroom. Notice that these kinds of explanations are ones that cross the boundary between the system (classroom) and the environment. If the boundary is relatively fragile or porous, the behavior of professors and students is likely to be affected by these *non-systemic* factors.

And so it is with the international system and its boundary. In general, the systems approach argues that the structure of the system will determine patterns of behavior. To the degree that the boundary between the international system and its environment is "firm," the power distribution will be the major determinant of behavior. Otherwise, environmental features will play a role, and the "environment" of the international system is quite broad. It includes all aspects of domestic politics, economics, and social events. With respect to policy makers, it may include personality, institutions of government, and the processes by which individuals make decisions. As you might expect, the real question is the degree to which these environmental features intrude on the operation of the system.[35]

We can depict the systems approach as follows:

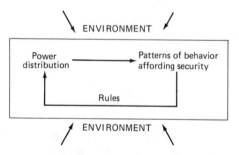

If the boundary between environment and system is relatively strong, state behavior is the response to the threat posed in the distribution of power. Those responses sort themselves into patterns, which in turn create "rules" or expectations about behavior. As long as states adhere to the rules, the distribution of power is likely to persist, thus continuing the cycle. Where the boundary is weak,

[35]What one chooses to identify as a systemic characteristic (such as the distribution of power) as opposed to environmental features is often a matter of discretion. Most incorporate some aspect of power; others include such things as regime characteristics (e.g., authoritarian or nonauthoritarian) and status (the prestige accorded the various actors). I have defined these as environmental features in order to facilitate the analysis.

pressures from the environment may lead states to violate the rules, which, if unchecked by other states, may bring about a change in the distribution of power. Such a new structure will presumably foster a new set of patterns and rules.

CONCLUSION

We have come to the end of a quick look at the five approaches that populate this book. I did not try to be exhaustive with the description of any one, for in the following chapters, I shall present each in operation. Each chapter begins with an historical account of world politics in a particular decade and ends with the application of various scientific approaches to major events or issues of that time period. I hope you are primed with questions and comments. I also hope the remaining chapters will add detail and insight and deal with some of your questions. And there will still be a host of questions that will remain unanswered. That is the challenge left for you.

This method of presentation may leave the impression that these five approaches are distinct. How different are the scientific approaches from each other? You may have noticed that the *subject* of the analysis changed in important ways.[36] When we looked at the domestic and environmental factor approach, our subject was the *state* broadly considered; we examined characteristics of the state such as its geographic location, its cultural images, its form of government. When we moved to policy making and policy makers, the subject became *individuals* (such as Stalin or Sadat) and the *process* by which individuals make policy. Interaction analysis, in contrast, had as its subject the *interaction* between two or more states. Finally, systems analysis identified a *characteristic* common to all the states (power) as its subject.

The usefulness of seeing different types of subjects (and their corresponding different types of analysis) should not blind us to the connections between the approaches. Domestic public opinion that demands noninvolvement in world politics, for instance, may create pressures on policy makers to create a particular foreign policy. In turn, the foreign policy of any given state will comprise one-half of the interaction process, and the interactions of many states become systemic patterns and rules.

It often happens, however, that we assume that one approach describes and explains world politics better than other approaches. When we single one approach out, we are saying that this approach seems to provide the most convincing analysis of the situation. We do not reject other approaches, but relegate them to secondary positions. We often do so by assuming that the concepts embedded in those secondary approaches are held constant or have only minimal impact. For example, systems analysis does have a tendency to assume that domestic factors have minimal impact by positing the existence of a strong boundary. Conversely, the policy-making approach often treats the international system as a given. From this view, an unchanging system forms a background for

---

[36]See J. David Singer, "The Level-of-Analysis Problem in International Relations," in *International Politics and Foreign Policy*, ed. James Rosenau, pp. 20–29.

decision makers whose perceptions of power or personality, rather than the actual distribution of power, may be all-important.

In later chapters I will explore some of the ways we might integrate the four "scientific" approaches. It seems to me to be premature to argue that they can be—for only modest efforts exist in that direction—nor is it entirely clear that they should be. Regarding the connection between the *"scientific" approach* and the *historical approach*, I can summarize some of the convergences and disjunctions between the two. The historian often works with a hypothesis—a guess or hunch—about what happened and why. She or he brings evidence to bear on the hypothesis and fashions an apt conclusion. In doing so, the historian assumes that events unfold in succession, each event building on other events. The characteristic style of history is the descriptive narrative of those events. Those events are usually grouped into "themes" of like events, such as American Cold War foreign policy, Hitler's diplomacy and wars of aggression, decolonization in Africa, and the Japanese-American struggle for control in the Pacific. The historical approach assumes that the explanation of any event is based on prior events. What happened yesterday accounts for what happens today. This is true even though things "change." Change itself is usually treated as synonymous with history.

These two assumptions can be depicted in general terms (see Figure 1-4). The historical description reports the change over time of particular characteristics thought to be important. Theme #1 in the diagram might be the aid that the People's Republic of China has provided foreign revolutionary movements. Theme #2 might be the American government's attempt to isolate the People's Republic of China. The explanatory framework for the historical approach draws explanation from prior events. The decline in Chinese support for revolutionary movements in the early 1970s, for instance, might be explained by the need to recover from the chaos of the Great Proletarian Cultural Revolution, the singular lack of success in exporting revolution, and the emergence of the Soviet Union as a direct military threat.

FIGURE 1-4   The Historical Perspective

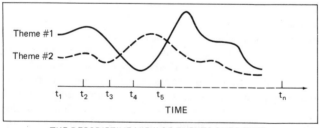

THE DESCRIPTIVE VIEW OF EVENTS OVER TIME

THE EXPLANATORY FRAMEWORK

Turning to the scientific approach, it is important to note that the scientific approaches to world politics are not ahistorical. There is a tradition of the use of historical materials and of the concept of time in studies of world politics. The interest of the scientific approaches is to use historical materials to develop and test generalizations about particular classes of events. Such classes of events might include the "use of violence by states," the "nature of alliance patterns," and "the perceptions held by policy makers." Such generalizations might include observations that in the twentieth century, the use of violence by states has remained relatively constant[37] and that in times of crisis, decision makers perceive fewer options available to their states.[38]

We can represent these kinds of assertions by the diagram given in Figure 1-5. Note that the scientific approach often attempts to draw conclusions about a particular type of event by drawing on different parts of the historical record. In addition, Figure 1-5 indicates the most common way in which any scientific approach "explains" some aspect of world politics. It hypothesizes (and often tests the hypothesis) that one particular class of events is related to another particular class of events. Changes in one class of events (the greater rigidity in alliances, for instance) are thought to produce changes in the other class of events (perhaps less

FIGURE 1-5   The Perspective of the Scientific Approaches

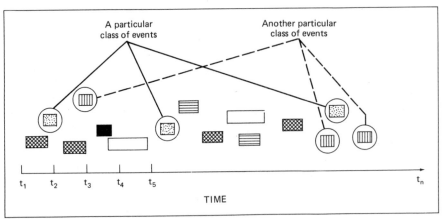

THE DESCRIPTIVE VIEW OF CLASSES OF EVENTS OVER TIME

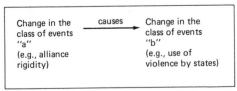

THE EXPLANATORY FRAMEWORK

[37]J. David Singer and Melvin Small, *The Wages of War, 1816–1965: A Statistical Handbook* (New York: John Wiley, 1972), p. 188.

[38]K.J. Holsti, "Perceptions of Time, Perceptions of Alternatives, and Patterns of Communication as Factors in Crisis Decision Making," *Peace Research Society Papers*, 3 (1965), 79–120.

use of violence by states). The test of that hypothesis may rely on information drawn from various parts of the historical record.

As I suggested earlier, each of these two main approaches may be a very powerful device for understanding world politics. Each has its own limitations. You, however, are reasonably well equipped with a variety of intellectual tools to confront world politics since the turn of the century and, more important, in your own lifetime. In the end, the best approach or approaches are those that give you the capacity to see more and to see more clearly. Obviously that is a matter for you to decide.

CHAPTER TWO

1900–1909_____
The first and last decade
of progress?

PART I:
DIPLOMATIC HISTORY[1]

Preparing for a new year and a new century, the editorial writers for *The New York Times* looked back over the past one hundred years. The nineteenth century, they noted, was born in the violence of the Napoleonic wars. In spite of such an unhappy beginning, all was ending well. The nineteenth century was a period "marked by greater progress in all that pertains to the material well-being and enlightenment of mankind than all the previous history of the race; and the political, social, and moral advancement has been hardly less striking." The new century promised "a still brighter dawn for human civilization."[2]

Such progress did not mean that conflict had been banished from world politics or that it should be. "Through agitation and conflict," argued *The New York Times*, "European nations are working toward an ultimate harmony of interests and purposes, and bringing awakened Asia into the sweeping current of progress." At some point "the kindly earth shall slumber, rapt in universal law." Until that time of harmony, states prepared for conflict; yet even here, the new century promised to keep conflict limited: "while armaments and defenses have

---

[1]For general treatments, see A.J.P. Taylor, *The Struggle for Mastery in Europe* (Oxford: Oxford University Press, 1954); René Albrecht-Carrié, *A Diplomatic History of Europe since the Congress of Vienna* (New York: Harper & Row, Pub., 1958); and Nazli Choucri and Robert North, *Nations in Conflict* (San Francisco: W.H. Freeman & Company Publishers, 1975). Several analyses of European politics focus on the causes of World War I, among which see Luigi Albertini, *The Origins of the War of 1914*, trans. and ed. Isabella Massey (London: Oxford University Press, 1952) and Sidney Bradshaw Fay, *The Origins of the World War* (New York: Macmillan, 1929).

[2]*The New York Times*, December 31, 1899, p. 20. © 1899 by The New York Times Company. Reprinted by permission.

been increased, they have become avowedly a means of preserving peace by deterring from war. . . .''

As the old century drew to a close, it appeared to reasonable men and women and to their political leaders that while no millenium was at hand, the more destructive methods of resolving conflicts had been relegated to museums. The world's nations had found ways to move "the kindly earth" closer to a world order based on peace and law. How realistic were such expectations?

Prologue to the Twentieth Century

In 1900 the inhabitants of the major states in Europe could look back upon a remarkable period of peace in Europe. Since 1871, with the end of a short war between France and Prussia, during which Prussia created a unified German state, there had been no war in Europe that had involved two major powers. To be sure, the thirty years of peace had seen numerous conflicts and threats of war between the major powers. No major power was exempt from the possibility of war. In each crisis, however, the states in conflict resolved the issues before hostilities took place.

While peace may have been preserved in the relations between the *major* powers, the same thirty years saw numerous wars and conflicts between lesser states, between major powers and lesser states, and between the major powers and non-Europeans who would suffer the last great wave of European imperialism. More than half of the years after 1871 would see the use of force in the European-Mediterranean area alone. Many other conflicts occurred in Latin America, Africa, and Asia. For those peoples who felt the violence, "peace" simply did not exist. The historical approach to world politics, however, usually concentrates on the major powers and draws conclusions about political relationships as if the major states were the only ones that mattered. This concentration is a result of the cultural bias of a European heritage and a reflection of the belief that major powers defined the nature of world politics (because they had the power), and other states and peoples were constrained by that fact to act in very limited ways. To say that peace characterized world politics in the last three decades of the nineteenth century is to make an accurate but incomplete statement.

Two Central Characteristics   *The creation and dissolution of alliances.*[3] Leaders of states felt that alliances with other states were essential for national survival. International conflicts constantly occurred, and one's opponent of the moment would probably be both powerful and aligned with other powerful states. Prudence dictated having similar friends. Alliances also seemed likely to prevent the outbreak of war, because no one could be sure that the gains reaped by war between alliances would outweigh the costs. The case of Germany illustrates this pattern of major-power diplomacy. Consider Germany's relations with Russia. Between 1871 and 1899, Germany and Russia were either aligned or worked with each other on four different occasions, and were neutral or hostile towards each other on four other occasions. In contrast to this pattern of alternating support and conflict, Germany and Austria became alliance partners in 1879 and

---

[3]For discussions of alliances during this period, see William Langer, *European Alliances and Alignments, 1871–1890*, 2nd ed. (New York: Knopf, 1962).

never disavowed the alliance (which would last until 1918). Such an alliance was neither inevitable nor without its tensions. Germany had decisively defeated Austria in a seven weeks' war in 1866. Moreover, the periodic German understandings with Russia were troublesome to the Austrians, because Russia and Austrian interests in the Balkans were often at odds.

You might also examine the question of alliance relationships by picking a particular year and determining who stood with Germany. In 1895, for instance, Germany had defensive alliances with Austria and Italy (The Triple Alliance), and collaborated with France and Russia on colonial matters. Only England was outside the network of states supporting (and receiving support from) Germany. Only five years earlier, Germany, in addition to the alliance with Austria and Italy, had a modest accommodation with England but stood estranged from Russia and France. This pattern of both relatively long-lasting relationships and some alternation of alliance partners and opponents is characteristic of most of the major states of the period—except for Great Britain, as we shall see.

Imperialism and colonial empires. Another major feature of the latter half of the nineteenth century was the expansion of European and American control and influence throughout the world.[4] Part of this expansion was imperialistic: the major powers established political control over peoples outside the territory of the major power. With the creation of colonies, the major power and its citizens determined to one degree or another the social, economic, and political practices of the society they dominated. Resistance was common, and most of the major powers participated in military campaigns of conquest and repression against the colonized.

Some weak states were able to fend off a would-be imperialist power, as the Ethiopians were able to do in the face of Italian imperialism. Other weak powers such as Persia were able to use the rivalry of two major powers (in this case Britain and Russia) to forestall colonization. Other weak states accepted the political control of a major power in return for autonomy in domestic affairs. In these protectorates, the weak state gave up its right to conduct foreign policy independent of that of the major power.

One step removed from colonial status was that of a "sphere of influence." A sphere of influence was a definition applied principally *by the major powers.* It designated a weak state that was expected to give greater weight to the political advice of a particular major power and to allow the citizens of that major power greater economic privileges within the sphere. Spheres of influence did not have the binding nature that colonialism had. A colony was created through force and was recognized by all major powers as "belonging" to the colonizers. Any attempt to change the situation without the consent of the colonizer usually meant war. A sphere of influence, on the other hand, could be contested by other major powers with less risk of war. The indigenous government also retained some capacity for determining who might exercise that influence. Some spheres of influ-

---

[4]For general discussions of imperialism and colonial empires see George Lichtheim, *Imperialism* (New York: Praeger, 1971); Raymond Betts, *Europe Overseas: Phases of Imperialism* (New York: Basic Books, 1963). Classic studies include V.I. Lenin, *Imperialism: The Highest Stage of Capitalism* (New York: International Publishers, 1939); Joseph Schumpeter, *Imperialism and Social Classes* (New York: Augustus Kelly, 1951); J.A. Hobson, *Imperialism*, 3rd ed. (London: Allen and Unwin, 1938); Grover Clark, *A Place in the Sun* (New York: Macmillan, 1937); and William Langer, *The Diplomacy of Imperialism* (New York: Knopf, 1951).

ence were long-standing—since the 1820s, for instance, the United States had proclaimed a sphere of influence in Latin America (Monroe Doctrine). How much actual control the major power exercised depended upon time and circumstance; American dominance in its Latin American sphere, for instance, decreased the further south one went.

The major powers of the late nineteenth century generally perceived colonies and spheres of influence as normal and necessary parts of world politics. They rationalized the exploitative aspects of imperialism as being part of "the white man's burden" to bring "civilization" to the "lesser races." Behind the moralism stood the presumed benefits of empire—a demonstration of prestige, capability, and commitment. Imperial powers were emulated; they were assumed to be great powers. Such prestige was a foreign policy resource, encouraging others to give way in conflict situations. The adage that "the sun never sets on the British empire" metaphorically reflects some of the clout the British government carried in the chancelleries of Europe. In terms of capabilities, colonies gave unqualified access to raw materials and to a market for manufactured goods; such access promoted an expanding economy within the ruling state. Colonies also necessitated the development of standing armies, navies, and merchant marines to protect and exploit the colonies, thereby enhancing the military status of the state. And finally, a colonial possession was a clear indication that a state had defined its national interests in a global way, that it was concerned with developments abroad, and that it would fight to protect its interests.

In an important way, political leaders defined colonies as a necessity for survival. Chapter 1 pointed out that there is no world government which can protect the individual states. They must look to their own capabilities to provide that security. But in an uncertain world, who is to say what kinds of capabilities in what amounts are sufficient to provide that security? Political leaders (and military men) must try to answer those questions in a discriminating fashion—their own budgets and resources are always limited. A government must work with some notion of what is sufficient. In 1900, colonial possessions were defined as part of the criteria for survival. A prudent statesman found it difficult to reject that definition of security, especially as other great powers appeared to have raised their flags on the mast of colonial expansion. And who would want to align with a state so deficient in power or will as one lacking that critical ingredient of power? Thus we would expect that the prevailing notions of what might help ensure survival would encourage states to pursue policies of colonial expansion in 1900 (or nuclear development in the 1970s and 1980s).

As citizens of the late twentieth century, we are likely to find these perceived needs for colonies as fallacious and foolish. How could men and women reasonably entertain such beliefs? Not all did. Some of the political elite saw little political gain in the scramble for colonial control. Many intellectuals saw the race for colonies as but a perpetuation of the exploitation of the working class by the capitalists. Most of the political elite and their supporters among the voters, however, saw colonial expansion in positive terms: prestige, capability, commitment. In many ways, those ideas are still important motivations for political leaders.

Colonialism had its acknowledged darker side as well. Exploitation by foreigners engenders protest and revolt. In June, 1900, for instance, nationalistic Chinese rose against Westerners who were rapidly dividing China into multiple

TABLE 2-1   Colonial Holdings

MAJOR POWERS	COLONIAL HOLDINGS PRIOR TO 1870 (SQUARE MILES)	COLONIAL HOLDINGS CREATED AFTER 1870 AND HELD IN 1900 (SQUARE MILES)	SPHERES OF INFLUENCE IN 1900
Great Britain	9,100,000	3,300,000	China, Persia
France	200,000	3,500,000	China
Russia*	6,200,000	900,000	China, Persia
Germany	0	1,000,000	China
Italy	0	200,000	
United States*	0	153,000	Latin America
Austria-Hungary*	0	0	
Turkey*	860,000	0	

*What constituted a colonial holding for these states is open to question. Their expansion was often contiguous to the state itself and imperialism would often lead to direct incorporation of the territory into the state. The American march to the West and the Russian march to the East have these characteristics.

Source: For colonial holdings of Great Britain, France, Germany, and Austria-Hungary, Nazli Choucri and Robert C. North, *Nations in Conflict* (San Francisco: W.H. Freeman, 1975), p. 37; for Turkey, *The Statesmen's Yearbook, 1899* (New York: Macmillan, 1899), pp. 1078–80.

spheres of influence. This so-called Boxer Rebellion was but one of many violent manifestations of emerging nationalism. Conflict between masters and subjects, however, did not attract the attention that the conflict between rival colonizers did. The fear that competing claims would lead to a major European war animated much of late nineteenth century diplomacy.

Although the creation of colonies and spheres of influence was a gradual process, the results were uneven. Table 2–1 indicates in a general way how well the imperial "race" had been going up to 1900. By the turn of the century, very little of the world was open to colonial expansion or the direct growth of major powers by annexation of adjacent territory. Indeed, once the long-standing spheres of influence have been excluded (principally the American sphere in Latin America and the European and Japanese spheres in China) there was not much left for colonization. Those who were behind in the race for empires were at an obvious disadvantage. Or, to put it differently, the world in 1900 had three major features: (1) what was left to colonize had acquired a number of rival claimants, (2) an *expansion* of the amount of land that might be colonized or annexed depended upon the *collapse of existing states or empires*, and (3) the jockeying for spheres of influence would intensify.

World Politics: 1900–1909

In 1900, Europe was the cockpit of world politics (see Map 3–1). What happened in many parts of the world depended upon what happened in Europe. To be sure, there were states outside of Europe that exercised some influence in the world arena. The American government had insisted on its policy of no European intervention in Latin America, confronting Britain in 1895 over the boundary between Venezuela and the British colony of Guiana, and in 1902, protesting a British, German, and Italian naval blockade of Venezuelan ports. In addition to protecting its sphere of influence, the United States became a colonial power in its own right. It defeated a weak Spain in a four-month war; by the treaty of Paris (December, 1898), Cuba became an American protectorate, and Puerto Rico, Guam, and the Philippines became American colonies.[5]

In the Pacific, the Japanese state began to emerge as a regional power. In 1894–1895, Japan defeated China in a six-month war. The peace treaty made Korea independent of China (and a sphere of Japanese influence) and ceded Formosa to the Japanese. Germany, Russia, and France blocked Japanese acquisition of any Chinese territory on the mainland. The European powers feared that a mutually destructive race to dismember China would result. They held no tender regard for the territorial integrity or political independence of China, however. Their preferred goals were to create their own spheres of influence. Some of the European states such as Russia had greater ambitions, though cloaked temporarily behind support for mutual spheres of influence. When the Boxers rose in revolt, Russia used the occasion to move troops into Manchuria; it seemed the first step in the absorption of another large territory into the Russian Empire.

Foreign Policy Interests of Britain and Germany   I indicated earlier that Britain did not fit the alliance pattern typical of the behavior of the other European states.[6] Historically, British governments had become active on the continent to prevent any one nation from establishing predominance. If that meant supporting one alliance in order to maintain a balance of power in Europe, its leaders did so. Otherwise, Britain studiously avoided permanent entangling alliances, resting its security on the English Channel, the Royal Navy, and the perennial conflicts that kept Europe divided.

At the turn of the century, British concerns did not center on the continent, but elsewhere. In the eastern Mediterranean, Britain controlled the Suez Canal, which linked England with its Asian empire, particularly India. In 1882, Britain had occupied Egypt in order to ensure that there would be no challenge to the canal and the maritime "lifeline" to the east. These colonial interests often forced Britain to consider temporary agreements with other states to protect its far-flung empire, for challenges to British imperial interests were never-ending. France and Britain had been on the verge of war over control of the Sudan (the Fashoda incident, 1898). British threats compelled France to give up its claim to the Sudan, but created enormous enmity for Britain. British attempts to dominate the Boer republics in South Africa led to friction with Germany, which intensified when warfare began between the Boers and the British government (1899–1902). German interests in China also clashed with British interests. Russia and Britain had a long-standing history of conflict over spheres of influence—China (Man-

---

[5]For descriptions of American policy, see Charles Campbell, *The Transformation of American Foreign Relations* (New York: Harper & Row, Pub., 1976); Ernest R. May, *American Imperialism* (New York: Atheneum, 1968); Frank Freidel, *The Splendid Little War* (Boston: Little, Brown, 1958).

[6]For British policy, see Kenneth Bourne, *The Foreign Policy of Victorian England, 1830–1902* (Oxford: Clarendon Press, 1970); C.J. Lowe and M.L. Dockrill, *The Mirage of Power* (London: Routledge & Kegan Paul, 1972); A.N. Porter, *The Origins of the South African War* (New York: St. Martin's Press, 1980).

churia), Afghanistan, and Persia were areas of relatively continuous diplomatic dueling.

Imperialist goals clearly threatened to embroil the British in conflict with other European powers, which might not remain localized in the colonial territories but escalate to hostilities between the European powers themselves. Alliances would be useful for the British in that circumstance. In addition, the British government feared that the French, Russians, and Germans would make common cause against them; such a combination could bring an end to English colonial expansion and might even force a withdrawal. The government could prevent such a coalition by reaching an agreement with one of the powers. If an alliance with one of the three were impossible, an agreement on colonial issues would at least help defuse the situation. Joseph Chamberlain, the British Colonial Secretary, took the lead in trying to secure some *rapprochement* or understanding with Britain's opponents. He tried to sound out the Russians and, after getting no response from the Tsar's government, turned to the Germans.

The German Kaiser, William II, had his own interests to pursue.[7] He had long envisioned a continental league of states, including Russia and France, two states allied with each other against Germany. To William, such a league would preserve the European peace. France would give up its desire for revenge against Germany for the Franco-Prussian war and its loss of the provinces of Alsace-Lorraine to the new German state. Russia would be constrained from challenging Austria-Hungary or Turkey. The former was an ally of Germany; the latter, a state with which Germany sought to cultivate friendly relations. Italy, a member of the Triple Alliance with Germany and Austria-Hungary, would complete the league. England did not fit easily into the Kaiser's grand design. England had no territorial interests *per se* on the continent, so there was no guarantee that Britain would be willing to use force to ensure the status quo. Moreover, the nature of the British military establishment made it an ally of dubious merit. Britain had invested its resources in a navy that was as strong as the combined navies of the next two most powerful states. As a consequence, it had a very small land army. What William needed was an ally with an army, for Germany's principal concern was a war against Russia and France. In addition to these deterrents, there was the German government's dislike of British aggression against the Boer republics.

Although he saw little reason to respond to the British, William felt that he could use their offer in his attempt to draw Russia into his league. He wrote to his cousin, Nicholas II, Tsar of Russia, in May, 1898; "Now I ask you, as my old and trusted friend, to tell me what you can offer me, and what you will do for me if I refuse the British offer."[8] Nicholas, however, was one step ahead of the Kaiser. "Three months ago," he replied, " . . . England handed us over a memorandum containing many *tempting* proposals trying to induce us to come to a full agreement upon *all the points* in which our interests collided with hers." Nicholas said that he had rejected the British offer, which he found to be so out of character

---

[7]For German policy, see Erich Brandenburg, *From Bismarck to the World War* (London: Oxford University Press, 1927).

[8]Quoted by Fay, *Origins*, Vol. 1, p. 131. Copyright 1928, 1930 by Macmillan Publishing Co., Inc., renewed 1956, 1958 by Sidney Bradshaw Fay.

''that I must say, we were quite amazed.''[9] He drew the conclusion that England was weak and sought to block Russia's imperialist goals through an agreement. The Kaiser reached similar conclusions.

Chamberlain pursued the possibility of an Anglo-German alliance over the next three years (1899–1901), often at odds with his own prime minister and foreign minister. Negotiations with the Germans did produce some agreements on specific colonial questions, but the alliance remained beyond the British grasp. The British proposals reinforced the German government's perception of British weakness and of its inability to defend its empire without help. The Russians had rejected British overtures; the Fashoda incident would keep the French hostile to the British. In time, the British would have to make a much better offer to Germany for its support. The Kaiser decided to wait.

Thus at the turn of the century, we find two divergent trends: British attempts to establish—for the first time in memory—a more intimate relationship with a continental power, and a German attempt to create a concert of continental powers to preserve the territorial status quo in Europe and keep peace. The Kaiser and his entourage were not acting out of altruism alone. Peace would help preserve the momentum of German economic development. France would have to drop any plans for a war of revenge against Germany and recovery of Alsace-Lorraine. As there was little or no room for the expansion of the German state on the Continent, the status quo would at least keep other states, such as Russia, with the potential for expansion from doing so. The league idea would give Germany relatively stable alliances, even with potentially hostile states. Moreover, to take the lead in creating such a league would allow Germany to define league goals and acceptable behaviors. The power to define an institution's characteristics usually translates into a power to dominate the institution.[10] Germany's ''grand design'' for Europe would not be at the expense of major German interests. On the other hand, it was not necessarily at the expense of the key interests of the other major powers.

Britain's search for an alliance upset the German calculations; it was not clear how Britain might fit into such a Europe. Britain's newness to the realm of continental politics compounded matters. It had its reputation as an ''outsider'' to overcome. Its statesmen were not schooled in the demands of ''entangling alliances'' and the bargaining that preceded and continued in such alliances. It had traditionally reserved for itself a maximum of flexibility in its dealings with other states. A desire for flexibility is the very antithesis of what states seek in creating alliances. The goal of an alliance is to bind a partner irrevocably to one's defense and to use the presence of an alliance partner to further one's own bargaining leverage. The very division in the British government on the issues of alliances, and with whom, did not encourage consistency in British policy or the rapid development of an understanding of how alliance politics differed from traditional British diplomacy.

---

[9]*Ibid.*, p. 132.

[10]One of the themes in Fritz Fischer's analysis is that Germany consistently sought hegemony in Europe. While this may be the case, it is not atypical of major-power behavior and certainly not characteristic of Germany alone. See his *Germany's Aims in the First World War* (New York: W.W. Norton & Co., Inc., 1961, 1967).

As we have seen, the change in the British approach to Europe had an impact on European perceptions of British policy. The Tsar saw British proposals as a trick to ensnare the Russians and to contain Russian expansionist policy. British behavior on colonial agreements reinforced these perceptions. In August, 1898, for instance, the Germans and British agreed to a division of the Portuguese colonial territories if Portugal defaulted on its loans from the two powers. The Germans then found the British arranging further loans to keep the Portuguese government solvent, thus preventing the division of territories, which Germany sought. The following year the British renewed their defensive alliance with Portugal, raising German suspicions that Britain had negotiated with Germany only to tie German hands but leave British flexibility unimpaired.

The Interests of the Other Major Powers[11]   At the turn of the century, the *Russian state* looked to the expansion of its empire into China. German power on its western frontier was held in check by the alliance with France. Traditional Russian interest in the Balkans and the Straits connecting the Black Sea to the Mediterranean were on the back burner. *Austria-Hungary*, on the other hand, could never take its eye off the Balkans. The Balkans had been part of the Turkish empire, but Turkish power was crumbling, leaving a number of small, weak, independent states and the possibility of more territory slipping out of Turkish control. The Austrians had been given political and military control over the Turkish provinces of Bosnia and Herzegovina (1878), although Turkey was still the legal sovereign. The expansion of Austrian control added more dissidents to the multinational empire of Austrians, Hungarians, Czechs, and other peoples.

Serbia was the principal weak power in the Balkans. Its leaders desired the creation of a "Greater Serbia," a state that would include the Serbs still under Turkish rule, those in Bosnia-Herzegovina under Austrian control, and those in the independent state of Montenegro. Such a goal was tailor-made for conflict with Austria-Hungary and Turkey. It also held enormous potential for conflict with Bulgaria and Greece. The overlapping of cultures and peoples in the Balkans was so great that any Serbian nationalism and a policy goal of a "Greater Serbia" was sure to collide with Bulgarian and Greek nationalism and their goals of expanding the territory of their states. Until 1903, the Serbian government maintained amicable relations with the Austrians and looked southward at Turkey as the area for building "Greater Serbia."

For the *French government*, domestic politics often overshadowed foreign policy. The French Third Republic had been rocked by the Dreyfus affair. Alfred Dreyfus had been falsely convicted of treason, and the French army protected the real culprits in order to protect the honor of the army. The effort to exonerate Dreyfus brought to the surface of French politics the unsettled issues of religion and support for republican government. Though distracted by the turmoil, French governments pursued a policy of colonial expansion and flirted with a *rapprochement* with Germany. It is hard to tell how important the recovery of Alsace-

[11]For the other states, see Hugh Seton-Watson, *The Decline of Imperial Russia 1855–1914* (New York: Praeger, 1952); Arthur May, *The Hapsburg Monarchy* (Cambridge: Harvard University Press, 1951); René Albrecht-Carrié, *France, Europe, and the Two World Wars* (New York: Harper & Row, Pub., 1961).

Lorraine was in French thinking. The military weakness of France encouraged the government to shy away from direct confrontations with Germany. No prominent French politician, however, dared abandon the idea of the recovery of the provinces.

The British Search for an Alliance   Unsuccessful in their search for an alliance with a European power, the British found the Japanese willing![12] Both states were worried about Russian expansion into China (the Russian army still occupied Manchuria). In addition, Japan wanted European recognition that Korea lay within its sphere of influence. Britain wanted to ensure that Japan, the major naval power in the western Pacific, would not threaten the extensive British commerce and colonial holdings in Asia. It was a marriage of convenience that held a moderate amount of risk for Britain. The alliance stipulated that if one partner became involved in war with another state, its ally would remain neutral. If, however, a *second* state entered the conflict, the alliance partner was obligated to declare war. A Russo-Japanese war would not involve Britain unless France (Russia's ally) declared war on Japan. Britain would then be expected to declare war on France and Russia, even though the cause of the war (such as conflicting colonial ambitions in China) might have had no relevance for British foreign policy goals. That was, and has always been, one of the penalties of an alliance: the potential that one's alliance partner can drag one into an unwanted war.

Treaties and agreements, however, are not self-executing. If a second state declared war on Japan, Britain would not mechanically enter the hostilities. Its government would need to make a set of decisions: to go to war, to mobilize and deploy British military forces, and to commence military operations against the enemy. A government may decide to renege on its commitments, but the governments of major powers are generally loath to do so. For one thing, the prestige and credibility of the state are damaged. An alliance with such a state becomes an unrewarding, even dangerous, relationship. Therefore, the offending state may find itself without allies and less able to ensure its own survival. Second, the failure to honor a commitment may lead to the weakening or defeat of one's former partner and the incorporation of the capabilities of that former partner into those of the victorious state. Such changes in capabilities may prove very threatening. Few leaders have accepted Lenin's aphorism that "treaties are like pie-crusts, made to be broken." On the other hand, because the refusal to honor treaty commitments carries such negative consequences, many treaties contain explicit escape clauses. For example, the second Strategic Arms Limitation Treaty (SALT II) between the United States and the Soviet Union stated, "Each party shall, in exercising its national sovereignty, have the right to withdraw from this treaty if it decides that extraordinary events related to the subject matter of this treaty have jeopardized its supreme interests."

Some governments will attempt to gain the best of all possible worlds, getting defensive commitments from others but offering little in return. Italy is a case in point. In June, 1902, Germany, Austria-Hungary, and Italy renewed

---

[12]See Ian Nish, *The Anglo-Japanese Alliance* (Westport, Conn.: Greenwood Press, 1966); and Malcolm Kennedy, *The Estrangement of Great Britain and Japan* (Berkeley: University of California Press, 1969).

their Triple Alliance for another six years. This alliance was defensive, obligating each partner to come to the aid of the others in case of war. Italy's main concern was protecting itself from France. The Italian government did not see much reason to become involved in a Franco-German war. It saw no reason to become involved in a war with Russia on behalf of its alliance partners. Indeed, the Triple Alliance seemed particularly confining for Italy. It prevented Italy from forcefully raising the issue of the Austrian Tyrol, which Italy claimed. German interests in cultivating good relations with Turkey hampered the ability of Italy to pursue its colonial ambitions in northern Africa (Tripoli and Cyrennaïca) which were parts of the Turkish empire. Italian colonial interests did collide with those of the French, and France was the main continental threat to Italy. Italy therefore entered negotiations *with the French*, pledging not to go to war against France even if France "as a result of a direct provocation" attacked Germany. Both pledged respect for their evolving colonial interests—France in Morocco, Italy in Tripoli/Cyrennaïca. All this came four months after the renewal of the Triple Alliance, which pledged an Italian declaration of war if France attacked Germany.

The German government faced a dilemma. Obviously Italy was not a partner to be trusted in a crisis; as the Kaiser noted, Germany had to "write this 'ally' off as smoke!"[13] However, an ally on paper was better than an ex-ally joining some rival alliance. Even a paper alliance reduced the likelihood of aggressive Italian moves to settle the border question with Austria-Hungary. The best one could do in the case of creeping defection from an alliance was not to speed up the process. And, as a reaction, Germany had to ensure the loyalty of its remaining alliance partner, Austria-Hungary.

The Anglo-Japanese alliance was, for the British government, a promising start, but Japan was far removed from the European cockpit and from the areas of British imperial interest in Africa and South Asia. The search for a continental ally continued, with France the only major state not yet approached.[14] This was a project personally favored by King Edward VII, who used his own charm and personal diplomacy to encourage the two governments to begin talks. From the tentative beginnings of an exchange of visits of the two heads of state in the summer of 1903, there emerged an agreement a year later (April 1904) between Britain and France settling all colonial issues. This "entente," or understanding, on colonial issues encouraged both parties to cooperate with each other in their bilateral relations.

Once again, Britain had taken a risk. It had defused French hostility that emerged during the Fashoda incident and had secured French acceptance of British domination of Egypt and the Sudan. Britain in return had recognized a French sphere of influence over Morocco—the first step in the creation of a French colony. And it was Morocco where German economic and political interests had staked a claim. Britain had coupled itself to French colonial goals. More important, Britain was "learning" that the obligation of an ally is *not to be flexible, but to be committed.* The British government now perceived that to preserve an un-

---

[13]Quoted by Fay, *Origins*, Vol. 1, p. 151.

[14]For the formation of the Entente, see George Monger, *The End of Isolation* (London: T. Nelson, 1963); Paul Rolo, *Entente Cordiale* (New York: St. Martin's Press, 1969); Samuel Williamson, Jr., *The Politics of Grand Strategy* (Cambridge: Harvard University Press, 1969).

derstanding or an alliance, one had to stand foursquare with one's partner on the issues that seemed unimportant to one's own immediate interests. But this was a case of overcompensation. The British government accepted the obligations of an alliance but failed to recognize that an alliance is beneficial *as long as the alliance partners exercised some restraint on each other.* Neither partner could allow the alliance to become a vehicle in the blind service of one state's immediate interests.

The First Moroccan Crisis[15] As you may have guessed, France and Germany did move into conflict over the status of Morocco. How that conflict emerged and resolved itself is instructive. Kaiser William told his ministers that Morocco was unimportant as long as there was an "open-door" policy. An "open door" meant that no one nation would have economic privileges at the expense of other nations. The term was popularized by the American Secretary of State, John Hay, when he tried to get the European states to accept the principle of the open door for China (1899).[16] Open-door policies were generally espoused by those who were politically or militarily weak in the particular area.

The Kaiser's ministers, however, feared Germany would be shut out of Morocco altogether. They were also puzzled by the Anglo-French entente, for it was out of character for the British and seemed fragile, given past Anglo-French hostility. The possibility of an alliance between France and Britain raised serious implications as well. French land power and British naval power might threaten German interests. French gravitation toward Britain would reduce French interest in belonging to a German-led federation. Conversely, the Anglo-French tie threatened to get Britain *into* the federation, but without Germany's stipulating the conditions. For these reasons, the advisors wanted the Kaiser to make an issue over Morocco in order to safeguard German economic interests *and to break the Anglo-French connection.* That it would break was expected: German experience with British diplomacy "proved" that Britain insisted on keeping its hands untied.

The Kaiser appeased his advisors with a compromise. Germany would not directly challenge the French, but would quietly try to prevent French control over Morocco by encouraging the Sultan of Morocco to reject French demands. That did not satisfy all the Kaiser's advisors. The German Chancellor (Prime Minister), Bernhard von Bulow, set out to force a more visible declaration of German interest. The Kaiser was sailing from Germany to Corfu in the Mediterranean. Von Bulow unofficially spread the word that the Kaiser would stop at Tangier on the Moroccan coast. He then persuaded an angry William to do so, in order not to have Germany and the Kaiser lose face now that the European press was reporting that the visit would occur. The Kaiser had a high regard for his own prestige. Moreover, for the Kaiser *not* to visit Tangier would be a clear signal to the French that Germany would not actively support even its economic interests in Morocco.

[15]For details, see Eugene Anderson, *The First Moroccan Crisis* (Chicago: University of Chicago Press, 1930).

[16]For American policy toward China, see Marilyn Young, *The Rhetoric of Empire* (Cambridge: Harvard University Press, 1968); Michael Hunt, *Frontier Defense and the Open Door* (New Haven: Yale University Press, 1973).

The Kaiser's dramatic landing and entry into Tangier in March, 1905, touched off the Moroccan crisis. The Kaiser reiterated German support for Morocco's independence and the open-door policy. The French government removed its foreign minister for bringing France so close to a war with Germany over Morocco. The French accepted a German proposal for an international conference on Morocco, and the French prime minister indicated to the German ambassador that unity between France and Germany was the cornerstone of peace in Europe. The Kaiser's ministers felt vindicated; a vivid display of Germany's interest preserved those interests and caused the French government to draw closer again to Germany.

Or did it? Was the entente between Britain and France broken? Both German and French behavior worried the British. For the Germans to acquire part of Morocco meant British control over the straits of Gibralter would be weakened. For the French to back away from the German challenge meant that Britain had an irresponsible ally capable of getting Britain into trouble. That the French were moving back toward the Germans made things worse, for Britain's sole European ally of any weight was seemingly drifting out of a budding alliance.

To counter the drift and bolster the French, the British government requested that the two states hold exploratory talks *about military preparations* that both should undertake in case of war with Germany. The entente of a year before stood on the verge of transforming itself into a defensive military alliance. Once again, the British were quickly learning the art of commitment. Although the French government refused to oppose the Germans, the military talks started in January, 1906, after the crisis had passed. British Foreign Minister Edward Grey avoided any formal guarantees to the French, but allowed the conversations to carry to the point that the British had developed plans to send an expeditionary force to the Continent in case of war between France and Germany. Thereupon, the British war minister began a major reorganization of the British army to ensure that it had the capability to deploy rapidly.

The German attempt to split the entente had, in the long run, actually solidified it. The development of joint military plans for the operation of British forces on the continent of Europe would create enormous pressures for seeing such plans as unavoidable commitments to France. Britain was becoming rigidly committed to France, in practice as well as in spirit. The target of the alliance was Germany. And the international conference on Morocco, held in 1906, generally confirmed French paramountcy in Morocco.

If the Kaiser's ministers were puzzled by the entente between France and Britain, the Tsar and his ministers were outraged. France, Russia's ally, had signed an agreement with Britain, a state which the Tsar had rejected as an ally and which challenged Russian interests in Asia. This anger was reinforced as Britain and Russia came close to war in October, 1904. Russia and Japan had gone to war in February, 1904, over the control of Korea and Manchuria (discussed below). Russia ordered its Baltic Sea fleet to the Pacific to cope with the Japanese navy. While steaming through the North Sea at night in October, 1904, the Russian commander ordered his ships to open fire on what he thought were Japanese torpedo boats. The Russians shot up a British fishing fleet. The British government deemed this an enormous provocation and ordered its navy to bring the Russian fleet to bay. The French stepped in to pacify the situation; the Russian fleet was allowed to continue (only to be sent to the bottom by the Japanese navy). Nonetheless, for the Russian government, the connection between France and England was dangerous, as was the tie between Japan and England. The Tsar needed a better alliance.

To that end, in late October, 1904, he entered negotiations with the Germans (who, you will recall, saw Russia as an integral part of their European league). Both sides accepted a provisional agreement to aid each other in case of an attack, but the negotiations stalled on the Russian insistence that France be consulted. The Tsar was not about to antagonize the French, his one existing alliance partner. The German prime minister, for his part, did not want to be consulting with France at the same time that he challenged France over Morocco.

The success of German policy in Morocco, the French government's movement toward Germany, and the unending series of military debacles the Russians suffered in the war with Japan encouraged the Kaiser to try once again to get the Russians into an alliance.[17] He met Nicholas at Bjorko in July, 1905, and the Kaiser found the Tsar had a similar perception of the state of the world. Both concluded that France no longer wanted to recover Alsace-Lorraine; otherwise, France would have risen to the challenge Germany had made in Morocco. "Our talk then turned on England," the Kaiser reported to Chancellor von Bulow, "and it very soon appeared that the Tsar feels a deep personal anger at England and the King."

> He called Edward VII the greatest "mischief-maker" and the most dangerous and deceptive intriguer in the world. I could only agree with him, adding that I especially had had to suffer from his intrigues in recent years. . . . He has a passion for plotting against every power, of making "a little agreement," whereupon the Tsar interrupted me, striking the table with his fist; "Well, I can only say he shall not get one from me and never in my life against Germany or you, my word of honor upon it!"[18]

William produced the provisional treaty of 1904 and Nicholas signed it. Russia and Germany pledged to defend each other in Europe. The continental league was taking shape. As William later graphically wrote the Tsar:

> The Dual Alliance between Russia and Germany combining with the Triple Alliance gives a quintuple alliance well able to hold all unruly neighbors in order to impose peace, even by force, if there should be a power hare-brained enough to wish to disturb it (i.e., England, from any agreement with whom France must be detached). Marianne [France] must remember that she is wedded to you [Russia] and that she is obliged to lie in bed with you and eventually to give a hug or kiss now and then to me [Germany], but not to sneak into the bedroom of the ever-intriguing *touche à tout* on the Island [Britain].[19]

---

[17]For the Bjorko agreement, see Bernard Oppel, "The Waning of a Traditional Alliance," *Central European History*, 5 (1972), 318–29.

[18]Quoted by Fay, *Origins*, pp. 173–74; William to von Bulow, July 25, 1905.

[19]Quoted by Albertini, *Origins*, Vol. 1, p. 160; William to Nicholas, July 27, 1905.

The Kaiser's words about enforcing the peace against "unruly neighbors" is not a reflection of his idiosyncracies. That particular image is one that is bound up with a league of nations such as the Kaiser sought to organize. Such a league uses its collective power not only to defend itself, but to force would-be trouble-makers into line before they could seriously endanger the peace.

The league died a quick death. The two monarchs did not reckon with the reactions of their respective ministers. Von Bulow was worried about the provisions of the agreement and probably angry that the Kaiser had conducted the negotiations without any advice from his ministers. Von Bulow threatened to resign, a threat that the Kaiser feared. Nicholas was told by his foreign minister that the agreement would rupture the existing Russian alliance with France and that France would not enter a multilateral alliance. France indeed refused, even though Germany made concessions on the agenda of the forthcoming conference on Morocco to demonstrate its interest in the inclusion of France.

Problems for Germany began to mount. Reports of Anglo-French military discussions reached Berlin, and the German ambassador questioned the British war minister. He denied that a military convention existed, said he knew of no informal talks, and asserted that "at any rate, no English officer has been authorized by the English government to prepare military arrangements with a French military person for the eventuality of war." "Magnificent lies!" the Kaiser raged.[20] The British disavowal reinforced William's image of Britain as the untrustworthy troublemaker. The minister's evasions (or lies, if you will) are not confined to the British diplomatic style. An old saying has it that a diplomat is someone who is sent abroad to lie for the good of his country. Diplomats do provide evasive answers from time to time. Indeed, one of the reasons the British took the indirect approach with the French was to give them the ability to deny that anything *official* had been done, and, presumably, if a crisis loomed over the issue, to be able to disavow the talks and the planning as not being government policy. Most states, however, avoid the repeated use of lies as a diplomatic practice because of the enormous hostility it can create, as well as the enormous damage it can do to the credibility and prestige of the state.

William's suspicions of British deceit and skill increased in August, 1907, when Russia and Britain announced an agreement settling their conflicts in Asia.[21] Just two years earlier, the Tsar had pledged that Britain would not get "a little agreement" from him. How is it that the two rivals had struck a bargain? Britain had used the French alliance with Russia as its entrée to St. Petersburg. Britain was still shopping for continental friends and agreements to protect its colonial empire. The Russian Foreign Minister, Aleksandr Izvolsky (in office since May, 1906), also desired an understanding between Russia and Britain.

Izvolsky was an adventurous foreign minister. After Russia's defeat by the Japanese and the collapse of its expansion into China, he turned his attention to

---

[20]Quoted by Fay, *Origins*, Vol. 1, pp. 212–13. Cable of January 31, 1907. After the war, the German government published the diplomatic documents using the cable texts that had the Kaiser's comments. One version in English is *Outbreak of the World War: German Documents Collected by Karl Kautsky* (New York: Oxford University Press, 1924).

[21]On the Anglo-Russian accord, see Rogers Churchill, *The Anglo-Russian Convention of 1907* (Cedar Rapids, Iowa: Torch Press, 1939).

the Balkans and Turkey. Russia was too weak militarily and politically (having been wracked by an unsuccessful revolution in 1905) to take what it wanted. It had to rely on diplomacy and a powerful coalition supporting its interests. The Japanese had to be held in check in the Pacific while Russia looked westward; the British alliance with Japan might accomplish that if Britain and Russia were allies. The Turks had to be persuaded to meet Russian demands; the British had traditionally supported the Turks and now needed to be bought off. The Tsar and the Russian military were generally opposed to the turn toward England. They disliked the terms of the agreement that Izvolsky negotiated with the British. In the end, the Tsar gave in, and the two states settled the status of Tibet, Afghanistan, and Persia, the recurring causes of friction between them.

Security Fears in Europe   The Tsar told the Kaiser that the Anglo-Russian agreement was not directed at Germany. The German government publicly accepted this interpretation. Privately, there began a gnawing fear that Germany was being encircled by a hostile coalition. A German-led federation of European states now seemed out of the picture for the future. The issue for Germany seemed to be more the survival of the German state itself. It was to become a very corrosive fear.

To keep that fear in check and to provide for the security of the state, governments have relied on armaments and organized military establishments. These obviously form the basis for the defense of the state, but their possession constitutes a potential threat to others, and thus may degrade the possessor's own security. Security, however, is more than a matter of the presence of armaments. It is also a matter of relative strength. In general terms, prudent leaders would prefer to be numerically stronger than their opponents. Such an ideal situation is usually not obtainable in full measure because of resource limitations (such as limited manpower, technology, or tax revenues to divert to military purposes), engrained habits of thinking (such as an inability to conceive of using women in industry to replace men who could then be drafted into the armed forces), and preferred military doctrines (such as the British emphasis on sea power at the expense of its army).

In general, we might say that statesmen have four policy choices they can make regarding military power[22]: (1) They can accept *inferiority* and seek protection through neutrality or alliance. (2) They can seek *parity* with a potential opponent and secure a margin of safety by means of alliances with others. (3) They can seek *superiority*, thus having the margin of safety in their own hands. (4) Finally, they can seek *sufficiency*, which is a point between inferiority and parity such that the state, while it cannot win a war, has sufficient power in concert with others to prevent an opponent from winning. As you might imagine, determining just what is "sufficient" is an imprecise art. Without confidence in the yardstick to determine sufficiency, leaders often either accept inferiority or grimly push for parity.

---

[22]For contemporary discussions of parity, superiority, and sufficiency, see Robert Jervis, "Why Nuclear Superiority Doesn't Matter," *Political Science Quarterly*, 94 (Winter 1979–80), 617–33; and Alain Enthoven and Wayne Smith, *How Much is Enough?* (New York: Harper & Row, Pub., 1972).

In addition to domestic economic or political restraints, a government faces two other factors that make security decisions difficult. First, security involves a *relationship* with others. The actions of others affect the choices one makes and the consequences of those choices. For instance, if the British chose a policy of naval supremacy and Germany adopted a policy of naval parity with Britain, the two states would find themselves in an energetic arms race, the British making a stream of decisions to stay ahead of the Germans, the Germans making a stream of decisions to catch up.

The second obstacle to easy security decisions concerns the application of technology to warfare.[23] The industrial revolution of the nineteenth century was a revolution in the application of capital, labor, management, and technology to production. The revolution made change a permanent feature of economic life. Technology held the promise to make certain kinds of weapons or military formations more powerful. A large army with rifles could now be held off by a smaller army equipped with machine guns as well as rifles. One might gain parity or superiority through a *qualitative shift* in use of technology. Technology also raises troubling questions of how one state's power could be compared to another's. For instance, in 1905, the British began the construction of a new type of battleship, called the *Dreadnought*. Was one Dreadnought worth three, five, fifty of the older kinds of battleships? Would an even faster but less well-armored ship be equal to a Dreadnought?

The revolution in armaments which technology made possible increased fears for the security of the state. It took only a few years to construct the first Dreadnought, threatening to give Britain a naval superiority that could never be challenged. But technology also held other unexpected problems. A state had to produce new weapons in order to acquire the benefits of technology, yet that very production created a bind. To produce quantities of today's weapons always carried the possibility of being stuck with a pile of obsolete weapons by tomorrow's standards. Not to produce raised the likelihood of inferiority in the face of a state that chose to produce those weapons. Thus, there was an incentive to defer the application of today's technology but to mimic the decisions of others closely.

Technology was also very unsettling because it showed the most wanton disregard for national borders. Technological secrets were impossible to keep, as the advances of science were generally open to any nation with the capital and trained manpower. The implication was paradoxical: a state could achieve a short-term advantage from the application of technology to military capability. But in the "long run" (five years or less!), the application would be common among the great powers. And, ironically, the state that pursued a policy of superiority could find that its superiority vanished overnight when it introduced a new weapons system. The Dreadnought did this for Britain. Both Britain and Germany started at much the same position in the race to construct the new battleships; all Germany needed to do would have been to match British construction to maintain naval parity. Of course, the enormous British superiority of older

---

[23]For a discussion of technology and war, see Bernard Brodie and Fawn Brodie, *From Crossbow to H-Bomb*, rev. ed. (Bloomington: Indiana University Press, 1973). For a prophetic view, see I.S. Bloch, *The Future of War in Its Technical, Economic, and Political Relations* (New York: Doubleday & Mc-Clure, 1899).

ships remained, but an older ship was not the equal of a Dreadnought. Thus, British Dreadnoughts made Britain's own extant fleet obsolete.

We can well imagine that leaders and others sought a way to make the complexities of security more manageable. One such mechanism would be an arms control agreement, or at least some ceiling on numbers of arms. The ability to take those first steps might lead to subsequent steps on dealing with technology or even reducing the number of arms in each nation's inventory. President Theodore Roosevelt had called for a peace conference in October, 1904, to discuss, among other things, armaments. It was finally held in the summer of 1907 at the Hague.[24] The British, then holding the edge in Dreadnoughts, sought an agreement that would have ensured British superiority. The Germans, determined to achieve sufficiency if not parity, blocked all proposals on arms limitations. British proposals were, in German eyes, in keeping with the intrigue against Germany.

The German navy was a central British concern.[25] The German leadership recognized it to be such, and took great pains to point out that the size of the German navy (built and building) was not great enough to challenge Britain. Moreover, Germany had no desire to challenge Britain on the issue. Indeed, the Kaiser and von Bulow recognized that, in building the fleet, which was provocative to the British, they must get "through the next few years with patience, avoiding incidents, and giving no obvious reason for annoyance."[26] Ultimately, however, the Kaiser expected his fleet to be translatable into bargaining power vis-à-vis the British.

The German naval program was quite visible; the government submitted legislation to the German parliament for the construction of certain numbers and types of vessels. British ship-building went through a similar public process. The activity of one side spurred the activity of the other. In 1908, a new German Navy Law established a construction rate of four Dreadnoughts a year between 1908 and 1911, and two a year for the period 1912–1917. The nationalist press in Britain and those political leaders wanting expanded British naval construction called the German decision tantamount to a declaration of war. From their perspective, the Germans needed no such large navy. Britain had no hostile intentions and Germany had no far-flung empire to protect. The British Parliament voted to build four ships a year and four more if the German program continued. The Kaiser now came under pressure from his foreign ministry to *scale down* the German program because it was too costly and provocative. William protested that ". . . if they want war, let them begin it; we are not afraid of it."[27]

The Kaiser's truculent mood was not matched by his civilian ministers. In early 1909, Chancellor von Bulow considered the possibility of an agreement

[24]For a partial examination of the Hague conference, see A.J. Morris, "The English Radicals' Campaign for Disarmament and the Hague Conference of 1907," *The Journal of Modern History*, 43 (September 1971), 367–93.

[25]On the Anglo-German naval race, see Jonathan Steinberg, *Yesterday's Deterrent* (New York: Macmillan, 1966); and Arthur Marder, *From the Dreadnought to Scapa Flow* (New York: Oxford University Press, 1961).

[26]Von Bulow to William, December 26, 1904; *German Diplomatic Documents, 1871–1914*, trans. E.T. Dugdale (New York: Harper & Row, Pub., 1930), Vol. 3, p. 213.

[27]Comments on cable from Metternich to von Bulow, July 16, 1908; *ibid.*, pp. 288–89.

with Britain that would reduce the German naval program in return for British *political concessions*. He thought that the transfer of British colonies to Germany and a pledge of British neutrality in case of a continental war would be a suitable quid pro quo. The German naval chief, Admiral Tirpitz, threatened to resign if von Bulow pushed the program. Von Bulow backed away, but continued to urge a slowdown of naval construction. He resigned in June, 1909, but the new Chancellor, Theobald von Bethmann-Hollweg, also made it a point to push for some accommodation with Britain on the subject of naval arms limitations. He, like von Bulow, saw peace in Europe as a central goal of German foreign policy. The talks concerning naval arms limitations continued fitfully into the next decade.

Crisis in the Balkans[28]   After 1903, a new Serbian king emphasized the nationalist dream of a Greater Serbia and began to reorient Serbia toward Russia. Austria-Hungary, its southward expansion hampered by the presence of Serbia and concerned that Serbian nationalism might disrupt its restless multinational empire, began to conclude that Serbia had to be destroyed or the Serbian regime converted into one responsive to Austrian interests. Austria-Hungary had, for instance, instituted a trade embargo on Serbia to bring pressure on the regime. This is not unusual; most major powers have insisted that small states on their borders not challenge the interests of the larger state. In the early 1960s, for instance, the United States tried to remove Fidel Castro of Cuba by indirect means (and failed); it was more successful in changing the regime in the Dominican Republic (1965), as were the Soviets in Czechoslovakia (1968). In all cases, the larger power saw the weaker as a threat to its vital interests.

To this evolution of Balkan politics we now add Russia's renewed interest in the region following the settlement of the Russo-Japanese war in 1905. Foreign Minister Izvolsky decided to raise the issue of the Straits (the Bosphorus and Dardanelles) that separate the Black Sea from the Mediterranean. An international treaty among the great powers closed the straits to all warships during peacetime, preventing redeployment of Russia's Black Sea fleet to European waters to make up for the crippling losses at the hands of the Japanese. The more fundamental issue was who would control the Straits. The territory was Turkish, and for Russia a weak Turkey was better than a strong foreign power. It was not as good, however, as direct Russian control. Izvolsky dusted off existing plans to seize the waterway, but the other ministers objected that Russia could not become engaged in a war so soon after the war with Japan.

Izvolsky sounded the British out on their willingness to revise the Straits agreement to allow the passage of Russian warships. The British government neither wanted to revise the treaty nor to alienate the Russians, now a potential ally. It therefore used the common ploy of saying that all the other signatories had to be consulted first; the hope was that *others* would object, deflecting Russian anger from Britain. Izvolsky travelled to Vienna. Austria-Hungary agreed, but wanted in return to annex Bosnia and Herzegovina. That would alienate the Serbs, who saw the provinces as part of Greater Serbia. Izvolsky felt the Serbs could be propitiated; he therefore accepted the proposal in September, 1908, and went on to

---

[28]See Bernadotte Schmitt, *The Annexation of Bosnia* (New York: Howard Fertig, 1970).

Rome and Berlin. He got their agreement in principle to a revision of the Straits treaty; Italy and Germany were to be compensated later in a similar manner to Austria.

While on the way to Paris, Izvolsky learned that the Austrians had announced the annexation of Bosnia and Herzegovina. They had what they wanted, while Russia was still trying to get the major powers to agree in principle to what it wanted. Izvolsky accused the Austrians of treachery. The Serbs were incensed as well, but willing to allow the Austrian *fait accompli* to stand if Serbia were given compensation. Equally angered was the Kaiser. The Austrians had not warned him in advance, yet they had acted under the protection of German military power. If Russia chose to contest the annexation, Germany would be dragged into war. Even without war, German relations with Russia and Britain were bound to be damaged, for both were likely to regard Germany as the instigator of the Austrian action. This is one of the liabilities of being the ally of a weaker state; the first assumption made by others is that the weaker state only acts on the directive, or with the blessing, of the stronger. The annexation also threatened German relations with the Turks, whose territory irrevocably passed into the Austrian empire. The Kaiser decided to let the Austrians get out of the crisis alone.

Once again, however, Chancellor von Bulow stepped in. Germany, he told the Kaiser, had no choice but to stand behind its alliance partner. Austria-Hungary was the only loyal major power ally Germany had. Italy was an ally in name only. Russia had an ally in France and a growing relationship with Britain. German security interests were at stake. The Kaiser gave in: Germany would rescue the Austrians. Germany demanded great-power approval of the Austrian annexation. Gone were the days of attempting to fashion a comprehensive settlement that would have knit Europe closer together. Time was critical, because the Austrian government was now looking for a way to go to war against Serbia in order to decide the future of the Balkans. Both states had mobilized forces, and the Serbs seemed to be of a mind to initiate hostilities, perhaps with the intention of forcing Russia to support them.

.   The Russians insisted on a conference to deal with all the issues. Von Bulow told the Russians in March, 1909, to either accept the German solution or Germany would "let things take their course." It was an ultimatum, but the Russians felt themselves too weak to "let things take their course." They accepted the Austrian annexation, and the other powers fell in line. Russia and the other powers coerced the Serbs into accepting the solution. Izvolsky told the Serbs to wait; their day would come, and at that time a strong Russia would be at their side.

The Balkan crisis of 1908–1909 was a trial run for a more momentous Austro-Serbian confrontation five years later. This first crisis had helped push Russia into closer ties with the British and led to an extensive reorganization of Russian armed forces. It created an expectation in St. Petersburg that, at some point, there would be a major confrontation between the Slavic and Germanic states. The Austrians, rewarded by success, concluded that they now had the handle on the Serbs, on the Russians, and most important, on their ally, the Germans. The Kaiser had committed himself to supporting a reckless ally even on issues of minimal concern to the German state. It was an open question whether "through agitation and conflict European nations are working toward an ultimate harmony of interests and purposes,'' as *The New York Times* editorial had proclaimed ten years before.

PART II:
SCIENTIFIC APPROACHES TO WORLD POLITICS

Systems Approach

Power in 1900   We start with the proposition that politics among nations rests on a never-ending concern for who has the capability to hurt the interests of the state. We assume that the predominant patterns of world politics are the responses of major states to ensure their survival. We expect those patterns to be responsive to the way power (and hence the source of threats to survival) is distributed among the states of the world.

If you were alive in 1900 and were asked to identify the distribution of power in the world, how would you perform the analysis? Would you begin by counting the number of men in each state's armed forces or battleships in the navy? The amount of grain harvested that year? The popular support enjoyed by the government? All these ways of assessing power are reasonable. Power clearly is not just military capability, although that obviously plays a major role. It includes economic factors (such as the productiveness of the economy and the generation of capital), access to resources, a skilled and unified population, a high level of technology, and so forth.[29] Generally, we might define power as the ability to harm, hinder, or help the interests of other states. The ability to place an embargo on trade with other states, for instance, reflects an economic capacity to hurt, while a higher tariff might hinder, and granting foreign aid might help. Recall, however, that having the capacity to do something does not necessarily mean that a state will use such capabilities or that they will be employed successfully. What it does mean is that those with such capabilities do constitute a potential threat to the well-being of other states.

Once we have identified the ingredients of power we think important, we need to devise some way of measuring a state's power. How powerful is Germany? Much work in political science has gone into constructing such yardsticks; many aspire to a precise quantitative measure.[30] What might you count? Military manpower, battleships, tons of grain? Governmental tax revenues, number of patents issued, energy reserves? The list is long. I have settled on three that I believe provide a succinct overall measure of power in 1900: crude steel production, population, and political stability. *Crude steel production* represents the pres-

[29]For a discussion of the elements of national power, see Hans Morgenthau, *Politics Among Nations*, 3rd ed. (New York: Knopf, 1964), pp. 110–48.

[30]There is an extensive literature about measuring "power," although much of it stresses the military component. See, among others, Wayne Ferris, *The Power Capabilities of Nation-States* (Lexington, Mass.: Lexington Books, 1973); Klaus Knorr, *Military Power and Potential* (Lexington, Mass.: Heath, 1970); Klaus P. Heiss, Klaus Knorr, and Oskar Morgenstern, *Long Term Projections of Power* (Cambridge: Ballinger, 1973); and Melvin Small and J. David Singer, "The Diplomatic Importance of States," *World Politics*, 25 (July 1973), 577–99.

ence of a modern economy capable of organizing capital, resources, and labor and utilizing the product. It signals an advanced technology and the ability to equip a modern military establishment. It depends upon continuing access to critical raw materials such as iron ore and coal. *Population* is the pool of individuals available for a state's armed forces and forms the domestic marketplace for the economy. *Political stability* allows the central government to mobilize resources and population and direct them into the arena of world politics.

I want to form some composite estimate of the *relative* power of the states in 1900. How powerful was Germany compared to France? The Triple Alliance of Germany, Austria-Hungary, and Italy to the Triple Entente of Britain, Russia, and France? To make these kinds of comparisons, I identified the percentage of the world's total population and steel production that a state has. Thus, in 1900, Germany produced 23 percent of the world's crude steel. It had 5 percent of the world's population. How does political stability enter the picture? Political stability affects the power that population provides. A large population and a politically unstable society provide very little power. Governments cannot mobilize the society effectively in the pursuit of foreign policy goals: indeed, they often must devote their resources and attention to maintaining domestic control. To express this connection between population and political stability, I first devised an estimate of the degree of political stability in the state over the last ten years (see Table 2-2). I then multiplied this "stability score" by the state's percentage of world population. For instance, China in 1900 had approximately 40 percent of the world's population, but an unstable political system (scored as .2). Therefore, the contribution of population to Chinese power is equal to 8 percent.

The power of any state can therefore be determined as follows:

$$\text{power} = \frac{\begin{array}{c}\text{percent of}\\\text{world's}\\\text{steel}\\\text{production}\end{array} + \left(\begin{array}{c}\text{political}\\\text{stability}\\\text{score}\end{array} \times \begin{array}{c}\text{percent of}\\\text{world's}\\\text{population}\end{array}\right)}{2}$$

The division by two allows the power score to fit the range of 0 to 100 percent. Normally, therefore, the power of all states will total 100 percent; however, because of the effect of political stability, in practice, the power of all states will be less.

TABLE 2-2   Political Stability

CONDITION	POLITICAL STABILITY SCORE
1. State in civil war, anarchy	0
2. Several major uprisings; coups; major deterioration of governmental authority	.2
3. Major uprising; coup; assorted lesser outbreaks	.4
4. General strike; agitation or tension in the political system; government paralysis	.6
5. Agitation; recurring changes in incumbents	.8
6. No real challenges	1.0

TABLE 2-3 Basic Power Levels in 1900

MEASURE	WORLD	US	UK	RUSSIA	FRANCE	GERMANY	AUSTRIA-HUNGARY	ITALY	BELGIUM	JAPAN	CHINA
1. Million metric tons of crude steel	27.7	10.2	4.9	2.2	1.54	6.4	1.1	.1	.6		
2. Percent of world steel		37%	18%	8%	6%	23%	4%	0%	2%	0%	0%
3. Million inhabitants in independent states	1024	76	40	136	39	46	42	30	6	41	403
4. Percent of world population in independent states		7%	4%	13%	4%	4%	4%	3%	1%	4%	39%
5. Political stability in past decade		.8	1.0	.6	.6	1.0	.6	.4	.6	1.0	.2
Power*		21	11	8	4	14	3	1	1	2	4

*Power $= \dfrac{\#2 + (\#5 \times \#4)}{2}$

Sources: For steel, Duncan Burn, *The Steel Industry, 1939–1959* (Cambridge: Cambridge University Press, 1961), Table 105; for population, *World Almanac 1901* (New York: Press Publishing Co., 1901), p. 363; for political stability, William L. Langer, *An Encyclopedia of World History*, rev. ed. (Boston: Houghton Mifflin, 1948).

With this method, we can turn to the "real world" of 1900 and measure state power. Table 2–3 identifies the major powers of the approximately 50 independent states in the international system. The United States is the most powerful state, followed by Germany, Britain, Russia, France, China, Austria-Hungary, and Japan. Obviously, power was not evenly distributed (except among a large number of powerless states).

Three non-European states have power that is in the same league with the European major powers: the United States, China, and Japan. Does this make them major figures of world politics during the first decade of the twentieth century? We would expect not. At this time, world politics is the politics of *Europe* and European states. This is true both historically and because the main arena of power is in Europe where approximately 50 percent of the world's power is concentrated. No other region comes close, although North America clearly constitutes a secondary arena. Therefore, to have a direct impact, American or Chinese or Japanese power must "reach Europe."

To ask what power these states had in world politics is to ask about their *projectable power*.[31] I estimated projectable power in terms of the *days* it took to transport war material (i.e., the capability to hurt) from the state to the arena of world politics. For the United States, in 1900, it took approximately six days to cross the Atlantic by ship.[32] Therefore,

$$\text{projectable power} = \frac{\text{power}}{\text{days needed to deploy power}}$$

The projectable power of the United States is on the order of four; its capacity to influence world politics in 1900 would be at the level of an actor like France and Austria-Hungary. Of course, European states suffered this erosion of power the further they went from the European "cockpit" of world politics.

Figure 2–1 depicts the distribution of power in world politics at the turn of the century. The size of the circles represents the power of each state. I will call this particular distribution a "ladder-like" system. The question we now need to wrestle with is, What particular patterns of world politics emerged as a consequence of this particular distribution of power?

Identifying Systemic Patterns   I must confess to you that not much work has been done on the identification of the patterns of behavior in such a system. Political scientists have traditionally described the period as being one with a "balance of power." A "balance of power" system usually means that each of the major states of the system has relatively equal amounts of power. (Rival alliances are likely to be in balance as well.) Political scientists have developed extensive analyses of the patterns of behavior typical of such a "balance of power" system.[33] They do not seem appropriate here.

[31]For an interesting discussion (and argument about differing abilities to project power), see Albert Wohlstetter, "Illusions of Distance," *Foreign Affairs*, 46 (January 1968), 242–55.

[32]For speed of transportation, see W.S. Woytinsky and E.S. Woytinsky, *World Commerce and Governments* (New York: Twentieth Century Fund, 1955), p. 308.

[33]See in particular Morton Kaplan, *System and Process in World Politics* (New York: John Wiley, 1957); M. Kaplan, *Towards Professionalism in International Theory: Macrosystem Analysis* (New York: Free Press, 1979); see also Raymond Aron, *Peace and War* (New York: Praeger, 1968) and Kenneth Waltz, *The Theory of International Politics* (Reading, Mass.: Addison-Wesley, 1979).

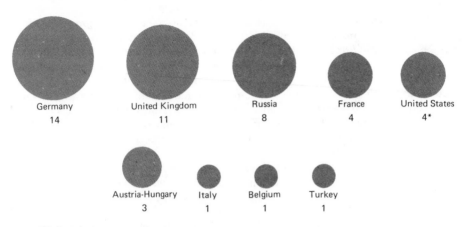

*Projected power

FIGURE 2-1   **Power Distribution in 1900**

Therefore, it is up to us to hypothesize likely patterns of behavior. How might we do so? If you think about it, there are three general methods you might use to generate hypotheses: analogy, logic, and example.[34] In Chapter 1, I used the analogy of the classroom to generate hypotheses about behavior in a system in which one actor monopolizes power. Are there similar situations outside of world politics that display a configuration of power similar to the ladder-like system? If there are, then we might hypothesize that their common patterns of behavior may be found in world politics. The drawback with analogies is that we can never be sure how apt the analogy is. For instance, to what degree can the classroom and the international system be treated as the same type of phenomenon?

Alternatively, we might seek hypotheses through logic or reasoned argumentation. We begin with a set of givens and assumptions. For instance, we have as a given this particular distribution of power. We assume that the major actors all have a strong interest in security. We derive a reasoned set of patterns that would meet that security objective in light of the constraints set by the power distribution. This method forces us to be clear in our assumptions about how and why states behave as they do. It allows us to articulate what seem to be the best strategies for attaining the security goal. On the other hand, it may have no connection with how states really behave, or it may confine our thinking to our own, ingrained perspectives.

Finally, we might take the example of the historical record contained in Part I of this chapter. We would hypothesize that the events of the years 1900–1909 are in fact the patterned behavior that results from the ladder-like distribution of power. One major drawback of the "example" approach is that we cannot be sure whether we have *patterns* of behavior. We do have behavior, but it may be difficult to determine in a ten-year period whether it happens repeatedly enough to establish a pattern. The Kaiser's attempt to build Russia and France into a co-

---

[34]There are two other major methods of hypothesis construction: the use of existing theory to derive hypotheses and the use of experimentation. Both are considered in a later chapter.

alition while excluding Britain did seem to happen often enough for me to call it a pattern, but you may be less convinced. Second, we cannot be sure if the pattern is the *result of the distribution of power* among the states or the result of other factors (such as Britain's insular position, the reputed impetuousness of the Kaiser, or the French desire for revenge against Germany). You will recall that this is a question of the *boundary* between the international system and nonsystemic factors. And third, if we use the events of the decade to form the hypothesis, we really cannot turn around and say that those same events prove the hypothesis. We would have to look for other decades with similar distributions of power, and they may not be all that prevalent.

Each approach has its limitations, none of which is particularly crippling at this point. I say that because of our particular goals: we are trying to hypothesize the consequences of a particular distribution of power. A hypothesis is a guess or hunch about the world. In particular, it is a guess about the relationship that may exist between two or more different factors. In our case, one factor is the distribution of power; the other, patterns of behavior. A hypothesis may be true or false, but we do not know which at the start of our inquiry. Thus any method that gives us a "reasonable" hunch about a relationship should be used. In a subsequent chapter, I will discuss the testing of hypotheses when we are concerned about truth and falsity.

I discuss below some of my hypothesized consequences of a ladder-like distribution of power. Before you read mine, you ought to stop *now* and devise some hypothesized patterns of your own. You have the historical material available in the first part of this chapter. As to analogies, could the distribution of power be like that of a company (owner, manager, foreman, worker) or that of a family (father, mother, children by age)? What patterns emerge in those circumstances? For logic, ask yourself, "If I were the leader of country X, what would I do in this situation?" Try your hand at the analysis now. This is much of what political scientists try to do as a matter of course. It is the first step in a systematic inquiry on any subject in the political realm.

Patterns of Behavior in a Ladder-like System   As you probably noticed, the patterns may vary, depending upon the states you considered. Weaker major actors will probably display different patterns of behavior than the stronger. Therefore, we are likely to come up with a diverse set of statements. (One of the reasons political scientists have focused on a "balance of power" system is because of the neatness of the description. If all major actors were relatively equal in power, each should behave similarly.)

What patterns might prevail? I have used logic and historical examples in the following analysis. Suppose power is distributed in the following ideal way:

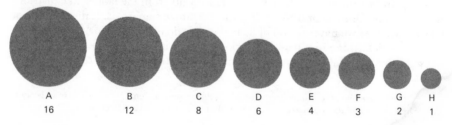

A	B	C	D	E	F	G	H
16	12	8	6	4	3	2	1

I have used letters to designate the states because it should not matter which state is Germany or France. States respond to power distributions, according to this approach. Put yourself in A's position. Who has the power to hurt A? No single state is more powerful. Does B pose a threat? One rule of thumb in military conflict is that when power is balanced, victory in war will depend on such things as luck, leadership, and striking first, but defeat is as likely as victory. From a survival standpoint, B's power is worrisome rather than threatening. Beyond B, the other states are too weak to form any kind of individual threat.

A threat to the survival of A would emerge if the other states formed an alliance. In the hypothetical system, the coalition would have a power of 36, more than twice A's power, greatly increasing the odds of victory for the coalition in a power confrontation. Logically, A might deal with this threat in four ways: (1) by increasing its own power, (2) by organizing a league of states, (3) by aligning with B, or (4) by fracturing the alliances of others. The first pattern is one we would expect of all states. The increase of power might be accomplished internally (such as by weapons innovation with the Dreadnought) or externally (the acquisition of new territory or resources through imperialism or conquest, for instance). For most states, however, "self-help" schemes alone are not likely to provide security. State A must prevent a coalition of opponents from emerging. A league of states organized by A would allow A to gain a measure of control over the policy of each member state and thereby enhance its security., Historically, we find Germany attempting to do just that. Failing to hold Russia or France, Germany became more dependent upon the weak states it had attracted—Austria-Hungary and Italy. On the other hand, Germany had not attempted to align with Britain, which forms the third route to security. The combined power of A and B would make them secure against any coalition of major powers. (A coalition of *all* other independent states would be overwhelming in the abstract, but in practice the power of most states is miniscule and would be effectively consumed in the coordination of their behaviors with the large powers.) Lastly, German behavior in the Moroccan crisis and the various attempts to get the Tsar to sign an agreement accord with the fourth pattern; if other methods fail, A must try to splinter any other coalition.

Although these responses by A to the threat of an opposing coalition are likely, the ladder-like system probably conspires to prevent success. As most of the other states must fear A, there will be a constant incentive to form an opposing alliance, one that will resist A's attempts to split it. Moreover, it is unlikely A can establish a close relationship with B. When B itself "looks down" the ladder, it sees no *individual* state threatening it. Looking "upward" there is the threat of A, and the only way to balance A is through an alliance with a weaker state. Alliance with A is unattractive because B's security rests principally on the forbearance of A from attacking. States usually seek a stronger guarantee for their security. Alliance *against* A is the answer. Besides, it gives B the opportunity to influence its weaker allies.

In a ladder-like system, therefore, we would expect alliances to form around the two most powerful states. For the other states, the range of policy choices is limited. The weakest (States E to H) will probably seek alliance with the most powerful states. If one is to be dominated in an alliance (which is inevitable for the weak), getting the most for one's subordination makes sense. That leaves the middle powers (C and D, or Russia and France, historically). While they have an incentive to align, they alone are not secure from A (or possibly B), especially as the weaker states have gravitated towards A (and B). As a consequence, it is unlikely that C will form the basis of a third alliance network. The two will seek security with A or B. From the perspective of the systems approach, world politics in a ladder-like system will polarize into two alliance networks centering on A and B.

In ladder-like systems, it is also probable that the rival alliance networks will be relatively evenly matched. States A and B form the core of the two alliance networks, furnishing bases for the alliances that are not greatly unequal in terms of power. Further, we would expect that the other major powers would find it difficult to flock to one alliance network to the exclusion of the other. Not only do those weaker powers have to defend themselves against A or B, *but equally from each other.* For E to be in an alliance with A may not protect it from C or D if they too are in alliance with A. In that alliance, State E must trust to the forbearance of C and D, or the restraint A might put on C or D, and that may be too much insecurity for E. Alliance with B may be more attractive. These calculations probably encourage the development of a *balance* among alliance networks. Historically, we find that during the decade a rough balance did prevail: Triple Alliance, 18; Triple Entente, 23.

I am sure you thought of other patterns, perhaps including a crucial question of the likelihood and nature of war in such a system. I will resume the analysis in the next chapter. Why should we be concerned with power distribution and patterns? Political science is interested in *compact* descriptions and explanations of how states behave. The historical analysis of world politics in the first decade took many pages. The systems approach takes relatively few. Second, systems analysis should be applicable to any international system. Therefore, our findings for one historical system should give us clues to how other systems of the same description should operate. If in the 1980s, for instance, the international system takes on a ladder-like configuration of power, you are ready to make some informed predictions about how and why contemporary states and their leaders will be impelled to act. For now, however, we have only hypotheses, rather than proven relationships. *If* they were demonstrated to be true, we would then be able to continue the systems analysis by saying that such patterns become the "rules" for the system. Leaders will feel pressure to duplicate those patterns because they do in fact provide a measure of security to the major states.

Policy-Making Approach:
The Russo-Japanese War of 1904–1905

The systems analysis of the preceding section explored world politics from a macro (large-scale) viewpoint. An alternative way of looking at world politics is to examine one or two states instead of all of them and to concentrate on a particular issue over a short period of time. Instead of assuming that what drives policy makers stems from the nature of the power distribution, we might focus on the pressures and demands that arise within a state that are resolved through a policy-making process. This particular case study is of Russian policy making in 1902–1905 regarding the Far East, and of Japanese decisions regarding war with

Russia.[35] Why did war occur there in the first decade of the century? What does this case study suggest about policy making? These are the questions we want to tackle.

The Far East had been a relatively recent area of Russian penetration (see Map 4-1). In 1858–1860, Russia forced China to cede the Maritime Province to Russia, making Manchuria the next area for the expansion of the empire. In 1895, Japan defeated China, forcing China to grant independence to Korea (so that it could become a Japanese sphere of influence) and to cede Chinese territory to the Japanese. The European powers fell over each other to secure what they wanted. Russia forced China to "lease" Port Arthur and surrounding territory to Russia for 25 years. In addition, Russia secured Chinese permission to build a rail line across Manchuria to Vladivostock and to build a line connecting Harbin to Port Arthur. The rail line and the corridor of land adjacent to it were for all purposes Russian, protected by Russian police and administered by Russian officials. During the Boxer Rebellion, Russian troops moved out of the rail corridors and occupied Manchurian cities.

The Japanese had similar imperial interests in the region. In Korea they began construction of a rail line that would aid the penetration of Korea by Japanese business interests and, where necessary, by Japanese military forces. The weak Korean government tried to fend off the imperialist states. It gave both Russian and Japanese lumber interests the right to exploit the forests in northern Korea. While such ploys did raise tensions between the two states, they also encouraged them to accelerate their penetration of Korea.

To the Japanese, Russian penetration of Korea was undesira. le. Korea was in the Japanese sphere of interest and therefore closed to others. On the other hand, the Japanese felt that the open door should prevail in Manchuria, giving everyone equal access to commercial opportunities. It was the familiar refrain of "what's mine is mine and what's yours is negotiable." The other European powers—except Russia—also felt that the open door should prevail in Manchuria. Russian military occupation was a cause for concern. The powers insisted that the Russian government clarify its intentions regarding Manchuria—a diplomatic way of warning the Tsar's government about creeping annexation through prolonged occupation.

Russian Policy Making   The Russians thus had two major considerations before them. The first was to avoid a confrontation with the major powers. To that end, the government announced in April, 1902, that it would withdraw Russian forces from Manchuria within 18 months. To show its good faith, it made a token withdrawal of some forces from Manchurian cities. The second issue was how to deal with the Japanese and the direct rivalry in the Manchurian-Korean area. There was general agreement within the Tsar's government that Manchuria was destined to become Russian territory. There was no consensus on methods or on timing, however. Nor was there agreement on Korea. It was not clear

---

[35]The sources for this analysis are John A. White, *The Diplomacy of the Russo-Japanese War* (Princeton: Princeton University Press, 1964) and Shumpei Okamoto, *The Japanese Oligarchy and the Russo-Japanese War* (New York: Columbia University Press, 1970).

whether the possession of Korea was necessary for the protection of a Russian Manchuria, nor was it clear whether Korea was a profitable place for Russian commercial activity.

Russian policy makers did not doubt that Japan constituted Russia's major opponent in the Far East. How should they respond? In general, there are two broad types of responses a state can make to a threat: appeasement and challenge. *Appeasement* is a policy of trying to reduce a threat to one's state by offering the threatening state things that it values. Such things might be territory (possibly someone else's territory!), raw materials, finished products, or support against a third state. The hope of appeasement is that the threat will be disarmed or deflected. To respond with a *challenge* is to court war. By refusing to accede to the demands of the threatening state or by indicating that the state will resist the other's attempts to secure its goals, a government hopes to deter the threatening state from acting. It was not clear how and on what issues Russia might appease or challenge.

There is another problem that confronted the Russian leadership (and confronts every leader, no matter the particular issue). Domestically, even when insulated from public opinion as the Tsar and his ministers were, leaders must demonstrate to critical audiences that they have the capacity for leadership. Otherwise, power is taken from them; in electoral democracies by the ballot, in oligarchies by the bureaucracies, and in authoritarian regimes by the bullet. Therefore, pervading the substance of every particular policy issue ("What are we going to do with the Russian troops in Manchurian cities?") is the leadership issue ("How will our policy decisions affect our ability to govern?"). While the Tsar was the "autocrat of all Russias," the monarchy's control of the society was precarious. Powerful and potentially ungovernable forces were afoot among the peasantry and the emerging proletariat. The Tsar's ministers themselves represented powerful contending forces of the traditional landed order and the rising capitalist entrepreneurs. The consensus in St. Petersburg tended to be that taking the initiative rather than timidity would ensure the leadership's status.

What foreign policy options were available to the Russian government in 1902–1903? Three seemed central, and each found some support within the Russian government.

1. *Immediate annexation of Manchuria.* With Russian forces now in occupation of the major cities and with the railroad offering access to much of the interior, annexation was feasible. Annexation would end the pressure for an open-door policy. Russian businessmen argued that they could not compete effectively with European and Japanese business interests under an open-door policy. The other states would denounce the act, but they would carve China up in consolation. Japan in particular would seize Korea; that would be acceptable. If the dismemberment of China was inevitable, the proponents of this position argued, it was better for Russia to get what it wanted first, than to have to scramble in competition with others.

2. *Gradual absorption in collusion with the Japanese.* Russian troops would be withdrawn from Manchuria, although the paramilitary Russian railway guards would remain in the railway zone. The Chinese government would be pressured into granting monopoly power to Russian enterprises. This would kill the open door, but make the Chinese government shoulder much of the blame. The Manchurian economy would be integrated into the Russian economy, and a creeping political annexation

take place. To gain Japanese acceptance, the Russian government would permit, if not actually encourage, Japanese penetration into Korea in a similar fashion.

3. *Move toward the annexation of Manchuria and contest the Japanese sphere in Korea.* Manchuria without Korea was indefensible, the supporters of this option argued. Korea provided a needed buffer zone to protect Manchuria. This option would directly confront the Japanese, but because Japan had *its* eye on Manchuria, the confrontation would take place when and how Russia chose. Korea would complete Russia's historic march to the east. Russia would demand more rights in Korea and rush the settlement of the existing concession areas in Korea by bringing in soldiers doubling as colonists.

As you can see, each of the options emphasized challenge or appeasement to some degree toward various states. Each of the options was proposed and defended by important individuals and groups in the Russian government. What did the Tsar and his ministers decide to do? Chapter 1 suggested that there are two different models of the policy-making process—the rational model and the political model. The rational model would suggest that the Russian policy makers debated the options in light of the goals they established (e.g., the national interest of the Russian state or the maintenance of their ability to govern) and selected the option that maximized their chances of securing their goals.

Does the evidence support such an interpretation? It does not. First, the policy kept changing—a sign that the rational process may not have been at work. Second, the policy contained contradictory elements. The Russian government decided to withdraw its military forces from the cities, but to station them in the railway zone. It opted to work for a gradual annexation of all of Manchuria. It decided to accept Japanese predominance in Korea—but to hold on to and expand its concession area in the northern part of Korea. It was with the Japanese that the contradictions were most evident. They were to be both appeased and challenged. Was this policy the product of irrational minds? The answer appears to be that in this case, the policy was the product of *politics*, rather than irrationality. That is, policy represented the *compromises* that satisfied enough important Russian policy makers. Some aspect of a particular policy maker's favored option was attached to an aspect of an option favored by someone else. The finance minister got the other ministers and the Tsar to accept Japanese control over Korea. The foreign minister won the right to keep the Russian concessions in Korea. It was more important that these two powerful policy makers (and the large bureaucracies they headed) support the decision because they had a stake in it than it was to avoid the contradictions. To tell the Russian foreign minister that the Russian concessions in Korea must be abandoned in order to support the decision to accept Japanese predominance is to ask him to abandon a position he feels is vital to Russian interests.

The Japanese View   Once policy is made, the other state becomes aware of it, but often does not see or comprehend the politics that created the policy. From the Japanese perspective, there *was* a sharp contradiction in Russian behavior. The Russians *said* they accepted Korea as a Japanese sphere. They *acted* otherwise, solidifying their control over their concession area in northern Korea. The Russians agreed to withdraw their forces; they moved them into the railway zones in Manchuria. How did the Japanese deal with these contradictions? Japanese diplomats began to look at the Russian behavior to discover the "real goals" Russia was pursuing.

In effect, the Japanese assumed that the Russian government was acting as the rational model postulated. Many policy makers assume that the other state makes policy according to the rational model. Therefore, the perception of contradictions means only that one really has not uncovered the truth about an opponent's intentions. From the Japanese perspective, pledges to withdraw military forces from Manchuria (but garrisoning them in the railway zone) and assurances that Korea was to be a Japanese sphere (coupled with active Russian exploitation of its concession) were part of a Russian plot to tie Japan's hands while closing the open door in Manchuria and driving Japan out of Korea. The Russian policy was perceived as a devious but powerful challenge. The Japanese government reacted by attacking Russian forces at Port Arthur in February, 1904.

The Japanese decision for war came after a protracted struggle within the Japanese government. The Japanese emperor, cabinet, and various advisory groups had reached a consensus that Korea was to be Japanese. There was little agreement about Manchuria and relations with Russia. The debate polarized the policy makers. One faction advocated an agreement with Russia that would give Manchuria to the Russians and Korea to the Japanese. Such a policy would meet immediate Japanese foreign policy goals and preserve the peace in the region. The opposing faction argued that war was the only realistic alternative. A Japanese Korea would never be safe if Russian forces stood on the border. Japan had to expel Russia from Manchuria (although not necessarily to make Manchuria a colony or sphere of influence). Pessimists in this group felt that war between the two states was likely and that Japan needed to strike before Russia got stronger. Russian forces in the Far East were among the worst in the Russian military establishment, and reinforcements and supplies had to be pushed through the bottleneck of the Trans-Siberian railway, a single track line connecting all of eastern Russia with the European center.

As long as Japan was at peace, did the anti-war faction dominate? Not necessarily. Even among polarized policy makers there are pressures for compromise. At an imperial conference in June, 1903, the Japanese emperor, government, and advisors agreed to raise the issue of Korea and Manchuria with the Russians by inviting them to negotiate an understanding. *That* part of the decision reflected the preferences of the anti-war faction. However, the conference also expressly stipulated that Japan would "be firmly resolved to achieve its objectives whatever the costs."[36] The pro-war faction was thus given a pledge that the war option would remain available if negotiations failed. Because the war option had been deferred rather than rejected, the pro-war faction had an incentive to criticize the government's policy. Every Russian demand—negotiations always feature demands—encouraged the pro-war faction and allowed them to "demonstrate" Russian aggressiveness and untrustworthiness. In January, 1904, after several months of inconclusive negotiations, the Russians tabled a new series of stiff demands. At this point, the anti-war faction collapsed, and an imperial conference agreed to go to war to resolve the future of Korea and Man-

---

[36]Quoted by Okamoto, *Japanese Oligarchy*, p. 77.

churia, even when the Japanese military estimated that the odds were only even for defeating the Russians.

The distribution of power (Table 2–3) indicates that Russia was four times as powerful as Japan. Yet in terms of *projectable power*—it took approximately twelve days to ship supplies on the Trans-Siberian railroad—Russia could deploy about half a point of power compared to Japan's two. As we might expect, the war did go well for the Japanese.[37] The Russian Pacific fleet was bottled up in Port Arthur. The Baltic fleet, sent in relief, went to the bottom at the battle of Tsushima Straits (May 1905). Japanese ground forces laid siege to Port Arthur and captured it in January, 1905. Japanese armies invaded Manchuria and inflicted defeats on the Russians. Japanese armies, however, were never able to inflict a crushing defeat on the Russians, and they could not reach the heart of Russian power. As each week went by, Russia moved more and more men and supplies on the Trans-Siberian railroad. Casualties were heavy on both sides and war costs were, for the time, astronomical. Both states fought the war on foreign loans; the foreign creditors refused to fund a prolonged war. In addition, the Russian government was distracted by abortive popular uprisings in 1905. The Japanese contacted President Theodore Roosevelt and asked him to propose peace talks. Roosevelt did so, and the Russians and Japanese met at Portsmouth, New Hampshire, in August, 1905. The peace treaty of September, 1905, recognized Japanese dominance over Korea, ceded Port Arthur to the Japanese, and caused the evacuation of Manchuria by all foreign troops. Riots broke out in Japanese cities; many had expected far more benefits, as the Japanese press had reported nothing but victories. And Teddy Roosevelt won the Nobel Peace Prize.

[37]For the war and its conclusions, see David Walder, *The Short Victorious War* (New York: Harper & Row, Pub., 1973).

CHAPTER THREE

1910–1919_____
Europe wanders into hell

PART I:
DIPLOMATIC AND MILITARY HISTORY[1]

Pre-War Diplomacy

German Initiatives   In the aftermath of the Bosnian crisis of 1908–1909, the major powers sought to stabilize the Balkans. Russia reached an agreement with Austria-Hungary in February, 1910, to preserve the status quo. The Russians looked eastward again; the Chinese Revolution of 1911, which brought republican government and forty decades of turmoil to China, offered new opportunities. Russia also negotiated with the Germans. In November, 1910, the foreign ministers of the two states reached a colonial agreement regarding their interests in Persia and Turkey.

The Germans were interested in taking the negotiations one step further. The German foreign minister, Kiderlen, offered to remove German support for Austria-Hungary's expansionist goals in the Balkans, thereby accepting Russian predominance in the region. There was a price, of course. Kiderlen wanted the Russians to publish a statement that Russia did not support the British policy of hostility to Germany. Such a declaration (coupled with the colonial understanding) would strain Anglo-Russian relations to the breaking point; precisely Kiderlen's goal. The Russians would only go so far as to give the Germans a verbal,

---

[1]See note 1 of Chapter 2 for major sources. As the world war dominates this period, see also Joachim Remak, *The Origins of World War I* (New York: Holt, Rinehart and Winston, 1967); Walter Laqueur and George Mosse, eds., *1914* (New York: Harper & Row, Pub., 1966); Fritz Fischer, *War of Illusions* (New York: W.W. Norton & Co., Inc., 1975); Winston Churchill, *The World Crisis* (New York: Scribner's, 1923–29); Dwight Lee, *Europe's Crucial Years* (Hanover, N.H.: University Press of New England, 1974).

private pledge not to support British aggressiveness against Germany. At this point in the talks the subject leaked to the press. Both sides quickly let the matter drop.

The effect, however, was much as the Germans had hoped. The British began to look on the Russians with suspicion and anger. Obviously their understanding with Russia did not preclude Russia's making decisions injurious to Britain. Indeed, the de facto alliance between Britain and Russia seemed to be a device by which the Russians hoped to tie British hands but to keep theirs unfettered. It was a galling point for the British, who had specialized in such maneuvers in the past.

At about the same time that Kiderlen tried to detach Russia from England, other German officials, especially the Kaiser, worked on Britain. By the second decade, the Kaiser had lost his enthusiasm for a continental league of states. France and Russia were likely to be Germany's opponents, not partners. The Russians—or Slavic people in general—now appeared to be quite alien to the Kaiser, whose racism was well developed. "I am," he told the British ambassador, "all for the white man against the black, whether they be Chinese, Japanese, niggers, or Slavs."[2] Increasingly, therefore, the Kaiser saw Britain as the one major power with whom Germany might develop close relations. In chiding the British ambassador for the British relationship with France and Russia, William painted another picture:

> You ought to be with us. What is perpetually in my mind is this: The Greeks and Romans each had their time; the Spaniards had theirs and the French also. The Latin races have in fact had their fair share of power and influence in the world. It is now for the Anglo-Saxons and Teutons to come to the front; not to be striving against each other and quarrelling over petty questions, but to join hand in hand and lead the world.[3]

Rhetoric alone rarely carries the day, however. The Kaiser and Chancellor Bethmann tried to produce a close working relationship by offering Britain a naval agreement that would guarantee supremacy to the British navy. The price of a naval agreement was a "political understanding" with Germany. Britain was to agree not to join in any hostile actions against Germany; specifically, in case of war between France and Germany, Britain was to remain neutral.

The German offer was attractive. Britain would protect its national security at a reasonable cost. A long-term naval arms race with Germany would be both expensive and dangerous. The cost would be the denial of the entente with France, which Britain had labored to construct. Wanting naval arms limitation but also wanting to avoid the price, Britain proposed resolving the arms issue first and, with regard to a political understanding, giving Germany an understanding of the same type as that existing between Britain and France—one with no *formal, written* commitments. Some in the British government did not want to grant even that much. "It is difficult to imagine," noted one diplomat, "any formula for an

---

[2]Quoted by Ambassador Goschen to Foreign Minister Grey, October 16, 1910; in *British Documents on the Origins of the War,* ed. G.P. Gooch and Harold Temperley (London: H.M. Stationery Office, 1930), VI, p. 351.

[3]Goschen to Grey, March 12, 1911; *ibid.,* p. 601.

understanding with Germany which would not fetter our freedom of action and disturb the minds of France and Russia.''[4] Relations with allies often produce an uncertainty in how to deal with opponents. In this case, Britain had to forego one foreign policy goal (limiting German naval construction) to keep hold of the other (a working alliance with France).

For the Germans, a pledge as vague as that offered by the British was out of the question. If Germany were to accept a limit on her fleet that would guarantee its inferiority, declared Chancellor Bethmann, and "should . . . Germany be forced into war by provocation on the part of a third Power, she must have the certainty of not finding England on the side of her opponents.''[5] As you might expect, both sides continued to negotiate for an agreement that would be mutually acceptable but in practice would restrict the other power most. There seemed to be no clear path to such an agreement.

Crisis Diplomacy in Morocco and the Balkans

The first Moroccan crisis (1905) had been settled by the Algeciras agreement which recognized French predominance in Morocco but accorded economic rights to the citizens of other powers. In spite of the agreement, France continued its policy of gradual colonization. In March, 1911, Moroccans in the city of Fez began a revolt against the French. The French advised Germany that they would intervene with military force in Fez.[6]

Foreign Minister Kiderlen became uneasy. French military forces and a native revolt were the ingredients to create a French colony. Germany would lose her commercial rights and suffer a decline in her prestige because France had unilaterally broken the Algeciras agreement. Germany, Kiderlen decided, had to receive compensation from France if the Moroccan status quo were changed. However, Germany could not *request* compensation—that was a sign of weakness—yet if Germany remained silent, the French would disregard German interests. How might Germany show its interest in the matter and force the French to offer compensation? The Kaiser's visit to Tangier in 1905 provided the precedent. Kiderlen recommended that Germany send warships to Morocco. The Kaiser temporized; he agreed in principle with the dispatch of ships but withheld the order to move them to Moroccan waters.

Actually, Kiderlen misjudged the French. The new government of Prime Minister Caillaux, having inherited the military intervention in Morocco from the previous government, judged the *absence* of any German response to be most ominous. Caillaux also saw Morocco as the stumbling block to his personal goal of creating better relations with Germany. To resolve the impending crisis, the French privately proposed in June, 1911, to compensate Germany by giving her territory in the French Congo.

The Germans were pleased; the Kaiser in particular. Germany had gotten what it sought by doing nothing, least of all by threatening the peace. The French were told that the idea was acceptable, and Germany awaited a specific proposal.

---

[4]Critique appended to the German proposal of August, 1909; *ibid.*, p. 284.

[5]Quoted by Goschen, November 4, 1909; *ibid.*, p. 308.

[6]For the second Moroccan crisis, see Ima Barlow, *The Agadir Crisis* (Chapel Hill: University of North Carolina Press, 1940).

A week went by without a French response. Kiderlen saw the delay as part of the French strategy to get Morocco for nothing. He importuned the Kaiser to activate the display of force. The Kaiser agreed, but kept the display limited to one small gunboat, the *Panther*. When it dropped anchor at Agadir, Morocco, on July 1, the second Moroccan crisis began in earnest. To the European states, the one gunboat threatened war.

The threat of war naturally forced the alliance partners of France to check their gunpowder. The Russian military told the Tsar's government that Russia was unprepared for war. Russian diplomats hurriedly told the French *and the Germans* that Russia would not go to war to support French colonial interests. So much for the eastern ally! In Britain, France's remaining hope, the government was divided. Some wanted to back France to the hilt; that is what an alliance commitment meant. Others argued that Germany was due compensation and that German patience had been sorely tried. Still others saw a threat in any agreement *between France and Germany* that might lead to better relations between the two. The government debated but rejected the idea of sending British warships and settled instead on verbal warnings that if Germany stayed in Morocco, Britain would also demand compensation. A nice but puzzling compromise. British and French military staffs, however, continued to work out contingency plans for the transport of British troops to France in case of war.

The Moroccan problem had become an immense headache for the French. Russia was standing aloof. Britain seemed supportive, but the French knew that Britain and Germany were discussing a general political understanding. Such a settlement could be at France's expense. It seemed clear to the French that they had to reach a bilateral accommodation with Germany. The Kaiser had reached a similar conclusion. He ordered that no further threats be made to the French, even when it became clear that the French were prepared to cede only portions of the French Congo rather than the entire colony. William had become distressed at how close Germany had come to either a diplomatic surrender or having to use force. He authorized acceptance of the French offer of two sections of the Congo as territorial compensation in return for the creation of a French protectorate over Morocco. Negotiations continued for several months, and a final settlement was reached in November, 1911.

A.J.P. Taylor has suggested that the Agadir crisis marked a change in the attitude of the European states.[7] To this point, "crisis diplomacy" had been a prominent feature of world politics. Crisis diplomacy emerged when the possibility of a major-power war hung over Europe. Most policy makers, however, assumed that diplomacy would resolve the crisis. Some accommodation could and would be found, because no one wanted war. Yet there was irony in this. As no one wanted a general war, a state had the incentive to probe the status quo in the pursuit of its interests. The risks were manageable; crisis diplomacy would rescue the brash if they miscalculated. Each challenge to the status quo, however, tended to produce a crisis, and crisis seemed to follow crisis *because of the very success of crisis diplomacy*. Each crisis also helped to divide the states into the two alliance systems, rigidifying the alliances and making any crisis a potential clash of alli-

[7]A.J.P. Taylor, *The Struggle for Mastery in Europe 1848-1918* (Oxford: Oxford University Press, 1954), p. 473.

ances rather than of individual states. Not unnaturally, a new attitude developed that "it might be better to settle this once and for all." And that attitude had its own pressures: if the leaders of Russia believed that the leaders of Germany felt that it was time to settle things, then Russia had to settle things *first*, so that Russia might benefit from taking the initiative. A "pre-war spirit" emerged and would not take long to flower.

Each successful probe of the status quo encouraged emulation by others. In September, 1911, reacting to the French example, the Italians invaded the Turkish province of Tripoli (modern Libya). The major powers held their collective breath. A defeat for the Turks might cause things to come unglued in the Balkans. No state, however, could afford to alienate the Italians by actively supporting the Turks. A relatively weak power such as Italy could probe the status quo with scant concern.

The Italian example in turn encouraged three small Balkan states to use similar tactics.[8] Serbia, Greece, and Bulgaria each believed in their right to rule territory inhabited by kinfolk but separated from the state by "unjust" international boundaries; these territories were known as *irredenta*.[9] But more than reuniting a divided nation was at stake. Each of the small Balkan states subscribed to the major-power belief that national survival depended upon one's own power, and power was a function of the size of the state. Each therefore thought in terms of a "Greater Serbia," "Greater Greece," and "Greater Bulgaria." The pressure of irredenta and national expansion caused them to look southward. The three Balkan states formed a series of alliances and plotted an attack on the crumbling Ottoman Empire.

The Russians had encouraged the development of the alliances in order to create a bulwark of states to oppose any further *Austrian* expansion. The Balkan states, of course, had other interests, but it is not uncommon to find large and small states acting in concert but for quite different reasons. And with grave risk to the large state. Any change in the Balkan status quo would produce a reaction from Austria-Hungary.

After placing demands on the Turks, which were refused, the three Balkan allies declared war on Turkey in October, 1912. In two months the allies had broken the Turkish forces. The Serb army reached the Adriatic Sea. The Bulgarian army stood at the gateway to Constantinople. The Russians and Austrians found themselves in an interesting position. The Russians did not like the prospect of a Bulgarian army situated on the Straits. Russian policy was to have a weak Turkey govern the Straits if Russia could not govern it. Austria-Hungary faced a more disturbing dilemma. The government was split on the issue of how to deal with Serbia. One determined faction wanted to cripple the power of the Serbian state either by war or by keeping Serbia hemmed in. The other major faction, led by Foreign Minister Berchtold, favored a policy of conciliation. They would allow Serbia to hold its newly conquered territory; in the long term, perhaps Serbia would join the Austro-Hungarian Empire. The decision reached by the divided

---

[8]See Ernst Helmreich, *The Diplomacy of the Balkan Wars* (Cambridge: Harvard University Press, 1938).

[9]The term comes from the *Italia irredenta* or "Italy unredeemed" and came to stand for any territory outside a state but linked to it ethnically or historically and thus claimed by that state.

government was to accept most of the Serb territorial gains but demand Serb withdrawal from the Adriatic coast. Access to the Mediterranean would give too much power to the Serb state and there would be greater agitation by Slavs in the Austro-Hungarian empire for union with Serbia.

The Austrian demand for Serb withdrawal triggered the now-familiar set of pledges. The Russian government, perhaps embarrassed by its erratic performance in the 1909 crisis, pledged to support Serbia if Austria attacked. The French fell in behind the Russians but, not wanting to go to war over the Balkans, they stipulated that they would enter the war only if Germany intervened. Germany gave its support to Austria, although the Kaiser worried that Austria now had the ability to get Germany in a war over a small stretch of land along the Adriatic coast. The British, on the other hand, pushed for a diplomatic settlement. By May, 1913, British persistence and threats paid off; the belligerents ceased fighting and Turkey gave up territory to the three Balkan states. An independent state of Albania was created on the Adriatic coast to deny Serbia access to the sea.

Two days after reaching the settlement, the three Balkan states went to war against each other! It was a familiar problem. The division of the spoils was unsatisfactory. Greece aligned with Serbia to take territory from the Bulgarians. Once Greece and Serbia attacked Bulgaria, Turkey joined in to recover the land it lost to the Bulgarians several months before! And Bulgaria's northern neighbor, Romania, sensing an easy acquisition, attacked the hapless Bulgaria in order to advance *its* territorial aspirations.

Bulgarian forces gave ground everywhere. The Serbs used the moment to seize northern Albania. With the war party in Vienna growing stronger, Austria issued another ultimatum to the Serbs in October, 1913. The Russian government, fearing that Austria really meant to "settle things," wavered and then urged the Serbs to withdraw from Albania. Serbia, in a bitter mood, did so. A peace treaty ended the second Balkan war.

The Serb government now grimly accepted the fact that Serbia had to deal with Austria if Serbia were to survive. To deal with Austria, Serbia needed the total commitment of Russia. To get that commitment, Serbia needed a situation in which the Russian government could not retreat. In Austria, the faction that wanted to destroy Serbia began to look for a pretext. Even the Kaiser—hesitant about war and anxious about Austrian rashness—found himself saying that it was "now or never" for Austria to deal with Serbia.

British Policies of Détente   Morocco and the Balkans provided the tense background for the Anglo-German negotiations. German naval construction continued. The British government sought some formula to assure Germany that Britain would "make no unprovoked attack upon Germany and pursue no aggressive policy towards her."[10] The British Foreign Minister Edward Grey repeatedly told the Germans that Britain could not make any pledge of neutrality in case of war between France and Germany. Privately, Grey admitted to some of his colleagues that even if France and Russia made an unprovoked attack on Germany, Britain could not stand by if Germany stood on the verge of crushing

---

[10]Grey's draft formula, presented to the German Ambassador, March 14, 1912; in *British Documents*, ed. Gooch and Temperley, VI, pp. 713–14.

France. Hardliners in the British foreign ministry opposed any formula at all, arguing that Germany would keep the peace only if the Germans knew Britain would *not* be neutral. However, the British government did search for a formula *and* subsequently offered to consider concessions on colonial issues.

How might we characterize British policy toward Germany in the several years before the outbreak of World War I? It appears that, in the main, Grey had settled on a policy of *détente* with Germany.[11] That is, he sought a reduction in tensions between the two states, rather than some comprehensive, formal understanding that an alliance might entail. When *specific* issues could be settled by negotiations (and the colonial issues were a case in point), Britain would do so. When not, Britain would endeavor to keep open the lines of communication. Détente was possibly all Grey could work for, given the conviction that Britain had to avoid alienating France. The interests of Britain and Germany probably did not diverge greatly, but could find no common expression. Détente was a logical response. Détente allowed for the maintenance of one's alliances, the buildup of one's own armaments, and at least a dialogue with a potential opponent.

Unfortunately, a policy of détente may not have much of a future. Chapter 2 suggested that a state can respond to threats by either appeasement or challenge. A détente policy is a "middle" option. It warily offers concessions on a quid pro quo basis to resolve specific issues that appear ready to be resolved. Appeasement policies, on the other hand, offer major unilateral concessions to the threatening state to acquire the "good will" of the threatening state or a pledge of "peaceful behavior." Détente policies, like challenge policies, see armed strength as necessary for peace; but unlike challenge policies, they do not use threats of force to wring agreement or concessions from the other state.

A policy of détente may be under constant pressure to shift toward the appeasement or challenge policy options. The historical experience of the second decade suggests three conditions when such a shift is likely:

1. Too many small conflicts not initially involving the two states "spill over" to create tension between them. Morocco and the Balkans were two such conflicts.

2. The strength of hardliners remains undiminished by the success of détente policies. The British hardliners, for instance, argued that Germany would make use of an unscrupulous mixture of conciliation and bullying to "dictate terms to every Power."[12] Their arguments formed an unceasing chorus challenging the détente policy of the government.

3. The opposing state does not respond with détente policies. The Kaiser tended to view his policy options toward Britain as either appeasement or challenge. The German attempts at appeasement (as the Kaiser interpreted them) had turned out badly. Challenge was to be his favored response: ". . . only ruthless, manly, and fearless defense of our interests impresses the British and is finally forcing them to seek a rapprochement; but never the so-called accommodation, which they merely

[11]For contemporary analyses and applications of the concept of détente, see Coral Bell, *The Diplomacy of Détente* (New York: St. Martin's Press, 1977); G.R. Urban, ed., *Détente* (New York: Universe, 1976); Theodore Draper, "Appeasement and Détente," in James Schlesinger, *Defending America* (New York: Basic Books, 1977), pp. 3–21; and Richard Rosecrance, "Détente or Entente?" *Foreign Affairs*, 53 (April 1975), 464–81.

[12]Minute by Eyre Crowe, a senior Foreign Office official, April 6, 1912; in *British Documents*, ed. Gooch and Temperley, VI, p. 739.

take for flabbiness and cowardice . . . England is turning to us not in spite of, but because of my Imperial Navy!!''[13]

The British policy of détente and the German policy of "ruthless defense" of German interests would face the critical test in 1914. In a tragic sense, both failed.

The Great War

Sarajevo and the Rush to War   On June 28, 1914, the heir to the Austro-Hungarian throne, Archduke Franz Ferdinand, drove through the streets of Sarajevo in the Austrian province of Bosnia.[14] Members of a Bosnian terrorist group with links to Serbia attacked the motorcade and killed Franz Ferdinand and his wife. The faction in the Austrian government that wanted to crush Serbia now won over or silenced its opposition. The Austrians consulted the Kaiser and Chancellor Bethmann, who pledged to back Austria. The Germans, you will recall, had fallen into a pattern of supporting Austria and not attempting to enforce restraint. However, if events followed the course of recent history, crisis diplomacy would resolve the issue.

Three weeks after the assassination, on July 23, Austria-Hungary delivered an ultimatum to Serbia calling for the Serbs to suppress all anti-Austrian agitation in Serbia and to allow Austrian police officials to enter Serbia to manage the operation. Such demands were designed to ensure Serbian rejection; no sovereign state willingly permits such interference in its internal affairs. Much to Austria's consternation, the Serbs appeared to accept most of the points and agreed to have neutral arbitration settle the question of the entry of the Austrian officials. Crisis diplomacy had triumphed again. Or had it? The Austrian government had decided on war. The Germans had pledged support and had not retracted it after the Serbs had made their concession. On July 28, Austria-Hungary declared war on Serbia, but made no major attack.

In the following days the world watched St. Petersburg.[15] Would Russia mobilize—that is, call up its enormous military reserves and send its forces to the borders of Austria-Hungary ready to begin offensive operations? The Germans, wanting to avoid having to enter a war in support of Austria's Balkan interests, warned the Russians that mobilization meant war with Germany. Germany was attempting to *deter* Russian action against Austria by threatening Russia, just as it had done in the Bosnian crisis of 1908–1909. For two days, July 29 and 30, the

---

[13]Noted on dispatch of October 10, 1913; in *German Diplomatic Documents,* ed. E.T. Dugdale (New York: Harper & Row, Pub., 1931), Vol. IV, p. 300.

[14]Numerous specialized studies of the assassination exist; see, among others, Vladimir Dedijer, *The Road to Sarajevo* (New York: Simon & Schuster, 1966); Joachim Remak, *Sarajevo* (New York: Criterion, 1959); and Bertha Pauli, *The Secret of Sarajevo* (Englewood Cliffs, N.J.: Prentice-Hall, 1965).

[15]Barbara Tuchman's study, *The Guns of August* (New York: Macmillan, 1962), picks up the events at about this point. Her book also demonstrates the point that decision makers sometimes respond to the historian's viewpoint. President John Kennedy recommended that his staff read Tuchman, as he had long been impressed by the "miscalculations" of 1914 and the need for leadership to be constantly aware of the potential for unforeseen disaster; Theodore Sorensen, *Kennedy* (New York: Harper & Row, Pub., 1965), p. 513.

Tsar and his ministers wrestled with the dilemma. They were agreed on the defense of Serbia. How could they avoid German intervention? After changing his mind several times, the Tsar ordered full mobilization.

The Kaiser, facing the prospect of a massive Russian army set to invade Germany, ordered German mobilization on July 31 and declared war on Russia on August 1. Germany's problem now became France. The German war plans called for beginning an offensive operation *against France* in case of war with Russia, based on the assumption that France would honor its alliance commitment to Russia. On August 3, Germany declared war on France and began the attack by *invading Belgium!* (These plans are discussed below.) The British government had been divided on the issue of war and there was some reluctance to support France. The German invasion of neutral Belgium—a state whose neutrality Britain and Germany had guaranteed by treaty and whose territory on the English Channel was strategic—brought a British declaration of war on Germany on August 4. Italy and Romania defected from the Triple Alliance and declared their neutrality. The Great War had begun.

Once the political leaders ordered war, the military commanders began military operations according to plans developed years earlier and for which the troops had been trained.[16] The proverbial fog of battle and human factors would, of course, produce deviations from the plan, but in the main the opening blows of the Great War came from the planning books. The German military plan, named after its originator, General von Schlieffen, assumed that the German army could not strike the Russians and the French simultaneously. Therefore, Germany had to concentrate its men on one front, hold the other with far fewer forces, and completely defeat first one state, then the other. States facing enemies on two or more fronts have usually relied on such an approach. Israel, for instance, in 1967 and 1973, chose to deal with its Arab opponents, Syria and Egypt, in this manner. In 1914, the Germans chose to concentrate against France first, because Russian mobilization was predicted to be slower than French mobilization.

The Germans felt they had to deliver a quick, *decisive* blow to the French army before the Russian steamroller began to move. Viewing the terrain, it became clear to German planners that an attack across the common Franco-German border would only throw German forces into the teeth of the French defensive network (see Map 3–1). To avoid French defenses, von Schlieffen planned to march through Belgium, bypass the French flank, pass behind Paris (thus capturing the French capital), and swing around to face east. The maneuver would encircle a major part of the French army along the Franco-German border.

The German plan, though audacious, was firmly rooted in a central tactical concept of combat: to command the enemy's rear areas. The German plan proposed to pass around the left flank of the French army and sweep behind it, thus

---

[16]See Tuchman, *Guns*; for the war itself, see B.H. Liddell Hart, *The Real War 1914–1918* (Boston: Little, Brown, 1930); Cyril Falls, *The Great War* (New York: Putnam's, 1959); John Terraine, *The Western Front, 1914–1918* (Philadelphia: Lippincott, 1965); Correlli Barnet, *The Swordbearers* (New York: Morrow, 1964); Norman Stone, *The Eastern Front* (New York: Scribner's, 1975). There are many specialized studies of the war. The reader might begin with Alan Moorehead, *Gallipoli*, rev. ed. (London: Hamilton, 1967); Alistair Horne, *The Price of Glory: Verdun 1916* (New York: St. Martin's Press, 1963); and Leon Wolff, *In Flanders Fields* (New York: Viking, 1958).

MAP 3-1   Europe During World War I

cutting its supply and communication lines. A modern army depends upon the continuous delivery of food, ammunition, and men to the front lines. Without these supplies, the best trained and led armies collapse. The massive envelopment of a major portion of the French army would cut off part of the French army, crush it with superior forces, and then turn on the weaker surviving portion. France was to be defeated in six weeks.

There were important risks in this military plan, as there are in any employment of force against a major power. Von Schlieffen's plan could be thought of as a hammer blow. The shaft of the hammer lay along the Franco-German border; the head (where the bulk of the German divisions would be concentrated) was opposite Belgium. To give the head of the hammer the crushing power it needed, the number of divisions in the south (the shaft) had to be kept low: Although those divisions were in defensive fortifications, there was a real risk that a French offensive might break through the German line at this point. General von Moltke, von Schlieffen's successor, felt the risk unacceptable and therefore moved divisions from the north to the south. In doing so, Moltke ran the risk that the hammer blow would be too weak to break the French.

The second major risk was political. What would be the consequence of the strike through Belgium? If France were defeated quickly, German forces would be removed from Belgium and an apology given. Von Schlieffen had also nursed the hope that once the French saw the German buildup along the Belgian border, they would invade Belgium first in order to gain a better defensive position (and to fight on Belgian rather than French soil!). A German invasion might provoke British entry, but as Britain had a small army, its entry did not seem likely to prevent the rapid destruction of France.

The French were not blind to the possibility of a German attack through Belgium. What is seen by one side is often seen by the other—but in different ways. Such a German strike would play havoc with the French war plan, which was to drive across the common border with Germany. It was more convenient, therefore, to assume that the Germans would attack only through the *southern* part of Belgium; therefore the French line did not have to extend to the left very far. Moreover, any German offensive would develop slowly because heavy forests covered much of southern Belgium. In short, nothing was allowed to interfere with planning for the major French offensive directly into Germany.

Taking the offensive against Germany was something new for French military thought. Up until 1910 or so, the French war plan called for the French to sit in their defensive positions and allow the Germans to throw themselves into the jaws of death. Led by General Foch, the French reevaluated their thinking and became convinced that courage and spirit would carry their *attacking* troops to victory. An offensive would also recover the lost provinces of Alsace and Lorraine. Unfortunately, the French failed to calculate the enormous firepower that the machine gun gave the defenders, especially when attacked frontally as the French proposed. It was a recipe for slaughter.

If the Western front promised to see simultaneous offensives from Germany and France, defense was the word in the East. The Germans planned to remain on the defensive, counting on a slow Russian mobilization. The Russians, for their part, planned to remain on the defensive against the Germans until their mobilization had been completed several months after the start of the war. They did, however, plan to attack the much weaker Austrians while mobilization proceeded.

The British, in accordance with the discussions begun in 1906, planned to send their small regular army of six divisions to France to fight on France's left wing. On the high seas, the British prepared to close off the oceans to the Germans. However, contrary to its traditions, the British navy decided not to seek out the Kaiser's navy for a decisive engagement. Defensive techniques—mines and submarines and heavily defended German harbors—led the naval commanders to minimize their risks by choosing to wait upon the Germans to seek battle. British numerical superiority (and later the ability to decipher German naval messages) was expected to carry the day. The German navy in fact ventured forth only once to give battle (Battle of Jutland, May 31 to June 1, 1916 which ended in a draw). However, except for its submarines, the German fleet rode at anchor in German ports thereafter.

The Stalemate in the Trenches   With these plans in hand, the major powers sallied forth to give battle. And the plans began to unravel. The Germans brushed aside the Belgian army and struck the British and French with the head of the hammer. The Entente line began to retreat. At the same time, the French attack into Alsace-Lorraine collapsed in front of the German defenses. Frantically, the French called on their Russian allies to attack and thus force Germany to disengage on the Western front. The Russians agreed and began a premature two-pronged drive into Germany.

The Germans responded to the early Russian attack by diverting divisions to the East, reducing the strength of the hammer blow even more. As the hammer swung round, the Germans found that it would not reach Paris now, so they decided to pass east of Paris and complete their encirclement of the Entente left flank. In so doing, the German right flank became exposed to the French forces pouring into Paris for the defense of the city. The French counterattack on the German flank began in September, 1914. Soon, the German forces were retreating northward away from the Marne River. The hammer stroke had failed.

At about the same time, the Germans met the oncoming Russians. They concentrated their forces against the Russian army advancing in the south, routed it (Battle of Tannenberg, late August) and did the same against the northern force (Battle of the Masurian Lakes, mid-September). 200,000 Russians became prisoners of war, and the loss of weapons and munitions crippled the Russian war machine before it could become effective. Russian manpower reserves were so vast, however, that the human losses were made good and a new line formed, which held the German attack. Only against the Austrians did a Russian offensive make much headway, but that, too, came to an end when German reinforcements appeared in the Austrian line.

Meanwhile, on the Western front, the Germans had withdrawn to a line along the Aisne River and repelled French attacks. Each side then sought to get behind the other's flank, only to find itself faced with a flanking countermove. By the end of the year, a line of trenches ran from Switzerland to the English Channel. A winter offensive by the British and French resulted in failure. A new kind of war had appeared in the West (and, as a paler reflection, in the East). Everywhere there was front rather than flank. Everywhere there were barbed wire and machine guns, which made direct frontal assaults by infantry an enormously costly proposition.

As winter of 1914 settled in, the military on both sides began to ponder what seemed to be a stalemate in the making. For the Entente powers, any stalemate was unacceptable. The success of the German army in the first months had led to the occupation of French, Belgian, and Russian territory. Entente political leaders urged their military commanders to recover the territory, sometimes out of a blind patriotism, sometimes out of a recognition that the Entente was in a weak bargaining position with the Germans as long as Germany had suffered no major territorial losses. The Entente military leaders needed little prodding. They had been schooled in the notion of the offensive and believed that the defense does not win wars. Stalemate became as much an enemy as the enemy.

As a consequence, Entente military leaders became wedded to the notion that the answer to the stalemate was the *breakthrough*. A massive artillery barrage and wave after wave of infantry would assault a sector of the enemy front line with such concentrated force that the defenders would be pulverized. Sheer force would create a hold in the enemy line. Into that breach would pour more infantry and, more important, cavalry. The cavalry would sweep to the enemy's unprotected rear while the infantry would strike the flanks and begin to roll up the enemy line. Entente armies on the continent would pursue these military policies during 1915, 1916, and 1917. The names of the resulting battles, such as Somme and Passchendaele, remain today as symbols of human bravery and frightful casualties. No breakthrough occurred. The powers of defense seemed to contain and crush the attackers. The front line hardly moved on the Western front during those years.

Stalemate for the Germans had a different complexion. They continued to assume that they could not stage simultaneous offensives on the Eastern and Western fronts. On one front, therefore, they had an interest in *prolonging* a stalemate and sought to maximize the power of the defense. On the other, they had to cope with trench warfare. They did have two quite different fronts to choose from. The weaker Russian front became the area for testing evolving German ideas on how to break the Western stalemate. This did not mean they avoided the frontal assault in the West. Indeed, in 1916, they began a particular type of operation in the West that was an attempt to rationalize costly direct assaults. This strategy was called *attrition*—forcing the opponent to accept battle essentially for the purpose of killing large numbers of its forces at less cost than the attacker suffers. It was a brutal business. Its goal was to bleed the opponent so heavily that the political leadership would seek peace rather than endure the pain of further attrition. The bad policy of costly frontal assault did not become good policy just because planners found a new justification for doing what they had been trained to do.

In February, 1916, the Germans began the attrition campaign against the French strong point at Verdun, which the French political leadership felt it essential to hold. The Germans kept up a relatively continuous bombardment and a series of attacks on the French line. French units were sent into Verdun, mangled, and replaced by new units. By December, 1916, after Germany called off the attempt and the French recovered the lost ground, there were some 500,000 French casualties, 400,000 German. Verdun remained French. The Germans abandoned the strategy.

The Entente took longer to learn. The French had made attrition part of their policy in 1915. Along the Somme River, the British began to experiment with attrition in the summer of 1916. There was no strategic point such as Verdun, so the British would stage limited assaults and wait for the German counterattack to try to cause the large casualties. In these battles and in the attempts to achieve a breakthrough, Entente casualties remained greater than German casualties, but the Entente military commanders knew that the Entente's manpower reserves were superior to Germany's; the Entente would therefore still win the "attrition race." The political leadership in France and Britain, faced with staggering casualties, became more dogmatic about waging the war to the end. The men in the trenches, however, grew less committed to the pursuit of a bitter end.

In 1917, after a disastrous French offensive, many French divisions mutinied, refusing to go "over the top." By 1918, the British government had adopted the expedient of holding up its reinforcements to France to prevent the British field commander, Douglas Haig, from pursuing the attrition strategy. It could not find the political courage or unity to sack Haig or to insist on a policy change. The military argued that there were few alternatives.

Tactical and Strategic Innovation   This is not to say that leaders grimly prosecuted the war without considering the cost or that innovation was absent. Some political and military officials argued that defensive firepower was so great that stalemate would continue until the attackers could avoid that firepower. Generally, the opponents of massive frontal attacks fell into two groups—those who stressed *tactical* (battlefield) innovation and those who stressed *strategic* innovation.[17]

The tactical innovators accepted the traditional argument that the war would be decided on the existing fronts; the battle had to be waged directly against enemy forces. One group of tactical innovators sought to apply *technology* to warfare in order to blunt the power of the defense. Infantry leaving their trenches to attack an enemy trench line had to cross the appropriately named No Man's Land—ground churned up by artillery fire, laced with row on row of barbed wire, and raked by machine guns. The human body was particularly vulnerable in such a situation. The Entente answer was to develop an armored vehicle carrying machine guns and running on continuous tracks that could cross broken ground and trenches. The tank (as it was named) promised to produce the breakthrough and to provide a powerful means to exploit that breakthrough. The tank emerged fitfully from the drawing boards. It was not until late 1917 that there were sufficient numbers and an effective doctrine of use to convert the promise of a breakthrough into a possibility for the Entente powers.

Another technological innovation was the application of poison gas to warfare. The Germans made use of it in 1915, first on a trial basis on the Russian front and then as a part of an attack in the West. A gas attack on the trenches nullified the defense by exterminating it or forcing it to flee. The Germans, however, had not forseen or planned for the success of the gas, and did not have the troops ready to exploit the breakthrough. The Entente quickly added gas to its arsenal and both sides developed gas masks, which generally restored the balance to the defender.

The other type of tactical innovator sought new ways of using the existing technology of war. What needed to change was *how* military leaders sought their battlefield objectives. One could not avoid the frontal assault, but perhaps one could avoid the traditional slaughter associated with it. It is worthwhile to take several paragraphs to compare the traditional views on the assault and compare the innovations first systematically made by the German army. It is worthwhile

[17]For a general review of innovation and strategy, see George Quester, *Offense and Defense in the International System* (New York: John Wiley, 1977); Bernard Brodie, *War and Politics* (New York: Macmillan, 1973). For various aspects, see, among others, Moorehead, *Gallipoli;* B.H. Liddell Hart, *The Tanks,* 2 vols. (New York: Praeger, 1959); Richard Gibson and Maurice Pendergast, *The German Submarine War, 1914–1918* (New York: R.R. Smith, 1931); and John Ellis, *The Social History of the Machine Gun* (New York: Pantheon, 1975).

because *how* men chose to fight had a profound impact on their subsequent international behavior, both diplomatic and military. The traditional method of assault was long used by the British and French, who advanced *yards* in return for thousands of casualties. That method left a whole generation of citizens and political leaders with the firm conviction of "never again." This war-bred pacifism was to plague those two states when they faced the totalitarians during the 1930s. In addition, the method encouraged British and French leaders to think of the defense as dominant—even when they had·observed in the last months of the war that the tank, new German tactics, and the airplane had swung the balance back to the offense.

Second, this example suggests how hard it is for organizations to innovate, whether it be in military or in foreign policy. Humans in organizations are *trained* to think and act in prescribed ways. In adversity, some organizations cling more rigidly to what they *know* well (even though it works poorly) and resist efforts to adopt the unfamiliar. Even when innovation takes place, those new ideas may be undercut by the traditional assumptions. The familiar may prove to be extraordinarily resistant to extinction.

To get a feeling for this form of innovation, imagine yourself as a British field commander with eleven divisions under your command. Your orders are to assault the German lines, break through and swing to the right to join up with a simultaneous French assault further south. The traditional method, and the one you have been trained to follow, is to begin the offensive with a lengthy artillery bombardment. Shelling of the German trenches and barbed wire entanglements (to cut holes in the wire to allow your infantry to advance) may last three days and be followed by forty eight hours of intense bombardment. In that five-day span, the Germans have assumed that an assault will occur and have been bringing reinforcements in by rail from quiet sectors of the front. At H-hour, eight divisions in the line go "over the top" of their trench works and push forward toward the German wire and trenches. Word reaches you that most of your forces have reached the first line of German trenches, although one division has penetrated into the second line of defenses while two are being held up by German strong points. As commander, you have three divisions in reserve. What do you do at this point?

If you were following the British army's doctrine (and you *are* because you have risen through the ranks precisely because you learned well), your next step is to *halt* the division making the most headway. If it pushes on, it may lose contact and become surrounded. You then throw your reserves at the spot where German resistance is the *greatest*—that is, to aid the stalled divisions in their attempt to reduce the German strong points. They make some headway, but the advanced division is hit by the inevitable German counterattack and withdraws, forcing the divisions on its flanks to fall back to avoid being struck on their flanks. By evening of the hypothetical battle, the British line has advanced some 500 yards. Perhaps 20 percent of your attacking force has become casualties. And a new German trench line lies before you, with a new one in construction beyond that.

The Germans were the first to integrate several evolving ideas on how to do the assault better and to *train* their forces to use the new tactics. First, there was no prolonged bombardment to alert the enemy to the coming offensive and to allow them time to reinforce the sector. An intense barrage of several hours prior to the attack provided the preparation. Second, units that penetrated the enemy lines were to become the leading edge of the attack. The points of resistance (such as the strong points holding up your two divisions) were to be bypassed. Reserves were to be pushed forward to support the units which had *penetrated furthest*. Second-line units would move in to reduce the bypassed strong points. These tactics were spectacularly successful in 1918. In March, April, and May, 1918, in three separate offensives, German forces operating without tanks created huge holes in British and French lines, advancing upwards of 40 *miles* in days.

The irony of the German approach was that these offensives were directed by a General, Erich Ludendorff, who underestimated the ability of the tactics to end the stalemate and who could not shake himself free of the traditional methods of assault. Ludendorff held his lead forces back while concentrating his reserves to destroy the strong points. Ludendorff had the agony of seeing the "offensive to end the war" contained by the power of the defense. Yet it was clear in 1918 that the tactical innovations involving tanks and assault methods had restored mobility to the battlefield.

How well did the *strategic* innovators fare? They were not concerned with fighting battles but with the conduct of the war as a whole. They rejected the assumption that war had to be fought primarily on the preexisting battlefields. Strategic innovators planned to avoid the stalemate on a strongly defended front by opening *a new front* where the enemy was weaker. Thus, at the beginning of 1915, some British military men and civilians (notably Winston Churchill, the naval minister) advocated an attack on the Gallipoli Peninsula of Turkey. Turkey had entered the war on the side of Germany in October, 1914. Seizure of Gallipoli and the conquest of Constantinople would probably drive the Turks out of the war and would provide a direct supply line to the Russians (who needed arms and munitions desperately). Serbia could be reinforced with an Anglo-French army as well.

Strategic innovations—especially when proposed by civilians—usually raise a spirited debate. So it was in the British government. The result was a patchwork of compromise and foot-dragging. A naval bombardment of the Turkish forts guarding the Straits began in February, 1915, but ended in March with some success and some losses. It also alerted the Turks. An initial landing of British troops began in late April, with additional landings in August. The operation failed; the troops never got beyond the landing zones. Delay, weak forces, and timid commanders—all symptoms of a heavily compromised policy—meant that real Turkish weakness overcame Entente ineptness. The British did successfully withdraw their forces from the peninsula at the end of the year. That was the only bright spot. The episode so tarnished the reputation of the strategic innovators (Churchill was fired) that the traditionalists in Britain faced no further challenge to their policy of hurling men against well defended trenches.

There were two other major areas of strategic innovation—the political and the naval. The Germans, for instance, in February, 1915, announced a submarine blockade of Britain. This new naval front struck where Britain was the weakest—the protection of its merchant marine—and did hold the promise of crippling British ability to sustain its war effort. The British blockade of all maritime commerce destined for Germany had a similar sort of purpose: to wage war on the economy and civilians of its opponents. We shall return to this strategic innovation in a moment.

Political warfare, the second strategic innovation, attempts to undermine the will and capacity of the government and *civilian* population to prosecute the war by encouraging crippling dissent *behind the front*. In March, 1917, a bread riot occurred in Petrograd (formerly called St. Petersburg, but Russified as a patriotic measure).[18] It was a spark that ignited pervasive discontent against the Tsarist regime and with the four million casualties in a war that increasingly seemed to have no point. Spontaneously, Russian workers, soldiers, and the urban middle class rose to overthrow the Tsar and install a parliamentary regime. The new regime pledged to honor the Tsar's alliance commitments and his war. The British and French insisted upon it. The war, however, now lacked popular support.

The Germans recognized the volatility of the situation and sought to exploit it. They contacted a Russian revolutionary stranded in Switzerland and offered him safe passage to Russia. V.I. Lenin was attractive to the Germans because he and his Bolshevik party advocated unilateral Russian withdrawal from the war. To that point, the war in the East had been inconclusive. In 1915 (and 1917), the Germans launched major offensives, driving the Russians back, taking thousands of prisoners, but never delivering the crushing blow. Russia was too vast, its transportation network too weak, and manpower too great to break easily. And it could count on its allies to draw off German troops.

Lenin accepted the German offer and arrived in Petrograd in April, 1917. After an unsuccessful coup attempt in July, the Bolsheviks toppled the parliamentary regime in November, 1917. True to his program, Lenin agreed to an armistice with the Germans in December. In March, 1918, the Bolshevik government accepted the Treaty of Brest-Litovsk, in which Russia lost the Ukraine, Poland, Finland, and the Baltic provinces, but gained peace with Germany. With Russia out of the war, the Germans moved their divisions westward for the final reckoning with the British, French, and newly arriving Americans.

Political warfare proved in the end to be another strategic innovation that Germany's opponents could wield as well. With the entry of the United States into the war (April 1917), President Woodrow Wilson's repeated calls for a new world order and the triumph of political democracy became harnessed to the Entente's war effort. The insistence that the Entente would discuss peace only with the representatives of the German people, and not the Kaiser or his government, fueled the revolutionary agitation in Germany in the fall of 1918. The political collapse of Germany contributed more to the ending of the war than the status of the battlefield in November, 1918. And in that lay an irony. The German military avoided having to surrender, leaving that up to the *political* leadership of the new German republic. That fact maintained the prestige of the military and the belief that civilians had lost the war.

---

[18]For studies of the Russian Revolution, see E.H. Carr, *The Bolshevik Revolution 1917–1923*, 3 vols. (New York: Macmillan, 1950–1953); George Kennan, *Soviet-American Relations, 1917–1920*, 2 vols. (Princeton: Princeton University Press, 1956–1958); Richard Ullman, *Anglo-Soviet Relations, 1917–1921*, 2 vols. (Princeton: Princeton University Press, 1961–1968); John Wheeler-Bennett, *The Treaty of Brest-Litovsk and Germany's Eastern Policy* (Oxford: Clarendon Press, 1939); and John Bradley, *Allied Intervention in Russia* (New York: Basic Books, 1968).

Coalition War and the Search for Allies   The character of the war and its tempo were also a consequence of its coalitional nature. You will recall that the Russians launched a premature offensive in 1914 to weaken the German drive into France. The British operation against Gallipoli was partially a response to a Russian plea for pressure on the Turks. In 1916, the French again called for an early Russian offensive to reduce the pressure on Verdun. The Russians responded with an offensive that routed the surprised Austrians but also depleted Russia's ability to sustain the war effort. The British loyally attacked when the French ran into trouble; the Germans did the same for the Austrians. Allies were vital, yet the demands of the alliance could prove to be devastating, as they did for the Russian regime.

Obviously, it was in the interests of both sides to expand their alliance networks or, failing that, to keep neutral states from joining the war on the other's side. Japan declared war on Germany in August, 1914, and seized the German Asiatic possessions. Turkey joined the Triple Alliance in October, 1914, while Italy declared its neutrality and then went over to the Entente in May, 1915. The addition of new members to the alliance brought problems as well. A weak state, for instance, brought its weakness into the alliance. That weakness invited attack by the enemy, which forced the stronger ally to divert resources to fend off the attack. For instance, in October, 1917, the static Italian front collapsed (the Battle of Capporetto) and Britain and France had to rush divisions to northeastern Italy to bolster the line. Similarly, when Romania entered the war on the side of the Entente in 1916, German forces quickly conquered Romania, creating a new avenue of attack into Russia and making the hard-pressed Russians man a longer defensive line.

On the other hand, when a strong state entered a wartime alliance, its very power meant that the original alliance partners had to accommodate the interests of the new state. The French and the British disagreed with several of Wilson's wartime and post-war goals. They could not, however, afford to alienate the Americans in 1918 because they recognized that the formula for victory had two mandatory features—tanks and Yanks. At the same time, their own domestic political situations did not permit them to abandon their own war goals for which so many had died. The most divisive issues were put on ice until victory, when presumably the Yanks would not be needed.

Was it inevitable that the United States, the last neutral major power, become involved in the war?[19] This total war between most of the world's major powers created a growing tension between neutrals and belligerents. The British gradually imposed a tight blockade on shipping to Germany. The United States and other neutrals protested that neutrals had the right to sell "peaceful" commodities such as foodstuffs and cotton to any nation. The British, seeking to choke the German economy, declared more and more commodities as contraband and therefore to be seized by the Royal Navy. The Germans countered with

---

[19]For American participation, see Ernest May, *The World War and American Isolation* (Cambridge: Harvard University Press, 1959); Daniel Smith, *The Great Departure* (New York: John Wiley, 1965); David Trask, *The United States in the Supreme War Council* (Middletown, Conn.: Wesleyan University Press, 1961); Edward Coffman, *The War to End All Wars* (New York: Oxford University Press, 1968).

a submarine blockade of the British Isles in early 1915. This was not a "torpedo on sight" blockade, but did lead to the sinking of passenger liners, most notably the British ship *Lusitania* in May, 1915. The deaths of Americans and the novel cruelty to noncombatants led to a series of strong American protests. Chancellor Bethmann was able to force a more circumspect submarine policy on the resisting German navy. With its fleet bottled up, the submarine campaign was the only active, systematic way in which the navy could fight.

By early 1917, the German government reversed itself and announced an end to the restrictions on U-boat warfare. A year of stalemate in the West (and some promise of change in the East) encouraged the Germans to push this innovation to the hilt. They expected a hostile American reaction, but assumed that, even if the United States declared war, the Americans could not mobilize and deploy their forces in time to change the outcome.

The American government did declare war (April 1917), ending two and a half years of attempting to be neutral "in thought as well as deed." President Wilson had made an effort to ensure neutrality, but he himself was not neutral. One month after the start of the war he told his confidant Edward House that "if Germany won it would change the course of our civilization and make the United States a military nation"[20]—a most regrettable event in Wilson's eyes. The dynamics of the war left no room for major power neutrality, and Wilson's distaste for the German cause helped begin the tilt in favor of the Entente. The renewed submarine offensive was the last straw.

American entry into the war proved to be quite uneven and almost as tardy as the Germans expected. The navy, traditionally the first line of defense, was ready to help break the back of the German submarine offensive. The American army and fledgling air force, on the other hand, were small and poorly equipped. An enormous expansion of the armed forces began, but it was not until August, 1918, that American ground forces appeared at the front in significant numbers. If the war had continued into 1919 (as everyone expected), two million Americans would have been in the trenches on the Western front; and those Americans were fired with naïve patriotism in contrast to the war weariness of all the other belligerents.

As it happened, the Americans saw only four months of sustained combat, although there was nothing "easy" about the combat they did see. They arrived in force as the last of the great German offensives of 1918 was being contested. In July, the Entente powers went over to the offensive, a strategic position they did not relinquish. They had belatedly changed their tactics as well. They had given up long preparatory bombardments; tanks were used in large numbers; and as an offensive began to falter in one sector, instead of using reserves to win the day, a new offensive was begun in another sector.

The Germans found themselves being driven back on the Western front. General Ludendorff in August, 1918, reluctantly told the Kaiser that Germany could not win the war; then in late September, after more battlefield reverses, he advised the Kaiser that Germany stood on the verge of losing the war. Ludendorff recommended that Germany arrange an armistice with the Entente powers

---

[20]House diary entry reprinted in *The Papers of Woodrow Wilson*, ed., Arthur Link (Princeton: Princeton University Press, 1979), vol. XXX: 1914 p. 462. Copyright © 1979 by Princeton University Press.

that would stop the fighting but leave Germany in control of the occupied territories. When the government publicly requested such an armistice on October 4, the news stunned the German public and political leaders. They had read—and believed—the newspapers that had spoken of the coming German victory. Their world seemed to crash in upon them, and a wave of defeatism washed over Germany. Entente propaganda helped the pot boil.

Ludendorff, however, recovered his nerve. He calculated that a stiff German resistance and some withdrawals from occupied territory would force the Entente into a negotiated peace, but the defeatism that he had helped launch several weeks earlier undercut his plans. In addition, there came the abrupt surrenders of Turkey and Bulgaria in October and the discussion of Austrian surrender terms with the Entente. During the first week in November, revolution broke out in German cities and in military barracks. With Wilson in the lead, the Entente insisted on conducting armistice negotiations with a democratic government. The Kaiser abdicated and fled to neutral Holland; civilian leaders proclaimed a republic on November 9.

The day before, a delegation of German political leaders met with General Foch, who represented the Entente states. Foch offered the Germans an armistice if Germany withdrew from all occupied land (including Russian territory), permitted Entente occupation of western Germany up to the Rhine River, and turned over to the Entente a large number of ships, trains, and trucks. The German representatives had hoped for a cease-fire in place. The Entente demanded a preliminary surrender. With Germany in political collapse, however, the German representatives saw no alternative but to sign the armistice. The guns fell silent at 11:00 A.M. on November 11, 1918, some 30 million casualties (10 million deaths) since those dramatic days of August, 1914.[21]

Peace Again   The victorious Entente leaders gathered in Paris the following January to decide the political outcome of the war.[22] Their first order of business was to reach an agreement among themselves about the world they wanted to shape. During the war, the European states had signed secret treaties and made pledges to divide up the spoils of war and to reaffirm certain practices various states felt necessary (such as Britain's unilateral determination of who could use the high seas). The United States, however, had not been a party to such agreements; indeed, Wilson's declaration of American war aims (the Fourteen Points) expressly rejected such secret agreements. In particular, Wilson demanded that peoples should have the right to determine for themselves who would rule them and that some league of states be created to safeguard the hard-won peace.

His idealism (as it was called at the time) collided with the "old politics" of the European powers. The French wanted to cripple Germany by breaking it up into separate states and by saddling the Germans with a huge indemnity. Britain also insisted on an indemnity to pay for the Entente costs of the war and to keep

[21]See R.E. Dupuy and Trevor Dupuy, *The Encyclopedia of Military History* (New York: Harper & Row, Pub., 1970), p. 990, for estimates of casualties by country.

[22]For studies of peacemaking, see Arno Mayer, *Politics and Diplomacy of Peacemaking* (New York: Knopf, 1967); Richard Watt, *The Kings Depart* (New York: Simon & Schuster, 1969); Thomas Bailey, *Woodrow Wilson and the Lost Peace* (New York: Macmillan, 1944); Harold Nicolson, *Peacemaking, 1919* (Boston: Houghton Mifflin, 1933).

control of German productivity. Both wanted to acquire Turkish and German colonial holdings. Italy wanted Turkish and Austrian territory (which it had been promised as a reward for its entry into the war on the side of the Entente).

The peoples of the Balkans and central Europe clamored for the creation of separate states reflecting their own particular national identities. Unfortunately, ethnically dissimilar people were mixed together in many areas. Wilson's policy of national self-determination was warmly applauded as long as it favored the state-building interests of one particular group over another. In addition, there were the issues of power (more territory) and defense (territory with defensible terrain), which encouraged the leaders of the major ethnic groups to think as expansively as possible. After all the juggling, and with much smoldering resentment, the new states emerged: Poland from Russian, German, and Austro-Hungarian territory; Finland and the Baltic republics of Latvia, Lithuania, and Estonia out of Russia; Austria, Czechoslovakia, and Hungary out of a shattered Austro-Hungarian empire; Yugoslavia from a consolidation of Bosnia and other portions of the Austro-Hungarian empire, along with Serbia and Montenegro. It was a new Europe that greeted the beginning of the third decade of the twentieth century (see Map 3–2).

However momentous the redefinition of Central Europe was, the principal problem for the Entente powers was the future of Germany and the means to ensure that a new world war would not occur again. In the negotiations among the victors which took place between January and May, 1919, Wilson found that he had to make a choice between many of the Fourteen Points. Even though the force of American arms helped carry the day on the battlefront, the other Entente powers would not accept the entire American program. Wilson decided to fight most vigorously for his League of Nations proposal, seeing in it a more permanent and pervasive force for peace. The League would be empowered to investigate, recommend solutions, and use force if necessary to quell any threat to world peace. On other issues, notably vis-à-vis Germany, the President did not insist on his viewpoint if it endangered his proposal for the League.

Thus the Entente agreed to saddle Germany with reparations (the amount to be fixed at a later conference); to force her to return Alsace-Lorraine to France and portions of her territory to the new Polish state; to limit the German army to 100,000 men with no tanks or aircraft and the navy to six warships and no submarines. Wilson was able to prevent the division of Germany, but had to agree to a fifteen-year occupation by the Entente powers of Germany west of the Rhine and a perpetual demilitarization of the area. In return for British and French concessions on the indemnity and the status of Germany, and to allay French and British fears that a League of Nations could not restrain a resurgent Germany, Wilson signed a defense treaty with Britain and France. The United States pledged to come to the aid of the two states in case of a German attack. That was a startling departure from American foreign policy traditions.

On May 7, 1919, the German delegation learned of the terms of the peace treaty for the first time. The victors gave them the option of accepting the terms or having the war resume. After a bitter debate, the new socialist government in Germany accepted the "dictated" Treaty of Versailles. Similar treaties were forced on Austria, Hungary, Bulgaria, and Turkey (although a subsequent revolt by nationalist Turks and a war against Greece brought about a substantial revision of the treaty with Turkey in 1923).

EUROPE 1919

NEW INDEPENDENT NATIONS

ALLIED OCCUPATION ZONE
(British, French, American)

0   100   200   300 miles

20°

Gulf of Bothnia

FINLAND

Helsinki

Ladoga

Petrograd

NORWAY

SWEDEN

10°

60°

Oslo

Stockholm

Tallin

ESTONIA

North Sea

Riga

LATVIA

U.S.S.R.

DENMARK

Baltic Sea

Memel

LITHUANIA

Kaunas

Copenhagen

Danzig

EAST PRUSSIA

NETHERLANDS

Hamburg

Elbe

Berlin

Vistula

Warsaw

Amsterdam

GERMANY

POLAND

BELGIUM

Brussels

Cologne

Leipzig

Oder

LUX.

Coblenz

Dresden

Cracow

Kiev

50°

SAAR

Mainz

Dnieper

Rhine

Prague

CZECHOSLOVAKIA

FRANCE

Munich

Danube

Vienna

SWITZERLAND

AUSTRIA

Budapest

Geneva

HUNGARY

Odessa

Milan

ROMANIA

Marseilles

Belgrade

Bucharest

Black Sea

Adriatic Sea

YUGOSLAVIA

Danube

ITALY

Sofia

BULGARIA

Rome

Constantinople

Naples

Tirana

GREECE

Aegean Sea

TURKEY

ALBANIA

40°

30°

Mediterranean Sea

MAP 3-2   Europe in 1919

The Entente powers—except for Bolshevik Russia—signed the Versailles Treaty. All the major signatories—except the United States—ratified the treaty, thus bringing it into force. Under the American Constitutional procedures, the United States Senate has the power to ratify or reject any treaty. Debate in the Senate lasted from July, 1919, to March, 1920. Opponents of the treaty objected to becoming inextricably entangled with the affairs of Europe. The Senators supporting the treaty failed to attract the necessary two-thirds of the votes, and the treaty failed. The Senate similarly failed to ratify the military alliance with France and Great Britain. In rejecting the Versailles Treaty, the Senate had rejected the League Wilson had woven into the terms of the peace treaty. The Republican victory in the Presidential election of 1920 confirmed the American withdrawal from a position of leadership in world politics.

In many other countries, the new peace began on a bitter note as well. While the League of Nations began operations without the United States, the scars of war and political unrest were everywhere. French Premier Clemenceau—who had insisted on squeezing Germany at the Versailles peace conference—went down to electoral defeat in 1920 because he appeared *too lenient* with Germany. One figure captures much of the French feeling. If you were a French male between 20–32 years of age in 1914, the odds were better than 50-50 that you would not have lived to see the peace.[23] In Germany, the socialists and moderates incurred the hatred of nationalistic Germans for accepting the Versailles *"diktat."* The new government of the Weimar Republic was buffeted by revolutionary uprisings from the left and military coup attempts from the right. Britain in 1920 had a civil war on its hands in Ireland. Russia, too, was convulsed by a civil war (1918–1920) and annoyed by small-scale military intervention by the Entente powers. Gradually the Bolsheviks defeated the disunited opposition forces, stumbled into a short and unsuccessful war with the Poles (1920), and then found sporadic urban and rural uprisings dogging their attempt to create a socialist state.

The decade that ended in 1919 saw unprecedented changes in world politics. Four great empires (the Russian, German, Austro-Hungarian, and Turkish) had collapsed and untried republics took their place. The first socialist state had emerged in Russia and had inspired revolutionary movements around the world. Europe itself was physically torn, politically and psychologically divided. America, militarily unscarred, economically dominant, and politically disillusioned, withdrew back into its hemisphere. Things were settled, and yet unsettled.

PART II:
SCIENTIFIC APPROACHES TO WORLD POLITICS

Systems Approach

In the last chapter, we examined the structure of the international system of 1900. Table 3-1 reports the power held by the major powers among the 50 or so independent states that compromised the system ten years later. Figure 3-1 de-

---

[23]William Langer, ed., *An Encyclopedia of World History*, rev. ed. (Boston: Houghton Mifflin, 1948), p. 976. Reprinted by permission of Houghton Mifflin Company.

TABLE 3-1 Basic Power Levels in 1910

MEASURE	WORLD	US	UK	RUSSIA	FRANCE	GERMANY	AUSTRIA-HUNGARY	ITALY	BELGIUM	JAPAN	CHINA
1. Million metric tons of crude steel	58.94	26.1	6.4	3.5	3.4	12.9	2.1	.7	1.9		
2. Percent of world steel		44%	11%	6%	6%	22%	4%	1%	3%		
3. Million inhabitants in independent states	1189	92	45	160	39	65	49	32	7	54	439
4. Percent of world population in independent states		8%	4%	13%	3%	5%	4%	3%	1%	5%	37%
5. Political stability in past decade		1.0	1.0	.2	.6	1.0	.8	.6	.8	.8	.4
Power*		26	8	4	4	14	4	1	2	2	7

$$*\text{Power} = \frac{\#2 + (\#5 \times \#4)}{2}$$

Sources: For population and political stability, see Table 2–3; for population, *The World Almanac, 1912* (New York: Press Publishing Co., 1911), p. 587.

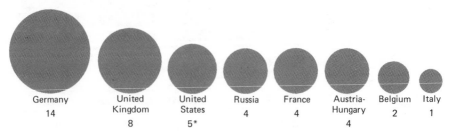

Germany	United Kingdom	United States	Russia	France	Austria-Hungary	Belgium	Italy
14	8	5*	4	4	4	2	1

*Projected power

FIGURE 3-1   Power Distribution in 1910

picts the relative strengths of the major powers (American power is projectable power).

Compared to the previous decade, the structure has not changed radically; we would expect continuity in the patterns of behavior. The diplomatic history of the second decade both illustrates some of the patterns hypothesized in Chapter 2 and suggests some possible additions. The Kaiser, for instance, turned away from the idea of a continental league of states and put greater emphasis on the creation of an arrangement with England. In rejecting the league of states approach, Germany gave up an interest in collective problem solving and enforcement of norms. In their place, Germany stressed bilateral relations and, increasingly, unilateral threats to deal with perceived troublemakers. Britain, however, was not willing to accept a subordinate position in an alliance with Germany if it could achieve greater security and influence in a rival alliance. Perhaps détente is all the second most powerful state can offer the most powerful.

While the ladder-like system persisted, a trend emerged. The relative power of Britain and Russia declined, while that of Germany increased. If this trend had continued, Germany might have become a state in a class by itself: the most powerful state in the system, with twice as much power as its nearest rival. A state in such a position may experience a change in its concern about alliances. We would not expect it to spurn its alliance partners, but it may be less likely to fear defection by the weaker states. What it may now fear is that *weakness* on the part of its alliance partners may lead other states to challenge its weaker allies, which would drag the strong power into an unwanted conflict. During the July, 1914, crisis, when the Austro-Hungarian government wavered on the question of war with Serbia, German diplomats dropped pointed hints that Germany would have to reevaluate its alliance with Austria-Hungary (i.e., renounce the alliance) if that nation did not act like a major power and quickly attack Serbia.

In terms of the two historic alliance systems of the period, we see that the Triple Entente's power (16) is more or less in balance with that of the Triple Alliance (19). Here again, however, there has been a shift. In 1900, the balance stood in favor of the Entente (assuming British membership) at 23, as opposed to the Triple Alliance's 18. If the trend in the balance were to continue into the future, the world would look increasingly ominous to the Entente powers. That possibility may have forced the Entente powers to regard their alliance partners as indispensible. The other side of the coin was that Germany had a very great incentive to attempt to split Britain off from France and Russia—a policy Germany followed up until August of 1914.

War in a Ladder-like System
Was World War I the product of a particular distribution of power? Did its nature, duration, and outcome display patterns we would expect in such a system? Alternatively, was the war more a product of *environmental* factors—such as the rise of a "pre-war spirit," the Russian government's felt need to back the Serbs after having backed away previously, the war plans of Germany, and so on? Or did these environmental factors *reinforce* a systemic pressure for major-power conflict during these two decades?

Before we tackle these questions, it would be wise to keep certain points in mind. First, international conflict is a normal occurrence in the relations among states, no matter the power distribution. The question here is whether a particular type of system encourages *total war*—a war of high intensity, involving most (if not all) major powers, of prolonged duration, and encouraging states to seek the destruction of their enemies. Second, the systems approach cannot explain specific events. For instance, it cannot tell us why the war began in August, 1914, following the assassination of Franz Ferdinand, rather than in 1911, with the second Moroccan crisis, or in 1913 during the Balkan war, or toward the end of the decade because of some colonial incident between Britain and Germany. It cannot do so (1) because the systems approach deals with *patterns*, which themselves are a summation of a *variety* of state behaviors, (2) because we have no way at present of isolating the effects of system structure from all the other environmental features. The systems approach should, however, estimate the *likelihood* of a war, and its characteristics.

Given the polarization of alliances and the relatively equal distribution of power between them, war seems *unlikely* between the major powers. Without a clear power advantage, only the costs of war are certain; victory is not. The outbreak of war, therefore, does not seem to be explicable in systemic terms. Does the approach do any better estimating the *type* of war likely to occur? Yes, indeed!

I would hypothesize that *in times of crisis or major-power war in polarized alliance networks, states will rigidly support alliance partners*. The disparity in the power of *individual* states means that one state might be easily defeated if its alliance partners did not come to its aid. Russia, for instance, faced defeat at the hands of Germany if its Entente allies backed out of their commitments. And the addition of Russian capabilities to a victorious Germany would make Germany clearly the dominant state in the international system, which would pose enormous new hazards for France and Britain. Thus the slogan for states in this system must be "my ally right or wrong." When two major powers become involved in war, the structure propels the two alliance networks to become involved as well.

In a ladder-like structure, wars will be prolonged and intense. The balance of alliance power and the rapid involvement of the alliance networks make a quick military victory improbable. Thus the structure works against a short war. The structure also discourages an early negotiated settlement as well. Each state needs to ensure the continuation of the alliance network, for in a war its survival rests on the willingness of others to fight on its behalf. Each state must therefore show its complete and unflagging commitment to its allies *and* insist on a similar commitment from them. The clearest and most irreversible means of demonstrating such a commitment is to call for complete victory ("we won't stop fighting until the other side is destroyed"). Others in the alliance will feel constrained to do likewise in order to receive the alliance's protection. To demand victory on the battlefield is to demand a long, intense war when power is evenly distributed as it is in a ladder-like system.

In summary, then, I would hypothesize that a ladder-like system would produce total war if and when war occurred between any two major powers. Thus the systems approach might help us better understand, and possibly predict, the nature of warfare in world politics. And (anticipating the discussion in the next chapter) total war in a ladder-like system is likely to have very disruptive consequences for the distribution of power in such a system. Large-scale violence may demolish the weaker major powers and reduce or elevate the stronger. We might expect, therefore, that the 1920s would present a new distribution of power and a new set of power-induced behaviors.

Policy-Maker Approach:
The Kaiser and the 1914 Crisis

In Chapters 1 and 2, I explored two different ways of viewing the process by which states make policy: as a process that displays the characteristics of rational decision making, or as a process of political bargaining. In each approach I emphasized the *group* basis of policy making. Now I want to focus on a single individual involved in the policy making. In doing so, these questions become central:

> What role did the individual's *personality* play in his or her perception and behavior?
>
> How did the individual's *perception* of the policies of others, of the national interest of his or her own state, and of his or her own personal interests affect behavior?
>
> How much *influence* did the individual have on the day-to-day and long-term policy making?

By and large, most recent scholarship on the war has concluded that the policy makers in 1914 were singularly unfit to cope with the crisis. Luigi Albertini, the most painstaking of the historians of the causes of the war, castigates all the policy makers in every country as being short-sighted, dull-witted, wavering, overly emotional, duplicitous, scheming, and the like.[24] Is it just a quirk of history that 1914 was so unfortunate to have such dangerous people in power in all the major powers simultaneously? Or have we too easily fallen prey to the argument that a terrible war *must* be the product of terribly flawed policy makers?

I do not want to suggest that the policy makers of 1914 (or of any other year) were paragons of virtue or wisdom. I would suspect, however, that many, if not all, were of average competence—just as the leaders of today's states are. The problem with our analysis of World War I has been a misleading richness of information *and* the assumption that policy is made by the rational model. In the 1950s, a group of political scientists began to reexamine the documents pertaining to World War I, employing hypotheses drawn from social psychology. Their

---

[24]Albertini, *Origins*.

findings suggest that the leaders of the major powers often perceived events and acted like the average individual under stress.[25] We want to go one step further by applying the political model of policy making. How do individuals in a *political* process respond? This brief case study, then, focuses on the Kaiser during July and early August.[26] Its purpose is to illustrate the role of personality, perception, and influence in the politics of policy making.

Personality   Personality can be thought of as "the relatively stable organization of a person's motivational dispositions."[27] The Kaiser's physical deformity has often been hypothesized as a central determinant of his personality. A difficult birth marked him with a withered left arm, and, at least in childhood, a difficulty in maintaining his balance. He was raised in a family and royal tradition that stressed the importance of an imposing stance: to appear manly, proud, and resolute. The birth defects and the cultural expectations combined to make him strongly conscious of the image he presented to the world, and yet perpetually uncertain of how well he maintained that image.

Irrespective of cause, three major dispositions appear in the Kaiser's personality. The first was *self-centeredness*. The Kaiser often defined issues in terms of himself, personalizing them to the point that they became challenges to his own personal worth and manhood. It was very difficult for him to distinguish between his personal interests and those of the German state. When he attempted to mediate the crisis between Austria-Hungary and Serbia, for instance, he saw it as a personal effort, one that could be abandoned if he felt he had been personally deceived. The second major disposition was a tendency toward *paranoia*. The Kaiser assumed that other states were capable of treachery. When they acted contrary to imperial or German interests, that was proof of their treachery. When interests coincided, the Kaiser suspected that they acted in fear of Germany or that they had masked their true intentions.

While these two dispositions may encourage aggressiveness and hinder meaningful cooperation, they do not inevitably lead to conflictual behavior. A self-centered individual may be quite cautious because failure reflects directly on his or her own self-worth. Similarly, paranoia may increase a leader's perception of the risks involved and thus induce a measure of caution. These "positive" consequences of his dispositions were not missing in the Kaiser's history. Fifty-

---

[25]See, among others, Ole Holsti, "The 1914 Case," *American Political Science Review,* 59 (June 1965), 365–78; Ole Holsti, Robert North, and Richard Brody, "Perception and Action in the 1914 Crisis," in *Quantitative International Politics,* ed., J. David Singer (New York: Free Press, 1968), pp. 85–119.

[26]This study draws primarily on the materials in Albertini, *Origins,* Michael Balfour, *The Kaiser and His Times* (New York: W.W. Norton & Co., Inc., 1972), and Alan Palmer, *The Kaiser* (London: Weidenfeld and Nicolson, 1978).

[27]H.J. Eysenck, W. Arnold, and R. Meili, eds., *Encyclopedia of Psychology* (New York: The Continuum Publishing Co., 1972), Vol. II, p. 383. For introductions to the subject of personality and politics, see Fred Greenstein, *Personality and Politics* (Chicago: Markham, 1970); Jeanne N. Knutson, ed., *Handbook of Political Psychology* (San Francisco: Jossey-Bass, 1973); Alan Elms, *Personality in Politics* (New York: Harcourt Brace Jovanovich, 1976); James D. Barber, *Presidential Character,* rev. ed. (Englewood Cliffs, N.J.: Prentice-Hall, 1977); and Joseph de Rivera, *The Psychological Dimension of Foreign Policy* (Columbus, Ohio: Chas. E. Merrill, 1968). The classic early study is Harold Lasswell, *Psychopathology and Politics* (Chicago: University of Chicago Press, 1930).

six years old in 1914, William II had been Kaiser since 1888. No newcomer to world politics, he had managed the affairs of state with perceptiveness and some skill. He had followed a consistent path of preserving and enhancing German prestige and power in world affairs; but when push came to shove, William had consistently sought to keep the peace.

The third disposition of the Kaiser's personality also had differing consequences. Initially flexible in his thinking, under pressure, he would slip into rigidity and then fatalism. In the latter stages, he easily absolved himself of the responsibility for his own actions on the premise that others had left him no choice. Following the assassination at Sarajevo, he wanted the Austrians to act quickly to settle the problem of Serbia and Slav nationalism in the Balkans. He assumed that the conflict could be "localized" and Russia kept neutral. After the Austrians delayed sending the ultimatum for three weeks, and Russia had pledged support for the Serbs, the Kaiser took a new tack. He instructed his diplomats to tell the Austrians to occupy Belgrade, the Serb capital, as a hostage. He himself would lead a mediation effort to negotiate an end to the crisis.

On July 29, William plunged into his mediation effort, spurred on by a cable that came during the night from the Tsar requesting his mediation. William replied that he was pressing the Austrians to reach an understanding with the Serbs and requested that Russia exercise the greatest restraint (i.e., avoid mobilization of its forces). Restraint was the order of the day, and that message was transmitted to all foreign capitals.

The hopefulness of the 29th turned sour on the 30th. A new telegram from the Tsar contained the fateful lines: "the military measures which have now come into force were decided five days ago."[28] To William, operating under enormous stress, the words were a revelation. The Tsar had already ordered partial mobilization. And he had done so *before* he had requested William's mediation. William was incensed at this personal treachery. Russia was free to strike Austria while Germany was busily tying Austria's hands. William declared his mediation effort over. Losing his earlier flexibility, the Kaiser did not bother to ask what "military measures" the Tsar had referred to. He would have discovered them to be an alert of the standing army, not a mobilization of reserves. However, on the 31st, he learned that the Tsar had indeed ordered general mobilization. The Kaiser, at the urging of his advisors, sent an ultimatum to Russia: end Russian general mobilization in 12 hours or Germany would mobilize. It was all stick (the threat of war) and no carrot; the ultimatum carried no promise that Russian interests might be safeguarded or that Germany would attempt mediation.

In these two days, the Kaiser had slipped into rigidity and then fatalism. Now the traits of self-centeredness and paranoia helped reinforce his inability to think creatively about the crisis. Looking ahead, the Kaiser grimly said, "The whole war [then pending] is plainly arranged between England, France, and Russia for the annihilation of Germany. . . . God help us in this fight for our existence, brought about by falseness, lies, and poisonous envy!"[29] He bitterly told

---

[28]*Outbreak of the World War: German Documents Collected by Karl Kautsky* (New York: Oxford University Press, 1924), p. 342.

[29]*Ibid.*, p. 351.

Nicholas that, because of Russian mobilization, "the whole weight of the decision lies solely on you[r] shoulders now, who have to bear the responsibility for peace or war."[30] Germany had done what it could honorably do. And the real villain? It was England, "this hated, lying conscienceless nation of shopkeepers."[31] England had relentlessly sought Germany's destruction and had created such an ingenious trap that, thanks to "the stupidity and ineptitude of our ally," Germany had been snared in a world war. William gloomily saw Germany's destruction as likely. As we know, the Russians refused to bow to the ultimatum. Heavy with emotion, the Kaiser signed the order committing Germany to mobilize and proceed directly to an attack on France. Relatively flexible crisis management had given way to "letting events take their course."

Perception   Perception refers to the way individuals see and interpret the world about them.[32] Personality helps shape perception, as does experience, training, and membership in particular groups. Three key perceptions stand out in the Kaiser's case.

Encirclement by rapacious neighbors. The idea of Germany's being at the center of things (as it was industrially and geographically) also fostered the belief that Germany was the target of its neighbors' concerted actions. The Entente symbolized the threatening combination. The Kaiser's perception was commonplace in Germany. Moreover, William perceived Germany as being the peaceful power, while the Entente was waiting for the opportune moment to damage German interests. In such a world, the temptation to strike first became a powerful one.

The use of force against smaller states was a normal part of world politics. The Kaiser's initial encouragement of an Austrian war on Serbia fit his perception well. Unruly states were to be punished by major powers: "[British foreign minister] Grey is committing the error of setting Serbia on the same plane with Austria and other Great Powers! That's unheard of: Serbia is nothing but a band of robbers that must be seized for its crimes!"[33] The military response by the great powers to the Boxer Rebellion in China was a reaffirmation of this principle.

A fait accompli is a useful device. William believed that the conquest of Serbia soon after the assassination would change the status quo quickly enough to prevent intervention by others, particularly the Russians. Successful, limited actions force other states to go through the agonies of having to decide whether to escalate the now-resolved conflict into a major power war. Inertia usually leads to a grumbling acceptance of the new status quo. The Austrian annexation of Bosnia-Herzegovina in 1908 demonstrated the efficacy of the *fait accompli.*

[30]*Ibid.*, p. 360.

[31]*Ibid.*, p. 350.

[32]See Robert Jervis, *Perception and Misperception in International Politics* (Princeton: Princeton University Press, 1976) for a general review and analysis. For more specialized treatments, see Ole Holsti, "Cognitive Dynamics and Images of the Enemy: Dulles and Russia," in David Finlay, Ole Holsti, and Richard Fagen, *Enemies in Politics* (Chicago: Rand McNally, 1967), pp. 25–96; Dina Zinnes, "The Expressions and Perception of Hostility in Prewar Crisis: 1914," in *Quantitative International Politics,* ed. Singer, pp. 85–119; and Dean Pruitt, "Definition of the Situation as a Determinant of International Action," in *International Behavior,* ed. Herbert Kelman (New York: Holt, Rinehart and Winston, 1965), pp. 393–432.

[33]*Outbreak: Kautsky Documents,* p. 163.

These perceptions—which were held by the Kaiser's ministers as well—led the German government to spur Austria on in its confrontation with Serbia. They also meshed well with the Kaiser's personality: a romantic and realist appreciation of the bold stroke (a "manly gesture"), a concern for how others might try to use the situation against Germany, and a flexibility as long as the issue concerned only the future of the weak Serb state. Yet the situation worsened; the image of a beleaguered Germany haunted the Kaiser.

Influence on Policy   The Kaiser relied on his advisors to tell him how he should act to maintain the image and prestige of the German state and his own rule. He castigated them when their suggestions failed. A minister's life was made more uncomfortable by the Kaiser's impetuosity, by his obstinancy one day and erraticness another. How did a minister handle the Kaiser; meeting his interests, yet preserving constancy in state policy? Chancellor Bethmann, for instance, served at the pleasure of the Kaiser, not the German parliament. Bethmann had to act on his own when necessary because the Kaiser expected results, and, on the other hand, hold up orders of the Kaiser when they seemed ill-conceived because William would not accept failure. When William had no position on an issue, he had to be furnished with one; when the sovereign had a "clearly" wrong view, it had to be changed. And when the sovereign was prone to become emotional and change direction easily, the sovereign's minister had to conduct policy in spite of the sovereign.

When a leader's advisors believe that they may have to act on behalf of the leader, the leader must often engage in a political battle to shape policy. That is, a leader must seek *influence* within her or his own government—to get others to accommodate the leader's interests and preferences in the formulation of the state's foreign policy.[34] In the week after the assassination, the Kaiser and his advisors were in general agreement. William approved the Austrian plan to submit an ultimatum as a pretext for war, even himself suggesting demands he felt the Serbs could never accept. He, like his advisors, continually worried about the foot-dragging of the Austrians in sending the ultimatum. His ministers, needing little encouragement, kept up a steady pressure on the Austrian government for quick action.

However, the Kaiser's capacity for influence was undercut by his decision to leave for a planned three-week vacation aboard his yacht. His departure on July 6 probably reflected his belief that there would be no crisis and that by appearing uninvolved, Germany could keep the affair localized. His absence from Berlin gave his ministers more leeway to make their own decisions and to prevent the Kaiser from reversing himself. By the time William returned from his cruise on the 27th, the Austrians had delivered the ultimatum (23rd) and broken relations on the 25th without consideration of the Serb reply. Under intense pressure from the German foreign ministry, the Austrians had agreed to declare war on Serbia on the 28th, thus creating the condition the Russians said would bring them in.

---

[34]"Influence" (like its compatriot "power") is one of the key concepts of political science. For good general introductions, see Jack Nagel, *The Descriptive Analysis of Power* (New Haven: Yale University Press, 1975), and David Bell, *Power, Influence and Authority* (New York: Oxford University Press, 1975).

The Kaiser was apparently not told by Bethmann of either the German pressure for a declaration of war or the Austrian commitment to begin war on the 28th.[35] The Kaiser was told, however, that the Austrians could not begin full-scale military operations against Serbia until August 12. William felt optimistic about the future because there were, in his view, two weeks to find a solution; the critical thing was to keep Russia from mobilizing, for Russian mobilization would necessitate German mobilization, and that necessitated war (and an attack on France, given the Schlieffen plan).

Bethmann withheld other information as well. The historical record suggests that, as in times past, the Kaiser's advisors were attempting to force William to follow certain lines of policy they believed he "really" wanted, or would want if he were not so emotional. In a *political* context, policy makers must operate in a complex environment, trying to reconcile the contending pressures of what each sees as the best policy, the policy the state has followed to this point, and the expectations other powerful policy makers have. The selective use of information is a time-honored device in the resulting policy battles. After all, the German government had struggled to buck up the Austrians. Why run the risk of having the Kaiser change his mind and call off the Austrians, who seemed reluctant to move anyway? At least the declaration of war would be a point of no return.

The Kaiser's advisors were correct in their concern about William's steadfastness. On July 28, he read the text of the Serb reply of the 25th to the Austrian ultimatum (the delay in its delivery to the Kaiser was probably intentional). William viewed the Serb reply as an adequate response and told his foreign minister that there were no grounds for war. Austria might occupy Belgrade in order to ensure Serb compliance with Austria's demands, but Austria was to go no further. He then would lead the mediation effort. This, then, became German policy. (But Bethmann delayed dispatch of these orders until he had heard that the Austrians had indeed declared war on Serbia. By that time, he was not about to give Austria an excuse to back out.)

The Kaiser's struggle to influence policy continued even after mediation failed and he had signed the order for German mobilization. After William signed the order, the war minister and General Moltke hurriedly left the palace to start the mobilization process, fearing that the Kaiser might reverse himself. And so he did! A cable arrived soon thereafter reporting that the British had agreed to remain neutral and keep *France* neutral as well, as long as Germany did not attack France. The Kaiser rejoiced. There would be no two-front war; the reckoning with Russia would go on unimpeded. The point now was to stop the attack on France. Moltke was summoned and told to reorient all his forces eastward against the Russians. The general refused, arguing that mobilization had been worked out to the man and to change plans would disrupt everything, leaving a mob rather than an army to defend Germany from either the west or the east.

The Kaiser repeated the order, and again Moltke refused. The Kaiser's ministers began to look for a way out of this tense confrontation. The decision that emerged was a compromise. The German government would accept the British offer and not attack France (the Kaiser's preference) but Britain would have to use all measures including force to ensure French neutrality (Moltke's

---

[35]Albertini, *Origins,* II, p. 441.

preference). Moltke won the right to continue the mobilization as planned, building up forces on the border with Belgium and France. France would be invaded if the agreement with Britain fell apart. The Kaiser accepted this unworkable compromise because he could neither force Moltke to yield nor find the courage in a crisis to relieve him from his command.

The irony of all this was revealed late on August 1, when a new message arrived from Britain. There had been a misunderstanding of the British position; there was no offer of neutrality. Perfidious Albion again! A chagrined Kaiser ordered Moltke to proceed as planned against France. The Great War was on.

We have observed that the Kaiser's influence varied, and that at critical points (such as the confrontation with Moltke) he did not have undisputed control over policy. A decision maker who is absent from day-to-day policy decisions (either by choice or by being unaware of an issue) can be influential only on broad questions (e.g., do we encourage Austria to act?), and from time to time on specific details when precise orders are given ("Tell the ambassador to deny the allegation"). Middle-range policy questions, such as *how* Austria should deal with Serbia, are less likely to be influenced by the absent political leader. Subordinates will operate under the broad mandate given by the leader (Serbia is to be dealt with). Subordinates are likely to avoid encouraging the leader to consider middle-range policy questions, and are likely to make selective use of information to that end.

Directly involved in policy making again, the political leader is likely to find that his or her influence is conditioned and constrained by the middle-range policy decisions already made by subordinates. William, for instance, had to work with the fact of an Austrian declaration of war, which gave him far less leeway in establishing the terms for mediation efforts. Indeed, the top political leader's influence on policy may be limited increasingly to "yes" or "no" decisions. The Kaiser found himself with such choices as send or not send an ultimatum to Russia, mobilize or not mobilize. In these cases, the political leader's choice is likely to be swayed by the momentum established by past decisions—in this case, toward more threatening, more irreversible German action. The more destructive aspects of personality and perception may also reinforce the momentum. The leader's influence may realistically be quite limited. Finally, as the confrontation with Moltke suggests, a leader can insist on some modification of critical decisions, but even there, influence was constrained by prior decisions about how mobilization was to be accomplished.

Interaction Approach:
Game Theory and Ending the War

How do wars end? Why does a war end at one point in time rather than another? The common sense answer to both of these questions is that wars end when and because one side conquers another. That is, the victor destroys the loser's capacity to resist. Traditionally, that has meant destroying the opponent's military establishment and physically occupying the territory of the opponent. The Allied victory against Germany *in 1945* comes the closest to meeting this common sense view. In most other wars of the twentieth century, wars have ceased before that point was reached. World War I is such a case. The Turks,

Bulgarians, Austrians, and Germans capitulated *before* conquest occurred. They might have elected, as the Germans did in 1945, to fight on to the bitter end. Why did they capitulate before conquest?

The other side of the question is why the Entente powers chose to wage war so long in spite of the minimal gains. Why did they persevere in spite of enormous casualties and a growing war weariness? Why did they not seek some negotiated settlement with the Germans or Austrians? Prior to American entry, Wilson made repeated calls for such negotiations. Why did the Entente prolong the war?

A Prisoner's Dilemma Game   The game theory approach introduced in Chapter 1 offers us an abstract tool to explore some of these questions. You should recall that the approach is not empirical; it suggests possible answers (hypotheses) by analogy. Let us suppose that for both Germany and the Entente powers there are two policy options: "not fight" and "fight." The situation is presented in Table 3–2. In each of the cells, there is a summary statement of the outcome of the policy choices made by each player. The mutual choice of the "fight" option produces the "war" outcome. "Appeasement under pressure" is illustrated by Lenin's attempts to take Russia out of the war. He chose to retreat on the battlefront and to negotiate with the Germans, relinquishing large sections of the Russian empire. Peace, on the other hand, occurs when both sides refrain from using violence against each other.

Let us further assume that both sides would suffer from the "war" outcome and both would benefit from the "peace" outcome (both relatively common perceptions at the time). If, on the other hand, one side chose "fight" and the other "not fight," the appeaser would suffer a relatively large loss and the aggressive state would reap a gain. Furthermore, assume that a prolonged war would mean that both sides would continue to suffer. Remember that in game theory, "gaining" and "suffering" refer to the utility of the particular outcome for the player, which we denote with numerical values. Table 3–2 represents the situation between Germany and the Entente powers in July and August, 1914, as well as in November, 1918.

**TABLE 3–2   Policy Options and Outcomes
in a Great War Game**

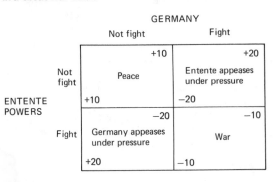

The values in the table conform to the classic "prisoner's dilemma" of game theory.[36] Its critical feature is the presence of a dilemma. Looking at the table, it is clear that both sides benefit from peace (each gets +10), which depends upon their both selecting the "not fight" option. Conversely, both suffer (each loses −10) from the war outcome, a result of their both picking "fight." That should settle matters. Neither side has an incentive for war, or if by mistake war did occur, both sides would quickly move to end it.

Unfortunately, the values are such that neither side can really afford to remain at peace, and both will continue the dreary business of butchering each other once war begins. Thus the dilemma of benefitting from peace but feeling compelled to wage war. To see why this is so, take the part of the German player. As a rational player, you would want to minimize your losses and, where possible, maximize your gain; the "fight" option does that best (−10, +20 respectively). If you choose "not fight," the Entente player can get a better result for the Entente position by "fighting," which produces the largest loss for you (−20). Similarly, you can do the same by fighting when the other side picks the "not fight" option. To guard against becoming the "sucker," both sides will "fight," producing the *undesired outcome for both*. In the historical context, in late July, 1914, the Kaiser wanted peace, but feared that if he continued to act as a mediator ("not fight") and the Russians mobilized ("fight"), Germany would become the "sucker." Wanting peace, but fearful of losing a great deal if other players did not pick peace, the Kaiser opted for war, which seemed to involve less loss. Similarly, to try to "call the war off" while the other side continues to fight, produces the "sucker" result again. The Entente and Germany will continue to damage each other because it is the best strategy possible. Prolonged wars are "reasonable," even though not in the best interests of either side!

Trust and Signalling   Now you might argue that the players are not compelled to "fight." They can both *agree* not to fight and thus produce the mutually beneficial outcome. Could Germany *trust* the Entente powers to follow through on such an agreement when they can get a larger payoff by double-crossing Germany (+20 instead of a +10)? Could Germany *trust itself* not to succumb to temptation and double-cross the Entente? Could the Entente trust Germany? Game theory leads us to the question of trust and the conditions under which states can trust each other even when one side wants to capitulate.

Suppose you were to play the game with someone else. What might we learn by your experience that might help answer these questions of trust, untrustworthiness, and the ending of wars? Let us further suppose you are required to bring $100 to play the game. Any negative results mean that you would pay the bank; positive results would mean that the bank would pay you. (Our analogy is that states always "bring" their resources to an issue, and their actions enhance or diminish those resources.) Finally, in this experiment you do not know how many turns will take place in this game, just as policy makers do not know how long an issue will confront them.

You are simply asked to write down "fight" or "not fight" and your opponent does the same thing. The choices are compared and the results imple-

---

[36]See Steven Brams, *Game Theory and Politics* (New York: Free Press, 1975), p. 30.

mented. It *is* a bit artificial to begin the game with no knowledge of any past events and with only the payoff values in the cells to guide you. Nonetheless, the common pattern between you and your opponent is likely to be one or two initial turns in which you both cooperate for peace. Then one of you will select "fight," either to gain more or because you fear the other will select "fight." In this example you have decided to break the peace. Once one selects "fight," both of you will do so for a series of turns. Table 3–3 illustrates this argument.

You can project the game beyond the sixth turn to see that you (and your opponent) will keep losing. The outcomes will eat away your resources to the point where you are distinctly worse off than when the war began. To continue the war is the road to ruin, *yet to try to get out (stop fighting) unilaterally will ruin you even faster!*

Experiments have suggested that one side can *as a deliberate policy* choose "not to fight," knowing that it will suffer the sucker's penalty.[37] It can do it again, knowing it is likely to suffer the penalty. But it has signalled a willingness to cooperate. Continuing with the example in Table 3–3, you have been appeased twice by your opponent, but you have continued to pick the "fight" option. Suppose, however, you decide to take your opponent up on the possibility of cooperating. You choose "not to fight" on turn 9 — only to find your opponent "fighting," which makes *you* the sucker (see Table 3–3). Was this a trap? Or was the opponent's choice of "fight" a warning to you that you had to reciprocate in order not to go back to the mutually punishing war? You decide to test your opponent once more by selecting "not fight." To your relief, the opponent chooses "not fight" as well. Warily, you continue to pick "not fight," as does your opponent.

TABLE 3–3   Moves in Prisoner's Dilemma Game

YOU			OPPONENT		
TURN #	CHOICE	VALUE OF RESOURCES	CHOICE	VALUE OF RESOURCES	
0		$100		$100	
1	NF	110	NF	110	pre-war cooperation (peace)
2	NF	120	NF	120	
3	F	140	NF	100	double-cross; war begins
4	F	130	F	90	
5	F	120	F	80	attrition
6	F	110	F	70	
7	F	130	NF	50	signalling and negative
8	F	150	NF	30	response
9	NF	130	F	50	signal responded to
10	NF	140	NF	60	and reaffirmed
11	NF	150	NF	70	peace
12	NF	160	NF	80	

[37]For an interesting experiment on strategies in a prisoner's dilemma game, see Robert Axelrod, "Effective Choice in the Prisoner's Dilemma," *Journal of Conflict Resolution,* 24 (March 1980), 3–25, and "More Effective Choice in the Prisoner's Dilemma," *ibid.* (September 1980), 379–403.

Thus it does seem possible to turn away from mutually punishing choices, even when on any single turn the rational player would choose to fight. Perhaps being caught in the attrition process and seeing a very bleak future encourages a reevaluation and leads to the signalling. Perhaps this game parallels the German-Russian front in late 1917 and early 1918, when Lenin attempted to leave the war, and the Western Front in October and November, 1918, when Germany sought to leave the war.

Two observations about falling into hell and getting out again. Your opponent faced a hard choice after turn 6. In an "attrition race," an opponent would "go under" when she or he reached zero. You would still have $40, which is far less than what you began with, but at least the war *and its losses* would end with the destruction of the opponent. Obviously, war over the long run is a disastrous proposition for your opponent. (A player out of a game is a leader out of office and without a country!) But for your opponent to begin signalling by "not fighting" *only accelerates the rush to the point of collapse.* Caught in an attrition situation, a state has only a particular range of resources that can support such signalling. Begun too late, signalling only hastens the extinction of the state (and increases the resources of the opponent).

The second point concerns the initial resources the players bring to the game. We assumed an equal distribution of resources. That may not often occur. For instance, in August, 1914, the Entente had 180 divisions, and Germany and Austria-Hungary had 145. The power analyses provide other evidence of resource inequalities. Different levels of resources may force different long-term strategies on the players. For instance, when there is a great difference between the players (say $100 to $20), the player with $20 has no margin for error; that player probably must "fight" from the start, because being the "sucker" means immediate extinction. When there is a difference in resources, but the weaker state (or coalition) is not in the danger zone regarding resources, the players may have more flexibility. Yet even here, it is likely that both will persist in the mutual punishment of attrition because neither side sees an immediate need to begin signalling, especially with the initial higher costs involved in signalling. In fact, if both begin with relatively large resources, both may accept attrition for a relatively long time. The American entry was important in this regard, because it kept the Entente powers away from their critical margin and ensured that the Germans would lose the attrition race.

One other point is relevant. The resources held by an opponent are difficult to calculate. In the game, you may know that your opponent has brought between $80 and $120, and your opponent has similarly imprecise information about you. In that case, neither you nor your opponent will know where the collapse point lies for the other. Hence, neither will know which player is close to being forced out of the game. Does one pursue an attrition strategy fueled by the hope that the opponent will collapse first or that the opponent will become convinced that *you* can last longer and therefore he or she must begin the signalling process?

Game theory and the prisoner's dilemma game have generated some insights and further questions regarding the outbreak, continuation, and termination of war. They suggest that two sides will choose to fight if the loss for being the sucker and the reward for being the double-crosser are greater than the rewards for war or peace, respectively. Furthermore, the *fear* that the other will double-cross is enough to make one pick the fight option. The outbreak of war becomes just a matter of time in such an environment. War will continue, even though both sides recognize the costs, because (a) there are hopes that attrition will drive the opponent out of the war first and (b) to signal for peace involves even stiffer costs. Such a war may indeed terminate when one side is exhausted and cannot prevent the conquest of its territory. Equally (or perhaps more) possible, one side may attempt to signal a willingness to return to the condition of peace in the hope that the other will respond. If successful, some form of compromise or capitulation ends the fighting, rather than conquest. Either way war ends, this particular type of game clearly suggests that the war will be prolonged and very costly in human lives.

CHAPTER FOUR

1920–1929
A hopeful peace?

PART I:
DIPLOMATIC HISTORY[1]

The Security Issue

The Great War of 1914–1918 discredited many of the traditional assumptions about world politics. Alliances and large military establishments now seemed to be the cause of war and insecurity. Yet if one rejected the traditional politics of alliances, secret treaties, and force, how might security be ensured? After the war to end wars, the question of security had become more vexing. Weakened states such as Germany and the Soviet Union feared invasion, while the victors feared a war of revenge by the defeated. At the same time, the very idea of security was changing. In the two decades before the war, "security" often meant the protection of a particular regime such as the Czarist regime or Kaiserdom. Even in democracies, security referred to the state or the empire, sometimes to the "nation," that mythical entity of people whose "place in the sun" had to be safeguarded. Romanticism and empires, however, had died in the trenches; war reached the home front. Now the individual citizen became the yardstick by which security was judged. Did the woman or man in the street feel secure? Political leaders sought to present themselves as the best architects of *personal security*.

[1]General sources include Sally Marks, *The Illusion of Peace* (London: Macmillan, 1976); Gordon Craig and Felix Gilbert, eds., *The Diplomats, 1919–1939* (Princeton: Princeton University Press, 1953); Hans Gatzke, ed., *European Diplomacy between Two Wars* (Chicago: Quadrangle, 1972); Jon Jacobson, *Locarno Diplomacy* (Princeton: Princeton University Press, 1972); Raymond Sontag, *A Broken World* (New York: Harper & Row, Pub., 1971); E.H. Carr, *German-Soviet Relations between the Two World Wars* (Baltimore: Johns Hopkins University Press, 1951). Contemporary, detailed reporting can be found in the yearly *Survey of International Affairs*, ed. Arnold Toynbee (Oxford: Oxford University Press); documentary sources include *Documents on British Foreign Policy*, first series (London: Her Majesty's Stationery Office, 1958 +).

At rock bottom, "security" meant having no future world war. That did not mean that individuals or leaders invariably rejected the usefulness of force, just that a war of all against all was intolerable. How might the states prevent such a war? How might conflict be managed to resolve the contentious issues of the day without such a war? And how might all this be done with a citizenry who demanded security but, burdened by the costs of one war, were reluctant to "bear any burden, pay any price" for that security?

The central answer for this decade was the League of Nations.[2] It began operations in January, 1920. By April, 40 states (the victors or neutrals in the war) had joined. Each was represented in the League Assembly. The Council of the League, on the other hand, initially had five permanent members (the United States, Britain, France, Italy, and Japan) and four elected members. The American failure to ratify the Versailles Treaty reduced the permanent powers to four.

The states joining the League entered a system that proposed to keep the peace by formal procedures for the resolution of conflict and by the threat of collective sanctions on the warlike. The Covenant creating the League gave the Council most of the power in these matters, making the League an instrument of major-power politics. This is not surprising. Major powers rarely create supranational institutions they cannot control. And as the power of the League rested on the capabilities of the major powers, they had an interest in ensuring that the League acted in their interests. Thus, for the League to act effectively, the major powers had to act. As a safeguard to prevent the League from being used against one of its major-power members, the Covenant required a unanimous vote of the Council for most sensitive issues.

Each League member pledged to behave in certain ways. Article X of the Covenant obligated members to "respect and preserve as against external aggression the territorial integrity and existing political independence of all members of the League." The Covenant was at heart a general commitment to the status quo. It spoke in the language of an alliance, but this was an alliance writ large, one encompassing all peace-loving states. Such a "concert of power" presumably would keep the peace, and do so cheaply. "When all unite to act in the same sense and with the same purpose," Woodrow Wilson had declared, "all act in the common interest and are free to live their own lives under a common protection."[3]

We call this *collective* security—the willingness of all member states to come to the aid of another in case of aggression.[4] Because of that willingness, aggression was unlikely. Any state that contemplated aggression would have to reckon on the collective opposition by the League. The League was empowered to de-

[2]For studies of the League, see Francis Walters, *A History of the League of Nations* (London: Oxford University Press, 1952); George Scott, *The Rise and Fall of the League of Nations* (New York: Macmillan, 1973); Byron Dexter, *The Years of Opportunity: The League of Nations, 1920–1926* (New York: Viking, 1967).

[3]Address to the Senate, January 22, 1917; *President Wilson's State Papers and Addresses* (New York: The Review of Reviews Co., 1918), p. 356.

[4]For discussions of the concept of collective security, see Inis Claude, *Power and International Relations* (New York: Random House, 1962); Marina and Lawrence Finkelstein, eds., *Collective Security* (San Francisco: Chandler, 1966); Otto Pick and Julian Critchley, *Collective Security* (London: Macmillan, 1974); Ernst Haas, *Collective Security and the Future International System* (Denver: University of Denver, 1968); Gwendolen M. Carter, *The British Commonwealth and International Security* (Westport, Conn.: Greenwood, 1971).

clare economic sanctions, which reflected a general belief that in an interdependent world, the threat to a state's trade was enough to enforce restraint. In addition, the League had the power "to recommend to the several Governments concerned what effective military, naval or air force the members of the League shall severally contribute to the armed forces to be used to protect the covenants of the League" (Article XVI). Whether the members would act together remained to be seen.

The Kaiser's dream of a continental league had been fulfilled, without the Kaiser or Germany. But the League of Nations had two critical differences. Its *membership* was global, not continental, and all members were to be protected, even those in Asia (such as China and Japan)—states far removed from the full influence of European power. Moreover, the League defined its *interests* in global terms. Article XXI insisted that "any war or threat of war, *whether immediately affecting any of the members of the League or not*, is hereby declared a matter of concern to the whole League, and the League shall take any action that may be deemed wise and effectual to safeguard the peace of nations."

The irony of the "League idea" was that it might lead to the very things that it hoped to prevent. First, it became extremely difficult to ignore any conflict. No use of force could remain a purely local matter. Given the recent past, we would predict a host of conflicts and a number of wars in any given year. These were now to be added to the agenda of world politics for consideration by all the powers. This was a recipe for crisis diplomacy—a technique that worked for years but failed awesomely in August, 1914. Second, globalization tended to trivialize world politics. The affairs of small states were put on par with those of the powerful. This met some standard of equality, perhaps, but it encouraged the loss of a sense of proportion. Insignificant issues could become major crises; important issues could be lost in the welter of problems. As a consequence, frustration and impatience among members of the League might grow—they would be confronted with more irreconcilable conflicts, in the full glare of publicity, with many more interested parties trying to shape a solution. A growing resignation and indifference to events would be a logical result. And finally, as the League clearly specified standards of behavior, failure to uphold those standards because of indifference or resignation would be visible and devastating. States that might be restrained would now have clear indications that standards would not be enforced. Peace would become a very fragile commodity.

These limitations on the effectiveness of the League are endemic to any international organization that attempts to deal with conflict between nations. One method of reducing the strain on the organization and its members is to create mechanisms for the peaceful resolution of conflicts. Indeed, such mechanisms were imperative for an organization that was designed to safeguard the status quo. Where traditional diplomacy was insufficient, the League offered arbitration, judicial settlement, and Council deliberation.

Arbitration has had a long, although erratic, history in world politics.[5]

---

[5]For specific studies see Max Habicht, ed., *Post-war Treaties for the Pacific Settlement of International Disputes* (Cambridge: Harvard University Press, 1931): Manley Hudson, *By Pacific Means* (New Haven: Yale University Press, 1935); Julius Stone, *Legal Controls of International Conflict* (New York: Holt, Rinehart & Winston, 1954). Between 1907 and 1972, the periodical *International Conciliation* appeared monthly.

States in conflict invite a third, disinterested party to resolve the conflict by making an award to one or both of the disputants. While such awards in principle are to be based on the merits of the case, in practice they often are compromises—something for both sides. With regard to judicial settlement, the Covenant of the League established a Permanent Court of International Justice (popularly called the World Court). It was to resolve conflicts based on the application of international law by a panel of distinguished jurists.[6] That law stems from three main sources: treaties and conventions (such as the Versailles Treaty or the convention outlawing gas warfare); the commonly accepted practices of states (such as the sanctity of embassies and diplomatic personnel); and the assertions of prominent jurists and scholars who have tried to systematize legal thinking. States in conflict, however, often have little interest in arbitration or juridical settlement. Such procedures produce results that are often at variance with the power of the disputants. If power can give a "better" result, why throw such an advantage away by voluntarily submitting to arbitration or the rule of law? Few states bother to do so. The inability to compel a state to submit to arbitration or adjudication further reduces the utility of such procedures.

Action by the Council of the League, on the other hand, did not depend upon permission from the parties in conflict. The Council could make an inquiry and issue a report with recommendations. Such a report would carry weight because it expressed the views of the major powers. League resolution of international conflicts was therefore a form of major-power intervention. Additionally, the very threat of major-power intervention, symbolized by the League, may have encouraged restraint.

How well did the collective security system of the League and its various mechanisms for conflict resolution work during the 1920s? Central Europe proved a testing ground. In that region, peoples, political movements, and states clashed over control of territory. Where the major powers had no pressing interests, the League became involved in these conflicts and helped shape peaceful solutions. Where major powers were involved, or the smaller states had major-power backers, the League remained discretely in the background, and diplomacy, threat, and force resolved the issues. At the time, the continuation of traditional politics did not seem threatening to the League, as they seemed part of the debris of the Great War, to be tidied up as quickly as possible. Whether League politics would replace the more traditional forms depended upon agreement among the major powers—agreement to prevent conflict among themselves, and to remain united toward the other states of the world.

The League also championed disarmament as a way to ensure that there would be no future world war. The Versailles Treaty disarmed Germany and pledged the victors to reduce their armies as well. Public hostility to large defense

[6]For general studies of international law, see Richard Falk, *The Status of Law in International Society* (Princeton: Princeton University Press, 1970); Louis Henkin, *How Nations Behave: Law and Foreign Policy*, 2nd ed. (New York: Columbia University Press, 1979); Percy Corbett, *Growth of World Law* (Princeton: Princeton University Press, 1971). For an attempt to relate the systems approach to international law, see Morton Kaplan and Nicholas Katzenbach, *The Political Foundations of International Law* (New York: John Wiley, 1961). For the World Court, see Manley Hudson, *The World Court* (Boston: World Peace Foundation, 1934); John Gamble and Dana Fischer, *The International Court of Justice* (Lexington, Mass.: Lexington Books, 1976); Michla Pomerance, *The Advisory Function of the International Court in the League and U.N. Eras* (Baltimore: Johns Hopkins University Press, 1973).

expenditures made arms reductions politically attractive. The security fear, however, discouraged unilateral reductions, which might give other states a preponderance of power. The solution seemed to be negotiation, yet to appear eager for reductions seemed to undermine one's bargaining position.

The United States broke the logjam. During the war, the Congress had authorized a massive expansion of the navy. Those ships would be deployed in the 1920s. Secretary of State Charles Hughes persuaded President Harding to call for naval arms reduction talks in Washington, and to consider two other pet concerns of the United States: the Anglo-Japanese alliance and the future of China.[7] In the opinion of the American navy (and of the British as well), the next naval war was bound to be with Japan. The prospect of Britain's having to honor its alliance commitment to Japan in such a war was disturbing. Moreover, Japanese imperial interests, which had accelerated during the war, seemed to be on a collision course with the continuing American policy of an economic open door in China and the maintenance of Chinese political and territorial integrity.

The delegations gathered in Washington in November, 1921, expecting to endorse general principles but avoid the difficult details. Secretary Hughes surprised them with a broadside—a point by point proposal to stop naval construction for ten years, break up ships then under construction, and sink some of those afloat. He further proposed that the battleships be kept in a ratio of 10-10-6, with the Japanese having approximately six tons for every ten tons of British or American warships. The British grudgingly accepted parity with the United States. They could ill afford a naval race with the world's wealthiest nation. After strenuous bargaining, the Japanese accepted the Hughes proposal. They also agreed to replace their alliance with Britain with an agreement between themselves, Britain, France, and the United States to maintain amicable relations and to confer with each other if a conflict arose. And everyone endorsed open doors and integrity for China.

The Washington Conference was a resounding success, giving impetus to future League efforts at disarmament. Yet neither disarmament, nor the selective participation of the United States in world politics, nor even the League itself, framed the major issue of the decade. The key question was the future of Germany. Even in defeat, Germany held center stage.

The German Problem

The Versailles Treaty had stipulated that Germany had to reduce its army to 100,000 men, remove its forces from the Rhineland (which was to become a permanently demilitarized zone), and make coal and timber deliveries to France. The allies also required Germany to pay war reparations for the devastation its armies had caused; France was to receive approximately half of the reparations, whose total amount would be established at a later conference. Germany in 1920 did not meet its obligations in any of these areas. German failures spilled over into the economies and politics of the victorious nations.

---

[7]See Thomas Buckley, *The United States and the Washington Conference* (Knoxville: University of Tennessee Press, 1970); Roger Dingman, *Power in the Pacific* (Chicago: University of Chicago Press, 1976). Breaking the Japanese code helped reinforce the American negotiating position; see David Kahn, *The Codebreakers* (New York: Macmillan, 1967), Chapter 12.

To illustrate the complexities that statesmen had to wrestle with, consider the following representation of Franco-German relations:

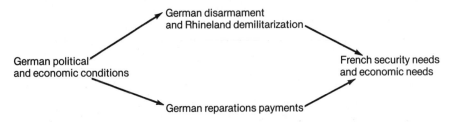

France needed reparation payments to begin the process of reconstruction without massive taxation of its own citizens, now politically impossible. Reparations would also promote French security by retarding Germany's return to economic power and would be a constant reminder to the German people of the cost of the war their leaders had (in French eyes) unleashed. The enforcement of disarmament and neutralization of the Rhineland (see Map 3-2) would prevent an attack on France, whose population of 40 million would always be inferior to Germany's 60. A small army with no reserves would give Germany a very short sword. And the demilitarized zone would deprive Germany of a shield against an invasion by the French army.

Unfortunately for France, its security and economic goals contradicted each other. A disarmed Germany had trouble quashing insurrection, which played havoc with the German economy, which in turn hindered payment of reparations. The Allies rejected German requests for a larger army. The French insisted (even to the point of a punitive occupation in April, 1920, of four German cities) that no German troops enter the Rhineland, even when insurrections there threatened the delivery of coal to France. And the more military pressure France applied to ensure its security, the more inflamed German nationalism became, forcing the German government to delay coal deliveries and reparations payments.

You might expect that French security interests would benefit from a weak German government, one incapable of mobilizing German patriotism and resources to threaten France. Yet, as British Prime Minister Lloyd George pointed out to his French counterpart, without a relatively *strong* German government, there would be no adherence to the terms of the Versailles Treaty. Hundreds of thousands of rifles, for instance, had passed into the hands of German civilians since the armistice. Those civilians, under the auspices of the various local German governments, began to organize militias in contravention of the Treaty. Such militias could rapidly become a reserve system for the new German army, the Reichswehr. If the German government was not strong enough to disarm the militia units, Lloyd George said, the Allies would have to do it, and the costs of doing so would outweigh the reparations the Allies would receive. Even more bluntly, if Germany had no effective government, France would receive no reparations at all. France was discovering that the victor needs the vanquished, and in that need lies no little power for the defeated state.

Unfortunately for France, this was not the end to the complexities and contradictions. Reparation payments depended on restoration of the German economy, and the consensus was that only through foreign loans and investments could Germany regenerate itself. Foreign investors, however, saw great risks in loaning money to Germany. Domestic disorder was worrisome, and if the communists came to power, everyone expected them to repudiate foreign debts just as the Bolsheviks had done. Moreover, as the French began to calculate the total amount of reparations they would demand, the confidence of foreign investors slumped. A large reparations figure would constantly siphon German funds off to pay France, rather than provide a lucrative return for foreign investors. But without foreign loans, France might not receive any reparations. It was a highly frustrating business (or lack of it!).

Gradual Revision of the Versailles Treaty   Successive German governments insisted that the Versailles Treaty had to be revised. The British government began to reach a similar conclusion, grew less concerned with French interests, and showed increasing distaste for coercing Germany. As the British could prevent the French from using the League to force German compliance, the French very soon looked to the traditional forms of world politics. The government quickly established working relations with Poland and then a mutual defense treaty in February, 1921, creating the old two-flank threat to Germany. In March, France occupied more German cities in response to Germany's failure to make interim reparations payments.

Allied tensions over Germany were paralleled by conflicts between Britain and France that had been submerged by the waves of war. Allied dissension now gave the German government greater leeway to whittle away at the restrictions imposed by the Versailles Treaty, without exposing a disarmed Germany to Allied retaliation.[8] Nationalism, both public and governmental, pressed Germany invariably in that direction. Security, for the Germans, was a dicey business. It rested in the main on (1) persuading some or all of the Allies that revision was in their best interests, or (2) making the enforcement of the provisions of the treaty more costly than the loss engendered by Germany's failure to meet the provisions.

Traditionally, of course, states formed alliances for security. Germany, however, had unique problems. France and Belgium had no interest in defending Germany. Poland, given German territory to create access to the Baltic, sought protection from Germany. Britain might be conciliatory, but would not put itself in the position of defending Germany from French arms. And with the triumph of the Republican Party in November, 1920, the United States repudiated political entanglement in Europe. That left only Soviet Russia, another international pariah whom the Allies had tried to strangle. Yet the socialist factions that controlled the German government rejected Bolshevism, and the Bolsheviks detested the renegade German socialists. The powerful German capitalists and Reichswehr leaders had similar hostile feelings for the Soviets. But as you might expect, mutual hostility did not prevent an exploration of common interests.

---

[8]For general discussions of Weimar's policies, see Erich Eyck, *A History of the Weimar Republic* (Cambridge: Harvard University Press, 1962), 2 vols.; David Felix, *Walter Rathenau and the Weimar Republic: The Politics of Reparations* (Baltimore: Johns Hopkins University Press, 1963); Hans Gatzke, *Stresemann and the Rearmament of Germany* (Baltimore: Johns Hopkins University Press, 1954).

A working relationship between Germany and Soviet Russia might elicit more restraint and reasonableness from the other powers. Lloyd George had warned the French that tightening the screws on Germany might drive them into the arms of the Bolsheviks, foreign or domestic. Lloyd George also wanted to expand British trade with Soviet Russia, something a German-Russian relationship might undermine. Equally important, a Soviet-German relationship might lead to the circumvention of both the Versailles restrictions on the German military and the Western economic boycott of Soviet Russia. Germany would provide manufactured goods and the capital and the expertise to build armament plants in Russia. In return, the German military could train its units in Russia in the use of tanks and aircraft, those forbidden weapons of modern war. Informal military cooperation between the two states did begin in 1921. In April, 1922, the two states signed the Treaty of Rapallo, in which they formally recognized each other, codified trade arrangements, and repudiated debts and reparations. The Treaty proved to be a diplomatic sensation. The military cooperation proceeded secretly.

The Rapallo agreement could provide no real security for Germany, however, because it could not deal with Germany's overwhelming economic problems. In May, 1921, after much internal squabbling, the Allies announced that Germany owed 50 billion gold marks (approximately $12.5 billion) as reparations, payable over 36 years. If Germany did not accept the figure, the Allies threatened to occupy the Ruhr, a key industrial area of Germany. Germany knuckled under to the ultimatum. The prospect of such a monetary outflow (tremendous at the time) set off a round of serious inflation in Germany. In May, 1921, the American dollar bought approximately 60 paper marks. By November, the dollar was worth 260 marks.[9]

In July, 1922, the German government requested a moratorium on reparations payments in order to protect its eroding economy. The French, fearing another blow at the Versailles Treaty, refused. The United States exacerbated the situation by asking when the Allies would begin to repay the debt owed the United States. If the United States insisted on British payments, Britain would have to ask France to repay its British loans in order to pay American banks. France in turn would have to insist on German reparations payments in order to meet the British loans. The British government sought to defuse the impending financial and political crisis by proposing an across-the-board cancellation of outstanding loans and reparations. The United States government refused. By August, 1922, the dollar bought 1000 German paper marks; by November, 7000 marks.

In January, 1923, the Allies met to consider another German plea for a moratorium. By this time, Germany had already failed to make some of the required payments and coal and timber deliveries. The British government indicated support for a moratorium. On January 11, France and Belgium responded by sending their troops into the Ruhr to force German payments or, failing that, to extract the money and coal by direct management. For the French govern-

---

[9]F.S. Northedge, *The Troubled Giant: Britain among the Great Powers* (New York: Praeger, 1966), pp. 178–79.

ment, this seemed to be the last opportunity to protect the Versailles Treaty, especially as Britain no longer seemed willing to use any force.

Anti-Allied movements mushroomed over Germany. The German government ordered passive resistance by German workers in the Ruhr, forcing France to take over the costly business of administering the area. The German government subsidized the idle workers by printing more money. Inflation rocketed upwards; by the end of the year, 4 *billion* paper marks to the dollar.[10] It literally took a basket of money to buy a loaf of bread. The collapse of the economy began to reverberate throughout the society. Communist uprisings, ordered by Moscow, occurred, and a politician from the nationalist right, Adolf Hitler, unsuccessfully attempted in November, 1923, to use the chaos to seize power in the German state of Bavaria.[11]

The strain toppled the German government in August, 1923. A new coalition led by Gustav Stresemann ordered an end to passive resistance and through drastic reforms began to stabilize the economy. Although Stresemann lost the chancellor's position in November in another cabinet shuffle, he remained as foreign minister. His policy goals became Germany's: to revise the Treaty, split the Allies by accommodating Britain, and restore German strength.

Franco-Belgian occupation of the Ruhr did split the Allies. Britain denounced the action. The government sought to prevent future occupations by the creation of a process that would ensure payment. An American proposal of the preceding August now looked more attractive. American banking, industrial, and farm interests had a large stake in a prosperous Germany. If the overtly "political" issues could be removed from the reparations dilemma, the new Coolidge administration felt comfortable in having an American, Charles Dawes, chair a committee of experts to formulate a reparations scheme. The Dawes committee concentrated on how much Germany could afford to pay each year. In April, 1924, it recommended initial payments averaging 1.3 billion gold marks a year ($320 million), far less than the 2.5 billion called for in 1921. In addition, the Committee recommended a loan of 800 million gold marks to Germany (half of it from American banks) and a pledge to use no further military coercion. After extensive debate, Germany and the Allies accepted the proposal.[12]

The Dawes plan marked a turning point in post-war politics. It began the process of breaking the link between the economic issues and the issues of security and political power in Europe. France was fast losing a weapon with which to coerce Germany. Britain and the United States would resist any future French claims that German foot-dragging on reparations was politically motivated, or that such behavior threatened the entire Treaty structure. German reparations were to be discussed in terms of economics. While reparations remained a palpable sign of Germany's status as a defeated state, Germany had successfully

---

[10]Charles Kindleberger, *The World in Depression: 1929–1939* (Berkeley: University of California Press, 1973), p. 36.

[11]Among the conspirators was General Ludendorff; see Harold Gordon, *Hitler and the Beer Hall Putsch* (Princeton: Princeton University Press, 1972).

[12]For works on the Dawes Plan (and its successor, the Young Plan), see John Wheeler-Bennett, *The Wreck of Reparations* (London: Allen & Unwin, 1933); Charles Harris, *Germany's Foreign Indebtedness* (London: Oxford University Press, 1935); Stephen Schuker, *The End of French Predominance* (Chapel Hill: University of North Carolina Press, 1976); Felix, *Rathenau*.

brought about a reduction in yearly payments (a precedent for the future), and in so doing, made much more likely the eventual reduction in the total reparations bill. Finally, the Dawes plan encouraged a new set of linkages in the economic realm, one that made the United States a critical element:

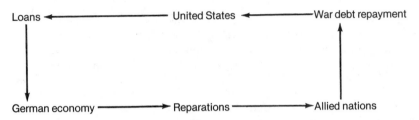

It is likely that most political leaders and diplomats were relieved to see the reparations issue "depoliticized." Economic issues as a rule have been difficult for such individuals to grasp. The Dawes plan, for instance, had a complicated arrangement for generating reparations from the German government's budget, bonds, and excise and customs duties. Once available, another set of complex provisions covered the transfer of monies out of German hands into foreign accounts. These were matters for business and financial experts. As long as economic issues were intimately tied to politics and foreign policy, political leaders and diplomats had to include economic experts in their deliberations and deal with economic advice they could not challenge, and whose political ramifications they could not clearly see. It seemed better (and certainly easier) to assume that there was no permanent connection between economics and foreign policy and to allow technicians to resolve the details.

Locarno and the Paris Peace Pact   Britain not only sought to isolate economics from politics: frightened by the political implications of the Ruhr occupation, the government considered ways of disengaging from Continental affairs. Could Britain rely on the League to keep the peace? No one was sure whether the League could or would recognize aggression when it occurred, or whether the members (including Britain) would respond collectively. A short-lived Labor government in Britain proposed in October, 1924, that a state rejecting arbitration and going to war be branded an aggressor and sanctioned by the League (the so-called Geneva Protocol). Canada, Australia, New Zealand, and South Africa chose to exercise their new autonomy from Britain by opposing the proposal. The Australians, intent on safeguarding a "whites only" immigration policy, feared that the arbitration clause would allow Asian nations to "meddle" in Australian internal affairs. More telling was a Canadian official's comment: "We live in a fireproof house, far from inflammable materials."[13] This was the crucial problem of collective security. Why should governments far from fires pledge in advance to run the risk of being burned to death putting out others' conflagrations? And more insidiously, if Germany defaulted, and France refused arbitration and occupied more of Germany, would Britain have to put out that "fire" by sanctioning its French ally? New elections in Britain in November, 1924, returned the

[13]Statement by Senator Dandurand, October 2, 1924; quoted by Carter, *British Commonwealth*, p. 117.

Conservatives to power; they rejected the Protocol. They could not, however, wish away the basic flaw in the collective security system.

The French response to the limitations of collective security and the perennial German problem wavered in the face of political instability. Between 1920 and 1929, there were eighteen different French governments. Some continuity prevailed in the foreign ministry: there were only six foreign ministers, two of whom held office for relatively long periods. Raymond Poincaré, who had been President of France during the Great War, epitomized the hard line. Germany was, in Poincaré's view, "the 'hereditary enemy' across the Rhine [which] must be 'kept down' by a program of treaty enforcement, military alliances with the new states of Central Europe, and a strong army."[14] The occupation of the Ruhr reflected Poincaré's position, including his willingness to antagonize Britain in order to suppress Germany. The occupation was generally a failure; German inflation began to spill over into France. New elections in May, 1924, removed Poincaré from power, and after several reshufflings of the cabinet, Aristide Briand became foreign minister in April, 1925 (and remained in the post until 1932).

Briand was the antithesis of Poincaré. For Briand, security vis-à-vis Germany would not come at the point of a bayonet. Security rested on a rapprochement with Germany, an understanding that would give the Germans incentives for peaceful relations. The tie with Britain would be reinforced; the League bolstered. In some ways, Briand's was a policy of default. Coercion and a rigid insistence on the Treaty provisions had failed.

Stresemann responded favorably to Briand's policy of appeasement. A statesman who seeks a *gradual* revision of the status quo finds it relatively easy to take the appeasement offered and provide concessions in return. Stresemann could scale back the demands to change the status quo, thus appearing moderate. He could permit the expansion of the "Black Reichswehr" (the part of the German army that evaded the Versailles limitations), but keep it unobtrusive. More positively, he offered to guarantee the status and inviolability of Germany's western borders with France and Belgium. That meant voluntary German acceptance of the Versailles Treaty provisions that gave Alsace-Lorraine to France and the small Eupen-Malmedy district to Belgium. It meant there would be no German attack across the frontiers. In addition, Stresemann agreed to keep the Rhineland demilitarized. In return, Stresemann asked for a similar guarantee for the German frontier, which would prevent France or Belgium from invading Germany as they had in 1923.

Stresemann's proposal found favor in London and Paris. The British government of Stanley Baldwin agreed to a *guarantee* of the frontier against aggression. For France, this was a de facto alliance with Britain in case of a German attack; for Germany, insurance of no further intervention. A lasting peace seemed at hand in the West. The effect in the East was more ambiguous. Would France come to the aid of Poland in case of a German attack on that state? If France were inhibited by a frontier agreement with Germany, the Franco-Polish alliance would mean little to Poland. Briand insisted that Germany make a similar pledge

[14]Richard Challener, "The French Foreign Office: The Era of Philippe Berthelot," in *The Diplomats*, ed. Craig and Gilbert, p. 53.

for its borders with Poland and Czechoslovakia. Germany refused, and Britain showed no interest in the Eastern problem. The best France could obtain was a German agreement to sign arbitration treaties with both states. The powers also agreed that the time had come for Germany to enter the League.

The three states hammered out these agreements during the summer and fall of 1925, and signed the Locarno Treaty in October. The "spirit of Locarno" promised a new future. The Allies ended their attempt to dominate Germany. While significant limitations existed (such as on the Reichswehr), Germany regained much of its diplomatic status as a great power. Germany had accepted its western borders and agreed to arbitrate disputes in the East. Britain had become a balancer again, not tied to either France or Germany, but to a general settlement in the West. Germany's entry into the League strengthened the institution.

While it would be correct to say that Locarno strengthened the collective security system, it did not end the traditional politics. France negotiated new mutual defense treaties with Poland and Czechoslovakia. It decided to build a massive (therefore expensive) fortification system from Switzerland to the Belgian border. The Maginot Line, as it was called, reflected French conclusions about how the next war would be fought. The hope was that it would deter or defeat any German attack.

Locarno completed the peaceful revision of Versailles. Thus, by 1926, the major patterns in world politics had shifted from a strong overlap between the security, economic, and political fields, each of which had Germany subordinated to the Allies, to a condition of less linkage and greater equality for Germany. Figure 4–1 depicts this change. The separation of the three fields made the rest of the decade remarkably untroubled. No state could easily translate an advantage in one field into power in the other. France, for instance, could not use reparations as a device to cripple German political power. Germany could not use reparations as a wedge to change its military position. "Decoupling" allowed incremental adjustments, all of which tended to favor a return of Germany to its former position of power, but at the same time, gave the Germans an incentive to keep the peace. Appeasement proved to be an apt policy.

Appeasement, however, did not extend to all matters. The most notable exception was German disarmament. The League did sponsor a series of arms talks in the last half of the decade to disarm the Allies to a level commensurate with Germany's. At the center of the difficulty in reaching any agreement was the asymmetry in the military balance.[15] The well-armed insisted that they could disarm only when foolproof collective security arrangements had been made. For the French in particular, there seemed to be no compelling reasons to disarm and many dangers in doing so. For the poorly armed, on the other hand, disarmament by others was a *precondition* for their security. Alternatively, they could rearm, but the French rejected this out of hand for Germany. The German government of the 1920s probably would have preferred the disarmament of others to

---

[15]For general treatments of disarmament and arms control, see Norman Angell, *The Great Illusion, 1933* (New York: Putnam's, 1933); John Wheeler-Bennett, *The Disarmament Deadlock* (London: Routledge & Kegan Paul, 1934); Duncan Clarke, *The Politics of Arms Control* (New York: Free Press, 1979); James Dougherty, *How to Think about Arms Control and Disarmament* (New York: Crane, Russak, 1973).

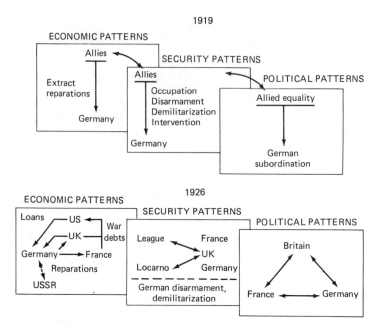

FIGURE 4-1   Decoupling of Issue Arenas

German rearmament, if for no other reason than the prevailing economic ortho-doxy, which held that spending for the military weakened the economy, some-thing Germany could scarcely afford. The Allied pledge in the Versailles Treaty to draw up and implement arms reductions remained a dead letter. That same treaty perpetuated the military weakness of Germany. It was unlikely that the vi-olation of one provision could long coexist with general adherence to the other. The question of German remilitarization, therefore, was not so much a matter of When?, but To what end?

While arms reduction talks lumbered ahead, the French continued to work on their own security system. In addition, Briand saw a need for more political cooperation (a belief that culminated in his proposal at the end of the decade for a United States of Europe). These two themes apparently encouraged him to pro-pose in April, 1927, that the United States and France agree to renounce war as a policy option in their relations with each other. The American Secretary of State, Frank Kellogg, was suspicious; neither state had contemplated war with the other. The proposal appeared to be the first step toward the creation of a defen-sive alliance, something that the United States had rejected in 1920. However, Briand had made his proposal public; an American refusal to consider such a pro-posal would be politically unwise. After waiting more than half a year, Kellogg made a counterproposal: "it has occurred to me that the two Governments, in-stead of contenting themselves with a bilateral declaration of the nature suggested by M. Briand, might make a more signal contribution to world peace by joining in an effort to obtain the adherence of all of the principal powers of the world to a declaration *renouncing war as an instrument of national policy.*"[16]

Briand acceded to the proposal and the two governments found a positive response from the other states. In Paris in August, 1928, the major powers, including Germany, Japan, and the United States, signed such a treaty (called variously the Pact of Paris and the Kellogg-Briand Peace Pact). Eventually, 65 states, including the Soviet Union, ratified the treaty, which renounced war as a part of their foreign policies but did not abrogate the right of self-defense. Many signatories stipulated exceptions. The United States, for instance, declared "self-defense" to include the defense of Latin America, as set forth in its Monroe Doctrine. The British made similar reservations regarding their colonial empire. The largest loophole, however, was the absence of any enforcement provisions in case of violations. That was the very reason it was attractive to the United States!

Was the Pact of Paris just a paper pledge, part of both the hope and the illusion that emerged with the Locarno conference? We know with hindsight that Germany, Japan, and Italy would soon use war or the threat of war as a mainstay of their foreign policies, and that the Western democracies would act as if the letter and spirit of the Paris Peace Pact still restrained them, even in the face of such aggression. One should, however, be slow to leap to that particular conclusion. The Pact was a departure from traditional world politics. It established a new standard by which to judge proposed policy and thus became another pressure operating on governments. It was a means to enhance the workings of a collective security system; if states pledged and expected mutual self-restraint in foreign policy, the need to enforce collective security would be less frequent. Systems of self-restraint do provide an incentive, however, for a state to show *less* restraint, if it believes that the other states will be inhibited. But that seemed to be a small risk to run when all major powers, as Wilson hoped, "act in the same sense and with the same purpose."

Locarno, Kellogg-Briand, and the Covenant did not mesh perfectly (the League still permitted war under certain circumstances), but together they helped create a new set of attitudes, expectations, and institutions that tried to make peace and security compatible. We have seen that more traditional practices of world politics lurked beneath this surface, but they now had to defend their presence when they emerged. Heading into the 1930s, the prospects for having no repetition of the Great War seemed bright. Indeed, the spirit of the time continued the erosion of "the German problem." The Versailles Treaty called for Anglo-French occupation of the Rhineland until 1935. German Foreign Minister Stresemann raised the issue of earlier withdrawal when he came to Paris to sign the Peace Pact. The French agreed to do so if there was a final settlement of the reparations issue. The Dawes plan had only devised a formula for yearly repayments, with no total indebtedness indicated. Once again, a committee of experts met, chaired by Owen Young, an American. The Young Report eventually became the settlement of the reparations issue. Germany would make specified payments until 1988. France and Britain in turn agreed to withdraw all

---

[16]Kellogg to French ambassador, December 28, 1927; *Foreign Relations of the United States, 1927* (Washington: Government Printing Office, 1942), Vol. II, p. 627 (emphasis added).

troops from the Rhineland in 1930. When that was accomplished, only the disarmament issue remained.

The New Imperialists

While war between the major powers did not disfigure the third decade of the twentieth century, threats to the peace were plentiful. The Greeks, for instance, with the encouragement of Lloyd George's government, attacked Turkey in 1920. A savage war went on for two years, ending with the Turks' pushing the Greeks off the Turkish coast. Britain in its empire, especially India, relied on force to deal with rising nationalism. It responded to the agitation for independence by Mahatma Gandhi and Mohammed Ali and other nationalists with jailings and in some cases indiscriminate violence (as in the Amritsar massacre of April, 1919). British officials, however, had to answer for their policies, making a policy of aggressive imperialism hard to sustain. The restraints in Japan and Italy were far less.

In October, 1922, Benito Mussolini, an ex-socialist but now head of the Fascist party, led a peaceful coup that ended democratic government in Italy and established an authoritarian regime. Mussolini took the post of foreign minister in the new government and dedicated himself to carry forward the old regime's interest in colonial expansion. The Versailles Treaty, however, had created new limitations on imperialism. The Treaty did not permit the simple transfer of German or Turkish colonial areas to the victor states. Instead, various victor states were to administer those territories as "mandates" and were to prepare the inhabitants for self-rule. While the allocation of territories generally conformed to the Allies' wartime plans to share the spoils, the Treaty had begun to codify the emerging view that imperialism was an unacceptable form of international politics.

More important at the time, weak independent states had flocked to the League. Any attempt to make imperial holdings out of those League members would mean aggression and the prospect of confronting the League collective security system. To be an unsatisfied imperialist state in the 1920s meant frustration and, as long as the imperialist ambitions remained, a willingness to take risks.

Frustration was certainly Mussolini's suit. The Versailles Treaty was a disappointment: no mandates, and the creation of the Yugoslav state, which not only blocked Italian expansion down the Adriatic coast, but also gave to Yugoslavia territory Italy claimed as *irredenta*. Albania, long a target of Italian imperialism, remained independent. Mussolini tested the waters in 1923 by seizing the island of Corfu from Greece. The League skirted the issue (Italy was a permanent member of the Council) but great-power diplomacy and pressure brought restoration of the island to Greece. Mussolini became more circumspect (and careful to remain friendly with Britain); whether his caution would grow was problematic.

Japanese imperial interests during the decade exhibited a similar caution. The Chinese mainland had long been the area of interest, absorbing Japanese goods and investments, and economic penetration of Manchuria had accelerated after the Russo-Japanese war. The Japanese army garrisoned the Kwantung peninsula on which Port Arthur stands and the railway zone linking Port Arthur to Harbin (see Map 4–1). The Chinese revolution of 1911 and the civil war that fol-

MAP 4-1 The Far East in World Politics

lowed, fueled as they were by nationalism, began to erode the Japanese position (as it did all foreigners'). Initially, the Japanese government reacted cautiously to the chaos in China. In Manchuria, it supported Chang Tso-lin, the warlord who controlled the territory and seemed willing to protect Japanese treaty rights in the area. Chang stood in opposition to the Chinese Nationalists under Chiang Kai-shek, who were slowly expanding control over the rest of China.

After 1927, a new Japanese government sought to have China formally divided between Manchuria under Chang and China under Chiang. Marshal Chang Tso-lin had other plans; he prepared to move south from Manchuria to conquer China. The Japanese government ordered its forces in Manchuria, the Kwantung Army, to disarm Chang's troops to prevent such an attack. It rescinded the order when Chang agreed to confine his interest to Manchuria.

Now it was the turn of the Kwantung Army leaders to be upset. They saw Chang as the obstacle to their particular goal—to make Manchuria into a Japanese colony. Ordered not to disarm the Marshal's troops, they decided to deal with him by blowing up his train, which they did in June, 1928. The murder worsened the situation. Chang's son, Chang Hsueh-Liang, proved to be an effective leader, and to the dismay of the Japanese, pledged his allegiance to the Nationalist government of Chiang Kai-shek. To break the Japanese hold on the Manchurian economy, the young Chang proposed an ambitious program of Chinese investment and railroad building in Manchuria. And everywhere, the Japanese could see the rising tide of Chinese nationalism threatening to push them off the mainland.

If the checks to Japanese imperial interests were not enough, the Japanese political system began to collapse. The Japanese army high command protected the murderers of Chang, partially because many favored making Manchuria a colony and partially to prevent civilian control over the military. The civilian political leaders did not dare push the issue. It was an ominous development—Tokyo might be cautious in its foreign policy; the officers of the Kwantung army had less reason for restraint.

A Small Cloud on the Horizon

When President Herbert Hoover delivered the traditional Armistice Day address on November 11, 1929, he could say, with some reason, "The outlook for a peaceable future is more bright than for half a century past." He called for a new diplomacy, which sought "to build the spirit of good will and friendliness, to create respect and confidence, to stimulate esteem between peoples."[17] Such a diplomacy has a very modern echo to it. In fact, it had begun to emerge in Europe in the 1920s. Americans had an annoying habit of not noticing things. Of course, Americans did notice the unrest in the New York stock market, which had been hit with a massive wave of selling in October, 1929. Informed opinion judged this to be a self-correcting pause in the American economy. Few, if any, saw any connection between this ripple in the American economy and world politics. After all, statesmen had labored mightily to divorce economics from politics. The Pact of Paris was to be the symbol of the future, not the cruder issues of profits and losses.

[17]*Public Papers of the Presidents: Herbert Hoover, 1929* (Washington: Government Printing Office, 1974), pp. 375, 378.

PART II:
SCIENTIFIC APPROACHES TO WORLD POLITICS

Domestic and Environmental Factor Approach:
The Impact of Marxism on Russian Foreign Policy

When the Bolsheviks seized power in Russia in November, 1917, they believed they had ushered in a new chapter of world history. When no other socialist revolution succeeded, the Bolsheviks had to write that chapter alone. Marxism, they believed, gave them an incomparable advantage, for it was a scientific method of analyzing history unavailable to capitalist leaders. It could correctly identify the central issues, estimate the correlation of forces, and devise the most appropriate response.

Marxism began as the historical and theoretical writings of Karl Marx, a revolutionary socialist, and his fellow socialist Friedrich Engels, a factory owner. While there were other fertile socialist minds, Marx's and Engels' works became a key force in socialist thought and action. Latter-day adherents, such as Lenin and the Bolsheviks, adopted and reworked this Marxism. We can describe Marxism as an *ideology*—a set of beliefs that are stated as general principles from which one deduces specific applications. The beliefs are resistant to evidence and rebuttal. To those beliefs an individual makes a passionate commitment. Lenin's comment about bread catches the perspective of the ideologue—the individual who knows the world through the ideology: "As for bread, I, who had never been in need, never gave it a thought. . . . Fundamentally, my ideas upon the class struggle for bread were reached by political analysis. . . ."[18]

As students of world politics, we want to know what role ideology plays in world politics. I shall explore this question in terms of the *domestic and environmental factor approach*. This approach suggests that individual decision makers are neutral transmitters of external pressures or forces that shape policy. What a state does is the result of those impersonal forces. In this case, I hypothesize that, if we know something about the ideology of Marxism, we do not need to know anything about individual decision makers. This can be represented as

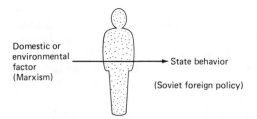

The substitution of one decision maker for another should have no effect. More broadly, the hypothesis suggests that when Marxist ideology is dominant in sev-

---

[18]V.I. Lenin, quoted by Robert Payne, *The Life and Death of Lenin* (New York: Simon & Schuster, 1964), p. 361. For general discussions of ideology, see Giovanni Sartori, "Politics, Ideology, and Belief Systems," *American Political Science Review*, 63 (June 1969), 399–405; Robert Putnam, "Studying Elite Political Culture: The Case of 'Ideology,' " *American Political Science Review*, 65 (September 1971), p. 661; Willard Mullins, "On the Concept of Ideology in Political Science," *American Political Science Review*, 66 (June 1972), pp. 498–510.

eral states, their foreign policies will be similar. If the hypothesis holds true, we should have a relatively powerful tool for understanding why some states behave as they do: specific ideas dictate specific policies.

Note that I have spoken of a *hypothesis*. At this point, I do not know if there is a relationship between ideology and foreign policy. There might be none; while ideology may have important functions in a society, the *shaping* of foreign policy may not be one. If we find no consistent linkage between policy and ideology, we will have to conclude that ideology does not explain much about a state's behavior.[19] On the other hand, the hypothesis may be correct. If it is, we need to think of *ways* ideology might be linked to foreign policy. Two suggest themselves:

1. *Ideology dictates policy*: Ideology provides a clear and compelling blueprint for state behavior. For example, the ideology may call for the conquest of other states.

2. *Ideology establishes a range of acceptable behaviors*: While not providing a blueprint, ideology may allow a number of different policies but also rule out others. For instance, ideology may permit behavior toward a certain state to range from hostility to 'correct diplomacy,' but prohibit any consideration of an alliance. Leaders therefore would have some leeway; forces other than ideology would shape their choices, except for the prohibited behaviors.

Let us assume for the moment, however, that Marxist ideology dictates policy. What blueprint does the ideology provide? While it is difficult to identify a core to which all Marxists might repair, we can at least suggest some of the ideological tenets that many Marxists would feel comfortable with.[20] For a Marxist, the central issue of human life is who will benefit from the society's economic system. The system is exploitative when the benefits of the system go to a small, favored class. In the capitalist societies, the exploiting class consists of the capitalists or bourgeoisie who own the factories and businesses (the means of production). Exploiting classes control the government (the state) and use it to protect their privileged position. The domestic and foreign policies of states, therefore, are in the service of the dominating class. Those who do not own the means of production constitute the underclasses, who must exchange their labor for an inequitably small share of the benefits generated by the economy.

Marxism postulates change as the fundamental characteristic of history. As technology changed, the nature of the economic system would change, releasing forces that would lead a progressive class to replace an outmoded one. Thus in France, Britain, and Germany in the recent historical past, the bourgeois class had supplanted the feudal class, bringing economic modernization to the nineteenth century. The next stage in the transformation of history would be the inev-

---

[19]As a general rule, a single case study can neither validate nor invalidate a hypothesis. Ideally, we want to examine as many cases as possible. A case study does allow us to refine the hypothesis and under special circumstances, perform some types of tests; see Harry Eckstein, "Case Study and Theory in Political Science," in *Strategies of Inquiry*, ed. Fred Greenstein and Nelson Polsby (Reading, Mass.: Addison-Wesley, 1975), pp. 79–137 (Vol. 7 of *Handbook of Political Science*).

[20]For general introductions to Marxism, see George Lichtheim, *Marxism,* 2nd ed. (New York: Praeger, 1965); Bertram Wolfe, *Marxism* (New York: Dial, 1965); Robert Tucker, *The Marxian Revolutionary Idea* (New York: W.W. Norton & Co. Inc., 1969); Melvin Rader, *Marx's Interpretation of History* (New York: Oxford University Press, 1979); David McLellan, *Karl Marx* (New York: Harper & Row, Pub., 1974).

itable replacement of the bourgeois class by the working class (the proletariat). The dictatorship of the proletariat would "expropriate the exploiters." By abolishing private property, which gave an individual the opportunity and power to exploit others, all exploitation would be ended, and the benefits of the economy would be distributed equitably.

Until 1917, the triumph of the proletariat was only a Marxist prediction. The great, divisive debate among Marxists was how the transformation would occur. Marx had said through violence. Some Marxists saw the possibility of a nonviolent evolution toward a socialist society through the growing power of socialist political parties. The radical Marxists scoffed at such notions; capitalism would not willingly consent to its extinction. Lenin carried the radical position a step further. He argued that a disciplined, secret revolutionary party had to lead the proletariat—such a party was necessary to aid the proletariat in seeing its true class interests in spite of the soothing capitalist propaganda, and to mobilize and spearhead the attack on the bourgeois state. When that revolutionary party, the Bolsheviks, triumphed in Russia in November, 1917, it remained in power to become the leading element in the struggle to create a socialist society.

What blueprint for foreign policy did Marxism provide the Bolsheviks? Three broad areas present themselves for discussion: relations with the capitalist states, relations with oppressed peoples, and the requirements for modernization. For each of these areas, I will suggest what ideology might dictate and compare that with the historical record of Soviet foreign policy from 1918 to 1925.[21]

Ideology and Relations with Capitalist States   Ideology would suggest that the world was divided into two camps: the capitalist states and the socialist state. There could be no long-term community of interests between, as Lenin repeatedly said, the handful of individuals who now exploit one and one-quarter billion people and the Russian people who had abolished exploitation. Indeed, the interest of the capitalist states would be to suppress, if not destroy, this new homeland of proletariat. The ideology would depict Soviet Russia as surrounded by hostile states whose every move, however benign on the surface, must necessarily be treated with suspicion.

In 1917, one of those hostile states, Germany, was waging war on Soviet Russia, and Russia was aligned with other capitalist powers. "This war," Lenin argued, drawing explicitly on Marxism, "was waged in order to decide which of the insignificant [i.e., bourgeois] groups of the biggest states—the British or the German—was to secure the opportunity and the right to rob, strangle, and exploit the whole world."[22] Socialist Russia could not promote the interests of the rival capitalist cliques. Withdrawal from the war, even at the heavy cost that the Brest-Litovsk treaty extracted, seems clearly the result of ideology. Any Marxist government would have done likewise.

[21]For a discussion of Marxism, Lenin, and early Soviet policy, see Bertram Wolfe, *An Ideology in Power* (Briarcliff, N.Y.: Stein & Day, 1969); E. H. Carr, *The Bolshevik Revolution* (London: Macmillan, 1950–1953), 3 vols.; Teddy J. Uldricks, *Diplomacy and Ideology* (Beverly Hills, Cal.: Sage, 1979); Richard Debo, *Revolution and Survival* (Toronto: University of Toronto Press, 1979); Adam Ulam, *Expansion and Coexistence*, 2nd ed. (New York: Praeger, 1974).

[22]Report to the Second Comintern Congress, July, 1920; V. Lenin, *Selected Works*, Vol. X: *The Communist International* (New York: International Publishers, 1938), p. 181.

Unfortunately, the historical record is ambiguous. Many prominent Bolsheviks opposed Lenin's peace proposal. They demanded a defensive, revolutionary war as long as Germany attacked or insisted on the territorial dismemberment of Russia. Lenin's opponents considered themselves good Marxists, well grounded in the tenets of the ideology. The debate among the Bolsheviks suggests that on some fundamental aspects of relations with capitalist states, ideology offered no clear blueprint. On the other hand, Lenin's opponents advocated a conventional policy in response to the war; Lenin proposed a radically different one. We might suggest that, for Lenin, ideology *expanded* the range of policy options for consideration.

Let us assume that ideology clearly said to end Russia's participation in the war. How do we know that Lenin's position came from the ideology and not some other source? Would not a pragmatic, realistic leader have acted as Lenin did? Russia was collapsing economically, its major cities were in turmoil, the soldiers were deserting, and all the while, the German army pushed through the disintegrating defenses. Peace, even at a high price, may have been the only real alternative to German conquest or complete social disintegration. The non-Bolshevik regime that replaced the Tsar fell precisely because it tried to continue the war. From this perspective, Brest-Litovsk was the product of circumstance, not ideology. Only those *most* captivated by ideology pursued the romantic notion of a revolutionary war of defense.

Suddenly what might have appeared to be a clear case turns very murky. The difficulty of attributing cause to ideology is made worse by the very nature of ideology. Ideology *claims* to provide guidance about appropriate behavior. Therefore, ideologues have a great incentive to insist that whatever is done *is* in fact *inspired* by ideology. After all, why bother with ideology if you could make decisions based on tea leaves or conversations with political scientists? No matter how the debate turned out between Lenin and the proponents of a defensive war, the winner would *describe* policy as being in line with the ideology. Perhaps if we had access to the transcripts of the debates, diaries of the key decision makers, or a chance to interview them, we might better gauge the impact of ideology. Unfortunately, ideological states are the most reticent about providing access to such materials.

There do seem to be, however, some clearer instances of the impact of ideology on relations with capitalist states. When Leon Trotsky became the first Soviet Foreign Minister, in November, 1917, he reportedly said that all he had to do was issue some revolutionary proclamations and then close up shop. The rest of the world would follow the example of the Russian revolution and thereby create a global proletarian commonwealth. The need for capitalist diplomacy would end. Trotsky soon learned that diplomacy could not be avoided, and Narkomindel, the Soviet foreign ministry, began to grow in size. Nonetheless, ideology appears to have influenced the *style of diplomacy*. "The first Narkomindel representatives thought of themselves not merely as diplomatic agents accredited to one of the bourgeois states, but as representatives of the revolutionary Russian working class to the proletariat of the country to which they were sent."[23] Thus, after Brest-Litovsk, the newly established Soviet diplomatic mission in Berlin became

---

[23]Uldricks, *Diplomacy*, p. 155.

a center for revolutionary agitation against capitalist Germany. We might hypothesize, therefore, that ideology may have a more pronounced impact on *diplomatic style* than on policy, at least in the early years of an ideological regime. I say "early," because Narkomindel diplomats soon began to act much like everyone else's diplomats, as we shall see.

Another sign that ideology had an impact on foreign policy came with creation of the Communist International in 1919.[24] The Comintern, as it was called, was to be a permanent organization representing all communist parties—those parties that adopted the organization and perspectives of the Bolsheviks (who changed their name to the Communist Party). The Bolsheviks initially enjoyed predominance but not exclusive control over the Comintern. However, requirements for entrance into the Comintern stipulated that a foreign communist party give "unconditional support" to the Russian socialist state. The Comintern thus evolved into a vehicle for the promotion of the interests of the Russian government. The British Communist Party, for instance, could be instructed to mobilize British dock workers to obstruct the loading of munitions destined for enemies of the Russian state.

Did the Comintern add an ideological element to Russian foreign policy, or did "state interests," grounded in considerations far removed from ideology, swallow up the Comintern as well? The evidence is mixed. As an organization, the Comintern did recruit a higher proportion of ideologues, individuals who would presumably lobby to make ideological values and perspectives a part of policy. And there was the rub. Comintern directives (such as to British dock workers) dealt with the domestic affairs of other states. Capitalist states took offense at such violations of international norms and rejected as arrogant sophistry the Soviet government's claim that the Comintern was an independent organization like the International Red Cross, not under the government's control. (Lenin himself was one of the Russian delegates to the Comintern.) To the degree that the Soviet government wanted good relations with capitalist states, the Comintern and its members had to be muzzled. The Comintern's ability to inject ideology into policy considerations consequently declined as the Russian state decided to promote good relations.

Ironically, as the impact of ideology on relations with capitalist states decreased, ideology continued to have a role regarding relations with the political left in capitalist nations. The Socialist left which chose to work within the capitalist political system raised serious ideological issues for the communist movement. In Lenin's view, "socialists" of such ilk "are better defenders of the bourgeoisie, than the bourgeoisie itself. Without their leadership of the workers, the bourgeoisie could not have remained in power."[25] When the Comintern forbade its members to form alliances with such parties and ordered vigorous political offensives against them, we were probably seeing the most clearcut case of the impact of ideology on the substance of policy. Such hostility had no immediate foreign policy

---

[24]Studies of the Comintern include Julius Braunthal, *History of the International* (New York: Praeger, 1967), 2 vols; James Hulse, *The Forming of the Communist International* (Stanford: Stanford University Press, 1964); Kermit McKenzie, *Comintern and World Revolution* (New York: Columbia University Press, 1963).

[25]*Selected Works*, X, p. 196.

consequences for Soviet Russia, but in the long run (as the 1930s would amply demonstrate), Soviet Russia would pay dearly for this ideological purity.

Ideology and Relations with Oppressed Peoples   Perhaps the most long-lasting impact of ideology on Russian foreign policy was in its identification of the natural allies of the Soviet state. While capitalist governments clearly were the enemy, the allies were the proletariat of those capitalist states, the peoples of the colonial world, and nations (such as China) under imperialist seige. In early Bolshevik thinking, the German proletariat was crucial. The German economy had reached the most advanced stages of capitalism (and therefore by definition had the most revolutionary proletariat). Revolution in Germany would add the most powerful capitalist state to the socialist community. In contrast, Russia was economically a primitive state where the transition to socialism would be difficult and the power to protect the socialist experiment weak in the extreme. Therefore, argued Lenin, drawing on the ideology, " . . . the task of transforming the dictatorship of the proletariat from a national one (that is, existing in one country and incapable of determining world politics) into an international one (that is, a dictatorship of the proletariat governing at least several *advanced* countries and capable of exercising decisive influence upon the whole of world politics) becomes a pressing question of the day."[26] The spread of communism seemed to be an ideological imperative. Unfortunately, and in spite of covert assistance by Soviet Russia, the German proletariat failed to seize power.

One of the problems in supporting proletarian liberation in Germany after the war was the presence of the new Polish state, which blocked direct contact between Russia and Germany. Relations between Poland and Soviet Russia would test how strongly the ideology would shape Soviet foreign policy as opposed to the pressures of traditional Russian nationalism and expansionism. In 1919, Polish troops drove the Red Army out of areas claimed by both states.[27] After a winter lull, the Poles attacked the Ukraine in April, 1920. In June, the Red Army began a counterattack in the Ukraine and into the disputed territory in the north. Soviet troops soon reached the Polish frontier established by the Allies at Versailles. Was this the opportunity to liberate Poland itself? The Russian field commander, Marshal Tukhachevsky, in his order for the advance, trumpeted the ideological answer: "Over the dead body of White Poland shines the road to world wide conflagration. On our bayonets we shall bring happiness and peace to toiling humanity."[28] The "Red Bridge" from Russia to Germany was about to fall into place.

Other Bolsheviks pointed out that France supported Poland and that the capitalist states might use a Russian offensive as the pretext for assaulting Soviet Russia. The then Soviet War Minister, Leon Trotsky, insisted that Russia call off the offensive and accept a British offer to mediate. Pragmatism came before the ideological concerns of liberating the Polish proletariat and reaching Germany. Lenin had initially adopted a cautious position as well—a defensive war

[26]From "Preliminary Draft of Theses on the National and Colonial Questions" (1920), in *Lenin on Politics and Revolution*, ed. James Connor (Indianapolis: Pegasus, 1968), pp. 317–18 (emphasis added).

[27]For the Russo-Polish war of 1919–1920, see Norman Davies, *White Eagle, Red Star* (New York: St. Martin's Press, 1972).

[28]Twenty-seven-year-old Marshal Tukhachevsky's Order of the Day; *ibid.*, p. 145.

against Polish aggression. When the offensives of 1920 routed the Polish army, Lenin now called for a "frantic acceleration of the offensive"; he was all for "thrashing the Poles"; Warsaw had to be taken "at whatever cost."[29] Liberating the Poles (or even Germans) from capitalism seemed to recede as a goal; the war was now more a nationalist endeavor, much as a capitalist state might pursue. The Poles, however, rallied to defend Warsaw and to drive the Red Army back to the border. A negotiated settlement in October, 1920, ended the attempt to spread revolution or national power by the bayonet. A pensive Lenin commented in the spring of 1921, "Soviet Russia can only win if it shows that it only carries on war to defend the Revolution . . ., that it has no intention to seize land, suppress nations, or embark on an imperialist adventure."[30]

The Polish war indicated that while *ideology* might identify new allies in the capitalist world, other forces might produce policy less in keeping with the ideology. Would similar forces distort the relations between the Soviet state and peoples suffering from imperialism? Those peoples seemed natural allies, although the level of romanticism increased as the distance from Moscow lengthened. Nikolai Bukharin, a leading Bolshevik theoretician (and later head of the Comintern), declared that " . . . the large industrial states are the *cities* of the world economy, and the colonies and semi-colonies its *countryside.*" Just as the Bolsheviks did in Russia, the Soviet state should create "a great united front between the revolutionary proletariat of the world 'city' and the peasantry of the world 'countryside.' "[31] In pursuit of that front, Comintern agents appeared in all parts of the world, and the Soviets gave political and military training to nationalist leaders.

But who exactly was to receive support? Anti-imperialist leaders in the colonial world were often wealthy, educated, and privileged. They often tried to repress or undercut the activities of the local communist party. Should the Soviets aid such nationalists? The pious Soviet response was that "we communists should, and will, support bourgeois liberation movements in the colonial countries only when these movements are really revolutionary, when the representatives of these movements do not hinder us in training and organizing the peasants and the broad masses of the exploited in a revolutionary spirit."[32] In practice, however, the Comintern often subordinated the interests of the local communist party to the promotion of good relations with the nationalists. The results could be disastrous, as when Chiang Kai-shek's Nationalists massacred party members in Shanghai in 1927.

The reason for the subordination was usually the estimate of which force, the nationalists or communists, could do the most to weaken the capitalist powers. Ideology provided little guidance. Pragmatism suggested working with the nationalists, who were usually stronger than the party. Nonetheless, the critical impact of Marxist ideology, greatly reworked by the Bolsheviks, lay in its sug-

---

[29]Lenin's cables to Trotsky, in *The Trotsky Papers*, ed. Jan Meijer (The Hauge: Mouton, 1971), Vol. 2, pp. 227, 249, 257.

[30]Quoted by Davies, *White Eagle*, p. 266.

[31]Report to the 12th Party Congress, April, 1923; quoted by Stephen Cohen, *Bukharin and the Bolskevik Revolution* (New York: Knopf, 1971, 1973), p. 149.

[32]Lenin, "Report to the Comintern," July, 1920; *Selected Works*, Vol. X, p. 241.

gestion that all dependent peoples were potential allies and that Soviet Russia, unhindered by any imperial interests of its own, could support some form of meaningful liberation.

That it *should* support liberation was clear. However, if Soviet Russia wanted amicable relations with capitalist powers, it might have to deny even that commandment. Certainly the capitalist states would see the issue in those terms. In 1920, when a Soviet trade mission was about to arrive in London for talks, the British foreign minister sketched for his cabinet colleagues the line he would take: "We can hardly contemplate coming to . . . [the] rescue [of the Soviet economy] without exacting our own price for it, and it seems to me that that price can far better be paid in a cessation of Bolshevik hostility in parts of the [Asiatic] world of importance to us, than in the ostensible interchange of commodities. . . . "[33]

Modernization, Ideology, and Foreign Relations   The central concern of the Bolsheviks after the revolution was the creation of a modern economy within a socialist framework. During the civil war (1918–1920), the party enforced "war communism," which fell most heavily on the peasants. Although they had been given title to the land as a consequence of the revolution, the peasants now had to deliver their crops at artificially low prices, at times at no price, to the state. The industrial workers could thus be fed cheaply and a surplus created for export. By 1921, the civil war had ended, but war communism continued, and the economy of Soviet Russia worsened at an alarming pace.

Those who stressed making economic practices match ideological principles (as in war communism) now found themselves on the defensive. The lack of success implied that Marxist ideology might be at fault, that it did not provide the blueprint for successful modernization. Such a conclusion was (and is) unacceptable to ideologues. How does one resolve the tension between ideology and experience? For the Bolsheviks, the answer was to assume that the ideology was correct, but that the timing and application were faulty. War communism was the correct policy during the civil war; now, however, it was inappropriate and had to be replaced by policies that did not alienate the peasantry and that encouraged greater industrial output. In 1921, the Party accepted Lenin's New Economic Policy (NEP) which returned many capitalist features to urban and rural life. The change to the NEP accelerated the growing caution in Soviet foreign policy. Instead of avoiding entanglement with capitalist economies, Soviet diplomats sought loans and trade with the capitalist states. The Comintern increasingly became an embarrassment; revolution abroad went onto the back burner.

The requirements of economic development had created a denial of ideological principles internally and externally, and yet the NEP received justification in ideological terms, as did war communism, as did every turn in Soviet foreign policy. Is ideology nothing more than inspiration and rationalization, to be discarded when it conflicts with reality? Possibly. Marxists, however, have long insisted that Marxism is programmatic—that its principal interest is devising ways in which the proletariat might lose their chains of enslavement. As long as the goal of a communist society remains untampered with, why cannot the means be as flexible as the situation dictates? Lenin consistently argued that in domestic

---

[33]Lord Curzon, May, 1920; in *Documents on British Foreign Policy*, Vol. XII, p. 724.

and world politics, the Party had to be prepared to compromise where necessary, to conciliate, to take two steps backward for one forward. Tactically, then, ideology may suggest optimal behavior (that which is most clearly in line with the ideology such as support for proletarian revolution), may identify new types of revolutionary behavior (such as the Brest-Litovsk Treaty), and may allow "old, capitalist type policies" where necessary.

If this sounds like rank opportunism, you would be in agreement with some Bolsheviks to the left of Lenin, who argued that an ideological state simply could not do anything that happened to be expedient. Lenin himself denounced the moderate socialists who had made themselves apprentices to the bourgeoisie. How was Lenin's approach any different than that of these "renegade" socialists? Lenin argued that socialist *opportunism* made compromises *for gain*; Bolshevik *realism* made compromises *out of necessity*. Realists sought foreign loans, for instance, because they had no choice: "The rule of the proletariat cannot be maintained in a country laid waste as no country has ever been before—a country where the vast majority are peasants who are equally ruined—without the help of [foreign] capital . . . This we must understand."[34]

A Blueprint for Policy?   Whether or not we find Lenin's distinction convincing, it seems clear that ideology was not the exclusive driving force behind Soviet foreign policy, nor did it provide a blueprint. We might hypothesize that the same holds true in later periods as well. In a discussion of how one might evaluate proposed tactics, Lenin himself suggested three forces shaping policy rather than one: Marxism, political experience, and argument (logic).[35] We might say that ideology tolerates a variety of acceptable behaviors, yet given the contradictory policies possible, such a conclusion does not mean very much. Perhaps we might say that ideology makes certain behaviors more unlikely (such as traditional imperialism) but not impossible.

Rather than rely on these assessments, we can use the case study to supply us with more focused hypotheses about the role of ideology in the formulation of any state's behavior:

1. Ideology may encourage a "we-them" view of world politics with attributions of long-term hostility to "them." "We" may now include a number of people whom traditional views of world politics did not consider or treated as hostile.

2. Ideology may encourage a diplomatic style at variance with the traditional norms. Such a style is less likely to be inhibited regarding involvement in the domestic affairs of other states.

3. Ideology may encourage the creation of organizations devoted to its service (such as the Comintern) which may advocate policies in conflict with those of the state apparatus.

4. Ideology may encourage a diversion of attention from world politics to factional struggles with polities (as between the Comintern and the moderate socialists).

5. Ideology may encourage consideration of unconventional policies.

[34]Lenin, "Introducing the New Economic Policy," March, 1921; in *The Lenin Anthology*, ed. Robert Tucker (New York: W.W. Norton & Co., Inc., 1975), p. 508.

[35]"In Support of the Tactics of the Communist International," July, 1921, *Selected Works*, Vol. X, p. 283. Similar conclusions are drawn by Bertram Wolfe, *Ideology*, p. 346, and Richard Debo, *Revolution*, p. 420.

We began this analysis of the role of ideology through the perspective of the domestic and environmental factor approach. The choice of that approach was essentially arbitrary; that is, we do not have a set of methodological laws that states that "ideology" must be considered in this fashion. In fact, the relative impreciseness of our knowledge really implies that we should consider ideology in terms of each of the scientific approaches. For instance, what is ideology's role in bargaining? Does an ideological state have more leverage in negotiations because it can insist it would never agree to something that would violate its ideological principles? Alternatively, you may have sensed in the study of early Soviet foreign policy that ideology was part of the political debate within the government. Did ideology give an advantage to holders of particular policy preferences? In the next section on the systems approach, we will ask how ideology relates to the international system. Notice how quickly our conception of the role of ideology expands by our asking different questions. That is one of the beauties of the scientific approach.

International Systems Approach

An Equilateral System   In 1910, the distribution of power in the international system resembled a ladder. After the Great War, power in the European arena had a different aspect (see Figure 4–2). Two words of caution. First, this particular power structure speaks only about world politics in the European context. Second, power is measured differently than in the two previous chapters. Some words of explanation: What constitutes power is unlikely to remain constant over a century. The development of nuclear weapons and intercontinental delivery systems vividly makes the point. The measurement of power has to this point been in terms of steel production, population, and political stability. To this, I now add the percent of the world's energy production each state accounts for. This new measure captures important changes in fuels (generally the increasing use of petroleum), in technology and transportation, and in the overall strength of the economy. In military terms, the consumption of energy reflects a nation's war potential in terms of overall production and the likelihood of being in the forefront of two key military revolutions: the mechanization of the ground forces and the emergence of military aircraft capable of having a decisive influence on the battlefield.[36]

The second caution concerns *where* power might be exercised. Table 4–1 reports the overall power scores. American power has continued to grow; since

FIGURE 4-2   Power Distribution in 1920

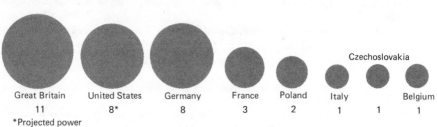

Great Britain	United States	Germany	France	Poland	Italy	Czechoslovakia	Belgium
11	8*	8	3	2	1	1	1

*Projected power

[36]The formula for computing power scores is (Steel + energy + [Population × Stability])/3.

TABLE 4–1 Basic Power Levels in 1920

MEASURE	WORLD	US	UK	GERMANY	FRANCE	USSR	POLAND	CZECHO-SLOVAKIA	ITALY	BELGIUM	JAPAN	CHINA
1. Million metric tons of crude steel	71.4	42.1	9.1	8.4	3	.2	1.0	1.0	.8	1.2	.8	0
2. Percent of world steel		59%	13%	12%	4%	0%	1%	1%	1%	2%	1%	0%
3. Million inhabitants in independent states	1167	106	44	60	39	132	27	14	37	8	59	400
4. Percent of world population in independent states		9%	4%	5%	3%	11%	2%	1%	3%	1%	5%	34%
5. Political stability in past decade		1.0	.8	.2	.8	0	.8	.8	.8	.8	.8	0
6. Energy production in million metric tons of coal equivalent	1566	776	247	190	48	27	31	23	1	23	32	23
7. Percent of world energy production		49%	16%	12%	3%	2%	2%	1%	0%	1%	2%	1%
Power*		39	11	8	3	1	2	1	1	1	2	0

*Power = $\dfrac{\#2 + (\#4 \times \#5) + \#7}{3}$

Sources: For steel and political stability, see Table 2–3; for population, *The World Almanac for 1924* (New York: New York World, 1924); for energy, Joel Darmstadter, *Energy in the World Economy* (Baltimore: Johns Hopkins University Press [for Resources for the Future, Inc.], 1971), Table II. (Energy data are 1925.)

1900 it has doubled, and in 1920 the American state is almost four times as powerful as its nearest rival. American power tipped the balance in the Great War and American bankers became the world's bankers. That is clear evidence that the main arena of world politics is expanding westward to include the North American continent. In an Atlantic arena (Europe and North America), the United States is clearly the dominant state. On the other hand, the American government's return to normalcy and rejection of the League meant that, for most issues, world politics remained centered in Europe. American power in such issues suffered erosion from distance, putting it on par with Britain and Germany.

The power position of the European states deserves comment. Overall German capabilities remained strong in spite of the war. Perhaps they remained strong because of the war—the basic economic and social structures of Germany were not damaged, as were those of many of its opponents. However, the Versailles Treaty created a demilitarized Germany, so we must note that Germany had very little capacity to threaten military action and little capacity to defend itself if attacked. Yet even being declawed did not mean that Germany was subjected to a continuing escalation of demands and punitive actions by the victors. The occupation of the Ruhr in 1923 was the high point in coercion. From then on, the lack of comparable military power counted for less and less. On most issues Germany was a major power of the first rank. French power benefitted little from the war and its outcome. Russia had but a fraction of its pre-war power. Austria no longer counted, but states such as Poland and Czechoslovakia emerged from the debris of empires and constituted the new but weak major powers of the 1920s. And Britain stood at the top of the heap.

While the fortunes of various states are of interest, the key question for systems analysis is the structure of the overall system and behaviors that are likely to result from such a structure. The system of the 1920s had a triumvirate of major powers of the first rank (Britain, Germany, and the United States) and a lesser constellation of weaker minor powers. In such a system, would we expect behavior quite different from that of a ladder-like system? The answer is a cautious "maybe." In comparing 1920 to 1910, we can still see the outline of a ladder-like structure, but now power has begun to shift disproportionately (but equally) to a few of the major states.

We can imagine that an ideal system of this type might look like Figure 4–3. This ideal case, which I call an "equilateral system," is likely to produce quite distinct behaviors. The more the historical system approximates this distribution, the more its behaviors are predicted to be in line with the ideal system's behaviors. I will take the liberty of pointing to historical behaviors as *examples* of structurally induced behavior; you should not assume that their use is invariably appropriate.

Would we logically expect states to polarize into two rival alliance systems? In a *ladder-like system*, states looked "above and below" to assess their security problems. Rival alliances were the result. In an equilateral system, *states of the first rank* "look sideways" to judge the threat. No single state constitutes a threat. Two states in an alliance *would* pose a threat. Therefore, a systemic rule of behavior would be "at the least, prevent an alliance between the other two states." One way to accomplish that would be to create an alliance first; hence the second rule: "Seek an alliance with either."

12   12   12   2   2   1   1   1

FIGURE 4–3   An Ideal Equilateral System

As each first-rank state follows these rules to protect its security, they all will now engage in a never-ending process of attempting to break and make alliances. The equal distribution of power means that no state is a more attractive alliance partner than another. Thus no state can guarantee that it will not be odd-state-out if an alliance forms. Even when states attempt to build an alliance expressly for aggression, this problem will remain. No state can guarantee that it will not be the target of attack by an alliance, because equal power gives no clues about who should align with whom.

It seems reasonable to hypothesize that the structure would impel the first-rank states to find ways to avoid the ''alliance scramble'' altogether. The safest way to do this would be to create an all-encompassing alliance—a nascent collective security system. In order to ensure that the first-rank states would not secretly try to negotiate a bilateral relationship, each would insist on a permanent institution (like the League), which would daily demonstrate a commitment to collective security. In addition, first-rank states would provide pledges of having no aggressive intentions. This is because to wage war successfully against an equal power, the state needs an alliance. To renounce war (as did the Kellogg-Briand Pact) is to reaffirm the agreement not to seek alliances. From this perspective, the League, Locarno, and Pact of Paris were not illusions, but reasonable responses to power in the post-war world.

This is not to say that the patterns of behavior dissolved all threats to the security of the major powers or necessarily made for a peaceful world. The permanent institution (such as the League), which embodied collective security, could pose a threat if a state captured control of it and was able to direct institutional resources and powers against others. In short, the ''alliance of all'' had to be real enough to prevent the competition for alliance partners but be *relatively toothless* in order not to threaten one of the first-rank states. The League's requirement for unanimity in its critical decision making and its failure to develop military power of its own illustrate the pressure to be toothless. President Hoover simply reflected American naïveté about world politics when he said that the League would ''apply force to compel other states to be reasonable.'' The League's function in the 1920s was not to police others, but to short-circuit the alliance formation process.[37]

---

[37]The League was founded under another set of conditions: when the United States was fully engaged in Europe and the arena of world politics had moved westward. The League, therefore, was a product of a structure that had a clearly predominant power. We might hypothesize that a League-like institution is the device the predominant power uses to police the rest of the system—a point made in Chapter 6. With the American retreat from world politics in the 1920s, the League would have to take on other characteristics in order to accommodate the new distribution of power.

Where did the lesser major powers fit into this world? Individually, each of the first-rank states was much more powerful than the lesser major powers. In systemic terms, collective security is designed to protect the strong, *not the weak*. Would the weaker states seek security by gravitating toward the first-rank states? Such a relationship would provide some security, but result in a subordination of the weaker state's interests to those of its protector. It would appear that the lesser major powers would do better by creating an alliance among themselves, for collectively they would be in rough balance with a state of the first rank. The French alliance network with Poland, Czechoslovakia, and Belgium is illustrative of this rule.

Even without such an alliance, the lesser major powers may not be in constant peril. The lesser powers could reasonably expect that states of the first rank would not sit idly by while one of the first-rank states attempted to become more powerful by conquering a weaker state. The security interests of the powerful would provide protection. However, the first-rank states would have less interest in conflict between lesser powers themselves and between lesser powers and the very weak states of the world; successful warfare would be unlikely to create a threat out of such weak initial power levels. Soviet Russia's conquest of Poland, for instance, would not produce a threat. In the equilateral system, weaker states have greater autonomy from the powerful than in a ladder-like system. Crises and war between weaker states will not necessarily drag in the powerful. This may prevent a total war from occurring, but it will also produce less restraint on the behaviors of the lesser states such as Italy or Japan.

Would we then conclude that the equilateral system is essentially *stable* and *peaceful*? When a system is able to preserve its power structure over a relatively long time, we call that system *stable*. Stability does *not* mean an absence of conflict, nor an unchanging power level for a particular state. It does mean that the overall distribution of power changes little and that the rules of the system tend to protect that overall distribution of power. These conditions were met in a ladder-like system when peace prevailed. Those same rules drove the system to instability when war broke out. The rules of the equilateral system suggest systemic stability and the prevalence of peace among the first-rank states, even when lesser powers are in conflict.

The Environment of the 1920s

Certainly all the rhetoric of the 1920s spoke of a peaceful world, of the outlawing of aggression. But in that lies a problem. The rhetoric and the treaty obligations committed everyone to refrain from war *and*, for League members, to react to *any* conflict likely to endanger world peace. Was this universal application of the rules a product of the system? I would argue that it was *not*. Rather, the impetus to apply rules globally came out of the Anglo-American liberal tradition so deeply embedded in domestic politics and symbolized by Woodrow Wilson. By definition, therefore, I am saying that some features of the *environment* (a particular view of politics derived from domestic politics) got past the *boundary* between environment and system and affected systemic *behavior*.

Recall that these words are simply concepts that allow us to discuss world politics effectively. The concepts of ''environment'' and ''boundary'' force us to ask what factors other than the distribution of power are likely to profoundly affect the operation of the system. More precisely, we must ask, "How does an environmental feature affect *either* the power of states *or* the patterns of international behavior?"

Regarding power, we can postulate a *systemic* rule that says that in *any* system, *all states will seek to maintain or increase their power vis-à-vis other states.*[38] Lenin, for instance, echoed the view of every government when he spoke of "our aspiration to rise again from enslavement to independence, and our unbending determination to ensure that at any price Russia ceases to be wretched and impotent and becomes mighty and abundant in the full meaning of these words."[39] The system drives states to enhance their power. *How effectively they are able to mobilize their own power internally is an environmental question.*

The Bolshevik revolution was an environmental event. The ideology, political organization, and skills of the leaders gave Russia a radically different set of tools with which to mobilize Russian power. We have seen how the crush of circumstances forced the regime to rely on the NEP to hold Russia together. In 1928, however, Josef Stalin had solidified his control over the Party and had inaugurated the first Five-Year Plan for the forced industrialization and agricultural collectivization of Russia. Only the 1930s would show whether these environmental events would drastically enhance Russian power. In the 1920s, Russia remained weak.

Other economic events occurred in the 1920s that suggested great potential for affecting power distributions. The sudden drop in American stock market prices in October, 1929, raised the possibility of a collapse in that nation's economy. Such events might easily feed into the international system because of their connection with power.

Environmental events can also "leak" through the boundary to affect the patterns of behavior directly. The Versailles Treaty, for instance, linked the economics of reparations to diplomatic relations between states. When the German economy faltered (an environmental event), Germany failed to make reparations payments, which brought the issue into the realm of world politics, upsetting the evolving patterns of cooperation among the major powers. The effort to isolate reparations issues in the 1920s (as in the Dawes and Young Plans) was an attempt to reestablish a boundary so that fluctuations of the German economy would not "spill over" into the operation of the international system.

When you think about it, there may be thousands of environmental events that *may* have an effect on the operation of the system. Millions of other events (such as your reading these lines) are unlikely to affect the system, because the boundary isolates them from the system. This section closes with a brief look at *ideology* as an environmental characteristic that might interfere with or reinforce the operation of the system.

Ideologies often reject the current pattern of state behavior as unjust and rapacious, dedicated to the enrichment of a few, and destined to be replaced by better patterns. A world of such ideological states may play havoc with the rules of the system and thereby endanger the security of the major powers. In the 1920s, there were two ideological states, Soviet Russia and Fascist Italy. In the

---

[38]Morton Kaplan, *System and Process in International Politics* (New York: John Wiley, 1957).

[39]"The Chief Task of Our Day," March, 1918, in *Lenin*, ed. Tucker, p. 434.

case of Soviet Russia, Marxism did enter into Soviet foreign policy in terms of supporting anticolonialism and aiding proletarian movements and other forms of subversion through the Comintern. In spite of this penetration of the boundary by the ideology, there was little impact. Why not?

In the 1920s, the ideological states had little power. Their deviation from the rules was not likely to upset the prevailing patterns of behavior, and the major powers would pressure the ideologues into acting in an acceptable manner. Britain, for instance, used trade to encourage Soviet restraint in subverting Asia. The counterpressures of the system (coupled with the emerging domestic requirements for economic development in Russia) helped restore the boundary between the system and the environment. Ideology continued in Russia, but the leadership decided to keep it out of foreign affairs. The question for the future would be how resistant the boundary would be if ideologues controlled a powerful state.

Rejection of system-induced patterns of behavior is not the only destabilizing aspect of ideology. Ideologies generally narrow an ideologue's perspective of the world. The Marxist "two-camp" view may fatally over-simplify world politics, especially as the camps are defined in terms of values (capitalist versus socialist) rather than power. The system functions inefficiently—has more trouble producing security for the major powers—when perceptions of power are distorted. Fortunately, perhaps, major ideologies of the twentieth century have all been power-oriented so there has been no major power that has rejected power as a central part of politics. (Americans and their leaders have rhetorically insisted that American foreign policy had replaced power with principles; all those principles, however, have rested on a bedrock of power.)

Ideology can also destabilize the system by distorting perceptions. The ideological state may define other states' behavior according to the dictates of the ideology rather than the realities of the situation. The Bolsheviks' assumption of continuing capitalist hostility toward Soviet Russia would make more difficult the operation of an equilateral system if the ideologues controlled one of the first-rank states. Such a state would probably resist the formation of a collective security system, because the system would reduce the antipathies between capitalist first-rank states and encourage them to turn collectively against the Soviet state. Marxist ideology, when it entered the international arena, would suggest a policy of dividing the other powers, rather than seeking some form of cooperation.

Indeed, early Soviet foreign policy had this particular bias. In 1923, when Stresemann began to conciliate the Western powers, the Comintern ordered an uprising by the German Communist Party. (It proved abortive.) Soviet Russia not only attempted to prevent the inevitable (in systemic terms), but also chose to risk irreparable damage to the relations with the only major-power friend it had. Once again, however, the weakness of the Soviet Union prevented misperception from undermining the systemic patterns. The 1930s would tell a different story.

In systemic terms, the 1920s were relatively peaceful, cooperative, and stable. The environment was generally supportive. The boundary kept unsettling events out of the international political arena and those states that would disrupt the system were too weak to affect it. Nothing in systemic terms suggested that the next decade would be one of chaos.

CHAPTER FIVE

1930–1939 _____
Night and fog

PART I:
DIPLOMATIC HISTORY[1]

Economic Collapse

Much of world politics during the 1930s centers on the problem of Germany and Adolf Hitler. However, the three years prior to his coming to power in January, 1933, decisively demonstrated that the hopes of the 1920s were not to be. While Hitler destroyed the peace, he did not destroy the conditions necessary for peace, foremost of which were economic stability and the effectiveness of the collective security system embodied in the League of Nations. Those conditions acquired terminal diseases in the first months of the decade.

Economic issues had been a central part of the politics of the 1920s. Now questions of reparations and war debts dissolved into insignificance as the capitalist system itself began to break down. The booming American economy of the

---

[1]General sources for the 1930s include F.S. Northedge, *The Troubled Giant: Britain among the Great Powers* (New York: Praeger, 1966); A.J.P. Taylor, *The Origins of the Second World War* (New York: Atheneum, 1962); Gerhard Weinberg, *The Foreign Policy of Hitler's Germany* (Chicago: University of Chicago Press, 1970); Raymond Sontag, *A Broken World* (New York: Harper & Row, Pub., 1971). For contemporary accounts, see the Royal Institute of International Affairs, *Survey of International Affairs* (London: Oxford University Press). For documentary sources: *Documents on International Affairs* (London: Oxford University Press); *Documents on German Foreign Policy, 1918–1945* (Washington: Government Printing Office) [cited hereafter as *DGFP*]; *Documents on British Foreign Policy, 1919–1939*, 2nd series, ed. E.L. Woodward and Rohan Butler (London: Her Majesty's Stationery Office) [cited hereafter as *DBFP*]; *Nazi Conspiracy and Aggression* (Washington: Government Printing Office), 8 vols., 2 supplements.

1920s had attracted increasing numbers of domestic and foreign investors.[2] Deprived of new capital, European economies began to falter in the last years of the decade. The decrease in American investment in Germany threatened to curtail reparations payments, heretofore made possible by American loans. In October, 1929, the stock market boom ended in the United States, and by April, 1930, the American economy slid into the worst depression in a century. Those with capital and those who had to make decisions regarding production turned exceedingly cautious. The purchase of raw materials ceased, drying up the trade of materials-exporting states. Production was reduced, throwing workers out of jobs, which meant they would be less able to buy finished goods exported by foreign states. No further loans were made, cutting off foreign investment as well as domestic industrial expansion. As a result, the American economy worsened week by week, drawing the economies of other states into a similar downward spiral. By 1931, the industrial decline threatened to spread to the financial sector; panicky depositors began to withdraw funds from banks, fearing they would lose their money if they did not. The run on the banks overwhelmed some institutions, threatening to undermine the financial structure of societies.

The central feature of the Depression that concerns us most is the uncertainty it created. An economy does not crash "to the bottom" all at once. It spirals down, never clearly telling its victims that it has reached bottom. In the United States, for instance, "time and again it appeared that conditions were so bad that they could not get worse, but they did. Each winter from 1930 to 1933 was worse than the one before it."[3] Uncertainty produced pessimism. If the American economy, the marvel of the age, was vulnerable to disaster, where did economic security lie? The uncertainty also produced demands by the public that the political system do something, anything, to fix the economy. The economic crisis eroded confidence in parliamentary democracy. There was a real question whether it could cope with the problems besetting societies. For the first time since the war, authoritarian regimes not only appeared understandable but attractive to many individuals. Hitler's Germany seemed to end unemployment and restart a broken economy; around the world, political movements and some governments emulated the apparent wave of the future. Authoritarian regimes stressed nationalism and spoke in the rhetoric of struggle and force. Those domestic images began to spill over into thinking about world politics.

These momentous changes in the environment of world politics undermined expectations about a peaceful future. The authoritarians of the right spoke of dismantling the old order. Marxist predictions of the final crisis of capitalism and impending global class war seemed half fulfilled. Instead of cooperation, leaders and citizens began to think of conflict as the normal pattern of world politics. The beliefs embodied in the Kellogg-Briand pact—sincerely held five years earlier—sounded hopelessly utopian if not utterly naive. When leaders began to

---

[2]For accounts of the depression see Charles Kindleberger, *The World in Depression, 1929–39* (Berkeley: University of California Press, 1973); John K. Galbraith, *The Great Crash* (Boston: Houghton Mifflin, 1955); Joseph Davis, *The World Between the Wars, 1919–1939: An Economist's View* (Baltimore: Johns Hopkins University Press, 1975); Robert Ferrell, *American Diplomacy in the Great Depression* (New Haven: Yale University Press, 1957); Burton Klein, *Germany's Economic Preparations for War* (Cambridge: Harvard University Press, 1959).

[3]Davis, *World Between the Wars*, p. 295.

stress the primacy of national needs and the necessities of survival, no matter the pain they may cause others, the arguments had a plausible ring to them. Even those who rejected such views often saw foreign affairs as an annoying distraction to the task of saving the state and the society.

The change in how people thought of world politics quickly appeared in world politics, which seemed to confirm the aptness of the new beliefs. We can summarize some of those instances:

1. *The rejoining of economic, political, and security issues.* In 1931, the German and Austrian governments proposed the creation of a customs union that would end restrictions on trade between the two, but maintain a common set of restrictions on foreign imports. The French strenuously objected to this as a violation of the Versailles Treaty. In May, 1931, the leading Austrian bank, Credit-Anstalt, stood on the verge of collapse. The French held up an international loan designed to save the bank until the Austrian government renounced the customs union. Credit-Anstalt failed and the reverberations spread throughout Europe, pushing the continent fully into depression. Once again, the French used loans to failing German banks as a way of extracting German pledges not to implement the customs union. The French had reverted to economic leverage to restrict German power and to uphold the sanctity of the Versailles Treaty.

Similarly, economic crisis reopened the reparations issue. By the spring of 1931, it was clear Germany would default on its June payment, which would force a political response from the victor states. And if Germany did not pay, the victors would not pay the United States the upcoming war debt installment the American government demanded. President Hoover, at the last moment, however, proposed a one-year moratorium on reparations and war debts. Europe gratefully accepted, and the following year, the European states met at Lausanne and agreed to what amounted to a cancellation of the war debt and reparations. The United States refused to accept the decision but chose not to challenge it. Thus, by 1932, this particular connection between economics and politics had finally terminated. Germany had ended that legacy of Versailles. Bitter feelings persisted, however.

2. *The collapse of economic cooperation.* One common response to the Depression was to try to isolate the state from the woes of the rest and to prevent others from regaining prosperity at one's expense. Autarky became something of a prized condition, for not only did it mean economic self-sufficiency, but it reduced the chances of political manipulation (as the French had done in the Credit-Anstalt case). For those states with natural resources or undeniable access to them, autarky was in reach. For the rest, such as Japan, Germany, and Italy (each, incidentally, lacking petroleum), autarky implied grabbing. As to making sure that no one else recovered at one's own expense, the Americans led the way. President Hoover, for instance, signed into law the Smoot-Hawley Tariff Act (June, 1930), which made it much more difficult to sell foreign goods in the United States. Three years later, President Roosevelt torpedoed a League-sponsored international economic conference by insisting on the right to make unilateral decisions regarding the American economy.

3. *Arms and economics.* Following the common wisdom of the times, most governments reduced their expenditures and at the same time tried to increase

their allocations for unemployment benefits. Military expenditures fell under the ax, and the flagging disarmament talks received new impetus. The initial exception to the common wisdom was Japan, which accepted budget deficits and continued military spending. The pre-Hitler German government fell some place in between, keeping military expenditures stable but reducing the budget by cutting social welfare. Hitler, always conscious of the public mood, undertook deficit financing to expand social services as well as to build the military. Germany and Japan did not count on military expenditures as the cure to the Depression, however. Expansion of the military was in keeping with their foreign policy aims. At least their governments were not so entranced by economic orthodoxies as to postpone such an expansion.

In sum, the Depression ensured that states would rediscover the issues that divided them, find new causes of complaint against each other, and assume that conflict, however unfortunate, was their common lot. And it caused statesmen to look to domestic politics rather than foreign politics. The collective security system now had to function under crippling limitations. Its survival depended upon relative harmony among the great powers and a continued concern for world politics.

Collective Security Falters

It fell to the Japanese to infect the collective security system with creeping paralysis. It easily might have been someone else. There would always be challenges to a collective security system that had a global mission. We have seen that in the 1920s Japanese economic and imperial interests clashed with growing Chinese nationalism. Furthermore, foreign policy questions had divided the Japanese government, and that division had promoted insubordination among the military. In the fall of 1931, events came to a boil.[4] The Japanese military feared that the civilian government would cave in to economic and Anglo-American pressures for restrictions on land and air forces at the upcoming League disarmament conference scheduled for February 1932—just as it had done at a 1930 naval disarmament conference. The government's lack of resolution regarding Manchuria was another worrisome point. The Chinese Nationalists in the spring of 1931 had announced their intention to recover the rights of sovereignty that foreign powers had stolen from imperial China.

Plots for a military coup became common in Japan, and the military elite refused to suppress the plotters, either out of sympathy or fear. And if insubordination was rife in Tokyo, it was far worse in Manchuria among the 10,000-man Kwantung Army on garrison duty (See Map 4–1). Assuming that only they had the courage to preserve Japanese rights in China—to say nothing of making Manchuria a colony—officers in the Kwantung Army decided on a *fait accompli*. On September 18, 1931, they detonated an explosive on the Japanese-owned South Manchuria railroad and, claiming they were under attack by Chinese troops, proceeded to order the occupation of Mukden and other cities along the rail line.

[4]See Sadako Ogata, *Defiance in Manchuria: The Making of Japanese Foreign Policy, 1931–1932* (Berkeley: University of California Press, 1964); and Takehiko Yoshihashi, *Conspiracy at Mukden* (New Haven: Yale University Press, 1963).

The government of Prime Minister Wakatsuki faced a dilemma. Could it end uncontrolled military adventurism, protect Japanese interests, placate the major powers, and avoid a messy confrontation with its own military establishment? Kwantung Army officers were determined not to be thwarted this time. Ignoring government suggestions, they continued to expand the area of Manchuria under occupation and encouraged sympathetic inhabitants to establish local governments under the Army's protection. This process would continue until February, 1932, when the Army announced the formation of the independent state of Manchukuo, with Henry Pu-yi, heir to the Chinese throne, as emperor.

At the beginning of the incident, China had appealed to the League, putting collective security on trial. How did the League respond?[5] Initially, it agreed with the Japanese not to take up the issue if Japan withdrew its forces and opened negotiations directly with the Chinese to resolve the general problem of Manchuria. League members agreed to the Japanese proposal because no one saw the issue as immediately fundamental to their interests, no one wanted a foreign crisis on top of an economic one, and many agreed with American Secretary of State Stimson that harsh League action would undermine the influence of the Japanese moderates.

When it became apparent that no one would or could control the Kwantung Army, the United States and other powers began to suggest deadlines for compliance. The Japanese government, fighting for time to bring its military into line, proposed a League commission of inquiry to investigate the initial incident at Mukden and to make recommendations for a general settlement. The League members agreed in December, 1931. However, Prime Minister Wakatsuki was forced from office in December. Military officers assassinated his successor in their drive to reform the Japanese political system and annex Manchuria. The new government of Admiral Saito, in tune with the expansionists, recognized Manchukuo in September, 1932, and signed an agreement making Manchukuo a puppet state under Japanese protection. The imperialists were appeased.

In October, 1932, the Lytton Commission reported to the League that Japan had not acted in self-defense, nor was Manchukuo created by the will of its inhabitants. It recommended the reorganization of Manchuria as an autonomous territory of China, with no Chinese or Japanese forces, and protection for Japanese economic interests. The League slowly debated the report and, over strong Japanese protests, accepted it in February, 1933. For teeth, the League endorsed the American refusal to grant diplomatic recognition to Manchukuo. Thereupon, Japan quit the League, charging its members with failure to recognize the requirements for a durable peace in Asia. Thus emerged the question: would the League powers, by and large satisfied with imperial holdings they had carved out with power, insist that Japan behave in a different fashion in an area that was of secondary importance to them but of primary interest to Japan? And if they insisted, would they be willing to use war against Japan in order to restore the status quo to Manchuria? It seemed mad to even think it. Ironically, the preservation of peace seemed to suggest that the League had failed.

Had collective security and its guardian, the League, failed? Not necessarily. The League had forced the international community to recognize and become involved in the conflict between China and Japan. It had formally upheld

---

[5]For details, see Christopher Thorne, *The Limits of Foreign Policy* (New York: Putnam's, 1973).

the position that new norms of international behavior could not be disregarded in the face of power. These were two of the foundations on which the League rested. The third foundation, the power to employ collective coercion, was not called upon. This suggests that the success of the League was in the area of *deterrence*. The seven year struggle (1927–1932) within the Japanese government over Manchurian policy indicates that the League did have some deterrent power.[6]

And when deterrence fails? Clearly the League failed to defend China from Japanese imperialism. When deterrence failed, the *individual* League members had to decide on enforcement. As there was no mechanism to compel states to defend China (precisely because no state wanted to be compelled on a potential life-or-death decision), the members looked to each other to lead the way. Leaders are often scarce in such circumstances. But even prior to the need to make the hard decision about enforcement, the League failed. The Lytton commission took nearly a year to produce a report, which, when submitted, had had the potential to be an acceptable compromise—*in 1931*, when Wakatsuki was looking for a way to rein in the Kwantung Army but still safeguard Japanese interests. The report was completely overtaken by events. It proposed to a Japanese government heavily influenced by the military and now possessing Manchuria that it give everything up. Collective security had contracted a mortal illness.

Hitler Completes the Destruction of the Versailles Treaty

Between 1933 and 1937, Japan's policy in Asia ceased to be of much interest to the major powers. It was not as openly aggressive, and the League had rather clearly indicated that as long as Japan had limited ambitions, the major powers would look the other way. Besides, the political hotspot had become Europe once again.

The League-sponsored disarmament talks of 1932 foundered on German insistence on equality (everybody disarmed or Germany rearmed) and French demands for a foolproof security system before any change in the status quo. When the talks resumed in February, 1933, conditions had changed. Germany in effect owed no reparations. But that was a minor matter compared to Hitler's accession to the Chancellorship on January 30, 1933.

It had been a remarkable rise to power.[7] Elections in September, 1930, made the Nazis[8] the second strongest party in the Reichstag. By the spring of 1932, Hitler was a strong contender for the Presidency, losing in a run-off to the incumbent, the war hero von Hindenburg. Hitler's popular support far outweighed that of the chancellors who preceded him. In addition to the electoral pursuit of power, the armed units of the Nazi Party (the Storm Troops) maintained a reign of terror in the streets against the socialist and communist parties

---

[6]Ogata, *Defiance,* p. 176.

[7]Studies of Hitler are numerous. Among the best are Alan Bullock, *Hitler: A Study in Tyranny,* rev. ed. (New York: Harper & Row, Pub., 1962, 1964); Joachim Fest, *Hitler,* trans. Richard and Clara Winston (New York: Harcourt Brace Jovanovich, 1973, 1974); John Toland, *Adolf Hitler* (New York: Doubleday, 1976).

[8]Although I shall use the term "Nazi," the correct title of the party was National Socialist German Workers' Party (also known by its initials, NSDAP).

and their street armies. Hitler's appointment as Chancellor in a coalition government of Nazis and right-wing politicians seemed both inevitable and impossible (he had pledged to destroy the Weimar political system).

Hitler was not someone to escape the attention of foreign diplomats. While probably few had read his book, *Mein Kampf*[9] before his accession to power, his and the party's ideas were relatively well known. The British Ambassador, for instance, reported the 1930 Party program:

> The final aim is a 'greater Germany,' to achieve which the programme demands the consolidation of all Germans into one great German state, equal rights for the German people with other nations [which was a known euphemism for remilitarization], the abolition of the Treaties of Versailles and Saint-Germain, and space and colonies to feed the nation and absorb the surplus population.[10]

In a highly publicized trial, Hitler declared that the means by which he would fight against Versailles "will be regarded as illegal . . . in the opinion of the world."[11] It seemed clear that a new and disturbing element had entered world politics.

Or had it? Hitler's arrival in power and his rapid development of a stranglehold on the state forced diplomats to ask the kinds of questions we have addressed earlier in this book: what role would Hitler's personality and perceptions play in shaping German foreign policy? What would be the role of Nazi ideology? Did Hitler come to office with fixed ideas, derived from his youth and young adulthood, regarding world politics? Between 1923 and 1926 he had written, for instance, that Germany would seek a reckoning with France, "the most terrible enemy," which "constitutes in its tie with the aims of Jewish world domination an enduring danger for the existence of the white race in Europe." And that Bolshevism must be eradicated, as it was a tool for Jewish world domination. That only in the East could Germany acquire the land necessary to become a world power, and in that acquisition, it was force that determined the boundaries of states. That "in the predictable future there can be only two allies for Germany in Europe: England and Italy."[12] Were these the embittered fulminations of a young, nationalistic, anti-Semitic German who could not, as many other Germans could not, accept the outcome of the war? Would maturity blunt the edges? Would he, as the leader of 60 million people, allow his personal craving for power to mold every decision he made?

How would the diplomats assess the contribution of Nazi ideology?[13] If ideology can be said to provide a way of looking at the world, Nazi ideology might contribute these elements: An orientation toward power and its use, a use based

---

[9]Adolf Hitler, *Mein Kampf,* trans. Ralph Manheim (Boston: Houghton Mifflin, 1943, 1971; UK: Hutchinson, 1943, 1971).

[10]Ambassador Rumbold's report, October 31, 1930; *DBFP*, 2nd series, Vol. I, p. 527.

[11]Rumbold report, September 26, 1930; *ibid.*, p. 516.

[12]The most extended discussion of foreign policy comes in *Mein Kampf*, Vol. II, Chapters 13–15. The quotations are from the Manheim translation, pp. 624 and 625, respectively. Translation © Houghton Mifflin. Reprinted by permission of Houghton Mifflin Company.

[13]For Nazi ideology, see *Mein Kampf;* George Mosse, ed., *Nazi Culture* (New York: Grosset & Dunlap, 1966); Horst Von Maltitz, *The Evolution of Hitler's Germany* (New York: McGraw-Hill, 1973).

on a social Darwinism that national (ethnic and racial) survival went to the strong and ruthless. A belief that national necessities drove the affairs of nations and that the only moral responsibility of leadership was to provide for the survival of the nation. A belief that non-Aryan peoples were inferior, and therefore destined for expulsion, exploitation, and extermination. A belief that a sinister, monolithic force (world Jewry) coordinated all the efforts to destroy Germany. Would these components of the ideology twist and bend German foreign policy in particular ways?

As that diplomat in 1933, what might you predict about Hitler's future behavior? Unfortunately, our knowledge of what Hitler actually did predisposes us to see all of his subsequent behavior prefigured in his personality, perspectives, and ideology. As a diplomat of the time, however, you would have been more likely to reason as did a German foreign ministry official: "When they have the responsibility the National Socialists are naturally different people and pursue a different policy than they proclaimed before. It was always like this, and it is the same with all parties."[14] And if you had been a student of Soviet ideology and foreign policy (as you became in the last chapter!), you also might have some reservations about ideology's dictating policy.

Indeed, Nazi and communist ideology in the early 1930s shared the characteristics of extremes in rhetoric, apparently more limited in application. Ironically, for all the touted power of Marxism as a guide to behavior, Soviet policy makers badly misjudged Hitler. The Comintern, reflecting Stalin's view, assumed Hitler's tenure would be as short as his predecessors'. In the early 1930s, the Comintern pushed its fight with the noncommunist left; the German communist party was ordered not to join the socialists in an anti-Nazi front. Indeed, at times it was ordered to support Nazi political positions. Even after Hitler as Chancellor ordered the suppression of the German communist party, the leadership felt sure that (as their slogan went), "After Hitler, Our Turn."

Of course, with the acuity of hindsight it is easy to say, "How foolish it was not to recognize that Hitler would do what he said he would." Much of the scholarship on Hitler's foreign policy now takes this view. A.J.P. Taylor has been one of the few to challenge the popular thesis.[15] This contrary view argues the following: Hitler's foreign policy had many of the same roots as Stresemann's—to break the shackles of Versailles. That would be a given for any German leader. Hitler departed from his predecessors in raising the threat level in the demands for revision, in an unwillingness to make meaningful concessions in return for revision, and in speaking of a territorially expansive Germany. Were these departures but tactical variations designed to give him more leverage to destroy Versailles? For instance, talk of "space in the East" may have been designed to increase the willingness of the victor states to accept a union of Germany and Austria. Alternatively, the expansionism in Hitler's perspective stemmed not so much from personal idiosyncrasy or ideology but a strategic orientation available to anyone: caught between Anglo-French power in the West and swelling Soviet power in the East (a product of the 1930s), it was "natural" that Germany would seek to push its frontiers outward. There was little room in the West (Netherlands

---

[14]State Secretary Bulow's letter of February 6, 1933; *DGFP*, series C, Vol. I, p. 21.

[15]Taylor, *Origins.*

and Belgium, perhaps) but much in the East (Poland and Central Europe as a shield against the Soviets).

One might suggest (as I will do in a moment) that Hitler's broad goals can be identified. However, that does not mean that his foreign policy at a particular moment was dictated by those goals (as the rational model of policy making would have it), or that Hitler "had things all planned out." The historical record simply is not clear—one can see fluctuations in view, denial of deeply rooted convictions, and a strikingly impromptu nature to much of his policy making. We also know that Hitler was a consummate liar. But *when* he lied is more difficult to establish. He told a French interviewer (who brought up those awkward statements about France in *Mein Kampf*):

> You want me to correct my book, like a man of letters bringing out a new and revised edition of his works. But I am a politician. I undertake my corrections in my foreign policy, which aims at an understanding with France.[16]

Was this a sincere (although perhaps transitory) goal, or was it a tactical expedient, reflecting German weakness but not a denial of an intensely held desire to destroy French power? This and similar evidence can be read various ways. I will have to leave it to you to form your own conclusions. What follows is my interpretation.

Hitler Remilitarizes Germany   Hitler had three amorphous aims: remilitarization, incorporation of all Germans into the Reich, and territorial expansion. Remilitarization had priority; in February, 1933, Hitler told his cabinet that "the next five years in Germany had to be devoted to rendering the German people again capable of bearing arms."[17] His initial estimates were that Germany could not mount a fundamental challenge to the Versailles system for ten years; subsequently 1943 cropped up in his conversations as the year in which force would be the predominant element of policy. Until then, Hitler would have to talk of peace while Germany regained its strength in a way that would not cause a coalition to form that would attack Germany. To ensure against such a coalition, Hitler, like the Kaiser and the Weimar diplomats before him, sought to keep the East divided from the West, Britain from France, and Poland from the Soviet Union.

Hitler, however, did not control the timetable of world politics, which would thrust Germany into conflict with the powers at its own pace. The issue at the moment was the reconvened disarmament conference. Hitler insisted that the "heavily armed states" begin reductions at once. The French refused; with Hitler in office, they insisted on the formula of "security first, then disarmament." In addition, 1935 began the "lean years" when the lowered birth rate occasioned by the Great War would shrink French manpower by half the strength needed to maintain the French army at current levels. Hitler ordered the Ger-

[16]Interview with Bertrand de Jouvenel, February 21, 1936; *Documents on International Affairs, 1936*, p. 21.

[17]Cabinet minutes, February 8, 1933; *DGFP*, series C, Vol. I, p. 36.

man delegation home and then announced in October, 1933, Germany's withdrawal from the League itself.

German withdrawal was a clear, almost provocative signal of German intentions regarding arms. When no forceful response came from the West, Hitler gloated to his advisors that the West was too divided to take a stand. And, he said, they would reopen the disarmament dialogue. They did so, agreeing to consider a large German army, an air force, and tanks, thereby formally acknowledging that the Versailles limitations were dead. By the end of 1934, however, the talks had run aground.

Relations with neighboring states also forced themselves to the fore. Hitler reversed a decade and a half of hostility toward the Polish state by signing in January, 1934, a ten-year nonaggression treaty. While this decision protected Germany's eastern flank, it worried the French, who now had doubts about their Polish allies. France strengthened the alliance with Czechoslovakia and—worse for Germany—began talks with the Soviet Union for a defensive alliance. In the fall of 1934, with France leading the way, the Soviet Union entered the League, that bastion of bourgeois interests.

The major difficulty for Germany at the time, however, lay in the south with Austria. Hitler's coming to power encouraged Austrian Nazis to step up their agitation. The Austrian government attempted to destroy the local Nazi movement and turned to Mussolini for protection. Mussolini did not want to see *Anschluss*, the union of Germany and Austria, for that would bring German power to his borders. His warning to Germany, echoed by Britain and France, and pressure from German diplomats who feared alienating Germany's small neighbors, led Hitler to moderate (but not end) German support for the Austrian Nazis. In fact, the Austrian movement (and its counterpart in Czechoslovakia where three million Germans lived) was not under Hitler's tight control. In July, 1934, the Austrian Nazis attempted a coup. Although the Austrian Chancellor died, the Austrian army and other paramilitary formations remained loyal to the new Chancellor, Kurt Schuschnigg. Mussolini mobilized forces on the Austrian frontier to make it clear that Germany would pay a price to rescue the failing coup. Hitler did nothing.

Encouraged by this success, the French and Italian governments began talks to resolve their differences and lay the groundwork for the containment of Germany. There was a price for Italian cooperation in protecting Austria and the League's norms—no challenge to Italy's imperial ambitions. The target was to be Ethiopia (Abyssinia). In December, 1934, Italian and Ethiopian forces clashed sporadically on the border between Ethiopia and Italian Somaliland. Ethiopia appealed to the League, forcing Britain and France into another dilemma. The League settled on relatively prompt mediation of the border dispute. Given the nature of Italian interests, mediation meant concessions by Ethiopia.

The involvement of the League produced friction between Italy and France and Britain. Hitler took the opportunity in March, 1935, to make public something that had been under way for some time, the creation of a German air force. The French quickly announced that military service would be extended an additional year (to enable France to get through the "lean years"). Hitler used the French announcement to declare that Germany was resuming conscription and would build a 500,000-man army. Versailles was crumbling.

Britain, France, and Italy held a hurried conference at Stresa, Italy, to decide on the next step. They condemned Germany's unilateral rearmament and agreed to act collectively in the future. No one was keen to apply sanctions, least of all Britain. The British still hoped to reach an arms agreement with Hitler, especially regarding aircraft. Aerial bombardment of heavily urbanized Britain would be devastating; projections spoke of 750,000 casualties in the first month of such attacks. Already the government had begun to expand the Royal Air Force to counter the suspected German buildup. The government's attempt to end this arms race floundered on Hitler's demand for parity with Britain's air force. As a sop, Hitler offered to restrict the German navy (also expanding) to 35 percent of the British navy. The two states signed such a treaty in June, 1935. There was a real question of whether the "Stresa Front" still existed. The French looked to the East. In May, the French and Soviets agreed on a mutual assistance treaty, and the Soviets signed a similar agreement with Czechoslovakia. Equally important, in August the Comintern ended its policy of attacking the left and called for a broad united front against fascism and war.

Italy, the third element of the dissolving Stresa Front, also wanted to avoid a confrontation with Germany. It had begun sending divisions to Eritrea and Somaliland in preparation for the conquest of Ethiopia. War clearly was in the offing. A number of states (including the United States) declared an embargo on arms sales to both Italy and Ethiopia. Such actions aided Italy, as it produced its own arms while Ethiopia did not. England and France had no easy road out. They pledged to uphold the Covenant, but they agreed that military sanctions were out of the question—who wanted to make a European war out of a colonial conflict?

Mussolini ignored requests and warnings, and, rejecting last-minute League mediation proposals, ordered the offensive to begin in early October, 1935. The Italian government proclaimed that it would add Ethiopia to its colonial empire in spite of the Western powers' "attempt to commit against them [the Italian people] the blackest of all injustices, to rob them of a place in the sun." And more ominously, "To sanctions of a military character we will reply with orders of a military character."[18]

No one could deny the League was on trial. The Council did label Italy as an aggressor in October, 1935, and voted to apply an embargo in November on arms, loans, and trade—but not on oil. Without foreign oil, Mussolini's war machine would stop. The inclusion of oil, however, might be taken by the Italians as an act of war. But when Italy ignored the sanctions, the League had to think oil. To avoid this, the British and French foreign ministers, Samuel Hoare and Pierre Laval, concocted a compromise—a division of Ethiopia between Italy and Haile Selassie, the Ethiopian emperor. The two governments supported the plan until it leaked to the press. The British public rose in protest of the Hoare-Laval betrayal of the principles of the League. This was the old problem—peace or

---

[18]Mussolini's statement of October 2, 1935; *Documents of International Affairs, 1935,* Vol. II, p. 170. For studies of the conflict, see George Baer, *The Coming of the Italian-Ethiopian War* (Cambridge: Harvard University Press, 1967); Angelo Del Boca, *The Ethiopian War, 1935–1941,* trans. P.D. Cummins (Chicago: University of Chicago Press, 1969); G. Baer, *Test Case: Italy, Ethiopia, and the League of Nations* (Stanford: Hoover Institution Press, 1975).

principles, now made more anguishing by the fact that to insist on principles would doom any prospect of maintaining the containment of Germany. Yet while the public clamored for principles, it rejected war as the ultimate protector of principle. Hoare and Laval left office in disgrace, the League rejected the oil weapon, and Italy completed the conquest of Ethiopia in late April, 1936. All sanctions ended that summer.

The Ethiopian crisis gave Hitler another opportunity. The failure of sanctions and the Hoare-Laval plan suggested that the League powers were impotent. On March 7, 1936, as the League debated oil sanctions, Hitler sent weak army units into the demilitarized zone along both sides of the Rhine. Prepared to order a withdrawal, he spent an anxious week waiting for the British and French to respond. The French military proved more timid than their German counterparts (who tried to talk Hitler out of the operation) and the British government had no appetite for a confrontation with both Italy and Germany. The League delivered the expected condemnation and that was that. Germany was unshackled.

Collective security, Neville Chamberlain told the British parliament, "has been tried out and it has failed to prevent war, failed to stop war, failed to save the victim of aggression."[19] The League receded into the background of world politics. The status-quo powers, Britain, France, and the Soviet Union, now had the responsibility to protect the system if they chose to. But to do that, they had to decide which norms of behavior they would uphold (even at the cost of war), what commitments they would make to each other, and how they would communicate and coordinate their intentions. The League, for all its weaknesses, had done these critical things for its members. The next three years marked the hesitating attempt by the three powers to restructure their perceptions and relations. They failed, and failed tragically.

The Lull Before the Storm   The British and French had some reason to believe they might be successful in protecting the status quo. Hitler had reached the end of the unilateral moves he could make. The next challenge would have to be against a neighbor. That was another matter, as German Foreign Minister von Neurath explained to the American ambassador.

> Von Neurath said that it was the policy of the German Government to do nothing active in foreign affairs until "the Rhineland had been digested." He explained that he meant that until the German fortifications had been constructed on the French and Belgian frontiers, the German Government would do everything possible to prevent rather than encourage an outbreak by the Nazis in Austria and would pursue a quiet line with regard to Czechoslovakia. "As soon as our fortifications are constructed and the countries of Central Europe realize that France cannot enter German territory at will, all those countries will begin to feel very differently about their foreign policies and a new constellation will develop," he said.[20]

While German challenges to the status quo did temporarily cease, world politics continued to drag states into confrontation. In July, 1936, right-wing

---

[19]Speech of June 10, 1936; *Documents on International Affairs, 1935,* Vol. II, pp. 487–88.

[20]Memorandum of conversation with William Bullitt, May 18, 1936; *Nazi Conspiracy,* Vol. VII, p. 890.

military commanders rose against the leftist Spanish government.[21] The government requested arms from France and the Soviet Union. The rebels appealed to Germany and Italy. Hitler made a snap decision to allow the use of German aircraft to ferry rebel troops from Spanish Morocco to Spain, and soon Germany and Italy became the major suppliers of the insurgent forces (including, eventually, aviators and troops who "volunteered" for service). France and Britain adopted a policy of neutrality, including a ban on arms sales. The Soviets supplied the government in response to German and Italian support for the insurgents. This not-so-covert activity took place while delegates from all the powers met in London in September, 1936, to supervise an embargo that all publicly supported. Except for several international volunteer units, the Republican government waged war with its own forces and limited Soviet aid. The result was a slow and brutal civil war, which would grind on until March, 1939, with perhaps 700,000 deaths. The carnage ended with the triumph of the fascist forces under Francisco Franco.

The Spanish Civil War helped consolidate the ties between Germany and Italy. In October, 1936, they created the Rome-Berlin Axis, an agreement to coordinate their diplomatic activity. In November, the Germans and Japanese signed the Anti-Comintern Pact, a thinly disguised warning to the Soviet Union (which Italy joined a year later). The growth in diplomatic clout of the authoritarians and their efforts to coordinate policies began sending shock waves through Europe. East European nations became far more solicitous of German interests. In the West, Belgium renounced its military alliance with France (October 1936) and opted for armed neutrality. The Belgian government's reasoning was impeccable: the League offered no protection; changes in warfare, especially the tank, truck, and airplane, meant a small state could be conquered before its allies could react; British and French policy clearly demonstrated a reluctance to risk mortal injury to defend a small state.

In addition to the defections of the weak, 1937 marked the crippling of the Red Army (or so it appeared in the West). Stalin had initiated a wave of purges, first within the Communist party, and then spreading out into the diplomatic, intelligence, and military hierarchies of the Soviet state. The top leadership of the Red Army was murdered. The purges rolled on into the society, as Stalin consolidated his hold on everything he could grasp.[22] How effective, Western leaders had to ask themselves, would the Soviets be in an anti-German coalition? If we allied with a weak Soviet Union, an inviting target for the Germans and Poles, would we not get pulled into war? In addition to these strategic hesitations were the old anticommunist feelings of others, reawakened by the brutality of the purges. Britain and France seemed alone.

If Europe remained somber but quiet in 1937, the same cannot be said for the Far East.[23] The establishment of Manchukuo had not ended the activities of

[21]For the Spanish Civil War, see Hugh Thomas, *The Spanish Civil War*, 3rd ed. (New York: Harper & Row, Pub., 1977); Dante Puzzo, *Spain and the Great Powers* (New York: Columbia University Press, 1962); Vincent Brome, *The International Brigades* (New York: Morrow, 1966).

[22]On the purges, see Robert Conquest, *The Great Terror* (New York: Macmillan, 1968).

[23]Studies of Sino-Japanese relations include Marius Jansen, *Japan and China* (Chicago: Rand McNally, 1975); James Crowley, *Japan's Quest for Autonomy* (Princeton: Princeton University Press, 1966); John Boyle, *China and Japan at War, 1937–1945* (Stanford: Stanford University Press, 1972); Dick Wilson, *When Tigers Fight* (New York: Viking, 1982).

the Kwantung army or Japanese business interests in the area of north China between Peking and the Manchukuo frontier. The Japanese army had sent units in the area to break up concentrations of local Chinese military power and to suppress banditry. They encouraged pro-Japanese Chinese to establish local regimes that would create an effective buffer zone between Nationalist Chinese power and Manchukuo. While some had further imperialist ambitions, many—including the Tokyo government—probably were ambivalent about the correct policy toward China. That China had to be responsive to Japanese interests was agreed. How one secured that responsiveness was unclear.

Chiang Kai-shek's Nationalist government, with its capital in Nanking, tried to accommodate the Japanese in the north China plain. Chiang was more intent on making himself master of China, and in his eyes that first meant the extermination of the Chinese communists.[24] In the 1930s, Chiang's military operations had driven the communists from central China into the northwest (Yenan). He proposed to mount another operation at the same time that the Japanese stated demands which would give Japan clear authority in Chinese politics. In desperation, Chiang's subordinates, including Chang Hseuh-liang, kidnapped him and extracted a pledge for a truce in the civil war and for resistance to the Japanese.

It was but a matter of time for warfare to resume between the two states. In July, 1937, Japanese and Chinese troops clashed at the Marco Polo Bridge, outside of Peking. Local Japanese commanders ordered their troops forward to establish security perimeters; Chinese Nationalist forces fought back. In Tokyo, the government agreed to allow a widening of the war. Perhaps force was all that would bring the Chinese to reason; failing that, Japan could install its own regime, which would accept the Japanese definition of Asian politics. Extensive air attacks and landings on the coast began, with Shanghai falling in November and Nanking in December. In December, 1937, a new Chinese Republic announced its existence in Peking, under the protection of Japan.

The Chinese appeal to the League brought the League's condemnation of Japan. The Americans offered to help find a settlement, and the Pacific powers invited Japan to a conference. Japan refused, insisting on bilateral talks with the Chinese. The Nationalists sought arms from the Soviets and the West, which gradually began to arrive, although hindered by increasing Japanese control of the coast. China's suppliers had to be circumspect in their involvement, for they did not want a confrontation with Japan nor an interruption of trade with Japan. Nonetheless, Japan's adventurism in China threatened Western economic and imperial interests and Soviet strategic interests. The end of an independent though weak China did not meet with their approval. In addition, Chinese publicists and Japanese brutality led to increasing public support for some form of aid to China.

The Japanese war against China would continue through 1945. The Nationalists retreated to the interior, making Chungking the wartime capital. The Japanese found it difficult to control all the territory nominally behind their lines

---

[24]See Franklin Houn, *A Short History of Chinese Communism* (Englewood Cliffs, N.J.: Prentice-Hall, 1967): Robert North, *Moscow and Chinese Communists*, 2nd ed. (Stanford: Stanford University Press, 1963); Edgar Snow, *Red Star over China*, rev. ed. (New York: Grove Press, 1968).

or to develop a logistics system that would allow them to penetrate and hold the interior. And there was the problem of defending Manchukuo from the Soviets. During July and August, 1938, Soviet and Japanese forces fought briefly on the eastern Manchukuo frontier. In 1939, from May to August, the two fought an intense but localized war on Manchukuo's western frontier. Japan's Asian program, fitfully crafted into a view of a new order for all of Asia, seemed destined to collide with other powers. With whom and when remained the questions that perplexed many capitals, not the least Tokyo.

The Journey into Hell Begins Anew   War in Spain and China created the distracting backdrop for the final chapter of peace in Europe. In November, 1937, Hitler met with his military leaders and foreign minister to outline future German policy. For Hitler, the central issue was Germany's need to acquire territory for agricultural resources and raw materials. Only Europe offered such space, yet all space had a master. "Germany's problem," he continued, "could only be solved by means of force and this was never without attendant risk." He did not specify the space he had in mind, but did say that he wanted preparations made for a lightning stroke to seize Austria and Czechoslovakia. His generals protested that Germany was not ready for war, nor could it afford to be at war with both France and Britain. Hitler had to argue repeatedly with his generals "that almost certainly Britain, and probably France as well, had already tacitly written off the Czechs and were reconciled to the fact that this question would be cleared up in due course by Germany."[25]

Hitler's aggressive outlook stemmed from his sense that time was running out. Germany had to solve the territorial problem by 1943 to 1945 at the latest. The rearmament programs of France, Britain, and the Soviet Union (triggered by German rearmament) would reach full stride in the not-too-distant future. Time would allow the three to discover the means to effect his containment. Finally, he was convinced that he alone mattered, and he understood that he was mortal. The problems of *lebensraum* ("living space") had to be solved ". . . in his lifetime. Later generations would no longer be able to do it. Only he himself was still in a position to."[26]

By February, 1938, Hitler set about making a lightning strike into Austria and Czechoslovakia possible. He dismissed his hesitant military commanders and reorganized the military to bring it more under his control. He then tightened the pressure on Austria to facilitate a takeover when the opportunity arose (a subject discussed in some detail in a subsequent section). In March, after the Austrian government attempted to display its independence, Austrian Nazis began riots throughout Austria. Hitler, who had not counted on precipitous developments, wavered, but entrusted the problem to Hermann Goering, a long-time confidant and air force commander. Goering ordered German troops into Austria on March 11. The invasion went uncontested by Austrian forces, and two days later Hitler stood in Vienna. The Reich had suddenly expanded; *Anschluss* had occurred. Mussolini earlier had indicated he would not defend Austria. Brit-

[25]Hossbach memorandum, November 10, 1937; *DGFP,* series D, Vol. I, pp. 29–39.
[26]Speech to Nazi party officials, October, 1937; quoted in Fest, *Hitler,* p. 536.

ain and France were not prepared to go to war against Germany to restore Vienna's independence.

The stunning Austrian success led Hitler to believe that he might destroy the multinational Czech state without outside interference as well. Claiming that German-speaking Czechs in the Sudeten region were being tortured, Hitler demanded a speedy resolution of the problem.[27] Under pressure from Britain and France, the Czech government presented four plans to the Sudeten Nazi leaders to protect minority rights. Each was rejected. German troop movements in September reinforced Hitler's declaration that he would settle the issue shortly. The Czechs checked their allies. The Soviets had no direct access to Czechoslovakia, and it was unlikely that Poland would give transit privileges to the Red Army. Moreover, the Soviets indicated that the Czechs' first recourse had to be the League. Thus the brunt of the defense of Czechoslovakia would have to be borne by France. But French military doctrine stressed the defensive, staying under the protection of the Maginot Line. How could France aid Czechoslovakia then? Perhaps through air bombardment of German cities. But what France could do to German cities, Germany could do to French cities (and worse, given the superiority of the German air force). Was Prague worth the destruction of Paris? And would airpower alone save Czechoslovakia?

The cruel dilemma again: Peace or principles? But the principles were not those of the League, but the principles of power. Could a state remain secure for long if it did not honor an alliance commitment? Hitler assumed that the desire for peace would again overwhelm principles, even these. The French, for a moment, took a deep breath and declared their unhappy duty to honor the commitment. Then other voices, most notably those of the British government, warned of the catastrophes of war, and the French government panicked.

The stage was set for Neville Chamberlain, the British Prime Minister since mid-1937. Chamberlain believed peace to be necessary and obtainable. He would accept changes in Czechoslovakia's frontiers as long as the process of change was peaceful. He was not for peace at any price, but for peace if at all possible. (The slow pace of British rearmament encouraged caution as well.) In September, 1938, with war a seeming inevitability, Chamberlain proposed a meeting with Hitler to settle the Czech problem. (The series of meetings the two leaders held are discussed below.)

At a final conference in Munich in late September, 1938, Hitler and Chamberlain were joined by Mussolini and the French prime minister. They announced that they had agreed on a phased cession of the Sudetenland to Germany, to be completed by October 10. Chamberlain had concluded that this was far less a price for the Czechs to pay than to be attacked by Germany. It certainly seemed a low price to pay for Britain. And Hitler had said several times that this issue was the last of German territorial demands. This appeasement policy, Chamberlain's successor to the failed collective security policy, assumed that each redress of the aggressor's grievances reduced the latter's interest in advancing other grievances. The Czechs, neither consulted nor supported, complied with the requirements of the new policy.

[27]The extensive literature on the Czech crisis includes Keith Robbins, *Munich, 1938* (London: Cassell, 1968); Laurence Thompson, *The Greatest Treason* (New York: Morrow, 1968); John Wheeler-Bennett, *Munich* (New York: Duell, Sloan and Pearce, 1948).

Stalin, watching from the sidelines, saw that the West's appeasement policy could really only be directed eastward, moving German power toward the Soviet Union. Britain and France appeared to accept the remainder of the Czech state's becoming a satellite of Germany. They seemed unconcerned that the rest of central Europe might go the same route. Cautiously, in the spring of 1939, Stalin began to look for some way to explore with Hitler the possibility of an understanding between the two states.

Stalin's mounting distrust of the West came at an awkward time. In mid-March, 1939, German troops occupied western Czechoslovakia ("invited" by the government) and entered the eastern areas at the behest of Slovak nationalists who proclaimed their independence from Prague. The uproar in Parliament forced Chamberlain to suspend the appeasement policy and revert to more traditional power politics—the unilateral guarantee to small states. On March 31, the British and French governments announced that they would guarantee the territorial integrity of Poland; on April 13, that of Romania. On April 7, Mussolini seized Albania, to which Britain responded with guarantees for Greece and Turkey. The guarantees shifted the security calculus for the Soviets. The West, in effect, had agreed to protect the western approaches to the Soviet Union. An alliance with the West became less attractive (or put another way, Stalin could ask a higher price for his pledge to come to France's or Britain's aid). And cutting the other way, Poles and Romanians rejected the idea of bringing the Soviets into an alliance because they assumed that to have Red Army troops on their soil meant the Bolshevization of their societies. Having made the guarantee, Britain and France had little leverage to get the Poles or Romanians to agree to Soviet participation. The idea of some understanding with Hitler grew more attractive to Stalin with each passing month.

The Attack on Poland   Hitler had been edging in that direction as well. With the Czech matter settled, he turned to the Polish dilemma. On coming to power, Hitler initially saw Poland as a partner in a crusade against communism. Versailles, however, had created perpetual irritants. It gave to Poland German land to create access to the sea; this "Corridor" isolated German East Prussia from Germany proper. In addition, the German city of Danzig became an international city to provide the Poles with a major seaport. Hitler determined to regain those areas, but apparently was undecided about the future of the Polish state.

The Poles rejected the German demands for the incorporation of Danzig into the Reich and a German-controlled transportation corridor through the Corridor. Polish intransigence and the British guarantee helped push Hitler into a new line: the Polish state was to be destroyed and the Soviets accommodated. The latter was necessary because the British and French made a belated effort to negotiate a defense agreement with the Soviets. Hitler could not run the risk of a two-front war if the West actually honored its Polish guarantee.

By August, Soviet diplomats carried on negotiations with both the West and Hitler. The Germans made the better offer, asking for Soviet neutrality, pledging not to attack the Soviet Union, and agreeing that when the destruction of Poland occurred, the Soviets would receive Polish territory. The Germans also recognized a Soviet sphere of influence along the Soviet frontier from Finland to Turkey. Moreover, an understanding with Germany would ease the crisis in the

Far East, where Japanese and Soviet forces had been engaged since May. The Soviets would have a secure flank if the Japanese chose to escalate the fighting, and German pressure on its Japanese ally might end the fighting all together. The Soviet Union and Germany signed their Non-Aggression Pact on August 23, 1939. (The territorial provisions were in a secret annex.)

Hitler scheduled the attack on Poland for August 26. He was reasonably confident the West would not act. At worst, they would sever relations and embargo trade with Germany. As he applied pressure to the Poles during the summer, he found Chamberlain's government restating its guarantee for Poland but also declaring that the issues were negotiable. Various British officials even speculated on a favorable settlement of German colonial demands and on large loans to Germany! Appeasement had not died! Hitler in return spun out promises of a German guarantee for the British empire and of keeping Japan from damaging British interests in Asia. What was a British guarantee to Poland worth if connected with offers to negotiate? Hitler did delay the offensive into Poland in response to last-minute British proposals, but on September 1, the German army stormed into Poland.

Initially, Hitler seemed correct in his judgment that Britain and France still valued peace too highly to fight. Chamberlain accepted Mussolini's call for an international conference to negotiate an end to the Polish war. He finally sent an ultimatum to Hitler calling for an end to the German attack only when his ministerial colleagues threatened to turn against him. When Hitler received it on September 3, he was stunned, but the die had been cast. Britain went to war on the 3rd, as did France. 1919 to 1939 had been only a twenty-year truce.

In two weeks, the German army and air force had crippled Polish resistance.[28] On September 17, Soviet forces invaded eastern Poland. Flushed with success against a weak opponent, Hitler called for a political settlement with Britain and France. War in the West was not in his thinking. Neither the German military nor the economy was prepared for a protracted war. The real issue was eastern expansion. Moreover, the longer the war in the West, the more tempting it would be for Stalin to ignore the nonaggression treaty. The Western Allies did not reject negotiations, but they refused to treat with the Hitler regime. Finding he could not achieve a political solution, Hitler set November 12 as the date for a lightning strike into the West. It was an updated von Schlieffen Plan. His generals strenuously objected, but in the end it was bad weather that forced repeated postponements. The reckoning with France would have to wait for the spring.

The Allies—France, Britain, and the Commonwealth—looked to the long haul. French forces manned the Maginot Line, Britain delivered its several divisions, and everyone waited. Instead of *Blitzkrieg* (lightning war), it was "sitzkrieg," a "phony war." British bombers raided German targets—dropping propaganda leaflets. The password was to build up. Italy clung to neutrality; Mussolini had tried to dissuade Hitler from attacking Poland, pleading that Italy could not be ready for war until 1942.

Only the Soviet Union remained active after the fall of Poland.[29] It forced

---

[28]For the opening days of the war, see Hanson Baldwin, *The Crucial Years, 1939–1941* (New York: Harper & Row, Pub., 1976).

[29]See Max Jakobson *The Diplomacy of the Winter War* (Cambridge: Harvard University Press, 1961); Allen Chew, *The White Death* (East Lansing, Mich.: Michigan State University Press, 1971).

Estonia, Latvia, and Lithuania to permit Soviet air and naval bases on their territory. Stalin was going to use the time and the provisions of the Non-Aggression Pact with Germany to create a forward shield against German power. The Finns also received a set of demands calling for boundary changes to move the border away from Leningrad in exchange for Soviet territory. The Finns refused. Soviet forces attacked on November 30, 1939. The Finns appealed to the League, which expelled the Soviet Union! For several months, the Finns beat back the Soviet attack.

Europe and Asia were hurtling toward a fateful rendezvous with destiny.

PART II:
SCIENTIFIC APPROACHES TO WORLD POLITICS

Interaction Approach:
The Bargaining Model and Hitler's Foreign Policy

Like all the scientific approaches, the bargaining model provides a systematic method to describe and explain the behavior of states. It assumes that much of world politics is a process by which two or more states search for a mutually acceptable solution to a conflict. That is *not* to say that bargaining encompasses all of world politics. It does not; but bargaining can be thought of as part of a continuum occupied by two other forms of world politics, *coercion* and *problem solving*. Table 5–1 illustrates the argument.

While each type of interaction has distinctive characteristics, there is no sharp break between them. For instance, even when coercion occurs, we are still likely to find bargaining. This bargaining usually concerns the conditions for the

TABLE 5-1   Three Principal Components of an Interaction Model

COERCION	BARGAINING	PROBLEM SOLVING
◄──────────────────── *INTERACTION CONTINUUM* ──────────────────►		
Unilateral behavior to secure state goal (e.g., Italian attack on Ethiopia)	Multilateral search for accommodation of conflicting state goals (League disarmament conference)	Multilateral search for efficient solution to a common goal (Anglo-French staff talks on deployment of British forces in Europe)
Force others to bear costs	Mutual acceptance of some cost	Perception of minimal costs compared to large, mutually shared benefits

◄────────── Increase in perception of the issue in conflictual terms

Increase in perception of the issue in coordination terms ──────────►

◄────────── Increase in number and intensity of threats

Decrease to absence of threats ──────────►

use of force. For instance, once Germany attacked Poland, both Germany and Britain sought to keep the war limited, especially in preventing air raids on urban areas. Similarly, Hitler warned that if the Allies used poison gas (as Italy had in Ethiopia), Germany would respond in kind. As we observed in the First World War, the fighting itself may terminate through bargaining. Finally, as we shall shortly see, the *threat* of war can be a potent weapon in bargaining.

At the other end of the continuum lies problem solving.[30] Problem-solving interactions probably constitute a large part of international relations, especially among friends. They emerge when states perceive a *common* threat, necessity, or opportunity, and interact to coordinate their response. Arranging state visits of leaders, international monitoring of maritime pollution, and coordinating disaster relief activities are examples. Bargaining may still occur, but often deals with peripheral issues such as whether the leaders will discuss certain topics, or whether multinational corporations are to participate in maritime monitoring, or whether relief activities should be coordinated by the United Nations. These sub-issues are peripheral when the states remain committed to the discovery and implementation of the most efficient solution to the broader issue. When the sub-issue moves to center stage, it is a sign that one or more states feel that the efficient solution may be detrimental to their interests.

Our interest in this section is bargaining rather than coercion and problem solving. This form of interaction occurs because the states in conflict do not believe that they can, by their own actions, meet their individual goals at a price that each is willing to pay. Furthermore, each recognizes that an agreement will involve some cost (although each would like to minimize that cost). Indeed, even the act of negotiating may involve a cost: Chamberlain told Hitler that " . . . he was being accused in certain circles in Great Britain of having sold and betrayed Czechoslovakia, of having yielded to the dictators and so on, and on leaving England that morning he had actually been booed."[31]

With the bargaining approach as a guide, we will look at Hitler's negotiations in 1938 concerning Austria and Czechoslovakia. To do that, we first need to examine some of the assumptions inherent in the approach.

1. *Rationality and goals.* The model assumes that the state has established goals and acts in the bargaining process in ways designed to accomplish those goals. Bargainers may make poor choices of goals, miscalculate their tactics, or prove inept in the implementation of the tactics. The model accepts such "failings" as natural; it only insists that state behavior is purposive, not necessarily successful.

2. *The goal of a negotiated settlement.* The goal of bargaining is a negotiated settlement. However, a state may participate in the bargaining process to camouflage its choice of force as the real means to achieve its goal. Bargaining is used to "soften up" or weaken the opponents, or to convince others that force is justi-

[30]For the concept of problem solving, see William Coplin, *Introduction to International Politics,* 2nd ed. (Chicago: Rand McNally, 1974), pp. 258–83. For a general treatment of the bargaining-coercion connection, see Thomas Schelling, *The Strategy of Conflict* (New York: Oxford University Press, 1963). For an application of the bargaining model to the period, see William Newman, *The Balance of Power in the Interwar Years* (New York: Random House, 1968).

[31]Godesberg conference, September 22, 1938; *DGFP*, series D, Vol. II, p. 875.

fied. This is bargaining in *bad faith*; the goal is to distract. One of the great problems of historical interpretation is whether Hitler negotiated in bad faith. Unfortunately for students of bargaining, the evidence is often ambiguous. One common tactic in bargaining is to stall, to delay in responding, or to reiterate the same position time and again. Does this mean that the state is not interested in a negotiated solution? Or does it mean that the state seeks to persuade its opponent that the latter must make the concession if there is to be a settlement? The former is bargaining in bad faith; the latter, seeking bargaining leverage.

3. *Bargaining leverage.* The bargaining process entails the mutual communication of demands. The costs involved in agreeing to the other's demands are usually more than a state can readily agree to. What, then, produces a settlement? Both states make a mutual attempt to manipulate the perceptions of the other. *Leverage* occurs when a state comes to believe that it cannot hope to get anything better, that it may get something worse if it rejects the other's proposal, and that no agreement is more costly than the other's proposal.[32]

From the perspective of this approach, much of world politics is the continuous search for bargaining leverage. Each state tries to demonstrate its commitment to its position and to encourage flexibility on the part of the other. The tactics are legion, the very stuff of world politics. The Kaiser disembarks at Tangier to demonstrate German interest; the Tsar mobilizes forces to dissuade Austria from attacking Serbia; Chamberlain declares a guarantee for Poland. And, as both sides usually act simultaneously, bargaining is continuous interaction to manipulate perceptions.

4. *Audiences.* Negotiators may meet alone in locked rooms, but they always negotiate in front of some audience. Political leaders from democracies must worry about the audience of voters: Chamberlain kept pointing out to Hitler how he was placing his political career on the line by attempting to negotiate an end to the Czech crisis. (Notice how that very statement is an attempt to create leverage.) Hitler, too, argued that he had to be responsive to the German public (and may have honestly held the belief). In addition to the public, all leaders negotiate before particular groups, most notably the political, military, economic, and bureaucratic elites. Hitler, for instance, was not sure of his generals' loyalty (with good cause; several planned a coup). What he did in the negotiating realm had to "play well" with them. Finally, the leaders and citizens of other states constitute another important audience, usually labelled "world opinion." That audience of allies, neutrals, and opponents draws conclusions about how one negotiates and for what. The reaction of that audience may be crucial, as Chamberlain discovered when he found Stalin agreeing to a nonaggression pact with Hitler after watching British bargaining behavior.

The two cases that follow illustrate these arguments in more detail. They concentrate on the attempt to create bargaining leverage in face-to-face negotiations. In this stage of the process, bargaining involves the words and demeanor of the negotiators, and that will be our focus.

---

[32]Adapted from Glenn Snyder and Paul Diesing, *Conflict among Nations* (Princeton: Princeton University Press, 1977), p. 23.

Case I: Austria, February–March, 1938   After the failure of the 1934 Nazi coup in Austria, Hitler accepted what he termed the ''evolutionary'' approach to *Anschluss*. Germany would maintain pressure on the Schuschnigg government to allow political activity by the Austrian Nazis and the gradual entry of Nazis into the Austrian government. Sooner or later, Austria would request incorporation into the Reich. Schuschnigg had tried to hinder Nazi activities, and while he felt it expedient to take Nazis or sympathizers into the government, he gave them no positions of authority. In early 1938, Nazi terrorism increased, and Schuschnigg responded with increased police repression.

Faced with the events in Austria, Hitler invited Schuschnigg to meet him at the Fuhrer's mountain retreat at Berchtesgaden on February 12, 1938. Hitler's goal was to get the Austrian Chancellor to reaffirm his willingness to permit the ''evolutionary'' approach to continue.[33] Given Austria's military and financial weakness, Hitler apparently concluded that face-to-face negotiations would reinforce the bargaining leverage that Germany already possessed.

We can identify four tactics Hitler used to create the leverage that gave Schuschnigg little choice:[34]

1. *The claim of being in step with history*. The talks began at 11:00 A.M. For two hours, Hitler repeatedly stressed that his was an ''historic mission'' and that he was absolutely determined to end Austria's ambivalent relationship to the Reich. A bargainer who cites external forces, such as history, nature, or God, tries to persuade the other that the demands are driven by unstoppable forces. The choice is between making concessions and being crushed. Moreover, leaders marching with history have no need to make concessions themselves.

2. *Unalterable demands*. After a break for lunch, Schuschnigg received a list of formal demands. Hitler declared,

> There is nothing to be discussed about it. I will not change one single iota. You will sign it as it stands or else our meeting has been useless. In that case I shall decide during the night what will be done next.[35]

This was demonstrating a commitment to his position, an ultimatum (with a very short deadline!), and a threat all rolled into one. Schuschnigg had to decide whether to reject the demands in the belief that Hitler had *not* uttered his final word or that the costs of not signing (invasion?) were smaller than those of signing (the probable but slow demise of independent Austria).

3. *The ''reasonableness'' of the demands*. In the morning, Hitler had denounced Austria's ''unfriendly policies,'' trumpeted Germany's great power status, and gave every impression that he was determined to achieve *Anschluss*. During the morning, Schuschnigg repeatedly asked what specific demands Hitler had. Hitler avoided the question—what better way to get the Austrian to expect the worst? Lunch followed, where the talk was of Hitler's interest in cars, build-

---

[33]A definitive statement about Hitler's goals is impossible to make, even with the capture of tons of German documents; this is my interpretation based on *DGFP*. For another, see Norman Rich, *Hitler's War Aims* (New York: W.W. Norton & Co., Inc., 1973), 2 vols.

[34]Drawn from Schuschnigg's memoirs, *Austrian Requiem*, trans. Franz Von Hildebrand (New York: Putnam's, 1946), pp. 3–27. A briefer version appears in a statement made for the Nuremberg war crimes trials; *Nazi Conspiracy*, Vol. V, pp. 709–12.

[35]Schuschnigg, *Austrian Requiem*, p. 24.

ings, and the like. Hitler then left Schuschnigg alone for two hours to worry. Thus, when the demands were presented, they seemed moderate in that they called "only" for the release of jailed Nazis, the right of the Nazis to participate in the Chancellor's political movement, and the appointment of Seyss-Inquart, a Nazi, as Minister of the Interior (which controlled the police). In fact, the demands had the look of a concession.

4. *The threat of violence and a wish to avoid it.* The element of threat was ever present. "Who knows?" Hitler mused. "Perhaps you will wake up one morning in Vienna to find us there—just like a spring storm."[36] Then, he warned, the Austrian National Socialists would exact a terrible revenge for the oppression they had suffered. When Schuschnigg referred to foreign supporters (the only real counterthreat he had to create leverage), Hitler mocked the idea. Austria would stand alone if war came, he asserted. Italy now stood with Germany, England was not interested, and France had lost its opportunity in 1936 when he reoccupied the Rhineland. Having paraded the reasons why he "knew" Austria to be defenseless, Hitler assured the Austrian that he preferred to deal with the issue without force. He had done so in Germany and the people had responded with love and trust.

Hitler stage-managed the talks to emphasize the potential for violence. When he greeted Schuschnigg on the steps to his resort, he was flanked by General Keitel, the Chief of High Command of the German armed forces, the local military commander, and a prominent air force general. During the day, the generals talked of their war experiences; the air force general, for instance, had commanded the German air units in the Spanish Civil War, air units that had a reputation for the terror bombing of cities. And Hitler was not above play acting. When Schuschnigg balked at one of the demands, Hitler abruptly dismissed him and loudly called for General Keitel.

Schuschnigg accepted Hitler's demands—and declined Hitler's offer to stay for dinner. The Austrian government implemented the agreement. But Schuschnigg was not done negotiating. On March 9, he called for a nationwide referendum to determine whether Austrians wanted "a free and independent, German and Christian Austria." Hitler was enraged by what he considered to be Schuschnigg's violation of their agreement. Aided by rioting Austrian Nazis, he set in motion the process that would lead to the military invasion on the 12th. Goering, in charge of the operation, forced the Austrians to appoint Seyss-Inquart as Chancellor and then had Seyss-Inquart request German troops to prevent a civil war in Austria. The occupation had the requisite gloss of legality.

Case II: Czechoslovakia, September, 1938   In April and May, 1938, Hitler ordered and signed plans for a lightning attack on Czechoslovakia, designed to produce success in four days to "convince foreign powers of the hopelessness of military intervention." However, "the idea of strategic attack out of the blue without cause or possibility of justification is rejected. Reason: hostile world opinion which might lead to serious situation."[37] Hitler was content to allow things to "evolve" to provide the opportunity and pretext. The Czechs, wanting

---

[36]*Ibid.*, p. 16.

[37]Memorandum of April 22, 1938; *DGFP,* series D, Vol. II, p. 240.

to demonstrate their determination not to be another Austria, partially mobilized their army with British and French support. An enraged Hitler decided to destroy the Czech state and set October 1, 1938, as the deadline. The "mistreatment" of the Sudeten Germans became the thrust of the propaganda and diplomatic offensive.

On September 13, Chamberlain decided to inject himself and Britain directly into the mounting crisis by offering to fly to Germany "with a view to trying to find a peaceful solution." Hitler could not ignore the dramatic offer. Chamberlain's position, however, was relatively weak. The French had succumbed to British councils of doom and wanted to avoid war, and on September 7, the politically well-connected *Times* of London had called for cession of the Sudetenland to Germany. Hitler could assume with some confidence that this is what Chamberlain would offer (or accept). Knowing what the opponent would offer and that the opponent's main ally demanded a peaceful solution encouraged Hitler not to offer much initially and to escalate his demands to see if he could get more. What he needed from the negotiations was both a free hand with the Czechs and a means to keep Britain neutral. This was bargaining in bad faith regarding the Czech issue, but very real bargaining regarding Britain's role.

Chamberlain met with Hitler three times: at Berchtesgaden (September 15), Godesberg (September 22–25), and Munich (September 29–30). Here the German leader had to negotiate with a firm individual, representing a major power. Would he seek leverage as he had against Schuschnigg? He would. In addition, we see other tactics emerging. In the discussion that follows, I shall keep the analysis in a roughly chronological order. Thus, at the first summit meeting at Hitler's mountain retreat, we can observe:

1. *The control of the agenda.* The negotiator who establishes the agenda or context for the bargaining often creates leverage. Chamberlain wanted to first deal with Anglo-German relations. Hitler refused. He won the point of making Czechoslovakia the prime topic by declaring that the situation was very grave and a crisis was at hand. The implication—it was either war or Hitler's agenda.

2. *Claims of being bound by public expectations.* Hitler insisted that "he could neither remain silent nor inactive in a situation in which the whole German nation expected energetic action and plain speaking from him."[38] This attempt to demonstrate commitment asserts that if the bargainer does compromise, he or she will face political punishment from key audiences. Chamberlain may not have been swayed. The image of "dictator" undermines the argument—a point not lost on Hitler, who declared he was not a dictator.

3. *Demands both "reasonable" and unalterable, yet colored by violence.* Hitler stated his demands in general terms in order to avoid tying his hands (how could he then ask for more if Chamberlain seemed pliant?) and to assess what might trigger British intervention. The three million Germans in Czechoslovakia, he said, "must be enabled in all circumstances to return" to the Reich, and Czechoslovakia could not be a "spearpoint" thrust into Germany (alluding to its military alliances with France and the Soviet Union). This problem had to be solved in short order. "He would face any war, and even the risk of a world war, for

---

[38]Memorandum of September 15, 1938; *ibid.*, p. 788.

this. Here the limit had been reached where the rest of the world might do what it liked, he would not yield one single step.''[39]

We might call this the blackmail style of negotiating. The rational opponent presumably would accept the ''modest'' demands rather than endure the pain of another world war. Of course, such a war would be painful for Germany as well. Why did Hitler's threat seem *credible?* Germany's rearmament gave it the capability to fight. Hitler's past foreign policy had risked war repeatedly. He seemed willing to do so again. Chamberlain subsequently told his Cabinet that ''it was impossible not to be impressed with the power of the man. He was extremely determined and would not brook opposition beyond a certain point.''[40]

Chamberlain proposed the cession of the Sudetenland and the neutralization of Czechoslovakia. Hitler accepted and then boldly demanded that Chamberlain give immediate approval to the cession and neutralization! Chamberlain said he could only give his personal approval but would seek his Cabinet's, French, and Czech concurrence. Hitler had been quite successful. He had gotten Chamberlain's approval for two conditions he felt the Czechs simply could *not* accept: the loss of the heavily fortified Sudeten territory and neutralization. When the Czechs refused to accept the demands, Germany would have its pretext for war and Britain would probably sit on its hands. France would not act without Britain; the Soviets would wait on France. It was unlikely that any state would go to war against Germany to liberate Czechoslovakia.

Hitler's plan foundered. The Czechs yielded to British and French threats to abandon them if they did not accept the agreement. For Hitler to abide by the agreement meant receiving only a part of Czechoslovakia and facing a probable British pledge to defend the remainder. To renounce the agreement would stigmatize him as a ''bad faith'' negotiator and probably commit Britain to the defense of all the Czech state. Hitler prepared another tactic for Chamberlain's return visit at Godesberg:

4. *Re-open an ''agreement in principle'' with demands regarding implementation.* Hitler told Chamberlain that the Czechs had to meet the claims of the Hungarians and Poles living in Czechoslovakia as well as the demands of dissident Slovaks in Czechoslovakia. And that German forces were to occupy the territory by the end of the week. And that no Czech state property could be removed or destroyed. In fact, a week's time meant that much private property would have to be abandoned. Convinced that he had found the point where the Czechs would have to say ''no,'' Hitler offered the concessions to keep Britain neutral: if the Czechs agreed, Germany would not object to a British guarantee for the ''rump'' Czech state; in fact, said Hitler, Germany had ''no interest'' in the rest of the state.

Chamberlain with bitterness reproached Hitler and stressed the political cost he had incurred in agreeing to cession. He announced that the time limit was unacceptable. They had come to an impasse.

5. *Audience reaction may provide leverage.* In the midst of the second Godesberg meeting, word came that the Czechs had mobilized. ''Now, of course,'' Hitler

---

[39]*Ibid.*, p. 790.

[40]Quoted from *The Chamberlain Cabinet* by Ian Colvin (New York: Taplinger, 1971; and London: Victor Gollancz Ltd., 1971), p. 152. © 1971 by Ian Colvin. Reprinted by permission.

said, "the whole affair was settled." He reiterated that his demands were "indeed his last word and that, moreover, he must repeat that the Czech mobilization compelled him to take certain military measures."[41] Chamberlain, faced with the possibility of war in the morning, was relieved to get Hitler to "concede" that there would be no invasion of Czechoslovakia as long as negotiations continued. So rewarded, Chamberlain left in good spirits to convey the new demands to the French and the Czechs.

The third set of meetings at Munich, now joined by Mussolini and French Premier Daladier, ratified the details hammered out at Berchtesgaden and Godesberg. Hitler now had to accept the compromise he had sought to avoid; only the Sudetenland would enter the Reich. He did so because Mussolini feared war and because Chamberlain seemed willing to consider it. Prior to Munich, British emissaries warned Hitler that if Germany attacked Czechoslovakia and if France fulfilled its treaty obligations, Britain would support France. Not the most forceful of threats, but at least an indication that the risk of war with Britain increased measurably if Hitler chose not to accept the settlement Chamberlain offered. Hitler also agreed that German occupation of the area would take until October 10, but he insisted that occupation begin on the 1st (his deadline!). However, the Western guarantee to Czechoslovakia was so conditional (e.g., the Czechs had to satisfy the Polish and Hungarian claims) that it had no meaning. Hitler's options were not closed at Munich.

Conclusions About Bargaining   What general conclusions might we draw from these two episodes? One set might consider the practical: how should one negotiate with a Hitler? Those kinds of "lessons" are examined in the next section. The other set has to do with bargaining leverage. Two general comments emerge:

The threat of force can be a powerful tool in bargaining. If the threat is credible (backed by capability and will), other states face a cruel dilemma. They can accept the demands, egregious as those demands may be, in order to avoid the horrendous cost of war. (Remember that World War I set the standard for measuring cost for these diplomats). Schuschnigg and Chamberlain believed Hitler would carry out his threats. The Austrian case seemed to confirm the threat.

In such circumstances, the more irrational Hitler appeared, the more credible his threat to unleash a world war.[42] But Chamberlain found it difficult to believe that Hitler was irrational, that he would knowingly start another war. To explain the seeming irrationality, Chamberlain decided that Hitler was intensely emotional regarding *race*. That led him to the comforting belief that Hitler's goals were limited, designed to "return" German folk to the Reich. Hence, appeasement was realistic, even in the face of an apparent willingness to trigger a second world war. Other British leaders concluded that Hitler *was* mad or on the verge of insanity. From that assumption came an equally crippling conclusion—too much of a "hard line" in response might drive him over the edge into a war no one

---

[41]*DGFP*, pp. 901, 902.

[42]See Schelling, *Strategy*, pp. 16–18.

wanted.[43] How could Chamberlain respond to such irrational behavior, respond in such a way as to preserve the peace (avoid war) but still not succumb to blackmail?

We know that Chamberlain's response was appeasement. Appeasement may be an effective bargaining tactic: giving up something today (Czech territory) in return for long-term control over behavior ("no more territorial demands"). Appeasement, however, cannot help but tempt the other negotiator. If the appeasers backed away on this, would they not also back away on another issue? In fact, appeasement may activate goals long thought of as "impossible dreams." Appeasement as a bargaining device *may* work when the bargainer has clearly established that certain things are not negotiable. It was commonly assumed, for instance, that Britain would not negotiate a major change in the status of Belgium or the Netherlands. Appeasement as a bargaining process may also work when it takes up the negotiable items one by one but does not hand them over quickly or with carte blanche. It makes the "aggressor" work for each one by dickering over the *conditions* under which change is to take place.

In this light, Poland was a *departure for both Hitler and the appeasers*. In 1938, Hitler had been forced to accept appeasement. In 1939, he rebelled at the slowness of the process and fixed on an attack on Poland. "I'm only afraid," he told his generals, "that at the last minute some son of a bitch will make a proposal for mediation."[44] The British response to the Polish crisis was more ambiguous. The guarantee attempted to take Poland out of the class of negotiable items and make it as nonnegotiable as the status of Belgium. Yet continued British willingness to discuss Danzig and the Corridor undermined those efforts. Britain had the worst of all possible worlds: the failure to deter an attack on Poland and the need to go to war to uphold the credibility of the claim that some things were not negotiable, *even if the defense of Poland itself was a mistake.*

Suppose Britain had been resolute earlier. Would Hitler have been exposed as a bluffer? As we shall see, Hitler's wartime behavior, as well as that of some Japanese leaders, suggested that when push comes to shove, some leaders will compel the nation to commit suicide. Just how does one deal with a Hitler?

POLICY-MAKER APPROACH:
THE LESSONS ADOLF HITLER TAUGHT

Decision makers, like all of us, view the world through a series of images.[45] Those images help provide an interpretation of what is occurring and why: what are foreign leaders after? Can they be trusted? Does power dictate behavior? Does ideology? We students also ask those questions, but we are more likely to do it con-

[43]The discussions of the British Cabinet are illuminating in this regard; see Colvin, *Chamberlain Cabinet*, pp. 150–73.

[44]Speech to military commanders, August 22, 1939; *Nazi Conspiracy*, Vol. III, p. 585.

[45]For general studies of images and perception, see Robert Jervis, *The Logic of Images in International Relations* (Princeton: Princeton University Press, 1970); R. Jervis, *Perception and Misperception in International Politics* (Princeton: Princeton University Press, 1976); Ernest May, *The "Lessons" of the Past* (New York: Oxford University Press, 1973).

sciously and to understand that the answers may vary depending upon the approach we employ. Such approaches are learned from books (I hope you have been paying attention!) and from experience. We call such learning the socialization process.[46] It is also likely that an individual's personality helps shape images; devious individuals may, for instance, assume that everyone is untrustworthy.

While each individual has some unique socialization experiences, individuals within a political culture may have a relatively uniform socialization process. Moreover, by the 1930s, newspapers, radio, and motion pictures combined to produce in the political elites of many nations a common set of images regarding a particular aspect of world politics: dealing with an Adolf Hitler. The Second World War, as it affected the lives of millions on the various battlefields and millions behind the lines, helped to reinforce the images and spread them to many of the common citizens. The defeat of Germany, the capture of German archives, and the Nuremburg war-crime trials created a permanency to the images that is unique in this century.

Coupled to the lessons Hitler taught was the sorry record of the Western democracies. Chamberlain, his rolled umbrella, and Munich became symbols of the disastrous appeasement policy. Many felt an individual and collective guilt for not standing up to Hitler. The guilt and symbols provided a fertile soil in which the images would flourish. The general hypothesis, therefore, is that the lessons of the 1930s were powerful causal agents acting on individual decision makers. In this section I will sketch the lessons; the following three chapters will explore the consequences.

The lessons are reported in Table 5–2 and are divided into two parts: the goals and methods attributed to a Hitler-like leader and the desirable response. Unlike ideology, these images tended to be rules of thumb, reflecting what seemed to be hard-won common wisdom. At heart, these *orientations* asserted that aggression *à la Hitler* is an orchestrated, long-standing plan, implemented in a series of steps. In this view, it was inconceivable that a Hitler would make decisions and fashion goals on the spur of the moment, reacting to other states in a game of guesswork and improvisation.

The lessons Hitler taught about how to respond might be summarized as "alliances, confrontations, no negotiations; and to have peace, prepare for war." Those lessons may be erroneous—this chapter suggested that other interpretations of Hitler's behavior are possible. But if women and men believed the lessons to be true, they would act as if they were true. Some very powerful leaders did put great stock in such images. President Harry Truman, for instance, flying to Washington in June, 1950, to deal with a North Korean invasion of South Korea, reflected:

> In my generation, this was not the first occasion when the strong had attacked the weak. I recalled some earlier instances: Manchuria, Ethiopia, Austria. I remembered how each time that the democracies failed to act it had encouraged the aggressors to keep going ahead. Communism was acting in Korea just as Hitler, Mussolini, and the Japanese had acted ten, fifteen, and twenty years earlier. I felt certain

[46]On socialization, see Stanley Renshon, *Handbook of Political Socialization* (New York: Free Press, 1977); Jack Dennis and M. Kent Jennings, *Comparative Political Socialization* (Beverly Hills, Cal.: Sage, 1970).

TABLE 5-2　The Lessons Hitler Taught about World Politics

GOALS AND METHODS OF A HITLER-LIKE LEADER	THE DESIRABLE RESPONSE
1. Aggressor leaders have infinite rather than finite ends (usually described as "world conquest"). No concession ever satisfies them.	1. No appeasement. Refrain from negotiations.
2. Although aggressor leaders are fixed in their goals, they are flexible in tactics. They wait in readiness to fall on a victim who finds itself defenseless.	2. Deny the opportunity for easy success by leaving no one defenseless. Small states in particular need allies who are clearly and completely linked to the defense of the small state.
3. Aggressor leaders bargain in bad faith. They pocket concessions and give worthless paper pledges in return.	3. Make no concessions unless aggressor leaders make substantial, practical concessions first. Demand such concessions as the price for engaging in negotiations.
4. Aggressor leaders will dupe the allies of the victim into the dirty work of forcing the victim to surrender. The Czechs were prepared to fight. Their allies insisted on capitulation.	4. Under no circumstances pressure an ally to make concessions to an aggressor leader.
5. Political parties having ties to aggressor leaders are inevitably the creatures of the aggressor. They are indirect but effective tools of aggression.	5. Reject the idea that such parties can reflect the real aspirations of the people. Work to uproot them.
6. As aggressor leaders amass more power, they become more difficult to defeat. At some point, war may ensue and it takes more blood and treasure to defeat the aggressor than if the aggressor had been challenged earlier when it had less power.	6. Rise to every occasion to block the increase of aggressor leader's power. Be prepared to use force.
7. War ultimately comes because the aggressor leader miscalculates. Hitler attacked Poland because he did not know that Britain and France would respond. War therefore *is* avoidable.	7. To prevent war, one must make the threat of war a part of one's foreign policy. That threat must be credible.

that if South Korea was allowed to fall Communist leaders would be emboldened to override nations closer to our own shores. If the Communists were permitted to force their way into the Republic of Korea without opposition from the free world, no small nation would have the courage to resist threats and aggression by stronger Communist neighbors. If this was allowed to go unchallenged it would mean a third world war, just as similar incidents had brought on the second world war.[47]

[47]*Memoirs of Harry S. Truman: Volume Two: Years of Trial and Hope,* pp. 332–33. Doubleday & Company, Inc., copyright © 1956 by Time Inc.

Fifteen years later, President Lyndon Johnson pondered the agony of Vietnam:

> Dean Rusk expressed one worry that was much on my mind. It lay at the heart of our Vietnam policy. "If the Communist world finds out that we will not pursue our commitments to the end," he said, "I don't know where they will stay their hand."
>
> I felt sure they would *not* stay their hand. If we ran out on Southeast Asia, I could see trouble ahead in every part of the globe—not just in Asia but in the Middle East and in Europe, in Africa and Latin America. I was convinced that our retreat from this challenge would open the path to World War III.[48]

The image of a Hitler-type leader did have a major ambiguity, however. How, in the hurly-burly of world politics, could one recognize aggressor leaders early enough? Not all could be expected to have Hitler's distinctive mustache (although it would seem that there was some connection between mustaches and aggressor leaders!). How the major powers identified the aggressor and brought the lessons into play is the subject of the next chapter.

SYSTEMS APPROACH:
COLLECTIVE SECURITY, APPEASEMENT, AND WAR

World politics underwent momentous changes during the 1930s. How much did the nature of the international system contribute to those changes? In what ways? Table 5–4 reports the power scores for the major powers for the years 1930, 1935, and 1939. Table 5–3 summarizes the power scores over time in the European cockpit of world politics.

Over the two decades, there has been a significant surge of Soviet power. German power grew in the 1930s, while that of Britain and France remained stable. Projectable American power declined, undercut by the Depression. If these trends were to continue, we would predict that much of world politics would revolve around a German-Soviet struggle for control of Europe. How it might turn out is not clear, but it is significant that German growth in part rests on the expansion of its territory, while Soviet power growth was internally generated.

TABLE 5-3   Power Distribution in Europe, 1920–1939

YEAR	GERMANY	UK	USSR	US	FRANCE	ITALY	POLAND	CZECH	BELGIUM
1920	8	11	1	8*	3	1	2	1	1
1930	9	8	6	6*	5	1	2	2	2
1935	10	8	9	5*	4	2	2	1	2
1939	13	8	11	5*	4	2	1	—	2

*Projectable Power

[48]Lyndon Johnson, *The Vantage Point* (New York: Holt, Rinehart and Winston, 1971), pp. 147–48.

TABLE 5–4 Basic Power Levels in 1930

MEASURE	WORLD	US	UK	GERMANY	FRANCE	USSR	POLAND	CZECHO-SLOVAKIA	BELGIUM	ITALY	JAPAN	CHINA
1. Million metric tons of crude steel	93.6	40.7	7.3	11.4	9.3	5.8	1.2	1.8	3.3	1.7	2.3	—
2. Percent of world steel		43%	8%	12%	10%	6%	1%	2%	4%	2%	2%	0%
3. Million inhabitants in independent states	1370.5	124	43	65	42	161	32	15	8	41	65	453
4. Percent of world population in independent states		9%	3%	5%	3%	12%	2%	1%	1%	3%	5%	33%
5. Political stability in past decade		1.0	.6	.4	.8	.8	.4	.8	.8	.4	.6	0
6. Energy production in million metric tons of coal equivalent	1847	766	262	232	48	58	48	30	26	2	36	24
7. Percent of world energy production		41%	14%	13%	3%	3%	3%	2%	1%	0%	2%	1%
Power		31	8	9	5	6	2	2	2	1	2	0

TABLE 5-4 (cont.) Basic Power Levels in 1935

MEASURE	WORLD	US	UK	GERMANY	FRANCE	USSR	POLAND	CZECHO-SLOVAKIA	BELGIUM	ITALY	JAPAN	CHINA
1. Million metric tons of crude steel	98.0	26.1	8.9	16.2	6.2	9.5	.9	1.1	3.0	2.2	4.6	—
2. Percent of world steel		27%	9%	17%	6%	10%	1%	1%	3%	2%	5%	0%
3. Million inhabitants in independent states*	1370.5	124	43	65	42	161	32	15	8	41	65	426
4. Percent of world population in independent states		9%	3%	5%	3%	12%	2%	1%	1%	3%	5%	31%
5. Political stability 1930–1934		1.0	.8	.4	.6	.8	.8	.8	.8	1.0	.8	.4
6. Energy production in million metric tons of coal equivalent	1466	620	211	161	49	107	29	20	25	2	35	27
7. Percent of world energy production		42%	14%	11%	3%	7%	2%	1%	2%	0%	2%	2%
Power		26	8	10	4	9	2	1	2	2	4	5

*The same population figures are used in each table, adjusted for territorial changes.

TABLE 5-4 (cont.) Basic Power Levels in 1939

MEASURE	WORLD	US	UK	GERMANY	FRANCE	USSR	POLAND	BELGIUM	ITALY	JAPAN	CHINA
1. Million metric tons of crude steel	135.6	47.1	13.2	25.5	7.8	18.5	1.9	3.1	2.3	6.6	—
2. Percent of world steel		35%	10%	19%	6%	14%	1%	2%	2%	5%	0%
3. Million inhabitants in independent states*	1370.5	124	43	79	42	161	32	8	41	65	426
4. Percent of world population in independent states		9%	3%	6%	3%	12%	2%	1%	3%	5%	31%
5. Political stability 1935–1939		1.0	1.0	1.0	.6	.8	.6	.8	1.0	.8	.4
6. Energy production in million metric tons of coal equivalent	1867	726	231	277	49	177	40	30	3	52	30
7. Percent of world energy production		39%	12%	15%	3%	9%	2%	2%	0%	3%	2%
Power		27	8	13	4	11	1	2	2	4	5

*The same population figures are used in each table, adjusted for territorial changes.
Sources: See Table 4–1; for population, League of Nations, *Statistical Year-Book of the League of Nations*, 1931/1932 (Geneva: League of Nations, 1932), Table 2.

(The Soviet case suggests that the Marxist regime had been able to use ideology as an effective tool for rapid power growth.)

Such descriptions of individual state power would help us fashion an explanation if we were employing the domestic and environmental factor approach— Does the growth of German power encourage a more aggressive German policy? We might also use them with a policy-maker approach—Did Hitler's perception of rapidly growing Soviet power dictate his policy choices? Or in a bargaining approach—Does the power differential help account for the outcome of Hitler and Chamberlain's negotiations? I must leave it up to you to explore those avenues, for the section title says I am to use the systems approach.

What does the power distribution in the international system look like? At first glance, the first half of the 1930s appears to be a continuation of the 1920s' "equilateral system," while the second half has the characteristics of the pre-1914 ladder-like system. Two reservations need to be noted regarding this conclusion, however. First, the system of 1930 differs significantly from that of 1920 in terms of the number of principal major powers. Second, the change in the distribution of power in the 1930s came relatively quickly and without the dramatic clarity that war often provides. Would the major powers be able to respond correctly to these rapidly changing conditions?

Why should the number of states make a difference?[49] The rules of a *three-state* equilateral system are a clear function of numbers: each state needs to prevent the other two from aligning while it attempts to produce an alliance with one of the others. As each adheres to the rule, they work in vain, driving each of them to accept a collective arrangement involving all three. The patterns of such a system worked to prevent the necessity of alignment and developed ways to prevent an inequality of power from emerging—disarmament and arms control conferences are symptomatic.

In a *five-state* equilateral system, on the other hand, there must be another calculus regarding power. The possibility still exists of two states aligning against a third, but now the third has the possibility of balancing that alliance with one of its own. Indeed, it *must* seek such an alliance. In addition, one state may be able to remain aloof from two rival alliances, siding with one or the other on occasion, as power considerations dictate. Because each state has more flexibility, the states are likely to be much more self-centered. The rules in this "balance of power" system will reflect this condition:[50]

1. Increase individual power, by negotiation if possible, by force if not.
2. Align to oppose a state or coalition threatening to become predominant, changing alliance partners freely to fulfill this rule.
3. Treat all principal major actors as acceptable partners.

A policy promoting collective security is out of place in a "balance of power" system. States *need separate alliances*, not an all-encompassing agreement.

---

[49]A point nicely argued by Morton Kaplan, *System and Process in International Politics* (New York: John Wiley, 1957), pp. 34–35; five "essential actors" are necessary to preserve the stability of a "balance of power system."

[50]*Ibid.*, p. 23 (adapted).

States need to be able to permit the individual use of force to preserve and enhance power, not collectively agree to outlaw it. They also need to avoid becoming involved when power issues are not at stake, rather than be compelled to defend the status quo everywhere. *In sum, the balance of power system could not support the League,* which crumbled in 1931 in the Far East and died in Ethiopia because the League rules were not those of the system. The League persisted, however, through its own inertia, and in doing so, pressured states to deviate from the rules of the system in order to uphold those of the League. Neither Britain nor France could see that Italy's imperialism in Ethiopia did *not* threaten their security or the peace of the world (no matter how morally reprehensible it was); both had difficulty in making concessions to pre-Hitler German governments regarding military capabilities and a customs union with Austria. How different Germany might have been if its nonfascist leaders had won some of the concessions that a balance of power system may allow. Or if the British and French governments had early on drawn the conclusion that in a balance of power system, rearmament rather than arms control is the systemic demand.

As it happened, Western leaders did begin to do these things. The problem was that the system continued to change (in part because they had failed to follow the rules) so that they were acting *as if a balance of power system prevailed when in fact, in the late 1930s, the system was ladder-like* in terms of the distribution of power. The ladder-like system has its own set of patterns. How well did the last half of the decade match the patterns we identified in the 1900s and 1910s?

1. *The strongest state will attempt to organize a league of states under its direction.* This systemic rule reinforced Hitler's own image of a German-led Europe. (Europe under German conquest did become a collection of state-like entities, all looking to Berlin for guidance and for arbitration of local disputes.)

2. Failing to create its own league, *the strongest state may attempt to convert the next most powerful into an ally.* Hitler's nonaggression pact with his bitter ideological foe, Stalin, made the two states quasi-allies, although neither felt that the agreement would last.

3. *The weakest major powers will drift into an alliance with the strongest.* This seems to hold reasonably well for Poland (1934) and Italy (1936) and partially for Belguim, which ended its alliance with France and opted for neutrality (1936).

4. *The middle powers will align and seek an alliance with the second most powerful state, thereby creating two rigid alliance systems. No other alliances will form.* Britain and France did slowly move toward the creation of a tie with the Soviet Union (Franco-Soviet defense treaty of 1935; 1939 military talks). They lost the alliance race, however. In the fall of 1939, the power balance was 26 (Axis states of Germany and Italy plus the Soviets, given the agreement to divide Poland) to 13 (Britain, France, Poland).

Stalin was not entirely at fault for failing to recognize the long-term necessities of a ladder-like system. Germany actively sought his neutrality. France and Britain were dilatory in pursuing an active alliance. (Chamberlain felt awkward in dealing with Red Russia—the boundary between the system and environment was weak in crucial ways!) Besides, Britain and France had thrown away part of their protection by sacrificing Czechoslovakia. The sacrifice of Czechoslovakia is understandable in a ''balance of power'' system; the equilateral structure is not upset, and with fluctuating alliances, the strengthened power is likely to be in one's own alliance now and again. In a ladder-like system, however, appeasement by the middle rank powers is madness if it enhances the power of the predominant power or the coalition it heads. In a ladder-like system, appeasement is the policy option of *the most powerful* state.

Can systems analysis suggest a reason for British and French behavior, or must we say that environmental factors such as Chamberlain's personality or a general aversion to war overrode systemic rules? It is probably the latter. I would hypothesize that the relatively slow, consensus-building nature of politics in democracies makes them ''late'' in bringing their policies in line with the rules of the system. The pressure of weakened economies also forced them to divert their energies and attention from world politics to domestic politics. The inattentiveness and lateness is probably not critical in a slowly changing system. In a rapidly changing one, they may prove fatal. The antifascist coalition came within a hair's breadth of losing—a tragic penalty to pay for the failure to heed systemic demands. If that penalty *were* extracted, the United States would have an enormous debt to pay. As it was, American blindness to the demands of the system was as culpable as the outdated responses of Britain and France.

We leave the systems approach and the decade with another war on our hands. Does a ladder-like system spawn such wars? We would need more cases in order to draw a conclusion, and we still need another approach to account for why the second war begins on September 1, 1939, on the Polish-German frontier. Based on the historical record, however, we would expect the war to be of long duration and intense; all major-power neutrals will be drawn in at some point; and a new international system will emerge in its aftermath.

CHAPTER SIX

1940–1949

Hell again
and a peace called war

PART I:
DIPLOMATIC AND MILITARY HISTORY[1]

The Second Great War

The leaders of the belligerent states spent the winter of 1939–1940 huddled over map tables, planning the spring campaigns. The Soviets renewed their winter offensive against Finland and began to drive the Finns back. The Allied

[1]General studies of the war include Peter Calvocoressi and Guy Wint, *Total War* (Harmondsworth, England: Penguin, 1972); Basil Liddell Hart, *History of the Second World War* (New York: Paragon Books, 1970, 1979). The politico-military element can be found in James Burns, *Roosevelt: The Soldier of Freedom* (New York: Harcourt Brace Jovanovich, 1970); Robert Britzell, *The Uneasy Alliance* (New York: Knopf, 1972); John Wheeler-Bennett, *The Semblance of Peace* (New York: St. Martin's Press, 1972). Memoirs include W. Churchill, *The History of the Second World War*, 6 vols. (Boston: Houghton Mifflin, 1948–1953); Walter Warlimont, *Inside Hitler's Headquarters, 1939–1945* (New York: Praeger, 1964); Dwight Eisenhower, *Crusade in Europe* (Garden City, N.Y.: Doubleday, 1948). Source materials include J.R. Butler, ed., *History of the Second World War*, various volumes (London: Her Majesty's Stationery Office); *The United States Army in World War II*, various volumes (Washington: Government Printing Office); Samuel E. Morison, *History of the United States Naval Operations in World War II*, 15 vol. (Boston: Little, Brown, 1947–1962); B.H. Liddell Hart, *The Other Side of the Hill* (London: Cassell, 1948); *Nazi Conspiracy and Aggression*, 8 vols. (Washington: Government Printing Office, 1946). Post-war studies include Herbert Feis, *From Trust to Terror* (New York: W.W. Norton & Co., Inc., 1970); Walter LaFeber, *America, Russia, and the Cold War* (New York: John Wiley, 1972); B. Ponomaryov, ed., *History of Soviet Foreign Policy* (Moscow: Progress Publishers, 1969); Adam Ulam, *The Rivals* (New York: Viking, 1971); and William Gamson and Andre Modigliani, *Untangling the Cold War* (Boston: Little, Brown, 1971). Memoirs are plentiful, such as Harry Truman, *Memoirs* (Garden City, N.Y.: Doubleday, 1955, 1956); George Kennan, *Memoirs* (Boston: Little, Brown, 1967, 1972); and James Forrestal, *The Forrestal Diaries* (New York: Viking, 1951). Documents include *Foreign Relations of the United States* (Washington: Government Printing Office) [hereafter *FRUS*].

powers, principally Britain and France, began to see in Finland and Scandinavia an answer to their strategic problem of attacking Germany. They ruled out a direct offensive across the Franco-German border as too costly; a strike through neutral but armed Belgium would be politically and militarily unwise. Plans to land in the Balkans to seize Romanian oil centers or in the Caucasus to seize Soviet oil centers received active consideration. Indeed, the Allied plans are striking in that they contemplated making the Soviet Union an active belligerent on the side of Germany. These plans reflected the influence of the strategic innovators of World War I, who sought the indirect route to defeat Germany. Winston Churchill, the proponent of the Gallipoli campaign, had become First Lord of the Admiralty in September, 1939, giving a powerful voice to the innovators.

Churchill persuaded Chamberlain and the French to spread the war to neutral Norway by mining its waters to block German ships; to seize Norwegian ports and rail lines to prevent Swedish iron ore from reaching Germany (through the ice-free port of Narvik); and *to send supplies and troops to Finland* (see Map 6–1). In mid-March, however, the Finns accepted Soviet peace terms, but the Allies decided to go ahead with the Norwegian operation, now scheduled for April. Not surprisingly, the *German* admirals had also pressed for a Norwegian operation to expand bases for their submarines, to protect iron-ore supplies, and to forestall a rumored British operation in Scandinavia. And they, like Churchill, were too restless to accept the routines of blockade and submarine warfare. Hitler preferred a neutral Scandinavia, but in February he became convinced that Britain planned to violate Norwegian neutrality with the connivance of the Norwegian government. Hitler set April 9 as the date for an air and sea invasion of Norway. In London, April 8 became the date for the mining of Norwegian waters. The belligerents were about to collide.

Hitler, however, had more ambitious plans. The army had planned to attack France by way of Belgium—the von Schlieffen plan embellished with tanks and aircraft. The Allies counted on such an attack, positioning their best and most mobile forces along the Belgian border, ready to rush into Belgium to shatter the German offensive and then invade the Ruhr, a strategic industrial area of Germany. On January 10, however, a German military plane mistakenly landed in Belgium, and Belgian police discovered the plans for the German attack. Hitler scrapped those plans and accepted an innovation proposed by younger officers: instead of attacking from the north through Belgium, German armor would pass through the Ardennes forests of Belgium and strike westward to the English Channel, cutting off the French and British units along the Belgian border. Slower moving infantry would then destroy the trapped units. Hitler set early May for the operation against the Low Countries and France.

Germany Triumphant   The German invasion of Norway began on schedule. Britain tried to send troops, but these were driven out by the better prepared Germans. The Norwegian debacle brought down the Chamberlain government; Churchill became Prime Minister on May 10. On that day, blitzkrieg struck Belgium, the Netherlands, and Luxembourg.[2] British and French units moved into

---

[2]For studies of the critical Scandinavian and French campaigns, see Alistair Horne, *To Lose a Battle: France 1940* (Harmondsworth, England: Penguin, 1969); Heinz Guderian, *Panzer Leader* (New York: Dutton, 1952); Richard Petrow, *The Bitter Years* (New York: Morrow, 1974).

MAP 6–1   The European Theater

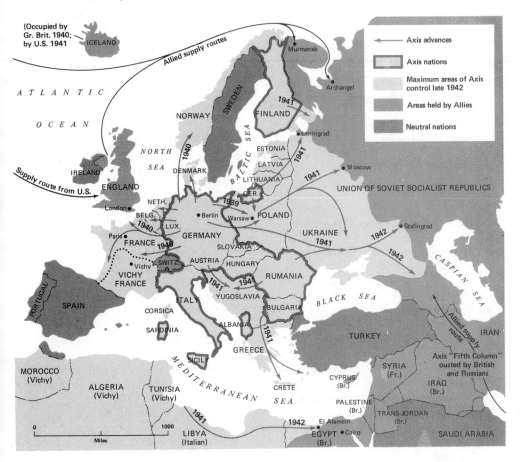

Belgium, making it easier for German *panzer* (tank) units to emerge from the "impassable" Ardennes forests and dash two hundred miles westward to the coast. On May 20, German tanks reached the Channel, encircling the Allied forces that had rushed into Belgium.

Mobility—that pipe dream of World War I—had returned to the battlefield. The rapidity of success, however, was unexpected, and Hitler and his generals found it difficult to divest themselves of the caution World War I had engrained in them. Looked at on a map, the armored blitzkrieg was the thin finger of vehicles that stretched from the Ardennes toward the Channel. (Germany had a total of ten armored divisions out of one hundred and thirty available.) An Allied counterattack could cut the finger off at the base (see Figure 6–1), immobilizing the tanks for lack of gasoline and rendering the entire force vulnerable to annihilation. Hitler twice ordered the tanks to halt so that the much slower infantry, marching on foot for the most part, could come up to protect the flanks from counterattack. He, like many of his generals, had difficulty appreciating the

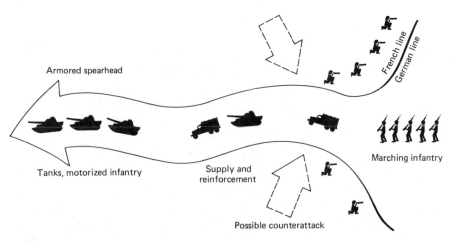

FIGURE 6-1   Armored Warfare: Breakthrough

enormous confusion, the breakdown of communication, and the paralysis in the minds of the French high command the panzers created.

The British and French mounted feeble counterattacks against the finger. German armor moved up the coast to encircle the trapped Allied units, who now were retreating toward Dunkirk. On May 24, Hitler ordered the tanks to stop and redeploy for the thrust into southern France. Goering's Luftwaffe (air force) was to of compel the encircled Allied forces to surrender. The British used the opportunity to send a rag-tag flotilla of boats to Dunkirk. In spite of Luftwaffe attacks, by June 4, some 300,000 soldiers (one third of which were French and Belgian) had left France to fight again. On June 5, the blitz struck the French lines, pierced them, and streamed south. Italy entered the war on the 10th. A new government under Pétain, the victor of Verdun in 1916, requested an armistice, which was granted on the 22nd. Northern France came under German military occupation, while Pétain governed the southern half from the new capital at Vichy.[3]

Blitzkrieg had made Hitler the master of Europe from Poland to the Pyrenees. It had failed, however, to provide a solution to the British problem. Hitler wavered. He ordered planning for a mid-August invasion of Britain,[4] but also contemplated a political settlement that would leave Britain and its empire unmolested in return for British acceptance of German hegemony in Europe. Publicly he declared,

> I feel I owe it to my conscience to make another appeal to reason in England. I do not speak up for reason as one who has been conquered and then pleads, but as a victor. I see no reason that makes the continuation of this struggle necessary.[5]

[3]See Robert Paxton, *Vichy France* (New York: Knopf, 1972); Richard Griffiths, *Pétain* (Garden City, N.Y.: Doubleday, 1972). For the tangled Vichy–US relations, see William Langer, *Our Vichy Gamble* (New York: W.W. Norton & Co. Inc., 1947).

[4]For studies of SEALION (the codename for the invasion of Britain), see Peter Fleming, *Operation Sea Lion* (New York: Simon & Schuster, 1957).

[5]Speech of July 19, 1940 to the Reichstag; quoted by Paul Schmidt, *Hitler's Interpreter* (New York: Macmillan, 1951), p. 186.

Hitler's bargaining style was to wait for the weak to offer specific proposals. Churchill roared defiance, declaring Britain would fight to the end to destroy Nazism.

Britain, however, was a diversion from Hitler's goal of acquiring "living space" in the East. The success of blitzkrieg led him to believe that he could turn on the Soviet Union with a reasonable prospect of success. In July, 1940, Hitler talked with his closest advisors about a fall offensive against the Soviet Union. Yet Britain was still at war with Germany, while the Soviet Union furnished needed raw materials as the nonaggression treaty stipulated. Uncertain, trying to preserve his options, Hitler accepted the advice of his naval and army advisors (themselves skeptical about an attack on Britain) to make the invasion of Britain dependent upon the Luftwaffe's establishing aerial supremacy over southern Britain. He ordered shipping collected in North Sea ports to carry the invasion forces and planning began for a spring 1941 invasion of the USSR.

One month after the Luftwaffe opened the "Battle of Britain" on August 13, the German leadership judged that it was unable to destroy the Royal Air Force and began to bomb London around the clock to produce a collapse in British morale.[6] The diminution of attacks on air bases and command centers saved the RAF from disintegration. On September 17, Hitler ordered the invasion of Britain postponed until spring. Goering ordered the Luftwaffe to raid British cities at night (the fabled Blitz), which only rallied Britons to the war effort.

The Battle for France and its outcome also had repercussions around the world. The Soviets drew the appropriate conclusions about blitzkrieg and annexed Estonia, Latvia, and Lithuania and seized the Romanian provinces of Bessarabia and northern Bukovina (June 1940) to expand their defensive perimeter. Hitler ordered the military occupation of Romania to protect Germany's major foreign oil source and by March, 1941, had "persuaded" Hungary, Romania, Bulgaria, and Yugoslavia to join the Tripartite Pact, the alliance created by Germany, Italy, and Japan. (The Pact had one particular target—the United States—and pledged the signatories to war on that country if it entered the war.) On the other hand, Pétain and Franco of Spain refused Hitler's requests to become active belligerents against Britain.

In the Far East, the fall of France accelerated the tension between the United States and Japan. The Japanese demanded that Vichy France allow Japan to station troops in northern Indochina in order to seal Nationalist China off from Western aid. When the French complied in September, President Roosevelt imposed an embargo on scrap iron and steel to Japan. This marked the opening round in America's declaration of economic war on Japan. Undeterred, the Japanese occupied southern Indochina. Roosevelt responded with an embargo on oil to Japan, which cut off 60 percent of its supplies, and a freezing of Japanese assets in American banks. Judging that the Americans were intent on not only blocking Japanese imperial expansion, but crippling Japan itself, their leadership opted for war. The decision to go to war (discussed in a following section) involved extensive debate in various Japanese cabinets, in large measure over the

---

[6]Studies of the Battle of Britain and Blitz are legion. See Derek Wood and Derek Dempster, *The Narrow Margin* (New York: McGraw-Hill, 1961); Francis Mason, *Battle Over Britain* (Garden City, N.Y.: Doubleday, 1969).

question of striking south (and colliding with British and American interests) or striking north against the Soviet Union. In April, 1941, Japanese Foreign Minister Matsuoka, acting on his own, negotiated a neutrality pact with Stalin. The embarrassed government accepted the pact (though it removed the foreign minister!) and lived up to it in spite of the enormous temptation to "go north" when Hitler attacked the Soviet Union. Matsuoka's impetuosity made a southward drive more probable and may have saved the Soviet Union from defeat in 1941.

The fall of France had also galvanized Roosevelt into heeding Churchill's warning that ". . . the voice and force of the United States may count for nothing if they are withheld too long."[7] The President persuaded the Congress to approve giving Britain fifty old destroyers in exchange for bases in British possessions in the Caribbean. The following spring, Congress accepted the policy of "Lend-Lease": the United States would openly supply Britain with arms, essentially at no cost. That meant the United States was an active but nonbelligerent opponent of Germany. By late 1941, the American navy was convoying British ships across the Atlantic and attacking German submarines in a unilaterally proclaimed maritime security zone. Yet Roosevelt, fearful of getting too far in front of public opinion, much of it bitterly opposed to war, refused to budge beyond a policy of everything short of war. He did hope, however, that his naval policies would force Germany to declare war on the United States.[8] At the same time, he sought to stave off a confrontation with Japan. He agreed in April, 1941, to a Japanese proposal to negotiate an Asian settlement. Roosevelt tried to make no concessions to encourage Japanese imperialism but still keep the talks going. It worked for nine months.

Finally, the fall of France directly expanded the hostilities by making Italy a belligerent. A battered Britain waited for larger Italian forces in Cyrennaïca (modern Libya) and Ethopia to attack Egypt and British East Africa. The Italian offensive began in September, to which Mussolini added an attack on Greece in October, in large part to ensure that Italy would share in the spoils in the division of the Balkans between Germany and Russia. The Italian army proved too weak. By December, the Greeks were attacking into Albania (Italy's base for the offensive) and the British routed the Italians in North Africa. Churchill, still hoping to defeat Germany at low cost, now made a fatal decision. He ordered British forces to Greece to open a Balkan front against the Axis. The Italians remained in control of western Libya.

Hitler in December, 1940, had approved the plans for the attack on the Soviet Union (Operation Barbarossa) and as spring approached, became more wedded to launching the undertaking. Italy's reverses in North Africa and the British threat in Greece (as well as Yugoslavia's sudden rejection of the Tripartite Pact) forced a change in plans. Two armored formations under General Rommel went to Africa, and major elements of the German army began an offensive in the Balkans on April 6. On April 17, Yugoslavia surrendered; on the 25th, the

---

[7]Churchill letter, May 15, 1940; *Roosevelt and Churchill: Their Secret Wartime Correspondence*, ed. Francis Loewenheim, Harold Langley, and Manfred Jonas (New York: Saturday Review Press/Dutton, 1975), p. 95. Reprinted by permission of The Sterling Lord Agency, Inc. Copyright © 1975 by Francis Loewenheim, Harold Langley, and Manfred Jonas.

[8]See Thomas Bailey and Paul Ryan, *Hitler vs. Roosevelt* (New York: Free Press, 1979); Burns, *Roosevelt.*

Greeks. British forces hurriedly left Greece and then the island of Crete, which fell to German airborne forces in May. To round out the disaster, Rommel drove the British back into Egypt in April. Churchill's policies were nearly bankrupt.

Then came the first watershed of 1941. The German attack on the Soviet Union on June 22 overnight created a new ally for Britain.[9] The question, however, was whether the USSR would survive the onslaught. Stalin had ignored warnings of the attack, and the Wehrmacht caught Soviet aircraft and divisions unprepared. It seemed to be France all over again. In fact, the German army was much like the one that attacked France the year before with essentially the same amount of armored striking power. The critical difference was space. Tanks could reach the English Channel by driving two hundred miles; Moscow lay six hundred and fifty miles from the frontier. The three "fingers of armor" that Hitler proposed to send into Russia might be swallowed up in that space before the decisive battles could be fought.

The "depth" of the Soviet Union posed the fundamental question: How was one to defeat the Soviet Union? When would the Red Army no longer offer effective resistance? When it was destroyed? When the political and military leadership was so disorganized that it could not command effective continuation of resistance? Or when the political leadership had decided that the costs of continued resistance far outweighed the terms the enemy offered? The more conservative German generals wanted to concentrate on the destruction of the Red Army by having the panzers break through the Soviet lines and envelop the enemy from behind. The more daring (especially those who led the tanks in the field in France) wanted to concentrate the forces for a drive on Moscow, to disrupt and disorganize and to prevent any strong secondary lines of resistance from forming. Faced with conflicting advice and his own conflicting views (a conservatism in military tactics but a need for quick victories), Hitler compromised. There was to be a series of encirclements, with infantry executing those near the frontier, the panzers at great depth. There was to be no single drive on Moscow.

The caution seemed to pay off. The successive encirclements cut off and overwhelmed one and one-half million Soviet soldiers and thousands of tanks. By October, the German armies had slashed more than four hundred miles into the Soviet Union. As in France, Hitler had ordered a halt to the onrushing panzers, this time to secure his southern flank. This respite, plus the rain (which created quagmires where roads had been) and the willingness of the Red Army to fight even when surrounded, kept decisive victory from Hitler. The Soviet mobilization system and the defense factories in the east continued to furnish new armies to make up the losses at the front. In addition, Stalin now accepted information from his espionage network in Japan that Japan would not attack; the divisions covering Manchuria raced westward.

On the Razor's Edge   Blitzkrieg stumbled to a halt on the outskirts of Moscow in December, 1941. With the divisions from the Far East, the Soviets counterattacked and drove the Germans back from the capital. Hitler ordered the new

---

[9]Of the many studies of BARBAROSSA and the Russo-German war, see Alan Clark, *Barbarossa* (New York: Morrow, 1965); Albert Seaton, *The Russo-German War* (New York: Praeger, 1971); Barton Whaley, *Codeword BARBAROSSA* (Cambridge, Mass. M.I.T. Press, 1973); Alexander Werth, *Russia at War* (New York: Dutton, 1964).

positions held at all costs, and the front stabilized in late winter. Blitzkrieg had failed; Hitler had a two-front war and there was no clear answer on how to drive either the Soviet Union or Britain out of the war. In North Africa, Hitler could send no reinforcements to Rommel during the summer. The British army, in spite of losing battles to Rommel, continued to receive the resources to continue the struggle; the Germans retreated into Libya.

On December 7, 1941, came the second watershed of the war. The Japanese staged a carrier attack on the American naval base at Pearl Harbor, Hawaii, which destroyed the Pacific battleship fleet, and Germany declared war on the United States. Why Hitler did so is unclear. It certainly sealed Germany's fate, giving Britain and the Soviet Union an indispensable ally. The war had become total in terms of both geography and organization. American power became available for deployment in Europe. The struggle now shifted from a war of surprise and movement to one of resources and time. It had become, as Russell Weigley has pointed out, a "gross national product war."[10] The victors would be those states who could bludgeon the opposition to death with a never-ending, timely supply of trained manpower and the implements of modern war. It was a global war of attrition. In such a war, the odds were against the Axis states. Their hope revolved around the question of timing. Could the Allied coalition be beaten separately before their combined resources overwhelmed the Axis states?

The year 1942 marked the struggle to control the timing of the war. German submarines took the war to the American coast with a vengeance, threatening to isolate Britain and curtail the projection of American power. The Japanese army and navy stormed through Southeast Asia (see Map 6–2). Malaya and Singapore fell in February, as did much of the Dutch East Indies. Organized American resistance in the Philippines ended in early May. Japanese entry into Burma—coupled with revolutionary appeals to Asian nationalism—threatened Britain's hold on India. In June, the German offensive resumed against the Soviet Union, now concentrated on a southern drive to complete the seizure of the Ukraine and to capture the oil wells of the Caucusus. By August, the panzer spearheads reached the Volga River at Stalingrad, and other units poured southward. That same month, Stalin listened in anger as Churchill told him that the Allies could not open a "second front" in Europe that year. The Red Army would have to bear the weight of Germany alone. And Rommel, now reinforced, again drove the British deep into Egypt.

By the end of the year, the battle of the clock had been won, if ever so barely, by the Allies. In June, 1942, using broken Japanese codes, American carriers ambushed a Japanese fleet attempting to take Midway Island; four Japanese carriers went to the bottom (one American carrier was lost), forcing the Japanese fleet to withdraw inside the Pacific perimeter of Japanese conquests. In November, American Marines landed on Guadalcanal in the Solomon Islands to begin an offensive that would ultimately carry American power to the Japanese home islands. In the Soviet Union, the battle for Stalingrad became a titanic struggle. The battle of attrition ended in November when Soviet forces attacked the Romanian divisions guarding the flanks of the German forces besieging Stalingrad.

---

[10]R. Weigley, *The American Way of War* (Bloomington: Indiana University Press, 1973), p. 146.

MAP 6-2   War in the Pacific

The Romanians, like the Hungarian and Italian divisions, were needed to release German units to form the spearheads. Their collapse left the German units surrounded. In late January, the German commander disregarded Hitler's orders to resist to the last, and surrendered. The tide had ebbed on the Eastern front. And in North Africa, a British offensive at El Alamein (October) and an Anglo-American landing on the North African coast (November) forced Rommel back into Tunisia. Now Hitler reinforced his forces there, only to increase the number of German troops who surrendered in May, 1943.[11]

The Destruction of the Axis   For the next two and a half years, the war had a repetitive quality to it, for it was essentially attrition writ large. A war of attrition was not attractive to Hitler. While he planned another Eastern offensive in 1943, he permitted German officials in neutral countries to approach Russian

---

[11]For the critical 1942 battles, see Alan Morehead, *The March to Tunis* (New York: Harper & Row, Pub., 1967); Walter Lord, *Incredible Victory* (New York: Harper & Row, Pub., 1967); John Erickson, *The Road to Stalingrad* (New York: Harper & Row, Pub., 1975).

diplomats with inquiries about a negotiated peace. German demands to retain captured Soviet territory produced a Soviet rejection. German policy, therefore, became one of holding on at all costs. For Stalin, on the other hand, attrition was the only way to recover the Motherland in this war (now called the Great Patriotic War in the Soviet Union). Churchill also had an aversion to attrition, wanting to avoid the bloodletting of 1914–1918. His solution was to confront Germany indirectly by operations against Italy, the Balkans, and Norway. However, he and Roosevelt in August, 1941, had pledged their nations to "the final destruction of Nazi tyranny," which made the indirect approach seem both misdirected and of little help to the Soviets, the only military power capable, until 1944, of keeping the Germans from winning.

The Americans had been spared the agonies of attrition in the First World War. Roosevelt and his military planners agreed that Germany was the main threat and thought of the war in terms of a massive buildup in Britain, an invasion of France, and an overwhelming drive into Germany. Churchill lobbied hard against this assault, getting the reluctant Americans to attack North Africa (1942) and Sicily and Italy (1943) instead. By 1944, the Americans could not be denied—nor could the Soviets, who for two years fought essentially alone. The invasion of France came in June, 1944.

The American view of the war was straightforward as well. As Roosevelt unilaterally announced at the Casablanca conference (January 1943), the United Nations (as they now called themselves) would insist on the "unconditional surrender" of the Axis states and on "the total elimination of German and Japanese war power." There would be no negotiations. To Roosevelt's mind, two generations of Germans had to live under the lash of palpable defeat before there would be real peace. Churchill had no quarrel with the aims. He did feel such a declaration was unwise because it encouraged the Germans to fight to the end. More important, the fixation on crippling German and Japanese power led Roosevelt and his military to avoid the question of *Soviet* power and where it would be at war's end. That concern became stronger for Churchill as the months went by.

The Japanese, with the bulk of their army tied down in China, had to rely on surprise and speed to expand the empire, now called the Greater East Asia Co-Prosperity Sphere to avoid the imperialist stigma. Knowing they could not force the United States to surrender, they sought to establish a defensive perimeter and make it costly enough for the Americans to retake the territory so that they would accept the new status quo. Such a strategy depended on their ability to replace ships (particularly carriers), aircraft, and pilots in order to fend off the American navy.

The United States vastly outproduced the Japanese and came to dominate the waters of the Pacific. As a consequence, General MacArthur could avoid major Japanese bases, land forces at other strategic spots in the Southwest Pacific, and cut the bases off. In this manner, he "leapfrogged" to the Philippines, which he invaded in October 1944 (Leyte) and January 1945 (Luzon). The American navy ran the war further to the east; they "leapfrogged" from island to island; the mid-1944 conquest of the Mariana Islands provided a base for air attacks on Japanese cities.

In Europe, the United Nations were on the offensive from 1943 on. A summer Soviet offensive surged forward, reaching Kiev by year's end. Anglo-American forces invaded Sicily in July, leading the Fascist elite to depose Mussolini and surrender to the Allies. Hitler, however, invaded Italy and blocked Allied progress in their drive on Rome. That campaign became a slugfest. Rome did not fall until June 1944, and Italy was not cleared of German forces until the spring of 1945.

In 1944, the Soviet steamroller began in January in the center and south. So ample were Soviet resources that they could attack a sector of the German line, force Hitler to commit his reserves there, then hit another sector of the German line. Hitler's insistence on permitting no withdrawals made successful defense less likely. Increasingly rigid, surrounded by yes-men, and (after the abortive attempt on his life in July, 1944) suspicious of the motives of his generals, Hitler assumed that the death of Germany was preferable to its subjugation.

The pressures on Germany became overwhelming in June with the Anglo-American landings in Normandy.[12] Hitler, convinced that the main landing would take place further east, had withheld panzer forces. In July, the American army broke through the defenses, and the German position in France collapsed. By September, the German border had been reached. And then the offensive bogged down, just as it had done on the Soviet front. Mobile forces would outrun their supplies, men and vehicles crumbled under the violence, and disagreements would emerge between commanders over whose forces should have priority. The rhythm of battle was buildup, strike, penetrate, overextend, pause, buildup, and renew the cycle. By year's end, Soviet forces had swept through Romania and were besieging Budapest and Warsaw. The next cycle of offensives in the East and West would carry the Allies into Germany. Hitler tried an offensive in the Ardennes in December, 1944, but the Allies beat down this "Battle of the Bulge."

In five months, Germany was overrun. By April, 1945, Soviet troops were in Berlin. Hitler ordered continued resistance and committed suicide (April 30) before the Soviets reached his bunker. His designated successor, Admiral Doenitz, ordered the surrender of all German forces on May 7. In the major German cities, scarred by Allied bombings, the lash of defeat was clear. With the occupation of the extermination camps,[13] the stigma of unforgivable evil settled on the Third Reich.

Peace Plans   How would the victor states handle Germany? How would they cope with the chaos in the newly liberated states? The answers would depend upon the cohesion of the Allied alliance and the congruence of their goals. As long as Germany was a threat, the alliance remained cohesive. Nonetheless, the failure to open a second front in 1942 and again in 1943 heightened Stalin's suspicions that the West sought the destruction of both German and Soviet power. Marxist ideology encouraged Stalin to interpret Western behavior in such nega-

---

[12]For Normandy, see Kenneth Macksey, *Anatomy of a Battle* (Briarcliff Manor, N.Y.: Stein & Day, 1974); Alan Wilt, *The Atlantic Wall* (Ames, Iowa: Iowa State University Press, 1975).

[13]On the German extermination policies, see Lucy Dawidowicz, *The War Against the Jews* (New York: Holt, Rinehart and Winston, 1975); Eugen Kogon, *The Theory and Practice of Hell* (New York: Octagon, 1973).

tive ways. Churchill and Roosevelt strove to convince him that military necessities forced the postponement.

The three leaders had met together for the first time in November, 1943, in Teheran.[14] There Churchill finally accepted the invasion of France as the primary Western task of 1944. Stalin, to demonstrate his commitment to the alliance, said the Soviet Union would be willing to enter the Pacific war after Germany's defeat. He did go on to state his view of post-war Europe: the Soviet Union would insist on the restoration of its June, 1941 frontiers. Post-war Poland would lose one third of its territory to the Soviet Union; Stalin proposed to compensate Poland with German land. Roosevelt, seeing the issue in terms of winning the war, felt that Poland would have to pay the price to keep the Soviets fully engaged.

When the three met again in Yalta in Soviet Crimea in February, 1945, Poland was again a central issue. Who would govern the liberated states? Stalin was determined that only Poles friendly to the Soviet Union would control the state, which meant communists or nationalists, such as Edward Benes of Czechoslovakia, who pledged themselves to intimate relations with the Soviets. Churchill and Roosevelt insisted that the Polish government be broadened to include Poles whom the West had sponsored as a government-in-exile. Stalin gave a general pledge to democratize the Polish government and political processes, but chose to do neither until the West demonstrated that it would push the subject more forcibly. Neither Churchill nor Roosevelt felt they could get more from Stalin as long as the war continued.

Churchill, however, had tried another gambit. He recognized that "who governed?" would be answered by "whose troops occupied the country?" The Western commitment to the invasion of France meant that the Soviets would be the liberators of much of the Balkans. To preserve a British presence there, Churchill proposed to Stalin in October, 1944, that the two agree on spheres of influence in the area. Stalin agreed to Churchill's plan to accord 90 percent predominance to the Soviet Union in Romania, 75 percent in Bulgaria, and 50 percent in Yugoslavia and Hungary. British influence in each would be the remaining percentage, and would be 90 percent in Greece. Roosevelt refused to accept the concept of spheres of influence. The West, therefore, had to demand freedom of choice in the liberated states which, for security reasons, Stalin refused to accept in practice. It was a recipe for continuing conflict.

The three were able to ratify plans for occupation zones in Germany and expectations of reparations to be extracted from Germany (mainly in the form of capital goods, such as machinery and raw materials). They furthered preparations for a United Nations organization, a project Roosevelt had underwritten and secured Congressional support for.[15] Roosevelt's idea was that effective power would be held by a four-power Security Council—the United States, Soviet Union, Britain, and China (with France added subsequently). The four

---

[14]For studies of the wartime conferences, see Herbert Feis, *Churchill, Roosevelt, Stalin* (Princeton: Princeton University Press, 1957).

[15]Studies of the founding and early work of the UN include Clark Eichelberger, *Organizing for Peace* (New York: Harper & Row, Pub., 1977); Trygve Lie, *In the Cause of Peace* (New York: Macmillan, 1954); Rosalyn Higgins, *United Nations Peacekeeping*, 3 vols. (London: Oxford University Press, 1969).

would act as the world's policemen to enforce their definition of peace on other nations. Stalin insisted on each of the policemen having a veto on action by the United Nations. Roosevelt finally agreed. The Soviet Union was too powerful to be left outside the United Nations. And Roosevelt had to ensure that Stalin would enter the Pacific war.

American military planners estimated that the war against Japan would take one and a half years after Germany's surrender, and produce an enormous casualty list as Americans invaded Japan proper. In the Pacific campaign, Japanese forces generally fought to the last rather than surrender, and during 1944, Japanese pilots began suicide attacks on American shipping with explosive-laden aircraft ("kamikaze"). No one was sure whether the millions spent to devise an atomic bomb would produce a workable weapon in time, or whether it would measurably affect Japanese policy decisions.[16] Roosevelt was gratified when Stalin agreed at Yalta to enter the Pacific war three months after Germany's surrender. (There was a price—return of Russian territory lost in 1905 and Chinese agreement to a Soviet base at Port Arthur.) In preparation for the final assault on Japan, American forces seized the islands of Iwo Jima and Okinawa, bringing American power to within four hundred miles of the Japanese home islands. The American air force began the systematic destruction of Japanese cities, killing tens of thousands of civilians.[17]

On April 12, 1945, Roosevelt died. Harry Truman, Vice President since January, clutched at the reins of government. Truman's advisors were divided on how to deal with Soviet failures to honor the pledges regarding governments in East Europe. Truman, brash but inexperienced, "got tough" with the Soviets rhetorically and won some cosmetic changes. He did not, however, order General Eisenhower to deploy the Allied forces in Europe for maximum political advantage. Stalin concluded that the rhetoric was for public consumption and that Truman, like Churchill, would be a realist about these things.

Truman journeyed to Potsdam, Germany, in July, 1945, for another summit conference.[18] While the conference was in progress, the British electorate refused to give Churchill's conservatives a majority in Parliamentary elections. The symbol of a defiant Britain was replaced by the leader of the victorious Labour Party, Clement Attlee. Only Stalin had survived the war. The conference hammered out general political, social, and economic prescriptions for all of Germany and ratified the temporary division of Germany into four occupation zones (France now having a zone). The leaders created a special four-power occupation zone in Berlin (which was otherwise completely surrounded by the Soviet occupation zone). Germany, by these decisions, was to be a unified, militarily weak, and heavily controlled state. While at the conference, Truman learned that a suc-

[16]For the Manhattan Project, see Leslie Groves, *Now It Can Be Told* (New York: Harper & Row, Pub., 1962); Stephane Groueff, *Manhattan Project* (Boston: Little, Brown, 1967); Martin Sherwin, *A World Destroyed* (New York: Knopf, 1975); Herbert Feis, *The Atomic Bomb and the End of World War II*, rev. ed. (Princeton: Princeton University Press, 1966).

[17]On the air war against Japan and Germany, see the various works of the U.S. Strategic Bombing Survey; Anthony Verrier, *The Bomber Offensive* (New York: Macmillan, 1969); William Craig, *The Fall of Japan* (New York: Dial, 1967).

[18]The Potsdam conference is described in Herbert Feis, *Between War and Peace* (Princeton: Princeton University Press, 1960); Charles Mee, *Meeting at Potsdam* (New York: Evans, 1975).

cessful atomic bomb had been tested and guardedly informed Stalin of the new weapon (Stalin's intelligence apparatus had kept him apprised). Truman ordered the bomb's use against Japan.

On August 6 and 9, the Japanese cities of Hiroshima and Nagasaki were destroyed (with approximately 90,000 deaths in each). The Soviet Union declared war on Japan as promised and invaded Manchuria. The Japanese quickly surrendered, and control of the Japanese state passed to the American military commander, General MacArthur.

In announcing the surrender, Truman declared that the war proved that "the spirit of liberty, the freedom of the individual, and the personal dignity of man" were "the strongest and toughest and most enduring forces in all the world." In addition, those qualities had "made us the strongest nation on earth."[19] Stalin's victory address, on the other hand, was devoid of ideology but reeking of power politics. Stalin explained why the Soviet Union attacked Japan:

> But the defeat of the Russian troops in 1904, in the period of the Russo-Japanese war, left grave memories in the minds of our people. It fell as a dark stain on our country. Our people trusted and awaited the day when Japan would be routed and the stain wiped out.[20]

Was the world rapidly going from peace to a confrontation between those who operated in terms of power and parochial security interests and those who preferred to be idealists?

The Slide into the Cold War

We commonly call much of the post-war period a "cold war" between the United States and the Soviet Union. A cold war is a state of conflict in which the states perceive each other as hostile and aggressive, pursue incompatible goals, and manifest relatively high-risk behaviors to protect their interests.[21] At the same time, however, they recognize there are common interests between them, principally the preservation of peace. This cold war did not emerge once the Japanese surrendered, but evolved during the next two to three years. It is difficult to say precisely when the peace turned cold, but when the leaders of the Soviet Union and the United States began to suspect that the other was another Hitler, a cold war could not be far behind, given the lessons Hitler had taught.

Stalin had watched the United States, a nonentity in world politics a decade before, become *the* global power with a continuing military, political, and economic presence in Europe and Asia. That much power, so close to the Soviet Union, constituted a threat. Stalin seemed unimpressed by atomic weapons—"atom bombs are designed to frighten those with weak nerves, but they cannot decide the outcome of wars because for this there definitely are not enough atom

[19]Statement of September 1, 1945; *Public Papers of the Presidents, Harry Truman, 1945* (Washington: Government Printing Office, 1961), pp. 256–57.

[20]Radio address, September 2, 1945; *Voices of History, 1945–1946*, ed. Nathan Ausubel (New York: Gramercy, 1946), p. 532.

[21]For discussions of the Cold War, both conceptually and historically, see Lloyd Gardner, *The Origins of the Cold War* (Waltham, Mass.: Ginn, Blaisdell, 1970); John Gaddis, *The United States and the Origins of the Cold War* (New York: Columbia University Press, 1972); Vojtech Mastony, *Russia's Road to the Cold War* (New York: Columbia University Press, 1979).

bombs.''[22] (American military planners had voiced similar conclusions.) It was the dynamism of the American state and its *capacity* to exercise power in various forms that made the threat. The enormous conventional military power of the Soviet Union rested on a society and economy torn by war and twenty million dead. That military power also gave power to Soviet generals and bureaucrats who ran the war machine. Stalin's dilemma was to demobilize his armed forces, to reduce the power of his subordinates, and to free manpower for reconstruction, but still not jeopardize Soviet security. For security, he could try to neutralize the West's power, or to build a security zone in Eastern Europe totally responsive to Soviet interests. He tried both and, as they were incompatible goals, failed in both.

Moreover, Stalin's thinking during the war had become more nationalistic; he had, after all, successfully rallied the people with calls to patriotism rather than to communism. The Soviet government had come to assume that Soviet power and contributions to the war had entitled the Soviet Union to expunge other ''dark stains'' of history. For all these reasons, Stalin was eager to establish Soviet spheres of influence in the world and, outside a few claims made for bargaining purposes (such as the demand to be given trusteeship over Libya), the sphere most sought was adjacent to the Soviet Union. Iran, Turkey, and Greece felt the pressure, as Finland and the Baltic states had six years before. Soviet forces had occupied northern Iran during the war while Britain and the United States occupied the southern half. The Soviets permitted the formation of a communist regime in their sector and prevented the Iranian government from reasserting control in the area after the war. The Iranian government appealed to the United Nations, and the American government supported Teheran. The Soviets withdrew their forces in the spring of 1946, and the autonomy movement was crushed. Turkey in 1945 was the recipient of Soviet demands for a return of Tsarist territory (Ardahan and Kars) and a military base in the Straits. The pressure continued for two more years, matched by American demonstrations of support for the Turkish regime. In Greece, the Greek communists reopened their sporadic civil war against the government, aided by supplies from Albania and Yugoslavia. British troops and economic aid helped to preserve a tenuous balance between the government and insurgents.

Containment   These Soviet activities provoked mounting concern in the West and a growing debate about Soviet intentions and appropriate responses. Churchill, out of office but unwilling to forsake his leadership role, told an American audience in March, 1946, that ''from Stettin in the Baltic to Trieste in the Adriatic an iron curtain has descended across the continent.'' From the American embassy in Moscow, George Kennan cabled a long analysis of Soviet foreign policy, which received wide circulation in the American government. Kennan argued that the Soviets saw no possibility of ''permanent peaceful coexistence'' with the West. ''At bottom of Kremlin's neurotic view of world affairs is traditional and instinctive Russian sense of insecurity.'' Added to this insecurity were the regime's fears: '' . . . Russian rulers have invariably sensed that their rule was relatively archaic in form, fragile and artificial in its psychological founda-

---

[22]Statement of September 24, 1946; *New York Times*, September 25, 1946, p. 3. © 1946 by The New York Times Company. Reprinted by permission.

tion, unable to stand comparison or contact with the political systems of Western countries." As a consequence, Soviet leaders "have learned to seek security only in patient but deadly struggle for total destruction of rival power, never in compacts and compromises with it."[23]

Kennan also suggested a Western response to Soviet policy:

> Soviet power, unlike that of Hitlerite Germany, is neither schematic nor adventuristic. It does not work by fixed plans. It does not take unnecessary risks. Impervious to logic of reason, and it is highly sensitive to logic of force. For this reason it can easily withdraw—and usually does—when strong resistance is encountered at any point. Thus, if the adversary has sufficient force and makes clear his readiness to use it, he rarely has to do so. If situations are properly handled, there need be no prestige-engaging showdowns.[24]

Kennan's analysis provided a framework and justification for the Truman administration's evolving confrontational policy with the Soviet Union. Soviet power, in a word, was to be *contained*. It is very likely that Soviet policy makers thought of the United States in similar terms: an archaic and fragile regime, a continuous attempt to destroy rival power, a responsiveness to the logic of power.

Containment, however, was a difficult policy orientation for American policy makers to accept, understand, or implement. Containment was a spheres-of-influence policy, accepting Soviet power where it now stood as in Eastern Europe, but pledging to keep it from spreading. That, in effect, necessitated an American sphere of influence which would quickly have to become global. Roosevelt had rejected spheres of influence, and for a while in the 1940s, prominent Americans (including Herbert Hoover) urged a no-spheres-of-influence policy based on the idea of an isolated "Fortress America." In addition, a containment policy spoke in terms of the calculus of *power* and *self-interest*. American decision makers still included "liberty, freedom, and the personal dignity of man" in their calculations—after all, they had just waged war for those ideals. Containment may at times have little to do with such ideals.

As a policy, containment emerged fitfully. In February, 1947, the British government informed Washington that it no longer could afford to support its client states in the Mediterranean and asked the United States to pick up the burden. Truman was ready, but felt the Republican-dominated Congress would balk at the cost. He chose to win support by stressing the threat of communism to free peoples. The Congress accepted his March, 1947, proposal to aid the governments resisting communist-backed insurrections (as in Greece) or direct communist threats from the Soviet Union (as in Turkey). The Truman Doctrine, as it became known, represented an uneasy compromise of containment of Soviet power in the interests of "free people."[25]

[23]Cable #511, February 22, 1946; *FRUS*, p. 699. Kennan expanded the analysis considerably for publication in *Foreign Affairs*, 25 (July 1947), 566–82. In this article, he spoke of the need to contain Soviet power, thus giving a semi-official definition of American foreign policy goals.

[24]*FRUS*, Vol. VI, p. 707.

[25]See Joseph Jones, *The Fifteen Weeks* (New York: Viking, 1955); Barton Bernstein, ed., *Politics and Policies of the Truman Administration* (Chicago: Quadrangle, 1970); Richard Freeland, *The Truman Doctrine and the Origins of McCarthyism* (New York: Knopf, 1972); John Gimbel, *The Origins of the Marshall Plan* (Stanford: Stanford University Press, 1976).

Encouraged by its success in getting $400 million out of a Republican Congress, the Truman administration launched a more ambitious project of helping the recovery of the European economy. Preventing an economic collapse in Europe was attractive to a wide variety of policy makers. Those who drew lessons from the 1930s concluded that peace depended upon economic prosperity. Others wanted to preserve flourishing markets for American goods. And others saw economic decay as a fertile breeding ground for communism. Beginning in May, 1947, Secretary of State Marshall encouraged all European states to devise a unified plan to meet the economic crisis and make a request for American aid. The Western European states responded favorably. The Soviet Union and the East European states refused to participate. Truman requested some $4 billion in aid. Congressional opposition was far greater than for the aid to Greece and Turkey, but ended in February, 1948, when the communists in Czechoslovakia staged a coup that placed that state irrevocably behind the "iron curtain."

By 1948, the division of Europe had reached a point of no return. Western Europe, now tied to the American economy, had lost interest in reaching some form of settlement with the Soviet Union. Stalin, seeing the West achieving unity (and doing so in the name of anticommunism), chose to make Eastern Europe the path to Soviet security. Soviet control in the satellites increased, which collided with indigenous nationalism. Tito of Yugoslavia, to that point a Stalinist *par excellence*, rejected Soviet dictation, and was read out of the Socialist camp in the summer of 1948. As a consequence, the Greek civil war ended, as Yugoslavia no longer wanted to antagonize the West by providing arms and sanctuary to the communist insurgents. For the first (but not the last) time, a socialist state began to look toward capitalist states for protection from other socialist states.

The American policy of containment had a much more curious history in Asia.[26] Truman had inherited both Roosevelt's goal to make China into a major power and the fact that a bitter civil war between Nationalists and Communists had survived the war with Japan. During the war, the American government had tried to promote a coalition regime of Nationalists and Communists so that all Chinese power could be focused on defeating Japan. With the war over, Truman dispatched General Marshall to China in December, 1945, to secure that elusive coalition government. Marshall created several truces and an agreement in principle on a new political system. Although both sides sought to use the negotiations to their best advantage, the Nationalists were most successful, combining the talks with military initiatives to wrest areas out of Communist hands. In August, 1946, Truman imposed an arms embargo on the Nationalists in order to increase Marshall's bargaining leverage, but Marshall had to abandon his efforts in January, 1947, and returned, denouncing the hard-liners on both sides. The Nationalist forces quickly reached the limit of their success, and in mid-1947, the momentum swung to the Communists. In two years, without significant Soviet aid, the Communists pushed the Nationalists off the mainland, leaving the island of Formosa (Taiwan) the last redoubt of Chiang Kai-shek. American policy was erratic during the time—ending the arms embargo in May, 1947, then trying to

---

[26]For the Chinese civil war and the American involvement, see Tang Tsou, *America's Failure in China, 1941–1950* (Chicago: University of Chicago Press, 1963); Herbert Feis, *The China Tangle* (Princeton: Princeton University Press, 1953).

curtail arms deliveries—all the while increasingly unhappy about but resigned to the "fall of China." With the establishment of the People's Republic of China in October, 1949, the American administration sat back "to let the dust settle." It decided not to defend Formosa or to arm the Nationalists on Taiwan. Mao Tse-tung and the victorious communists began the difficult process of social revolution, and asked only to be left alone.

In the swirl of world politics in the late 1940s, there still remained "the German problem."[27] While peace treaties were quickly negotiated for Germany's European allies, no one could find the formula for Germany that would satisfy the Soviets and the French regarding security, or the United States regarding both economic self-sufficiency for Germany (felt to be a key for European economic recovery) and its future as a noncommunist state. Under Washington's leadership, the Western powers agreed to integrate their three occupation zones, allow the revival of a German economy, and move toward German self-government. The Soviets were given the choice of cooperation on Western terms or isolation.

Stalin, fearful that the West would rebuild Germany and turn it on the Soviet Union, ordered disruptions in the flow of rail, water, and land traffic to the Western sectors of Berlin. That failed to communicate Soviet interests effectively. When the West took practical steps to separate the Soviet zone from theirs by a currency reform, Stalin responded in June, 1948, with a complete surface blockade of Berlin. Truman rejected advice that the West negotiate its way *out* of Berlin or force its way *in*. Instead, he ordered an increase of deliveries of supplies to the Western sectors by aircraft. One year later, the blockade came to an end; the airlift had proved successful and the West had made no essential changes in its position. The division of Germany was complete.

Militarily and politically, the division of the European continent as a whole was also complete by the summer of 1949. With quiet American encouragement, the British, French, Dutch, and Belgians signed a fifty-year defensive alliance (March 1948). In June, 1948, the United States Senate passed a resolution expressing the willingness of the Senate and the Administration to join a defense agreement with interested European states. In April, 1949, the North Atlantic Treaty Organization came into being, committing the United States to consider an armed attack against one of its allies as an attack against itself. NATO completed the transformation of American foreign policy; this was the peace-time entangling alliance that American policy makers heretofore had assiduously avoided. The one small counterpoint to the treaty commitment was that the American government conceived its role as one of providing money and arms for the defense of Europe, not troops.

An Uncertain Future   By the end of the decade, an old world had disintegrated, and a new, unsteady, and ambiguous world had taken its place. Leaders of the major powers spoke in terms of the probability of war and the threat of world conquest, yet neither the Soviet Union nor the United States maintained

[27]For Germany, see Jean Smith, *The Defense of Berlin* (Baltimore: Johns Hopkins University Press, 1963); Lucius Clay, *Decision in Germany* (Garden City, N.Y.: Doubleday, 1950); Peter Merkl, *The Origin of the West German Republic* (New York: Oxford University Press, 1963); David Childs, *East Germany* (New York: Praeger, 1969).

anything like the eleven- to thirteen-million-man military establishments they had to defeat the Axis. Both probably asked, "What the hell does the other want?" (as an American Senator asked of the Soviets), and both increasingly assumed that the answer might be, "Just what Hitler wanted." For the Soviet Union, 1949 was *not* a year filled with hope: the West was united. China was united for the first time in forty years, under communists to be sure, but communists who had acted independently of Soviet direction. Even the successful test of a Soviet atomic device in August was a liability, for it might provoke a preemptive American attack while the Soviets had few deliverable atomic weapons.

But if the confrontations between the Soviet Union and the United States captured most of the headlines, a fundamental revolution was also occurring outside the traditional arenas of world politics. The immediate post-war period marked the beginning of *decolonization* and the entrance of scores of new nations into the political arena.[28] The war had played its role. The Japanese had demonstrated that Asiatics could confront white regimes. Many Asian nationalists got their first taste of self-rule under Japanese tutelage. Others, such as Ho Chi Minh in Indochina, expressed their nationalism and organizing abilities in anti-Japanese guerrilla movements. Only the most reactionary could not gauge the temper of the colonized world. Churchill had refused to consider any change in the British colonial system. Prime Minister Attlee could, and under his government, British India gained its independence in August, 1947. Intense hostility between Muslims and non-Muslims, however, forced the partition of the colony into Pakistan and India. Hundreds of thousands died in the social chaos that accompanied partition, and disputed territory (as in the Kashmir) continued to inflame hostility between the two new states. By 1949, Indonesians had broken the Dutch hold in the East Indies, and Arabic peoples had forced a withdrawal of British and French political control in the Middle East. The state of Israel emerged in May, 1948, as Britain ended its attempt to rule Palestine. In spite of quick recognition of Israel by the United States and the Soviet Union, Arab armies attacked Israel but were driven off. Only in the French and Portuguese governments was there still a fixation on preserving an empire.

Independence for colonial peoples increased the number of actors in world politics and the number of conflicts. Territorial issues, irredenta, claims to leadership, personal ambitions—all those afflictions of the "old" states were visited on the new as well. Thus, as the "old" powers attempted to come to terms with their post-war environment, the stability of the colonial system unraveled, leaving new regimes to learn the possibilities and problems of world politics, still unfreed peoples to strive for independence, and the major powers to ponder how they related to the changing colonial world and what their interests were. Stalin, for instance, saw the world divided into two camps, socialist and capitalist, which encouraged him to classify Indian nationalist leaders as "running dogs of capitalism" rather than as men and women who paid allegiance to neither camp. (An American response is examined in a succeeding section.)

This confluence of the Soviet-American Cold War and the liberation of the colonial world would create more than two decades of distinctive world politics. As the two events became intertwined, the major powers became far less able

---

[28]Studies of decolonization include Rupert Emerson, *From Empire to Nation* (Boston: Beacon Press, 1960); Francis Hutchins, *India's Revolution* (Cambridge: Harvard University Press, 1973).

to make world politics serve their individual interests. That, indeed, was revolutionary.

PART II:
SCIENTIFIC APPROACHES TO WORLD POLITICS

Domestic and Environmental Factor Approach:
Weapons and the Japanese Decision for War in 1941

Discussions today of neutron bombs and cruise missiles naturally seem to raise the question of whether armaments increase or decrease the likelihood of war. In our historical analyses we have encountered a related question of whether arms races lead to war.[29] I want to pose a general question and turn to the Japanese experience for some clues. The question is: Do well-armed states initiate warfare precisely because they are well armed? As with the analysis of ideology, I begin with the hypothesis that arms have an impact on state behavior, irrespective of the individuals who formally make decisions:

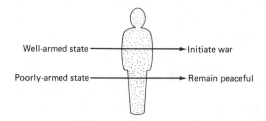

By the summer of 1941, Japanese political and military leadership had reached a consensus that Japanese expansion into Southeast Asia was vital for the economic survival and defense of Japan.[30] The question that remained was how to deal with the United States: by continuing the negotiations begun that spring to find a mutually acceptable accommodation, or to use force to move southward, even if it meant war with the United States? What role would weapons and their proposed deployment and employment play in answering that question?

We might begin with the general proposition that weapons by themselves force decision makers to perform a calculation that relates weapons to potential outcomes. In battle, so Confederate cavalry General Forrest once said, winning

[29]Arms race materials are plentiful: L.F. Richardson, *Arms and Insecurity* (Pacific Grove, Cal.: Boxwood Press, 1960); Samuel Huntington, "Arms Races," in *Public Policy*, ed. C. Friedrich and S. Harris (Cambridge: Harvard University Press, 1958), pp. 41–86; C.S. Gray, "The Arms Race Phenomenon," *World Politics*, 24 (October 1971), 39–79; Michael Wallace, "Arms Races and Escalation," *Journal of Conflict Resolution*, 23 (March 1979), 3–16.

[30]Basic sources for the 1941 decision include Robert Butow, *Tojo and the Coming of the War* (Princeton: Princeton University Press, 1961); David Bergamini, *Japan's Imperial Conspiracy* (New York: Morrow, 1971), Vol. II; Dorothy Borg and Shumpei Okamoto, eds. *Pearl Harbor as History* (New York: Columbia University Press, 1973); Nobutaka Ike, ed., *Japan's Decision for War* (Stanford: Stanford University Press, 1967); James Morley, ed., *Japan's Foreign Policy, 1868–1941* (New York: Columbia University Press, 1974).

went to the side that could "git thar fust with the most men." In its crudest form, the foreign policy calculation is "As we have more battalions (or battleships), we are likely to secure our policy goals in war"; or, "We have less, and are likely to lose." We would expect that when a state perceives a choice between war and peace, it would perform the calculation, and conclude as a Japanese general did: "We will go ahead if we perceive that conditions are extremely advantageous, and not go ahead if they are disadvantageous."[31]

How did the calculation appear to the Japanese? How advantageous were the conditions? As the Japanese navy was expected to bear the brunt of the war with the United States, I will concentrate on this aspect of the calculation.[32]

Weapons: 1. Japan had two battleships of the *Yamato* class (with more planned), which were faster and more powerful than any American ship.

2. Long-range, high-speed torpedoes for Japanese submarines and aircraft made American merchant and naval vessels extremely vulnerable. (The American navy had nothing comparable; its torpedoes of the time often bounced off a ship's side without exploding.)

3. Japanese naval aircraft, especially the Mitsubishi A6M "Zero," were superior to American naval aircraft and to many American land-based fighters.

Numbers: 4. Fleet strengths in the Pacific were relatively equal for Japan and the United States (counting the British Pacific fleet) except in the critical matter of aircraft carriers, where Japan had ten carriers to the American three.

Position: 5. The United States had to operate from distant naval bases, while the Japanese were better situated for naval combat in the western Pacific. The American colony and major military base in the Philippines was vulnerable to attack from Japan proper and from the Japanese colony of Formosa.

Strategy: 6. To use superior Japanese ground, naval, and air forces to seize the Philippines and force the American fleet to sail through hostile waters to relieve or recapture the islands. Submarines and land-based aircraft from Japanese islands in the Pacific would wage a war of attrition against the Americans. The unscathed Japanese main fleet would then engage the battered American fleet in a climactic battle.

7. In a daring addition to the plan (which only a few key leaders, including the Emperor, knew of until weeks before the attack), Japanese carriers would stage a lightning raid on the key American naval base at Pearl Harbor to destroy the battleships and carriers before they could even sail.

8. Even if the Americans did not try to relieve the Philippines, rapid Japanese naval and ground advances in Southeast Asia would create a security perimeter in which the Americans would gradually wear themselves down trying to batter their way through.

[31]Army Vice Chief of Staff Tsukada; Liaison Conference of June 26, 1941; in Ike, *Japan's Decision*, p. 63.

[32]Stephen Pelz, *Race to Pearl Harbor* (Cambridge: Harvard University Press, 1974), pp. 25–40; Clay Blair, *Silent Victory* (Philadelphia: Lippincott, 1975); Stephen Roskill, *The War at Sea* (London: Her Majesty's Stationery Office, 1954), Vol. I, pp. 560–61.

This estimation of naval power augered well; the estimates from the army were similar. By the fall of 1941, Japan's military leaders felt confident they could achieve initial victories over the United States and Britain, whose forces in the western Pacific were scattered (which meant the Japanese could concentrate theirs to have more "battalions and battleships" at critical points) while the American navy was concentrated but unsuspecting at Pearl Harbor. Clearly, then, our factor approach suggests that this equation was at work:

weapons————————→ calculated advantage ————————→ attack

Yet, this model predicts that any state that finds a favorable equation will attack. Many states should therefore be constantly at war, and that just does not accord with the historical record. In fact, in our case, the Japanese government still hesitated, even after the military presented their favorable conclusions. What might interfere with the operation of the model stipulated above? Some hesitancy may lie in the common belief that the gods of war do not always play by the equation. Indeed, the Japanese themselves had been numerically inferior in their 1904–1905 naval battles with the Russians, yet they had won. They attributed victory to superior morale and training. In 1941, they assumed they still had the edge in these matters, so they were less prone to worry about the mischief of luck and accident.

Hesitancy in the Japanese case came more from the uncertainty about the calculation projected into the future. Unlike their confidence of victory in the opening months of the war, the Japanese were more doubtful of success in a prolonged war, one in which the United States would be able to bring to bear "her impregnable position, her superior industrial power, and her abundant resources."[33] *And the leaders felt reasonably sure that the United States would wage a prolonged war.* Even the war hawks in the military conceded that "we must spare no efforts in seeking a way to settle the present difficult situation peacefully. . . . We must never fight a war that can be avoided."[34] It seemed, therefore, to be an uncertainty about the long run and a general feeling that peaceful avenues had to be exhausted first that encouraged hesitancy. That leaves us with the question, Why does a state conclude that peaceful solutions are *not* possible and war is *not* avoidable? There are many potential answers; our interest here is the role weapons might play. How might weapons encourage, if not force, a decision for war rather than allow diplomacy to grind on, or have the state reevaluate its goals, or encourage another, nonbelligerent tack? Four forces seem to be at work:

1. *Weapons create and maintain the prominence of the war option.* When nations are in conflict, armaments increase the visibility of the war option. In Japan, this visibility was enhanced by two factors: a history of intense political activism and policy advocacy by members of the Japanese armed services, and the control the services had over the appointment of the ministers of navy and war (and, in effect, over the cabinet itself). Weapons and the policies that employ them also

---

[33]Navy Chief of Staff Nagano, Imperial Conference of September 6, 1941; Ike, *Japan's Decision*, p. 139.

[34]Nagano, September 6, 1941; *ibid.*, p. 140.

carry the reputation of providing quick and decisive settlements—at least once Hitler had demonstrated that World War I need not be repeated. Compared to the indecision and painful slowness of diplomacy, weapons make a war option attractive. The availability of the war option and its attractiveness may encourage many to say, "The situation is urgent. We want it decided one way or another quickly."[35]

2. *Weapons engender a sense of machismo.*[36] The presence of weapons and the war option may encourage leaders to be more willing to take risks, to make "hard" decisions. In addition to psychological considerations,[37] there are social pressures. Leaders have reputations to maintain; failure to meet others' expectations reduces a leader's ability to command, something no leader readily wishes to lose. In the critical November 1st debate in the Japanese government on the war issue, Naval Minister Shimada (an admiral) tried to support the peace option. He suggested that Japan pursue a negotiated settlement right up to the date set for war. He was answered by the Army Vice Chief of Staff: "Please keep quiet. What you've just said won't do."[38] That such a rebuke could be voiced by a lower-ranking officer from another service and remain unanswered by other navy officers indicates how little clout Shimada had. The foreign minister suffered a similar fate. Those who do not "talk weapons" are often considered weak and their proposals worthless.

3. *Weapons create the perception that the opportunity for success is fast fading and the costs of not using weapons are fast rising.* Having weapons may create the impression that unless they are used now, the enemy will be stronger tomorrow. We observed one aspect of this in the analysis of World War I—Germany felt it had to strike first before its military power was overwhelmed by Russia and France. Japan's planners had similar fears; every month that went by, they argued, the naval balance would tip further against Japan as the American rearmament program reached high gear. "When can we go to war and win?" asked the Finance Minister. "Now!" roared Admiral Nagano. "The time for war will not come later!"[39] Waiting too long would, in this view, ensure the defeat of the Empire. Apparently Japanese decision makers clearly saw defeat only as a consequence of hesitation; at worst, selecting the war option now would produce a costly stalemate with the United States.

4. *Weapons lead attention away from careful consideration of goals and focus it on the use of the weapons.* The Emperor appears to have consistently held doubts about a successful outcome of war and tried to keep the government sensitive to such issues. In the end, however, he too appears to have succumbed to a fixation on the technical aspects of the proposed war. The raid on Pearl Harbor and the elaborate plans for the invasion of Malaya and the Dutch East Indies took creativity and energy in planning and preparation. The successful training of air crews to perform torpedo attacks in shallow waters fueled the impetus to stage the attack at

[35]Nagano, Liaison conference, October 23, 1941; *ibid.*, p. 186.

[36]Richard Barnet, *Roots of War* (New York: Atheneum, 1972), pp. 109–15.

[37]See L. Berkowitz and N. LePage, "Weapons as Aggression-Eliciting Stimuli," *Journal of Personality and Social Psychology*, 7 (1967), 202–7.

[38]Ike, *Japan's Decision*, p. 203.

[39]Liaison conference, November 1, 1941; *ibid.*, p. 202.

Pearl Harbor. Dealing with the technical questions of "Can it be done with these weapons?" made the leaders less likely to ask "should it be done?"

The Japanese sailed toward their rendezvous with destiny with this overall assessment, voiced by Emperor Hirohito:

> I will put my trust in what I have been told: namely, that things will go well in the early part of the war; and that although we will experience increasing difficulties as the war progresses, there is some prospect of success.[40]

Our brief study suggests that weapons themselves created pressure for war, in spite of the gloomy prognosis for long-term success.

Policy-Making Approach:
The State Department and the Response
to Vietnamese Nationalism in the 1940s[41]

French Indochina (Vietnam, Cambodia, and Laos) had the reputation of being one of the most exploitive colonial regimes (see map 7–2). During much of the war, the Vichy French conscientiously administered the colony under Japanese direction. Resistance to the Japanese came from the Indochinese themselves. In the forefront was the Viet Minh (Vietnamese Independence League), led by Ho Chi Minh, a member of the Indochinese Communist Party. The Viet Minh appealed to a broad spectrum of Vietnamese with its anti-Japanese, anti-French, pro-national liberation platform. As a military force, it amounted to little.

American military strategy bypassed Indochina. The political issues, however, could not be so easily avoided. Would the United States permit France to recover the colony when Japan surrendered? What stance would the United States take toward Vietnamese nationalists such as Ho and movements such as the Viet Minh? To explore and explain the American response, I will examine a critical component of the policy-making approach: the *organizations* in which and through which policy is made and implemented.[42]

An organization can be thought of as a collection of hierarchically arranged positions which communicate and process information. Information enters the organization, individuals make various kinds of decisions based on that information, and issue directives. The directives constitute the state's foreign policy. Organizations cannot, however, take the time to handle information, decisions, or directives as separate, unique things. There are neither the time nor the re-

---

[40]Imperial conference, November 5, 1941; *ibid.*, p. 236. As was the custom, the words were spoken by a court official.

[41]For studies in Indochina during this period, see Joseph Siracusa, "FDR, Truman, and Indochina, 1941–1952," in *The Impact of the Cold War*, ed. Joseph Siracusa and Glen Barclay (Port Washington, N.Y.: Kennikat Press, 1977), pp. 163–83; Ellen Hammer, *The Struggle for Indochina* (Stanford: Stanford University Press, 1966); Lucien Bodard, *The Quicksand War* (Boston: Little, Brown, 1967).

[42]For a careful exposition of the organizational model, see Graham Allison, *Essence of Decision* (Boston: Little, Brown, 1971).

sources. Instead, organizations create specific *routines* or standardized ways of handling information, making decisions, or implementing directives. Thus, in general, if we know an organization's routines, we can explain why policy is as it is, for policy itself is the mixture of organizational routines.

To illustrate this approach, I will concentrate on the Department of State and, to a lesser degree, the Office of Strategic Services (OSS), which was the forerunner of the Central Intelligence Agency.[43] In organizational terms, in 1945–1946, the Department of State had the general configuration depicted in Figure 6–2.

This kind of organizational structure is typical of bureaucracies that handle foreign policy. The French desk, for instance, is staffed by a group of professional diplomats (called Foreign Service Officers in the American organization) who handle matters relating to American relations with France. They report to the head of the Division of West European Affairs (WE), who also receives reports from the United Kingdom desk, the Spanish desk, and so forth. His or her superior is an Assistant Secretary of State for European Affairs, who receives reports from WE and others such as the Division of East European Affairs. Assistant Secretaries report to the Secretary of State or his/her deputies. As one goes up the chain of command, the volume of information decreases, issues become more general, and directives broaden. Most decisions are made at the lower levels of the bureaucracy, following general guidance from above. Decisions, as well as interpretations of information, are usually made in accordance with routines established in each bureaucratic layer.

FIGURE 6–2   Department of State

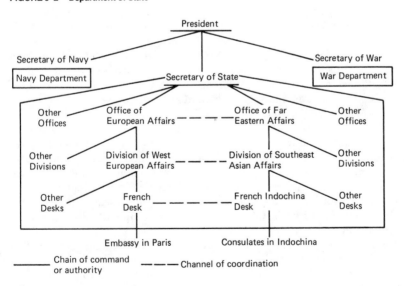

[43]Descriptions of the Department of State and the OSS can be found in Burtin Sapin, *The Making of United States Foreign Policy* (New York: Praeger, 1966) and Harris Smith, *OSS* (Berkeley: University of California Press, 1972).

Until the spring of 1944, the French desk and WE handled questions regarding the French colony of Indochina. They defined their principal mission as restoring France to its former status as a great power. Colonial questions were perceived in this light, which meant that WE favored the restoration of French colonial control. If there were to be a change in status of the colony, the French should be free to make the decision. In 1944, however, WE acquired a rival with the creation of the Division of Southeast Asian Affairs (SEA). The new French Indochina desk in SEA was given jurisdiction over Indochinese matters as well. SEA, searching for guidance in order to determine its mission (that is, its routine), took as its guidepost Roosevelt's known anticolonialist sentiments, his stated opinion that the Indochinese deserved something better than French imperialism, and a comment he had penned on a memo: "No French help in Indochina—country on trusteeship."[44] Its organizational goal became the promotion of independence for the colonies in the area on a relatively rapid timetable.

It is not uncommon to find different components of an organization sharing jurisdiction, as WE and SEA did in Indochina. Shared jurisdiction meant that neither could act without the concurrence of the other. Without concurrence, there could be no decisions. That in turn meant that American policy would either be a compromise or, failing that, a policy of drift (doing nothing more than had already been agreed on, even though circumstances might change dramatically). To compound matters, SEA and WE were under orders "not to kick their disagreements upstairs." The Assistant Secretaries of Far Eastern Affairs and European Affairs had enough to contend with without becoming involved in squabbles over Indochina policy. Roosevelt himself wanted to defer dealing with the matter until after the war.

We have seen that WE and SEA had quite different perspectives on Indochina. The more the respective offices dealt with the issues, the more sympathetic they became to the interests of the French and of the colonial peoples. As you might suspect, they found it difficult to bridge their different perspectives, and policy drifted. Thus in 1944–45, State generally avoided making decisions. Roosevelt remained content with a diplomatic policy that verbally supported decolonization, but he was increasingly reluctant to apply pressure, especially in ways that would alienate Britain.

Foreign policy, however, is never just the organizational response of a State Department or a foreign ministry. Other organizations enact routines abroad as well. One such organization was the OSS, an autonomous agency reporting to Roosevelt. Its mission was to conduct unconventional war against the Axis, and, as a part of its routine, it worked with anyone actively fighting the Japanese. OSS built (over French objections) an espionage-guerrilla-pilot rescue network in Indochina. By the spring of 1945, OSS agents had linked up with Vietnamese resistance units and Ho Chi Minh, providing weapons, training, and advice. Thus, if we looked at American policy behavior in 1945, we might conclude that it was to support Vietnamese nationalists and spurn the French.

When Roosevelt died in April, 1945, both WE and SEA scrambled to prepare position papers for the new President. Similar bureaucratic activities take

---

[44]Testimony of Abbot Moffat, former Chief SEA; Hearings, May 9–11, 1972; Committee on Foreign Relations, *Hearings: Causes, Origins, and Lessons of the Vietnam War* (Washington: Government Printing Office, 1973), p. 164.

place whenever an administration changes, because here is a chance to get the support of powerful figures for an organization's perspectives and routines. WE's draft on Indochina policy declared that while the United States should encourage liberalization, it "should neither oppose the restoration of Indochina to France . . . nor take any action toward French overseas possessions which it is not prepared to take or suggest with regard to the colonial possessions of our other Allies."[45] SEA's draft argued that peace and stability in Southeast Asia would depend upon granting self-government. If one did not accommodate the independence movements (and this meant pressuring the French), "the peoples of Southeast Asia may embrace ideologies contrary to our own or develop a pan-Asiatic movement against all Western powers."[46]

Once again, SEA and WE could not agree on a common draft, and when "kicked upstairs" to the Assistant Secretary level, the stalemate continued. No paper reached the President, and Truman remained unguided in these matters and unaware of the conflicting viewpoints. When the Japanese surrendered in August, war-making was no longer the order of the day. OSS terminated its routine of arming Vietnamese nationalists and became essentially a conveyor of information. Even that role ended in September, 1945, when Truman disbanded the organization (equating it with the Gestapo!). Without OSS activity, "drift" became the pervasive aspect of American policy.

Following Japan's surrender, Chinese forces occupied the northern half of Indochina to disarm the Japanese, while British forces occupied the southern half. The Viet Minh established a provisional government for Indochina. French officials, however, announced they would restore French control, by force if necessary. Pressed by events, the State Department reached a compromise policy position:

> U.S. has no thought of opposing the reestablishment of French control in Indochina and no official statement by U.S. Government has questioned even by implication French sovereignty over Indochina. However, it is not the policy of this government to assist the French to reestablish their control over Indochina by force and the willingness of the U.S. to see French control reestablished assumes that French claim to have the support of the population of Indochina is borne out by future events.[47]

The first sentence reflected WE's position; the second, SEA's. Examined closely, however, it still is a policy of drift, in that the United States would leave it up to the French and Vietnamese to decide the future of the colony. That might have been wise policy, but it was not the result of conscious decision making. It was the product of organizational stalemates.

One year later, however, State had a policy that was essentially anti-Vietnamese. While still uneasy about French reestablishing control by force, the American government had no interest in confronting France on the issue. What had happened? In part, the policy of drift had been "overtaken by events." With

[45]Draft memorandum with cover letter of April 20, 1945; Department of Defense, *United States–Vietnam Relations, 1945–1967* (Washington: Government Printing Office, 1971), Book 8, p. 7. (Cited hereafter as the *Pentagon Papers*.)

[46]Far East's memo of April 21, 1945; in *ibid.*, p. 11.

[47]Cable to New Delhi and Chunking, October 5, 1945; *ibid.*, p. 49.

the connivance of the British, French forces entered southern Indochina, ousted the Viet Minh, and recreated the colonial regime in the south (November). In the north, they negotiated with Ho and began a naval buildup in the surrounding waters. Ho also had to worry about the Chinese Nationalist troops in his country—China had a long history of imperialism in the region. He reluctantly adopted the philosophy that "it was better to sniff the French dung for a while than eat China's all our lives,"[48] and allowed the French to regarrison the north in place of the Chinese (March 1946). The Viet Minh government would continue while Ho and the French negotiated a definitive political settlement.

The March agreement allowed the State Department to open consulates in Saigon and Hanoi, giving the State Department direct access to information. Prior to this, State's information came from French and Chinese official sources (both hostile to Vietnamese nationalism and communism); from the OSS (generally sympathetic to Vietnamese nationalism but aware of Ho and the Viet Minh's links with communism); and from travelling American military personnel and occasional SEA officials sent on quick inspections. The picture they presented of Ho and the Viet Minh was mixed: nationalist, anti-French, friendly toward the United States, and communist or leftist. SEA's interpretation of the information followed a routine, probably best expressed this way:

> I have never met an American, be he military, OSS, diplomat, or journalist, who had met Ho Chi Minh who did not reach the same belief: that Ho Chi Minh was first and foremost a Vietnamese nationalist. He was also a Communist and believed that Communism offered the best hope for the Vietnamese people. But his loyalty was to his people.[49]

WE's approach was to reverse the emphasis: first and foremost a communist; secondly, anti-French.

In the summer of 1946, negotiations between Ho and the French collapsed and military clashes began. The French, wanting American support for the reconquest of the north, began to emphasize Ho's past (he had been a Comintern agent), his present communism, and his alleged subservience to the Soviet Union. These allegations, especially the last, could not be ignored. A directive went out in September instructing the consulates in Indochina to look for indications of communist activities and Ho's subservience to Moscow. To this point, the consulates' reports had not said much in this regard, but with the directive to establish a particular routine of information collection and interpretation, that changed. The Saigon consulate, relying on the French who controlled the south, reported evidence of increased communist activities and the possible presence of Chinese communists. By December (after the French opened their November offensive to reconquer the north), Saigon cabled: "Majority my contacts confirm generally development of Communist setup in FIC [French Indochina]."[50] The officials in the Hanoi consulate—closer to the scene and with a wider variety of contacts—

[48]Quoted by Jean Lacouture, *Ho Chi Minh*, trans. Peter Wiles (New York: Random House, Inc., 1968), p. 119.

[49]Moffat testimony, May 1972; Foreign Relations Committee, *Hearings*, p. 169.

[50]Cable of Vice Consul at Saigon, December 2, 1946, in *Pentagon Papers*, Book 8, p. 83.

found very little to report about Ho's contacts with communists! The information, nonetheless, seemed to confirm the view of WE that larger issues were involved than just those of colonialism and nationalism. Under pressure from WE and in the face of the new, Department-wide routine of containment that began to emerge, SEA's perspectives began to shift as well. In December, 1946, a new routine had crystallized. The Department identified something to be avoided: "Least desirable eventuality would be establishment [of] Communist dominated, Moscow-oriented state [in] Indochina."[51] That was a possibility, given "Ho's clear record as agent of international communism [and] absence [of] evidence [of] recantation [of] Moscow affiliations."[52]

With this new routine, organizations would develop information, make decisions, and issue directives in ways that would support the French colonial interests over Vietnamese (albeit communist) nationalism and increasingly condition the organizations to act as if the United States had an important interest in preventing communist rule in Vietnam. As we shall see, those routines made increased American involvement in the 1950s and 1960s an expected organizational output of American foreign policy. Did such routines characterize all American policy toward anticolonialist movements? The answer is "no, but. . . ." Generally, the routines supporting decolonization persisted. However, where communists were thought to be involved, the pressure was there to adopt the routine of "avoid the communist state at almost any cost." But the organizational model in the study of policy making suggests that routines will vary across the components of organizations. In particular components, a willingness to tolerate communists or leftists or anti-American nationalists may be relatively strong. Fidel Castro would come to power in Cuba in 1959 with support from sections of the Department of State.

Interaction Approach:
A Pattern Analysis of the Soviet-American Cold War

We have observed the growth of hostility between the Soviet Union and the United States in the post-war period. What brought on this Cold War between former allies, between leaders who, in Roosevelt's phrase, could talk "like men and brothers"?[53] Any one of the approaches we have discussed would provide a distinctive answer, and the subject has certainly fascinated scholars. The diplomatic history section suggested such causes as a clash between American idealism and Soviet power politics, and a mutual effort to contain each other's power and influence. The next section on the systems approach invites you to consider the Cold War as a systemic event. In this section, I will employ the *analysis of interaction patterns*.

It has often been said, with much lamentation, that American foreign policy is one of reaction—not of the political kind (although that argument has been

---

[51]Cable to A. Moffat, December 5, 1946; *ibid.*, p. 85.

[52]*Ibid.*

[53]Roosevelt's description of Teheran to Frances Perkins, *The Roosevelt I Knew* (New York: Viking, 1946), p. 85. From THE ROOSEVELT I KNEW by Frances Perkins. Copyright 1946 by Frances Perkins. Copyright renewed by Susanna W. Coggeshall. Reprinted by permission of Viking Penguin Inc.

made, too), but of the interactive kind. That is, as a democracy with a slow political process, the United States, more often than not, reacts to the behavior of other states rather than initiating policy. Conversely, authoritarian states, responsive to one or few leaders, are said to initiate more often than react. Many of the traditional explanations of the Cold War use this action-reaction model:[54]

SOVIET UNION

UNITED STATES

| Action |------------→| Reaction |

Block decisions on
German economy

Integration of Western
occupation zones

Taken a step further, we can add a "feedback loop" and create a chain of events:

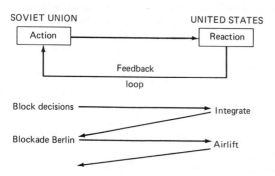

SOVIET UNION

UNITED STATES

| Action |------------→| Reaction |

Feedback
loop

Block decisions ————————→ Integrate

Blockade Berlin ←————— Airlift

If, on the other hand, you are attracted to what is known as the revisionist view of American foreign policy,[55] you simply switch the actors around: the United States, out to protect and expand its (capitalist) economic control, took the initiative in the post-war world, challenging a weak Soviet Union whose policies were thus reactions to the American thrusts.

Either way you choose to see the actors, the essence of the explanation is that every state's behavior is a reaction to another state's behavior. Before you become too certain that this is self-evident, note that this model rules out the importance of domestic and environmental factors (the American public's growing concern about domestic communism? the enormous damage suffered by the Soviet Union?); it rules out the importance of individual policy makers (Truman's pugnaciousness? Stalin's paranoia?) and the policy process (organizational routines? compromise policies?). Equally important, the model, as stated, does not help us get very far with a "scientific" analysis of world politics, because it does not search for *patterns*, the stuff from which we try to draw generalizations. As long as we treat each action and reaction as a discrete event, explained by the preceding event, we continue to employ the *historical* approach.

[54]Traditionalists include Feis, *From Trust*; Adam Ulam, *Expansion and Coexistence*, rev. ed. (New York: Praeger, 1974); Louis Halle, *The Cold War as History* (New York: Harper & Row, Pub., 1967).

[55]Revisionists include D.F. Fleming, *The Cold War and Its Origins* (Garden City, N.Y.: Doubleday, 1961); David Horowitz, *Free World Colossus* (New York: Hill and Wang, 1965); Joyce Kolko and Gabriel Kolko, *The Limits of Power* (New York: Harper & Row, Pub., 1972).

For a scientific approach, we need to identify action/reaction sequences that, in their general form, occur time and again in world politics. Figure 1–1 sketched one such sequence, called the "escalation pattern." That pattern can be depicted as:

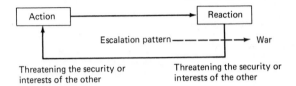

Another common pattern is that of an arms race:

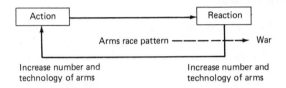

We use the terms "escalation" and "arms race" to describe the *interaction* between the states, an interaction dependent upon specific behaviors. The dashed line suggests that one type of interaction may eventuate in another pattern of interaction. "War" in this view is a particular pattern of interactions, having its own action/reaction sequence, and may itself produce other patterns:

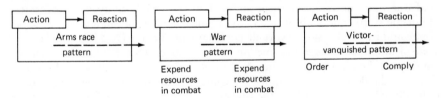

From this perspective, world politics is an enormous collection of patterned interactions, some stable (as the war pattern was from 1939–1945), others transforming themselves. Notice that the *explanation* of a particular pattern comes from the actions of the states, which in turn are predetermined by the behavior of the other in a predictable way. In addition, as the figure above implies, our understanding of world politics also necessitates an explanation of how and why one pattern becomes transformed into another.

Let us turn our attention to the *Cold War as a pattern of interaction*. What follows is a speculative illustration of the approach. It begins with the hypothesis that the Cold War was a consequence of an alliance of necessity during World War II. It further hypothesizes that there was an intermediate pattern between the wartime pattern and the cold-war pattern, in which both states in the interaction recognized that they were not allies who could get along "like men and brothers." Figure 6–3 summarizes the major types of behaviors we would expect to find in the transition period in a cold war.

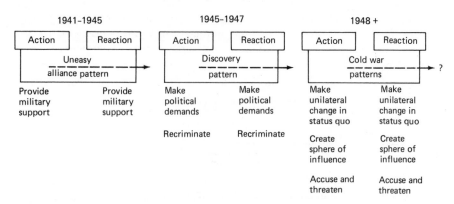

FIGURE 6-3   Pattern Analysis: Transition to the Cold War

A closer inspection of the historic post-war period provides more details of the particular action/reaction patterns that together comprise the overall patterns I have labelled "discovery" and "cold war." I selected two time periods for the analysis. Tables 6-1 and 6-2 provide those details. By extension, the hypothesis argues that these are the kinds of patterns we would expect to find between any two states on the road to or engaged in a cold war. Will, for instance, Chinese Communist and Soviet behavior show these characteristics in the coming decades?

Some of the patterns of the "discovery" period appear to set the stage for the Cold War, especially in terms of the mutual suspicions generated and the ambiguous nature of the status quo and each state's interests in the status quo. The cold-war patterns replaced suspicion with confirmed hostility and uneasiness about the status quo with an effort to organize spheres of influence in order to create and freeze the most favorable environment. Yet the Cold War was not devoid of attempts to negotiate meaningfully (Pattern IX). Diplomatic relations continued, the United States and the Soviet Union occasionally agreed on such things as the desirability of a quick recognition of the state of Israel, and "little" obligations were met, such as the Soviet return of the cruiser *Milwaukee*, which they had received as a part of Lend-Lease.

If we were to predict much of world politics in the next decade, pattern analysis would suggest that both states would:

1. make major proposals both for propaganda and for serious purposes;
2. continue to draw lines and express a commitment to defend certain areas of the world;
3. work to organize those areas into its own camp;
4. challenge the status quo; and,
5. make mutual adjustments for mutually nonrewarding situations.

We would make those predictions because our model says that states act in patterned ways in response to each other. As to when these "cold war" patterns might end and what would replace them, that remained a nagging question for statesmen and citizens. A "hot war" pattern appeared all too likely.

PATTERN	ACTION/REACTION SEQUENCE	RESULTANT	EXAMPLES
I. Truncated negotiation	1. Both express unhappiness at lack of agreement 2. New agreement in principle 3. Deadlock on specifics	A. Gradual production of partial agreement B. New status quo C. Suspicion of intentions	Peace treaties with Italy and minor Axis states
II. Implementation avoidance	1. Request implementation of previous agreement 2. Acceptance by other 3. Ineffective implementation by other	A. Status quo remains B. Suspicion of intentions	Soviet-sponsored governments in East Europe accept concept of democratization but control political process. US agrees to Soviet participation in occupation of Japan but keeps effective control in MacArthur's hands
III. Advance proposals	1. Propose x 2. Counter-propose y	A. Status quo B. Propaganda battles	July, 1946, proposals to deal with atomic weapons. US (Baruch) plan called for US retention of the bomb until an international agency had been created to prevent production of atomic weapons; Soviet plan called for abolition first, then controls
IV. Allege inappropriate behavior	1. Allege with regret inappropriate behavior by other 2. Deny and counterallege with regret	A. Suspicion of intentions	Both states declared themselves in favor of peace, sometimes said the other did as well, but "the United States is trying to impose its will on the Soviet Union" or "the Soviet Union has shown aloofness, coolness, and hostility to our proposals"
V. Unilateral challenge to status quo and response	1. Use position to change status quo 2. Protest by other 3. Consolidate change 4. Threaten 5. Restore status quo or slow down rate of change	A. Suspicion of intentions B. Fear C. Potentially uncontrolled or uncontrollable change in status quo	Soviet activities in northern Iran; US proposals for integration of German occupation zones

TABLE 6-2 Cold War Pattern: Soviet-American Relations in 1949

PATTERN	ACTION/REACTION SEQUENCE	RESULTANT	EXAMPLES
III. Advance proposals	1. Propose x 2. Counter-propose y	A. Status quo B. Propaganda battles	Atomic plans; Soviet proposal for a Big Five non-aggression pact brought US counter-proposal that USSR live up to UN Charter
Va. Unilateral challenge to status quo and response	1. Use position to change status quo 2. Protest by other 3. Consolidate change 4. Threaten 5. Continue consolidation	A. Competitive reordering of status quo B. Institutionalization	The integration of Western Germany; the political integration of Eastern Europe
VI. Institutionalization of opposition	1. Create or expand an entity and its functions 2. Create or expand a counter-entity and its functions	A. Mutual political iron curtains B. Demarcated spheres of influence	West creates West German state; Soviets create East German state. US agrees to integrate West Germany into European political structures; Soviets integrate East Germany into eastern economic system
VII. Harass	1. Take small, negative action 2. Protest, deny	A. Perception of unvarying hostility	US requests UN investigation of Soviet "slave labor systems"; Soviets periodically disrupt traffic to Berlin; indictment of Soviet trade officials in US
VIII. Line-drawing	1. Assert other has hostile intentions 2. Counter-assert and pledge to fight	A. Commitments made B. Prestige engaged; hostility perceived and projected	Truman pledged democracy's full support in the battle against communism; Soviet Defense minister called for high level of military preparedness in face of US policy of aggression; Truman declared US would not hesitate to use atomic weapons again
IX. Mutual agreement	1. Propose end to behavior costly to both 2. Agree	A. Removal of irritant B. Conclusion that other learned its lesson	Soviets proposed to end Berlin blockade in return for ending Western counterblockade against Soviet zone and calling of Foreign Ministers' conference to discuss Germany

Systems Approach: A New World

By 1939, power distribution had reverted to a ladder-like configuration. The states polarized (but not entirely as expected, given the Soviet defection from the Western allies), war began, and ground through six years. The historical approach indicated that it was not foreordained that the war would end with the destruction of Germany. Indeed, an examination of power distribution suggests how close the contest was:[56]

	Early 1940	Mid-1942	Mid-1944
Germany, Axis states, and German-occupied territory	18	26	21
Allied powers	12	27	29

World War II did have enormous consequences for the distribution of power in the post-war era. Germany and Japan no longer were actors in world politics; both were occupied, and Germany was dismembered. France and Britain had suffered six years of war; the Soviets, four. The critical change, however, was in the position of the United States. It had again entered European politics but, unlike in 1920, now resolutely refused to disengage itself. Given its innate power and new commitment to world politics, the arena of world politics shifted to the North Atlantic (and with less certainty into the Western Pacific). Equally important, the ability of the United States to project its power had expanded during the war. Its long-range bombers could reach Europe in a day; an atomic bomb gave each bomber enormous power to cripple another's society. Thus, in the post-war period, American power was relatively undiluted in the cockpit of major power politics. How would the power structure of 1947 appear?

As before, I have used the factors of steel production, energy production, population, and political stability to make such an estimate. Because of the nature of the war, I have modified the political stability scores to reflect what happened politically during and immediately after the war.[57] In addition, I added a new power factor: the percentage of the world's nuclear weapons that each state is able to deliver to strategic (as opposed to battlefield) targets. The only strategic delivery system at the time was the bomber, so the number of bombs *and* strategic bombers becomes the measure of the state's power in this area. Nuclear weapons and their delivery systems are unique elements of military power and have since 1945 given their possessor prestige. Equally important, they are also a gauge of the technological sophistication and resources of the state. They represent capabilities in such areas as theoretical and high-energy physics, computer systems, engineering (as in space exploration), and communication systems. Those aspects of power became increasingly important in the post-war period. Table 6–3 reports the calculation of power. Figure 6–4 makes its own graphic statement.

[56]Figures based only on steel production; from Duncan Burn, *The Steel Industry, 1939–1959* (Cambridge: Cambridge University Press, 1961), Table 105. I estimated the figures for German-occupied territory and calculated U.S. power as projectable (four days).

[57]Scoring of political stability as follows: country neither occupied nor directly attacked, no domestic turmoil: 1.0; country directly attacked but not occupied, no domestic turmoil: .9; attacked and partially occupied: .7; occupied, no major changes in pre- and post-war regime: .5; occupied, post-war change in regime: .3; civil war: 0.

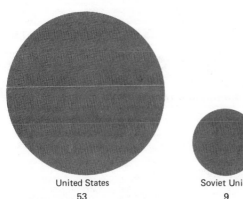

United States	Soviet Union	Great Britain	France	Poland
53	9	6	1	1

FIGURE 6-4   Power Distribution in 1947

This is clearly a system different from any we have observed so far. Even if we remove the nuclear power component, the gross disparity in power remains. Even if we assume that the power of Eastern Europe is there for the Soviets to do with as they will, Soviet power will not rise significantly, because of the weakness of those states. In this system, one state is clearly predominant, far overshadowing the other actors.

What set of rules might this structure dictate? I am going to leave it to you to answer that. Chapter 1 offered three ways one might construct a set of rules for any system. I'll review them here and point out some of the things that are striking to me:

1. What rules seem to be apparent in the *logic* of the structure? Does an extremely powerful actor (let us call it a "superpower") have certain incentives to behave in certain ways? Are there inhibitions? At this time, there are approximately sixty independent states. A coalition of all those states might theoretically balance the superpower, but imagine the difficulty in coordinating the policy and power of sixty states, or even twenty, or ten, each with a small fraction of the world's power.

2. Are there analogous power structures? Chapter 1 raised the possibility that the classroom approximates this distribution of power. What rules describe the classroom behavior for the teacher and any individual student? Are there possible applications to this international system?

3. Does the historical record illustrate state behaviors that may be in accord with system rules? Recall that all state behavior may *not* be in response to the system; environmental events may break through the boundary to compel states to act in opposition to the rules. The previous section described some particular patterns of behavior. Given this distribution of power in the post-war period, would you have predicted a period of "discovery" followed by "cold war?" Was the Cold War dictated by the system?

I confess that I have wrestled with these questions. My tentative answers appear in the next chapter. As you will see, this particular power structure will persist for some time, so the next chapter is a convenient place to talk about systemic explanations. Work out your own responses and we will compare notes later.

TABLE 6–3   Basic Power Levels in 1947

MEASURE	WORLD	US	USSR	UK	FRANCE	CHINA
1. Million metric tons of crude steel	106	59.5	13.1	12.7	4.3	
2. Percent of world steel		54%	12%	12%	2%	0%
3. Million inhabitants in independent states	1379	141	193	49	41	456
4. Percent of world population in independent states		10%	14%	4%	3%	33%
5. Political stability		1.0	.7	.9	.3	0
6. Energy production in million metric tons of coal equivalent	2475	1206	292	220	54	43
7. Percent of world energy production		49%	12%	9%	2%	2%
8. Nuclear weapons with strategic delivery systems	25–50	25–50				
9. Percent of deliverable nuclear power		100%	0%	0%	0%	0%
Power*		53	9	6	1	<1

$$*\text{Power} = \frac{\#2 + (\#4 \times \#5) + \#7 + \#9}{4}$$

Sources: For steel and energy, see Table 4–1; for population, United Nations, *Statistical Yearbook 1948* (Lake Success, N.Y.: United Nations, 1949), Table 1; for political stability, William Langer, *An Encyclopedia of World History*, 4th ed. (New York: Houghton Mifflin, 1968); for nuclear weapons and delivery systems, George Quester, *Nuclear Diplomacy* (New York: Dunellen, 1970), Chapter 1 and p. 295.

CHAPTER SEVEN

1950–1959
An uncertain coexistence at midcentury

Korea and the American Response

Josef Stalin had turned 70 in 1949. The Soviet media extolled him to the skies (perhaps beyond: "He was addressed as Father of the Peoples, the Greatest Genius in History, Friend and Teacher of All Toilers, Shining Sun of Humanity, and Life-giving Force of Socialism."[2]). The security organs tracked down those who did not echo this "cult of personality."[3] Yet Stalin had begun to show signs

---

[1]General studies include Walter LaFeber, *America, Russia and the Cold War*, 4th ed. (New York: John Wiley, 1980); John Herz, *International Politics in the Atomic Age* (New York: Columbia University Press, 1959); Charles Alexander, *Holding the Line* (Bloomington: Indiana University Press, 1975). Country studies include Alvin Rubinstein, *Soviet Foreign Policy Since World War II* (Cambridge, Mass.: Winthrop, 1981); John Gittings, *The World And China, 1922-1972* (New York: Harper & Row, Pub., 1974). For Europe, see Anton De Porte, *Europe Between the Superpowers* (New Haven: Yale University Press, 1979). For documents on American foreign policy, see *Foreign Relations of the United States* (Washington: Government Printing Office); other documents can be found in *Documents on International Affairs* (London: Oxford University Press). Memoirs include Dwight D. Eisenhower, *The White House Years* (Garden City, N.Y.: Doubleday, 1963, 1965), 2 vols.; Nikita Khrushchev, *Khrushchev Remembers*, trans. and ed. Strobe Talbott (Boston: Little, Brown, 1970) and N. Khrushchev, *Khrushchev Remembers: The Last Testament,* trans. and ed. Strobe Talbott (Boston: Little, Brown, 1974).

[2]From *Stalin: A Political Biography,* 2nd ed., by Isaac Deutscher, p. 609. Copyright © 1967 by Isaac Deutscher. Reprinted by permission of Oxford University Press, Inc. For other studies of Stalin, see Adam Ulam, *Stalin* (New York: Viking, 1973); Roy Medvedev, *Let History Judge* (New York: Knopf, 1971).

[3]Aleksander Solzhenitsyn, for instance, then an artillery captain in the Red Army, found himself under arrest in February 1945 for injudicious remarks he made about Stalin in letters to army friends. See *Gulag Archipelago,* Vol. 1 (New York: Harper & Row, Pub., 1973), pp. 18–20, 133–37.

of senility and paranoia, from time to time consumed with fear that his closest subordinates were either out to destroy him or were agents of the Western powers. He held equally somber views about world politics. "He lived in terror of an enemy attack," Nikita Khrushchev would recall. "For him foreign policy meant keeping the antiaircraft units around Moscow on a twenty-four-hour alert."[4] Only he could safeguard the Soviet state. "You'll see," he warned his subordinates, "When I'm gone the imperialistic powers will wring your necks like chickens."[5]

Such pessimism made world politics easier to manage. The Soviet Union stood against the world. Other states were assumed to be hostile. The resulting clumsiness of Soviet foreign policy was astonishing. Churchill put his finger on the mystery: "We may well ask why have they [the Soviet Union] deliberately acted for three long years so as to unite the free world against them?"[6] Even a leadership with notions of global conquest might have tried finesse before coercion.

That clumsiness had carried over into relations with the new socialist states. Tito had been driven closer to the West, and purge and exploitation became the predominant form of relations with the other states in Eastern Europe. Now Stalin had to cope with the Chinese communists. Mao Tse-tung and Chou En-lai[7] acknowledged Soviet leadership on matters of doctrine, but they were nationalist Marxists who had liberated their own country. They had come to power through mobilization of the peasantry rather than the industrial proletariat, which earned them Stalin's disparaging label of "margarine communists." (Some American decision makers had in the 1940s adopted a similar view of the Chinese as "agrarian communists," ostensibly interested in agrarian reform, rather than in the revolutionizing of Chinese society.) Stalin had thought little of their prospects during the civil war and had maintained relations with Chiang's Nationalist regime until 1949.

In spite of past Soviet coolness, the Chinese communists chose to "lean toward the Soviet Union." The United States had demonstrated its hostility by aiding Chiang during the civil war, and China would need aid to conquer Taiwan, Chiang's last redoubt. In December, 1949, Mao journeyed to Moscow to negotiate. It took two months for the Soviets to agree to terms calling for mutual assistance in case of aggression, eventual cession of Port Arthur and the Manchurian railroad to China, and $300 million in aid over a five-year period. (In 1949, the United States granted South Korea alone $120 million in foreign aid.) How the Soviet Union would benefit from the alliance would remain to be seen. It had immediate costs—when the United Nations did not expel the representatives of the Nationalist government and replace them with those of the People's Republic, the Soviet delegation began a boycott of all United Nations activities, including meetings of the Security Council.

[4]Khrushchev, *Khrushchev Remembers,* p. 393.

[5]Quoted, *ibid.*, p. 392.

[6]Speech at MIT, March 31, 1949; *The New York Times,* April 1, 1949, p. 10 © 1949 by the New York Times Company. Reprinted by permission.

[7]In the 1970s, the PRC adopted a new transliteration of Chinese to English, which changed the spelling of Chinese names. Mao and Chou, for instance, became Mao Zedong and Zhou Enlai.

The immediate problem for Stalin in 1950 was not China, however; it was Korea. After World War II, Korea (like Indochina) had been occupied by two powers to take the surrender of the Japanese: the Soviets north of the 38th parallel, the Americans to the south. After unsuccessful attempts to reach agreement with the Soviets regarding unification, the United States turned the problem over to the United Nations. Soviet refusal of access to its occupation zone led to the creation of the Republic of Korea in the south under the auspices of the United Nations in August, 1948. The Soviets countered with the Democratic People's Republic of Korea in the north a month later. Soviet and American forces withdrew amid demands by the two new governments that Korea be unified, by force if necessary.

In late 1949, Kim Il-sung went to Moscow to secure Stalin's approval for a Northern attack on the South, timed to coincide with an uprising in the South.[8] The time looked propitious. The United States had acquiesed in the collapse of Nationalist China, the regime in South Korea was weak, and since the summer of 1949, Soviet propaganda had endorsed armed struggle by communist parties to liberate their countries. Stalin, however, was wary, and sought to avoid having to make a decision by telling Kim to "think it over, make some calculations, and then come back with a concrete plan."[9] Kim produced a plan, using his Soviet military advisors. Once again, Stalin stalled by insisting that Mao be consulted. Mao, apparently drawing on the recent Chinese experience, assumed that the United States would not intervene, and gave his approval. Thus caught, Stalin gave in (perhaps encouraged by the American Secretary of State's announcement that Korea lay outside the American defense perimeter). He did order Soviet advisors withdrawn from North Korean units and probably told Kim that he was on his own.

On June 25, 1950 (Korean time), Northern forces began the assault.[10] Tanks formed the spearheads, and the North Korean airforce dominated the skies. The Truman administration, working closely with and often a step ahead of the United Nations, made incremental decisions to involve American forces in the fighting by week's end.[11] With the Soviets still boycotting the Security Council, the United Nations called on its members to support the Republic of Korea, and sixteen nations eventually fought under the UN flag, with the United States contributing the bulk of foreign forces. However, the initial external support was too weak to stop the North Koreans. Seoul fell on June 28, and by mid-August the remnants of the South Korean army and small UN detachments held only the area around Pusan (see Map 7-1). The question remained whether the Northern forces could complete the conquest of the peninsula before the superior resources of the United Nations participants came into play.

[8]See *Khrushchev Remembers,* p. 368. For a review of scholarly writing on the subject, see William Stueck, "The Soviet Union and the Origins of the Korean War," *World Politics,* 28 (July 1976), 622–35.

[9]*Khrushchev Remembers,* p. 368.

[10]For general studies of the Korean war, see U.S. Department of the Army, *United States Army in the Korean War* (Washington: Government Printing Office); David Rees, *Korea: The Limited War* (New York: St. Martin's Press, 1964); Allen Whiting, *China Crosses the Yalu* (New York: Macmillan, 1960); Isidor Stone, *The Hidden History of the Korean War* (New York: Monthly Review Press, 1952).

[11]Glenn Paige, *The Korean Decision* (New York: Free Press, 1968) contains a detailed reconstruction of American decision making.

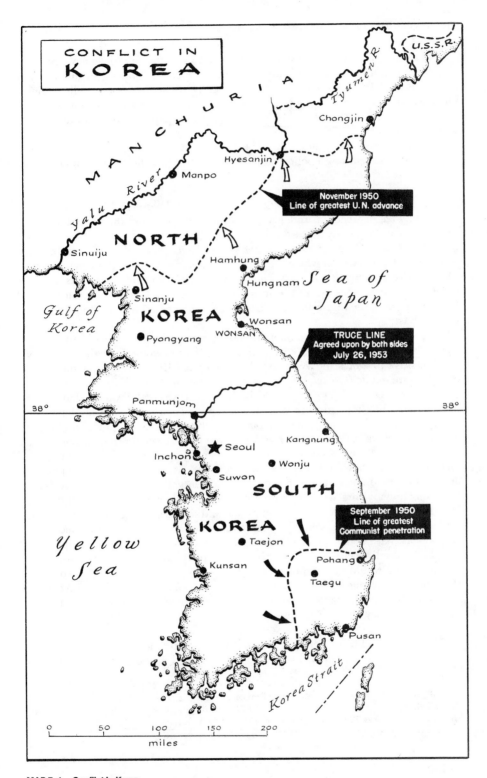

CONFLICT IN KOREA

November 1950
Line of greatest U.N. advance

TRUCE LINE
Agreed upon by both sides
July 26, 1953

September 1950
Line of greatest
Communist penetration

MANCHURIA

U.S.S.R.

Tyumen R.

Chongjin

Hyesanjin

Yalu River

Manpo

NORTH

Sinuiju

Hamhung

Hungnam

Sea of Japan

Sinanju

KOREA

Wonsan

Gulf of Korea

Pyongyang

WONSAN

Panmunjom

38°   38°

Seoul

Kangnung

Inchon

Wonju

Suwon

SOUTH

Yellow Sea

KOREA

Taejon

Kunsan

Pohang

Taegu

Pusan

Korea Strait

0   50   100   150   200
miles

MAP 7–1   Conflict in Korea

213

The invasion of Korea had come at a point when the American government had entered into a major reexamination of its policies. Spurred by the Soviet atomic test of 1949, Truman had ordered a study of its implications. The recommendations of the American foreign policy and defense bureaucracies emerged in the spring of 1950 under the label NSC–68 (the 68th paper of the National Security Council, a body set up in 1947 under the chairmanship of the President to coordinate foreign and military policies).[12] While evoking some pointed criticism by members of the foreign policy bureaucracy, NSC–68 reflected the official consensus:

1. *The American version of a "two-camp world."* "There is a basic conflict between the idea of freedom under a government of laws, and the idea of slavery under the grim oligarchy of the Kremlin. . . . "[13]

2. *The consequences of a cold war were identical with those of a hot one.* "The cold war is in fact a real war in which the survival of the free world is at stake."[14]

3. *Overwhelming regional Soviet power.* The report concluded that the Soviets in 1950 had the power to seize Western Europe, to isolate Britain and thus keep it from being used as a base for the liberation of the continent, and to attack the Middle East.

4. *Frightening timetables.* American policy makers began to think in terms of "periods of maximum danger" when the Soviet Union would have the capability and incentive to attack the West. NSC–68 predicted 1953–1954 to be the period of maximum danger (Korea led to a new prediction of 1951–1952).

5. *Long-term hope for the future.* If the Cold War was really war, and the crisis immediate, what hope did the West have, especially in its pursuit of a containment policy? Containment meant a *constant, patient* response to Soviet probes. It was a political war of attrition. How long would the American public accept the burden? Would they at some point grow tired and demand an end to resisting Soviet expansion? Or would they become "fed up" with such a "no-win" policy and encourage the leadership to seek a showdown with the Soviet Union? Truman and his advisors were determined to avoid either appeasement or World War III, but they had to offer to the public and themselves the prospect that, at some point, their efforts would be successful. The consensus within the administration was that during the 20–30 years of the containment "treatment," one of two things would occur: either the Soviet Union would "mellow," become conservative, and would have an interest in maintaining the status quo; or, because every totalitarian regime carried "the seeds of its own destruction," containment would produce such strains on the regime that it would crack it open and lead to its replacement by a more liberal one.

The bottom line of NSC–68 was to call for greatly increased defense spending (to go from a budgeted $13 billion to something on the order of $35–50 billion

---

[12]See Paul Y. Hammond, "NSC-68: Prologue to Rearmament," in Warner Schilling, Paul Hammond, and Glenn Snyder, *Strategy, Politics and Defense Budgets* (New York: Columbia University Press, 1962), pp. 267–378. For documentation, *FRUS 1950*, Vol. I, pp. 126–292.

[13]NSC-68, April 7, 1950; *FRUS 1950*, p. 239.

[14]*Ibid.*, p. 292.

in defense expenditures). Money is always a scarce commodity in any government. In fact, Truman was on an economy drive and was planning to *reduce* defense spending. Although Truman was in agreement with the policy perspectives of NSC–68, he remained unwilling to confront the fiscal implications. NSC–68 remained rhetoric. Until Korea.

"The profound lesson of Korea," noted Secretary of State Acheson, "is that contrary to every action preceding, the USSR took a step which risked—however remotely—general war."[15] Defense was in, not only because of the American commitment to the UN's action in Korea, but because "we are not justified in taking a gamble that the Kremlin is bluffing. The nation should therefore prepare for the contingency of total war with the Soviet Union in the immediate future."[16] The United States began to rearm and to assume that, to support containment, it had to threaten the Soviet Union directly with armed force. Stalin had created a truly dangerous foe. And he had attached the image of a Hitler-like state to the Soviet Union.

In Korea, the UN's command under General MacArthur had stabilized the front around Pusan. The familiar pattern of offensive surge followed by depletion of the North Korean striking force was accentuated by American control of the air over Korea, which made it increasingly difficult for the North Korean forces to build up men and supplies for another offensive against the Pusan perimeter. The Soviets concluded that the North had failed and the time had come for a negotiated solution. The American government, increasingly confident that it had won the battle for time, rejected the idea and began speaking of reunification, but not as the North had intended. Alarmed, Soviet officials (now attending UN functions) warned that "any continuation of the Korean war will lead inevitably to a widening of the conflict,"[17] and the Chinese stressed that their security rested on the security of the North Korean state.

The American government, however, took another view. It had confined itself to a limited war, fought only on the Korean peninsula (all of which was heavily bombed) with no attacks on the Soviet Union (the "real aggressor") or China. Within that area, the issue was to be settled by force of arms—unless the Chinese or Soviets intervened, in which case the Administration would not push the point. In addition, the Administration assumed that it would have failed disastrously in dealing with a Hitler-like state if it did not punish the aggressor. If North Korea survived, it would be a clear signal that there was little penalty attached to aggression, *even if it failed.* Finally (but not least), Truman and his advisors saw Korea as a place to deflect the domestic political allegations of having "lost China" and of being either "soft on communism" or heavily infiltrated by communists.

On September 15, 1950, MacArthur landed forces at Inchon, far to the rear of the front, and simultaneously began an offensive from the Pusan bridgehead. The North Korean army disintegrated and UN forces raced for the 38th parallel. The Chinese repeated their warnings and began a troop buildup in Manchuria. South Korean forces "tested the water" by crossing the 38th parallel

[15]Notes prepared for Congressional testimony; August, 1950; *ibid.*, p. 395.

[16]State Department Policy Planning Staff memo, December 9, 1950; *ibid.*, p. 464.

[17]UN delegate A. Malik, August 22, 1950; quoted by Whiting, *China Crosses,* p. 70.

on October 1. Chou En-lai relayed a message through the Indian government that China would intervene if American forces crossed the parallel. MacArthur opined that China was bluffing and Truman elected to reunify Korea by force. The Administration reassured China that it would not be attacked. On October 7, American forces entered North Korea.

Thus far the Chinese had failed to communicate effectively either their concern or the credibility of their threat to intervene. They made one last effort. Infiltrating units into North Korea, they staged several surprise attacks on South Korean and American forces during late October and early November, then broke off contact. MacArthur concluded that a Chinese offensive had failed and he could complete the conquest of North Korea by Christmas. He deployed his forces to maximize their mobility at the expense of security and hurried them northward. On November 26, the Chinese committed themselves to the war and began an offensive that shattered the poorly deployed United Nations command. It fell back in retreat, and a deep gloom settled on Washington. It was, as MacArthur said, an entirely new war.

The American administration decided that it would settle for a ceasefire and restoration of the status quo *ante bellum*. But it would not give up; Truman said that ''he wanted to make it perfectly plain here that we do not desert our friends when the going is rough.''[18] It did become rough as the Chinese drove the UN forces out of Seoul. However, the front again stabilized south of Seoul, and a counteroffensive by UN forces pushed the Chinese north of the 38th parallel. And there the UN drive lost both momentum and political support. The American government and its supporters in the United Nations now sought to call the war off. MacArthur, arguing that a nation should use its resources to win rather than squander them for a stalemate, publicly advocated attacking China. Truman dismissed him in April, 1951. The Chinese, after losing heavily in efforts to dislodge the UN forces, and the Soviets, seeing the growing menace of the American global response to Korea (discussed below) indicated their interest in a negotiated settlement. Talks began in July, 1951, and went on for two more years, as did the fighting. The American government insisted that the new frontier was to be the battle-line, a point finally conceded at the end of the year by the Chinese. The more intractable issue had been spawned by the war itself—return of prisoners of war. Caught in its imagery of free-world versus slave, the United States was loath to force the repatriation of captured Koreans or Chinese who said they did not wish to return to their homelands. The Chinese and North Koreans insisted on complete repatriation, and neither side found the way to break that deadlock for two years.

Korea had profound effects on world politics because it propelled the United States into a series of decisions which further committed the United States to conflict and a military response.[19] One of Truman's initial decisions in response to Korea was to put an American fleet between Formosa and the mainland to block any Chinese move to seize the island. The American government had reentered the Chinese civil war, this time as an active military participant. In

---

[18]Conversation with Prime Minister Attlee, December 5, 1950; in *FRUS*, Vol. III, p. 1726.

[19]For discussion of the consequences of Korea, see Robert Jervis, ''The Impact of the Korean War on the Cold War,'' *Journal of Conflict Resolution,* 24 (December 1980), 563–92.

addition, Truman ordered the modest aid program in Indochina converted into extensive military aid to the French in their struggle to destroy the Viet Minh. All expansion of "international communism," directed by Moscow, had to be opposed. The American military establishment expanded to accomplish this. Negotiations with the Soviets or their puppets would take place only when they were ready to make "retractions and adjustments" and when negotiations provided the West with "opportunities for maintaining a moral ascendency"—in other words, when there were Soviet concessions and a propaganda advantage to be had. The Cold War had become frozen.

Nowhere was this clearer than in Europe, which also bore the impact of the Korean war. (Europe had an influence on the Korean war as well; the fear that Korea was a trap to tie down American resources in Asia while the Soviets overran Europe helped ensure a limited war in Korea.) Korea made real the threat of a Soviet offensive and the need for remilitarization of the continent if Europe was to be defended. The Truman administration contributed American ground forces to Europe to bolster their defenses, to demonstrate its commitment, and to create a trip-wire in Europe—America had no choice but to be involved if the Soviets attacked. In addition, NATO moved from a paper alliance to a bureaucratic institution with missions ranging from the coordination of defense plans to the standardization of ammunition. The central issue, however, concerned Germany. Truman and his advisors saw the return of full sovereignty to Germany *and its remilitarization* as essential to the defense of Europe. Korea, in their eyes, gave them no option. In spite of the resistance of various European states (France in particular) and a variety of Soviet proposals suggesting a unified, neutral, and weakly armed Germany, the American government persisted. The Federal Republic of Germany, with its new Bundeswehr, entered the ranks of fully independent nations and NATO in 1955. The Soviets, faced with a historic enemy now rearmed and unreconciled to the "loss" of eastern Germany or the territory held by Poland, countered with the creation of the Warsaw Treaty Organization (WTO). This military alliance between the Soviet Union and Eastern Europe insured a continued Soviet presence in the area—and gave the East European governments a potential access channel to influence Soviet policy. The creation of WTO did not hide the fact that the Germans were again with arms.[20]

Military integration was not the only change in European politics during the decade. The idea of a political union gained increasing impetus. Pan-Europeanists initially avoided the political to concentrate on the economic. In May, 1950, Robert Schuman, the French Foreign Minister, proposed the creation of a European coal and steel community that would abolish restrictions (such as tariffs and quotas) on the movement of coal and steel across the boundaries of the member states. Its successful implementation among West Germany, France, Italy, Belgium, the Netherlands, and Luxembourg led to consideration of a general common market in Europe where all goods could pass freely across frontiers. After hard bargaining, the six states agreed in March, 1957, to create the Euro-

[20]For discussions of the integration of Germany into NATO and the emergence of WTO, see James Richardson, *Germany and the Atlantic Alliance* (Cambridge: Harvard University Press, 1966); Gordon Craig, "Germany and NATO," in *NATO and American Security,* ed. Klaus Knorr (Princeton: Princeton University Press, 1959), pp. 236–59; Robin Remington, *The Warsaw Pact* (Cambridge: M.I.T. Press, 1971).

pean Economic Community (the "Common Market"), which incorporated a customs union, mechanisms for integrating the economies of the members, and a supra-national authority given power to make decisions for the entire community.[21] The benefits of economic cooperation could not smother conflict. How, for instance, could a government allow its inefficient but politically powerful farmers to be bankrupted by more efficient farmers in a member state? Benefits were frequent enough, however, and fueled the spirit of New Europe sufficiently to make the EEC a going concern. Robert Schuman's plan of forging European unity, especially between France and Germany, had borne fruit. Britain, however, remained on the outside, concerned with preserving its sovereignty unfettered.

While Europe took its tentative steps toward political union and poured billions into defense, the Korean war ground on into 1953. Both sides struggled to convince each other that they would continue the war rather than accept the other's position on prisoners. In March, 1953, Stalin died. His successors, struggling against each other for power, wanted the war liquidated as soon as possible. The American Presidency also changed hands in January, as the Republicans under Dwight Eisenhower ended twenty years of Democratic dominance of American foreign policy. Various Republican orators had called for a more positive policy than containment. Eisenhower and his Secretary of State, John Foster Dulles, reviewed their options and settled on containment, but sought to give it more teeth. The new Administration quietly warned the Chinese that it would use atomic weapons rather than allow the fighting to continue in Korea. The Chinese, having lost perhaps 900,000 men, having delayed their own economic development program, having to pay the Soviets for war material delivered to Chinese forces in Korea, and now facing nuclear war with a timid ally at its side, accepted a UN plan for prisoner repatriation. In spite of the South Korean government's attempt to sabotage the agreement (there still were diehards who wanted reunification at any cost), an armistice was signed on July 27, 1953. Korea remained divided, and there was now a permanent American military presence on the mainland of Asia.

The Soviets Look for Peaceful Coexistence

Stalin's death loosened the shackles on Soviet policy; the struggle for power among his subordinates made for a real debate among policy options. Georgi Malenkov inherited Stalin's title as Premier (or prime minister) while Nikita Khrushchev became Party Secretary. With no tight hold on their own positions, the new leadership had to confront an ominous menace:

> The United States was then conducting an arrogant and aggressive policy towards us, never missing a chance to demonstrate its superiority. The Americans had the Soviet Union surrounded with military bases and kept sending reconnaissance

---

[21]For the development of the EEC, see Ernst Haas, *The Uniting of Europe* (Stanford: Stanford University Press, 1958); William Diebold, *The Schuman Plan* (New York: Praeger, 1959); Leon Lindberg and Stuart Scheingold, *Europe's Would-Be Polity* (Englewood Cliffs, N.J.: Prentice-Hall, 1970); Roy Pryce, *The Politics of the European Community* (London: Butterworth, 1973).

planes deep into our territory, sometimes as far as Kiev. We expected an all-out attack any day.[22]

The new Soviet government sought to defuse the danger it perceived by pledging strict adherence to treaties, respect for the rights of others, and "the observance of established international usages." Malenkov went on to declare, "At present there is no litigious or unsolved question which could not be settled by peaceful means on the basis of mutual agreement of the countries concerned. This concerns our relations with all states, including the United States of America."[23] While offers to negotiate were not new, this one came at a time when Malenkov was attempting to build a record of achievement in order to reinforce his position within the Soviet political structure. Stalin's policies had produced a series of disasters; Malenkov was attempting to chart a new course but run minimum risks. He held out to Yugoslavia, Greece, and Turkey the possibility of amicable relations. And to the Americans. It was now up to the American administration to pursue the possibilities of peaceful coexistence.

Eisenhower and Dulles chose not to. The image of a Hitler-like state and Dulles' own brand of strident moralism[24] made serious negotiations unwise, unless there were unilateral concessions from the Soviet Union first (a step Malenkov could not take because of the potential domestic political ramifications). The United States would talk, but would not change its bargaining position. Moreover, Dulles concluded that the Soviet offer to negotiate was a sign of weakness[25]—which it was. Dulles' conclusion was to keep the pressure on in hopes of cracking open the Soviet system. The Soviet leadership was unable to see that even though they might be willing to move away from a Stalinist policy, the West could not easily give up ingrained patterns of thought without some dramatic incentive to do so. A bitter Malenkov subsequently announced that American leaders seemed to

> . . . regard the Soviet Union's efforts to safeguard peace among nations, its concern to lessen international tensions, as a manifestation of weakness. It is precisely this preposterous assumption that explains the flagrantly unreasonable approach in certain U.S. circles to the settlement of international issues, and their policy of pressure and indiscriminate adventurism.[26]

The War in Indochina   As the two sought to define their relations, the prolonged struggle in Indochina neared its climax.[27] Neither the French nor the Viet Minh had been able to win a decisive victory, in spite of seven years of war

---

[22]Khrushchev, *Last Testament,* p. 220.

[23]Malenkov speech of March 15, 1953; *Documents on International Affairs 1953* (London: Oxford University Press, 1956), pp. 12–13.

[24]Studies of Dulles include Townsend Hoopes, *The Devil and John Foster Dulles* (Boston: Atlantic Monthly Press/Little, Brown, 1973); Louis Gerson, *John Foster Dulles* (New York: Cooper Square, 1967); Michael Guhin, *John Foster Dulles* (New York: Columbia University Press, 1972).

[25]Ole Holsti, "Cognitive Dynamics and Images of the Enemy: Dulles and Russia," in D. Finlay, O. Holsti, and R. Fagen, *Enemies in Politics* (Chicago: Rand McNally, 1967) pp. 25–96.

[26]Malenkov speech of August 8, 1953; *Documents 1953,* p. 29.

[27]For studies of the first Indochina war, see Ellen Hammer, *The Struggle for Indochina, 1940–*

and external support from the United States and China. American involvement had raised the question of whether, in the name of anticommunism, the United States would support colonialism. Caught between conflicting goals, the Americans pressed for enough decolonization to undermine the French military effort, but not enough to rally the Indochinese away from the Viet Minh. And because they found colonialism distasteful (as they later found friendly repressive oligarchies distasteful), the Americans denied that the issue was colonialism (or repression). "The real issue in Indochina," insisted Assistant Secretary of State Dean Rusk, "is whether the peoples of that land will be permitted to work out their future as they see fit or whether they will be subjected to a Communist reign of terror and be absorbed by force into the new colonialism of a Soviet Communist Empire."[28] To phrase the question that way ensured the American response.

In the first half of 1954, various French officials came to Washington to request more American involvement. The current innovation in the French strategy to defeat the Vietnamese insurgents was to establish strong points in rural areas and lure the Viet Minh into a climactic battle. At Dien Bien Phu, the French found that the Viet Minh had taken the bait, but were so strong that they threatened to overrun the base. The Eisenhower Administration pondered French requests for aid, canvassing the possibilities, ranging from air strikes from carriers to atomic bombs. Apparently committing itself to some action, the Administration then found the Senate Democrats (led by Lyndon Johnson) dubious and the British (once again with Churchill as Prime Minister) rigidly opposed to intervention. Eisenhower had to fall back on the diplomatic track.

In fact, an international conference on Indochina (and Korea) had been scheduled for the summer of 1954 by Soviet, American, French, and British foreign ministers. For the Americans, this was a part of their talk-if-we-have-to-but-no-concessions policy. The British were pushing for conferences, and the unstable French government was anxious to explore any way out of the agony of Indochina. The Vietnamese had been anxious as well. In early 1954, Chou Enlai reported to Khrushchev that "Comrade Ho Chi Minh has told me that the situation in Vietnam is hopeless and that if we don't attain a ceasefire soon, the Vietnamese won't be able to hold out against the French."[29]

When the conference opened in late April 1954, an interest in a negotiated settlement was exhibited by all parties except the Americans and the Vietnamese government sponsored by the French. When Dien Bien Phu fell on May 7, the French government committed itself to finding a solution at Geneva. The Soviets and Chinese insisted that Ho accept the compromise the French proposed—the temporary partition of Vietnam at the 17th parallel. The July 1954 agreement did that, and established the independence of Laos and Cambodia (see Map 7-2). Ho and the Viet Minh and a Southern nationalist, Ngo Dinh Diem, were to organize provisional regimes north and south of the 17th parallel, with elections two years later to create a unified state. Only the Americans and South

---

1955, (Stanford: Stanford University Press, 1966); Lucien Bodard, *The Quicksand War* (Boston: Little, Brown, 1967); Robert Randle, *Geneva, 1954* (Princeton: Princeton University Press, 1969). For documents, see *Pentagon Papers.*

[28]Speech of November 6, 1951; *Department of State Bulletin,* 25 (November 19, 1951), 822–23.

[29]*Khrushchev Remembers,* p. 482.

MAP 7-2   Southeast Asia

Within the map:

YUNNAN

CHINA

KWANGSI

KWANGTUNG

BURMA

Mekong

Clear R.

Red R.

Black R.

Phong
Saly

Dien
Bien Phu

NORTH

Hanoi

Haiphong

VIET

Samneua

Gulf of Tonkin

Luang Prabang

Thanh Hoa

HAINAN

Xieng
Khouang

NAM

Ha Tinh

Mekong

L A O S

Mekong

Vientiane

Dong Hoi

Cease-fire line,
July 22, 1954

Savannakhet

Hué

THAILAND

Danang

Pakse

Quang Ngai

Menam R.

Ayuthia

SOUTH

Bangkok

Pleiku

QuiNhon

Angkor

Sekong

VIET

C A M B O D I A

Nhatrang

Mekong

Dalat

NAM

Phnom
Penh

BienHoa

Gulf

Saigon

of

Siam

PHU
QUOC I.

Cantho

South

China Sea

0   50   100   150

MILES

105°

110°

20°

15°

15°

10°

10°

100°

105°

110°

Vietnamese representatives refused to sign; Ho was expected to sweep the elections, making the Geneva accords an agreement for the phased communization of Vietnam.

In the temporary peace that followed, Ngo Dinh Diem, with American assistance, proved capable of organizing the South, smashing his political opponents, and creating an army. He refused to hold the elections as called for. Ho for his part socialized the North (and repressed resistance), and when the South refused to hold the elections, began to activate the cadres of communists who had remained in the South. By 1957, a small-scale war of insurgency had bubbled up in the South, attracting not only Ho's supporters, but Vietnamese reacting to the growing repression and corruption of the Southern government. The United States responded with economic aid, arms, and advisors. American political and military leaders began to grapple with the problem of "counter-insurgency." And in Laos, the United States abetted the Laotian political right in undermining the accommodation the Laotian government had reached with Laos' communists. Insurgency emerged there as well by the end of the decade.[30]

Security in an Age of Uncertainty and Nuclear Weapons

Indochina, the Korean war, and the threat of a Soviet or Chinese invasion of neighboring states raised, for the Eisenhower government, the question of how containment, deterrence, and defense were to be implemented. The Soviets pondered similar questions. The mutual possession of nuclear weapons, now augmented by the development of the far more powerful hydrogen bomb, made such questions even more pressing. The American response took three forms. The first was an attempt to build a ring of states around the Soviet Union tied together in a NATO-like arrangement. By September 1954, Dulles had created the Southeast Asia Treaty Organization (SEATO), which bound the United States into a defensive alliance system with France, Britain, Australia, New Zealand, Thailand, the Philippines, and Pakistan. SEATO unilaterally announced that its protective cover extended over Laos, Cambodia, and South Vietnam. Taking a more indirect approach in the Middle East, Dulles encouraged Britain to take the lead in creating a similar organization (called the Baghdad Pact), which, by the fall of 1955, included Britain, Iraq, Iran, Pakistan (thus linking the Pact with SEATO), and Turkey (linking the Pact with NATO, which Turkey, along with Greece, had joined).

Second, the Administration sought to provide large amounts of aid to those "frontline states," both military supplies and economic aid to allow the recipient to devote its own resources to its defense establishment. For the cost-conscious Eisenhower, this made sense: ". . . while it cost $3515 to maintain an American soldier for a year, to maintain a Pakistani the price was $485, for a Greek, $424."[31] Third, because it would be economically prohibitive to station large American forces around the world (and politically costly, as the American public was unwilling to forego the search for the good life), and because small states could not defend themselves effectively, the Administration chose to brandish its

---

[30]For Vietnam between the wars, see Bernard Fall, *The Two Viet-Nams* (New York: Praeger, 1963); Jean Lacouture, *Vietnam: Between Two Truces* (New York: Vintage, 1966); Frances Fitzgerald, *Fire in the Lake* (Boston: Little, Brown, 1972).

[31]Eisenhower, *White House Years: Waging Peace*, p. 133.

nuclear capability. Dulles warned that in case of future communist aggression, the United States would feel free to deliver "massive retaliation" against an aggressor at the time and place of its own choosing. A conventional Soviet thrust into west Berlin might provoke a nuclear bombing of Moscow; a Chinese attack on Formosa, nuclear retaliation in Manchuria.

The Soviet response to the security issue continued to be caught up in the political maneuverings of the elite. In the spring of 1954, Premier Malenkov abandoned the Stalinist position on another world war. Instead of war's leading to a further expansion of the area ruled by the proletariat (just as the two previous world wars had), Malenkov concluded that civilization itself would not survive a nuclear world war. The nuclear weapons a state collected should therefore be sufficient to *deter* a nuclear attack, not to constitute an overwhelming stockpile. Not coincidentally, the money saved by avoiding a large nuclear weapons system could be devoted to an expansion of the goods available to the Soviet consumer and thereby enhance Malenkov's political position.[32] His numerous opponents (including Khrushchev) rejected this view, both because it was politically expedient to do so in the contest for power, and because Malenkov's proposal challenged orthodox thinking about defense and deterrence. How could "fewer" be as good as (perhaps better than) "more" nuclear weapons? Malenkov moved quickly into political impotence, although he was not removed from the premiership until February, 1955, when he was replaced by a Khrushchev ally, Nikolai Bulganin.

The 1950s was a period of intense interest in the role of nuclear weapons in world politics.[33] Political leaders, military men, and academics sought to discover that role. All were relatively equal in the search because of the novelty of the weapon and the inability to experiment with one's ideas except on paper. What emerged (more quickly in the United States) was a theory of defense and deterrence that generally became the framework for American and probably Soviet thinking. It had the distinction of being one of the few models of world politics that both academics and policy makers used with familiarity and conviction.

The basic assumption of this model was that nuclear warfare was very undesirable because of the potential for massive mutual devastation. The bombs that obliterated two Japanese cities had the equivalent of 20,000 tons of TNT. In the 1950s, the United States and the Soviet Union had not only stockpiled many such weapons in the kiloton range, they had produced fusion (hydrogen) weapons capable of delivering millions of tons of TNT explosiveness for each bomb. Megatons doomed any city to rubble.[34] Such a future was unacceptable to the possessors of those weapons.

---

[32]Joseph Nogee and Robert Donaldson, *Soviet Foreign Policy Since World War II* (New York: Pergamon, 1981), pp. 88–95.

[33]For discussions of nuclear weapons and world politics, see, among others, George Quester, *Nuclear Diplomacy* (New York: Dunellen, 1970) and Michael Mandelbaum, *The Nuclear Question* (Cambridge: Cambridge University Press, 1979); for Henry Kissinger's early contribution, see his *Nuclear Weapons and Foreign Policy* (New York: Harper & Row Pub., 1957).

[34]For reviews of the effects of nuclear weapons, see Jonathan Schell, *The Fate of the Earth* (New York: Knopf, 1982); Robert Lifton, *Death in Life* (New York: Random House, 1968); Ruth Adams and Susan Cullen, eds., *The Final Epidemic* (Chicago: University of Chicago Press, 1981); Arthur Katz, *Life After Nuclear War* (Cambridge: Ballinger, 1981); Nigel Calder, *Nuclear Nightmares* (New York: Viking Press, 1980).

As tactical (battlefield) nuclear weapons became available in the 1950s, the question would emerge whether the use of such weapons on the battlefield would escalate to a general nuclear war. There was no unanimity among those who thought about the problem; generally, however, most agreed that the use of any nuclear device would change how leaders thought about waging war. Crossing the nuclear "threshold" raised the *probability* of a general nuclear war, and that was undesirable. Nonetheless, the United States deployed them in Europe, and the Soviet Union targeted Europe with short-range missiles and bombers.

If nuclear weapons were not to be used, what would one do with those that existed—and might therefore be used? Neither side trusted the other enough or had enough accurate information about the capabilities of the other to negotiate an arms reduction. Indeed, during the 1950s, the distribution of nuclear weapons and delivery systems and information regarding capabilities were out of balance. The Soviet Union was inferior and knew it, while the United States assumed Soviet nuclear parity and relied on threats of retaliation as the means to prevent the use of nuclear weapons. This then was *deterrence* in the nuclear age: to induce the other side to believe that it would suffer mortal retaliatory damage, even if it struck first. Much of world politics for the next three decades was caught up in the attempt to *develop a capability* to retaliate and to *demonstrate the will* to fulfill a pledge to retaliate.

In the process, some of old "truths" about world politics began to crumble. Common wisdoms (and subsequent academic analysis[35]) indicated that arms races might be *necessary to prevent* nuclear war. Suppose that State X has a bomber force of 100 aircraft and State Y has the same. These constitute the vehicles of nuclear retaliation for both sides. If the leaders of State X calculate that a surprise raid of 75 bombers could, using nuclear weapons, destroy most of Y's bomber fleet, it may be tempted to strike. State X would still have 25 unused bombers to threaten Y's population, which presumably would be enough to compel Y to accede to X's demands. Even if several of Y's bombers survived, the punishment they could deliver would be "acceptable" to a leadership contemplating war. And perhaps Y would not even launch them in retaliation, because that retaliation would produce a far more devastating attack on its inhabitants by X's remaining aircraft. If the leaders of State X make this calculation and are prepared to act, *deterrence has failed,* because X no longer believes it will suffer a mortal retaliatory blow. If we are to preserve peace, how might such thoughts be banished from the minds of X's leaders? One answer has been to engage in an arms race— *to increase the number of bombers* so that even after a first strike, X would have to assume that Y would still have enough bombers surviving to cause unacceptable damage to X. How many more bombers (or later, missiles) would be enough? No one knew. Malenkov had argued for "not too many more." That seemed foolish to his peers. The novelty of deterrence and survival in the nuclear age favored large numbers.

The concern for deterrence became more pressing in 1957 when the Soviet Union put *Sputnik* into space and the United States followed with its own satellites. To orbit a payload meant that each had developed missiles with inter-

---

[35]Michael Wallace, "Arms Races and Escalations," *Journal of Conflict Resolution,* 23 (March 1979), 3–16, and 24 (June 1980), 289–92.

continental ranges. Unlike aircraft, a launched intercontinental ballistic missile (ICBM) could not be shot down before it reached its target. No defense was possible, other than trying to shield the target or to attack first—which meant unleashing a preemptive nuclear war. With the ICBM, the prevention of nuclear war rested squarely on the success of deterrence, which in turn was ultimately dependent upon the *opinions* of those who had the power to initiate nuclear war.

And where did this evolution in thought and capability leave the Eisenhower Administration's policy of "massive retaliation?" Was it *credible* that the United States would unleash nuclear war? In response to a strike on the United States, yes. But to punish Soviet aggression against Berlin or Chinese aggression against Formosa? The administration had no choice but to insist that it would so retaliate, as it was committed not to engage in another protracted, inconclusive, limited war like Korea, and had therefore reduced the size of the army. Others were much more dubious. The British and French governments decided to produce their own nuclear weapons to serve as a deterrent, in part because of the fear that the United States would rationally choose not to die a nuclear death to save Europe. (Questions of international prestige and the pressures of internal politics also encouraged this nuclear proliferation.) The irony of the credibility of "massive retaliation" was that it was so damned difficult to ascertain. If the Soviets refrained from aggression, was it because they feared "massive retaliation"? Or because they, for other reasons, had no intention of being aggressive? If you were a policy maker who had made "massive retaliation" a part of your policy program, you would have an incentive to believe that it worked and that this kind of threat-making should be an active part of your foreign policy repertory.

Against this backdrop of military preparation and planning, the major powers sought to define their relations with each other and with the weaker states, especially those emerging from colonialism. The British government had long advocated a summit meeting to begin the process of defining relations between the major powers (and thereby prop up a Britain whose power was eroding). Eisenhower and Dulles were reluctant. Khrushchev, increasingly dominant in the Presidium (the dozen or so top leaders of the Communist party) looked forward to a summit to legitimize the Soviet Union's great-power status and his own leadership position within the Soviet Union. In addition, it fit in with Khrushchev's leadership style of face-to-face meetings, of confrontation and winning over others. The price to get the Americans to the summit was a sudden Soviet agreement in early 1955 to end the occupation of Austria and allow its return as a sovereign but perpetually neutral state.

The summit conference of July, 1955, in Geneva is remembered for its "atmospherics" rather than for substantive agreements. Germany remained a bone of contention. Soviet suspicion killed Eisenhower's proposal for aerial reconnaissance to prevent surprise attack. Yet the meeting went well in terms of establishing a dialogue. Khrushchev felt encouraged, for the West seemed as fearful as the Soviets. Dulles, however, voiced a deep American pessimism: "Stalinism lives, though Stalin [is] dead."[36]

Dulles was partially right, and for Khrushchev, a living Stalinism was precisely the problem. As long as Stalin and his policies remained the yardstick, de-

---

[36]Speech notes, December 15, 1955, quoted in Hoopes, *Devil and John Foster Dulles,* p. 286.

viation from the Stalinist path would furnish ammunition to political rivals, who could claim that they alone were faithful to "the Greatest Genius in History." Malenkov had suffered the fate of deviation. Yet it was clear to Khrushchev that Stalinist policies regarding economic development, agriculture, and foreign relations were inefficient, if not self-destructive. More profoundly, Khrushchev and his supporters saw much of Stalin's behavior and his imprint on both the Party and society as deviations from the Leninist goal of a progressive and humane society. His solution was to denounce Stalin at the 20th Congress of the Soviet Communist Party in February, 1956.[37] This was generally well received by the party activists. Freeing himself of the yardstick, Khrushchev declared that "many roads to socialism" were possible (a bow to Tito and to other independent spirits), that socialism might be achieved through peaceful political processes such as elections, that peaceful coexistence was to be the goal of Soviet foreign policy, and that the Soviet Union would actively promote ties with the decolonizing world.

The denunciation of Stalin occurred at a closed session of the Congress, but its contents quickly spread as foreign delegations attending the Congress returned home (and then became public in the West when it was passed on to the American Central Intelligence Agency, who gleefully made sure it was available to anyone). The impact on Eastern Europe was immense. The satellite governments were run by little Stalins; their party rivals now had a very potent weapon with which to challenge the incumbents. De-Stalinization in the USSR also came at a time of mounting pressure in Eastern Europe for change.[38] Popular protest against the regime in Poland began in June, 1956, discreetly encouraged by Polish Communist Party factions who sought to replace their rivals. As the unrest spread, the Soviet leadership grew fearful that the protests would turn anti-Soviet and lead Poland out of the Warsaw Treaty Organization. Khrushchev and a Soviet delegation flew to Warsaw, threatened, cajoled, and blessed the candidacy of dissident Party leader Wladyslaw Gomulka to head the Polish Communist Party. The Party rallied behind Gomulka and restored order in Poland.

Hungary was another matter. Indeed, the success of the Poles fueled public protest against the Hungarian regime, which snowballed into violence, and by late October, growing anti-Sovietism. A new Hungarian government "was unable to follow Gomulka's course of playing off the people and Russia, winning restraint from each with the threat of the other."[39] Swept away, the regime announced the end of the Communist Party's monopoly on power and Hungary's neutralization and withdrawal from the WTO. After agonizing indecision, Khrushchev ordered a military invasion to smash the "counter revolution." It began on November 1, 1956, and in nine days crushed the poorly armed Hun-

[37]For a text of the secret speech and analysis, see Bertram Wolfe, *Khrushchev and Stalin's Ghost* (New York: Praeger, 1957).

[38]For descriptions of the events of 1956, see Bill Lomax, *Hungary 1956* (New York: St. Martin's Press, 1976); Béla Király and Paul Jónás, eds., *The Hungarian Revolution of 1956 in Retrospect* (New York: Columbia University Press, 1978); James F. Morrison, *The Polish Peoples' Republic* (Baltimore: Johns Hopkins University Press, 1968); Adam Bromke, *Poland's Politics: Idealism and Realism* (Cambridge: Harvard University Press, 1967).

[39]M.D. Donelan and M.J. Grieve, *International Disputes* (New York: St. Martin's Press, 1973), p. 132.

garian resistance. The dissident leadership was executed or jailed, and a new regime under Janos Kadar installed.

The West denounced the Soviet invasion and stoked the propaganda fires. No one was willing to risk war to save Hungary, but even Western diplomacy was hamstrung by a recrudescence of Western imperialism in the Middle East (as we shall see). Khrushchev paid a personal price for the unrest in the Soviet sphere; his power diminished, and in July 1957, his opponents held a majority in the Presidium and voted to dismiss him from his post as leader of the Party. However, Khrushchev refused to resign and hurriedly called a meeting of the Central Committee to the Party, a more numerous body to which the Presidium is subordinate—at least on paper. There Khrushchev had the votes. As the Party had no established procedures to resolve this conflict, the participants presumably calculated the power held by those who supported and opposed Khrushchev. On that basis, the vote of the Central Committee stood. Khrushchev's opponents went into retirement or minor bureaucratic positions, and Khrushchev now cemented his position by becoming the Premier as well as Party chairman. The tensions of de-Stalinization and Eastern Europe were not the sole causes of the revolt against Khrushchev within the party. His plans for economic decentralization had threatened the power of the bureaucracies managing the economy; his stress on missile development threatened the position of the Soviet airforce and ground forces, as well as the heavy industry bureaucracies who provided the weapons for those services. In combination, they brought his tenure into question.

The invasion of Hungary also forced the Soviets to acknowledge the limits of their diplomatic influence and the potential costs of coercion in controlling change in Eastern Europe. At what point might those limits and costs prevent the use of force by the Soviet Union? Why were they not high enough in 1956? The case of Hungary indicated that there *were* limitations on the Soviet's ability to manipulate or influence East European politics. There *were* costs to coercion: a damaged image, the need to devote more resources to ensure control and stability, and continuing resentment, if not hostility. Yet to refrain from intervention seemed to hold greater costs: the possible contagion of rebellion spreading to other East European states; the defection of the "iron triangle" states of the German Democratic Republic, Poland, and Czechoslovakia, which guarded the historic invasion route into Russia; the encouragement for the West to increase its pressure on the socialist camp now that Soviet weakness was clear. And for all its expediency in foreign policy, there was a question of principle—did the Soviet Union have an obligation to defend the socialist experiment? We find it easy to assume that American policy makers could respond to the idea of "aiding free peoples." Soviet policy makers probably had to wrestle with similar emotions.

In any event, the display of Soviet power kept Eastern Europe relatively quiet, but not passive. The Soviets found that they often had to bargain strenuously with the local leadership, who demanded a never-ending flow of Soviet aid. Khrushchev found that the Poles, for instance, constantly claimed to be in difficulty and were often able to get help from a chronically short Soviet economy.[40] This ability of the weak to extract concessions or place a major power in an awkward position is no new phenomenon in world politics. It was, however, rela-

---

[40]See, for instance, Khrushchev, *Last Testament,* p. 212.

tively new to the Soviets and Americans, but would become more familiar as decolonization continued and the number of participants (usually weak) in world politics increased.

Decolonization and the Third World

The 1950s brought the end to most of the colonial empires, as Table 7-1 indicates. The British generally accepted decolonization as inevitable and gradually relinquished control. The Belgians and French were more unwilling, while the Portuguese resisted for two decades. In 1956, Algerian nationalists began a war of liberation against France that, with its mutual savagery, brought public outcries in France, greater instability to French coalition governments, and finally, in the spring of 1958, the fear of a military coup. The crisis passed with the return of Charles de Gaulle to power (the war hero had served as President of France in 1945). Creating a new political system with a strong Presidency (the Fifth Republic), de Gaulle pledged to permit any French colony to leave the fold if it chose to do so—except for Algeria, for many de Gaulle supporters were bitter-enders in that regard. Table 7-1 shows the results. Those who wanted to retain Algeria had not counted on de Gaulle's political skills.

The American government applauded decolonization but seemed to fear the consequences. The newly independent governments were often unstable and unskilled—in Washington's eyes, the perfect breeding grounds for communist subversion. Moreover, many of the new states refused to see the world in the Cold War terms that the American government did. Dulles, in particular, argued that to opt for neutrality (as many did) in the struggle between good and evil was naïve and immoral. The attempt to create large military alliances was Dulles' way of implementing this version of a ''two-camp'' world.

TABLE 7-1   Decolonization: 1945–1965

IMPERIAL STATE	COLONY	INDEPENDENT STATE	DATE OF INDEPENDENCE
Great Britain	Burma	Burma	January 1948
	Cyprus	Cyprus	August 1960
	Gambia	Gambia	April 1965
	Gold Coast	Ghana	March 1957
	India	India	August 1947
		Pakistan	August 1947
	Palestine	Israel	May 1948
	Jamaica	Jamaica	August 1962
	Trans-Jordan	Jordan	May 1946
	Kenya	Kenya	December 1963
	Kuwait	Kuwait	June 1961
	Nyasaland	Malawi	July 1964
	Malaya, Sarawak, and Sabah	Malaysia	September 1963
	Maldive Islands	Maldives	July 1965

TABLE 7-1 (Cont.)

IMPERIAL STATE	COLONY	INDEPENDENT STATE	DATE OF INDEPENDENCE
	Malta	Malta	September 1964
	Nigeria	Nigeria	October 1960
	Sierra Leone	Sierra Leone	April 1961
	Singapore	Singapore	August 1965
	Somaliland (British and Italian)	Somalia	July 1960
	Ceylon	Sri Lanka	February 1948
	Sudan (Britain and Egypt)	Sudan	January 1956
	Tanganyika & Zanzibar	Tanzania	April 1964
	Uganda	Uganda	October 1962
	N. Rhodesia	Zambia	October 1964
France	Algeria	Algeria	July 1962
	French Equatorial Africa	Central African Republic	August 1960
		Chad	August 1960
		People's Republic of the Congo	August 1960
		Gabon	August 1960
	French West Africa	Benin	August 1960
		Togo	April 1960
		Niger	August 1960
		Senegal	June 1960
		Upper Volta	August 1960
		Guinea	October 1958
		Ivory Coast	August 1960
		Mali	September 1960
		Mauritania	November 1960
	Madagascar	Madagascar	June 1960
	Indochina	Kampuchea (Cambodia)	November 1953
		Laos	October 1953
		Vietnam	July 1954
	Lebanon	Lebanon	December 1946
	Morocco (French and Spanish)	Morocco	March 1956
	Syria	Syria	April 1946
	Tunisia	Tunisia	March 1956
Belgium	Ruanda-Urundi	Burundi	July 1962
		Rwanda	July 1962
	Belgian Congo	Zaire	June 1960
Netherlands	Netherlands East Indies	Indonesia	December 1949

The Soviets, on the other hand, had dropped the Stalinist view and could see the new nations and their nonalignment as a positive "zone for peace," a third world. Such changes did erode Western influence, which pleased those Soviet leaders who desired an expansion of Soviet influence for its own sake or for ideological reasons. And there were security and economic concerns much like those Eisenhower voiced; as Khrushchev said:

> There's no doubt that if the Afghans hadn't become our friends, the Americans would have managed to ingratiate themselves with "humanitarian aid," as they called it. *The amount of money we spent in gratuitous assistance to Afghanistan is a drop in the ocean compared to the price we would have had to pay in order to counter the threat of an American military base on Afghan territory.*[41]

By and large, however, the Soviet presence in the Third World was more the result of being invited in, and that often came because the Third World states found it useful to play the Soviets off against the West. Nowhere would this be clearer than in the Middle East. In July, 1952, young Egyptian army officers (including Gamal abdel Nasser and Anwar al-Sadat) staged a coup, which gradually constructed a revolutionary state under Nasser's leadership.[42] Externally, Nasser became the voice of Arab nationalism; internally, the promoter of economic development, for which he secured American and British agreement to finance a dam at Aswan on the Nile River. Then came Dulles' "pactomania." Nasser interpreted the Baghdad pact and American requests that Nasser join in the defense against international communism as Western *neocolonialism*—an attempt to reassert Western dominance over the region. At the same time, Egypt was moving into a confrontation with Israel and needed arms, something the United States was loath to supply because of its close ties with Israel and because Nasser rejected the alliance. In August, 1955, Nasser turned to Czechoslovakia (in reality, the Soviet Union) for arms. The Americans and British could find no way to bring Nasser to heel other than to cancel the dam project (July 1956). In response, Nasser nationalized the Suez Canal, bringing it under Egyptian rather than British control. British Prime Minister Eden resolved to deal with Nasser, whom he saw as another Hitler! He found allies in the French (Egypt supported the Algerians) and the Israelis (who had suffered from Palestinian raids mounted in Egyptian-controlled territory).[43] As the American government insisted on a peaceful resolution of the crisis, the conspirators did not divulge their plans. The Israelis attacked Egypt on October 29 (as the Hungarian crisis moved towards its climax). On the pretext that the fighting threatened the Canal (Israeli armored columns overwhelmed the Egyptian army in the Sinai), Britain and France ordered both sides to withdraw from the Canal area. When Nasser refused, Anglo-French forces attacked, although in a haphazard fashion. The operation ended on November 7, after Eisenhower indicated that he would shut off oil to the Allies

---

[41]*Khrushchev Remembers*, p. 508 (emphasis added).

[42]For studies of Egypt and Nasser, see Peter Mansfield, *Nasser's Egypt* 2nd ed. (Hammondsworth: Penguin, 1969); Raymond Baker, *Egypt's Uncertain Revolution under Nasser and Sadat* (Cambridge: Harvard University Press, 1978); Jean Lacouture, *Nasser* (New York: Knopf, 1974).

[43]For the Suez intervention, see Kenneth Love, *Suez* (New York: McGraw-Hill, 1969); Herman Finer, *Dulles over Suez* (Chicago: Quadrangle, 1964); and Donald Neff, *Warriors at Suez* (New York: Linden Press, 1981).

and allow their economies to collapse unless they withdrew. Similar pressure forced Israel to return all of the Sinai, but there the United Nations agreed to station neutral forces to patrol the Egyptian/Israeli frontier.

The attack heightened Nasser's prestige throughout the region. Soviet prestige also increased, as they had threatened Britain and France with a rain of rockets (*after* it was clear that the United States opposed the attack) and pledged volunteers to aid Egypt. The war made Soviet arms even more necessary for Egypt, and the Soviets agreed to fund the Aswan dam. The tie between Nasser's anti-Western nationalism and the Soviet Union disturbed Washington no end. When the Iraqi monarchy fell to a nationalist uprising in July, 1958, the Americans rushed troops to Lebanon, while Britain did the same in Jordan, to prevent internal tension from toppling two friendly regimes. In so doing, the United States moved one step closer publicly to equating radical or leftist nationalism with either communism or subservience to communism. Under Eisenhower, the CIA had covertly helped to bring down such nationalists in Iran (1953) and Guatemala (1954),[44] and the Lebanese operation seemed a further evolution of the policy.

The Chinese response to the Third World meant primarily dealing with their nonsocialist neighbors, and that was often colored by historic territorial claims. India, a strong supporter of the People's Republic from its founding, watched with growing concern in October, 1950, as the Chinese announced a return of Chinese control over Tibet. That brought the Chinese to the Indian frontier and ended the forty-year sphere of influence over Tibet that India had inherited from the British. Minimal garrisons of Chinese forces and a good deal of local autonomy in Tibet kept Tibet from endangering cordial relations. In April, 1954, India and China signed a declaration of the ''five principles'' (*panch shila*) to govern their relations: mutual respect for each other's territorial integrity and sovereignty, mutual nonaggression, mutual noninterference in each other's internal affairs, equality and mutual benefit, and peaceful coexistence. These principles were endorsed by a meeting of Third World leaders the following year in Bandung, Indonesia, and subsequently became an accepted norm of state relations for many states. In the case of China and India, the principles foundered in the face of old problems. The border between India and China/Tibet was open to dispute; each state claimed the same territory on the basis of British and imperial Chinese government claims. Neither side was willing to compromise, and the dispute worsened in 1958–1959, as Tibetans revolted against the Chinese. A Chinese campaign of suppression sent refugees into India. Skirmishes along the border began, and, with the rigidity displayed by both sides, the potential for a major clash grew.

The end of the decade also brought China into tension with the Soviet Union and into a confrontation with the United States.[45] The future of Taiwan and the construction of a socialist society in China were the principal preoccupation of

[44]For discussions of American involvement in Iran and Guatemala, see David Wise and Thomas Ross, *The Invisible Government* (New York: Random House, 1964).

[45]For ''triangular politics,'' see David Floyd, *Mao against Khrushchev* (New York: Praeger, 1964); John Fairbank, *The United States and Chinese,* 3rd ed. (Cambridge: Harvard University Press, 1971); J. Kalicki, *The Pattern of Sino-American Crises* (Cambridge: Cambridge University Press, 1975). A Soviet view can be found in O. Borisov and B. Koloskov, *Soviet-Chinese Relations* (Bloomington: Indiana University Press, 1975).

the Chinese leadership, itself heavily factionalized, often dividing roughly between the "experts" (those who stressed pragmatism and efficiency) and the "reds" (those, like Mao, who gave priority to the revolution in the lives of the people). Both accepted the need to liberate Taiwan and to rely on the Soviet assistance for modernization. The debate was essentially over priorities and means to accomplish the ends. In Mao's view, Soviet missile development in 1957 confirmed his view that the "correlation of forces" had shifted in favor of the socialist camp and that socialist states could take more risks under the protection of the Soviet nuclear umbrella. In addition, the Soviet agreement to provide assistance in constructing Chinese nuclear weapons would soon give China an independent umbrella. While strategically bold, Mao was tactically cautious (whether from personal inclination, careful calculation, or the "natural" result of compromise among competing factions is not clear). He reopened the Taiwan issue in August, 1958, by an extensive bombardment of Quemoy, a Nationalist-held island off the city of Amoy (see Map 4–1). This action may also have been part of a plan to mobilize the Chinese citizenry for an ambitious modernization program (the Great Leap Forward).

Eisenhower quickly pledged to defend Taiwan and any place else presumed to be vital to the defense of Taiwan. Quick and resolute action was the prescription for dealing with a Hitler-like state, an appellation the Chinese had acquired in Korea. Rapid augmentation of the American fleet in the area (there since Truman's 1950 decision), the readying of nuclear weapons, and naval escort of Nationalist shipping to the vicinity of Quemoy were all signals of American commitment. The Soviets pledged support to China in case of conflict with the United States, but made it clear that they did not want the Chinese to push the issue. The Chinese deescalated the crisis, but in their own manner—for instance, by shelling Quemoy on only odd-numbered days.

Soviet caution toward the West was irksome enough for the Chinese. In the following year, in the growing confrontation with India, the Chinese found the Soviets taking a neutral position, something the Chinese felt to be quite contrary to the Soviet role as ally and leading proponent of Marxism-Leninism. Soviet criticism of the Great Leap Forward (which proved to be a failure) smacked of intervention. By the end of the decade, the Chinese leadership appears to have concluded that the Soviets wanted China to refrain from provoking the West (hence, accept the status quo of Taiwan), while the Soviet Union both explored an accommodation with the West and raised the German issue again. Soviet interests were to take precedence over the interests of the socialist camp as a whole or China in particular. That was unacceptable.

The Soviets had become alienated as well. When Mao urged Khrushchev to be more aggressive toward the West, he would talk about the manpower advantage the socialist camp had and appeared unconcerned about Khrushchev's lectures on how nuclear weapons upset all those calculations. The Chinese appeared to be the kind of ally who could pull the Soviet Union into disaster. Moreover, as the circle of Soviet relations expanded (as with India), the Soviet Union experienced the dilemma of every large state with many friends; when those friends quarrel, what does one do to avoid alienating either or both? Neutrality proved to be ineffective. Finally, and most importantly, relations with the Western powers—those states with the ability to hurt, hinder, or help the Soviet Union—had to be regularized. Chinese objections brought Soviet actions to force the Chinese into acquiescence; in June, 1959, the Soviet Union terminated its aid for the Chinese nuclear weapons program and left the clear impression that all aid might be terminated if China did not hew to the Soviet line.

The Impending Crisis

By the end of the decade, Khrushchev was in a race against time with the West. At some point, they would discover that the Soviet Union was still greatly inferior to the West in terms of strategic nuclear delivery systems. Since 1956, the United States had sent high-altitude reconnaissance aircraft (the U-2) on flights across the Soviet Union. Though they tracked them by radar, the Soviets could not bring them down. Sooner or later, the compiled photographs would show few missiles and long-range bombers. How would the West exploit its strategic advantage? Eisenhower's massive retaliation policy risked nuclear war with a Soviet Union presumed to be equal in power. How much more aggressive might the Americans be when the truth emerged? The strategic dilemma was exacerbated by the growing American nuclear stockpile in Europe and growing German interest in having a voice in the use of such weapons. Khrushchev decided to resolve the dilemma by seeking to establish a working relationship with Eisenhower. He visited the United States in September, 1959, and Eisenhower prepared to return the visit the following year. While the visit produced mostly "atmospherics" and nothing approaching Roosevelt's response to Stalin, the exchanges probably reduced the tendency of each to view the other as a Hitler-like leader. (Dulles had left office in early 1959, dying of cancer.)

Khrushchev's second track was aimed at Europe. He wanted to get the West to recognize the post-war status quo: that Germany was to remain divided; that the socialist regimes in the East were there to stay; and that the borders, especially the contentious Polish-German boundary, were permanent. Berlin, however, remained a distracting problem. The Western presence and garrisons in two-thirds of the city served to keep alive hopes of a reunited Germany. More pressing was the escape route it provided many of the 150,000 East Germans who yearly fled to the West. That kind of exodus would continuously destabilize the German Democratic Republic. In November, 1958, Khrushchev warned that the status of Berlin had to change, and if the West refused to negotiate, the Soviet Union would give the East Germans control over access to Berlin. The Western powers in turn warned they would not accept this change, but proposed negotiations on the whole German problem. Diplomacy produced an agreement to hold another four-power summit in May, 1960, to discuss the issues. Perhaps the Cold War was drawing to a close.

Who would have known then that it would be Cuba rather than Germany that would bring the Cold War to a climax? American power (both economic and political) had insulated Latin America from world politics for much of the century.[46] In the post-war period, the United States had encouraged the generally conservative regimes in the hemisphere to work together to prevent "communist

---

[46]See Milton Eisenhower, *The Wine Is Bitter* (Garden City, N.Y.: Doubleday, 1963); John Mecham, *A Survey of United States-Latin American Relations* (Boston: Houghton Mifflin, 1965).

subversion," had subverted a leftist regime in Guatemala, and had supported strongmen and military juntas on the rather pragmatic grounds that "he may be an S.O.B., but at least he's *our* S.O.B."[47]

That did not mean, however, that the Eisenhower Administration was unwaveringly hostile to popular revolutionary movements, as the Cuban case illustrates.[48] Since 1933, Cuba had been ruled directly or indirectly, but corruptly and oppressively, by Fulgencio Batista, in collusion with foreign economic interests (essentially American). Fidel Castro, a 30-year-old, middle-class Cuban revolutionary, began his second guerrilla war on the Batista government in December, 1956. Given Castro's military weakness, the American position would be critical. Lower-level State Department officials were anti-Batista and cautiously sympathetic to Castro's cause, although many wanted a more traditional leader. The American ambassador also favored someone between Batista and Castro, especially as he became convinced of growing communist influence in Castro's movement. The Central Intelligence Agency's operatives in Cuba were the most supportive of Castro. The resulting American policy had many of the features of the American policy toward Chiang Kai-shek during the Chinese civil war: an insistence on changes in Cuba (such as the restitution of civil liberties, curbs on the police, and free election) backed by sanctions (such as suspension of arms deliveries and withholding spare parts to an American-equipped army).

In January, 1959, Castro entered Havana on the heels of the departing Batista and quickly adopted a socialist program for Cuba. Socialism was, and would continue to be, attractive to both revolutionaries and more traditional leaders in the Third World. Capitalism was intimately connected with colonialism or the economic dominance under which their nations had suffered. Socialism emphasized an economy under the control of the masses, working for the masses. This matched the political themes of the anti-imperialist, anti-oligarchic revolutionary leaders. But, most important, socialism as developed in the two most salient cases, the Soviet Union and the People's Republic of China, spoke in terms of a *command economy,* where decisions about production and distribution are made by the political leadership, who can use the economy as a means of furthering whatever goals they endorsed.[49] For Castro, socialism offered a means to restore the economy to Cuban hands through nationalization of foreign enterprises; to ensure the desired mix between manufacturing, export agriculture (sugar), and domestic agriculture; and to mobilize Cubans to support the new regime. A free-market, capitalist economy does not offer these political advantages.

"Socialism" was not well received in Washington; nor was expropriation of American firms or the execution of the losers, which often follows a revolution.

---

[47]Franklin Roosevelt's purported comment about Trujillo of the Dominican Republic; quoted by Robert Crassweller, *Trujillo* (New York: Macmillan, 1966), p. 213.

[48]For analyses of Cuba, Castro, and American policy, see Maurice Halperin, *The Rise and Decline of Fidel Castro* (Berkeley: University of California Press, 1974); Earl Smith, *The Fourth Floor* (New York: Random House, 1962); Philip Bonsal, *Cuba, Castro and the United States* (Pittsburgh: University of Pittsburgh Press, 1972); Herbert Matthews, *Revolution in Cuba* (New York: Scribner's, 1975).

[49]Robert Heilbroner, *The Making of Economic Society* (Englewood Cliffs, N.J.: Prentice-Hall, 1962), pp. 12–14. Heilbroner's discussion of the market economy and how unappealing it is to new nations is worth reading (pp. 14–16).

Castro paid a visit to the United States in April, 1959, speaking in moderate terms but clearly unwilling to stop the Cuban revolution. The Eisenhower administration quietly began to apply the label "communist" to the Cuban leadership and consider how the breach in the walls of containment might be rectified. And the American foreign policy bureaucracies drew a fatal lesson: unrest in the Third World, even when driven by liberal, progressive hopes, was likely to be exploited and then ridden by communists for their own purposes.

PART II:
SCIENTIFIC APPROACHES TO WORLD POLITICS

Systems Approach:
Cold War in an American-Dominated World?

Power in 1955 remained distributed much as it had been in the immediate post-war period, as Figure 7–1 and Table 7–2 indicate. This structure has two essential features. One state clearly predominates. The United States is more than twice as powerful as the next most powerful state. No coalition is likely to balance the power of the predominant state. Security calculations therefore are unlike either of the two systems we have seen in this century (the ladder-like and the equilateral). One state faces no threat to its security, while for all the rest, the traditional alliance offers no security.

FIGURE 7–1   Power Distribution in 1955

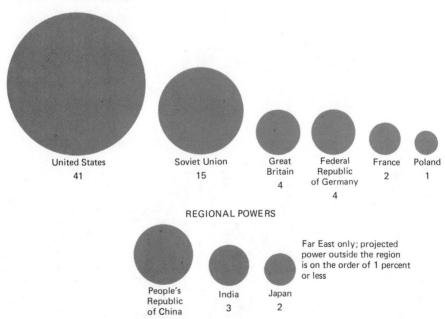

United States
41

Soviet Union
15

Great
Britain
4

Federal
Republic
of Germany
4

France
2

Poland
1

REGIONAL POWERS

People's
Republic
of China
7

India
3

Japan
2

Far East only; projected
power outside the region
is on the order of 1 percent
or less

TABLE 7-2 Basic Power Levels in 1955

MEASURE	WORLD	US	USSR	UK	FEDERAL REPUBLIC OF GERMANY[a]	FRANCE	POLAND	PRC	JAPAN[b]	INDIA[c]
1. Million metric tons of crude steel	265	105	45	20	24	12	4	3	9	2
2. Percent of world steel		39%	17%	7%	9%	5%	1%	1%	3%	—
3. Million inhabitants in independent states	2496	165	200	51	50	43	28	602	39	377
4. Percent of world population in independent states		7%	8%	2%	2%	2%	1%	24%	4%	15%
5. Political stability		1.0	1.0	1.0	1.0	.8	1.0	1.0	1.0	.8
6. Energy production (million metric tons of coal equivalent)	3480	1370	460	220	190	60	100	100	50	30
7. Percent of world energy production		39%	13%	6%	5%	2%	3%	3%	2%	1%
8. Nuclear weapons with strategic delivery systems	1750	1400	350	0	0	0	0	0	0	0
9. Percent of strategically deliverable nuclear power		80%	20%	0%	0%	0%	0%	0%	0%	0%
Power		41	15	4	4	2	1	7	2	3

a 1950–1955 only
b From 1951 with peace treaty restoring independence
c From 1947 with independence

Sources: For steel, political stability, nuclear weapons, and energy, see Table 6–3; for population, United Nations, *Statistical Yearbook, 1956* (New York: United Nations, 1956), Table 1.

These observations run counter to one of the most commonly held ideas about the postwar world; that it was *bipolar*.[50] "Bipolar" generally has meant that two states *of relatively equal power* dominated the world. Now it certainly is true that there was some *ideological* polarization (but even that ignores the presence of many states attempting to avoid either camp). And it is likely that leaders of both the Soviet Union and the United States saw advantages in talking about world politics as a struggle between the "slave" world and the "free" world. But ideological division does not mean equality of power. It is also true that leaders can *misperceive* distributions of power, as the Americans overestimated Soviet strategic nuclear capabilities. But it is clear that there were few misconceptions about power broadly conceived, and that is what Table 7–2 assesses. If one chose to view power in purely military terms, there was some balance between American nuclear weapons and larger Soviet land forces. Moreover, leaders of both states had an incentive to claim they were confronted by a militarily powerful adversary. But as defense expenditures by the two states reveal, whatever military balance there may have been in the late 1940s disappeared in the 1950s, thanks (in large part) to Korea.[51]

We can conclude that for the period 1945–1959, there was an overall *imbalance* in power. I shall designate this system as *monopolar,* defined as any structure of power in which one actor is more than twice as powerful as the next most powerful state and has more power than can be balanced by a coalition of all other major powers. It is important to be able to distinguish a monopolar system from a bipolar system, because we would expect the rules for a bipolar system, (where two states equally monopolize power) to be quite different from a system in which only one state clearly dominates.

Just what might those rules be? The last chapter asked you to develop such rules and suggested three possible methods to do so. Let me sketch my thinking and then list the rules I hypothesize to be consequences of a monopolar system. I considered the interaction patterns discussed in Chapter 6 and the diplomatic history related in this chapter. Soviet behavior toward Iran, Greece, Turkey, Berlin, and Korea constituted challenges to the American position. Would we have expected such behavior from a state as weak as the Soviet Union in the face of overwhelming American power? As a Soviet leader in a monopolar world, I believe I might have been much more cautious and far less provocative. My initial reaction, therefore, was that Soviet behavior was not the result of systemic pressures, but the consequence of environmental factors—such as Stalin's habit, created by years of domestic political infighting, to seek the destruction of rival centers of power. Alternatively, it reflected desperate Soviet bargaining responses in an attempt to deal with a perceived Hitler-type American state.

What if we said, however, that Soviet behavior in the late 1940s was the product of the momentary *military balance?* Challenge then might be expected, as

[50]For discussions of bipolarity, see Joseph Nogee, "Polarity: An Ambiguous Concept," *Orbis,* 18 (Winter 1975), 1193–1225; David Rapkin, William Thompson, and Jon Christopherson, "Bipolarity and Bipolarization in the Cold War Era," *Journal of Conflict Resolution,* 23 (June 1979), 261–95; Richard Rosecrance, "Bipolarity, Multipolarity, and the Future," *Journal of Conflict Resolution,* 10 (September 1966), 314–27.

[51]George Modelski, "World Power Concentrations: Typology, Data, and Explanatory Framework" (Morristown, N.J.: General Learning Press, 1974), p. 10.

might restrained American responses, given the fact that neither could easily overwhelm the other. The fact is that Stalin never saw power purely in military terms, and his successors threatened to attack American allies in 1956, supported the Viet Minh in Indochina, and in 1958–1959 demanded the status of Berlin be changed—all in a period of military *imbalance.*

If Soviet behavior seems hard to reconcile with the structure of the system, consider American behavior. Given its clear domination, what was to prevent the use of such power to undermine, cripple, or destroy the weaker states, including the Soviet Union? If you have trouble imagining such possibilities because the United States did not do these things, or because it does not seem capable of such ruthlessness, then consider a system in which the Soviet Union is the lone super-power, or perhaps more bluntly, Nazi Germany. Remember that from the per-spective of the systems approach, states behave according to power distribution, irrespective of who the actors are, as long as the boundary seals the environment off from the system. Did systemic pressures fail to influence American behavior? Why did it not run amuck in a relatively defenseless world?

A host of answers should be deluging you, but let me try a systemic expla-nation. *Let us assume that post-war American and Soviet behavior adhered to systemic rules.* Systemic rules reflect each major power's search for security. In a monopolar world there is no threat to the security of the superpower. On the other hand, the second most powerful state (abbreviated hereafter as SMP state) lives under con-stant threat of destruction from the superpower. Stalin may have been paranoid, but an SMP state may have no choice but to keep anti-aircraft units on constant alert. It must constantly be oriented to power politics. For the rest of the major powers, there were two constant, unanswerable threats to their security. What rules would optimize security for the states in such a system?

Rule 1. Seek to maintain or increase the state's power. For the weak major powers, there is no prospect of overtaking the superpower, and only a modest prospect of balancing the SMP state. They can only hope to maintain their power. From the system perspective, we can suggest that the cooperative relations among West European states in the post-1945 period were a result of the realization that terri-torial expansion could not significantly change their power position. At the other extreme, the superpower is not driven to increase its power, because such an in-crease provides little or no extra security. It will be interested in *maintaining* its power predominance, for that ensures its survival. The SMP state, on the other hand, may wish to increase its power as a means of enhancing deterrence against the superpower. It cannot realistically achieve a balance in the short run, but it can hope to increase the costs that the superpower would incur if it attacked the SMP state.

Rule 2. The superpower and weak major powers will insist on the status quo regarding power. As long as the status quo remains, the superpower has ensured its predom-inance at very little cost. In addition, the possession of great power may encour-age superpower leaders to think of their state as embodying the interests of all states, of great power conferring responsibility for the larger community of na-tions.[52] (In fact, as the superpower monopolizes more power, it does become *the*

---

[52]Compare Robert Osgood, "Reappraisal of American Policy," in Robert Osgood, et al., *America and the World* (Baltimore: Johns Hopkins University Press, 1970), p. 10.

center of the world defined in power terms.) In that community, which the super-power symbolizes, the status quo preserves both its own interests and, by exten-sion, those of the larger community as well. From this perspective, although the United Nations was a product of historical inertia, American domestic images, and the like, it fit into an American-dominated world, because it was a device for maintaining the status quo. In this world, the weak major powers accept the status quo; they have little choice. It is their ticket to survival.

Rule 3. Weaker major powers will gravitate toward the superpower. As no coalition can protect the weak major powers from the superpower, they can at least protect themselves from the SMP state. They become satellites who surrender some de-gree of their sovereignty to the superpower for some degree of security. NATO was not an accident of history, nor was American participation in NATO a re-sponse to its having learned its lessons; these were system-induced behaviors.

Rule 4. The SMP state will probe to discover where and how it can increase its power without provoking retaliation by the superpower. For the SMP state, the status quo is dangerous and has to be modified in order to enhance its security. Yet the status quo is protected by the superpower. Thus, the SMP state must discover where the superpower is most intensely committed (and thus avoid those areas) and which methods of testing the status quo are most provocative (and thus avoid those actions). Probing is therefore a necessary, *system-induced behavior,* not the result of an expansionist historical tradition or an expansionist ideology. It is *secu-rity-seeking* behavior for a state with few options.

Rule 5. The superpower will respond to probes with restraint. The American gov-ernment had the option of shooting its way into Berlin or attacking China with nuclear weapons after its entry into the Korean war. Or doing nothing. The sys-tem *forced* the superpower to respond because of the latter's commitment to the status quo. It also forced it to do so *with restraint* because, even if the probe were successful, success *could not change the distribution of power to a significant degree* and overreaction would damage the community (and hence the superpower's inter-ests). In addition, the SMP state does not counterescalate because of the demon-stration of commitment by the superpower. All parties kept the war confined to Korea; the United States refrained from bombing supply bases or airfields in Manchuria or Siberia. The Soviets kept hands off, and the Chinese did not attack American airbases in Japan or the maritime supply route to Korea. The Chinese did label their troops "volunteers," to minimize the appearance of escalation.

In summation, in a monopolar world, we would expect challenge and re-sponse, occasional limited wars, globalist intervention by the superpower, and general displays of restrained hostility between the SMP state and the super-power. In other words, a cold war. Drawing on this one historical example, we can hypothesize that a cold war will characterize any monopolar system.

You might consider this additional example. It is possible to consider *regions* as having their own systems: a specific regional distribution of power and corre-sponding rules. State behavior in the region should be responsive to the subsys-tem if (a) the boundary prevents intrusion of the environment, and if (b) *the re-gional subsystem is relatively isolated from the international system.* That last requirement will always raise problems, as we shall see when we examine the Middle Eastern regional subsystem in the next chapter. For the moment, assume that the socialist camp (Eastern Europe, the Soviet Union, and the People's Republic of China) is relatively isolated from the international system. Here is another monopolar world: a superpower (the USSR), a SMP state (the PRC) and the remainder of weaker states.[53] The Soviet Union has not run amuck there—it did not incorporate Eastern Europe into the Soviet state as the Tsars had done in their expansion of the Russian state or as the Soviet state did with the Baltic republics in 1940. (Constitutionally the Soviet Union is a collection of separate republics; thus its structure would *encourage* the addition of a Polish Soviet Socialist Republic to the Union.) When the Soviets intervened, as in Hungary, they did not destroy the state, and generally seemed to try to avoid coercive intervention. The tension in that regional subsystem might aptly be called a cold war.

As you have been reading this argument, you may have found yourself saying "yes, but." Let me try to categorize the kinds of challenges or objections that might be leveled against the systems approach and its application.

1. *The hypothesized systemic rules are incorrect.* For instance, the preponderance of power enjoyed by one state might well have allowed for this systemic rule: *the superpower will appease the SMP state rather than confront it.* After all, change cannot damage the security of the superpower, nor can appeasement lead to world war, because the far weaker SMP state would not risk its existence. If this rule *were* correct, then American behavior was clearly at variance with the rules. Dulles' pactomania, his willingness to go to "the brink of war," and constant confrontation with socialist states came from *environmental* sources, such as the image of a Hitler-type state, rather than systemic pressures.

2. *The hypothesized systemic rules are correct, but actual behavior does not accord with the rules.* Singling out examples such as the Berlin blockade may seem conclusive, but are those representative of all Soviet and American behaviors? Malenkov's 1953 call for negotiations and subsequent attempts to improve relations with Yugoslavia, Greece, and Turkey can be seen as attempts to reach a mutually agreeable end to the Cold War. Similarly, the American efforts to reunify Korea or to contain radical Arab nationalism do not seem to be lessons in restraint. Indeed, the fearfulness that American decision makers demonstrated during much of this time suggests that they failed to see the security that their predominance gave them—or that environmental forces overrode systemic pressures.

3. *The very conception of power is flawed, because it does not take into account the changes wrought by nuclear weapons.* Nuclear weapons did add enormous destructive power to a nation's military forces. They compressed the time it took to destroy an opponent from months or years to minutes. Moreover, they permitted the destruction of an opponent's civilian society without defeating or even engaging the opponent's armed forces. Indeed, a nation that *lost* on the battlefield might still destroy the "winner's" society.[54] When decisions about the life or death of nations had to be made in minutes and when power could not be used to protect the homeland, might we not expect states to behave quite differently, no matter the distribution of power? Might not a few nuclear weapons become the "great equalizer" of nations?

---

[53]Compare Thomas Robinson, "Systems Theory and the Communist System," *International Studies Quarterly,* 13 (December 1969), 398–420.

[54]Thomas Schelling, *Arms and Influence* (New Haven: Yale University Press, 1966), pp. 18–26.

Perhaps. A brief look at the hypothesized rules of the monopolar system, however, suggests that nuclear weapons may *reinforce* rather than undermine systemic pressures:

1. *Maintain or increase power.* All major powers will attempt to develop nuclear weapons and efficient delivery systems.
2. *Status quo orientation.* Nuclear powers will seek to prevent the proliferation of nuclear-armed states[55] and to control escalation situations by clinging to the status quo. The threat of nuclear war also consolidates the perception of community, for the effects of nuclear war would not be confined to the targets.
3. *Gravitation toward the superpower by weaker major powers.* Weaker states can have a nuclear sting, but a sting can also be a provocation. As Britain coupled its atomic weapons to its strategic V-bomber force in the late 1950s, it felt *more* vulnerable to a Soviet attack, because such weapons forced the Soviets to *see* Britain as a primary target in a nuclear war. Having a weak nuclear force made the protection of the United States all the more necessary.
4. *Probing.* For nuclear weapons to deter probing behavior, the SMP state would have to believe that the superpower would unleash such horrendous punishment for a comparatively small transgression of the status quo. Such a threat is incredible. Many probes will remain undeterred by nuclear weapons.
5. *Restrained response.* The superpower has no incentive to overreact with nuclear weapons because the results for its security pale next to the potential cost of using nuclear weapons. Monopolar worlds do not encourage harsh superpower behavior; the presence of nuclear weapons makes this even more true.

The rules for any system remain hypotheses, for which we should expect to find plausible counter-hypotheses. The strength of the boundary between system and environment remains open to conjecture. When can we be more precise about which hypothesis is correct? The next chapter gingerly picks up that question.

Interaction Approach: Pattern Analysis Revisited— The Cold War Gets Older, But Does It Get Colder?

Chapter 6 provided an initial look at the interaction patterns of the Cold War. I drew on the historical record for that *qualitative* description of the interaction and its results. By "qualitative," I mean that the description told you *what* happened, using verbal symbols such as "propose" and "counter-propose." Social scientists have also employed another method to describe political phenomena. Here their interest is to measure how much *change* there has been in particular phenomenon, and to do so using numbers rather than words. This *quantitative* approach attempts to find ways to *measure* such things as the number of proposals presented by the United States or the degree of fear manifested by the Soviet Union. This section examines two different ways in which we might measure *the intensity of the Cold War* over time.

---

[55]For analyses of proliferation, see Richard Rosecrance, ed., *The Dispersion of Nuclear Weapons* (New York: Columbia University Press, 1964); William Bader, *The United States and the Spread of Nuclear Weapons* (New York: Pegasus, 1968); "Nuclear Proliferation," *Annals of the American Academy of Political and Social Science,* 430 (1977).

Chapter 6 defined a "cold war" as a state of conflict in which states perceive each other as hostile and aggressive, pursue incompatible goals and take risky actions, but acknowledge a common interest in preserving the peace between them. The cold-war patterns of behavior reported in Table 6–2 capture those elements, but they do not tell us whether some behaviors predominated over others, or if, over time, the behavior was uniform. To get at those aspects of cold-war interaction, I will examine the *level of hostility* shown toward the other state. The time period is 1948 to 1962 (why 1962 was chosen will become clear in the next chapter). In a cold war we would expect rather high levels of hostility. How might we describe the actual level of hostility in some precise manner?

"Event-interaction" analysis is one commonly employed method.[56] Students of world politics using this approach count the number of different types of behaviors that are reported in a standard news source such as *The New York Times* or *Facts on File.* Figure 7–2 summarizes the data of this type collected by William Gamson and Andre Modigliani.[57] Gamson and Modigliani are concerned with the behaviors of the two alliances (the American-led Western states and the Soviet-led socialist camp), so their findings speak to *coalition* interaction, rather than state interaction. They classify actions as refractory (behavior that increases disagreement), conciliatory (behavior that reduces disagreement), or neutral. We can measure changes in the Cold War by asking what proportion of the behavior of the two coalitions has been hostile (refractory).

For the entire time period, the overall behavior of the coalitions in their interactions was hostile, sometimes at a quite high level. Although the fluctuations in hostility make it more difficult to generalize about the Cold War over time, there does seem to be a cyclical nature to the hostility, approximating a wave:

A second measure of hostility is that developed by Kjell Goldmann, who determined how often the Soviet coalition and the American coalition asserted that war was likely in Europe and that the other coalition had hostile or threatening intentions in Europe.[58] Goldmann calls this an indication of *tension* in Europe. The results appear in Figure 7–3. Once again, we see the outline of a wave in the levels of Cold War tension. This wave characteristic has been noted in other aspects of the relationship between the two states, most notably the arms race.[59] The data suggest that this particular cold war, and (by extension as a hypothesis), all cold wars, are characterized by regular alterations in the level of hostility. The

[56]See Charles Kegley, Jr., ed., *International Events and the Comparative Analysis of Foreign Policy* (Columbia: University of South Carolina Press, 1975); and Edward Azar and Joseph Ben-Dak, eds., *Theory and Practice of Events Research* (New York: Gordon & Beach, 1975). Some principal scholars in the field include Charles McClelland (World Event/Interaction Survey), Rudolph Rummel (Dimensions of Nations), and Edward Azar (Conflict and Peace Data Bank).

[57]William Gamson and Andre Modigliani, *Untangling the Cold War* (Boston: Little, Brown, 1971).

[58]Kjell Goldmann, "East-West Tension in Europe, 1946–1970," *World Politics,* 26 (October 1973), 106–25.

[59]Paul Smoker, "The Arms Race: A Wave Model," *Peace Research Society (International) Papers,* 4 (1966), 151–92.

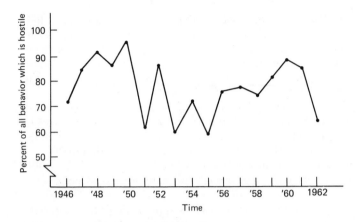

FIGURE 7-2   Inter-Coalition Hostility, 1946–1962

two measures obviously deviate from this general proposition to some degree, but the wave model provides new insights. Historically, the summit conference in Geneva and the "spirit of Geneva" appear to mark the *end* to a period of lessened tension rather than the beginning of a new period of relaxation.

Furthermore, the interactions appear to remain in the hostile range, rather than escalating to hot war or "declining" into a less conflictual pattern. Why

FIGURE 7-3   Inter-Coalition Tension, 1946–1962

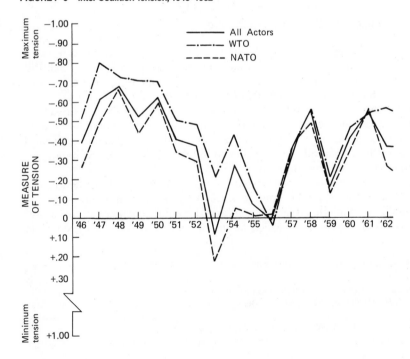

should this be the case? Why, indeed, should there be a more or less regular alteration in levels of hostility? Let's begin with the question of why alterations occur. You might hypothesize any number of reasons—Stalin's death decreases Soviet rigidity or increases the divided Soviet elite's need for international calm; Dulles' death reduces American rigidity in a similar way. Alternatively, new advances in weapons systems, such as the introduction of the ICBM in 1957, might trigger an increased hostility. Notice, however, that these proposed explanations come from other approaches (the policy makers and the environmental-factor approaches, respectively). While historically these features may account for the "wave" in the cold war, we should look for explanations embedded in the interaction itself.

We might hypothesize that, in a cold war, while hostile action is met with hostile action, the response is likely to be of slightly greater intensity or of slightly greater frequency. Both states have an incentive to "up the ante." However, at some point both states or coalitions see themselves approaching the war threshold, a threshold neither wants to cross. To avoid that possibility, the states reciprocally scale back their hostile actions and "down the ante" in that regard as well. As they approach the cooperative range of behaviors, the states become fearful that they are being taken advantage of (or both try to take advantage of the cooperativeness of the other), and the reciprocated hostile actions mount again.

If this scenario is correct, we would expect the Cold War wave to wash into the next decade, with 1962 marking the point of another upward climb in hostility levels. Whether it does so is grist for the next chapter.

Domestic and Environmental Factor Approach:
Public Opinion and the Korean Intervention

American foreign policy officials insist that, to be successful, foreign policy must flow from the people.[60] After all, that is a fundamental premise of a political democracy—leaders are responsive to citizens. Yet as one long-time student of public opinion has noted, "It is ironic, not to say frustrating, that groups of specially affected citizens seem to have ways of getting a grip on limited-impact issue-areas, such as agricultural policy or savings-and-loan regulations or auto safety standards, while the 'really important questions' of war and peace, life and death, which belong to us all, seem to elude our grasp and to be in the hands of a higher and more mysterious imperative."[61]

Scholarly research has not resolved the irony. Dexter Perkins identified a number of cases where public opinion seemed to be very influential,[62] while Melvin Small has concluded that " . . . a careful reading of American history reveals few clearcut situations in which public opinion has forced a President to

---

[60]See William Chittick's interview results, *State Department, Press and Pressure Groups* (New York: Wiley-Interscience, 1970), p. 99.

[61]Bernard C. Cohen, "The Relationship Between Public Opinion and the Foreign Policy Maker," in *Public Opinion and Historians,* ed. Melvin Small (Detroit: Wayne State University Press, 1970) p. 65

[62]D. Perkins, "The Department of State and American Public Opinion," in *The Diplomats 1919–1939,* ed. Gordon Craig and Felix Gelibert (Princeton: Princeton University Press, 1953), pp. 282–308.

adopt foreign policies that he himself opposed."[63] Yet a study of more recent public opinion found a general congruence between opinion and governmental policy on three of four different policy issues. But Robert Weissberg warned that "the questions of influence and causality are beyond the scope of our analysis."[64] On the other hand, Ralph Levering argues that public opinion is most influential when the political elite is divided.[65]

Like so much of our study of world politics, we have hypotheses rather than conclusions to offer. Our previous studies of ideology and weapons have provided us with a range of possible models of the relationship between public opinion and foreign policy:

Possibility I: The Deterministic Model

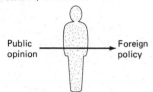

The nature of public opinion determines the nature of foreign policy.

Possibility II: The Independent Model

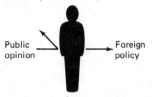

Decision makers operate independently of public opinion and make policy in response to either other factors or their own perceptions and preferences.

Possibility III: The Expanding Options Model

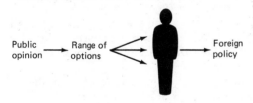

Public opinion does not dictate policy but suggests a greater range of viable choices that have support.

Possibility IV: The Narrowing Options Model

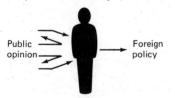

Public opinion decreases the number of options available to decision makers but does not dictate a single choice.(If it did, Possibility I would be the appropriate model.)

[63]M. Small, "Public Opinion," in *Encyclopedia of American Foreign Policy,* ed. Alexander De-Conde (New York: Scribner's, 1978), Vol. III, p. 845.

[64]Robert Weissberg, *Public Opinion and Popular Government* (Englewood Cliffs, N.J.: Prentice-Hall, 1976), pp. 138–68. See also Alan Monroe, "Consistency Between Public Preferences and National Policy Decisions," *American Politics Quarterly,* 7 (January 1979), 3–19.

[65]R. Levering, *The Public and American Foreign Policy 1918–1978* (New York: Morrow, 1978), p. 31.

Possibility V: The Manipulation Model

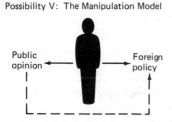

Public opinion ←——→ Foreign policy

Decision makers make policy and attempt to mold public opinion in the hope of having it support the chosen policy.

In such a model, the term "public opinion" means an expression of attitudes and knowledge held by a particular group (in this case, adult citizens) about a particular issue (such as the desirability of granting American aid to Egypt to build the Aswan dam), an event (such as the Anglo-French-Israeli attack on Egypt), or an individual or collection of individuals (such as Nasser or neutralist leaders in general).[66] Students of public opinion lean toward Models II and V, which see policy makers as unresponsive to public opinion, or toward Model IV, which depicts public opinion as setting limits.[67] Those limits may be in terms of the "great veto" public opinion can exercise to block initiatives by an administration and the "electoral club" that threatens to punish transgressions of the limits that opinion will tolerate. Or the public may constantly press decision makers to select the least costly, least disruptive policy.

In support of the unresponsiveness and limitations models, scholars often point out the general ignorance and lack of interest the public displays about world politics. For instance, in early 1950, 42 percent of respondents to a poll could not correctly say what the term "cold war" meant, or replied that they "didn't know." One year later—with the Korean war prominent in the news—45 percent were still unable to do so.[68] Moreover, public opinion on foreign policy is often characterized as unstable and inconsistent, responding to "moods" that sweep the public. Conversely, others have found that in times of crisis, the public rallies behind the President and, given the President's enormous access to the media, the President is often able to shape that unstable or inconsistent opinion to suit his policy.

If we were to take a specific example of foreign policy, which of the five models would be most applicable? The example which I shall report is the American decision to intervene in the Korean war. What impact did public opinion have? To answer that, we first need to know who had what opinion in June of 1950 and how that opinion was communicated.

[66]See, among others, Philip Converse, "Public Opinion and Voting Behavior," in *Nongovernmental Politics*, ed. Fred Greenstein and Nelson Polsby (Reading, Mass.: Addison-Wesley, 1975), pp. 75–169; V.O. Key, Jr., *Public Opinion and American Democracy* (New York: Knopf, 1968); W. Lance Bennett, *Public Opinion in American Politics* (New York: Harcourt Brace Jovanovich, 1980).

[67]See Michael Leigh, *Mobilizing Consent* (Westport, Conn.: Greenwood Press, 1976); Kenneth Waltz, "Electoral Punishment and Foreign Policy Crises," in *Domestic Sources of Foreign Policy*, ed. James Rosenau, (New York: Free Press, 1967), pp. 263–92; Gabriel Almond, *The American People and Foreign Policy* (New York: Harcourt Brace Jovanovich, 1950); William Caspary, "The 'Mood Theory,'" *American Political Science Review*, 64 (June 1970), 536–47; and John Mueller, *War, Presidents and Public Opinion* (New York: John Wiley, 1973).

[68]Gallup polls of February 26–March 3, 1950, and January 1–5, 1951; in George Gallup, *The Gallup Poll, Public Opinion 1935–1971*, Vol. II (New York: Random House, 1972), p. 897 and p. 963, respectively.

MECHANISM OF COMMUNICATION	WHOSE OPINION
Mail and telegram	Opinion of those who are willing and able to make their opinions known
Representatives ("opinion leaders")	Individuals such as lobbyists or legislators who claim to reflect the opinions of specific constituencies and who may mold that opinion
Media	Opinion of the writers, possibly reflecting readership opinion; media may mold that opinion
Public opinion polls	Opinion of a more or less random sample of individuals who are said to reflect the opinion of the public

By and large, what we know of public opinion comes from the polls. *What* is reported as opinion, however, is often determined by the interests of the polling organizations (or by the people who commission the polls) and is affected by *how* the poll questions are asked. The opinions reflected in the polls in the six months prior to the Korean War have these characteristics:[69]

1. The public did not believe another war involving the United States was likely in the short run, but divided equally about the possibility of being drawn into another war in the next five years.
2. Most of the public felt that the Soviet Union was trying to build itself up to be the ruling power of the world, an opinion which presumably would allow the administration to intervene in Korea under the guise of containment. The public, however, did not insist on a confrontational policy. Indeed, two-thirds supported negotiations with the Soviets for arms control, even though a clear majority doubted negotiations would be successful.
3. The public was initially reluctant to spend more for defense. In March, 1950, only 23% of the respondents agreed that the administration was spending too little for "the army, navy, and airforce" in Truman's tight, pre-Korea budget. At the end of the month, however, 63% of the public favored an increase in military spending.[70]

The fluctuation of opinion on defense spending and the inconsistency of wanting negotiations with a state seeking to rule the world and expecting failure are examples of what some have called the confused nature of public opinion. Such confusion would provide no guidance to a leader willing to respond to public opinion, and carte blanche to a leader unresponsive to public opinion. Before we conclude, however, that the confusion of public opinion undermines any potential for influence, we might do well to consider Lance Bennett's observations.[71] Opinions, Bennett argues, always occur in a *context*. For instance, between the first and second polls done in March on defense spending, the highly respected General Dwight Eisenhower had testified that the United States had

[69]The following conclusions are drawn from the polls reported in *Gallup Poll*.

[70]Gallup polls of February 26–March 3, 1950, and March 26–31, 1950; *ibid.*, pp. 897–98 and p. 906, respectively.

[71]Bennett, *Public Opinion*, pp. 43–95.

disarmed too much. His testimony may have helped shift the debate on defense spending out of the traditional manner of thinking about the defense budget ("How much can the economy and federal government afford to spend?") and into an emphasis on security ("How much do we need to protect the nation?"). Moreover, the first March Gallup poll asked about spending for the three military services. Those services had repeatedly and publicly attacked each other's budgets and plans in the preceding years, alleging that budget requests by the other services were for "selfish" purposes. In the second poll, Gallup asked if spending on *national defense* should be changed. "National defense" carries different connotations. Had the public changed its mind about defense spending? Perhaps. An equally likely conclusion would be that the public responds to different cues in different ways without changing opinion.

Bennett also questions the inconsistency argument. Is favoring negotiations with the Soviet Union inconsistent? If we impose *our* notions of consistent opinions, it might be. Bennett argues that it would be better to probe to see how individuals integrate opinions. The public, for instance, may assume that "talking is always better than not talking" and that talking is one way to dissuade the Soviet Union from believing it can become the ruling power of the world. (Such opinions may be naïve; they are not necessarily inconsistent.)

Thus there may be constancy and consistency in public opinion, enough so to "send a message" to the political leadership. At the same time, it should be clear that by manipulating various symbols (such as "national security"), political leaders can alter the public's appreciation of an issue. Similarly, the leadership can present new ways of integrating opinions, such as arguing that any negotiations with a Hitler-like state lead to disaster. This is not to suggest that public opinion is uniform. Often it is split into partisan factions with conflicting prescriptions. When respondents were asked, "For the future, which one of these three things do you think it most important for the United States to do?", they divided rather equally:[72]

1. Rely mainly on the UN organization and do what we can to make it more effective   28%
2. Rely mainly on our alliance with other democratic countries, and work toward closer unity with them   27%
3. Rely mainly on our own armed forces, and stay out of world affairs as much as we can   38%

Even if opinion determined policy, how would these three conflicting views translate themselves into policy? Such divisions pose political problems for a President. A choice of one direction may alienate two-thirds of the public. In this particular case, a sizeable number of Americans appeared to support isolationism, a policy that Truman was convinced would bring on World War III. Perhaps his ambivalence toward the implications of NSC–68 can be found in the contradictory preferences among the public. Perhaps when a President can avoid

---

[72]National Opinion Research Center Poll, March 1951; reprinted by permission of the publisher from *Public Opinion Quarterly*, 15 (Summer 1951), 399. Copyright 1951 by The Trustees of Columbia University.

choosing (as Truman could before June), divided public opinion encourages a President to drift.

The willingness to avoid choice may also be compounded by an inability to manipulate symbols, definitions of the situation, or integrating principles. That inability may stem from the low respect the public accords the political leadership. Gallup has long asked, "Do you approve or disapprove of the way X is handling his job as president?" Truman's rating showed a steady erosion from the high of 69-percent approval in January, 1949, to 37 percent in March, 1950.[73] Might not a president be tempted to take bold action in order to rebuild his political support and to increase his control over the contours of public opinion?

Truman's popularity in the months before the Korean war was entangled with the erratic fortunes of the Republican Senator from Wisconsin, Joseph McCarthy.[74] McCarthy had declared that the State Department had been infiltrated by communists, that Secretary of State Acheson was a dupe of the communists, and that Truman's policy was one of foul appeasement. McCarthy was big news, seeming to strike a responsive chord among some of the public and many of the Congressional Republicans, whose ability to wreck Presidential programs was of growing concern to Truman. In all, we might say that the absence of public support, coupled with the McCarthy challenge, might predispose Truman to respond vigorously in the face of the North Korean attack.

But he may have responded vigorously for other reasons. How did Truman look on public opinion and the mechanisms by which it reached him? Did he listen to it? Do policy makers, as a rule, listen? During the mid-1960s, Bernard Cohen interviewed American Foreign Service Officers. He found that the FSO's did monitor the opinion of particular groups, but they tended to believe that public opinion should follow, rather than lead, decision makers and that the job of the leadership was to mold public support for the policy.[75]

Truman, like any other President, acknowledged his obligation to serve the public interest. But was he to be responsive to "public opinion"? In this area he held some strong opinions of his own:

1. Organized mail campaigns did not reflect public opinion. "I think that is propaganda." " . . . when I was in the Senate, I never paid the slightest attention to propaganda messages, and I used to get them by the thousands."[76]

2. Polls did not reflect public opinion. Ever since the polls indicated that he would lose the 1948 election, Truman disregarded them.

3. Polls were clearly wrong when they contradicted administration policy or hopes. When told that a poll indicated a majority of Americans expected war in the next five years, Truman snapped, "I don't agree with that at all."[77]

[73]Polls of January 8–13 and February 26–March 3; *Gallup Poll*, Vol. II, pp. 890–903.

[74]For studies of McCarthyism and foreign policy, see Athan Theoharis, *Seeds of Repression* (Chicago: Quadrangle Books, 1971); Richard Freeland, *The Truman Doctrine and the Origins of McCarthyism* (New York: Knopf, 1972); Robert Griffith and Athan Theoharis, eds., *The Spectre* (New York: New Viewpoints, 1974).

[75]Cohen, *Public's Impact.*

[76]News conference of July 12, 1951; *Public Papers of the President: Harry S. Truman, 1951* (Washington: Government Printing Office, 1965), p. 388.

[77]News conference of June 1, 1950; *Public Papers: 1950,* p. 450.

4. Critical opinion voiced by opposition politicians was not worthy of consideration. "There are no issues on which these people can attack the administration," Truman insisted. "Now, when the opposition has no issues on which to fight, their next step is misrepresentation and smear. And that is what is going on."[78]

5. The public's opinion would be the same as the President's when all the facts were known.

Truman's view of "public opinion" and the mechanisms by which it might be transmitted suggest that the decision to intervene in Korea was made with little reference to public opinion. His own memoirs do not mention public opinion or hint that it had an impact. Glenn Paige's detailed reconstruction of the decision reports that at the end of the initial meeting between Truman and his advisors (June 25), the "Under Secretary of State . . . said, 'I'd like to talk about the political aspects of the situation.' The President snapped back, 'We're not going to talk about politics. I'll handle the political affairs.' "[79] The President's refusal to discuss politics and his initial reaction "to hit them [the North] hard" leads Paige to conclude:

> In the Korean decision the President is seen as not being pushed into militant decisions by a bellicose public opinion or as being incited by war cries of a few opposition legislators. In fact, perhaps partly as the result of surprise and shortened time for coalescence and effective expression of public opinion, he seems almost to have been in a position of momentary suspension from it. His anticipation of what would be popularly acceptable rather than any organized expression of popular will seems to have been crucial.[80]

This brief study of one decision corresponds best to Model II, independence from public opinion. There are overtones of Model V as well: when the public got "the facts," they would approve Truman's policy. Yet we also have to recognize that this was a decision made in a crisis situation, in which Presidents and others may have less time to consider public opinion. Truman's views on public opinion and its mechanisms for expression suggest that *non*-crisis decisions might show the same results. Until we look at such examples, we cannot be sure. And, until we can assess the impact of public opinion in other states, our generalizations will apply only to one country.[81] Nonetheless, our hypothesis suggests that the public's impact will be circumscribed. In looking ahead, would this be true for another President who found himself in another war? Is it likely to be true today?

---

[78]News conference of September 20, 1951; *ibid.:* 1951, p. 531.

[79]Paige, *Korean Decision,* p. 141.

[80]*Ibid.,* pp. 304–5. For three other case studies from the Roosevelt-Truman period, see Leigh, *Mobilizing Consent.*

[81]For comparison, Karl Kaiser, "The Role of Public Opinion in West German Foreign Policy," in *West German Foreign Policy: 1949–1979,* ed. Wolfram Hanrieder (Boulder, Col.: Westview Press, 1979).

CHAPTER EIGHT

1960–1969_____
Détente for some,
war for others

PART I:
DIPLOMATIC HISTORY[1]

The Cold War Bears Fruit

Soviet Politics and Policy   The growth of Soviet power and the expansion
of its interests continued to pose new difficulties for the Soviet leadership. Having
diplomatic relations with more nations increased the possibility that when states
were in conflict, Soviet policy would alienate one, if not both. States at some distance from the Soviet Union escaped the influence proximity brings, but distance
did not seem to diminish their ability to manipulate the Soviets. Nasser of Egypt
proved quite adept at this, as did Fidel Castro. When American pressure
mounted against socialist Cuba, initially by curbing Cuban sugar exports to the
American market, the Soviet Union agreed to buy the sugar, which the Soviet
Union did not need. Castro's subsequent request for protection was met by Soviet arms, ultimately including nuclear missiles. Each step committed the Soviet
Union to the success of Castro. Of course, Soviet aid gave the Soviets a channel
for influence, but that did not guarantee leverage. When Nasser was asked if he
were not mortgaging his country to the Soviet Union because of its extensive aid
program to Egypt, the Egyptian President replied,

---

[1]Major sources for the period include many of the sources given in footnote 1 of Chapter 7.
For the American Presidents, see Theodore Sorensen, *Kennedy* (New York: Harper & Row, Pub.,
1965); Arthur Schlesinger, Jr., *The Thousand Days* (Boston: Houghton Mifflin, 1965); Lyndon Johnson, *The Vantage Point* (New York: Holt, Rinehart and Winston, 1971); Doris Kearns, *Lyndon Johnson
and the American Dream* (New York: Harper & Row, Pub., 1976); *The Annual Register* (New York: St.
Martin's Press) is a good source of reporting and analysis on a state-by-state basis.

It is not as complex as you seem to think. When you are in debt to somebody, you are always in a strong position. Debtors are always stronger than creditors.[2]

If Soviet involvement did not guarantee influence, the Soviets must have noted with irony that the Americans thought it did. Americans tended to assume that communism and unrest had some link to Moscow. A plaintive Khrushchev once wrote to an American journalist:

About our "calling off" the Communist Party in your country or elsewhere. If you will forgive me for saying so, you make it sound as though I had a pack of dogs at my disposal that I could call off just by whistling them to heel. I just want to assure you that I have no special whistle that can send Communists scurrying in this direction or that.[3]

The control Stalin wielded over the world's communist parties was a thing of the past. The Sino-Soviet schism split those parties as well; pro-Moscow and pro-Peking factions often directed their combative energies against each other. And other groups emerged to challenge the traditional revolutionary party's claim to be the leading edge of revolution.

All major powers found themselves in a world in which the number of internal conflicts had grown significantly. The number of violent internal political changes had doubled in the decade since the mid-1950s.[4] Most, if not all, internal strife found its genesis and sustenance within the existing societal divisions in a state. Nonetheless, internal violence could drag other states into the turmoil. With a doubling of new states in the international system, most laboring with internal tensions, world politics increasingly penetrated domestic politics of many societies, and, in turn, was affected by domestic cleavage.

In this relatively novel world, the Soviet Union had to navigate and at the same time try to find the stable relationship with the United States Khrushchev had sought for several years. This proved difficult. An increase in the number of issues confronting the Soviet Union divided the Soviet Communist Party even more and kept alive the question of Khrushchev's tenure. Numerous Western scholars have attempted to classify the various participants in Soviet politics and their foreign policy preferences.[5] Vernon Aspaturian identifies two common coalitions within the Party.[6] Although these coalitions usually emerge in the never-

[2]Interview with Arnaud de Borchgrave, *Newsweek*, 73 (February 10, 1969), 36. © 1969 by Newsweek Inc. All rights reserved. Reprinted by permission.

[3]Khrushchev to Norman Cousins, August 1963; *Saturday Review* (October 30, 1971), p. 35. © 1963 Saturday Review Magazine Co. Reprinted by permission.

[4]William Whitson, "The Global Security Environment of 1977," in *Foreign Policy and U.S. National Security*, ed. W. Whitson (New York: Praeger, 1976), p. 10.

[5]See, among others, H. Gordon Skilling and Franklyn Griffiths, eds., *Interest Groups in Soviet Politics* (Princeton: Princeton University Press, 1971); Frederick Barghorn, *Politics in the USSR* (Boston: Little, Brown, 1966); Jerry Hough, "The Bureaucratic Model and the Nature of the Soviet System," *Journal of Comparative Administration*, 5 (August 1973), 134–68; and Gordon B. Smith, ed., *Public Policy and Administration in the Soviet Union* (New York: Praeger, 1980); for a case study, Robert Slusser, *The Berlin Crisis of 1961* (Baltimore: Johns Hopkins University Press, 1973).

[6]Vernon Aspaturian, "Internal Politics and Foreign Policy in the Soviet System," in *Approaches to Comparative and International Politics*, ed. R. Barry Farrell (Evanston, Ill.: Northwestern University Press, 1966), pp. 240–87.

ending debate over the allocation of economic resources, they appear to have significant foreign policy orientations as well. The "security-productionist-ideological" coalition is composed of the security sectors of the military, police, and defense industry; the heavy industry sector; and the ideologues and party bureaucrats. The "domestic" coalition is composed of those government and party units concerned with consumer goods, agriculture, welfare, and public services. The first coalition has a vested interest in maintaining an emphasis on defense and preparedness. It stresses the existence of foreign threats to the Soviet Union and is willing to accept and at times promote a state of international tension. This coalition's image of the United States depicts a monolithic ruling elite that has a pervasive hostility toward the Soviet Union and is prone to aggression.[7] The "domestic" coalition seeks to expand the Soviet citizens' benefits from the economy. It shows less concern about the existence of foreign threats and is disinterested in, or rejects, the desirability of a state of international tension. Its image of the United States sees two contending elite groups: the "sober" leaders and the "aggressive" leaders (often called "madmen"). The latter are hostile; the former recognize Soviet power and the need for accommodation.

The party chairman typically has policy preferences in common with both coalitions, as well as an interest in maintaining elite cohesion. How he resolves the conflicting demands is probably a function of personality, political style, and the balance of power in the Politburo. Khrushchev was willing to experiment with policy and had a personal commitment to improving domestic standards (as opposed to the "metal eaters" of the heavy and defense industries). His hold on power and his political style of confrontation combined, as we shall see, to give him tentative victories in the policy debates, but with significant reservations. Khrushchev probably did not stand alone as the bridge between competing policy preferences. Those party officials charged with overseeing foreign policy and the government's foreign policy bureaucrats probably found themselves divided but desiring a policy consensus. Indeed, the division of foreign policy responsibility within the party (different secretariats charged with supervision of relations with socialist regimes, with nonsocialist regimes, and with nonruling communist parties) increased the likelihood of debate and the incentive to shape a compromise.

We might expect Soviet policy to show three different "faces," depending upon the nature of the internal politics:

1. *Coalition dominance.* When one coalition dominates, its perspectives and preferences will receive emphasis in policy. Policy will have a relatively high degree of consistency. Continuing policy dominance by a coalition depends upon continued success; the losing coalition has a powerful claim to set policy in case of failure. (This in itself may be an implicit compromise between contending coalitions).

2. *A compromise policy.* Divergent preferences become reconciled into a policy that shows contradictory elements. Policy failure reopens the debate but most likely leads to another compromise, because both coalitions are tarred with the brush of failure.

3. *A policy of drift.* Neither coalition dominates, but no acceptable compromise emerges. Policy continues in the form of standard operating procedures of the various organizations that comprise the state.

[7]See Christer Jonsson, *Soviet Bargaining Behavior: The Nuclear Test Ban Case* (New York: Columbia University Press, 1979).

In the last chapter, we saw how Khrushchev leaned toward the domestic co-alition and sought some preliminary understanding with the United States on the questions of nuclear testing and the status of Germany. He prepared to receive Eisenhower at the summit in Paris; then both would tour the Soviet Union. Khrushchev, along with the "domestic coalition," had set the Soviet Union on the route to détente. He needed to demonstrate to the other coalition that the pol-icy would protect Soviet security concerns.

One of those critical "accidents" of history upset the political applecart. On May 1, 1960, two weeks before the opening of the Paris summit, an Ameri-can U-2 reconnaissance aircraft took off from Pakistan for a flight over the Soviet Union. Unlike in previous missions over the past four years, engine trouble and Soviet air defenses brought the plane down. Khrushchev was in an awkward po-sition; to raise the issue would jeopardize the summit. To remain silent would forego what propaganda and bargaining leverage the incident placed in his hand. Moreover, his domestic opponents pointed to the overflight just prior to the sum-mit as an example of fundamental American hostility, something Khrushchev's policy denied. Khrushchev announced the downing of the plane and the capture of its pilot, Francis Powers, but put the blame on the American military rather than on Eisenhower. This ploy failed, as Eisenhower accepted full responsibility and defended the violation of Soviet air space as necessary to ensure American se-curity.

The affront to Soviet prestige, let alone Khrushchev's reputation, would have been enough to scuttle the summit, which Khrushchev did. More signifi-cantly, the policy failure swung the balance to the "security" sector, and Khrushchev swung that way as well. Khrushchev, however, apparently won agreement to postpone any new actions until after the American Presidential election; perhaps a new face in the White House could salvage a policy of accom-modation.

An election year in the United States contributes its own impact on Ameri-can foreign policy. The Republican Administration had an incentive to give its candidate, Vice President Richard Nixon, the legacy of a popular policy. In the furor of the U-2 incident and the growing concern over Cuba, the Administra-tion fell back on the habitual "resistance to international communism." By the end of the year, the Administration had imposed an embargo on American goods to Cuba and began the training of Cuban refugees for an invasion of Cuba. The tension level between the United States and the Soviet Union reached such a level in September, 1960, that Soviet leaders worried that NATO forces might try to sink the Soviet ship carrying Khrushchev to New York to address the United Na-tions.[8]

The United Nations had always been an arena of confrontation between the United States and the Soviet Union, but the evolution of the institution had changed the nature of that confrontation.[9] The post of Secretary General, espe-cially under its current incumbent, Dag Hammarskjold of Sweden, had achieved

---

[8]Khrushchev, *Last Testament*, p. 463.

[9]Inis Claude, *The Changing United Nations* (New York: Random House, 1967); David Kay, *The New Nations in the United Nations* (New York: Columbia University Press, 1970); Leland Goodrich, *The United Nations in a Changing World* (New York: Columbia University Press, 1974).

autonomy from the major powers. Hammarskjold had gradually carved out a role as a mediator between contending states and as a supplier of United Nations forces to keep hostile forces separated. All his skills were needed when the Belgian Congo (present-day Zaire) achieved independence in July, 1960.[10] Within days, the Congolese army mutinied, the central government splintered into rival factions, and mineral-rich Katanga province seceded. The intervention of Belgian forces to restore order triggered a Congolese appeal for United Nations action. The Security Council ordered the Belgians to withdraw and created a United Nations force to take their place. Major-power cooperation quickly eroded as political factionalism increased in the Congo. The Western powers supported the moderate faction in the central government; the Soviets and Egyptians supported a radical faction; all opposed secessionist Katanga, which enjoyed the support of Belgium and some Western economic interests. As in all internal conflict, the activity of an outside agency could not be neutral. Even *inactivity* would help one faction over the others. Hammarskjold's efforts aided the moderates. Khrushchev's response was vitriolic. He called on Hammarskjold to "muster the courage to resign" and warned of "tremendous damage to the cause of peace and international cooperation" if the United Nations remained dominated by "the imperialist group of countries." His solution was a *troika*, three Secretaries General representing the West, the Socialist camp, and the Third World.

This challenge to the United Nations was tied to a more general challenge to the West. Before the United Nations, Khrushchev declared:

> It has been said that Khrushchev is preaching rebellion. I am not preaching rebellion, because the question of rebellion against an undesirable order of things in one or another country is decided by the people itself. All I said was that, if the colonialists do not grant independence and freedom to the colonial peoples, then there is nothing for the peoples of the colonial countries to do but to rise against this shameful oppression, and all honourable people should stretch out their hands to help those who are fighting for their human dignity, against robbery, against the colonialists.
>
> . . . the freedom-loving peoples of the Soviet Union stretch out their hands to help the peoples who are rebelling against the colonialists, for their freedom and independence.[11]

In January, 1961, Khrushchev's rhetoric escalated to a pledge of support for wars of liberation "fully and without reservations." And the pledge covered states such as Cuba, which were not colonies in a formal sense.

The new Kennedy administration saw this as a declaration of global guerrilla war. While calling for a renewed dialogue with the Soviets, American rhetoric escalated as well. There was the pledge of defense: "Let every nation know, whether it wishes us well or ill, that we shall pay any price, bear any burden, meet any hardship, support any friend, oppose any foe to assure the survival and

---

[10]See Crawford Young, *Politics in the Congo* (Princeton: Princeton University Press, 1965); Stephen Weissman, *American Foreign Policy in the Congo, 1960–1964.* (Ithaca, N.Y.: Cornell University Press, 1974).

[11]Speech to the United Nations, October 3, 1960; *Documents on International Affairs, 1960* (London: Oxford University Press, 1964), p. 25.

success of liberty.'' And there was a gloomy view of the near future: ''Each day we draw nearer the hour of maximum danger''; ''the tide of events has been running out and time has not been our friend''; and ''we must never be lulled into believing that either power [USSR or PRC] has yielded its ambitions for world domination.''[12] The United States began to rearm in time with the rhetoric.

Kennedy had inherited from the Eisenhower administration the preparations to topple Castro. He permitted the invasion by Cuban exiles to take place in April, 1961, at the Bay of Pigs. Castro's forces easily handled the invaders, and he and the Soviet leadership marvelled that no American forces intervened to save the day. Neither believed the United States would let the matter lie. The Soviet leadership saw no way out; their prestige had become linked to Cuba. They decided to deter a subsequent American attack by making large deliveries of conventional arms. That in turn increased American domestic pressure on Kennedy ''to do something about Cuba.''

Kennedy and Khrushchev did agree to meet in Vienna (June 1961) to explore areas in which they might agree. There were few; both needed a concession from the other without having to make one in return. Khrushchev reactivated the German issue, calling for a peace treaty recognizing the two Germanies and ending Western occupation of Berlin. As a countermove, Kennedy reinforced American units in Germany and Berlin in October. The German Democratic Republic quickly threw a wall up around West Berlin to prevent thousands from fleeing socialism, and Soviet and American tanks staged a war of nerves in Berlin's streets. The crisis subsided as neither side took a further step, but the animosity and incompatible interests remained.

The Cold War seemed to have a momentum all its own, and these clashes had a dreary familiarity. They obscured but could not hide the forces let loose or accelerated by the Second World War, which began to remold world politics. France became the fourth nuclear power in February, 1960, and gave Algeria its independence in July, 1962. The de Gaulle government then threw itself into European politics, attempting to reduce the American role. Decolonization gathered steam. Blacks in South Africa began to protest racial segregation (apartheid) and newly independent African states took up the cause of freedom there and in Southwest Africa (Namibia), the old League mandate controlled by South Africa. Wars of liberation began in the Portuguese colonies of Angola and Mozambique. In the Congo, the moderates gained the upper hand, and United Nations forces ended the secession of Katanga by force. (Hammarskjold died in an airplane crash in the Congo in December, 1961; his successor, U Thant of Burma, received support from all parties, putting the Soviet call for a troika on the back burner.)

Moscow and Peking continued to conduct their backstage verbal war. An anti-Mao position apparently united the Soviet leadership, but they could not get other socialist states or the communist parties of the world to censure the Chinese. Indeed, the search for ''votes'' probably gave the other parties and states greater leverage with the Soviet state. In the end, the Indian problem forced each

---

[12]Kennedy Inaugural of January 20, 1961, and State of the Union of January 30, 1961; *Public Papers of the President, John F. Kennedy, 1961* (Washington: Government Printing Office, 1962), pp. 1 and 22–23.

to make critical choices. In 1961, India began to move troops into areas along the frontier China claimed. In October, 1962, the Chinese attacked, drove the Indians back for miles, and then themselves withdrew.[13] The Soviets joined the West in providing military aid to India. The following year, China began a series of public denunciations of the Soviet Union for betrayal of Marxism-Leninism ("Soviet revisionism") and questioned the status of portions of the Sino-Soviet frontier. The Soviets responded with the hostility that ideologues find natural. Along the 4000-mile frontier between the two states, small but hostile incidents occurred with growing frequency.

Change also occurred among the leaders of nations. For the first time since the end of Queen Victoria's reign (1903), women occupied political positions that gave them direct influence on the state's foreign policy. In 1960, Sirima Bandaranaike became Prime Minister of Sri Lanka (Ceylon), to be followed by Indira Gandhi in India (1966) and Golda Meir in Israel (1969).[14] Bandaranaike and Gandhi had entered politics as adjuncts to males (the former's husband was Sri Lanka's Prime Minister from 1954–1959; the latter's father, Jawaharlal Nehru, was the Indian Prime Minister from 1947–1964). Meir, on the other hand, had long been active in Zionist and Israeli politics, and had served as Israeli ambassador to Moscow, Minister of Labor, and, from 1955–1966, Foreign Minister.

They each came to the prime ministership as the choices of male political leaders who wanted to use a popular name, yet control the government behind the scenes. Once in office, these women developed their own political following, displayed a leadership style that emphasized control of the political apparatus, and insisted on charting their own paths. Bandaranaike, for instance, was an active participant in conferences of nonaligned states and tried to serve as a mediator in various conflicts, including the 1962 Sino-Indian war and the Congo crisis. Bandaranaike and Gandhi insisted on nonalignment as a foreign policy principle, but often showed greater sympathy for the Soviet position. Meir, inevitably enmeshed in the Arab-Israeli struggle and Israel's dependence on the United States, had far less flexibility.

Did the entrance of women into key positions affect world politics? The evidence is too sparse to advance any conclusions. To tackle that question, we would need answers to three preliminary questions. First, are there *politically relevant* biological, psychological, and attitudinal differences between men and women?[15] Such differences may exist, but will they characterize the women who emerge in positions of authority? Second, do male leaders' perceptions of their female counterparts in other states lead them to behave differently? Finally, we would have to

---

[13]Neville Maxwell, *India's China War* (New York: Pantheon, 1970).

[14]For materials on these women, see Robert Kearney, *The Politics of Ceylon* (Ithaca: Cornell University Press, 1973); A. Jeyaratnam Wilson, *Politics in Sri Lanka, 1947–1973* (New York: St. Martin's Press, 1974); J.A. Sethi, *India in Crisis* (New Delhi: Vikas Publishing House, 1975); Henry Hart, "Indira Gandhi," in *Indira Gandhi's India*, ed. H. Hart (Boulder, Col.: Westview Press, 1976), pp. 241–73; Golda Meir, *My Life* (New York: Putnam's, 1975).

[15]For discussions of women and foreign policy, see Ole R. Holsti and James N. Rosenau, "The Foreign Policy Beliefs of Women in Leadership Positions," *Journal of Politics*, 43 (May 1981), 326–41.

decide how potent *any* individual is in shaping policy. If impersonal forces determine state behavior, gender is not politically relevant.

The Cuban Missile Crisis   Soviet-American relations took a new turn in 1962. The spring and early summer found the Soviet leadership confronting a mounting set of problems. In 1961, the American government made public what the Soviet leadership had known for some time: the Soviet Union was strategically vulnerable to an American nuclear attack: 100 intercontinental American missiles to 20 Soviet ICBM's in 1961, with a worsening balance projected in 1962. The initial Soviet lead in ICBM development had evaporated as the Soviets experimented with a wide variety of missile types while the United States rushed the production and deployment of two types, Titan and Minuteman. The German problem remained unresolved, with growing American commitment to a modernization of West European defenses and a sharing of control over tactical nuclear weapons with the Federal Republic of Germany. Cuba remained under threat of invasion. The Chinese were alleging Soviet disinterest in protecting the interests of the revolutionary movements of the world. Mixed in with those problems was never-ending Soviet debate about the allocation of resources. Defense is expensive. Soviet agriculture, always a weak but vital link in the Soviet economy, needed a massive infusion of funds if it were to preserve the Soviet standard of living. And over all these issues hung the ambiguity of how the United States would "bear any burden and pay any price."

To cope with these problems, the Politburo agreed upon an awkward compromise: medium- and short-range nuclear missiles would be secretly deployed in Cuba.[16] For some, it seemed to resolve a number of dilemmas. Khrushchev, in retrospect, defended his advocacy of deployment by saying "the main thing was that the installation of our missiles in Cuba would, I thought, restrain the United States from precipitous military action against Castro's government. In addition to protecting Cuba, our missiles would have equalized what the West likes to call 'the balance of power.'"[17] Shifting the balance would be done quickly and cheaply, thus allowing the agricultural and consumer sectors to avoid budget cuts to fund a crash ICBM program. Perhaps deployment might give the Soviets a bargaining chip in the negotiations about the future of the Germanies and German access to nuclear weapons. Deployment might blunt Chinese allegations of timidity and revisionism. In sum, deployment gave partial satisfaction to a number of interests. But as deployment might also damage interests, there was opposition as well. The deployment of missiles in Cuba would make them easy prey for the Americans if they decided to invade Cuba. It was improbable that the Politburo would order the launching of those missiles in case of an American invasion, because of the devastation likely to rain down on the Soviet Union. If deterrence failed, therefore, the opponent would acquire sophisticated Soviet war materiel (and Soviet personnel) at modest cost. Moreover, the missiles would be provocative; they would *encourage* the Americans to think of an attack—the very

---

[16]See Graham Allison, *Essence of Decision* (Boston: Little, Brown, 1971) for the best analysis of policy making in the Cuban missile crisis. For presentations of the Soviet perspective, see *Khrushchev Remembers*, pp. 488–505 and *Last Testament*, pp. 509–14.

[17]*Khrushchev Remembers*, p. 494.

thing to be avoided. Furthermore, those who wished to lower the level of tension with the United States could see little merit in the proposal.

The decision that emerged had the earmarks of compromise. Missiles were to be deployed, but only sixty out of a much larger stockpile. Given the growing American ICBM arsenal and larger bomber force, this would not "balance forces," yet it would be enough to be provocative. Deployment was to be clandestine, but haphazard provisions were made to ensure secrecy. The missile sites in Cuba were built as they had been in the Soviet Union and without camouflage. Compromise decisions often leave such details uncoordinated because the more the group has to deal with details, the greater the delay in decision making, and the more likely the hard-won general compromise will unravel as the group confronts those awkward details. And how were the missiles to be used? The evidence suggests that that question was deferred to the future; as long as it need not be answered precisely, each of the various interests who supported deployment could assume that the missiles would be "used" to support their preferences. To establish any use now, even before deployment began, would tend to splinter the supporting coalition and give those who opposed deployment a single target to concentrate their objections on.

In October, 1962, an American U-2 overflight of Cuba detected the construction of the missile sites, confirming other (though less reliable) intelligence.[18] Kennedy had repeatedly declared the United States would not tolerate such offensive weapons in Cuba, and now in the secret strategy sessions, he declared that the principal issue was to force their withdrawal. The symbol of "nuclear weapons" encouraged the policy makers to be "tough" in their thinking; Secretary of Defense McNamara quickly backed away from his initial position that missiles in Cuba were strategically unimportant. For Kennedy, this was "a probe, a test of America's will to resist." Its purpose was to demonstrate American irresolution, fracture its alliances, and prepare for a probe "in a more important place."[19] Those advisors who argued for a diplomatic approach were generally dismissed as soft and unrealistic.

"Toughness," however, came in degrees. The military leadership and other advisors wanted an immediate attack on Cuba, if not to retake the island, then at least to destroy the missiles. Kennedy initially favored an air strike. Those opposed to the immediate application of force feverishly put together a plan for a naval blockade of Cuba as a first step. The compromise the President accepted was to implement the blockade, but to agree that unless there was a quick Soviet withdrawal, an armed attack would follow. On October 22, 1962, Kennedy publicly revealed the presence of missiles in Cuba and demanded their withdrawal. A blockade would go into effect two days later if the Soviets had not complied. And, if any Cuban-based missile were launched, the Soviet Union would receive nuclear retaliation.

The initial Soviet response was to reject the American demands. Missile-site construction quickened, and Khrushchev denounced American interference

[18]For the U.S. perspective, see Elie Abel, *The Cuban Missile Crisis* (Philadelphia: Lippincott, 1966); Allison, *Essence of Decision*; Robert Kennedy, *Thirteen Days* (New York: W. W. Norton & Co., Inc., 1969).

[19]Sorensen, *Kennedy*, pp. 676–77.

in the relations between two sovereign states and with navigation of the high seas. "I do not doubt," wrote Khrushchev to the President, "that if someone attempted to dictate similar conditions to you—the United States—you would reject such an attempt. And we also say—no."[20] The blockade began, and American military forces staged a massive buildup in the southeastern United States. At the end of the week, Kennedy, through his brother, warned that unless the Soviets complied, the United States would attack. Tactical and strategic military inferiority gave the Politburo little choice. Khrushchev tried to salvage what he could: the protection of Cuba and a token withdrawal of similar missiles from Turkey. Kennedy publicly pledged not to attack Cuba in return for withdrawal of the missiles and privately indicated that the missiles in Turkey (scheduled for withdrawal in any case) would go.

This week-long crisis marked a watershed in Soviet-American relations. Both leaders recognized that neither state could afford a repetition. Both echoed each other in their evaluations of the types of problems two nuclear powers posed for themselves and the world.[21] Neither state, however, chose to abandon nuclear weapons. In fact, both energetically sought to bolster their deterrent capability. The Soviets initiated a massive missile production program, one that emphasized both numbers and "throw weight"—missile jargon for large warheads, usually in the megaton rather than the kiloton range. The American government, ahead in numbers and increasingly convinced that it need not deploy missiles beyond a certain number, poured its resources into technological improvements, principally accuracy and multiple warheads on each missile. Both continued to believe that if another crisis came, only a powerful nuclear force would keep the peace and avoid capitulation.

Yet the missile crisis shifted the internal balance in both governments to seek to prevent crisis, to substitute restraint for challenge. By the end of the decade, the two states had negotiated an impressive number of agreements and had discussed others, as Table 8-1 shows. That momentum would carry over into the next decade, when more than thirty agreements of various types would be made in the first four years of the 1970s.

The period beginning in 1963 has been characterized by the West as one of détente, by the Soviet Union as a relaxation of tension. For American leaders, "détente" implied that neither state would challenge the status quo (because such challenges tended to produce tension between the two states). Furthermore, the Americans often assumed that the Soviets would be willing to cooperate in the protection of the status quo in order to avoid tension in bilateral relations with the United States. For the Soviet leadership, relaxation of tensions (like "peaceful coexistence") applied only to the relations between the two powers. The Soviets were not interested in preserving a global status quo and had both the realism to recognize that challenges to the status quo were inevitable and the self-interest to assume that change might enhance their influence at the expense of the West's. Certainly there was to be no truce in the ideological war. For a decade, these conflicting interpretations of what each owed the other did not undermine the funda-

---

[20]Khrushchev letter of October 24, 1962 (official translation); *Department of State Bulletin*, 69 (November 19, 1973), 639.

[21]*Ibid.*, see the letters exchanged during the crisis.

TABLE 8-1   Post-Cuban Missile Crisis Soviet-American Agreements

DATE	AGREEMENT	GENERAL PROVISIONS
June 1963	"Hot Line" Treaty	Establishment of a direct communications link between policy centers in Washington and Moscow
August 1963	Test Ban Treaty	No testing of nuclear weapons in the atmosphere, outer space, or under water (a multilateral treaty)
June 1964	Consular Convention	Permission to open consulates in each other's major cities
November 196€	Civil Air Transport Agreement	Opened the way for commercial air service by flag airlines
January 1967	Outer Space Treaty	Freedom of exploration, peaceful use of space, no orbiting nuclear weapons (a multilateral treaty)
July 1968	Non-Proliferation Treaty	No transfer of nuclear weapons to non-nuclear states or provision of aid in building such weapons (a multilateral treaty)
December 1968	Rescue and Return of Astronauts Agreement	Facilitate rescue and return (a multilateral treaty)
May 1969	Embassy Site Agreement	Reciprocal allocation of land free of charge for new embassies

mental premise that they could design mutually acceptable norms for their own interactions. That discovery, born of the Cuban missile crisis, was central to world politics in this decade. It marked the end of the Cold War.

Vietnam

But détente had to share center stage with the deepening American involvement in the Vietnamese civil war.[22] Kennedy had reaffirmed Eisenhower's commitment to preserve a non-communist South Vietnam (see map 7–2). In 1959, apparently after prolonged debate, the leadership of the Democratic Republic of Vietnam (DRV) ordered an armed struggle to begin in the South, but those who favored protecting the North's resources were able to restrict direct Northern participation for a time. The Southern insurgents, now under a communist-led coalition called the National Liberation Front (NLF), began to expand their influence gradually. The corruption and inefficiency of the government of the Republic of Vietnam under Ngo Dinh Diem provided little effective resistance, and often directed its energies against its noncommunist opposition. The American government searched for the key to defeating the enemy, which it labeled "Viet

---

[22]Studies of American involvement in Vietnam are numerous; see, among others, Robert Gallucci, *Neither Peace nor Honor* (Baltimore: Johns Hopkins University Press, 1975); Leslie Gelb with Richard Betts, *The Irony of Vietnam* (Washington: Brookings Institution, 1979); David Halberstam, *The Best and the Brightest* (New York: Random House, 1972); Francis FitzGerald, *Fire in the Lake* (Boston: Atlantic/Little, Brown, 1972).

Cong.'' How did one wage a war against guerrillas? The American military, providing advice and training to the Southern military forces, saw the answer in the conventional American formulas for waging war: find the enemy, fix them in place, fight them, and finish them off. Guerrillas, however, were often farmers by day, insurgents by night. Living in the midst of noncombatants, they proved difficult to find. They were difficult to "fix," because they defended no location. Guerrilla war in its opening stages is a war of constant harassment, of attrition against the political will of the regime and its supporters. The taking and holding of territory is not necessary to attack political authority. If guerrillas could not be fixed in a position, they would melt away, resume their civilian identity, leaving no one to be fought or finished off.

Some in Washington believed that the war had to be fought using political criteria: to mobilize the people to the regime's side and make the citizenry active opponents of the insurgents. Deprived of their protection and camouflage, guerrilla forces would either have to end the war or resort to conventional military operations, where the Southern army could deal with them. But how were the citizenry to be rallied to the government? American planners concluded that Ngo Dinh Diem had to be forced to undertake major reforms in such critical areas as taxation, landownership, and political participation and representation. But if the Southern government undertook reforms, it would likely alienate the wealthy elite, landowners, and military who ensured the survival of the regime in the short run. Caught between incompatible pressures, Ngo Dinh Diem chose to accept American demands for reform in principle, but delay their implementation. He judged that the Americans would not push the issue because they saw his government as preferable to the chaos that would follow if his supporters deserted him.

He was half-right. Those in the Kennedy administration who wanted to wage a political war persuaded the President to sanction a coup by South Vietnamese military officers. In November, 1963, the generals seized power, killing Ngo Dinh Diem. The result was political chaos in the government for months, growing NLF strength in rural areas, and a conclusion by Lyndon Johnson, the new American president, that encouragement of the coup was the worst mistake the United States made in Vietnam. The abandonment of the "political" approach to the war seemingly left the military option as the President's only choice. Johnson sought to avoid making choices while he ran for reelection in 1964. In August, 1964, however, after receiving word that North Vietnamese naval units had attacked American destroyers in the Gulf of Tonkin, Johnson rushed through an angered Congress a resolution authorizing the United States to resist aggression in Southeast Asia.[23] The resolution and his landslide victory in November gave Johnson some freedom to maneuver.

He turned his attention to the deteriorating situation in the South. "By the fall of 1964, in the judgment of non-aligned Vietnamese, U.S. and foreign missionaries, and numbers of Viet Minh, the National Liberation Front enjoyed the active, willing cooperation of more than 50 percent of the population in South Vietnam and a belief among the majority of the population in the inevitability of

---

[23]On the Tonkin Gulf incident, see Anthony Austin, *The President's War* (Philadelphia: Lippincott, 1971).

a Communist takeover."[24] The choice appeared to be between losing the war or vastly expanding the American commitment, which to this point had entailed arms, advisors, and some Americans in combat support roles (such as helicopter pilots). Johnson refused to be "the first President who lost a war." Moreover, he was troubled by the image of Munich and appeasement. "He had a theory that the United States was made to be misunderstood, that the U.S. system was essentially strange and hardly understandable to foreigners and that most of the ills that had befallen the United States in the world—World Wars I and II and Korea, for example—stemmed from miscalculation of American intentions and American will."[25] Intervention seemed to be the answer.

Yet intervention in principle left a lot unsettled in practice. How, when, where, to what degree? In the spring of 1965, the Administration agreed to begin a systematic aerial attack on North Vietnam. The Americans had always claimed that the North directed the war, but its participation over the years had evolved into a supply of men and material, generally by way of Laos and Cambodia (the "Ho Chi Minh Trail"). Like the Soviet decision to deploy missiles in Cuba, bombing the North partially satisfied a variety of policy makers. Some saw bombing as a way to destroy the North's capacity to wage war. Others saw it as a means of interdicting the flow of supplies to the battlefields in the South. Others saw it as a bargaining strategy, raising the cost of the war for the North so that Ho would call it off. Still others saw it as a way of signalling American resolve to the Soviets and Chinese, and to the South Vietnamese. And some, perhaps the President among them, saw bombing as the least costly way to keep the South from collapsing (while, at the same time, the Administration sought legislative support for its ambitious program to build a "Great Society" in the United States). Very few wanted to trigger Chinese entry or greater Soviet involvement, or to jeopardize détente.

The actual decisions regarding bombing were a series of compromises. Bombing would be relatively limited at first, with targets subject to Presidential approval. Critical areas (such as Hanoi and its port of Haiphong) often remained off limits. Pauses in the bombing were arranged for negotiation and propaganda. The bombing met none of the disparate goals. Perhaps no form of bombing could have an impact on a civil war or on a society which had invested twenty years in the struggle for independence. The willingness of the People's Republic of China and the Soviet Union to make good the material losses and to build a formidable air defense network in the North made bombing a costly choice as well.

Thus the Administration had to reevaluate its method of intervention. The apparent feasibility of direct military intervention had been demonstrated in April, 1965, when the United States used its forces to prevent alleged Castroite forces from seizing power in the Dominican Republic.[26] Increasing success by Vietnamese insurgent forces forced a decision in July, 1965, to deploy large American combat forces in Vietnam. By the end of the year, 180,000 Americans

[24]National Security Council Study Memorandum 1, 1969; quoted by Wallace Thies, *When Governments Collide* (Berkeley: University of California Press, 1980), p. 268.

[25]Philip Geyelin, *Lyndon B. Johnson and the World* (New York: Praeger, 1966), p. 44.

[26]Abraham Lowenthal, *The Dominican Intervention* (Cambridge: Harvard University Press, 1972); Jerome Slater, *Intervention and Negotiation* (New York: Harper & Row, Pub., 1970).

were in Vietnam, and an increasing proportion of the fighting fell to them. The DRV countered with the infiltration of its own military units.

> As a result, one suspects that, if anything, the Administration's policy of gradually increasing the pressures on the North actually had the effect of spurring the North Vietnamese to *increase* their efforts in the South in the hope of achieving a quick victory there or, at the least, strengthening their own bargaining position prior to an international conference (which, as we know, *they* thought the U.S. was seeking in order to extricate *itself* from the war).[27]

Direct military intervention shifted the power within the American Administration to those who saw the war in traditional military terms: find, fix, fight, and finish. Large "search-and-destroy" operations in areas of insurgent activity did produce major pitched battles as American forces collided with North Vietnamese units and larger NLF formations. The war became one of attrition, still with a political side, but increasingly familiar to American military men. By early 1968, the Americans demonstrated that they could prevent the military conquest of the South. Some policy makers entertained the hope that the corner had been turned and that "more of the same" might eventually win the war.

Johnson, unlike Truman, had been careful not to lose the war politically by losing the support of the American public. From January, 1965, with the start of the air war against the North, through the summer of 1965, Johnson was personally popular, and the public was willing to engage the nation in Vietnam, with a majority of Americans agreeing that the United States should use its military forces. Opinion was not averse to a negotiated settlement.[28] Johnson found, however, that while he consistently had a plurality of public support, there was a tireless, articulate, and energetic group of citizens who opposed American policy in Vietnam—either because it was undesirable or immoral (the so-called "doves") or because it did not go far enough (the "super hawks").

Johnson might have played the two dissenting extremes off against each other and stuck to what seemed to be the middle of the road. That proved difficult after February, 1968, when large insurgent units and DRV formations attacked major cities in the South and held them for brief periods. Although the communist forces were driven off with large casualties, this "Tet Offensive" (named for the Vietnamese holiday when it occurred) demolished the claim that the war was progressing well for the South and their American allies. Tet also brought into clearer focus the *political* element of the war: who would be willing to pay the greater cost to achieve its ends? After acrimonious debate, Johnson found many of his key advisors recommending deescalation. (It is possible that the "hawks" in the DRV also lost influence as well.)

Johnson ordered a partial bombing halt in March, 1968, and announced he would not be a candidate for President. He made the bombing halt complete in October, partially to aid Hubert Humphrey's campaign. The DRV accepted an American offer of negotiations, which began cautiously in May. By the time the

---

[27]Thies, *When Governments Collide*, p. 271.

[28]See George Gallup, *The Gallup Poll: Public Opinion 1935–1971* (New York: Random House, 1972), Vol. III, pp. 1921, 1922, 1929, 1940, 1955, 1967–69, 1971, 1977.

preliminary sparring over who would negotiate in whose name had ended and the Americans, DRV, NLF, and Republic of Vietnam began to discuss substance, Johnson had been replaced by Richard Nixon. Nixon accepted negotiations in Paris as a way of exploring this avenue to a settlement. He began small withdrawals of American forces (then in excess of 500,000 men) but concentrated on equipping the South Vietnamese forces with the resources the United States had demonstrated could at least keep the war in stalemate. Whether "Vietnamization" would preserve the South remained to be seen.

The response of the socialist bloc to American involvement in Vietnam was generally muted. The Soviets and Chinese underwent major political changes that directed attention toward internal rather than foreign politics. In October, 1964, Khrushchev lost the backing of the Politburo and was dismissed from his offices, which were filled by his erstwhile protegés Leonid Brezhnev (who became Party General Secretary) and Alexi Kosygin (who became Premier). The new leadership castigated Khrushchev for his "harebrained schemes" and set about dismantling a number of his domestic programs, which seemed to have been the catalyst for the revolt of his subordinates. Khrushchev's promotion of a policy of relaxation of tensions remained. The new regime moved cautiously in foreign affairs, reflecting both the inherent caution of new incumbents and the hesitancy of a collective leadership to raise issues that might have called into question the new power relationship in the Politburo.

Political change in China was far more dramatic.[29] Mao Tse-tung had found himself increasingly at odds with other members of the Chinese political elite, especially those who insisted on pragmatic approaches to modernization. For Mao, the transformation of Chinese culture was critical for the success of the revolution and economic modernization. Not only were the "experts" trying to call off the revolution, the Chinese Communist Party itself had grown comfortable with the status quo. In August, 1966, Mao persuaded the Party elite to launch the Great Proletarian Cultural Revolution, which emphasized mass mobilization and criticism of the Party cadres. Mao's opponents found themselves under attack; Liu Shao-chi, the President of the People's Republic, and Chen Y'i, the Foreign Minister, left office in disgrace. The Cultural Revolution soon rolled out of control, and the army had to step in to suppress fighting between various factions. The turmoil in China brought Chinese foreign policy to a standstill during the height of the Cultural Revolution (1967–1968). Verbal polemics did continue with Khrushchev's successors, and here and there the Cultural Revolution spilled out of Chinese embassies abroad, to the consternation or amusement of the more traditional-minded. Rhetoric was the chief ingredient of policy.

The domestic disruption in China and tensions between China and the Soviet Union hampered aid from the Socialist block to the DRV. Soviet shipments across China by rail were purposefully delayed and inadvertently held up by turmoil in major Chinese cities. As neither the Soviets nor the Chinese wanted a confrontation with the United States, the DRV remained on the battlefield alone,

---

[29]On the Cultural Revolution, see Charles Cell, *Revolution at Work* (New York: Academic Press, 1971); Jack Chen, *Inside the Cultural Revolution* (New York: Macmillan, 1975); Thomas Robinson, ed., *The Cultural Revolution in China* (Berkeley: University of California Press, 1971).

which accorded with Mao's rather pragmatic view that revolutionary forces had to be self-reliant.

By the end of the decade, Sino-Soviet tension reached the level of a localized border war. On March 2, 1969, Soviet and Chinese forces fought a two-hour battle for control of Damansky Island in the Ussuri River. On March 15, now augmented with artillery, armor, and airpower, the opposing armies staged day-long operations.[30] Neither side let the fighting escalate, but over the next several months, these localized border clashes continued. The Soviets unofficially asked what the American reaction would be if the Soviets attacked Chinese nuclear facilities. The Nixon Administration indicated that it would be negative. Subsequent negotiations between China and the Soviet Union marked a lessening of the tension. The potential for war between the two, however, would encourage momentous changes in the first half of the next decade.

The World Beyond Soviet-American Relations

American involvement in Vietnam and the caution shown in Soviet and Chinese diplomacy created a greater fluidity in world politics. The behavior of other states captured attention, not only because of the element of tension they injected in world politics, but also because the United States and the Soviet Union seemed to have lost the ability to keep crises from emerging or to resolve them quickly when they did. I shall conclude this chapter with three representative incidents: the civil war in Nigeria, the rebellion of alliance partners, and the Arab-Israeli war of 1967.

The Nigerian Civil War   The potential for civil war exists in any society. The power inherent in a modern, national government makes it a valuable prize to be captured. Control of the central government can enrich and secure the lives of some, and, conversely, can weaken if not destroy the lives of others. In a society divided strongly along social, ethnic, cultural, or class lines (as most of the societies of the newly independent states were), that inherent power of the state is both highly desired and feared for what it can do to groups within the society. Untested parliamentary methods and vague assertions about tolerance are not always enough to prevent the use of force to seize or evade the power of the central government—either in the United States in the 1860s or in Nigeria a century later.

Foreign states respond in a variety of ways to a civil war, but the common characteristic is that foreign governments will become involved. In some civil wars, such as in Vietnam or Spain in the 1930s, foreign powers decide that they have an important stake in who governs, and intervene to protect their interests. In other cases, they are pulled in by the contestants. Losing a civil war can deprive the losing side of life, liberty, and the future. To ensure against losing, the contestants seek to add foreign power to their own. When the indigenous government is relatively strong, it may be content with pledges of neutrality from for-

---

[30]Thomas W. Robinson, "The Sino-Soviet Border Dispute," *American Political Science Review*, 66 (December 1972), 1175–1202.

eign states. The insurgents, on the other hand, are invariably weaker when the war begins, and must secure outside support in order to survive. They search for a way to make their cause identical to those of foreign states. The government does likewise. Both also attempt to manipulate the international concern that emerges over the human tragedy that modern weapons create in any civil war.

Independent since 1960, Nigeria struggled to cope with three major ethnic/cultural divisions: Ibo peoples in the southeast, Yoruba peoples in the southwest, and an Islamic culture in the north.[31] In 1966, Nigeria experienced two military coups, which were judged by many Nigerians to be ethnically motivated: the first, to put Ibos in control of the state; the second, to create a northern-dominated state. Pogroms against Ibos in northern and western Nigeria encouraged Ibo military men in the east to arm the populace, and in May, 1967, to declare independence as the central government tried to reassert control. From 1966, when the Nigerian central government and the Ibo leaders sought arms and funds from abroad, to January, 1970, when the Ibo state of Biafra surrendered, much of the world was involved in one fashion or another. The United States declared an arms embargo, Britain sold light weapons to the central government, and France aided Biafra. Portugal, South Africa, and the white Rhodesian government (which had declared itself independent of British rule in 1965), provided aid for Biafra. The People's Republic of China gave Biafra rhetorical support. The Czechs sold arms to both sides until Biafra's declarations of independence, when the Soviet Union became the central government's source for heavy weapons and aircraft. Most African states supported the declaration made by their regional organization, the Organization of African Unity, opposing secession in any state. Four African states did recognize Biafra. Nongovernmental organizations, such as the World Council of Churches and the International Red Cross, provided relief supplies to civilians, which the central government tried to block because it feared that relief would only encourage further resistance by Biafra.

Foreign involvement did not convert the Nigerian civil war into a major issue of world politics, nor did it encourage a quick resolution of the fighting before 600,000 had died. Where the powers had been quick to involve the United Nations in the Congo in 1960, they now hung back but could not stay out.

European Allies Relations with alliance partners also manifested the symptoms of both declining major-power influence and an inability to disengage. French President de Gaulle withdrew French forces from the integrated NATO command and ordered all NATO forces to leave French soil; he did not renounce the treaty of defense, however. Viewing Britain as both a challenge to French influence and as an American protégé, de Gaulle twice vetoed British membership in the European Economic Community. (Within the EEC, de Gaulle threatened to destroy the organization unless French demands on economic policy were met.) In 1964 and 1967, Greece and Turkey—both NATO allies—moved to the brink of war over Cyprus, now an independent state, but populated by feuding Greeks and Turks. Pakistan, an American ally, improved relations with China

---

[31]See John De St. Jorre, *The Brothers' War: Biafra and Nigeria* (Boston: Houghton Mifflin, 1972); John Ostheimer, *Nigerian Politics* (New York: Harper & Row, Pub., 1973); John Stremlau, *The International Politics of the Nigerian Civil War, 1967–1970* (Princeton University Press, 1977).

and fought a brief war in 1965 with India. Generally, many American allies seemed unresponsive to American interests and resistant to American pressures.

The Soviets encountered similar problems. In Czechoslovakia, dissidents within the Czech Communist Party found themselves in the majority, and, with Brezhnev's blessing, replaced the conservative party chief with Alexander Dubcek in January, 1968. But Czechoslovakia's problems were economic as well as political; the command economy continued to stagnate. Dubcek and his allies began to reduce controls on the economy and then found a popular call for a similar reduction of controls on intellectual and political life. By the spring of 1968, censorship had ended, and the Party tolerated (if not encouraged) the development of groups free of Party supervision and their pressing of claims on the government.[32]

As the weeks passed, the Soviets demanded that the Czechs control antisocialist and anti-Soviet tendencies; the Soviet standard in this regard was an unchallenged position for the Czech Communist Party. Czech and Soviet officials met repeatedly during the summer, often with WTO military maneuvers occurring within and without Czechoslovakia. The Polish and East German parties worried aloud about the dangers of the Czech experiment. The Czech-Soviet meetings (including an extraordinary meeting of the two Politburos) would end with statements of mutual respect and with mutual misperceptions of how much leeway the Czech regime had. The Soviets were singularly unable to bring the Czech party into line. On August 28, 1968, they resolved the issue with military intervention. But even after the deployment of Soviet and other WTO troops, the reconstitution of an acceptable Czech regime took a year. The hostile NATO reaction, although limited to words and a suspension of various negotiations, compounded the costs of intervention—costs not incurred by the far bloodier suppression of the Hungarian revolt.

The Middle-Eastern War of 1967   The Middle East, however, provided the most vivid example of declining major-power influence. Nasser had alienated Syria and Iraq in his drive to assert leadership of the Arab world and had sent troops to fight in the Yemeni civil war. An Arab "cold war" was in full bloom in the early 1960s.[33] It spilled over to affect Palestinian politics. The Palestinian refugees began to organize in order to assert their claim to Israeli territory. The Palestine Liberation Organization (PLO) emerged in 1964 under Egyptian sponsorship; Al Fatah (under Yasser Arafat's leadership) had Syrian sponsorship. The rivalry to attract supporters and to begin the liberation of their homeland created an escalating guerrilla war against Israel. Israeli retaliation helped drive Egypt and Syria into an uneasy mutual defense agreement in November, 1966. The Soviets encouraged this development, as it was a way out of the "our-friends-are-enemies" dilemma.

By early 1967, as Figure 1–2 suggested, the interaction of Syrian-Egyptian

---

[32]H. Gordon Skilling, *Czechoslovakia's Interrupted Revolution* (Princeton: Princeton University Press, 1976); Galia Golan, *Reform Rule in Czechoslovakia* (Cambridge: Cambridge University Press, 1973); Jiri Valenta, *Soviet Intervention in Czechoslovakia, 1968* (Baltimore: Johns Hopkins University Press, 1979).

[33]Malcolm Kerr, *The Arab Cold War*, 3rd ed. (London: Oxford University Press, 1971).

rivalry and Arab-Israeli hostility produced a classic pattern of escalation.[34] Nasser found that each step he took—be it demanding the withdrawal of the United Nations forces on the Israeli-Egyptian frontier, closing of the Straits of Tiran to Israeli shipping bound for the port of Elath, or massing troops in Sinai—failed to compel the Israelis to capitulate, but created a position that would be impossible for him to back away from if he were to retain domestic and Arab support. Nasser had previously found (as other Third World leaders had) that being a "nuisance" forced the major powers to pay attention.[35] Kennedy had cautiously explored the possibility of improving relations; the Soviets had remained supportive in spite of the repression of Egyptian communists. Perhaps in this crisis Nasser felt that taking aggressive positions with no line of retreat would force the major powers to step in to defuse the crisis. Indeed, the Johnson administration did lobby hard with the Israelis to allow major-power diplomacy to deal with the closing of the Straits of Tiran.

Neither Soviets nor Americans wanted to become deeply involved in an intractable situation that might jeopardize détente between them. In truth, there probably was no solution that diplomacy could produce. To fulfill the demands of the Palestianians for a homeland meant the dismantling of the Jewish state or the cession of Arab territory. The long-voiced Arab pledge to destroy the Zionist state and the fervent Israeli pledge to defend it gave no room to the whisper of accommodation. As Nasser's actions escalated, so, too, did Arab propaganda. The Israelis began to fear that the destruction of Jews as well as the state of Israel stood at the top of the Arab agenda. War, even if undesired by most parties, seemed inevitable.

The Israeli coalition government was bitterly divided. In May, 1967, the Israeli military demanded a preemptive strike and half the cabinet agreed. The Prime Minister, Levi Eshkol, counseled patience and reliance on the United States to find a solution. Patience may be good policy, but proved bad politics as the Israeli public assailed the government's do-nothing policy in the face of possible annihilation. Eshkol enlarged the Cabinet to include the popular but hawkish war hero, Moshe Dayan, and as the Americans seemed unable or unwilling to provide a solution, the weight of Cabinet opinion shifted to war.

Hostilities began with a surprise Israeli air raid on June 5, 1967, which destroyed the Egyptian air force. With air supremacy over the Sinai, Israeli tank columns raced westward in classic blitzkrieg style, cutting off Egyptian units and reaching the Suez Canal on June 8. No effective Egyptian forces lay to the west. Unlike in the 1956 war, however, Egypt found it had reliable allies. On the 5th, Jordan and Syria entered the war. The possibility of a three-front war had been the central worry for the Israelis, because they could not maintain a military establishment large enough to defeat all three states simultaneously. Plans called for the defense on two fronts with the major blow against the third, and then redeployment to strike sequentially at the other two fronts. By the 8th, the West

---

[34]For studies of the 1967 war, see Michael Brecher, *Decisions in Crisis* (Berkeley: University of California Press, 1980); Walter Laqueur, *The Road to War* (Hammondsworth, England: Penguin, 1970); Edgar O'Ballance, *The Third Arab-Israeli War* (Hamden, Conn: Archon Books, 1972); Janice Gross Stein and Raymond Tanter, *Rational Decision-Making* (Columbus: Ohio State University Press, 1980).

[35]Miles Copeland, *The Game of Nations* (New York: Simon & Schuster), pp. 132–69.

Bank of Jordan (and Jerusalem) had been overrun by Israeli forces, and by the evening of the 10th, Syrian forces had been driven out of the Golan Heights.

Israeli strategy and policy stressed limited war. American and Soviet pressure gradually forced a cease-fire on the parties by June 10, thus ensuring the limited nature of the war. Israeli forces remained in occupation of Sinai, Golan, and the West Bank. After strenuous negotiations, the United Nation's Security Council in November endorsed a compromise peace plan; Resolution 242 requested Israeli withdrawal from "territories occupied in the recent conflict" in return for Arab "termination of all claims of belligerency and respect for and acknowledgement of the sovereignty, territorial integrity, and political independence of every state in the area and their right to live in peace within secure and recognized boundaries free from threats or acts of force."

While the United Nations worked to implement the resolution, Israel turned to the United States to resupply its military (de Gaulle had ended the French supply of aircraft) while the Egyptians and Syrians turned to the Soviets. Rearmed, and facing the prospect of well-equipped Arab armies again on its frontiers, the Israelis had less interest in Resolution 242 and more in retaining the occupied territories. Nasser, on the other hand, needed to recover at least Sinai, but had no military force and grew suspicious that the budding Soviet-American détente would effectively cement the status quo. In 1968, United Nations efforts to advance the peace process remained stalled.

Nixon committed the new American Administration to the regularization of relations with the Soviet Union and the achievement of peace in the Middle East. Indeed, he saw the two goals as interrelated. American and Soviet diplomats negotiated during 1969 to discover an acceptable "package" of Israeli withdrawal and Arab acceptance of Israel. Egypt kept the pressure on by shelling Israeli positions across the canal, and Israel retaliated. Palestinian guerrilla organizations, still not accepted as forces to be reckoned with, increased their raids into Israel. At the end of the year, both Israel and the Soviet Union rejected the American proposals.

Nixon had entered office declaring that "the greatest honor history can bestow is the title of peacemaker. This honor now beckons America." "I know that peace does not come through waiting for it," he added, " . . . there is no substitute for days and even years of patient and prolonged diplomacy."[36] While dialogues had begun, the Middle East and Vietnam loudly insisted that global peace was not about to break out.

PART II:
SCIENTIFIC APPROACHES TO WORLD POLITICS

Multiple Approaches:
The Third World, Capitalist States, and Political Economy

Each of the approaches employed in previous chapters has suggested a particular way of stating a question, identifying the central features for an analysis, and constructing generalizations that purport to describe and explain world poli-

---

[36]Inaugural address, January 20, 1969, *Public Papers of the Presidents, Richard M. Nixon, 1969* (Washington: Government Printing Office, 1969), p.1.

tics. As we rush toward the twenty-first century (and the end of this book), we need to make some comparison of how different approaches provide us with different insights into world politics. To do that, I shall consider the general topic of the relations between the industrialized capitalist states and the less developed nations of the world. We have observed some Third World nations become battlegrounds for major powers (Korea), battlegrounds among themselves (Middle East), and objects of the UN's attention (the Congo). With the wave of decolonization, the Third World and the industrialized states entered into a new era of diplomatic relations. How might we describe this new aspect of world politics? How might we explain it?

The general approach that I shall employ to deal with these questions is "political economy," an approach that assumes that there is an "intimate, dialectical interaction of political and economic forces."[37] "Dialectical," in this context, means that there is a tension within and between the political and economic characteristics of a society, a tension that constantly produces change in both areas; that change creates new tensions or exacerbates old ones. One of the most common variants of the political economy approach is Marxism, which postulates that the nature of the economic system determines the shape of political life in a society: its laws, institutions, ideas, values, and its foreign policy. As the tensions in the economic system resolve themselves, the nature of political life changes as well.

I will apply a Marxist viewpoint to a question of capitalist-Third World relations. A clarifying comment is in order at this point, however. Chapter 4 assessed the impact of Marxist ideology on the foreign policy of the young Soviet state. There I hypothesized that ideology helped account for Soviet foreign policy; ideology itself was a variable or factor that shaped policy in particular ways. In this chapter, we shall look on Marxism as an *approach* which itself *identifies* particular variables or factors and provides a reason for why and how those variables shape policy as hypothesized. I also need to make another distinction (which shapes the following discussion). I assume that there is a difference between an *ideologue* and a *social scientist*.[38] A social scientist is most likely to ask, "What evidence would lead one to believe that assertion to be true?" An ideologue, on the other hand, is most likely to ask, "Given this certain truth, what does it tell me about the situation?" The problem occurs when the social scientist adopts the ideologue's assumption. It is my belief that many of our generalizations about world politics are still only *hypotheses* awaiting confirmation and our "theories" are only orienting devices or approaches to the study of world politics.[39] This is as true for "political economy" as it is for anything else discussed in this book.

[37]Charles Kegley, Jr., and Pat McGowan, "Political Economy and the Study of Foreign Policy," in *The Political Economy of Foreign Policy Behavior*, ed. C. Kegley, Jr., and P. McGowan (Beverly Hills, Cal.: Sage, 1981), p. 8. See also David Blake and Robert Walters, *The Politics of Global Economic Relations* (Englewood Cliffs, N.J.: Prentice-Hall, 1976).

[38]A Marxist would argue that in making this distinction I am simply revealing my own ideological posture, firmly rooted in the liberal bourgeois tradition.

[39]There are many "tested" hypotheses, as a look at any political science journal will indicate. Susan Jones and J. David Singer have entitled their compilation of such fundings *Beyond Conjecture in International Politics* (Itasca: Peacock, 1972). We are probably at the "beyond-conjecture" stage, but we are nowhere near the "beyond-doubt" stage. Enormous problems with the validity and reliability of the evidence we use reduce the certainty of findings in world politics research; our conceptual problems—as evidenced by the variety of approaches—give no current theory strong empirical support.

Of course, for an ideologue, events *do* validate the theory. They do so because the ideologue's method ensures that result. First, she or he can make things true by definition. Marxist ideology, for instance, stipulates that a capitalist state *is* an imperialist state. A careful examination of American foreign policy to determine whether it is imperialist or not becomes unnecessary, because it *must* be an imperialist policy. Second, the ideologue can shape the evidence to fit the expectation. Lenin's injunction to see a class interest in every state behavior forces the ideologue to interpret what seems to be the most benign or altruistic actions (such as the gift of medical supplies to a nation rocked by an earthquake) as an expression of class (hence imperialist) interests. Third, the evidence that does not seem to fit easily with expectations can be ignored or dismissed if it is not reinterpreted. Earthquake relief and similar behaviors may not enter into an ideologue's thinking, or they may be dismissed as so small a part of American policy that they do not negate the basic imperialist thrust of American foreign policy.

Now it may be that the Marxist equation of capitalism and imperialism *is correct*, that *every* state behavior does serve class interests, or that altruism *is* overwhelmed by the magnitude of imperialist actions. The social scientist wants to establish "correctness" by *inquiry* rather than by *definition or selective interpretation* of the evidence.

Marxism is often singled out as the clearest case of where *assumptions* are equated with truth. You should recognize, however, that *any* of the approaches we have discussed can easily slip from hypotheses into doctrine, and evidence can be twisted to buttress that doctrine: the structure of power *does* determine patterns of world politics; *all* foreign policy *is* a contradictory compromise; weapons *do* produce aggressive state behaviors. I have assumed that we students of world politics are better served by exploring the *insights* various (and conflicting) approaches provide rather than insisting that any one of them provides "the truth."

Marxist Analysis I   A Marxist viewpoint regarding relations between capitalist states and Third World states can be considered along three lines, each corresponding to one of the general approaches we have investigated. From *the domestic and environmental factor approach*, the Marxist viewpoint would hypothesize that the nature of the ownership of the means of production will dictate a state's foreign policy. Lenin's *Imperialism, the Highest Stage of Capitalism* was for many years the central Marxist work on the foreign policy of capitalist states (although it itself drew heavily on John Hobson's *Imperialism*, a non-Marxist analysis but still in the realm of political economy). Today, there is a plethora of Marxist scholars writing about capitalist states, some hewing to the Leninist tradition, others revising the tradition substantially.[40]

The Leninist thesis accounted for imperialism by arguing that, as capitalism matured, capitalist monopolies acquired wealth (profits) that could not easily be reinvested in their own societies to make new profits. Overseas investment,

---

[40]See, among others, G. William Domhoff, *Who Rules America?* (Englewood Cliffs, N.J.: Prentice-Hall, 1967); James O'Connor, *The Fiscal Crisis of the State* (New York: St. Martin's Press, 1972); Immanuel Wallerstein, *The Capitalist World Economy* (Cambridge: Cambridge University Press, 1979).

however, would open up new areas for the exploitation of cheap labor and for the garnering of large profits. But in order to prevent competition from foreign capitalists, the state (which, recall, is the creature of the ruling class) carved out colonies where it could and spheres of influence where it could not. Behind this protective wall, capitalists had free reign. This exported exploitation led to the impoverishment of the inhabitants of the colonies. Today some Marxists argue that, not only were the capitalists of the mother country enriched, they also used the profits extracted from the colonial world to create affluence among some of the working class in their own industrial societies. That tended to mask the class conflict in those societies.

Exploitation in the colonial world was raw and undisguised, however. It led to a revolt of the oppressed, which brought about the wave of decolonization in the post-war period. Had imperialism therefore ended? Marxists argue that it has not. Instead of an expensive and politically costly apparatus of colonial control (governors, bureaucrats, and soldiers), capitalist states found they could control the newly independent colonies just as effectively through economic leverage. The capitalist's investments remained, as did the foreign factories. The economy of the new states remained tied to the economy of capitalist states: the new states needed markets in the capitalist state to sell their goods, principally raw materials and agricultural products; they needed the finished goods and financial capital of the capitalist states to undertake their own economic development. Their economic dependence meant weakness in other ways: the prices of their exports were generally low and unstable, while the prices of industrial goods were high and going higher; the capitalists imposed their terms for private investment or public foreign aid—chief of which was an insistence that the state's politics not harm capitalist interests.

With the penetration of a new state's economy, the capitalist state continued to exercise control by reducing the range of choices left to the leaders of the new state. In many cases, the leaders were unaware that they had little choice; it simply seemed "natural" to act in a certain way. At other times, the capitalist state would restate the economic "facts of life" to indicate the narrow range of choice:

> The Hickenlooper Amendment (which requires the President to suspend aid to countries that expropriate US property without prompt and effective compensation) was introduced in the US Senate at the urging of Harold Geneen, president of International Telephone and Telegraph, whose utility subsidiaries were being threatened in Brazil and Argentina. Shortly after the Amendment passed in 1962, a moderate government in Nicaragua was told the legislation would be applied against it if pending land reform legislation that would have touched United Fruit plantations were enacted. The next year Senator Hickenlooper rewrote the Amendment specifically so that it could be directed against Argentina's decision to void the contracts of US oil companies. At the same time US aid was cut off (without formal invocation of the Hickenlooper Amendment) for three years to Peru to try to force Fernando Belaunde Terry to settle with the International Petroleum Corporation on terms acceptable to Standard of New Jersey (now Exxon).[41]

[41]Theodore Moran, "Multinational Corporations and Dependency," *International Organization*, 23 (Winter 1978), 95.

In addition to governmental pressure, the evolution of capitalism brought a powerful new institution into prominence—the multinational corporation (MNC).[42] The MNC's primary interest is production, rather than exporting goods and capital. To produce profitably, it locates its factories in any nation that will have it. If the European Common Market's tariff makes American-made computers too costly in Western Europe, the American computer firm will build a plant in Italy and sell the Italian-made computer throughout the Common Market at a price competitive with indigenous products. The profits return to the MNC, usually headquartered in the United States. The economic power of such corporations as General Motors, Exxon, and General Electric is impressive. Their individual incomes from sales, licenses, and the like are often more than what many *governments* of the Third World spend. This economic power is harnessed, according to Marxist theorists, to support clear preferences: "they want the world of nations in which they operate to be as large as possible and . . . they want its laws and institutions to be favorable to the unfettered development of private capitalist enterprise."[43]

From this viewpoint, it is easy to understand the assertions by many Third World leaders that they were victims of *neo-colonialism*—colonialism without the visible structures of control.[44] The imperialism of the capitalist states may take new forms, but it remains the essential aspect of a capitalist foreign policy. Figure 8-1 summarizes the argument *in the idiom of the domestic and environmental factor approach*. During the 1960s, many Third World leaders spoke of breaking the neo-colonialist patterns and of redistributing the wealth of the Northern or industrialized states to the South (the impoverished Third World). Redistribution would rectify the wrong done by colonial exploitation and it would give the Southern states the economic autonomy to function as sovereign political entities in world politics.

Marxist Analysis II   A second version of the Marxist viewpoint corresponds with the *interaction approach*. It argues that we need to examine the relationship between the ruling class of the capitalist state and the ruling class of the Third World state. From that perspective, "in the pure case of neo-colonialism, the allocation of economic resources, investment effort, legal and ideological structures, and other features of the old society remained unchanged—with the single exception of the substitution of 'internal colonialism' for formal colonialism, that is *by the transfer of power to the domestic ruling classes* by their former colonial mas-

---

[42]For descriptions, see Raymond Vernon, *Sovereignty at Bay* (New York: Basic Books, 1971); J.M. Stopford and L.T. Wells, Jr., *Managing the Multinational Enterprises* (Englewood Cliffs, N.J.: Prentice-Hall, 1970); Robert Gilpin, *U.S. Power and the Multinational Corporation* (New York:Basic Books, 1975).

[43]Paul Baran and Paul Sweezy, "Notes on the Theory of Imperialism," in *Readings in U.S. Imperialism*, ed. K.T.Fann and Donald Hodges (Boston: Porter Sargent, 1971), p. 81.

[44]For studies of "neocolonialism" and its synonym, "dependency," see Samir Amin, *Accumulation on a World Scale*, 2 vols. (New York: Monthly Review Press, 1974); Andre Gunder Frank, *Capitalism and Underdevelopment in Latin America* (New York: Monthly Review Press, 1967); James Caporaso, "Dependence, Dependency and Power in the Global System," *International Organization*, 32 (Winter 1978), 13–43; Vincent Mahler, *Dependency Approaches to International Political Economy* (New York: Columbia University Press, 1980).

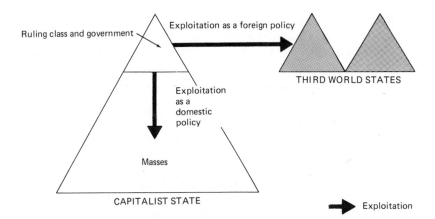

FIGURE 8-1   A Marxist Domestic and Environmental Factor Explanation for Relations between Capitalist and Third World States

ters.''[45] The ruling classes in both states share a common interest: exploitation of the inhabitants. As Richard Fagen has argued, ''what is increasingly clear is the fact that the majority of the elites speaking in the name of the South have from the outset been the spokesmen for, and in some cases even the direct creation of, national and international class interests quite satisfied with the existing world economic system if not with their share of the pie.''[46]

As Figure 8-2 indicates, the interaction between the ruling classes consists of a sharing of resources extracted from their respective societies. The underdeveloped state provides a flow of raw materials and profits. The capitalist state

FIGURE 8-2   A Marxist Interaction Explanation of Relations between Capitalist and Third World States

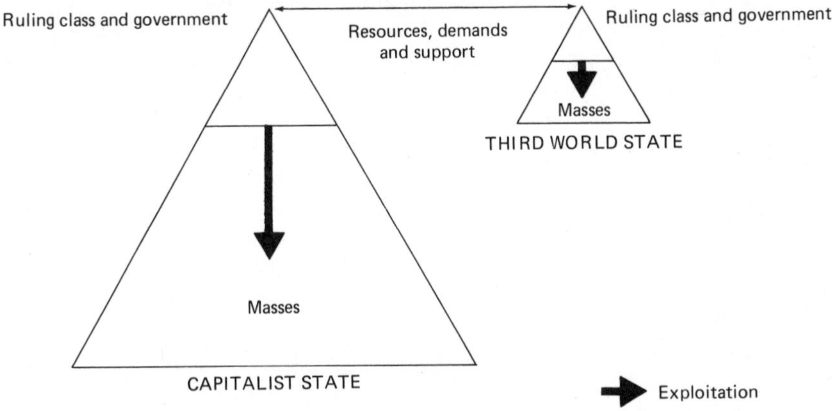

[45]James O'Connor, ''The Meaning of Economic Imperialism,'' in *Imperialism and Underdevelopment*, ed. R.I. Rhodes (New York: Monthly Review Press, 1970), p. 118.

[46]Richard Fagen, ''A Funny Thing Happened on the Way to the Market,'' *International Organization*, 32 (Winter 1978), 295.

provides a flow of foreign aid—goods and services paid for by its citizens which generally benefit the ruling class of the underdeveloped state. The small state provides an opportunity for investment and MNC operations, thus supporting the class interests of the capitalist state; the latter in return provides support for the indigenous ruling class with advisors, experts, and, from time to time, troops. However, because of the uneven level of economic development between the two states, there is not a complete identity of interests, often leading the elites of the Third World to demand more resources and support than the developed states are willing or able to give. In particular, Third World elites face more explosive situations because their nonmodern economic systems seem more exploitative, while their ability to repress citizen opposition is still underdeveloped. They need *external* resources to buy off or contain the opposition.

From this perspective, we would expect to find a general cooperativeness in world politics between states having similar ruling classes. Protection of the political status quo becomes the policy of both Northern and Southern states. Conflict in world politics would still exist, but similar ruling classes would have few options in pursuing that conflict. Neither would they be likely to do anything to jeopardize their control or the exchange of benefits. So threats to cut off contacts or to turn to the socialist camp would have little credibility. The threats that are made are addressed more to domestic audiences—*to appear* to confront the other state in order to bolster public acceptance for the necessity of continuing exploitation. On the other hand, the anger and reality of the threats between a capitalist state and a Third World *socialist* state would not be sham, for international politics there would consist of the resistance to efforts to reestablish exploitation. In those cases, the Marxist domestic and environmental factor approach may be more appropriate.

Marxist Analysis III   The third version of the Marxist viewpoint is similar to the *systems approach*. Instead of investigating the power structure as we have done, this approach identifies the predominant form of *economic organization in the world*. Capitalism has been dominant globally since the turn of the century. In a capitalist world economy, all noncapitalist systems "bend" or "distort" under the pressure of the dominating market-based economy. Immanual Wallerstein has argued that "there are today no socialist systems in the world economy any more than there are feudal systems because there is one world system."[47] Socialism, therefore, becomes *state capitalism*; the workers own the means of production in name only. A closed elite (the communist party) makes the essential decisions using the profits generated by the economy to enhance state (and elite) power. Only young revolutionary regimes might momentarily break some of the capitalist patterns, but they are compromised from the beginning and fall back upon capitalist methods eventually (as Lenin did with the NEP) or upon a state capitalism that becomes integrated into the global capitalist system, generally on the latter's terms.

This systems perspective would predict patterned political behavior in the manner of rules of the international system. As our particular concern is world

---

[47]I. Wallerstein, "The Rise and Future Demise of the World Capitalist System," *Comparative Studies in Society and History*, 16 (September 1974), 415. Published by Cambridge University Press. See also C. Chase-Dunn, "Comparative Research on World-System Characteristics," *International Studies Quarterly*, 23 (December 1979), 604.

politics involving the Third World, I will confine my attention to hypothesized rules for those states:

1. Developed states, irrespective of the classification of their economic system, behave similarly toward the Third World.[48] Soviet economic and military aid policies, for instance, will mimic those of the capitalist states.

2. Developed states will present a generally coercive face to the Third World states, much as the ruling class in a society presents to the workers. Developed states will compete but cooperate to ensure stability; intervention will take place on a relatively continuous basis.

3. The response of the Third World states may have a domestic analogue in the creation of unions and radical political movements. They may organize regional networks such as the Organization of African Unity (OAU), or production networks such as the Organization of Petroleum Exporting Countries (OPEC), or general networks specifically designed to confront the North on questions of wealth, such as the "Group of 77." Such networks have employed rhetoric, demands, threats, and (where they have some leverage, as OPEC does with oil) the withholding of services. The developed states have responded with "union-busting" activities— refusing to recognize such networks (the Soviets, for instance, argue that the grievances of the Third World belong on the doorstep of the capitalists, not theirs); by trying to lead the union (the Western capitalist states have tried to make the United Nations Conference on Trade and Development the company union to ensure that there will be no dangerous activity); and by trying to split organizations by insisting on bi- rather than multilateral relations (the United States has resisted demands that all aid be funnelled through international agencies rather than be given directly to the states it chooses to aid).

In the Marxist framework, at some point the exploited will rise and challenge the domination of the world capitalist system. How this is to occur and whether it would have the support of the working class of the capitalist states can only be guessed at. Nonetheless, the framework would predict a period of increasing political conflict between the North and South, culminating in a series of crises that would change the world order.

Other frameworks would furnish different perspectives, of course. Marxism and political economy do not have a monopoly on providing interesting hypotheses about the relations between developed states and less developed states. One alternative framework examines the similarities of the political elites of the "large" and "small" state to see if they have common experiences (in education, military service, or politics, for instance).[49] Shared experiences can create parallel perceptions, values, and thought processes; channels of communication, friendship networks, incentives for cooperation; and mutually acceptable mechanisms for resolving conflict. Interactions between large and small states are thus a function of socialization patterns. A second approach examines the *interdependence* between states.[50] It assumes that interaction provides channels for the *mutual manipulation* of state behavior. Some states have greater leverage in such situations,

---

[48]Walter Seabold and N.G. Onuf, "Late Capitalism, Uneven Development, and Foreign Policy Postures," in *Political Economy*, ed. Kegley and McGowan, p. 27.

[49]See Marshall R. Singer, *Weak States in a World of Power* (New York: Free Press, 1972).

[50]See Robert Keohane and Joseph Nye, *Power and Interdependence* (Boston: Little, Brown, 1977).

but that leverage is not necessarily determined by economic conditions. In fact, the economically more powerful state may be more easily manipulated, as Nasser's comment that "debtors are always stronger than creditors" suggests. These alternative hypotheses await confirmation as much as the hypotheses offered by political economists.

Testing Hypotheses   As Eliza Doolittle might sing, "Hypotheses! Hypotheses! Hypotheses!" When can we move beyond saying that we have a hunch about some aspect of world politics? In part, that is a methodological issue that is beyond the scope of this text. However, we do need to understand some basic methodological elements in order to cope with the growing literature on world politics that uses specialized techniques. More generally, whenever you and I try to advance a generalization about world politics, we are employing a methodology whether we recognize it or not. An awareness of some of the assumptions we may be making may help improve the quality of those generalizations.[51]

Consider how we might attempt to examine or test this hypothesis drawn from the Marxist analysis of the system: when the system has a particular characteristic (such as a global capitalist economy), developed states would act in a particular manner (such as "union-busting"). We can depict this hypothesis in this way:

SYSTEM CHARACTERISTIC

Global capitalism

DEVELOPED
STATE   Union busting
BEHAVIOR

Let us assume that the evidence we collect does support this statement. Can we conclude that the nature of the global economic system dictates state behavior? *Probably not.* During this century, there has been only one global economic system; that of capitalism. *If* there were another type of system, such as a socialist world economy, would the economically developed states act in a different manner? *If* a socialist world economy also engaged in union-busting, we would be less inclined to accept the hypothesis that the nature of the global economic system had a consistent impact on state behavior.

To amplify this point, consider this analogy. Ever since you fell into the clutches of the school system, you have been told that "hard work pays off." That assertion can be represented as follows:

WORK CHARACTERISTIC

Hard work

ACADEMIC RESULT   Good grades

Suppose we examined the work habits of the individual with the best grades in your world politics class and found that that person worked hard. Would we be

---

[51]For a discussion of methods, see Mary Grisez Kweit and Robert Kweit, *Concepts and Methods for Political Analysis* (Englewood Cliffs, N.J.: Prentice-Hall, 1981).

willing to say that the evidence confirmed the hypothesis? Probably not, and for two related reasons.

First, we have reason to suspect that there are cases where, in spite of hard work, individuals have failed courses; *or* cases where individuals barely opened a book all semester and still received good grades. We need to add these possibilities to our thinking:

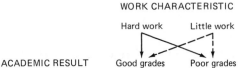

WORK CHARACTERISTIC

Hard work   Little work

ACADEMIC RESULT   Good grades   Poor grades

If an individual can get good grades or poor grades for hard work (or for no work), *it would be very difficult for us to believe that how hard one works is really the cause of the variations in one's grades.* We need some other explanation for the variation in grades. Similarly, *if* states behave in the same way in *different* global economic systems, we would find it hard to believe that the nature of the global economic system was really the cause of state behavior. We would need to look elsewhere for an explanation.

There is a second reason you might have been unwilling to accept the hypothesis linking work and grades based on one individual's record. There is simply too little evidence. As a general rule, social scientists would like to examine as many cases as possible before attempting to draw a conclusion. *And there lies the problem for testing the hypothesis that a capitalist global economy produces specific behaviors,* be they assertions about economic exploitation, foreign policy patterns, or the level of poverty in the Third World. We simply do not have any case of a modern global economic system other than that of capitalist domination. Political economists are quite right when they assert that this hypothesis cannot be tested as we might test the proposition about work and grades. You might note that a similar situation confronts the international systems approach I have employed in each chapter. The different distributions of power have not recurred with great frequency. It is therefore very difficult to demonstrate that the hypothesized system "rules" are accurate. In general, for either systems approach, we have the choice of seeing the hypotheses as only hypotheses or *accepting them as true on some other basis, such as intuition, faith, or political attractiveness.*

However, when we move away from the systems level, we have a greater ability to test hypotheses regarding economic structure and political behavior. I offer an example to conclude this section. One argument we encountered is that a capitalist state creates through its economic system an exploitative relationship with Third World states. Those states are said to lose control over their own economies and, as hypothesized here, over their foreign policies. Specifically, the more dependent a Third World state is on the American economy, the more it will comply in its foreign policy with the interests of the American government.[52] We can picture this hypothesis in more formal terms:

---

[52]This follows studies done by Neil Richardson, "Political Compliance and U.S. Trade Dominance," *American Political Science Review*, 70 (December 1976), 1098–1109; and Eugene Wittkopf, "Foreign Aid and United Nations Votes," *American Political Science Review*, 67 (September 1973), 868–88.

RELATIONSHIP TO THE US ECONOMY

		Little dependence	High dependence
FOREIGN POLICY COMPLIANCE WITH UNITED STATES	Little compliance	a	b
	High compliance	c	d

This table helps my analysis in a number of ways. It forces me to check to make sure that as the level of dependence changes, compliance changes, just as we saw it was necessary to check to see if changing work habits changed grades. Second, it helps me keep track of the evidence by forming categories into which I will place the cases. In this example, the cases are the (approximately) 35 independent states of Black Africa in 1968. Each state will go into one of the four cells of the table. Ivory Coast, for example, with its high dependence and high compliance goes in cell "d". Finally, the table helps me evaluate the evidence. In this example, when I finish sorting the states into their proper cells, *if the hypothesis holds true*, I would expect most of the states to be found in cell "a" (where little dependence correlates with little compliance) and cell "d" (where high dependence correlates with much compliance). If the evidence does so, then I have grounds for saying that economic dependence seems to have an impact on compliance and may help us explain why Third World states behave differently.

Note that I said I expected *most* of the states to fall in the two cells, not all of the cases. Social scientists have found that very little regarding human behavior strictly accords with any hypothesis. Therefore, when we say a hypothesis holds, we are really saying that for the bulk of the cases it holds. We often try to alert the reader to this restriction by speaking in terms of "tendency" or "probability."

Before I can actually test the hypothesis, I need to translate the concepts of "dependence on the American economy" and "foreign policy compliance" into more precise terms. Just how will I know if Nigeria is dependent or not, or whether it complies often or infrequently with the American government? I will investigate two types of *dependence*:

1. *Trade dependence*: the percentage of the state's total trade that is directed toward the United States. I would predict that the greater this dependence (and therefore linkage to the American economy), the greater the leverage the economic and political elites of the United States exercise over the dependent state. Its political compliance should be relatively great.

2. *Foreign aid dependence*: the total value of grants and credits provided by the American government. Such aid would make the state wish for its continuation, if for no other reason than to enrich the local elites. As capitalism is not altruistic, the donor nation will ask for something in return—in this case, political compliance.

The measure of *political compliance* used here is the degree to which a state's votes in the General Assembly of the United Nations coincide with those of the United States.[53] The data for these three variables appear in Table 8-2.

[53]Political compliance is measured by the Index of Agreement developed by Arend Lijphart, "The Analysis of Bloc Voting in the General Assembly," *American Political Science Review*, 62 (Decem-

TABLE 8-2   Data on Dependence and Political Compliance, 35 African States circa 1968

NATION	INDEX OF AGREEMENT	TRADE DEPENDENCE ON US (PERCENT OF TOTAL TRADE)	US ECONOMIC AID (THOUSANDS OF DOLLARS)
Botswana	.90	1%	65
Burundi	.41	34%	36
Cameroon	.51	9%	359
Cent. Af. Rep.	.61	18%	223
Chad	.50	5%	559
Congo(B)	.37	4%	0
D.R. Congo	.57	11%	16,065
Dahomey	.57	5%	345
Eq. Guinea	.49	n.a.	n.a.
Ethiopia	.55	34%	6,850
Gabon	.62	10%	325
Gambia	.90	2%	36
Ghana	.51	21%	16,846
Guinea	.38	13%	1,084
Ivory Coast	.79	12%	159
Kenya	.46	7%	2,624
Lesotho	.79	1%	50
Liberia	.68	31%	5,638
Madagascar	.68	n.a.	296
Malawi	.79	4%	8,137
Mali	.35	0%	1,105
Mauritania	.37	5%	n.a.
Niger	.60	4%	1,055
Nigeria	.47	8%	21,334
Rwanda	.57	4%	100
Senegal	.55	3%	322
Sierra Leone	.51	8%	1,104
Somalia	.43	6%	3,708
Sudan	.38	4%	337
Swaziland	.82	n.a.	n.a.
Togo	.60	2%	147
Uganda	.42	15%	2,050
Tanzania	.36	8%	2,508
Upper Volta	.46	3%	348
Zambia	.34	5%	1,214

Sources: For compliance, author's calculations; for aid, International Development Agency, *Foreign Assistance Program: Annual Report to the Congress, Fiscal Year 1968* (Washington: Government Printing Office, 1969); for trade, Donald Morrison et al., *Black Africa, A Comparative Handbook* (New York: Free Press, 1972), p. 148.

ber 1963), 909–17; the index $= [f + (\frac{1}{2}g)]/t$, where f = number of votes that the two states are in complete agreement, g = number of partial agreement (abstain-yes, abstain-no), and t = total number of votes on which the two states voted.

Table 8–3 reports the results.[54] I expected to find a high percentage of cases in cells "a" and "d". Instead, the evidence suggests the reverse: high dependence states tend to show *little* political compliance while those states with little dependence show *high* compliance.[55] The hypothesis as originally stated does not appear to hold true. While we would want to test other years and other states, using additional measures of dependence and compliance, before we claimed to have a definitive answer, we can sketch some tentative conclusions:

1.   The link between economic factors and political behavior may be much more complex than Marxist theory initially admits, or, while economic factors are important, they do not operate as the Marxist viewpoint suggests.

2.   Nasser's comment may provide a clue: dependence creates autonomy because "the debtor is always stronger than the creditor." But why is *low* dependence linked to *high* compliance?

3.   A Marxist might argue that states dominated by American capitalism will be given autonomy in some minor areas such as voting in the United Nations in order to disguise their continuing exploitation. But again, why is there high compliance where American capitalism is less dominant?

4.   Alternatively, a Marxist might argue that in Africa, the key is dependence on British or French capitalism and if one looked at those data, the hypothesis would be confirmed. Such an argument implies, however, that *different types of capitalism* have different types of impact on less-developed-state behavior.

5.   Alternatively, our problem may be the *causal assumptions* in the hypothesis. Instead of assuming that economics molds political behaviors, we might assume that political conditions cause economic behavior. That is, the American state directs its economic *bribes* (such as aid and trade) toward states out of step with it in order to win their political support. For those states already in line, such costly payments need not be as great. (The evidence supports this interpretation.)

6.   In a similar vein, African states seeking *more* American trade and aid (dependence) may offer political bribes such as compliance on UN votes. States already "enjoying" dependence need to offer fewer political favors. (The evidence also supports this interpretation.)

As you can see, even the availability of evidence does not end the questions or hypotheses about world politics. It probably increases them! Nonetheless, we are able to say that the original Marxist hypothesis is not accurate, given these particular data.

Systems Approach:
The International System and Regional Subsystems

International System   The distribution of power in 1965 (see Figure 8–3) looks much like that in the earlier post-war years. Table 8–4 provides the data. There has been some change, of course. Three states in the Asian region contin-

---

[54]In order to place the data from Table 8–2 into tabular form, I need to specify what is the dividing line between "little" and "high" for my variables. For Trade Dependence, it was 5.5 percent; for Aid Dependence, $400,000; for political compliance, .535. These "cutpoints" were chosen to equalize the marginals.

[55]See Richardson, "Political Compliance" for similar findings and further specifications. For results using UK as the capitalist power, see Richard Vengroff, "Neo-Colonialism and Policy Outputs in Africa," *Comparative Political Studies*, 8 (July 1975), 242–45.

TABLE 8-3   Test of Hypothesis of the Relationship Between Economic Dependence and Political Compliance

		TRADE DEPENDENCE ON THE UNITED STATES (percent of a nation's trade)				DEPENDENCE ON US FOREIGN AID (thousands of dollars)		
		Little	High			Little	High	
DEGREE OF POLITICAL COMPLIANCE	Little	44% (7)	62% (10)		Little	33% (6)	69% (11)	
	High	56% (9)	38% (6)		High	67% (12)	31% (5)	
		100%	100%	N = 32		100%	100%	N = 34

ued to increase their share of the world's power, but within the main arena of world politics, the United States remains dominant. Its power has continued to decline, and if the trend persists, the second most powerful state can hope to balance the superpower with a coalition of major powers. Indeed, those other major powers can also think of themselves as forming a collective "third force," as de Gaulle tried to encourage in the 1960s.

We would expect that the rules discussed in the last chapter would remain operative, although the erosion of the position of the superpower may encourage new emphases. In particular, we might expect the superpower to manifest greater concern for the status quo, for the trend in power distribution is running against

FIGURE 8-3   Power Distribution in 1965

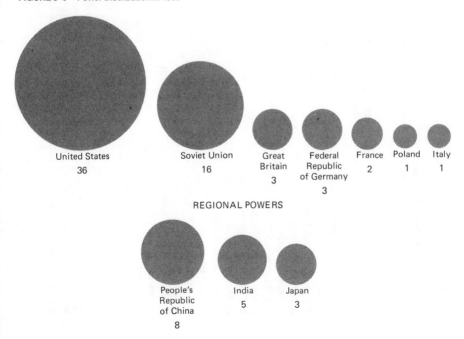

| United States 36 | Soviet Union 16 | Great Britain 3 | Federal Republic of Germany 3 | France 2 | Poland 1 | Italy 1 |

REGIONAL POWERS

| People's Republic of China 8 | India 5 | Japan 3 |

TABLE 8-4 Basic Power Levels in 1965

MEASURE	WORLD	US	USSR	UK	FEDERAL REPUBLIC OF GERMANY	FRANCE	POLAND	ITALY	PRC	INDIA	JAPAN
1. Million metric tons of crude steel	505.2	131.4	100.3	30.2	40.6	21.6	10.0	14	16.5	7.1	45.4
2. Percent of world steel		26%	20%	6%	8%	4%	2%	3%	3%	2%	9%
3. Million inhabitants in independent states	3295	195	231	55	59	49	31	52	700	483	98
4. Percent of world population in independent states		6%	7%	2%	2%	2%	1%	2%	21%	15%	3%
5. Political stability (1956–1965)		1.0	1.0	1.0	1.0	.6	.8	.8	1.0	1.0	1.0
6. Energy production in million metric tons of coal equivalent	5660	1749	993	191	186	70	128	20	323	61	62
7. Percent of world energy production		31%	18%	3%	3%	1%	2%	0%	6%	1%	1%
8. Nuclear weapons with strategic delivery systems		1980	491	50							
9. Percent of strategically deliverable nuclear power		79%	19%	2%							
Power		36	16	3	3	2	1	1	8	5	3

Sources: For steel production and population, U.S. Bureau of the Census, *Statistical Abstract of the United States, 1967* (Washington: Government Printing Office, 1967), pp. 862–64, 880–81; for nuclear weapons, Bruce Russett and Bruce Blair, eds., *Progress in Arms Control* (San Francisco: W.H. Freeman, 1979), pp. 6–7; for energy, see Table 4–1; for political stability, *The Annual Register* (New York: St. Martin's Press).

it. Overall, "cold war" would still remain the principal pattern in this weakening monopolar world. American intervention in Vietnam and the Dominican Republic are systemically induced responses to change in the status quo. The SMP state continued its probes, as in Soviet support for wars of liberation and the deployment of missiles to Cuba. The superpower, however, remained relatively restrained in response to probes and challenges to the status quo; it did not attack Cuba to remove the missiles, nor did it use its full range of power in Vietnam. Both the United States and the Soviet Union engaged in a nuclear arms race to maintain their power, yet at the same time, sought to introduce some stability in that area to prevent unwanted (risky) challenges. The United States refrained from overt intervention in some conflicts, such as the Congo or the 1967 Arab-Israeli war, as outside (i.e., Soviet) involvement remained minimal, but it did become involved because it defined conflict anywhere in the system as its concern. The SMP state, on the other hand, had an interest in manipulating conflict to increase the size of the coalition willing to support its interests (as in supporting the Arab states).

The striking feature of the monopolar world is the continued peace between the major powers. No other system in this century preserved peace for more than twenty years. My interpretation of the rules of the system suggests why this should be so in a monopolar world. No doubt nuclear weapons played a part in keeping the peace between the major powers (a point we shall examine in greater detail in the next chapter). Yet they were not used during the period of American nuclear monopoly, nor during the period of a "massive retaliation" policy, nor during the first years of the 1960s, when the strategic balance still strongly favored the United States. Nuclear weapons may be an environmental factor that does penetrate the boundary of the system to reinforce restraint, but they alone do not seem to account for the patterns of behavior.

If major-power war is unlikely in such a system, will the structure of power remain relatively stable? World Wars I and II created the potential for a monopolar world, although it was only after 1945 that technology and American interest ensured the emergence of such a system. Both wars partially created American dominance by the destruction of the power of others. As many of those states revived, American power would naturally diminish.[56] Equally important, the bases for power are not secret; they are knowable and transferable. The rate of diffusion of those bases has increased throughout this century; the economic development of parts of the Third World is a part of the process. A continuation of the power dominance of one state is unlikely, and thus *the structure of a monopolar system seems inherently unstable.* Fortunately, it changes incrementally rather than dramatically, allowing the states to identify the new rules as they evolve. Whether they do so is another matter, something we shall explore in the next chapter.

Regional Subsystem: The Middle East   In the last chapter, I introduced the concept of a regional subsystem in looking at the Socialist camp. Does a closer analysis of a regional subsystem help us understand politics on a regional level? Consider the Middle East: Egypt, Iraq, Israel, Jordan, Lebanon, Saudi Arabia,

---

[56]A.F.K. Organski and Jacek Kugler, "The Costs of Major Wars: The Phoenix Factor," *American Political Science Review*, 71 (December 1977), 1347–66.

and Syria.[57] The systems approach argues that we can understand the politics by knowing (a) the distribution of power, (b) the strength of the boundary between system and environment, and (c) the nature of the environmental forces that penetrate the boundary. To this we now must add (d) the nature and intensity of the penetration of the regional subsystem by the international system. In some cases, the interface between the two systems may be slight, creating an autonomy for politics in the regional subsystem. In other cases, the interface may be extensive and one system's behavior may be shaped by the rules of the other.

Our first step in the analysis is to measure the power structure in the region. The measures I have used for the international system are not applicable, so I have devised an alternative measure for regional power. The economic component of power is measured by the state's gross national product, the value of all goods and services produced in a year. The second measure is of military power, the amount of money spent on the military establishment. The third measure of population and political stability is similar to that used for the international system, except the population considered comprises only those who are literate. Table 8–5 provides the data.

On the basis of the structure, we would conclude that the regional subsystem approximates the *ladder-like* system we have observed in the international system. *If* the boundary were firm between environment and regional subsystem, and *if* there were autonomy between regional and international systems, we would expect politics in the region to adhere to the rules we have attributed to a ladder-like system. Did politics do so?

Systemic Rule

1. The most powerful state will attempt to organize a league of states (but will fail); it will seek an alliance with the second most powerful state (but will fail).

2. States will group themselves in two alliances around the two most powerful states, with the weakest joining the most powerful, the "middle" powers joining each other.

Regional Political Patterns

1. Egypt did attempt to create a league of Arab states, getting as far as a union of Egypt and Syria (the United Arab Republic, 1958–1961), but in the end failing. In the 1960s, Egypt never considered an alliance with Israel (but in the following decade did move in that direction).

2. The patterns were not in accord with expectations. Arab states refused to deal with Israel (although Lebanon and Jordan have from time to time acted more neutrally toward Israel). However, Saudi Arabia and Iraq have functioned as the rallying point for an anti-Egyptian alliance. The most durable alliances have been those of the Arab states directed against Israel.

---

[57]The actors of this sub-region are variously defined; see Michael Brecher, "The Middle East Subordinate System and Its Impact on Israel's Foreign Policy," *International Studies Quarterly*, 13 (June 1969), 118, for a useful discussion. For more general discussions of subsystems, see William Thompson, "The Regional Subsystem," *International Studies Quarterly*, 17 (March 1973), 89–117; L.J. Cantori and S. Spiegel, *The International Politics of Regions* (Englewood Cliffs, N.J.: Prentice-Hall, 1970); Bruce Russett, *International Regions and the International System* (Chicago: Rand McNally, 1967).

3. The alliances will be stable and relatively balanced in terms of power.	3. Alliances were fragile and, in the Arab-Israeli contest, not in balance.
4. The system may be war-prone; when war occurs, conflict is unlimited and a destruction of the power structure occurs.	4. War is common (every 8 years on the average) but is clearly limited in terms of territorial conquest, targets of military operations, and possibly the types of weapons brought to bear. The power structure has remained stable.

Some of the patterns we might expect to find in a ladder-like system do appear; others do not. How can we account for the clear deviations from the rules? Two things quickly suggest themselves: the presence of the state of Israel (an environmental feature that presumably blasts through the boundary) and external interventions (the intrusion of the international system). How do these factors distort the operation of the regional subsystem?

The systems approach assumes that leaders of states respond to the distribution of power and deemphasize other considerations. This was difficult for Arab leaders to do in Israel's case. Their nationalism and anti-imperialist backgrounds led them to see Israel not as just another power holder but as a culturally alien state, imperialistic in that it had driven Arabic peoples from their lands. To some, Israel was an outpost of the Western powers and their neocolonialist ambitions. And for others, there was a culturally engrained antisemitism. These perceptions made it politically difficult for an Arab leader to appear neutral toward Israel. This hostility toward Israel affected the foreign behavior of the Arab states, generally in opposition to the rules.

The systems approach suggests that when rules are violated, security diminishes for the states of that system. Given the power distribution, and denied the possibility of an alliance with Israel, the Saudis, Iraqis, and Syrians have a real security dilemma in the face of Egyptian power. In a malfunctioning system, they need to acquire additional power, and that can come only from *external sources*. Thus there is an incentive *to pull* the major actors of the international system into regional politics. The same holds for Israel; denied Arab alliance partners, it needs external power for survival. The regional subsystem thus gives up its autonomy. I must admit, however, that the monopolar international system rules discourage autonomy. The superpower defines itself as having a global community interest. The SMP state probes where it can. These combined pressures mean that the rules of the international system will propel the major powers into the region. We can suggest the following consequences:

1. The restraints on conflict found in the monopolar international system will intrude here, keeping war short and limited. Indeed, war in the regional subsystem will be terminated in large measure by pressure from the international system.

2. The Soviet need to probe involves them in the region, seeking influence among as many Arab states as possible. If the regional subsystem operated normally, this would not be possible because strong ties with Egypt, for instance, would promote hostile relations with other Arab states aligned against Egypt. The Soviet interest, therefore, must be to encourage Arab fixation with Israel in order to avoid the normal alliance polarization in the region.

TABLE 8-5   Power Distribution in the Middle East Regional Subsystem 1966

MEASURE	REGION	EGYPT	IRAQ	ISRAEL	JORDAN	LEBANON	SAUDI ARABIA	SYRIA
1. Gross national product in millions of US dollars	15673	5075	2235	3822	520	1250	1670	1101
Percent of regional GNP		32%	14%	24%	3%	8%	11%	7%
2. Military expenditures in millions of US dollars	2166	666	272	651	77	40	335	125
Percent of regional military expenditures		31%	13%	30%	4%	2%	15%	6%
3. Literate population in millions	16.1	7.8	1.3	2.3	.7	1.1*	1.3*	1.6
Percent of regional literate population		48%	8%	14%	4%	7%	8%	10%
4. Governmental stability (1956–1966)		1.0	.2	1.0	.8	.4	1.0	.2
Power**		37	10	23	3	4	11	5

*Estimate

$$**Power = \frac{\% \text{ GNP} + \% \text{ Military Expenditures} + (\% \text{ Literate} \times \text{ Governmental stability})}{3}$$

Sources: For GNP and military expenditures, United States Arms Control and Disarmament Agency, *World Military Expenditures, 1971* (Washington: Government Printing Office, 1972); for estimates of stability, *The Annual Register* (New York: St. Martin's Press); for literacy, U.S. Bureau of the Census, *Statistical Abstract of the United States, 1969* (Washington: Government Printing Office, 1969), pp. 859–60; 828–30.

3. The United States, in seeking to promote stability in the region, has focused on finding a settlement of the Arab-Israeli problem. Through the 1960s, while providing the external support for Israel, it pushed for Israeli restraint and gradual Arab acceptance of Israel. Such behavior accorded with the rules for a superpower and, if successful, would allow politics in the regional subsystem to parallel the rules of a ladder-like system.

4. Soviet and American activities in the region ensured that power distributions would remain relatively stable; the competitive arming of Arabs and Israelis is symptomatic. At the same time, as both powers began to consider ways to reduce the risk of confrontation between themselves, the possibility of mutual withdrawal from the region grew. As did the possibility of an imposed settlement.

CHAPTER NINE

1970–1979 _____
Détente and doubts

PART I:
DIPLOMATIC HISTORY[1]

Five Fundamental Changes

The eighth decade of the century brought a fundamental change in the character of world politics: those forces and factors spawned by the two world wars finally spent themselves or were consigned to the ashcan of history. Momentarily, leaders and citizens felt that a new era had dawned, as indeed it had. It was not the era of cooperation, as many expected, however, but an era of conflict that took new and unexpected forms. The short-lived era of détente between the major powers failed to achieve permanence. The instability in the political leadership of the United States and the People's Republic of China during the decade and the petrification of the Soviet leadership undermined détente before it had a chance to harden. The chaotic political change in the Third World provided a never-ending series of temptations to the major powers to seek local advantage against their rivals, even if such action hamstrung détente.

Between 1970 and 1973, five fundamental changes occurred that set the rest of the decade off from the decades that preceded it:

a SALT agreement, which ratified nuclear parity between the Soviet Union and the United States and in so doing affirmed the beginning of the *bipolar* age.

[1]Presently, the most valuable sources about world politics in the 1970s are memoirs and journalists' accounts. Henry Kissinger's memoirs, *White House Years* (Boston: Little, Brown, 1979) and *Years of Upheaval* (Boston: Little, Brown, 1982) are indispensable; see also Richard Nixon, *Memoirs* (New York: Grosset & Dunlap, 1978). Analyses of American foreign policy include Seyon Brown, *The Crises of Power* (New York: Columbia University Press, 1979) and Tad Szulc, *The Illusion of Peace* (New York: Viking, 1978). Other titles can be found in footnote 1 of Chapter 8.

a Vietnam agreement, which removed American military power from Southeast Asia and created inhibitions against similar American intervention elsewhere.

the discovery of common interests between the People's Republic of China and the United States, which necessitated a revision of their hostility of twenty years.

the negotiated end to World War II in Europe and a growing articulation of European interests.

a new Middle Eastern war, which demonstrated the vulnerability of Israel, the possibility of escalation, and the desirability of negotiations.

Each of these changes involved the United States and the Soviet Union, symptomatic of how much of conflict in world politics still revolved around these two states. In January, 1970, President Nixon declared that it was the goal of the United States to move "from an era of confrontation to an era of negotiation" with the Soviet Union.[2] The State Department was eager to negotiate; Henry Kissinger, Nixon's principal foreign policy advisor, was more cautious. Kissinger saw the Soviets as skilled negotiators, waiting to take advantage of American eagerness to end the Cold War by insisting on real American concessions in return for paper pledges from the Soviets. To bring the American foreign policy bureaucracies into line and to develop an American bargaining position, Kissinger stressed the notion of "linkage." "Linkage" made many claims: (1) the United States would judge Soviet behavior by what it did everywhere: Soviet interest in détente had to be matched by Soviet restraint in the Third World, for instance; (2) American willingness to reach agreement with the Soviets depended upon their acceptance of linkage; (3) The Soviets would be willing to do something on one issue in order to get an American concession on another issue.[3]

The two most intimately linked issues in 1970 were Vietnam and the nuclear arms race. Nixon and Kissinger had rejected a goal of military victory in Vietnam, settling instead on a negotiated settlement that would end American involvement yet preserve a noncommunist regime in the South. They sought to minimize the damage to the credibility of American pledges to defend its interests and allies. The growth of the Soviet nuclear stockpile, on the other hand, did not have the pressing immediacy that Vietnam had for American domestic politics, but the long-term prospects were more disturbing. The Soviet Union had reached numerical parity with the United States in ICBMs (both at approximately 1050 in 1970) and while the United States' advantage in bombers and SLBMs was substantial (approximately 650 to 100 SLBMs, 580 to 140 long-range bombers), Soviet missile production was continuing. No additions to the American inventory were planned, and given the costs of the Vietnam war and Congress's desire to cut defense expenditures, none were likely. If the American government insisted that the Soviets help the United States extricate itself from Vietnam by pressuring North Vietnam to make concessions, it might jeopardize any chance for arms limitations. On the other hand, to concentrate on bilateral relations exclusively might mean that the agony of Vietnam would continue.

[2]State of the Union message, January 22, 1970; *Public Papers of the Presidents: Richard Nixon 1970* (Washington: Government Printing Office, 1971), p. 9.

[3]For Kissinger's discussion of linkage, see *White House Years,* pp. 127–37; see also A. Stein, "The Politics of Linkage," *World Politics,* 33 (October 1980), 62–81.

For their part, the Soviets had no great desire to serve as a lobbyist in Hanoi for the Americans. Sino-Soviet rivalry for the allegiance of the world Marxist parties precluded any obvious pressure; besides, it was unlikely that the North Vietnamese would respond to Soviet dictation. An agreement on strategic weapons was attractive to the Soviet leadership as long as it prevented new American missile production and accorded the Soviet Union a political status equivalent to the Americans'. Moreover, the Soviet leadership wanted the West to ratify the outcome of World War II in Europe and begin the dismantling of its military power there.

These incentives were probably not enough to encourage the Soviet leadership to make concessions. Internal Soviet politics, however, had created their own pressures.[4] After six years of collective leadership—which meant an uneasy balance of forces at the top of the Party—Party Secretary Leonid Brezhnev and his partisans in the Politburo became increasingly dominant. While that made foreign policy more responsive to his direction, it also meant that he personally would bear the blame for foreign policy and domestic policy reverses. Three areas were particularly sensitive: agriculture, technology, and dissent. The aging Soviet economy and polity proved less responsive to central direction than the leadership desired. Nowhere was this more evident than the field of agriculture, where production, especially of grains, began to lag chronically behind the economic plans. While grain shortfalls did not mean physical deprivation, they did carry a potent message. Khrushchev's successors had pledged to better the life of the citizenry. Grain shortages would reduce the amount of meat and bread on the table and make the food queue longer—both signs of an ineffective system. The Party needed to avoid pushing the apolitical citizenry into opposition at the same time that political dissent in the Soviet Union was having a resurgence.[5] The Soviet leadership developed a growing interest in tapping the economic bounty provided by the capitalist states.

Brezhnev thus found himself in Khrushchev's position—trying to lead a party divided between the security-productionist-ideological coalition and the "domestic" coalition, yet cognizant of the need to meet the interests of the latter. The policy of the Soviet Union during the decade would be one of compromise, a compromise baffling to the West, which assumed that underlying all Soviet moves was a common (usually insidious) thread. The internal cohesion of the Politburo was high enough, however, to permit an evolution of Soviet attitude on various issues to match the changing American view.

We now need to look in depth at the five fundamental changes that took place in the early 1970s. As I treat each change separately, there will be a tendency not to see the interconnection between the issues. The brief discussion of the link between strategic arms and Vietnam is indicative of the complexities. Indeed, in retrospect it seems almost miraculous that the issues reinforced each other in a way to enhance the possibilities of resolution rather than conflict.

[4]For Brezhnev's rise to predominance, see John Dornberg, *Brezhnev* (New York: Basic Books, 1974); Archie Brown, "Political Developments," in *The Soviet Union since the Fall of Khrushchev*, ed. Archie Brown and Michael Kaser (New York: Macmillan, 1975), pp. 240–42.

[5]For studies of dissent, see Rudolf Tokes, ed., *Dissent in the USSR* (Baltimore: Johns Hopkins University Press, 1975); Abraham Brumberg, "Dissent in Russia," *Foreign Affairs*, 52 (July 1974), 781–98.

ABM, SALT, and Détente   After extensive Strategic Arms Limitations Talks (SALT), Brezhnev and Nixon signed two separate agreements regarding nuclear weapons in May, 1972.[6] One was a treaty limiting the testing and deployment of antiballistic missile systems (ABMs) to two sites. An ABM was the dream of military planners since the beginning of the missile age, and for some a nightmare as far as deterrence was concerned. Some *defense* against *bombers* carrying nuclear weapons was possible; interceptor aircraft and anti-aircraft systems might destroy the bomber before it reached its target. A nuclear warhead, lofted above the atmosphere by a missile and then plunging back down, was an object too small, moving too fast, to intercept and destroy. There was no active defense possible against incoming warheads. Or was there?

Suppose one aimed a missile at an incoming warhead by radar and high-speed computers, launched it, and detonated a nuclear device in the vicinity. Perhaps that would destroy the warhead. Both the United States and the Soviet Union poured money into ABM development and concluded that ABMs would not work. No one was sure whether the technology could adequately track and destroy an incoming strike of perhaps 1,000 warheads. Even a 90-percent success rate would mean enormous damage. A nation could overload any feasible ABM system by building more warheads. Indeed, the American government had stopped building missiles to develop multiple warheads, or MIRVs (Multiple Independent Re-entry Vehicles). One Minuteman missile would carry three MIRVs; the submarine-launched *Polaris* would carry ten warheads and decoys designed to baffle ABMs. Technology, economics, and countermeasures conspired to make ABMs mutually unattractive.

In addition to the infeasibility of ABMs, there emerged in American circles a fear that defensive systems such as ABMs would cripple deterrence. If an effective ABM system could protect one's ICBM retaliatory force, it could also protect one's population. Recall that one's population was the hostage held by the other nuclear state to ensure the nuclear good behavior of one's own government. The American or Soviet government, knowing that tens of millions of its citizens would die even it if struck first, would act prudently. However, if the ABM protected population centers, a government might be willing to take greater nuclear risks. The more American strategists considered the problem, the more threatening ABMs became.[7] Suppose, they said, that the Soviets thought the United States was about to perfect and deploy an effective ABM system. Now the Soviet Union would be vulnerable to an American first strike and have little ability to deter such a strike by threatening retaliation. Would the Americans succumb to the temptation to strike first? If the Soviets feared such a possibility (irrespective of American plans), they might attack first before the American ABM became effective. And worse, if the Americans suspected that the Soviets were fearful enough to seriously contemplate a first strike, then perhaps the United States had to strike first to preempt the Soviets. It seemed increasingly possible that an attempt to protect civilians might force policy makers to recalcu-

---

[6]For studies of SALT, see John Newhouse, *Cold Dawn* (New York: Holt, Rinehart and Winston, 1973); Duncan Clarke, *Politics of Arms Control* (New York: Free Press, 1979); Thomas Wolfe, *The SALT Experience* (Cambridge, Mass.: Ballinger, 1979).

[7]See Thomas Schelling, *Arms and Influence* (New Haven: Yale University Press, 1966).

late the nature of the situation and opt for nuclear war, even if it was not their desire. In 1914, spasms of fear and the recalculation had triggered German mobilization and the headlong plunge into war. Bringing ABM development to a halt seemed eminently prudent if one wished to preserve deterrence—which, after all, is a state of mind.

When arms limitations talks began in 1969, the Soviets proposed only that ABMs be limited. Watching the Soviet ICBM and submarine-launched ballistic missile (SLBM) buildup, Nixon insisted that any ABM limitation had to be coupled with a ceiling on missiles. In 1971, the Soviets accepted simultaneous negotiations. From that point on, Kissinger conducted the critical negotiations with the Soviet ambassador in Washington, bypassing the State Department and the Arms Control and Disarmament Agency, which conducted the formal SALT negotiations with their Soviet counterparts. The Soviets accepted the "two-track" negotiations because it gave them access to top American policy makers and gave them more room to seek a bargaining advantage. It also helped keep tensions within the Soviet bureaucracy under control: the Soviet military were extremely reluctant to disclose to *Soviet* diplomats information about Soviet nuclear weapons and delivery systems. Kissinger, for his part, dreaded the snail's pace the American foreign policy bureaucracies could impose on the negotiations by having to reach some common position. Kissinger made sure the American military would accept a ceiling on launchers by preventing MIRVs from becoming a subject of negotiation; the Joint Chiefs could simply fit more warheads on the existing missiles.

As it was, the United States did pay a price to bring Soviet missile production to a halt. The five-year interim agreement Brezhnev and Nixon signed in May, 1972, permitted the two states to have the following:

	UNITED STATES	SOVIET UNION
ICBMs	1054	1618
SLBMs	656*	740*
	1710	2358

*More SLBMs could be added if the ICBM strength was reduced proportionately for a total of 710 US SLBMs and 950 Soviet SLBMs.

The numerical imbalance and the ability of Soviet missiles to carry larger warheads raised fears that the SALT agreement of 1972 guaranteed a nuclear superiority to the USSR. The Nixon administration argued a doctrine of "sufficiency": the United States did not need to keep producing missiles beyond a certain point because enough of its delivery systems, soon to be armed with MIRV, would survive any Soviet first strike—a force sufficient to deter the Soviets. Liberal critics argued that, while SALT was a step in the right direction, it left uncontrolled a technological arms race that would seek to exploit ideas such as MIRV and make a mockery out of the idea of "arms control." Conservative critics charged that the real danger with a sufficiency doctrine was that it failed to recognize that a numerical imbalance might translate into an imbalance of *political* power favoring the Soviets. Kissinger looked to "linkage" to keep the Soviets from trying to translate any military advantage into a political one. If the Soviets wanted détente (especially after 1977, when the SALT agreement expired), they would have to exercise self-restraint.

Vietnam and the American Withdrawal   The American troop withdrawals that began in 1969 created a dilemma for the Nixon Administration. On the battlefield they reduced the ability of South Vietnam to prevent an expansion of communist-controlled territory. At the bargaining table, the unilateral nature of the reductions and the growing expectation of the American public that such unilateral withdrawals would continue encouraged the Democratic Republic of Vietnam to wait patiently until a renewed offensive would capture the South. Such an offensive would come from a series of North Vietnamese supply bases which dotted the Cambodian and Laotian border adjacent to South Vietnam. The governments of Laos and Cambodia were too weak to expel the North Vietnamese, and as the North kept the insurgent communist parties in Cambodia and Laos from going on the offensive against the two governments, an accommodation of sorts had been reached. Mutual restraint ended, however, in the spring of 1970, when a clique of Cambodian military and political leaders deposed President Norodom Sihanouk and tried to expel the North Vietnamese.[8] North Vietnamese and indigenous communist forces responded with counterattacks.

Events in Cambodia came at a time when the Nixon Administration was about to conclude that the bases in Cambodia threatened the shrinking American military presence and the prospects for Vietnamization—supplying the South Vietnamese forces with enough American weapons to make up for the loss of American firepower and mobility. Over the opposition of Secretary of State Rogers and Secretary of Defense Laird, Nixon ordered American ground forces to invade Cambodia along with South Vietnamese forces in order to destroy the sanctuaries and keep Cambodia from collapsing. (More on the policy making appears in Part II of this chapter.) The two-month operation (May–June 1970) did disrupt North Vietnamese plans, but unleashed a storm of protest in the United States (in which the killing of four students at Kent State University by the Ohio National Guard served as the emblem of the times).

The rebirth of vigorous dissent, especially among students, and the expectation of continuing troop withdrawals encouraged the United States to offer more concessions in order to negotiate an end to the war before the Americans had to abandon the Southern government. By the fall of 1971, the United States (and the reluctant South Vietnamese) had offered to withdraw unconditionally all American forces and end its bombing operations in return for a ceasefire and the return of American prisoners of war. The DRV did not have to withdraw its forces from the South, but the Americans assumed that a ceasefire would keep them relatively confined to the sparsely populated rural areas they then occupied. The DRV insisted, and the United States refused, that the Americans topple the South Vietnamese government and replace it with one acceptable to the DRV. Who would rule the South still remained the critical, unresolved question.

Both sides resorted to the battlefield in 1972 to force a solution.[9] In March, 1972, the North Vietnamese began an offensive across the demilitarized zone

---

[8]For events in Cambodia, William Shawcross, *Sideshow* (New York: Simon & Schuster, 1979).

[9]For the settlement, see Kissinger, *White House Years;* Gareth Porter, *A Peace Denied* (Bloomington: Indiana University Press, 1975).

that separated North and South Vietnam, driving the South Vietnamese forces from the region. Nixon ordered a resumption of full-scale bombing of the North, and the mining of coastal waters. These actions threatened Soviet and Chinese vessels and personnel, but both refrained from retaliation—Brezhnev was looking forward to the May summit meeting where SALT would be signed and the Soviet Union's status as an equal recognized; the Chinese, as we shall see, had the month before received Nixon in Peking and were loath to jeopardize the growing relationship with the United States. Nixon, for his part, worried that the intensified war against the North would jeopardize détente, but concluded that he could not duck the challenge.

The bombing and the partial success of South Vietnamese forces in expelling the North Vietnamese from the northern provinces led to a major change in the North's bargaining position. They dropped their demands that the United States topple the Southern government. Kissinger began another round of secret negotiations. There were two negotiating "tracks" here as well—one public, which went through the motions in Paris; one private, which featured the hard bargaining. By October, both sides had hammered out the details: a supervised ceasefire in place; an end to American military involvement; commissions that would seek to reconcile the warring Vietnamese parties but had no power to force a solution. The North agreed not to send more men to the South (although it could "replace" men and weapons). American prisoners of war would be returned. The stumbling block came when Kissinger tried to sell the plan to Nguyen Van Thieu, President of South Vietnam. The Vietnamese leader, fearing his regime would collapse without American participation in the war and with North Vietnamese units permitted to remain in the South, refused to agree to the settlement. Kissinger had to inform Hanoi that the scheduled signing of the agreement had to be postponed; Hanoi responded by announcing the terms of the settlement, and Kissinger, not to be outdone, declared, "We believe that peace is at hand."

The November election returned Richard Nixon to the White House with a strong mandate, but the new Congress was likely to end American involvement in the war, regardless of Presidential wishes. Washington passed the word to Nguyen Van Thieu that the South had to accept the terms or risk the loss of all American aid. Saigon gave in, but now it was Hanoi's turn to use the occasion to use the negotiations to destabilize the Southern regime. In December, the talks between the United States and the DRV collapsed. Nixon ordered renewed bombing of the North (in partial suspension since October), this time with B-52s. The attacks (December 18–30) evoked a wave of protests in the United States. The DRV agreed to renew negotiations, and on January 23, 1973, the October terms were signed by the belligerents in Paris. The war, which had cost 57,000 American lives and more than 700,000 Vietnamese lives,[10] had staggered to an end, although many saw the Paris agreement as a pause rather than a resolution of the Vietnamese civil war. Seventy percent of the Americans interviewed by the Gallup organization felt the North was likely to try again to conquer the South, but 80 percent expressed satisfaction with the Paris accords, and 71 percent said

---

[10]For Vietnamese military casualty figures, see John Mueller, "The Search for the 'Breaking Point' in Vietnam," *International Studies Quarterly*, 24 (December 1980), 497–519.

they would oppose any renewal of the bombing, even if the North did attack.[11]
The public's willingness to support intervention had greatly eroded.

The Sino-American Rapprochement   The early 1970s marked the convergence of American and Chinese thinking about their major common problem: the Soviet Union. The possibility of a Soviet attack on the PRC encouraged the Chinese to act as a traditional state might act. The Chinese supported the unity of bourgeois Europe and its expression in such institutions as NATO and the European Economic Community. They established relations with some of the more repressive or conservative noncommunist regimes, such as Greece, Spain, and Zaire. In October, 1971, the members of the United Nations, over the protests of the United States, voted to expel the Republic of China (Taiwan) and seat the People's Republic in its place. Chinese prestige and importance as a permanent member of the Security Council gave it additional security and created pressure on the government to behave in a relatively traditional manner.[12]

It was the American connection that made the difference, however, for only the United States had the power in Asia to thwart Soviet designs. After cautious and reciprocal gestures, the Chinese invited a receptive American government to send Henry Kissinger secretly to Peking to explore the basis for an understanding. Kissinger's trip in July, 1971, set the stage for President Nixon's journey to China in February, 1972. In private conversations between Nixon, Mao Tse-tung, and Chou En-lai, the Chinese indicated that they would respect the American definition of its interests in Korea and Japan and, as long as the United States was withdrawing from Vietnam, the Chinese would not intervene in the Vietnamese conflict. Kissinger, sitting in on these meetings, concluded that:

> . . . the leaders of China were beyond ideology in their dealings with us. Their peril had established the absolute primacy of geo-politics. They were in effect freeing one front by a tacit nonaggression treaty with us.[13]

Mao and Chou expected American reciprocity. In the Shanghai communiqué, which the governments issued at the end of the Presidential visit, both states agreed that "neither should seek hegemony in the Asia-Pacific region and each is opposed to efforts by any other country or group of countries to establish such hegemony." That common warning to the Soviet Union (and, as it would turn out, to the DRV) was coupled to an observation that "both sides are of the view that it would be against the interests of the peoples of the world for any major country to collude with another against other countries, or for major countries to divide up the world into spheres of interest."[14] Futhermore, the Chinese expected concessions with regard to Taiwan; Nixon committed the United States to the view that

[11]Gallup poll of January 25, 1973; George Gallup, *The Gallup Poll: Public Opinion 1972–1977* (Wilmington, Del.: Scholarly Resources, 1978), pp. 93–94.

[12]See Samuel Kim, *China, the United Nations, and World Order* (Princeton: Princeton University Press, 1979).

[13]Kissinger, *White House Years,* p. 1063.

[14]Shanghai Communique of February 27, 1972; *Public Papers of the Presidents: Richard Nixon 1972* (Washington: Government Printing Office, 1974), p. 378.

Taiwan is a part of China and pledged to withdraw American forces from the island as long as the People's Republic sought peaceful reunification.

The change in relations with China came at little cost to the United States. It gave the Americans a "card" to play against the Soviets, a de facto ally in the Pacific, and an increasingly isolated Hanoi. The China Lobby, which for twenty years had pressed a militant anticommunism on succeeding American administrations, was ignored by politicians and citizens alike. The Chinese political elite, on the other hand, paid a heavier price for détente with the United States. Lin Piao, Mao's heir apparent, tried in the fall of 1971 to stage a coup against the Chinese leadership to prevent the change in Chinese foreign policy. The plot failed, and Lin died as a plane carrying the fleeing conspirators crashed in Mongolia.[15] Mao remained in control, but his age and collection of opponents began to wear away at his leadership.

The Watershed in the Middle East[16]   American Secretary of State Rogers' attempt to achieve an end to the artillery and air battles across the Suez Canal finally came to fruition in a ceasefire (August 1970). Palestinian factions, fearing that everyone would accept the status quo, staged a series of spectacular hijackings of aircraft and increased pressure on Jordan's King Hussein to permit Palestinians to attack Israel from Jordanian territory. In September, Hussein tried to reassert control over Palestinians in Jordan, but found Palestinian armored units based in Syria invading Jordan. The American government prepared to intervene to support Hussein, but the Jordanian military routed the attackers and a subsequent coup in Syria improved relations with Jordan. The Palestinians were pointed back toward Israel.

The death of Nasser in late September, 1970, created a new fluidity in the region. The new government under Anwar al-Sadat, with a tenuous hold on power, set out to deal with the problem of Israel. In May, 1971, he signed a treaty of friendship and cooperation with the Soviet Union, which gave him greater access to Soviet arms with which to force a settlement. At the same time, he cautiously explored the possibility of a settlement imposed by the major powers, or even direct negotiations with Israel to exchange an end to the state of war with the Jewish state in return for the territories occupied by Israel after the 1967 war.

In 1971 and 1972, the Soviet Union publicly endorsed "measures other than political ones" to achieve an acceptable solution, but Sadat found that the Soviets were cautious in providing weapons in quantity or in sophistication to match the Israelis. On the other hand, the more visible the Soviets became in Egypt, the more the Americans decreased their pressures on the Israelis to negotiate and increased their deliveries of weapons. When Nixon and Brezhnev met in Moscow in May, 1972, they discussed general political issues as well as strategic arms. Their joint communiqué stressed "support for a peaceful settlement in

---

[15]See Michael Y.M. Kau, ed., *The Lin Piao Affair* (White Plains, N.Y.: International Arts and Science Press, 1975).

[16]Studies of the Middle Eastern conflict during the 1970s include Mohammed Heikal, *The Road to Ramadan* (New York: Quadrangle, 1975); Edward Sheehan, *The Arabs, Israelis, and Kissinger* (New York: Reader's Digest Press, 1976); Chaim Herzog, *The War of Atonement* (Boston: Little, Brown, 1975); William Quandt, *Decade of Decisions* (Berkeley: University of California Press, 1977).

the Middle East in accordance with Security Council Resolution 242.''[17] Sadat, angered by Soviet arrogance (Brezhnev had said the delay in arms deliveries was due to "paperwork"[18]) and hesitation, expelled Soviet advisors in July, 1972, as a warning. He did not break relations, and, as the United States seemed unwilling to force an Israeli withdrawal, Sadat reached a new agreement with the Soviets to acquire arms.

The war option became policy on October 6, 1973. Egyptian forces crossed the Canal in a surprise attack, while Syrian armor attacked Israeli positions in the Golan Heights. The attack found Israel only partially prepared, immobilized by overconfidence and an assumption that it could not attack first because of a negative American reaction. The Israeli fortifications along the Canal were quickly isolated as Egyptian armored formations moved into Sinai. The Egyptian plan, however, called for penetration into the Sinai to a depth of several miles, the establishment of a strong defensive line, and subsequently the destruction of the Israeli forces that tried to expel the Egyptians. This would avoid a war of movement, which favored the Israelis, and force them instead into a hopeless war of attrition. The plan proved tactically sound. The initial Israeli counterattack, delivered piecemeal, failed. Soviet-supplied antitank missiles proved to be answer to the armored attack.

The Egyptian plan strategically depended upon similar success on the Syrian front. There, the mountainous terrain aided the Israelis, who inflicted growing losses on the Syrian armored forces. On October 13, the Israelis completed their mobilization and began a powerful offensive against the Syrian forces; the road to Damascus suddenly seemed open. Syrian President Hafez al-Assad appealed to Sadat to resume the Egyptian offensive. Sadat agreed; it proved a mistake. Israeli armored forces blunted the Egyptian attack, found an opening in the lines, dashed to the Canal, and on the 16th, crossed it. Soon there was a growing Israeli force on the western bank, threatening to cut off all Egyptian forces in the Sinai and raising the possibility of a drive on Cairo.

The war had caught the Western powers by surprise; the Soviets had been advised only several days before the outbreak of hostilities. As long as Egyptian and Syrian forces were on the offensive, Sadat and Assad rejected Soviet and American proposals for a ceasefire. The intensity of the conflict quickly depleted the ammunition and spare parts of the combatants, which brought pleas for resupply. So strongly did the superpowers feel bound to their allies that they began massive airlifts to replenish the warring armies. That involvement permitted the war to continue and raised the probability of a superpower confrontation. The Israelis, in the process of encircling the Egyptian army in the southern Canal area, ignored a UN ceasefire resolution supported by the United States and the Soviet Union. Brezhnev warned that the Soviet Union would not permit the destruction of the Egyptians. The United States put its forces on alert to deter Soviet intervention and stepped up pressure on Israel to abide by the ceasefire. On the 25th of October, a fragile ceasefire took hold.

Sadat judged the war a success. Arab armies had, for the first time, made coordinated plans, seized the military initiative, and shattered the image of Is-

---

[17]Joint communiqué of May 29, 1972; *Public Papers: Nixon 1972*, p. 640.

[18]Anwar al-Sadat, *In Search of Identity* (New York: Harper & Row, Pub., 1978), p. 228.

raeli invincibility. Politically, he had demonstrated that the Middle East could be a cause of superpower confrontation, regardless of another 1972 Moscow summit pledge to "avoid military confrontations" and "to do everything in their power so that conflicts or situations will not arise which would serve to increase international tensions."[19] Therefore, if the United States wanted to protect Israel and preserve détente with the Soviet Union, it had to lead Israel to accept a settlement. Kissinger, now Secretary of State, threw himself into the tempest.[20] After shuttling between Cairo and Tel Aviv, Kissinger engineered an agreement between Egypt and Israel in January, 1974, which caused the withdrawal of all Israeli forces some five miles into the Sinai, giving Egypt control of the Canal for its entire length. In May, Kissinger's shuttle diplomacy produced a similar disengagement on the Syrian front. Further success eluded Kissinger until late 1975 (which will be discussed below).

The Oil Weapon   If Arab armies had demonstrated they could coordinate a military operation, the Arab oil states demonstrated that they could use oil as a weapon against the allies of Israel. In 1973, there were three converging trends that made oil a potent weapon. The first was the growing collective strength of the oil-producing states of the Third World, many of whom were members of OPEC (Organization of Petroleum Exporting Countries).[21] At its inception in 1960, this cartel gave little clout to its member governments, because privately owned, Western-based companies controlled the production and price of oil. Until the governments controlled production and price, oil was a potential, rather than a practical, weapon. The second trend emerged in the early 1970s. In 1972, for instance, the Arab members of OPEC announced a "creeping nationalization" of foreign oil companies, which would give them 51 percent ownership in ten years (most completed the process earlier). In June, 1973, Arab OPEC governments unilaterally announced a 12 percent increase in oil prices, which the oil companies accepted. Thus, before the war, Arab OPEC had created a political responsiveness of Western oil companies to Arab interests. Third, Saudi Arabia had experimented with oil as a political weapon. Before the war, it had used its oil revenues to help Egypt buy war material, and it had warned the American government that it would not permit an increase in oil production requested by the West unless the United States modified its position on Israel.

The oil embargo directed against the United States (and the Netherlands) by the Arab states reduced American oil imports by 25 percent and presaged a new feature of world politics.[22] Although the embargo was lifted in March, 1974,

---

[19]"Basic Principles of Relations Between the United States of America and the Union of Soviet Socialist Republics," May 29, 1972; *Public Papers: Nixon 1972*, p. 633.

[20]For shuttle diplomacy, see Kissinger, *White House Years*, and Sheehan, *Arabs, Israelis, and Kissinger*.

[21]OPEC members are Algeria, Ecuador, Gabon, Indonesia, Iran, Iraq, Kuwait, Libya, Nigeria, Qatar, Saudi Arabia, the United Arab Emirates, and Venezuela. See Mana Saeed Al-Otaiba, *OPEC and the Petroleum Industry* (New York: John Wiley, 1975); Oystein Noreng, *Oil Politics in the 1980s* (New York: McGraw-Hill, 1978); and Fariborz Ghadar, *The Evolution of OPEC Strategy* (Lexington, Mass.: Lexington Books, 1977).

[22]George Perry, "The United States," in *Higher Oil Prices and the World Economy*, ed. Edward Fried and Charles Schultze (Washington: Brookings Institution, 1975), p. 75. See also J. C. Hure-

the vulnerability of many industrialized nations was evident, as Table 9–1 shows. The experience led Arab OPEC and Iran to double oil prices unilaterally in December, 1973. That set the stage for OPEC as a whole to periodically raise the price of oil and trigger a round of global inflation. Not since the 1920s with the issue of reparations and the late 1940s with the issue of the Marshall Plan aid had economics become a central feature of world politics. Unlike in the past, when economic matters were the province of the major powers, oil economics arrayed a number of traditionally weak powers against major powers (and against a host of very weak states who needed oil for transportation and fertilizers but who could not afford the increased costs). By the end of 1974, OPEC states had amassed a surplus of some $60 billion, far greater than they could absorb in imports, although states such as Iran and Saudi Arabia acquired expensive military hardware. Those "petrodollars" often were invested in industrialized states, which implied that properties and businesses in the West would pass into the hands of Third World governments.

Those quiet, long-term effects were overshadowed by the more immediate changes in the definition of power. OPEC and other oil producers did *not* have a stranglehold on the economies of the nations, because the amount of dependence varied and because the oil-producing nations had a stake in ensuring the economic viability of the importing states. (Lloyd George had called attention to this relationship when France sought to strangle the German economy, yet still receive reparations.) Nonetheless, the nature of power—and therefore the complexion of world politics—changed because:

1. the threat to use force to compel the delivery of oil at reasonable prices was not credible. In part, this was because of the geographic dispersion of the world's oil regions (making a sudden seizure difficult) and the ease with which the facilities could be destroyed. Moreover, a use of force against a Third World oil state would probably

TABLE 9-1   Oil Vulnerability 1974

	CONSUMPTION (THOUSANDS OF BARRELS DAILY)	IMPORTS* (THOUSANDS OF BARRELS DAILY)
France	2,527	2,742
FRG	2,896	2,758
Italy	2,072	2,528
Japan	5,567	5,227
UK	2,160	2,585
US	16,646	6,088
USSR	6,480	—

*Imports may exceed consumption because of stockpiling

Source: United States Office of International Energy Affairs, *The Relationship of Oil Companies and Foreign Governments* (Washington: Government Printing Office, 1975), p. 203.

witz, , ed., *Oil, the Arab-Israeli Dispute, and the Industrial World* (Boulder, Col.: Westview Press, 1976); and Arthur Klinghoffer, *The Soviet Union and International Oil Politics* (New York: Columbia University Press, 1977).

rally the Third World against the aggressor, something no major power could blithely risk.

2. Soviet ties with OPEC states and its willingness to side with Third World states against the West raised the possibility that, unlike twenty years previously when all the Soviets could do was bluster when the British and French attacked Egypt, now they might be committed to the use of force to protect their allies.

3. the West was not united. Indeed, as we will see, the selective Arab OPEC boycott encouraged disunity in the West, and the United States found that it could neither lead nor dictate the European response.

The European Emergence   We have seen how Khrushchev had struggled to get the West's acceptance of the post-war borders of Eastern Europe, to accept the legitimacy of the socialist regimes, and to remove the thorn of Berlin. The Federal Republic of Germany, with Western backing, had resisted the Soviet demands. In 1969, with the election of a socialist government under Willy Brandt, the Federal Republic's stance changed. By the end of 1973, the two Germanies had recognized each other (thus accepting the division of Germany), the Federal Republic had established diplomatic relations with Poland and Czechoslovakia (accepting the post-war borders), and, in agreement with the Soviets and the West, established Berlin as an independent territory, linked to, but not part of, the Federal Republic. And in August, 1970, the Federal Republic and the Soviet Union signed a treaty of friendship. The ratification of the post-war status quo culminated in September, 1973, with the admission of the two Germanies to the United Nations, and a year later, American diplomatic recognition of the German Democratic Republic.

The acceptance of the status quo paralleled pressures to assert autonomy from American leadership. During the Middle East October War, European dependence on Arab oil encouraged the Europeans to keep their distance from the United States. The Germans and British, for instance, denied American requests to ship American weapons and ammunition stockpiled in those states to Israel. NATO refused to back the United States when American forces went on alert. The oil embargo and price increases further divided the alliance; the EEC announced that it would negotiate its own agreement with OPEC, leaving Kissinger to complain that at the very time that allied cooperation was most necessary, America's allies were forgetting the lessons of history.

Military policy rather than economics formed the most chronic cause of conflict, and, at the same time, cooperation within the Atlantic Community. As Congressional dissent about Vietnam mounted, and détente seemed more secure, the Nixon Administration faced the possibility that Congress would compel a reduction in American forces stationed in Europe. Nixon accepted a Soviet offer to discuss a mutual reduction in forces, correctly believing that Congress would not force a unilateral reduction if there was a possibility of reducing Soviet troop strength as well. The Soviets, for their part, did not want to see the Americans leave the Continent, for that would encourage the Germans to expand their military forces and consider the acquisition of nuclear weapons. The Europeans also wanted to keep an American military presence to deter a Soviet attack, but wanted a stronger voice in American nuclear weapons policies (increasingly a matter of domestic concern), and they wanted to decrease their military spending. Thus, when the Force Reduction Talks formally began in Vienna in 1973, there seemed to be a converging set of goals looking for a common means.[23] None was to be found, because, although each side insisted on a balance of forces when the process was completed, neither agreed on what withdrawals would have to occur to create that balance. Discussion within NATO was often as contentious, focusing increasingly on nuclear weapons, which had for years served NATO as its means of counterbalancing the greater armored strength of the WTO forces. As détente emerged and the Soviets reached military parity with the United States, Europeans began to question the feasibility of nuclear deterrence. Would the United States truly risk nuclear war with the Soviet Union to defend Europe?

Pressures for autonomy took another form in Eastern Europe. The new Czech regime hewed the orthodox path, while Romania took a maverick line in its foreign policy, but kept tight control internally. The Poles, on the other hand, remained in step with Soviet foreign policy, but found themselves improvising their domestic movements. In December, 1970, in the face of an economic slowdown and agricultural shortages, the Polish Communist Party announced increased food prices. Urban riots forced the suspension of the price increases, Gomulka lost the party chairmanship, and the Soviets agreed to underwrite the economy. The new leadership tried to persuade the citizenry to increase productivity and turned to the West for loans and machinery to modernize the economy. In 1976, the regime tried to raise prices but retreated after vigorous public protest. It became more dependent on the West and the Soviet Union for loans and food. Repression of the dissenting workers, intellectuals, and church leaders only encouraged the growth of anti-Party tendencies. The command economy in Poland was fast becoming a negotiated economy, which implied that at some point, groups in the society would demand a negotiated polity as well.

Détente Under Pressure

These five changes in no way encompassed the sum of world politics. Indeed, in a world of 150 nations, the volume of world politics grew exponentially. On the other hand, given the power of the United States and the Soviet Union much of those politics involved the two states. In spite of the growing reconciliation with the Soviet Union, the Nixon Administration worked to prevent the election of a Marxist, Salvador Allende, to the Presidency of Chile.[24] When India and Pakistan went to war in 1971, during which time India abetted the creation of Bangladesh out of eastern Pakistan, the major powers took sides: the United States and the PRC behind Pakistan; the Soviet Union behind India.[25] Nonethe-

[23]For the force reduction talks, see Christoph Bertram, *Mutual Force Reductions in Europe* (London: International Institute for Strategic Studies, 1972); John Borawski, "Mutual Force Reductions in Europe from a Soviet Perspective," *Orbis,* 22 (Winter 1979), 845–73.

[24]For studies of Chile and the 1973 coup, see Stefan De Vylder, *Allende's Chile* (New York: Cambridge University Press, 1976); Philip O'Brien, ed., *Allende's Chile* (New York: Praeger, 1976); James Petras and Morris Morely, *The United States and Chile* (New York: Monthly Review Press, 1975).

[25]See G.W. Choudhury, *The Last Days of United Pakistan* (Bloomington: Indiana University Press, 1974); S.M. Burke, *Mainsprings of Indian and Pakistani Foreign Policies* (Minneapolis: University of Minnesota Press, 1974).

less, it would be accurate to say that at the core of world politics, *the ability to cooperate* between the major powers had replaced the habit of confrontation. Nowhere was this more clearly expressed than in the "Basic Principles of Relations Between the United States of America and the Union of Soviet Socialist Republics," which Nixon and Brezhnev signed in May, 1972:

> They will proceed from the common determination that in the nuclear age there is no alternative to conducting their mutual relations on the basis of peaceful coexistence. Differences in ideology and in the social systems of the USA and the USSR are not obstacles to the bilateral development of normal relations based on the principles of sovereignty, equality, non-interference in internal affairs, and mutual advantage.
>
> * * *
>
> They will always exercise restraint in their mutual relations, and will be prepared to negotiate and settle differences by peaceful means. Discussions and negotiations on outstanding issues will be conducted in a spirit of reciprocity, mutual accommodation and mutual benefit.
>
> Both sides recognize that efforts to obtain unilateral advantage at the expense of the other, directly or indirectly, are inconsistent with these objectives. The prerequisites for maintaining and strengthening peaceful relations between the USA and the USSR are the recognition of the security interests of the Parties based on the principle of equality and the renunciation of the use or threat of force.[26]

What happened between 1972 and the end of the decade, when the habit of confrontation crept back into superpower diplomacy? Two circumstances, interrelated and feeding on one another, helped overburden détente before it too could become a habit: domestic political instability in the United States and the People's Republic of China and the growing internation conflict in the Third World.

Political instability caused the United States to lose its concentration and sense of purpose in world politics. The symptom of the time was the Watergate scandal; the practical consequence was a rapid turnover of leadership—four Presidents in eight years. During the early months of the 1972 Presidential campaign, seven men connected with Nixon's Committee to Re-Elect the President were caught inside the Democratic National Committee headquarters in the Watergate building.[27] After the election, increasing allegations that such operations were sponsored by Administration officials and that the President himself was involved in a "coverup" of involvement led to an unrelenting series of exposures, resignations, and firings. In July, 1973, a White House official dropped the bombshell—there were tape recordings of Presidential conversations. The Congress waged a long and ultimately successful struggle to acquire the tapes. As Nixon released batches of transcripts and tapes under this pressure, new questions emerged (as did a very unflattering picture of the private President and a concern of advisors and foreigners that their private conversations with the President might soon appear in public print). For a year, the President was under assault, devoting more and more time to protecting himself as close aides were sen-

---

[26]May 29, 1972; *Public Papers: Nixon 1972*, p. 633

[27]On the Watergate affair, see J. Anthony Lukas, *Nightmare* (New York: Viking, 1976).

tenced to jail and the evidence mounted that he was involved in the coverup. In July, 1974, the House Judiciary Committee recommended to the full House that the President be impeached. New transcripts showing unmistakable Presidential involvement melted whatever political support Nixon had in Congress. On August 7, 1974, he resigned.

Into the Oval Office moved Gerald Ford, a man elected by the public for neither the Presidency nor Vice Presidency. In August, 1973, the elected Vice President, Spiro Agnew, had resigned after being charged with accepting payoffs. Ford, then leader of the House Republicans, had been nominated by Nixon and approved by the Congress to fill out Agnew's term. An individual's hold on the Presidency remained tenuous. Ford had to fight to win renomination by his party in the face of a strong challenge by Ronald Reagan. Ford then lost to a novice in the arena of national politics, Jimmy Carter, who in turn faced a stiff challenge from a member of his own party for renomination (Edward Kennedy) and went on to lose to a relative novice in national politics, Ronald Reagan. Both Carter and Reagan had garnered support by appearing as outsiders, not habituated or bound by the traditional politics and policies of Washington.

As Presidential instability increased, the American Congress insisted on a broader role in policy making, usually in the direction of restricting American involvement in the world or setting conditions on that involvement. In November, 1973, the Congress overrode a Presidential veto of the War Powers Act and put time limits on the President's right to use the armed forces in combat without Congressional approval. At the end of 1974, the Congress took the laboriously negotiated Soviet-American trade agreement and added its own restriction: the Soviets had to liberalize their emigration policies (especially for Soviet Jews) in order to receive the most-favored-nation benefits of the agreement. The Soviets repudiated the treaty the following year. Moreover, the relatively frequent changes in Presidents meant that it took time for the inexperienced President to learn what had been bequeathed him, master the unfamiliar terrain of Presidential politics, develop a new course—only to find himself departing from office. Not only were the voters fickle; the traditional public support for the President had become more erratic, leaving less room for maneuver.

Chinese political instability, intense during the Cultural Revolution of the late 1960s, returned to the fore with Lin Piao's attempted coup and accelerated as the aging Mao and Chou En-lai struggled to control the party and state. In January 1976, Chou died; in September, Mao. The factions within the Chinese Politburo, increasingly split between moderates and radicals, settled on a compromise candidate for the posts of premier and party chairman. Compromise seemed essential as few wanted to return to the politics of the Cultural Revolution. A violent clash between the supporters of Chou and governmental officials had rocked Peking in April, 1976, touching off fears that the issue of succession might involve the masses. The need to confine politics to the elite put a premium on coup politics. The moderates moved first, arresting leading radicals, including Mao's wife, Chiang Ch'ing (the radicals were dubbed "the Gang of Four"). The coup against the radicals was also an attack on Maoism and Mao, yet the moderates had to move cautiously to dismantle what they considered to be Maoist obstacles that stood in the path of modernization. Teng Hsiao-p'ing (which in the new transliteration is written Deng Xiaoping), a modernizer and shrewd politician, emerged in 1977 as the driving force in the party. The triumph of the moderates did ensure continuity in the opening to the United States, but China paid a price. It lost much of its revolutionary aura, and in so doing, lost much of the power that symbols and ideas gave it. It became a traditional major power, of moderate influence, concerned more with internal industrial development and unable to exercise a global influence as it had through its status as *the* revolutionary nation in the post-World War II world.

Brezhnev, on the other hand, continued to shape the Soviet Politburo to reinforce his position. Committed to demonstrating the success of détente, he continued to press the United States for agreements showing the correctness of his policy choice. He visited the United States in June, 1973, agreed to begin negotiations for SALT II, and seemed willing to consider some of the restraints that "linkage" entailed. In November, 1974, he and President Ford met at Vladivostok to agree to a framework for SALT II. Each side would be limited to 2400 delivery systems (bombers now counted along with missiles) and no more than 1320 of them could carry MIRVs. The Soviets would have to reduce by some 100 delivery vehicles; the United States could *increase* its stockpile by 200. In practice, SALT II would permit an enormous increase in *warheads* as implementation of MIRV went forward: the 8,000 warheads available to American strategic forces in 1974 could grow to nearly 20,000; the Soviet's 2,500 warheads, to 11,000.[28]

Two unresolved issues bedeviled subsequent negotiations. Was a new Soviet bomber, called the Backfire in NATO parlance, a strategic system and therefore covered by the Vladivostok accord? The Soviets said "no"; the United States disagreed. How was the American cruise missile to be treated? The missile is 20 feet long, powered by a jet engine and able to use its onboard computers to fly a thousand miles at treetop level and deliver a nuclear warhead to a target with high precision. Cheap, they could be built by the thousands and launched from bombers, submarines, or on the ground (in Europe). Was each cruise missile a separate system (and therefore counted against the American limit of 2400) or actually a MIRV system when carried by bombers? The Soviets, without a comparable system, demanded an outright ban on cruise missiles. The United States objected, as it saw cruise missiles as a way of both protecting its strategic retaliatory capability and upgrading its nuclear forces in Europe.

These issues may strike you as technical trivialities, but in a time when the habit of cooperation had yet to form, they served as constant reminders of the conflict between the states. Moreover, there were critical implications behind each of the issues. From the American perspective, if an understanding could not be reached on the Backfire bomber, the Soviet Union would be allowed, perhaps even impelled, to build delivery systems that in the strictest terms did not violate SALT, but could be used strategically. Similarly, for the Soviets to accept the American position on cruise missiles meant that the United States could keep the letter of the agreement but still deploy cruise missiles to Europe (which was not covered by SALT) and thereby circumvent the spirit of SALT. Indeed, the existing American nuclear forces deployed in Europe, many able to reach Soviet cities in the eastern USSR, seemed a constant challenge to the SALT process.

[28]Stockholm International Peace Research Institute, *World Armaments and Disarmament: SIPRI Yearbook 1975* (Cambridge, Mass.: M.I.T. Press, 1975), p. 423.

Into the unresolved technical details stepped a new President, Jimmy Carter. Carter began his Presidency with a stinging rebuke of Soviet human rights practices and by publicly associating himself with prominent Soviet dissidents. That was not what Brezhnev defined as acceptable behavior. In that atmosphere of mutual indignation, Carter proposed major reductions in delivery systems and postponement of the cruise and Backfire issues. The sudden departure from the Vladivostok agreement struck the Soviets as negotiating in bad faith. Moreover, Brezhnev needed to control American nuclear technological advances such as cruise missiles; reductions could wait. And no SALT II treaty would quickly emerge to demonstrate the success of his policy line.

For two more years, the superpowers wrangled. When Carter and Brezhnev met in Vienna in June, 1979, to sign a SALT II treaty, they agreed to a sensible but awkward compromise that was prefigured in the 1974 agreement. Each side would be limited to 2400 systems now, 2250 within two years (Carter's reduction). There would be a three-year moratorium on cruise missile deployment (but not on testing). The Soviets agreed to station their Backfire bombers so as to make their use for intercontinental missions less likely. All that work went for naught, however, as changing circumstances in the Third World made the treaty politically unpopular in the United States.

The Third World Achieves Some Autonomy

What had happened? What made "détente" such an unpalatable symbol that Ford chose not to use the word in his 1976 campaign? Kissinger and Ford (not to speak of those who had less personal involvement with détente policies) had come to see Soviet behavior in places such as Africa as violating the requirements of linkage. For instance, the wars of liberation in Angola and Mozambique against Portuguese colonial rule came to abrupt end in 1974. A military coup in Portugal gave Portugal an erratic but functioning democracy dominated by the left.[29] The new government chose to decolonize. In Mozambique, a unified guerrilla movement received power from the Portuguese authorities. In Angola, three rival liberation movements grasped for the reins of power.[30] One faction, the Popular Movement for the Liberation of Angola (MPLA), controlled the cities on the coast and called on the Soviets to supply arms in order to suppress the other factions. When Cuba offered troops, the MPLA accepted. Kissinger insisted that the Soviets could not have détente with the United States while undermining the status quo elsewhere. Congress, however, prohibited either overt or covert support to the other Angolan guerrilla movements. Although denied American aid, the anti-MPLA factions received support from South Africa, Zaire, and the People's Republic of China. By the end of the decade, the MPLA had received recognition by the Organization of African Unity, support from 15,000 Cubans, continuing opposition from guerrillas in the south, private investment from the West, and aid from the socialist bloc. It was hard to demonstrate that the West's position had eroded, but it was clear that Soviet involve-

---

[29]See Rona Fields, *The Portuguese Revolution and the Armed Forces Movement* (New York: Praeger, 1976); Robert Harvey, *Portugal* (New York: St. Martin's Press, 1978).

[30]See John Marcum, *The Angolan Revolution* (Cambridge, Mass.: M.I.T. Press, 1969, 1978), 2 vols.; Arthur Klinghoffer, *The Angolan War* (Boulder, Col.: Westview Press, 1980).

ment had raised intense suspicions in Washington and a growing frustration over having no way to respond.

The frustration over Angola was nothing compared to that felt over Vietnam. Deprived of American firepower, the South Vietnamese government needed massive infusions of American economic and military aid. The Congress became increasingly resistant to providing either. The wounds inflicted by Watergate washed away Nixon's pledge to use American airpower if North Vietnam turned to overt aggression. In March, 1975, the DRV began its final military offensive, using tanks and motorized troops. The Southern forces disintegrated, and on April 30, DRV forces entered Saigon. The Americans had abandoned the capital and the cause of a noncommunist South the week before. Cambodia fell as well, and Laos accommodated itself to communist leadership. In one quick stroke, three dominoes had fallen.[31] (The frustrations eased a bit in May, after the new Cambodian government seized an American merchant ship, the *Mayaguez*, allowing the Administration the satisfaction of a forceful recovery of the ship and the crew.)[32]

The failure to prevent an insurrectionary victory in Vietnam and Angola persuaded the American government to take another approach: to force a negotiated settlement on governments and insurgents before the situation became so polarized that it prevented accommodation or before the Soviets or Cubans became involved. The approach appeared to work in Rhodesia and Nicaragua.

Rhodesia, ruled since 1965 by its five percent white minority, found a growing guerrilla war on its hands, while more moderate black leaders applied traditional forms of political pressure to secure majority rule. The independence of Mozambique gave the two Rhodesian liberation movements supplies and sanctuaries; the presence of Cubans in Angola raised questions about their possible involvement. Britain, legally still the ruler of Rhodesia, tried to keep Rhodesia isolated from the rest of the world until the whites agreed to a quick transition to majority rule. The Americans generally supported the British. In September, 1976, the white government agreed in principle but began negotiations with the moderate black leaders. A new coalition government of whites and blacks emerged in March, 1978, but the whites dominated the political process. The guerrilla leaders, Joshua Nkomo and Robert Mugabe, rejected this internal settlement, as did Britain and the United States, even though the guerrillas were receiving support from the Soviet Union and the People's Republic of China. The mounting losses from guerrilla operations and the unrelenting Anglo-American pressure forced a new agreement in December, 1979, which led to free elections and a majority rule government under Mugabe for the new nation of Zimbabwe.

In Nicaragua, a coalition of insurgents calling themselves Sandanistas (after an early Nicaraguan revolutionary who had, at one time, fought American Marines) worked to topple the Somoza family from its control of the state. Cou-

---

[31]For the fall of Indochina, see Weldon Brown, *The Last Chopper* (Port Washington, N.Y.: Kennikat Press, 1976); Alan Dawson, *55 Days* (Englewood Cliffs, N.J.: Prentice-Hall, 1977); Frank Snepp, *Decent Interval* (New York: Random House, 1977).

[32]See Roy Rowan, *The Four Days of the Mayaguez* (New York: W.W. Norton & Co. Inc., 1975); Richard Head, Frisco Short, and Robert McFarland, *Crisis Resolution* (Boulder, Col.: Westview Press, 1978).

pling political pressure with suspension of economic and military aid, the United States weakened the Somoza government at the same time that the Sandanistas seized major cities in Nicaragua. Somoza fled in July, 1979, and the United States quickly recognized the new government.

Underpinning American actions was an assumption that the Soviets would try to intervene wherever they could (or, at best, others would have an incentive to request Soviet intervention, which would prove difficult to refuse). And once in, the Soviets would be permanent fixtures. In fact, the Soviets did find themselves being *expelled*, not because of effective Western diplomacy, but because they had not found a means of preserving friendly relations with two states at war with each other. The Soviet Union, for instance, had established close relations with Somalia, trading arms for a Soviet naval base in Somalia. Somalia had long claimed the eastern region of Ethiopia known as the Ogaden. In September, 1974, a successful leftist military coup in Ethiopia toppled Haile Selassie, the emperor who had survived Mussolini's attack in 1935. Internal instability mounted, and the United States began interrupting military aid deliveries to Ethiopia. The new Ethiopian regime requested Soviet support and the Soviets agreed. In July, 1977, the Somali government ordered its forces to take the Ogaden before the Ethiopian military could solidify their control of the region. Soviet military aid to Ethiopia did not end, and Cuban forces began to appear in Ethiopia. Somalia expelled the Soviets from Somalia. By March, 1978, Cuban forces had helped Ethiopia recover the Ogaden, while Somalia turned to the West as its source of support. Ethiopia, in spite of Soviet aid and Cuban troops, continued on its own path.

The Soviet experience in the Middle East was similar. Egypt had sought American support, and Soviet influence remained confined to the provision of war materials to various Arab states. The United States, now committed to the peace process, understood that its continued influence in the region depended upon securing a settlement, which in the short run meant return of the lands occupied by Israel in the 1967 war. Kissinger was able to reactivate "shuttle diplomacy" in 1975, and that, along with demonstrative disruptions of aid and arms deliveries to Israel, produced in September a second Israeli pullback in the Sinai. International pressure on Israel had increased as well—in November, 1975, the United Nations General Assembly had labelled Zionism a form of racism. At the same time, the Palestinians were becoming more bitterly divided, and Lebanon fell into a four-cornered civil war (Christian Lebanese, Muslim Lebanese, Palestinians, and the government). Syria intervened to impose a ceasefire and Israel warned that Syrian entrance into southern Lebanon opposite the Israeli frontier would mean war.

New Light in the Middle East   These distractions slowed the peace process but could not prevent change. Just two months in office, President Carter announced that the United States endorsed the concept of a homeland for the Palestinians and negotiations with the PLO if it accepted United Nations Resolution 242. In June, 1977, Menachem Begin became the Israeli Prime Minister. Begin's coalition included religious parties who insisted on the retention of the West Bank, an area many had equated with a homeland for the Palestinians. Begin, trying to balance the demands of his coalition and pressures coming from the

United States, rejected the idea of a return of the West Bank or negotiations with the PLO, but announced himself in favor of negotiations in general.

Sadat's position, on the other hand, was worsening. (Chapter 1 contains more details on his decision making.) The American government was responsive to Egyptian requests for aid and diplomatic support, but the tie to Israel meant that Egypt would always take second place. Egypt had given up its war option in the years after 1973. Begin's government did not seem to be interested in a settlement, even for the Sinai, as members of his coalition spoke of retention of that territory as well. In November, 1977, half-seriously and half in sarcastic jest, Sadat declared he was ready to travel to Jerusalem to talk peace. The statement, heavily played up in the American media, forced Begin to issue the invitation. On November 19, Sadat arrived in Jerusalem, a city whose status was part of the conflict because part of it had been taken from Jordan in the 1967 war, and no major political party in Israel countenanced its return. Before the Israeli Parliament, Sadat renounced Egypt's state of war with Israel and his presence accorded recognition of Israel's right to exist and a willingness to begin normal relations. In return, he called for a return to the 1967 frontiers and creation of a Palestinian state. The following month, Begin met Sadat at Ismalia on the Suez Canal but the Israeli leader did not respond to the specific demands Sadat had made.

The Carter administration, after recovering from its surprise, began to press Israel for a response. In March, 1978, Begin rejected the idea of the return of occupied territory and even the idea of giving up Israeli settlements established in the Sinai. Sadat was under growing attack by Arab states who accused him of selling out or being willing to accept a partial rather than a comprehensive settlement. Carter concluded that only the United States had the resources to bring about a settlement—and the obligation, as Sadat had met the demands of Resolution 242, which the United States consistently supported. Carter invited Sadat and Begin to a summit meeting at Camp David, the Presidential retreat in Maryland. It was a high risk venture for each because, unlike for other summits, virtually nothing for this one had been agreed upon beforehand. Acting as a go-between and prod during the September summit, Carter pushed the two to agree on a framework for a comprehensive settlement and for a peace treaty between Israel and Egypt involving Israeli withdrawal from the Sinai and the establishment of normal, pacific relations. The signing of the Camp David accords was a remarkable achievement, but agreement on the implementation eluded the three. The December deadline they established to sign a peace treaty came and went. Carter had to throw himself into the breach once again. In March, 1979, he shuttled between Egypt and Israel, offered large sums of aid, twisted arms, and emerged with a peace treaty between the two states (which had the last Israelis leaving the Sinai in the spring of 1982). Sadat and Carter had less success in pushing Israel to deal with the question of the West Bank, beyond the Camp David agreement to negotiate some form of automony for the area. Most Arab states, including Saudi Arabia, which to this point had made large contributions to the Egyptian budget, denounced the Egyptian president.

The Israeli-Egyptian peace treaty demonstrated that the United States still had the capacity to engineer the resolution of conflict and that the American president, although hemmed in by restrictions, could still take risks. Yet the complexity of the world of the late 1970s and the reduced leverage that every major power had on events raised the question of whether the Middle East was an exception rather than the rule. 1979 brought with it three crises and a sputtering fuse that suggested that local events may be beyond the control of any major power, perhaps even beyond control of the states in the area. There was a crisis apiece for the United States, China, and the Soviet Union. The fuse was Poland, which involved the larger Atlantic community of nations.

Three Crises and a Sputtering Fuse   Toward the end of the decade, the Shah of Iran found his control of the Iranian state crumbling.[33] Pushing modernization, he alienated traditionalists who loathed the corruption of Iranian values. Pushing education, the Shah alienated students with a suffocating authoritarianism. Pushing land reform, he alienated the privileged. Periodic riots swept Iranian cities in 1978. The Carter Administration pressed the Shah to reduce his government's violations of human rights, leaving the Shah with American disapproval and sanctions if he repressed the opposition to his regime, and escalating challenges to his hold on Iran if he did not. The exiled religious leader, the Ayatollah Khomeini, continued to call for the destruction of the Shah. In January, 1979, denied American support, the Shah left Iran. The new government, unable to keep the army loyal and cohesive or to prevent Khomeini's return to Iran, crumbled in a week. Backed by a well-knit organization of Islamic clergy, the popular Khomeini became the de facto ruler of Iran, but had to share power with numerous mobilized groups, in particular, armed students.

On November 4, 1979, after learning that the Shah had entered the United States for cancer therapy, armed students seized the American embassy in Teheran, taking 63 Americans hostage (thirteen were subsequently released). The Carter Administration gradually increased pressure on Iran to release the hostages by embargoing oil and freezing Iranian assets in American banks. A rescue mission failed (April 1980). Secretary of State Vance resigned in opposition to the use of force, and Carter resigned himself to the onerous route of negotiations. In the last days of his Presidency, they were released. Carter was hurt politically by the crisis (possibly losing office because of it). It was easy, as Republican candidates did, to blame the difficulty on a weak Administration. The real question was whether any Administration could afford to pay the price of more forceful (and probably unsuccessful) measures.

As if Iran were not enough of an embarrassment for Carter, in December, 1979, the Soviet Union invaded Afghanistan. This was the first use of Soviet forces since World War II in areas not patrolled by the Red Army. Many interpreted the Soviet action as heralding a new period of aggressive interventionism by a state reaching superpower status. While this is possible, another interpretation is equally consonant with the available evidence: the Soviet Union intervened as a last-resort compromise between policy factions in the Politburo. Afghan governments have long understood it wise to pay deference to Soviet interests and sensitivities, and the Soviets have responded with aid and indifference to Afghan domestic politics. Domestic politics centered on contending elites, which increasingly took the route of military coups. In April, 1978, one such

---

[33]On Iran, see Amin Saikal, *The Rise and Fall of the Shah* (Princeton: Princeton University Press, 1980); Barry Rubin, *Paved with Good Intentions* (New York: Oxford University Press, 1980).

coup brought to power members of the two rival factions of the Afghan communist party. While the Carter Administration accepted this turn of events, regional and religious groups in Afghanistan did not, and they began to resist the central government. Rivalry among the communist factions produced another coup in 1979, more instability, and greater insurrectionary activity. The Soviets, supporting the government under attack, concerned that the West might try to wrest Afghanistan out of the Soviet sphere of influence, and fearful that the religious revival then sweeping Iran and parts of Afghanistan might spill over into the Islamic areas of the USSR, decided to restore the status quo with the use of its forces.

Fifty thousand Soviet soldiers quickly entered the country, first to free the Afghan army to pacify the country, and when the Afghan army proved ineffective and prone to desertion, to undertake the mission themselves. As expected in superpower intervention, the Soviets claimed that the Afghan government had requested it (although the head of the government died during the operation). Brezhnev pledged to withdraw the forces when stability returned and foreign interference in Afghanistan ended. Carter rejected the allegation of Western meddling and demanded an immediate withdrawal; the United States embargoed grain and technology sales to the USSR and forbade participation in the 1980 Moscow Olympics. SALT II and other steps toward détente were suspended (although both agreed to abide by SALT I, which had expired in 1977). Détente had reached a plateau, if not the road downward; and the old themes of the Cold War resurfaced: "History teaches perhaps very few clear lessons," warned Carter. "But surely one such lesson learned by the world at great cost is that aggression unopposed becomes a contagious disease."[34]

The American pressure did not remove Soviet forces. Once the Soviets intervened, more was at stake than the defeat of an insurrection. Soviet credibility, honor, and prestige entered the picture, just as it had in Vietnam for the United States. For the Politburo factions, which had finally agreed to intervention, there was no easy way to admit error. Brezhnev's proposals for a negotiated solution drew a quick American rebuff. Americans, from Carter to the newly elected Reagan Administration, found it difficult to think of a *negotiated* resolution to *aggression*; aggressors could not be rewarded for their behavior, and Soviet proposals certainly did not propose to punish the Soviet Union. Afghanistan and the Reagan election put Soviet-American relations on a new footing: while neither denied the importance of bilateral issues such as the prevention of nuclear war, each used issues outside of their direct relations as a measure of how trustworthy or honorable the other was. This was "linkage" with a vengeance. If the trend were to continue, two decades of experience would be reversed: cooperation between the two would depend first on the resolution of the indirect issues that divided them. Given the enormous complexity of those issues, the prospects for success seemed dim; a new cold war loomed on the horizon for the next decade.

The second invasion of 1979 did not cause consternation in Washington. The American government took quiet satisfaction in China's willingness to police

[34]Address to the nation, January 4, 1980; *Public Papers of the President: Jimmy Carter 1980–1981* (Washington: Government Printing Office, 1981), Book I, p. 24.

Southeast Asia. Conflict between Vietnam and China had a long history that even ideology and a common struggle against Western imperialism could not overcome. In 1978, Chinese living in Vietnam began to flee northward, claiming persecution by the Vietnamese government. Border incidents became common. At the same time, relations between Vietnam and communist Cambodia (renamed Kampuchea) worsened. Historic animosities, persecution of Vietnamese in Kampuchea, and the savagery of the Kampuchean government encouraged Hanoi to invade Kampuchea in December, 1978. Vietnamese forces captured Phom Penh in January, but were unable to suppress the Khmer Rouge forces, who fled to the Thai-Kampuchean border area. The defeated Kampuchean regime had the sponsorship of China. In February, 1979, Chinese armed forces invaded northern Vietnam, stayed a month, and then withdrew. The Chinese announced that they were there to teach the Vietnamese a lesson. The strategy was reminiscent of Korea, but thirty years made a fundamental difference: a socialist state was willing to punish the behavior of another fraternal socialist state by force.

Unlike the relatively sharply defined events in Iran, Afghanistan, and Indochina, the Polish situation seemed to be a collection of small events, erratically but inevitably moving states toward confrontation. The Polish economy was forever disintegrating, to be rescued by short-term expedients such as foreign loans, which would create new economic dislocations in the future. The Party tried to remain ahead of the public mood, but now found that its control of Polish life was melting: students were organizing, local trade union movements free of Party control materialized, and farmers—still owning their own land—began to form associations to bargain with the government. The election of Polish Cardinal Wojtyla as Pope (John Paul II) gave the Polish church great external support. In the mounting social ferment, Communist Party members themselves became active proponents of a participatory polity.

In July, 1980, the government tried again to raise prices. Workers responded with strikes throughout Poland, and then moved to coordinate their activities under an organization free of Party control. In September, the government recognized this new union, Solidarity, under the leadership of Lech Walesa. The Party purged its leadership to make itself more responsive to the citizenry, but it had to find a middle ground in order not to trigger Soviet intervention. The usual pressures emanated from Moscow; Brezhnev warned that in Poland, "the enemies of socialism, with the support of outside forces, are creating anarchy and endeavoring to turn the development of events into a counter-revolutionary channel."[35] There were references in the Soviet press to Czechoslovakia, and WTO forces staged maneuvers in and around Poland. Workers (joined by farmers) continued to use the strike as a means of furthering reform. Although the government negotiated for a while, in December, 1981, it declared martial law, disbanded Solidarity, and arrested Walesa and other dissidents. A year later, it rescinded some of the measures. Poland was creeping toward a negotiated polity. The question for the future was how long the Soviets could forbear.

[35]Speech to the CPSU Congress, February 1981.

PART II:
SCIENTIFIC APPROACHES TO WORLD POLITICS

Prologue: Putting Things Together

In Chapter 8, we explored how three different approaches might examine the relationship between industrialized capitalist states and the states of the Third World. Each approach provided a different set of answers, which is as we would suspect. How we see the world depends on our intellectual orientation to that world. But up to this point, I have treated the approaches as more or less distinct. The question naturally emerges of whether there is any connection between them. The answer is a cautious "yes." For instance, consider Soviet intervention in Afghanistan and the concept of "power," a concept at the core of political science. Table 9-2 shows how each of the four scientific approaches might discuss the event in terms of the concept.

Looking "downward" in Table 9-2 reproduces the kinds of analysis we have engaged in to this point. Can we profitably look "across"? Does a hypothesis or conclusion from one approach help deepen our understanding about the argument generated by a different approach? For instance, we might explore some of the possible connections between the approaches:

DOMESTIC AND ENVIRONMENTAL ———————► POLICY MAKER
FACTOR ANALYSIS ◄——————— AND POLICY MAKING

"power" as capability ———————► perceptions of "power"
◄——————— and "power" of individuals

One's own *capability* to intervene may create a *perception* that other states will have an incentive to intervene first, thus prompting one to intervene before others do so. Or the capability to perform certain operations (such as to stage a carrier raid on the American naval base at Pearl Harbor) may provide the holders of that capability (the carrier admirals) great influence in the councils of government. Alternatively, the power of various individuals may lead to policies that expand the capabilities of the state, as Hitler demonstrated in both the remilitarization of Germany and in his diplomatic clout. And certainly the *perceptions* of Soviet power by American leaders after World War II gave more power capability for the Soviet Union. You should feel equipped to sketch similar connections on your own, using concepts other than power.

All approaches acknowledge the possibility of some connection. The systems approach is perhaps the most explicit, with its incorporation of the concepts of "environment" and "boundary." Nonetheless, each approach assumes that these connections are not as influential in shaping world politics as the central factor the approach identifies. Therefore, every approach is incomplete, a simplification of a complex reality. Is it not possible to combine the simplifications into a more comprehensive approach? The answer is a cautious "maybe." Figure 9-1 attempts to link together all four approaches. It is not clear how much more we gain from such a combination. Not all approaches are equally adept at accounting for the same event or events. Systems analysis, for instance, does not handle

TABLE 9-2 Four Explanations of Soviet Intervention in Afghanistan, 1979

	SCIENTIFIC APPROACH			
	DOMESTIC AND ENVIRONMENTAL FACTOR ANALYSIS	POLICY MAKER AND POLICY MAKING	INTERACTION ANALYSIS	SYSTEMS ANALYSIS
How is the concept of "power" used?	"Power" is the capability to undertake an action; the existence of people, material, and logistical systems	Perceptions of "power" and the "power" of various individuals within a government	Exercise of "power" (compelling one state to do the bidding of another state)	Distribution of "power" among states
Explanation for Soviet intervention in Afghanistan	The availability of military forces capable of intervention creates an aggressive foreign policy	The fear of the power of a religious revival and the power of proponents of intervention led to intervention	The need to force the Afghan government to deal with the insurrection rather than stay preoccupied with its own factional struggles led to the intervention	In a bipolar world, superpowers intervene to enforce order on their periphery

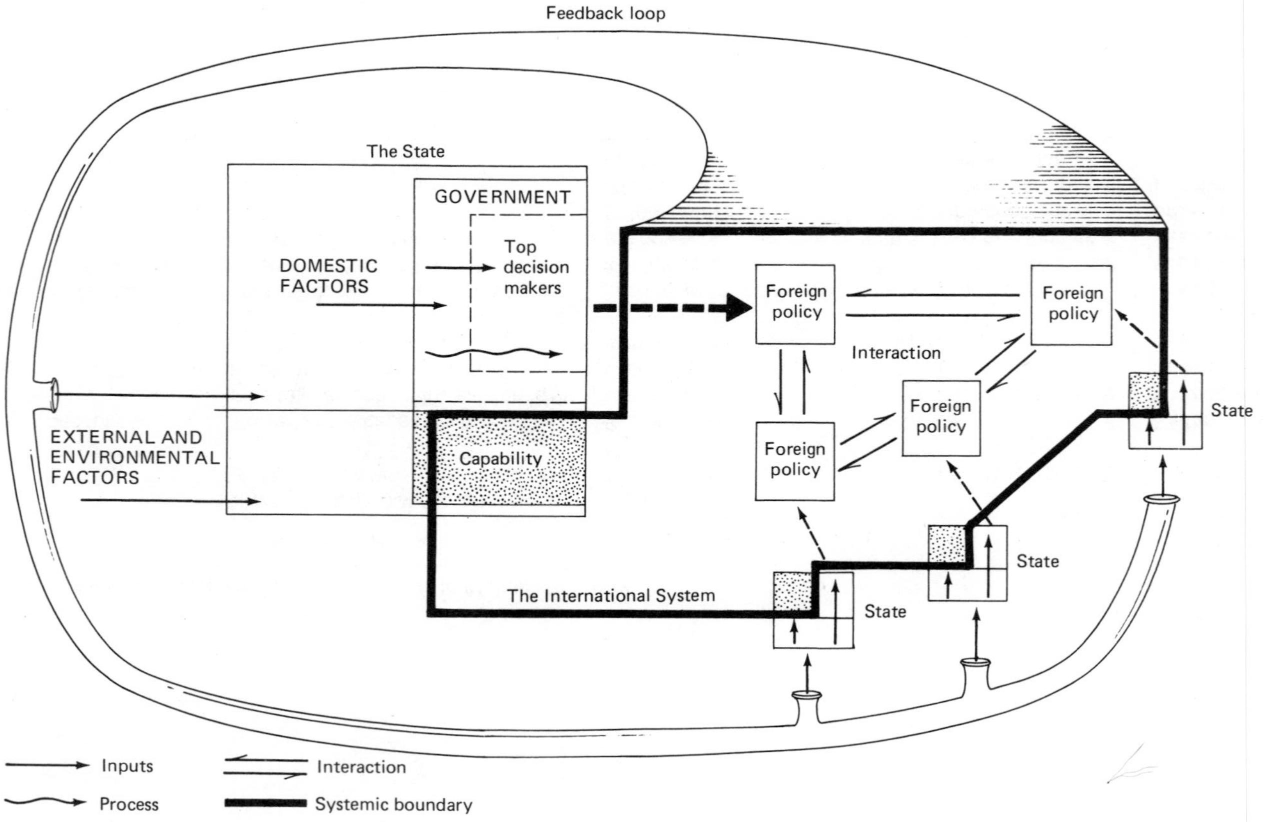

FIGURE 9-1 A Tentative Synthesis of Four "Scientific Approaches" to World Politics

single events well, because the approach concentrates on patterns. An event such as the Soviet invasion of Afghanistan may be typical of a pattern, or it may not.

Furthermore, combining the approaches may lead us back to the historical approach, where we become oriented to the specific event and lose interest in generalization. An explanation of the intervention in Afghanistan then becomes situation-specific: in December, 1979, the distribution of power encouraged (or did not inhibit) the use of force; the intervention was another step in the Soviet support for counter-insurrectionary activity; Soviet leaders increased support because at this time they feared the spread of religious nationalism; and the Soviet military had the capability of rapid deployment. There is nothing wrong with such a historical explanation. It does, however, encourage us to overlook some of the strengths of the scientific approaches.

Policy Makers and Policy Making:
The American Invasion of Cambodia, 1970

Individuals, Structure, and Process   The discussion of Kaiser William in Chapter 3 explored some of the ways personality might affect foreign policy. Beginning with the discussion of decision making in the Russo-Japanese war, I have developed the theme that policy is often a result of internal politics, rather than of rational choices.[36] In Chapter 6, I explored how the structure of the organizations may have affected the American response to Ho Chi Minh. This section takes another look at policy makers and policy making. In addition, it explores the *horizontal* connections between individuals, processes, and bureaucratic structures:

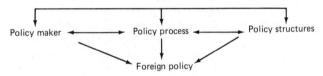

For example, let us suppose that in a particular state, the policy process is relatively open to the public. The media are active, institutions must make decisions publicly, and some key policy makers must stand the test of periodic elections. That policy process may force policy makers to act in ways that inhibit the expression of their personal characteristics in foreign policy.[37] We might represent this by using the size of the arrows to depict impact:

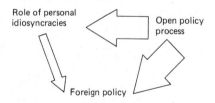

[36]There are other process models; for a sketch see Wilfrid Kohl, "The Nixon-Kissinger Foreign Policy System and US-European Relations," *World Politics,* 28 (October 1975), 1–43; and Lloyd Jensen, *Explaining Foreign Policy* (Englewood Cliffs, N.J.: Prentice-Hall, 1982), pp. 1–11.

[37]See Fred Greenstein, "Personality and Politics," in *Micropolitical Theory,* ed. Fred Greenstein and Nelson Polsby (Reading, Mass.: Addison-Wesley, 1975), pp. 1–92 (Vol. 2 of *Handbook of Political Science*).

How might this composite framework help us better understand the decision in April, 1970, to send American forces into Cambodia? The announced purpose was to destroy supply bases of the North Vietnamese regular army forces and National Liberation Front forces operating in South Vietnam. A successful operation, the American government argued, would forestall a DRV/NLF offensive, thereby permitting the withdrawal of American forces in safety, increasing the chances of success for Vietnamization, and inducing greater flexibility of the DRV at the negotiating table. Critics, however, charged that the Administration sought to widen the war in order to impose a military solution.

Policy makers are those individuals who occupy positions accorded the right and the power to order high-risk decisions for a state. The range of characteristics of policy makers which we might consider is quite varied.[38] I have selected three developed by James D. Barber (style, worldview, and character),[39] and to make this sketch manageable, I have confined the analysis to Richard Nixon and Henry Kissinger. Table 9-3 summarizes these two policy makers' characteristics.

Policy makers operate within structures: the networks of communication, authority, and command that handle the process of formulating and implementing policy. Some formal structures, such as the Department of State and the National Security Council, are the products of statute and tradition. Connections with other structures may be fixed by law, as is the connection between the top-ranking military officers who constitute the Joint Chiefs of Staff and the Presidency. More informal structures exist, often involving the advisors who surround the President.

The nature and volume of communication, authority, and command in such structures vary, often as a result of the structure itself. While the Secretary of State, for instance, is formally the President's chief foreign policy advisor, his or her organizational responsibilities may leave little time for face-to-face contact with the President to render such advice. For instance, a study done in January, 1965, of Secretary of State Rusk's time revealed that during the month, he met more than 200 times with foreign diplomats, his own staff, and members of Congress, but he had only 11 face-to-face meetings with the President.[40] Rusk's work week was six days a week, 14 hours a day, which is probably typical of recent Secretaries of State. Even with the long hours, he simply cannot be at the President's elbow whenever foreign policy matters reach the President's attention. On the other hand, the structure may give an advantage to the National Security Advisor. Having an office in the White House or directly across the street, with a small staff and no responsibilities to explain policy, the National Security Advisor has more time for access to the President.

Having identified individuals and structures, we can begin to sketch the interrelationships. For instance, Nixon reflexively assumed that the State Depart-

---

[38]See Alan Elms, *Personality in Politics* (New York: Harcourt Brace Jovanovich, 1976); Greenstein, "Personality and Politics"; Lloyd Etheredge, *A World of Men* (Cambridge, Mass.: M.I.T. Press, 1978); and Bruce Buchanan, *The Presidential Experience* (Englewood Cliffs, N.J.: Prentice-Hall, 1978).

[39]*The Presidential Character: Predicting Performance in the White House,* 2nd ed. © 1977, 1972 by James David Barber. Published by Prentice-Hall, Inc., Englewood Cliffs, N.J., pp. 7-8.

[40]"How the Secretary of State Apportions His Time," *Department of State Bulletin,* 54 (April 25, 1966), 651-54.

**TABLE 9-3   Personal Characteristics of Nixon and Kissinger
(Barber's Concepts)**

CHARACTERISTIC	RICHARD NIXON*	HENRY KISSINGER†
Style: An individual's habits of political action and relationships	S1. Dominate others	S1. Act alone to leave his mark
	S2. Avoid face-to-face disagreement	S2. Dominate others unless alienation of the powerful is likely
	S3. Make decisions when forced to do so and only after being reassured that he has studied the matter	S3. Treat others as inferiors unless their abilities merit their recognition as peers
Worldview: The expectations of what drives people and history and what should be done in the political realm	W1. Tough guys dealing from positions of power win	W1. Realism and intelligence produce success
	W2. Nixon-haters will attempt to sabotage any policy with his name on it	W2. Bureaucracies can be roadblocks
	W3. The US must meet its responsibilities and maintain the confidence of others that it will do so	W3. Create an acceptable world order by producing a balance between states
Character: An individual's orientation toward political life—active or passive, positive or negative	C1. Active-negative. Nixon invested enormous time and energy into politics but did not find it rewarding or enjoyable	C1. Active-positive. Kissinger invested enormous time and energy into his responsibilities and felt great pleasure with his successes and the combat of politics
	C2. Motivated to "protect himself against doubts of his goodness and doubts of his manliness" by remaining in control of himself, repressing his frustration and anger**	C2. Motivated to protect himself against doubts of the accuracy and wisdom of his perceptions and recommendations.

Sources: *For personality studies of Nixon, see Bruce Mazlish, *In Search of Nixon* (New York: Basic Books, 1972); Garry Wills, *Nixon Agonistes* (New York: Houghton Mifflin, 1970); James D. Barber, *Presidential Character*, 2nd ed. (Englewood Cliffs, N.J.: Prentice-Hall, 1978). †For a good introduction to the literature on Kissinger, see Harvey Starr, "The Kissinger Years," *International Studies Quarterly*, 24 (December 1980), 465–96. **James Barber, *The New York Times,* November 8, 1973, p. 47. © 1973 by The New York Times Company. Reprinted by permission.

ment was staffed by Nixon-haters. That assumption seemed to be corroborated for Nixon when he ran into the inherently conservative nature of bureaucracies. As Nixon's Secretary of State, William Rogers, recalled,

> When a new idea comes along, a Foreign Service Officer will tend to look at it in the light of all his experience, to insist that it be thought through carefully because it's hard to correct a mistake in diplomacy. I've seen the President talking to a Foreign

Service Officer, and I knew exactly what was going on through the President's head: "This guy is against me." Well, he's not, nor is he against new initiatives— he just wants to be careful.[41]

The choice of William Rogers reflected Nixon's view of the State Department. Rogers was a friend of the President, but had no experience in foreign relations. He was to keep the Department under control and responsive to Nixon. That Rogers soon became a persistent advocate of the State Department's position is vivid testimony to the power of the structure of an organization to make its leaders responsive to its internal demands. Nixon, in turn, became incensed at Rogers' behavior (it seemed disloyal) and avoided meetings with the Secretary when there was a possibility of disagreements surfacing (which was often quite likely).

In order to minimize the possibility of having to deal with such awkward scenes and to give himself the assurance that the "hard decisions" had been preceded by careful study, Nixon insisted on a structure to move issues toward decisions and implementation. National Security Advisor Kissinger, convinced from his scholarly studies of the need to control the bureaucracy and anxious to leave his mark on policy, proposed a structure that ensured his sitting astride the critical transmission points. The Nixon-Kissinger National Security Council had the structural features indicated in Figure 9-2.

The structure gave Kissinger the opportunity for influence and Nixon a mechanism to avoid disagreement. Differences would either be hammered out in the drafting stages or Nixon could listen to various disputed options at the NSC meeting but defer a decision until he was alone with Kissinger. In contrast to the access Rogers had to the President (an access restricted by the Secretary's many duties irrespective of his personal relations with the President), Kissinger's was quite high: in a typical day, he met with the President in the morning, at noon, and in the late afternoon, in addition to exchanging perhaps half a dozen phone calls.[42]

Finally, while the structure provides the arena for policy making, a *political process* furnishes the action. I should reiterate that the assertion that policies are made through a *political* rather than a rational process is only a hypothesis. We do not know how things are "really done." Chapter 1 offered two hypotheses by Charles Hermann that specified when one type of process was more likely than the other. I must say that I am persuaded that the political model is most apt when policy makers share power, a condition in both of Hermann's hypotheses and one likely to be present much of the time.

If we accept the proposition that the process is often political, then we can ask about the intensity and characteristics of the political process. How much does each actor have to negotiate? How is a winning consensus reached? And we can also ask how *characteristics* of the individuals and *structures* shape the process. Nixon wanted to avoid politics because he did not like opposition; the NSC structure was designed to weaken the State Department's control over policy. Hopes,

[41]Quoted by William Safire, *Before the Fall* (Garden City, N.Y.: Doubleday, 1975), p. 249.

[42]Mike McGrady, "Kissinger: Putting the Pieces Together," *Rochester Democrat and Chronicle*, December 3, 1972.

FIGURE 9-2 **Structure and Process of the National Security Council**

INITIATION →	WORK-UP →	REVIEW →	ADVICE GIVING →	PRESIDENTIAL DECISION →	IMPLEMENTATION
Decision made by Kissinger or Nixon that an issue needed analysis	Drafting of analysis and options by a working group from State, Defense, CIA, and staff members of the NSC who reported to Kissinger	Kissinger chaired a meeting of senior policy makers to review the draft	Formal NSC meeting for top decision makers to state their positions	Nixon's decision, with separate advice from Kissinger	Designated bureaucracies enact policy under monitoring by NSC staff

Adapted from Wilfrid L. Kohl, "The Nixon-Kissinger Foreign Policy System and US-European Relations: Patterns of Policy Making," *World Politics*, 28, no. 1 (October 1975), 1–43.

however, do not eliminate politics. Indeed, Kissinger suggests that Nixon saw this clearly: "If the NSC system of elaborating options interested him [Nixon] for anything, it was for the intelligence it supplied him about the views of a bureaucracy he distrusted and for the opportunity it provided to camouflage his own aims."[43] It is also possible to consider how the process and structure affect personal characteristics of leaders. Bruce Buchanan, for instance, argues that the pressures of the Presidency can distort an individual's self perceptions, erode moral inhibitions, and encourage "the use of secrecy, misrepresentation, and lying as weapons in the struggle for political success and survival."[44]

Cambodia, 1970   How might these observations about personal characteristics, structure, and process help account for the decision to invade Cambodia?[45] By the spring of 1970, the Administration had made a series of statements announcing withdrawals of American forces, something both the American public and the North Vietnamese came to expect. Secretary of Defense Laird wanted to accelerate the withdrawals so he could end the drain of defense monies to Vietnam. Secretary of State Rogers wanted American involvement to end quickly in order to quiet public unrest and clear the way for rapid progress on such issues as SALT and a Middle Eastern settlement. Kissinger, however, worried about American bargaining leverage in the peace talks if unilateral withdrawals continued. Another troop withdrawal announcement was due in April, 1970. With Nixon committed to continuing withdrawals, Kissinger and the top military leadership presented the President a plan to announce a large withdrawal of 150,000 more men over a year, but to make the bulk of the withdrawals toward the end of the time. The military had agreed on the understanding that the remaining American forces would not be endangered. Laird and Rogers learned of the decision at the last minute when they were 3,000 miles from the President.

The withdrawal announcement came on April 20, a time when Cambodia seemed to be on the verge of being overrun by the Vietnamese and their Cambodian communist allies. If Cambodia fell, the country would become one large supply base for DRV/NLF forces operating in South Vietnam. No "peace with honor" seemed likely in such circumstances. Nixon ordered the convening of an emergency NSC meeting on April 22. The President was convinced that something had to be done, but was concerned that "too much" might cause a domestic uproar and possibly trigger increased socialist camp support for the DRV. "Too little" might give him a rebellious military. The Joint Chiefs of Staff, encouraged by the White House, came with their pet projects: American incursions into Cambodia and Laos, amphibious operations to seal Cambodia off from the sea, and a loosening of the restrictions on bombing the North. Laird and Rogers urged that nothing be done (in fact, both had probably tried to undercut a previous Presidential decision to send arms to the new Cambodian government). Kissinger had positioned himself in the middle of the options, recommending that the South Vietnamese attack one of the sanctuaries in Cambodia. Nixon, searching for something, adopted Kissinger's position. The debate now focused

[43]Kissinger, *White House Years,* pp. 163–64.

[44]Buchanan, *Presidential Experience,* p. 7.

[45]Much of the following is drawn from Kissinger, *White House Years,* Shawcross, *Sideshow,* and news accounts.

on how much American support would be given the South Vietnamese. At this point, an actor with no institutional stake in the issues—and therefore likely to see the policy process in rational model terms—weighed in. Vice President Agnew

> . . . thought the whole debate irrelevant. Either the sanctuaries were a danger or they were not. If it was worth cleaning them out, he did not understand all the pussyfooting about the American role or what we accomplished by attacking only one. . . . If Nixon hated anything more than being presented with a plan he had not considered, it was to be shown up in a group as being less tough than his advisers. . . . He authorized American air support for the . . . [South Vietnamese] operation but only "on the basis of demonstrated necessity."[46]

The continued bureaucratic footdragging in supplying arms to Cambodia as directed by the President, and increasing leaks to the press about foreign policy decisions angered the President and gave the proponents of invasion another chance to persuade him. On April 24, Nixon discussed with the Joint Chiefs the possibility of using American forces. Neither Laird nor Rogers were invited. The military rushed to draw up plans but were hampered because they could not tell Laird, nor many subordinates, for fear of leaks. Kissinger, fearing a political storm if Rogers and Laird were not informed of the direction the President was moving, persuaded Nixon to at least appear to take counsel of his chief civilian advisors before making a decision. Nixon did so on the 26th, but ever anxious to avoid a confrontation, told Rogers and Laird that the military plans presented at the meeting were in case of an emergency. After they left, Nixon signed an order authorizing the use of American forces against one sanctuary in Cambodia while the South Vietnamese attacked another.

When Laird and Rogers received copies of the Presidential order, they demanded to meet with Nixon. Nixon listened impatiently to their objections. He had convinced himself that "you would have a hell of an uproar at home," even for a limited operation. "If you are going to take the heat, go for all the marbles. . . . Let's go after all the sanctuaries."[47] Rogers and Laird raised objections, this time procedural rather than substantive. Laird said the military opposed part of the operation (they did not) and Rogers wanted to tell a Senate hearing the following day that no decisions regarding Cambodia had been made. Kissinger suggested a twenty-four hour delay in the implementation of the order to give the two secretaries time to reconcile themselves to the Presidential decision. On the 28th, Nixon again repeated his order, but said that the record would show that he had acted contrary to their advice. Nixon then secluded himself for two days to retrace his thinking and write the speech announcing his decision to invade Cambodia—and to avoid requests for reconsideration. It was at this stage that Nixon did a formal assessment of the pros and cons of the operation; the decision-making process must *appear* rational. But at this point, he was locked into an agreement which the various bureaucracies had grudgingly accepted and in which he had invested a great deal of face.

Although American forces began the invasion on the evening of April 30 (Washington time), it remained a heavily compromised decision. The President

---

[46]Kissinger, *White House Years,* pp. 491–92.
[47]Quoted in Safire, *Before the Fall,* p. 103.

had spoken of clearing all the sanctuaries for good, but already an unnamed White House official (perhaps Kissinger) had publicly said that the operation would last no more than six to eight weeks, far too little time. Within two weeks, the military had received permission to stage eleven separate incursions, including an American-supported flotilla moving up the Mekong River. At the same time, the Administration forbade the use of American forces more than 21 miles into Cambodia. And the press, feasting on leaks, reported the high-level disagreements and how the structures for rational decision making had been repeatedly bypassed.

Personal characteristics, structure, and process combine to give us a clearer picture of the Cambodian decision. Nixon's worldview and his character made him prone to do something, especially when the Vietnamese increased their offensive in Cambodia after he had announced another major troop withdrawal. His insistence on dealing from a position of power and Kissinger's concern for preserving a balance predisposed them to a wider war. Moreover, not only were foreign enemies out to thwart the President, his own subordinates were in opposition. His active-negative character encouraged him to lash out against those who made his life unpleasant. Kissinger, more oriented by his character toward the pragmatic criterion of success, gradually leaned toward the incursion as a way of signalling commitment to the DRV. Neither man accepted the idea that public protests should sway policy.

An incentive to "do something," however, is not the same thing as policy, for policy is composed of tangible "somethings." The NSC structure was designed to provide a range of "somethings" for presidential consideration. It did that on the 22nd of April. The military provided a gamut of possibilities; Laird and Rogers proposed doing little or nothing. Nixon found his two Cabinet officers unresponsive to his needs. He was aware of their objections "that the Communists might respond with an attack on Phnom Penh, . . . that an attack on the sanctuaries would provoke 'deep divisions' in the United States, . . . that it might lead to a breaking off of the Paris talks, and . . . that the Communist side might attack across the demilitarized zone in Vietnam."[48] But doing nothing— even contemplating the collapse of Cambodia as Rogers seemed to—did not meet with his view of the situation. In 1962, as Chapter 1 pointed out, when President Kennedy informed Secretary of Defense McNamara that Soviet missiles in Cuba were a critical question for Kennedy, McNamara quickly dropped his recommendation to do nothing. In 1970, however, Nixon found his subordinates continuing to disagree with him and trying to change his mind.

The NSC structure thus ensured that the President would hear something of what he wanted to hear. From that point on, however, the structure became a liability in the President's eyes, for it promised the nay-sayers continued access to the high councils of government. Kissinger struggled to keep the structure in operation, in part because it gave him influence, in part because without a means of privately airing dissent, officials might go public. The structure, coupled with Nixon's difficulty in making decisions when faced with opposition, ensured that the actions Nixon would decide upon would incrementally increase (from no in-

---

[48]Quoted by Stewart Alsop, who saw Nixon's note pad reflecting his thinking; "On the President's Yellow Pad," *Newsweek,* June 1, 1970, p. 106.

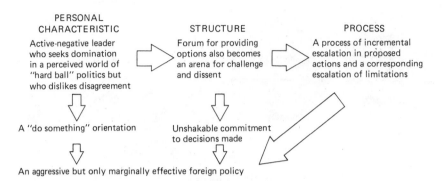

FIGURE 9-3   The Impact of Three Factors on the Cambodian Decision

volvement, to air support, to attacking one sanctuary, to attacking "all" sanctuaries) at the same time that the *constraints* on action (time and depth of the incursion) would increase as well.[49]

Put another way, Presidential characteristics and the structure forced a *political* resolution of the contending views. The "price" was a set of contradictions; Nixon took the "heat" for the incursion (far more than most expected), yet also made the operation less tenable. Equally contradictory, he encouraged the very politics he despised. This one, limited example suggests the kinds of relationships and consequences depicted in Figure 9-3.

Systems Approach: A Bipolar World

Once again, we need to determine how the world turns in terms of power. The distribution pictured in Figure 9-4 is quite unlike any we have seen in this century. The world is clearly no longer monopolar. It is *bipolar*: two states of relatively equal power, each of which is much more powerful than any of the other major powers. Both together cannot be balanced by any feasible coalition of states (Table 9-4 provides the data).

What would we expect to be the systemic pressures operating on the states of such a system? The logic of this kind of power distribution indicates that, for a superpower, only the other superpower constitutes a threat. This was a novel situation for the United States in that it had not had an equally powerful rival since 1945. It was novel for the Soviet Union as well, for it had never been the most powerful state or a superpower. Logic also suggests that, acting alone, neither state can hope for real gains in conflict with the other, as power is too evenly matched. We might expect both superpowers to have an incentive to find mutually acceptable understandings that would reduce the likelihood of confrontation. The SALT negotiations seem historically to fit these expectations, as do the "Basic Principles of Relations" signed in 1972. Détente seems a natural condition, at least in the relations between the superpowers.

[49]Leslie Gelb found a similar result in examining decision-making by Johnson on Vietnam; *The Irony of Vietnam* (Washington: Brookings Institution, 1979).

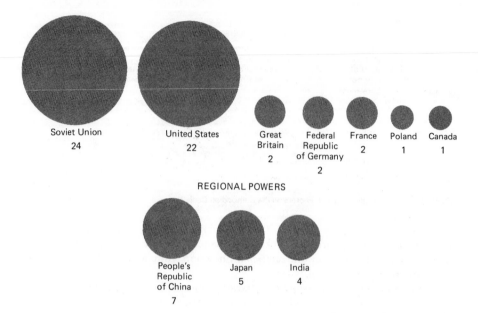

Soviet Union 24 · United States 22 · Great Britain 2 · Federal Republic of Germany 2 · France 2 · Poland 1 · Canada 1

REGIONAL POWERS

People's Republic of China 7 · Japan 5 · India 4

FIGURE 9-4   Power Distribution in 1975

Yet, at the same time, logic dictates that the superpowers have to be con-cerned with the behavior of other major powers. If most aligned with one super-power, the balance would shift heavily in its favor. Bipolarism gives each super-power an incentive to build an alliance network and maintain it, disrupt the unity of the rival alliance, and to tolerate a stance of neutrality by other states. Much of the discussion of bipolarism in the literature makes these points.[50] Historically, of course, the alliance systems of today are the product of an earlier (monopolar) era. The United States carried its NATO and Japanese alliances into the bipolar world, as the Soviets did their WTO alliance. The American opening to China is in line with systemic rules, for it moved the Chinese from neutrality into an incip-ient alliance with the United States. At mid-decade, in alliance with the United States were states whose power totalled roughly 40, while the Soviet alliance sys-tem totalled roughly 30. The specific power distribution and composition of alli-ances was, however, more an artifact of history than the operation of systemic pressures.

In a bipolar system, on the other hand, the alliance connections of very weak states (a large number of states in the 1970s) are immaterial. Even if all very weak states aligned with one superpower, the resources necessary to coordinate and control the behaviors of such states would very likely outweigh the increase in overall power the superpower would enjoy by such an acquisition. Superpowers in bipolar systems should be relatively disinterested in alignment patterns of the very weak, perhaps even willing to discourage additions to their alliance systems.

[50]See, in particular, Morton Kaplan, *System and Process in International Politics* (New York: John Wiley, 1964), pp. 38–39.

TABLE 9-4 Basic Power Levels in 1975

MEASURE	WORLD	US	USSR	UK	FEDERAL REPUBLIC OF GERMANY	FRANCE	POLAND	CANADA	PRC	JAPAN	INDIA
1. Million metric tons of crude steel	643.9	105.8	141.3	20.1	40.4	21.5	14.6	13.0	29	102.3	7.9
2. Percent of world steel		16%	22%	3%	6%	3%	2%	2%	5%	16%	1%
3. Million inhabitants in independent states (1977)	4124	217	259	56	61	53	34	23	866	114	626
4. Percent of world population in independent states		5%	6%	1%	1%	1%	1%	1%	21%	3%	15%
5. Political stability		.8	1.0	1.0	1.0	1.0	.6	1.0	.6	1.0	.8
6. Energy production in million metric tons of coal equivalent	8482	2049	1577	184	166	48	192	266	590	37	115
7. Percent of world energy production		24%	19%	2%	2%	1%	2%	3%	7%	0%	1%
8. Nuclear weapons with strategic delivery systems	4833	2138	2435	114	0	66	0	0	80	0	0
9. Percent of strategically deliverable nuclear power		44%	50%	2%	0%	1%	0%	0%	2%	0%	0%
Power		22	24	2	2	2	1	1	7	5	4

Sources: For steel, energy, and population, United Nations, *Statistical Yearbook 1978* (New York: United Nations, 1979), pp. 68, 335, 389–92; for political stability scores, *The Annual Register* (New York: St. Martin's Press); for Nuclear force levels, International Institute for Strategic Studies, *The Military Balance 1974–1975* (London: IISS, 1974), pp. 49, 73–77.

The demise of SEATO in the 1970s and the American willingness not to contest the triumph of the leftist forces in Angola, Zimbabwe, and Nicaragua are in line with systemic rules. (American concern about the future of El Salvador, Guatemala, and Afghanistan seem to be at variance with the rules; these cases are discussed below.)

Equally important, the shift in alliances of one or two major powers does not pose a threat to the superpower, for the addition or deletion of still relatively small amounts of power is not crucial to survival. Such shifts do, however, raise the possibility of *dominoes falling*—a series of alliance changes among major powers that fundamentally alter the overall power alignment. In a bipolar system, superpowers must seek to prevent the fall of major-power dominoes. We would expect that the Soviet Union and the United States would guard their European alliance structures by coercion where necessary, concessions where possible. The emphasis is likely to be on the latter, for in a crisis in a bipolar world, a coerced ally is probably no ally at all. Soviet restraint in the Polish crisis is suggestive of the new era of alliance politics.

This does not mean that superpower intervention is a thing of the past. Bipolarity mandates intervention when dominoes are likely to fall. The Soviet invasion of Afghanistan must be considered in the context of Poland and Eastern Europe. The demise of a Soviet-sponsored regime and its movement past neutrality into the opposition camp may encourage others to exit from Soviet alliance systems. Prudent leaders in a bipolar world will seek to prevent that. The Soviet Union is particularly vulnerable to such possibilities, because its alliance systems have been historically grounded on coercion more than on cooperative common interests. Nonetheless, the systems approach suggests the United States will not be immune to interventionary pressures. Such intervention, when it does occur, will be unlike past American intervention in Korea or Vietnam. Those were interventions in a monopolar world, where the lone superpower intervened to protect what it assumes to be a rule of the community—states are not to use war to cause political change. In a bipolar world, superpowers intervene to prevent a change in power distributions; security, not principle, is at stake.

If a bipolar world encourages both bilateral détente and greater fears about alliance relations, would we expect the ''cold war'' of a monopolar world to continue? Certainly recent diplomatic history suggests we may not have left the Cold War, and it is common to have scholars speak of a ''new cold war.''[51] Logic would suggest, on the other hand, that in a bipolar world, the superpowers would reach an understanding about spheres of influence (''yours'' and ''mine'') and about a large area that ''belongs'' to neither. In the latter, both would pursue specific interests of a ''business'' rather than a political nature. In the former, as both states have complementary interests, mutual accommodation and negotiated change is possible. ''Suspicious cooperation'' is more likely to be the logical character of bipolar politics than ''cold war.''

The recent historical record does not support these conclusions. That may be because the record is incomplete and the above observations are predictions,

---

[51]For discussions of a ''new cold war,'' see Robert Osgood, ''The Revitalization of Containment,'' *Foreign Affairs,* 60 (Spring 1982), 465–502; Michael Howard, ''Return to the Cold War?'' *Foreign Affairs,* 59 (Spring 1981), 459–73.

rather than conclusions drawn from evidence. On the other hand, the practice of world politics may be at variance with the logic of the power distribution because of the intrusion of environmental factors. (Again we see the incompleteness of any one approach and the utility of combining several!) It seems to me that the age of the current leadership of the superpowers may be a critical factor. Both Reagan and Brezhnev (before his death) were of an age when the practice of cold war was the habit, and their current orientation toward world politics follows suit.

On becoming President, Reagan said that he believed Soviet leaders when they declared that "their goal must be the promotion of world revolution and a one-world socialist or communist state." And he expected the worst from them in pursuit of that goal: " . . . they reserve unto themselves the right to commit any crime; to lie; to cheat, in order to obtain that and that is moral, not immoral, and we operate on a different set of standards, I think when you do business with them—even at a détente—you keep that in mind."[52] A month later he added "murder" as a Soviet practice.[53] The President's Secretaries of State and Defense echoed these themes, and pointed to (in their eyes) an unrelenting military buildup and Soviet intervention in the Third World as proof of the permanence of the Soviet goal. Brezhnev, for his part, was caught up with the military metaphor common to the second most powerful state in a *monopolar* world. In that world, the Soviet Union could never feel secure (and therefore could not cooperate or make concessions readily), but did feel compelled to expand its military apparatus and to manipulate conflict wherever it could in order to both probe and keep the superpower preoccupied.

The point is not whether Reagan's attitudes were grounded in fact or whether Brezhnev had cause to follow habit. The point is that such attitudes and behaviors are unnecessary in the bipolar world. They do not enhance the security of the superpowers; in fact, because they run counter to the (predicted) rules of the system, they are likely to degrade security. From the perspective of the systems approach, we would expect that time will press the two states into greater compliance with the rules sketched here, and that as long as the bipolar distribution of power persists into the future, superpower behavior will be shaped accordingly.

That's not the only prediction we might make about the future. The next chapter canvasses a number of possibilities for the next fifteen years and beyond.

[52]News conference of January 29, 1981; *Weekly Compilation of Presidential Documents,* Vol. 17, pp. 66–67.

[53]Interview with Walter Cronkite; *ibid.,* p. 232.

CHAPTER TEN

1980–2000
The future(s)

PREDICTION AS A GOAL

World politics continues to unfold in dramatic ways. Will the twists and turns of the drama be as unexpected as they have been to policy makers, and perhaps to you? Can we as students and citizens of the world better *predict* what lies ahead?

At this point in our study of world politics, we part company with many historians who feel that prediction is not possible using the tools of the historian. Events to them are explicable, but only in retrospect, after a careful sifting and weighing of the evidence. The social scientist, on the other hand, is less cautious about time. He or she seeks to make generalizations about a class of events that may come from different time periods. The future can be thought of as one of those time periods. Social scientists also assume that the hypotheses they construct may hold true in the future as well. A monopolar distribution of power in the future, for instance, may produce the kinds of behaviors we have observed in the past.

This chapter tries its hand at predicting the contours of world politics in the remaining years of this century (and beyond, in some cases).[1] What should we expect these predictions to do? Consider this simple analogy. When we flip a coin onto a flat surface, we can predict two possible futures: the coin will turn up either "heads" or "tails." Before we actually flip the coin, then, we can state relatively precisely the *range of possible outcomes*. Furthermore, we can specify the *probability of each outcome*: 50 percent of the time (a .5 probability) the outcome will be

---

[1]On the subject of prediction, see William Ascher, *Forecasting* (Baltimore: Johns Hopkins University Press, 1978); Bertrand de Jouvenel, *The Art of Conjecture* (New York: Basic Books, 1967); H. Ornauer, et al., *Images of the World in the Year 2000* (Atlantic Highlands, N.J.: Humanities Press, 1976); Daniel Bell, *The Coming of Post-Industrial Society* (New York: Basic Books, 1973); Robert Bundy, ed., *Images of the Future* (Buffalo, N.Y.: Prometheus Books, 1976).

heads; 50 percent of the time, tails. There is no "sure thing" here. The probability will never be 1.0 (100 percent) that the future will be "heads." Of course, I had to make assumptions. The coin is an honest coin and I cannot *control* the future and thereby ensure any particular outcome. The precision of prediction in world politics does not (and probably will never) reach the level of this analogy, but it remains a goal. In general, however, we expect a prediction to answer two key questions: What can the futures look like (the range of outcomes)? and, How likely are such futures (the probabilities of outcomes)?

How might these questions be answered? Would we, for instance, have been able to predict the Argentine seizure of the Falkland Islands (called the Malvinas by the Argentines) in April, 1982? One thing should be immediately apparent: we would have to know *to think* about the Falklands. (We *knew* in the coin-tossing example that a coin would be tossed.) Our surprise at much of what seems unexpected in world politics is not so much because we had no idea that such an event might happen, but because we did not consider an area or problem where such an event did indeed happen. Large states devote much of their diplomatic and intelligence resources to warning against such surprises.[2] Of course, policy makers may routinely disregard such warnings, for there are likely to be many of them, and no prediction of "trouble" can say that "trouble" is a "sure thing."

Let us assume that in early 1982, we had an interest in predicting the future of the conflict between Argentina and Britain over the Falklands. The islands, with 1,800 or so British subjects, had been under British rule since the 1830s, although Argentina never relinquished its claim to the islands.[3] We know how history worked out: in March, 1982, an Argentine civilian work party landed on South Georgia Island (600 miles east of the Falklands, but part and parcel of the issue of sovereignty) to dismantle an old whaling station. They had a right to the scrap metal, but they refused British orders to leave until they acquired official papers permitting them to be there. On April 2, 1982, Argentine armed forces seized the Falkland Islands and South Georgia from the small British garrisons. Margaret Thatcher, the British Prime Minister, declared that Argentina would either withdraw voluntarily or be expelled by force. After laborious negotiations failed, a British force landed and compelled the Argentine garrison to surrender on June 14, 1982.

What futures might we have predicted in early 1982? If we had predicted "no Argentine invasion is likely" (a probability of less than .1) for every year of the century through 1981, we would have an enviable record—100 percent accuracy! Indeed, in the short run, our best prediction about any aspect of world politics often is that the next year will be quite similar to this year. What would lead us to forsake such an estimable prediction? Would the scientific approaches have suggested that the probability of invasion in 1982 would be greater than .1? In what follows, I have taken a number of general propositions, asked how events in

---

[2] See J. David Singer and Michael D. Wallace, eds., *To Auger Well* (Beverly Hills, Cal.: Sage, 1979); and Thomas Belden, "Indicators, Warning, and Crisis Operations," *International Studies Quarterly*, 21 (March 1977), 181–98.

[3] A quick review of the tangled history can be found in H.S. Ferns, *Argentina* (New York: Praeger, 1969), pp. 253–60.

Argentina compared to those propositions, and then adduced a number of specific predictions.

Domestic and Environmental Factor Approach

General Proposition   High levels of economic and political instability drive a regime with uncertain legitimacy to either (a) take advantage of an opportunity to divert attention from the instability or (b) be more aggressive in order to bolster confidence or a belief in the regime's ability to "take charge."[4]

Argentine Case[5]   Since 1976, a four-man military junta (three officers representing each of the military services and a fourth as President) ruled Argentina. For several years following the 1976 military coup, the military and right-wing terror squads waged a war of repression against the left. Thousands died and thousands "disappeared." Political parties and labor unions were banned or brought under military supervision. Repression had eased in 1981, and the political activism of politicians and labor leaders increased, partly encouraged by the junta, which had vague notions about restoring civilian rule. In addition to trying to destroy the political left, the junta had made an effort to end rampant inflation and the chronic stagnation of the Argentine economy by decreasing government protection for inefficient Argentine enterprises. Five years of this "treatment" brought the unexpected collapse of large businesses, growing unemployment (uncommon in Argentina), a repeatedly devalued currency, and an inflation rate that hovered around 100 percent.

In terms of the polity and the economy, by early 1982, the regime had reached the point where it needed to garner greater support, which only citizens and nonmilitary political leaders could provide. Or the military could allow the civilians to govern, a prospect unpalatable to most military men at the time.

Predictions and probabilities

1. Undertake aggressive or high-risk foreign policy behaviors that would rally the public. (With whom is another matter. Relations with Chile were unsettled, and Brazil is a traditional rival.)   .5 probability
2. Devote attention internally to making the economic program work and building a new political structure to make civilian-run politics acceptable to the military.   .5 probability

Policy-Makers and Policy-Making Approach

General Proposition   The pressures of junta politics force military men in power to consider unconventional ways to ensure their own personal continuation in office, especially when traditional means seem unsuccessful.

---

[4]For discussion of the "diversion thesis," see Michael Sullivan, *International Relations: Theories and Evidence* (Englewood Cliffs, N.J.: Prentice-Hall, 1976), pp. 121–32.

[5]Sources for the Argentine case study include Gary Wynia, "Illusion and Reality in Argentina," *Current History*, 80 (February 1981), 62–65, 84–85; G. Wynia, "The Argentine Revolution Falters," *Current History*, 82 (February 1982), 74–77, 87–88; David Jordan, "Argentina's Military Commonwealth," *Current History*, 76 (February 1979), 66–69, 89–90; Peter Smith, "Argentina: The Uncertain Warriors," *Current History*, 78 (February 1980) 62–65, 85–86; Edward Milenky, *Argentina's Foreign Policies* (Boulder, Col.: Westview Press, 1978); *New York Times*.

Argentine Case   In November, 1981, the military elite had dismissed the current President, eight months in office, for failure to right the economy and to keep demands for political participation under control. His successor, moderate army General Leopoldo Galtieri, was under enormous pressure to avoid his predecessor's failings. Galtieri also represented a faction of the Argentine military that had generally taken the view that the military should create conditions for restoration of civilian rule. The opposing faction, to this point denied power, argued that the military should govern into the foreseeable future, creating a "strong and pure" Argentine society. A failure by Galtieri to demonstrate the validity of the moderate's approach would create strong pressures for his replacement by someone from the "duro" (hardliner) camp.

Predictions and probabilities

1. If internal conditions did not improve or worsened, Galtieri and other moderates would contemplate actions to continue their tenure; they would be willing to take high risks rather than do "more of the same," which seemed to spell the end to their hold on power.   .5 probability
2. The current leadership would be paralyzed by the enormity of the problems and make few changes.   .5 probability

Interaction Approach

General Proposition   In a game where there is a "have" state and a "have-not" state, and the issue revolves around what is "had" (in this case, British control of the Falklands), peace will prevail only as long as the "have" state structures the payoffs for the "have-not" state in a way that makes peace worth more than the use of force. The game table for this situation appears in Table 10–1.

Argentine Case   Britain and Argentina had negotiated for 15 years under the auspices of the United Nations. Various formulas had been presented, but at bottom, Britain refused to relinquish control over the islands as long as the inhabitants wished to remain under British control (as they did). The Argentines were unwilling to accept legal title but no real power (Austria-Hungary's relationship to Bosnia-Herzegovina was the analogy favored by the British). As the game table indicates, the "have" player has one strategy—to bargain to secure Argentina's acquiescence in the status quo.

TABLE 10-1   The Have-Not Game

"HAVE NOT" STATE (ARGENTINA)

		Take (use force)	Bargain (but refrain from use of force)
"HAVE" STATE (GREAT BRITAIN)	Give	+15 Cell 1 −20	+20 Cell 2 −15
	Bargain (but defend)	X Cell 3 −10	Y Cell 4 +15

For the "have-not" player, the critical issue is the values for **X** and **Y**. Unlike other games, however, where the values of one player are not easily manipulatable by the other, in the "have-not" game, the "have" state plays a crucial role in determining the values of **X** and **Y**. The "have" state can provide rewards for the choice of the "bargain" option by the "have-not" state. In 1970, for instance, Britain aided Argentina in the construction of two destroyers for its navy. And the "have" state can promise heavy costs for an attempt to take what is "had." Long-standing trade contacts between Britain and Argentina, for instance, would likely be ruptured by a use of force. Thus the "have" state can improve the likelihood of its desired outcome (cell 4) by making the value of **Y** greater than **X**.

Predictions and probabilities

1. As Britain reduces its capability to punish (by weakening the defenses of the Falklands) or fails to provide rewards for the "bargain option," the probability of the "take" option increases. As **X** becomes greater than **Y** . . .   > .6 probability

Systems Approach

General Proposition　The systems approach is quite limited in furnishing predictions in this case because the issue is quite removed from the cockpit of world politics, Argentina is a very weak state in the international system, and it is not clear how the regional subsystem would affect behavior. In terms of world power as we have measured it, British power (approximately 2) is absolutely greater than the fractional power of Argentina (less than .3). However, the Falklands' location suggests that *projected* power, principally by ship, is important.[6] From England and from the northeastern heartland of Argentina, British projected power in those terms is approximately .16 to Argentina's .12. In addition, Argentina must contend with its traditional rivals, a relatively weak Chile but a more powerful Brazil. On the other hand, the regional powers in Latin America might be willing to join Argentina in a confrontation with Britain. Unlike the other approaches, however, the systems approach in this instance gives us the weakest indication of why Argentine behavior *in 1982 would differ so markedly from the previous years*, when the same distribution of power presumably existed. Thus, in view of past behavior on this issue:

Predictions and probabilities

1. The distribution of power would encourage military action.   .1 probability
2. The distribution of power would discourage military action.   .9 probability

In looking at all these predictions, it is clear that no prediction would have identified an Argentine invasion of the Falklands as a sure thing. Nonetheless, the probabilities associated with a number of them should have caused some skepticism that "this year would be the same as the last." Granted, those probability values are arbitrary ones I assigned after the fact. I certainly made no prediction that 1982 would be different! Can we do better?

---

[6]British forces in the area included a hundred-man garrison and one ice breaker.

TYPES OF PREDICTION

Anyone can make predictions. In fact, everyone does. Policy makers do it continuously as a part of fulfilling their roles. That does not mean that everyone makes
the same kinds of predictions or predictions of the same quality. How are quality
predictions made? Quality often means accuracy, and there is the problem—if we
want to assess accuracy, we are condemned to wait until the time period of the
prediction has passed. What we need is a prediction about the accuracy of predictions!

Prediction methods fall into four broad types, which I introduce here and
elaborate upon below.

1. *Analytic method*: predictions derived from hypotheses (sometimes tested ones!) or approaches that speak of cause and effect. Knowing a presumed cause (such as war's
   being a live policy option), we can predict some future effect (such as an initial reliance on negotiations but a commitment to war if the opponent does not make
   quick, substantial concessions). This method was used in the "post-prediction" of
   Argentine actions against the Falklands.

2. *Extrapolation method*: descriptions of current trends are made and projected into the
   future.

3. *Intuitive method*: predictions derived from sensation or feeling rather than reasoning,
   or from "experience, intelligence, and good sense."[7]

4. *Goal-inspired method:* predictions derived essentially from a *preferred* future. Such a future is said to be inevitable or possible through conscious human choice. Once defined, that future logically implies other predictions.

In order to assess the potential quality of predictions generated by these
methods, I begin with the assumption that good predictions are as precise as possible regarding who, what, and where. A prediction such as "In the future, states
will be in conflict with each other," is trivial because it is too imprecise. Beyond
those expectations, I shall use three criteria to evaluate quality: specification
about time, the "goodness of fit" to known relationships, and the cogency of the
method used. The specification of time is important because it gives a gauge of
potential accuracy. In general, the further off the time period, the more unlikely
the prediction.[8] But without *any* specification of time, we should be suspicious, for
one can predict "rain" or "war" for the future and be right at *some* point.

"Goodness of fit" refers to how well the prediction meets our understanding of reality. To say, for instance, that the nation-state will soon disappear as the
principal actor in world politics strains credulity, because such actors have been
central for over three hundred years. On the other hand, goodness of fit cannot
be rigidly applied. Anything that is physically possible can occur; the prominence
of the nation-state may well shrink. We might feel such an occurrence has a low
probability, but we cannot deny its possibility. Furthermore, much of world politics seems unexpected; that is, before it does happen, it may fail our goodness-of-
fit criterion. That does not mean we should reject our criterion. Rather, it means

---

[7]Herman Kahn and B. Bruce-Briggs, *Things to Come* (New York: Macmillan, 1972), pp.
187–88.

[8]Ascher, *Forecasting*, p. 11.

that we need to have a variety of ways of seeing reality, each of which helps broaden our range of expectations. Both the scientific approach and the historical approach assume that the unexpected is an aspect of world politics momentarily not perceived in some pattern of relationships. As we become better students of world politics, the unexpected should diminish.

The third criterion for making some judgment about the quality of a prediction is in how convincing the method is. We cannot wait to see if the method "works." The method itself must encourage us to accept the prediction today. In the twentieth century, persuasiveness has often depended on how well a method could be described, its workings laid out for inspection. If we are dubious about the machinery, we are likely to be skeptical about what people *claim* will come out at the end. Remember, we will not know that Argentina invaded or that the coin turned up heads. All we will have are verbal assurances that those things are likely to happen.

Analytical Methods

How well do the four methods of prediction measure up to the criteria? The *analytic method* is strongest in its exposition of the method of prediction. In the examination of the Argentine case, we could see the reasons why various outcomes might be expected. "Goodness of fit" is also strong because predictions are integral parts of patterns we believe to exist. On the other hand, the method is relatively weak in terms of precision. As it deals with patterns and general concepts (such as "high-risk foreign policy behavior"), it often cannot lead to precise predictions (such as "a military operation to seize the Falklands"). It is weaker yet in specification of time. The method does deal with time by positing that the effect will follow cause,[9] but generally we have little means at present to gauge how much time will transpire between cause and effect. Long-term predictions are most suspect with this method. On the other hand, its ability to say, "if you find **A** occurring in the future, then **B** will probably follow" does give us some handle on possible events in the relatively distant future.

Extrapolation Methods

The *extrapolation method* is clear in its method. It relies on the discovery of regularities in the past for a particular phenomenon and then presumes that such regularities will continue in the future. Consider, for instance, the past history of world military expenditures, which is presented in Figure 10–1. What prediction would you make? There is a variety:

PREDICTION	PROBABILITY	DISCUSSION
Expenditures will continue to increase 2½ percent on the average through the year 2000	.7	Extrapolation of the trend. There may be momentary plateaus but growth will continue
Expenditures will level off or decrease	.2	No plateau in the capacity of the world's states to support armed forces seems in evidence

[9]Actually showing cause is a very difficult business; much of the study of world politics assumes that demonstrating a correlation between factors is tantamount to identifying cause.

| Unpredictable (not extrapolatable) changes in expenditures | .1 | No discontinuities in behavior seem likely |

Another example of prediction by extrapolation can be taken from Chapter 7 where we examined Cold War interactions and found a wave-like pattern. I argued, however, that the Cuban missile crisis created a discontinuity in the pattern such that cooperation was enhanced in the period thereafter, but conflict still remained. *If one assumes that since the late 1970s another discontinuity has occurred and we have returned to Cold War behavior*, then we can make the projection depicted in Figure 10-2. By this extrapolation, we would predict that the chances were quite good that the United States and the Soviet Union would cycle through periods of tension and relaxation, with the next "spirit of Geneva" coming at the end of the 1980s to be followed by a return to the "frostiness" of the Cold War.

Extrapolation can be done for the behaviors of single states as well. Frank Klingberg, for instance, has investigated changing American foreign policy moods, which he argues set limits on policy decisions. The chief moods are "introvert" ("a tendency to concentrate on domestic matters and to reduce military and political actions abroad") and "extrovert" (willing[ness] to support direct pressure, often military, on other nations to gain its ends").[10] The change in moods is cyclical, and produces this kind of pattern across the nation's history.[11]

FIGURE 10-1   World Military Spending Over Time

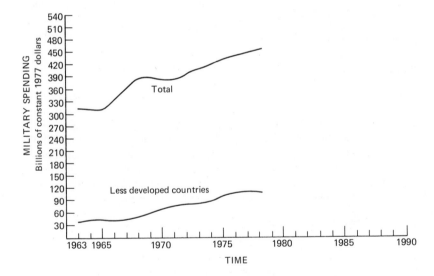

---

[10]Frank Klingberg, "Cyclical Trends in American Foreign Policy Moods and Their Policy Implications," in *Challenges to America: United States Foreign Policy in the 1980s*, ed. Charles W. Kegley, Jr., and Patrick J. McGowan (Beverly Hills, Cal.: Sage, 1979), p. 38. The argument first appeared in Klingberg, "The Historical Alternation of Moods in American Foreign Policy," *World Politics*, 4 (January 1952), 239–73.

[11]Klingberg, "Cyclical Trends," p. 38. © 1979 by Sage Publications, Inc.

PERIOD	INTROVERT	EXTROVERT
I	1776–1798	1798–1824
II	1824–1844	1844–1871
III	1871–1891	1891–1918
IV	1918–1940	1940–1966
V	1966–	

With "extrovert" periods lasting 27 years on the average, and "introvert" periods 21, we can extrapolate as follows:

PERIOD	INTROVERT	EXTROVERT
V	1966–1987	1987–2014

By this prediction, the United States is very likely to be an active ("aggressive") state in the international community: more likely to be militarily involved, expand its alliances, and bring a variety of pressures to bear to ensure the enhancement of its interests.

Obviously, extrapolation techniques are intimately bound to the question of time, for it is the pattern across time that gives the method its predictive power. Similarly, the goodness-of-fit with expectations is relatively strong; the predictions are expectations writ large. And in that lies a problem; the method assumes that the conditions that support a trend will continue into the future as well. Extrapolations often carry the unvoiced caveat, "all other things being equal." They rarely are, but the success of the method encourages its use. Finally, the method's main weakness is that it is not concerned with the *explanation* of why a trend occurs.

Intuitive Methods

Extrapolation and analytic methods rest on an empirical base that can be articulated. The *intuitive method*, on the other hand, produces predictions creatively without necessarily referring to empirical observations. Many such predictions are available at the supermarket checkout where tabloids abound with the predictions of psychics. Table 10–2 displays a representative set of predictions made about 1975. When I read these predictions at the time, I assigned a very low probability to each. Why? They seemed quite suspect according to the criteria. Time is clearly specified, which is to the good. But so much specificity (such

FIGURE 10-2   Extrapolation of Cold War Interactions

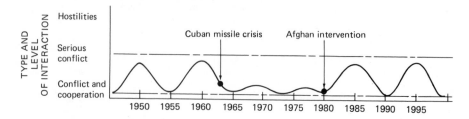

TABLE 10-2   Intuitive Predictions of World Politics

PSYCHIC	PREDICTIONS	
	SET A NEAR-TERM	SET B FAR-TERM
Criswell	"On February 11, 1981 a foreign power will attempt to bomb the U.S. with atomic weapons. The attempt will fail, but 50 people in Vermont will be killed."	"In 1985, a Caucasian woman, called the Lady of Light, will become leader, first of the Orient, then of the world."
Jeanne Dixon	Between 1975–1980, "there will be a major earthquake in the Middle East, which will inspire the enemies of Israel to invade it. This will result in an 8-year war.	"In 1999, the U.S. and its allies will be at war with Russia and its satellites. Russian missiles 'will rain down a nuclear holocaust' on the U.S. 'coastal cities, both east and west.' "

Source: David Wallechinsky and Irving Wallace, "The Psychics Predict," *The People's Almanac* (Garden City, N.Y.: Doubleday & Company, 1975), pp. 3, 5.

as ''February 11,'' for instance) should give one pause. On the other hand, Dixon's prediction for the near term has a generous six-year leeway; the long-term prediction—when we would expect the need for the leeway—specified a single year.

What about goodness-of-fit to known relationships? Consider Criswell's predictions. Given what we know about the quantities and characteristics of nuclear weapons, their typical targets, and some of the strategies associated with their threatened use, would an outcome of ''50 people in Vermont will be killed'' seem likely? Similarly, given the wave of anti-Western, anticolonial, anti-imperialist sentiment which has swept the Third World in this century, why would we expect Asians to follow Caucasian leaders? Moreover, no individual or state in this century has become the leader of the East (although Japan came close) and the prospects of world leadership seem even more remote. Finally, women have been particularly disadvantaged in acquiring leadership roles. Thus, while we cannot say that Criswell's predictions are or were impossible, they seem to be compounds of improbabilities. Dixon's predictions have more of an ''expected'' flavor: a Middle Eastern war, the nature of a nuclear exchange. Yet the prediction of an eight-year war rings improbable: it does not accord with historical experience for the region or for most wars of this century. On the criterion of goodness-of-fit, we have reasons for skepticism.

The number of improbabilities raises questions about how these predictions were derived. Intuition as a way of knowing is probably not amenable to explication. One simply ''knows.'' (Astrology's use of the position and motion of celestial bodies is explicable, but the reasons for interpreting a constellation in a particular way are not.) While it may be unfair to expect a psychic to make a case for his or her prediction based on an explication of the method, that is a criterion we cannot afford to give up.

Perhaps it is too easy to be critical of supermarket seers, although their frequency of appearance suggests the readership may take such predictions seriously. We do know that some leaders (such as Hitler and his propaganda minister Goebbels in the last months of the war) may clutch at the words of prophecy and astrology to convince themselves that success is probable. Certainly you and I have acted on the basis of intuitively derived predictions. But there is another form of the intuitive method that has been far better received and has had a pervasive impact on our lives: prediction that comes as a part of a literary work.[12] The exemplar is George Orwell's *1984*,[13] published in 1949.

World politics in 1984 revolved around three "superstates," Oceania (the English-speaking world), Eurasia (the USSR and Europe), and Eastasia (China and Japan). War was relatively continuous between them, but limited in nature, because after an initial use of nuclear weapons in the mid-1950s, the elites of the three states recognized their own impending demise and discontinued use of such weapons. War remained necessary to destroy resources that might enhance the life of the masses (and make them want more, including power) and to rationalize the need for authoritarian government.

Most of the fighting was confined to the northern ice cap and the "rough quadrilateral with its corners at Tangier, Brazzaville, Darwin, and Hong Kong." Fighting was done by "very small numbers of people, mostly highly trained specialists, and causes comparatively few casualties." The death of noncombatants in the quadrilateral, on the other hand, was commonplace: "such acts as raping, looting, the slaughter of children, the reduction of whole populations to slavery, and reprisals against prisoners which extend even to boiling and burying alive, are looked upon as normal, and, when they are committed by one's own side and not by the enemy, meritorious."[14]

In this world, changes in alliances could come with lightning speed. In the midst of Oceania's Hate Week against the enemy Eurasia, it was suddenly announced that Oceania was allied with Eurasia, at war with Eastasia, and it had always been thus. The government of Big Brother rewrote the past to bring memory in line with the current version of the truth. In controlling the past, it controlled the future and made it unimaginable—except to say that "If you want a picture of the future, imagine a boot stamping on a human face—forever."[15]

Orwell's reputation as both a writer and futurist is incomparably better than any psychic's. One is certainly struck by the quality of his creative vision even where it has proved wrong. Clearly, Orwell *wanted his vision to be wrong*, for it was a future to be avoided. But in 1950, how might we have judged that predicted future? Was it a good prediction? Orwell was relatively precise about time,

---

[12]See among others, Edward Bellamy, *Looking Backward* (1887); the novels of H.G. Wells, in particular *When the Sleeper Wakes* (1899); *The War in the Air* (1908); *The Shape of Things to Come* (1933); and Aldous Huxley's *Brave New World* (1932). See also Martin Greenberg and Joseph Olander, *International Relations Through Science Fiction* (New York: New Viewpoints, 1978).

[13]Excerpts from *Nineteen Eighty-Four* by George Orwell, copyright 1949 by Harcourt Brace Jovanovich, Inc.; renewed 1977 by Sonia Brownell Orwell. Acknowledgment to the estate of the late Sonia Brownell Orwell and Martin Secker & Warburg, Ltd. Reprinted by permission of the publisher.

[14]*Ibid.*, pp., 188, 187.

[15]*Ibid.*, p. 271.

so that criterion is adequately met. Is goodness-of-fit? Probably not, but perhaps more because our vision in 1950 was not as perceptive as the novelist's! Outside the realm of (Western) expectations at the time would have been such predictions as (1) a world dominated by three authoritarian superstates, (2) restraint in the waging of war, particularly nuclear war, (3) rapid alteration in alliances, and (4) conflict being confined essentially to the Third World. The predictions in Orwell's work that seemed most plausible were those that described life in an authoritarian state, for those dovetailed with the impressions of life in Hitler's Germany and Stalin's Russia. Orwell did try to sketch analytic reasons for his predictions (e.g., elite interests keep war both limited and continuous). In the main, persuasiveness is generated by his skills as a writer, diverting us from asking for fuller explanations and toward a feeling that "things just might happen that way."

Goal-Inspired Methods

Orwell's interest in encouraging his readers to avoid the future he predicted shares with the *goal-inspired method of prediction* a belief that the future is open to conscious human choice. The goal-inspired method, however, has an explicit preference for one future over others. That future, often called a utopia,[16] is said to be possible when humans work for it. Statements about preferred futures often come with *prescriptions* as well—what must be done to achieve the desired future.

Marxism is a classic form of a goal-inspired method of prediction. Reacting to the brutalities of early industrialization, Marx longed for a society in which exploitation and privation had ended. He needed to account for the existence of both, which he did by blaming both on the existence of social classes. However, given Marx's view of how progress occurred, social classes were also necessary to build the economic system that would allow the eradication of exploitation and privation. Based on an extrapolation from history, Marx predicted that through the clash of antagonistic social classes, a new order would emerge in which there would be no social classes—and therefore no exploitation—yet the economic base would provide enough for all.

From this general prediction, others emerged. In this excerpt from *The Communist Manifesto* (1848), Marx predicted a future for world politics:

> In proportion as the exploitation of one individual by another is put an end to, the exploitation of one nation by another will also be put an end to. In proportion as the antagonism between classes within the nation vanishes, the hostility of one nation to another will come to an end.[17]

You might well remark that Marx's predictions appear to employ analytic methods and extrapolations. How is this method of prediction any different from those? The central distinction lies in how we answer this question: How strongly

---

[16]See Frank Manuel, ed., *Utopias and Utopian Thought* (Boston: Houghton Mifflin, 1966); Melvin Lasky, *Utopia and Revolution* (Chicago: University of Chicago Press, 1976); David Plath, ed., *Aware of Utopia* (Urbana: University of Illinois Press, 1971).

[17]Karl Marx and Frederick Engels, *The Communist Manifesto*, in *Karl Marx and Frederick Engels: Selected Works* (New York: International Publishers, 1968), p. 51.

did the hoped-for-goal of a society without exploitation or privation shape the predictions? If a prediction emerged from the goal, then analytic methods and extrapolations are developed more *to support* a particular prediction than to create it. There are two other ways we might distinguish the methods. First, goal-inspired predictions make statements (actually hypotheses) about future conditions that have no contemporary referent. For instance, there is often no way of testing such a hypothesis about a world in which there are classless societies—at least at the time when the prediction is made—for such conditions then did not exist. Second, because the goal is so important, the prediction usually survives, even when logic or some evidence suggests that the prediction is unlikely to be true. Analytic predictions, on the other hand, are presumably less heavily freighted with values and emotional or political commitments. For instance, with Marx's prediction in mind, we might assume that each year a communist party is in power (which implies progressive steps toward a nonexploitative society) there would be a decrease in the hostility shown other states led by communist parties. The diplomatic history of China and the Soviet Union in the post-World War II period suggests that, if anything, as party control continues, hostility between the two states *increases*. If one believes that the evidence contradicts the premise of the prediction, one might have serious reservations about the goal of a "classless" society, for it may *enhance* conflict between peoples rather than reduce it. There is a natural tendency to assume that the goal-induced prediction is not wrong; only the methods or assumptions we use to develop the evidence are wrong. For instance, some have denied that in one or both communist states the proletariat rules or that classes have been abolished. Or one might claim that while the party represents the proletariat in a classless society, the economic backwardness of both states distorts their ability to interact in an amicable manner.

The goal-inspired method tends to develop predictions that have the ring of "ought" statements—what "should" be done in the future, rather than what "will" be done. The tendency to mix the normative (the "ought") with the empirical (the "is") has led many goal-inspired predictions to be rejected out of hand (as when we mutter "that's utopian" in disparagement). The criteria I have used, on the other hand, encourage a more respectful look at such predictions. Like the analytic method, the goal-inspired method is usually quite vague about time. In some cases, the prediction is held to be inevitable; in other cases, possible if humans work for it. Those imprecisions weaken the quality of the predictions. It is in the area of goodness-of-fit to expectations that goal-inspired predictions seem the weakest, however, because they are often at variance with traditional ways of thinking. Conflict between states, for instance, has been an inescapable part of world politics since the rise of the modern state system in the seventeenth century. Predictions of an end to state conflict seem implausible. The more the goal diverges from the current state of affairs, the more implausible the predictions will appear.

Paradoxically, the implausibility of the predictions may make them persuasive. If we extrapolate the trend of conflict between states into the future, we are left with the unhappy conclusion that all we can expect is more of the same. Goal-inspired predictions furnish both a hope (the future need not be like that) and a challenge to our assumptions about *why* things should be like that. And here is where the *method* takes on its own particular persuasiveness. It *insists* on an alternative future and, because it knows that it cannot persuade simply by exhortation, it builds (and rebuilds!) an elaborate theoretical structure to show *how* that future is obtainable. And because the *means* for getting from here to there, from now to then, are plausible, we often find ourselves assuming that the alternative future is not only possible (a world without state conflict *is* always *possible*) but quite probable as well.

These four methods of making predictions provide us with a battery of approaches to the future. No one of them is superior; each brings different strengths and weaknesses to bear. I personally favor the analytic and extrapolative methods, but one often uses all four. You should as well. Without a concern for futures, we may be futureless.

PREDICTED FUTURES FOR THE REMAINDER OF THE CENTURY: THE FRUITS OF THE SCIENTIFIC APPROACHES

We have already examined a number of predictions about world politics selected rather eclectically. One could go on forever, for the more than 150 nations in the world and the countless issues confronting them provide a near-infinite number of possibilities. To provide some focus to the discussion, I will provide predictions about world politics in general, and from time to time, about four specific subjects: (1) Soviet-American relations, (2) nuclear war, (3) North-South relations, and (4) the politics of the Middle East. (The choice of these four subjects represents something of a prediction—that these will be critical areas in the future for both our understanding of world politics and our lives as citizens of a state and inhabitants of planet Earth.)

System Predictions

The systems approach provides the most general and inclusive set of predictions about world politics.[18] If we extrapolate the current system into the future, we would predict a continuation of the bipolar world as indicated in Prediction 1 of Figure 10–3. However, when we look at the specific trends in power distribution since World War II, we find the following: (1) a shrinkage of American power, a growth of Soviet power; (2) a decline in the total power held by the superpowers; and (3) a leakage of significant power out of the North Atlantic cockpit into Asia. Suppose these trends continue; what alternative predictions might we make (see Figure 10–3)?

The *polar melt* prediction has superpower strength decreasing until four to five major powers share relatively equal amounts of moderate power (perhaps 15 points on the power score). Major-power behavior would most likely accord with the equilateral system rules. Specifically,

> *Prediction 2a*: Alliances of major powers will be common but membership will change over time.

---

[18]For power projections, see Klaus Heiss, Klaus Knorr, and Oskar Morgenstern, *Long Term Projections of Power* (Cambridge, Mass: Ballinger, 1973).

PREDICTION 1	PREDICTION 2	PREDICTION 3	PREDICTION 4
Bipolar power distribution Time: Present–2000+ Typical patterns: 1. Superpowers seek bilateral understanding 2. Create and safeguard alliance with major powers 3. Intervene to protect security interests	A polar melt US USSR  Equilateral system	Soviet decades USSR US Monopolar system	Déjà vu US USSR  A ladder-like system

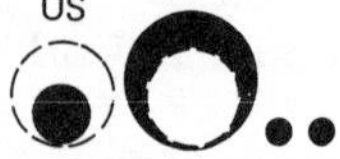

Estimated Probability of System Occurrence		PREDICTION 2	PREDICTION 3	PREDICTION 4
	1985–1990 .7	.2	.0	.1
	1991–2000 .5	.2	.1	.2
	2001–2010 .2	.3	.1	.4

FIGURE 10-3   Possible Power Distributions, 1985–2010

Prediction 2b: Threats and appeasement will be common. Major powers will use force to prevent one state or coalition from becoming predominant.

Prediction 2c: The inhibition on the use of nuclear weapons will weaken; nuclear exchanges may occur to demonstrate resolve, but will probably remain limited.

The *Soviet decades* prediction makes the Soviet Union the superpower in a monopolar world. We would expect the United States and Soviet Union to behave as they did during the post-World War II period, only the roles would be reversed.

Prediction 3a: The United States probes to determine the limits of Soviet tolerance; the Soviets respond with restraint but are heavily interventionary around the globe. The interaction would be of necessity a cold war.

Prediction 3b: Nuclear weapons will encourage restraint by the superpower. However, the Soviet Union will face the prospect of proliferation of the number of nuclear armed states, which would make its intervention more precarious. Therefore, the Soviet Union is likely to insist on a rule of nonproliferation and preemptively intervene in weak states to prevent it.

Prediction 3c: If there still exists an Arab-Israeli conflict that matches historic proportions, the Arab states with Soviet backing will defeat Israel and end the existence of the Jewish state.

The return of the ladder-like system (Prediction 4) would leave the century as it began. There is no way to predict which state would fall where, although I suspect that the United States and the Soviet Union would be the most powerful. In such a system,

Prediction 4a: The most powerful state will attempt to organize a new league of states (because the United Nations has become the stronghold of the numerous but weak states). As that will fail, it will attempt to reach an accommodation with the second most powerful state. A period of détente is likely but systemic pressures will produce two rival coalitions, one of the strongest and the weakest major powers; the other of the middle powers.

Prediction 4b: Conflict between states will result in wars of nerves between polarized alliance systems.

Prediction 4c: Nuclear weapons will be a part of the posturing in wars of nerves. If intercoalitional war occurs, massive uses of nuclear weapons are likely as the system encourages total war once war begins. Of the four alternative systems futures, a major nuclear exchange seems most likely here.

Figure 10–3 also assesses the probabilities of various power distributions over time. It sees bipolarity as the most likely power distribution in the near term, but increasingly unlikely after the turn of the century. After that point, I suspect the ladder-like system will be our future; that, I admit, is an intuitive hunch, based on an assumption that in human endeavors, a range of power distributions is more likely to be the mode than any other form. If that is the case, and we find the ladder-like system undesirable, what might we do about this future?

Interaction Predictions

As we move from the systems approach, our interests become narrower and more detailed. What we gain in detail, however, we lose in comprehensiveness. And we face a far greater number of aspects of world politics about which we might make predictions. The limitations of space compel me to use but one example from the interaction approach (although the earlier discussion of game theory in the Argentine case and the cold war ''wave'' pattern provided a range of examples). I will examine the patterned interactions among three pairs of states, the Soviet Union, the People's Republic of China, and the United States, and make a series of predictions through extrapolation. Historically, certain types of interactive behavior appear frequently in those relationships:

fragile alliance: recognition of the benefits of cooperation against a common opponent, including some control over the alliance partner's behavior; suspicion of hostile intentions of the partner; war planning does not identify partner as a principal target.

alliance in collapse: tentative identification of a partner as an opponent; perception that cooperation compels restraint on oneself yet confers license on the partner; war plans reevaluated.

cold war: assumption of hostile intention in all actions of the other, now deemed an ''enemy''; plans and targeting focus on the other.

bridge building: a dialogue to find areas of common interest where agreement might benefit both, but fears exist that dialogue may imply a willingness to make concessions on ''fundamental issues.'' War plans remain unchanged.

negotiation for self-regulation: mutual agreement to restrain activities in certain areas; formal attempts to deal with the threat of war. War plans remain unchanged, but interest in other contingencies increases.

interdependence: mutual agreements to exchange desired things (especially tangible goods); mutual acknowledgement that both have a stake in continuing the relationship; war plans see ''opponent'' in terms of an overall strategy or a response to a set of particular issues.

TABLE 10-3 Interaction Patterns Among the United States, People's Republic of China, and the Soviet Union

PAIR	TIME							
	1941–1945	1945–1947	1948–1952	1953–1957	1958–1962	1963–1968	1969–1974	1975–1980
US–USSR	Fragile alliance	Alliance in collapse	—————————— Cold war ——————————			Bridge building ⟶	Negotiation for self-regulation	Interdependence
US–PRC	Fragile alliance	Alliance in collapse	Limited hot war 1950–53	—————— Cold war —————⟶			Bridge building	Negotiation for self-regulation
USSR–PRC	*	*	Fragile alliance		Alliance in collapse		———— Cold war ————⟶	

*Soviet behavior toward the Chinese communist party was ambivalent during this period.

TABLE 10-4 Prediction for Relations Among the United States, Soviet Union, and People's Republic of China

PAIR	TIME					
	1981–1985	1986–1990	1991–1995	1996–2000	2001–2005	2006–2010
US–USSR	Competitive manipulation	Renunciation	Negotiation for self-regulation	Interdependence	Competitive manipulation	Renunciation
US–PRC	Interdependence	Competitive manipulation	Renunciation	Negotiation for self-regulation	Interdependence	Competitive manipulation
USSR–PRC	Cold war	Bridge building	Negotiation for self-regulation	Interdependence	Competitive manipulation	Renunciation

Over time, these types of interaction seem to form a stable sequence, as the historical summary in Table 10-3 suggests. At this point, I am not concerned with why a particular type of behavior occurs or changes for another. The trends in the table do suggest the following general predictions for any similar pair of states:

Prediction 5a: Fragile alliances collapse and lead to a cold war; that cold war lasts for an indeterminate period until interrupted by some event that lies outside the pattern of cold war behaviors (represented on the table by a darker line). The termination of the cold war initiates a sequence of improved reactions.

Prediction 5b: The change in types of behavior appears to occur on the average of five years (except for cold war).

Unfortunately, the evidence is ambiguous about what follows the "interdependence" type of behavior and whether its period would be approximately five years as well. One possibility is that, over time, interdependence blossoms to the point where a "security community" may emerge[19] or problem solving becomes the main pattern of interaction between the two states. More likely is the emergence of another fragile alliance due to some event the two states find mutually threatening. A nuclear exchange between weak states, confrontation by a unified group of Third World states, or a regional power acting in damaging ways may form such an event. The most likely stage following interdependence (probability of .6) is that of competitive manipulation. Having broken out of the cold war, neither state wishes to return to it, but both have an incentive to cheat on the other and in so doing will alienate each other. After a period of such manipulation, both would be likely to reduce contact with each other, and then gradually move back to the stage of negotiation for self-regulation—and begin the cycle again. Table 10-4 plots these occurrences and makes the assumption that the Sino-Soviet cold war will end as well (our historical example suggests that its duration is on the order of 15–20 years).

Using such a table, you can experiment with various combinations of occurrences. In doing so, you might consider this additional prediction:

Prediction 5d: When "cold war" describes the relationship in two pairs of states, while the third pair is engaged in some form of cooperative behavior, a limited war involving the "odd-state-out" and one of the others is probable. (See the 1948–1952 time period.)

Policy Makers and Policy-Making Predictions

The systems approach and pattern analysis assume that individuals make little independent contribution to the shape of world politics. The policy-maker and policy-making approach makes them central. Chapter 9 explored some of the characteristics of individuals, structure, and process that might enable us to pre-

---

[19]For the "security community" concept, see Karl Deutsch, et al., "Political Community and the North Atlantic Area," in *International Political Communities* (Garden City, N.Y.: Anchor Books, 1966), pp. 2–11.

dict certain policy outcomes. I shall restrict myself here to a familiar refrain. In arguing that individuals do matter, we have been dogged by the question of how they make policy. The two contrasting views are the political model and the rational model (you should be able to repeat this catechism by heart!):

Political model	Rational model
Individuals bring to the policy process competing perceptions, interests, goals, power	Individuals generally agree on the nature of the major issues, possible goals and options
and	and
policy is a process of continuing compromises.	policy is made through the selection of a goal and an efficient option that promotes the national (or elite) welfare.

We have discussed various conditions under which one model is more likely to occur than the other. I have suggested that the political process is usually operative in policy making when we examine the creation of specific decisions. That is, some debate, conflict, and compromise is likely to characterize all decisions. But we can also imagine that the scope and intensity of the debate varies, as does the degree of conflict, and thus, too, the nature of the compromises that emerge as policy. How much variation depends on the degree of consensus within a government. When certain assumptions are commonly accepted (such as the aggressive nature of the Soviet Union and the role of the United States as the leader of "free nations"), and certain policies are felt to be effective ("military strength provides political clout"), and certain viewpoints considered relevant or irrelevant ("the Joint Chiefs of Staff should determine a military response"), then the variation in the debate, the conflict, and the compromise will decrease. In that sense, a preexisting consensus on the nature of the issue, the goals, and the relevant options significantly narrows the politics of decision making. Under these conditions, the rational model probably best accords with the initial process of formulating policy.

When will such a consensus exist? Our diplomatic studies have suggested that authoritarian regimes may be better able to install a consensus, and that democracies, with fragmented power and pluralist interests, are less able to do so. On the other hand, we might imagine that as the number of diplomatic relations a state has increases, the state will need a larger bureaucracy. Large bureaucracies make coordination and control more difficult, and provide breeding grounds for differing perspectives. Certainly the problem of having relations with two states in conflict with each other (the usual condition of internationally active states) cannot help but foster competing convictions that weaken a consensus. The sheer complexity of world politics may cripple consensus.

Foreign policy leaders, however, have an interest in minimizing complexity, the fragmentation of power, and competing views. They would prefer a rational process because it usually accords them the right to choose (rather than the need to bargain). Similarly, they would like consensus if it accorded with their perspectives, for that narrows the range of debate and favors their own policy preferences. How might leaders make their world less complex and the policy process more manageable? They can attempt to lessen their involvement with a complex world (as the Chinese did during the Cultural Revolution); they can cast their lot with one state rather than try to maintain good relations with both (as Mussolini did in 1940 when he declared war on France); they can increase the level of terror in the society to stifle competing policy options (as Stalin did in the late 1940s). Yet these options are not easily invoked for most leaders.

They more often resort to changing and consolidating perceptions regarding the way the world "is" and what the nation should do in it. How is that to be done? Historically, we have identified two factors that might permit this: ideology and "lessons" learned from recent experience. (Public opinion may be a third, in that popularly accepted views such as "no more Sommes" for the British public after 1919, and "no more war" for the Russian public after 1945, or "no more Vietnams" for the American public after 1972 may effectively reduce the range of policy choice and policy politics.)

Ideology and "lessons" can form the basis for a consensus. The lessons Hitler taught, for instance, allowed identification of an aggressor state, the methods of such a state, and its long-term and short-term goals. Ideology served a similar purpose for the young Chinese and Soviet states. But we have seen that ideology did not rule out debate and disagreement in Lenin's Russia, nor did the "Hitler lessons" rule out debate during the early years of the Truman administration. Ideology and "lessons" initially stress what to look out for and what *not* to do (such as "don't appease an aggressor state"). Consensus, to be effective in reducing the policy debate, must also identify the "what should be done." Within five to ten years, the foundation established by the lessons and ideology and the trial and error of policy choices helped grind down dissent and debate, thus significantly narrowing the political process. Over time, however, new conditions and rude shocks to old verities are likely to erode the consensus and restore the political process to a full range of concerns.

These dynamics can be seen in particular issues. Consider the American government's changing policy toward nuclear weapons and arms control presented in Table 10–5.

Drawing on this information, I can advance several predictions:

Prediction 6a: Increased use or reference to ideology or "lessons of the past" by leaders enhances the probability of a rational process in policy making.

Prediction 6b: The more time has elapsed from the development of a consensus, the more probable the predominance of the political process.

Prediction 6c: Specific events are likely to shatter consensus and to refashion it.

Prediction 7: When the policy process is political, foreign policy is most likely:

to be inhibited and contradictory.

to be marginally responsive to opportunities and threats but able to avoid sudden destabilizing departures.

to be constantly challenged by losers in the internal policy-making process who use setbacks to force a change.

Prediction 8: When the policy process is rational, foreign policy is most likely:

to be composed of coordinated, reinforcing elements.

to be responsive to opportunities and threats if the consensus permits such responsiveness.

to be resilient during a number of setbacks (although this ability will deteriorate with time).

Predictions 6 through 8 suggest that the United States will, for some time into the future, continue to engage in a debate over nuclear policy. The controversy over whether to deploy the new MX missile and how to do it is illustrative, as is the public demand for a nuclear freeze. No new arms control agreement is likely during this period or immediately afterward, and the Reagan administration will continue to undertake a buildup of nuclear weapons, at the same time fielding a number of proposals on arms reductions. As to what event might create

TABLE 10-5   American Policy Toward Nuclear Weapons and Arms Control

TIME	DEGREE OF CONSENSUS AND POLICY PROCESS	POLICY REGARDING WEAPONS AND THEIR USE OR THE CENTRAL ISSUES IN DEBATE	ARMS CONTROL BEHAVIOR
1945–1956	Consensus (rational process)	Nuclear weapons will be used in war fighting and as a threat in diplomacy	Abolition only in accord with American proposals
	*Event: Launching of Sputnik and the demonstration that the USSR could deliver unstoppable nuclear warheads against the US		
1957–1962	Debate (political process)	How is the US to be protected and how can such weapons be used to achieve political ends?	Voice willingness to negotiate but undertake an arms buildup "to negotiate from a position of strength"
	*Event: Cuban missile crisis		
1963–1978	Consensus (rational process)	Nuclear weapons exist for deterrence	Negotiate controls on number and technology of weapons
	*Event: Continuing Soviet arms buildup and a belief that the USSR seeks to use nuclear weapons to secure political advantage		
1979–Present	Debate (political process)	When is a nation vulnerable? Is defense possible? Can nuclear war be managed and survived?	Voice willingness to negotiate but undertake arms buildup "to negotiate from a position of strength"

a new consensus and lead to a deemphasis of the political process, several possibilities suggest themselves: rapid nuclear proliferation among a number of states, the use of a nuclear device (accidental or intentional, but probably not by either superpower), or another "missile crisis" confrontation. The probability seems modest (but high enough) that the new "lesson" or consensus will be that nuclear weapons can be used in warfighting in limited ways (such as in space or in "local" conflicts).

Domestic and Environmental Factor Predictions

The last set of predictions I will offer using the scientific approaches comes from the domestic and environmental factor approach. As with the policy-maker and policy-making approach, I will single out but one area in which to make predictions: the impact of changes in ecological and economic systems on state behavior. You should feel anxious at this point to stalk through the forests of untouched questions.

The 1970s proved to be the decade when many people suddenly discovered that the ability of the earth to sustain life was problematic. In 1972, for instance, the Club of Rome's study, *The Limits to Growth*, concluded that "if the present growth trends in world population, industrialization, pollution, food production, and resource depletion continue unchanged, the limits to growth on this planet will be reached sometime within the next 100 years. The most probable result will be a rather sudden and uncontrollable decline in both population and industrial capacity."[20] In 1980, in response to a Presidential directive, a task force of the American government produced *The Global 2000 Report to the President*, which concluded:

> If present trends continue, the world in 2000 will be more crowded, more polluted, less stable ecologically, and more vulnerable to disruption than the world we live in now. Serious stresses involving population, resources, and environment are clearly visible ahead. Despite greater material output, the world's people will be poorer in many ways than they are today.[21]

While the quality of life may be worse in a global sense, suffering is not likely to be equally distributed, at least not initially. Some of the extrapolations from *The Global 2000 Report* that appear in Table 10–6 make the point. The rich are expected to get richer; the poor, more numerous. The urgency of world hunger and ill health has entered into world politics, as have the demands for a more equitable distribution of the wealth of humankind.[22]

---

[20]*The Limits to Growth: A Report for the Club of Rome's Project on the Predicament of Mankind*, by Donella Meadows, Dennis Meadows, Jørgen Randers, and William Behrens III. A Potomac Associates book published by Universe Books, New York, 1972. Pp. 23–24. For other studies see Mihajlo Mesarovic and Eduard Pestel, *Mankind at the Turning Point* (New York: E.P. Dutton, 1974); H.S. Cole, ed., *Models of Doom* (New York: Universe Books, 1973); Lester Brown, *The Twenty-Ninth Day* (New York: W.W. Norton & Co., Inc., 1978).

[21]Council on Environmental Quality and the Department of State, *The Global 2000 Report to the President* (Washington: Government Printing Office, 1980), Vol. 1, p. 1.

[22]For the dimensions of the problem, see Raymond Hopkins and Donald Puchala, eds., *The Global Political Economy of Food* (Madison: University of Wisconsin Press, 1978); Frances Moore Lappe and Joseph Collins, *Food First* (Boston: Houghton Mifflin, 1977).

TABLE 10-6   *Global 2000 Report's* Projections

	WORLD		MORE DEVELOPED REGIONS		LESS DEVELOPED REGIONS	
	1975	2000	1975	2000	1975	2000
Population in millions	4,090	6,351	1,131	1,323	2,959	5,028
Per capita income in constant 1975 US dollars	$1,473	$2,311	$4,325	$8,485	$382	$587
Grain production per capita in kilograms	312	343	575	850	180	220
(These are the Report's medium projections.)						

Source: Council on Environmental Quality and the Department of State, *The Global 2000 Report to the President* (Washington: Government Printing Office, 1980), Vol. 1, Tables 1, 4, 6.

Resource depletion is an environmental feature that has attracted particular attention, especially in the developed states.[23] Oil is often used as an illustration, as it underpins much of the economic life of industrial and non-industrial states. Figure 10-4 shows projected world oil production into the twenty-first century. Production declines because of the depletion of an unrenewable natural resource. The year in which the demand for oil exceeds supply depends on the growth rate in that demand. If demand does not increase beyond its current level, it would be approximately 2010 before a never-ending energy crisis would begin. A five percent yearly increase, on the other hand, means the crisis is approaching as you read these words.

FIGURE 10-4   Projected Oil Depletion Rates   Source: Council on Environmental Quality and the Department of State, *The Global 2000 Report to the President* (Washington: Government Printing Office, 1980), Vol. 2, p. 171.

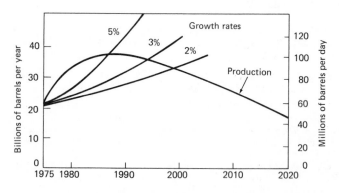

[23]For studies of oil depletion and consequences, see R.A. Werner, "Oil and U.S. Security Policies," *Orbis*, 21 (Fall 1977), 651–70: N. Choucri, "Analytical Specification of the World Oil Market," *Journal of Conflict Resolution*, 23 (June 1979), 346–72; R.R. Bowie, "Outlook for the 1980s," *Atlantic Community Quarterly*, 18 (Summer 1980), 218–25.

The functioning of capitalist economies has an intimate linkage to the eco-system. The United States, with five percent of the world's population, consumes from 30 to 40 percent of the earth's resources. An ecological crisis is likely to de-stabilize such high consumption economies, which, in turn, may destabilize other economies. That is one view of a coming economic crisis. Another type of predic-tion dispenses with the ecological catastrophe to argue that there are long- and short-term crises built into a capitalist system. For instance, the Russian econo-mist Nikolai Kondratieff in the 1920s pointed to a cyclical peaking of economic activity in Western industrial states every 45 to 60 years (1810s, 1860s, 1920s).[24] That would make the 1970s and 1980s the period of peak activity and transition to a substantially lower level of economic activity which would last into the twenty-first century.

Thus there are a number of predictions pointing to the next several decades as a period of crisis in domestic environments and economies of various states. Indeed, the probability of crisis is often depicted as increasing as each year passes. Not everyone agrees with these kinds of predictions, but we can make the following estimates:

> *Prediction 9a*: Major ecologic crisis such as depletion of a key resource,
> wide-spread famine, or catastrophic pollution by the year 2000.   .3 probability
>
> *Prediction 9b*: Major decline in the capitalist system's functioning by the
> year 2000.   .3 probability

Ironically, the linkage of such environmental and domestic factors to poli-tics, especially world politics, has not received systematic attention. As there have been no examples of global events in this century specified in 9a, and only the Great Depression meets the specification of 9b, this would be expected. There are, of course, speculations on the linkage between such events and world poli-tics. Jay Forester, for example, bases his predictions on the assumption that there are finite limits to growth in population size and resource use.

> Most countries are now acting as if their shortages could forever be met from the outside. But, as worldwide limits to growth are ever more closely approached, there is less slack in the world system. International trade has depended on such slack. Many countries have supported their population growth with imports. However, as every region becomes more densely populated, food and material surpluses decline and less is available to export to others. The time is approaching when each country must more and more meet its growth-induced needs from within its borders.
>
> If a country believes that solutions for its stresses can be found outside, then fail-ure to achieve solutions will naturally be attributed to others. When both the source of the problem and the potential solution are believed to lie across the border, war appears to be the only answer. . . . Only if each nation accommodates its needs to its own geographical capacity, can international tension be reduced.[25]

[24]N. Kondratieff, "The Long Waves in Economic Life," *Review of Economic Statistics*, 17 (No-vember 1935), 105–15. See also George Modelski, "Long Cycles, Kondratieffs, and Alternating In-novations," in *The Political Economy of Foreign Policy Behavior*, ed. Charles Kegley, Jr., and Patrick McGowan (Beverly Hills, Cal.: Sage, 1981), pp. 63–83.

[25]J. Forrester, "New Perspectives on Economic Growth," in *Alternatives to Growth-I*, ed. Den-nis Meadows (Cambridge, Mass.: Ballinger, 1977), p. 110.

Intensified conflict between states seems to be the most common prediction of the consequences of a major disruptive change in an environmental or domestic factor. That conflict is often pictured in terms of sudden military operations to seize land for its food or raw materials. On the other hand, we might also suggest that the initial response to such a crisis might be a perpetuation of the current patterns of world politics, because in an uncertain domestic climate, governments may cherish the stability of known international patterns. Even with continued crisis, most states may continue to look inward (or at least so the events of the early 1930s would suggest).

Prediction 10a: Greater aggressiveness in world politics.   .4 probability

Prediction 10b: Stable levels of aggressiveness, perhaps a decline.   .6 probability

Perhaps, however, we can develop these themes more fully by looking at the four areas of special concern. What difference might such a crisis make for *nuclear war*?

Prediction 11a: Non-nuclear states with the preexisting capability will go nuclear. Nuclear weapons will be seen as a relatively cheap measure of self-defense.   .5 probability

Prediction 11b: Increased threats and use of nuclear weapons by states other than superpowers or major powers. As there is a greater likelihood of wars of desperation, the belief that the rational calculus of deterrence will work is likely to erode.   .4 probability

Prediction 11c: Superpowers and major powers will use nuclear weapons as a means of dealing with the crisis. High levels of force have little utility for resolving the crisis for such states.   < .1 probability

The nature of *Soviet-American relations* may depend on the degree of symmetry with which the crisis affects each state. Does a socialist state have the greater capacity to restructure the operation of its economy and extract or encourage public compliance? The young Soviet state, aided by heavy doses of terror, avoided the capitalist's Depression in the 1930s, but neither youth nor terror exist now. Poland's inability to deal with its economy and the erosion of party control suggest the kinds of problems Soviet leaders will face. There is no reason to believe the American political or economic system could do much better.

Prediction 12a: Serious escalation of conflict between the US and USSR.   .2 probability

Prediction 12b: Increased mutual cooperation and problem-solving.   .3 probability

Prediction 12c: Looking inward produces a non-hostile reduction in contacts.   .5 probability

Expectations about increased conflict often center on the less developed states, either in their relations with the developed states or among themselves. In *North-South relations*, the South has demanded a more equitable distribution of resources. Such demands have been made more in rhetoric, although OPEC and Arab OPEC have used prices and an embargo to support some policy goals. In the aftermath of an ecological or economic crisis, the leverage of the South is likely to collapse. The demand for their resources is likely to drop and pleas for equity are likely to be ignored by governments struggling to preserve their own societies. The experience of the oil producers in the early 1980s is indicative. As demand from the industrial states decreased, OPEC fell into disunity, and even the disruption of oil deliveries because of the Iraqi-Iranian war that began in September, 1980, did not change matters. A world in crisis is likely to be a buyer's market.

> *Prediction 13*: With the onset of an ecologic or economic crisis, there will be reduced North-South interaction, leading to isolation of the South.   .7 probability
>
> *Prediction 14*: If the crisis is one of resource depletion and develops gradually, the producer nations will individually use their leverage for individual policy goals but not undertake collective action.   .6 probability

An isolated Third World would have to look to itself, yet its political fragmentation and uneven distribution of resources (from minerals to arable lands) work against coordinated or cooperative behavior. Fragile governments sitting on top of alienated, heterogeneous cultures are likely to devote most of their attention to preserving the polity.

> *Prediction 15*: Third World states in crisis will be internally oriented; the means for using external power will fall in disrepair.   .8 probability

However, states with well-equipped, professional military establishments may have their means of projecting power decay less rapidly. By "professional," I mean a military whose prime mission and preparation have been for the exercise of force in foreign politics, not for participation in domestic politics. Such military establishments are relatively few and far between in the Third World, creating pockets of projectable power surrounded by states with little defensive capability.

> *Prediction 16*: Third World states with professional military establishments will embark on regional aggression and build larger political entities. (As the Middle East has many such states, we might expect war to be a chronic condition there.)   .4 probability

WORLD POLITICS IN THE FUTURE

The dividing line between the "empirically" based predictions of the extrapolation and analytic methods and those generated by intuition is ambiguous at times. Many of the predictions you have just read reflect my sense of how things might occur; the incomplete development of explanations for several of them are symptomatic. The lack of tested hypotheses often forces us to rely on intuition if we hope to wrestle with the future.

In a similar fashion, the lack of integration of the four scientific approaches means that we must rely more on intuition for summary predictions about the state of the world in the coming decades. That should not deter us—and it hasn't!

What is, overall, the most probable future of world politics in the next several decades?

As I have said at several points, the best prediction is often that the future will look much like the present, but we know from historical experience that this is not always true. The probability does seem high, however, that world politics between now and 2000 will be *relatively unchanged*. Specifically, I would expect these patterns:

1. The two superpowers will interact with suspicion but continue to seek partial agreements regulating their behavior. No additional superpowers emerge.
2. Western Europe remains economically integrated, politically cooperative, linked by alliance and interest to the United States but anxious to influence US policy.
3. Eastern Europe goes through periodic unrest with various forms of Soviet intervention; a gradual liberalization in the economic sphere occurs.
4. North-South relations remain an uneven mixture. For the North, humanitarian concern, a search for influence to protect economic and political interests, and various types of intervention to support clients, remain the rule. For the South, trying to set the agenda to make politics and economics more responsive to the underdogs. Superpower confrontation in the Third World remains sporadic and of low intensity.
5. A variety of small wars of a duration measured in months will occur, encouraging collective action by the regional states and major powers or superpowers, often under the aegis of the United Nations.
6. Inequalities continue, but do not form the major calculus of world politics. Power does. Conflict and cooperation are as they have been

A world unchanged is also likely *not* to have certain features such as (1) a nuclear war between the powers having nuclear weapons in 1980 (United States, Soviet Union, China, Britain, France, and India), (2) conventional war in Europe, (3) a cohesive Third World, (4) sudden changes in the power distribution, or (5) a major deterioration in the norms of international intercourse. Those features are projections of what has *not* happened in the post-World War II world. On the other hand, there is a new element in the world at the end of the century that marks a distinct change from the post-war period. Liberation movements against colonial regimes are a thing of the past (except in Namibia and, in one sense, South Africa). Liberation movements such as the Viet Minh in French Indochina were the driving force of much of world politics, drawing in the colonial power and its allies, while the insurgents often drew in the socialist states. That era has passed; the *necessary* involvement of great powers has ended. In place of the politics of liberation stands the politics of internal political change. Possibly violent, possibly threatening great power interests, such changes do not constitute a direct attack on a great power and are likely to be far too numerous to encourage the kind of violent intervention we saw in the post-war period.

WHAT IS TO BE DONE?

A prediction of a world unchanged may sound moderately appealing, depending on where you happen to stand. Some of the predictions may have appeared far more unappealing, threatening some of the things you cherish. What should we do with a prediction? For what end should we wish to know the future? Karl Schuessler has argued that "the purpose of prediction . . . is to secure a measure of control over what otherwise would be less manageable circumstances." Therefore, "practically all predictions are potential instruments of social action, enabling the group either to facilitate a favorable outcome or to impede an unfavorable one."[26] Others have argued that the purpose of predictions is not necessarily to provide accurate forecasts, but to encourage a systematic exploration of various goals and options.[27] Still others see prediction as a way of giving greater prominence to current problems (as the *Global 2000* report attempts) to encourage people to consider the need for collective problem solving as a method of human and international relations. Each of these purposes serves a larger end—to raise our awareness that the future is a result of human choice. "The future is not an overarching leap into the distance," concludes Daniel Bell. "It begins in the present . . . for in the decisions we make now, in the way we design our environment and thus sketch the lines of constraints, the future is committed."[28]

These assertions about prediction imply an intimate connection with values. To seek a measure of control means to serve some values and hinder others. To provide a wider range of goals and options means that values will have to be invoked in making choices. "Problems" are precisely those things that threaten values. The critical question is where values should enter the process of making predictions. The goal-induced method makes them foremost.

One set of goal-induced predictions that has received much attention concerns the hope and expectation that *the state-centered nature of world politics will end.* The state system seems so natural to the twentieth century; I assumed when I began this book that you would not need to be reminded of its existence. In traditional parlance, a state is an entity that has a population in a particular territory under the control of a government. In juridical terms, the state is sovereign within its own boundaries and has equal standing with all other states. On those useful fictions some of world politics has taken shape. But we have seen that the state is also an efficient vehicle for the organization of power and its projection beyond the territory of the state. Power means inequality of standing, meddling in the affairs of others, and conflict. Power has been a more pervasive molder of world politics, and power is the property of the state.

And that, to many, is what was wrong. The acceptance (or worship) of the present state-centered system is unacceptable, argues Richard Falk, because it "accepts as virtually permanent the present structure of inequality, violence, oppression, misappropriation of resources, and poverty."[29] Falk asserts that the current state system is doomed to be replaced "during the next few decades." Saul Mendlovitz, one of Falk's co-workers, makes a further prediction:

> It is my considered judgment that there is no longer a question of whether or not there will be world government by the year 2000. As I see it, the questions we

[26]From F.K. Schuessler, "Prediction," in *International Encyclopedia of the Social Sciences*, David L. Sills, Editor. Vol. 12, p. 418. Copyright © 1968 by Crowell Collier and Macmillan, Inc.

[27]Ascher, *Forecasting*, p. 2.

[28]Daniel Bell, in foreword to *The Future of the U.S. Government*, ed. Harvey Perloff (Englewood Cliffs, N.J.: Prentice-Hall, 1972), p. ix.

[29]Richard Falk, *A Study of Future Worlds* (New York: Macmillan, 1975), p. 177. © 1975 by Institute for World Order, New York.

should be addressing ourselves to are, how it will come into being—by cataclysm, drift, rational design—and whether it will be totalitarian, benign, or participatory (the probabilities being in that order).[30]

Falk and others associated with the World Order Models Project[31] (WOMP) have devised possible and preferred worlds and tried to specify "transition steps" that would lead to a preferred future. In engineering the future, they use as their guideposts four values that they believe any future should safeguard:[32]

Minimization of large-scale collective violence.

Maximization of social and economic well-being.

Realization of fundamental human rights and considerations of political justice.

Maintenance and rehabilitation of ecological quality.

Their preferred world is one in which power is fragmented (hence a weakening of the state, perhaps its dissolution), but the resulting smaller units are joined together in networks of intense but nonexploitative communication and exchange. A world government would exist, but it "would have a role as a major articulator of problems and conflicts" and would aid the many constituent units of the world polity in devising solutions.[33] Violence would be the first element brought under control, but not by freezing the status quo, for that would probably violate the other values. Denuclearization, reductions in armed forces, and multinational peacekeeping operations would be characteristic.

Such changes would begin by the development of a new consciousness, which would develop its own political power. "No world order solution which presupposes the substantial modification of the state system" notes Falk, "can be achieved unless the advocates of the new system are aligned with important social and political forces within the existing world structure. Education and related strategies of persuasion can help to mobilize or even 'create' social forces committed to world order change."[34] Admittedly utopian, the WOMP future, its proponents argue, is a "relevant utopia" for it is consciously interested in being a self-fulfilling prediction: by demonstrating a more attractive future than the present, by insisting the present is doomed, and by providing the levers for change, the proponents hope their prediction will so mobilize individuals to work to create that future that it will come to pass.

None of the predictions I have presented in this chapter see the emergence of such a future as probable (nor do they see a totalitarian world government, for that matter). Nor does any Marxist-relevant utopia seem probable. But that does

[30]*Ibid.*, S. Mendlovitz, "Introduction," p. xxvi.

[31]For other WOMP projects, see Saul Mendlovitz, ed., *On the Creation of a Just World Order* (New York: Free Press, 1975); and Rajni Kothari, *Footsteps into the Future* (New York: Free Press, 1974).

[32]Falk, *Study of Future Worlds*, pp. 11–30.

[33]Johan Galtung, *The True Worlds* (New York: Macmillan, 1980), p. 382. © 1980 by Institute for World Order, New York.

[34]Falk, *Study of Future Worlds*, p. 277.

not mean that these predictions are impossible, or that we should become fatalists and take whatever comes our way. We owe it to ourselves as humans to work for a future in which the values we cherish find expression.

Some values, of course, are selfish and destructive; we have seen the havoc they wreaked in this century. Other values, in isolation quite unselfish and positive, may deny other values: if starvation in an unjust social order is not to be tolerated, can we outlaw violence, which may be the only way to prevent that starvation? Yet the outlawing of violence would seem to be desirable. I know of no easy solution to this dilemma. I would suggest there may be a future and a value to which we all can repair: a world where children are not fearful or in pain. Our minimal obligation as humans would be to work against probable futures that threaten this value.

Yet we are often afflicted by the immobilism inherent in the question, "What can *I* do?" Unfortunately, we have no sure answers, even if you change the stress to "*What* can I do?" I am convinced that what you and I and the four billion others who share the planet with us *can do* depends on the understanding and creativity we bring to the study and implementation of world politics. If you see world politics as essentially an art, practiced by artists, apprentice yourself to the diplomatic or military or international services to learn the art. You will need history and scientific approaches, for art must be a product of head as well as heart. The discovery of new forms takes the insight of thought as well as inspiration. As an artist, your hope for the future would find expression in the molding of world politics.

You might see world politics as choices made by elites, and the route to having a choice in the future is by membership in the elite. History and scientific approaches may enable you to demonstrate to those who control the entrance into that world that you see better than others, that you understand more deeply how things work. When choices are yours to make, history and scientific approaches may provide the vision to see well and the courage and compassion to choose wisely and humanely.

Alternatively, you might see world politics as the expression of the global culture we share as humans and of the disparate cultures we do not share. Those cultures are shaped by concerned and active individuals who are willing to pay the price to learn, think, and act. Those individuals serve as the critics for the artists and the elites, prodding them to raise their sights, their concerns, and their confidence. For them, for us, history and scientific approaches give us the power to be informed, creative, and compelling. The twentieth century began with presentiments of progress. Skeptical as we may be, we cannot reject that possibility on the eve of the twenty-first.

INDEX _____

(*Note*: Consult the Contents for general guidance to historical periods and approaches. Maps are indexed under *Maps*. The power of individual states appears in the tables indexed under *Power distribution*.)

ABM (Anti-Ballistic Missile), 293–294
Abyssinia (*see* Ethiopia)
Acheson, Dean, 215, 249
Action-Reaction (*see* Pattern analysis)
Afghanistan, 8, 39, 48, 230, 311–312, 315
Africa, ties to United States, 280–282 (*see also individual states*)
Agadir crisis (1911), 68–69
Agnew, Spiro, 305, 323
Albania, 71, 153, 187
Albertini, Luigi, 92
Allende, Salvador, 303
Alliance in collapse, 345–347
Alliance of necessity, 203–204
Alliance polarization, 59–60
Alliances, 34–35, 40, 43–44, 83
    honoring of, 42–43, 74, 82, 91–92, 152, 267–268
    necessity for, 34, 59–60, 90–91
    rigidity, 45, 69, 91, 326–328
    risks of, 42–43, 45, 52, 83, 90, 232
    as systemic patterns:
        in bipolar systems, 326–327
        in equilateral systems, 132–133, 170–171
        in ladder-like systems, 59–60, 90–91, 171
    in wartime, 83
Allison, Graham, 15

Alsace-Lorraine, 39, 41–43, 76, 86
Angola, 307
Anti-Comintern Pact, 149
Appeasement policy, 62, 72, 99, 114–115, 152–153, 162–163, 172
    definition, 62
Arab-Israeli conflict (*see* Middle East)
Arbitration, 106–107
Argentina, 331–334
Armored warfare, 79, 175–176, 179, 183, 299
Arms (*see* Weapons)
Arms control:
    conventional weapons, 50, 67–68, 107–108, 115–116, 140, 142, 145–147, 171, 303
    nuclear weapons, 205, 302–303, 350
        SALT, 293–295, 306–307, 312
Arms race, 12, 49, 171
    Anglo-German naval race, 50–51, 67–68, 147
    nuclear, 223–224, 241, 258, 260, 291, 294, 350
    pattern analysis of, 23, 203
Aspaturian, Vernon, 252
Assad, Hafez, 299
Atomic bomb, 185–187, 223 (*see also* Nuclear weapons)
Attlee, Clement, 185, 191

Attrition, in war, 78, 102–103, 180–182, 193, 262
   in prisoner's dilemma game, 102
Audiences, in bargaining, 22, 157, 160, 161–162 (*see also* Domestic audiences)
Australia, 113, 222
Austria, 139, 146, 225
   German seizure, 151, 158–159
Austria-Hungary:
   diplomatic history, 41, 51, 66, 70–71, 73, 85
   with Serbia, 51, 70–71, 73, 96
Authoritarian governments, 138, 202, 348

Backfire, 306–307
Baghdad Pact, 222, 230
Balance of power system, 55, 58, 170–172
Balkans, 41, 51, 66, 70–71, 86
Bandaranaike, Sirima, 257
Bandung Conference (1955), 231
Bangladesh, 1, 303
Barber, James D., 318
Bargaining, 21
   and appeasement, 163
   in bad faith, 155–156, 160–161
   commitment in, 21, 157–158, 160
   communication in, 21, 157, 216
   conditions for, 21, 156
   credibility, 22, 161
   and threats of war, 158, 160–161, 162
   during war, 155–156, 216–218, 264–265, 295–296
Bargaining leverage, 50, 77, 108, 157–162, 251–252, 295
   definition, 157
Bargaining tactics, 158–161
Bargaining theory, 21–23, 155–163
   and rationality, 156, 162
Baruch Plan, 205
Begin, Menachem, 309–310
Belgian Congo (*see* Zaire)
Belgium, 74, 76, 111, 114, 149, 174–175
Bell, Daniel, 357
Benedict, Ruth, 11
Benes, Edward, 184
Bennett, Lance, 247–248
Berlin, 185, 233, 256, 302
   blockade, 190, 206
Bethmann, Theobald, 51, 67–68, 73, 84
   relationship to William II, 96–97
Biafra, 267
Bipolar system, 237, 325–329, 343–344
Blackmail in negotiation, 161
Blitzkrieg, 154, 175–176
Boer War (1899–1902), 38
Bolshevik Party, 82, 88, 123
Bolshevik Revolution (1917), 82, 123
Bosnia-Herzegovina, 41, 51–52, 73

Bosnian crisis (1908), 51–52
Boundary, of system, 27, 58, 134–136
Boxer Rebellion, 36–37
Brest-Litovsk Treaty, 82, 121–122
Brezhnev, Leonid, 265, 292, 296, 299, 306, 329
Briand, Aristide, 114, 116–117
Bridge building, 345–347
Buchanan, Bruce, 322
Bukharin, Nikolai, 127
Bulgaria, 41, 70–71, 85, 177
Bulow, Bernhard von, 44, 47, 52

Caillaux, Joseph, 68
Cambodia, 220–221, 295, 308, 313
   American invasion of, 295, 318, 322–325
Canada, 113
Capability (*see* Power, as capability)
Capitalist states:
   economic cycles, 353
   and less developed states, 271–282
   and Soviet Union, 123–129
Carter, Jimmy, 305, 307, 309–312
Castro, Fidel, 201, 234–235, 251
Central Intelligence Agency, 226, 231, 234
Challenge, policy of, 62, 72
Chamberlain, Joseph, 39–40
Chamberlain, Neville, 148, 152–154
   negotiation with Hitler, 156, 157, 160–163
Chang Hsueh-liang, 120, 150
Chang Tso-lin, 120
Chiang Kai-shek, 120, 127, 150, 189
China (to 1949), 118–120, 140–142, 150–151 (*see also* People's Republic of China)
   civil war, 150, 189
   relations with Japan, 141–142, 150
   war, 38, 150–151
   relations with Russia, 61–63
   Revolution of 1911, 66
   as sphere of influence, 36–38
Chou En-lai, 211, 216, 220, 297, 305
Churchill, Winston, 81, 174, 191, 211, 220
   on iron curtain, 187
   spheres of influence, 184
   as wartime leader, 174, 177–178, 180, 182, 184–185
Civil war and foreign intervention, 149, 266–267
Club of Rome, 351
Coercion, 155, 227
Cohen, Bernard, 249
Cold war, 186, 345–347
   Arab, 268
   definition, 186
   measurement, 241–243
   pattern analysis, 242–244

prediction for, 337-338
public knowledge of, 246
Soviet-American, 186-191, 201-206,
    214, 216-217, 242-244, 256,
    260-261, 312, 328-329 (*see also*
    United States, relations with
    Soviet Union; Soviet Union,
    relations with United States)
as systemic behavior, 239, 285, 328
Collective security, 105
and equilateral system, 133, 170-171
limitations, 113, 117, 133, 140-142,
    148
operation of, 107, 115, 117, 134,
    141-142
Colonies, 35-37, 272-273 (*see also*
    Decolonialization; Imperialism;
    Neo-colonialism; Sphere of
    influence)
holdings (*table*), 37
Comintern, 125, 127, 144, 147
Command economy, 234, 305
Commitment:
in alliances, 91-92
in bargaining, 21, 157, 158, 160
and colonies, 36
Common market, 217-218
Communication:
in bargaining, 21-22, 44-45, 157, 216
in prisoner's dilemma game, 101
Communist International (*see* Comintern)
Communist Party, Soviet Union (*see* Soviet
    Union, internal politics)
Competitive manipulation, 346-347
Conflict in world politics, 6-10
classification (*table*), 9
and cooperation, 6-10, 138
and personality, 93-95
Congress, U.S., 188-189, 190, 296, 302,
    305, 307-308
Consensus, in government, 348-351
Containment, 188-191, 214-215, 218 (*see
    also* United States, relations with
    Soviet Union; Soviet Union,
    relations with United States)
Cooperation in world politics, 6-10, 138,
    155-156, 244, 276, 304
in prisoner's dilemma game, 101
Credibility:
in bargaining, 21-22, 161, 163, 301
in nuclear deterrence, 224-225
Crisis diplomacy, 69-70, 73
Criswell, 339
Cruise missile, 306
Cuba, 38, 234-235, 251, 256, 307-309
Cuban missile crisis, 17, 258-260
Cyprus, 267
Czechoslovakia, 86, 115, 153, 189, 268,
    303

1938 crisis, 152, 159-162

Dawes Plan, 112-113
Decision maker (*see* Policy maker)
Decision making (*see* Policy making)
Decolonization, 191, 198-201, 219-220,
    228-230, 256, 273, 307-308
De Gaulle, Charles, 228, 283
Democracies and foreign policy, 202, 348
Democratic Republic of Vietnam (North
    Vietnam), 261-265, 295-297,
    308, 313 (*see also* Ho Chi Minh)
Department of State, 197-201, 294, 320
organization (*illus.*), 197
Dependence, 279-282, 301
Depression of 1930s, 137-138, 139
consequences for world politics,
    138-140, 141
Détente, 260-261, 290, 307, 312, 325
definitions, 72, 260-261
as a policy, 72, 90
Deterrence, 25, 142 (*see also* Nuclear
    deterrence)
Diplomacy, 25
and ideology, 124-125, 129
and lies, 47, 145
Disarmament (*see* Arms control)
Discovery pattern, 204-205
Distribution of power (*see* Power
    distribution; International
    system, power)
Dixon, Jeanne, 339
Domestic and Environmental Factor
    Approach, 10-14, 121-122, 315,
    332
Marxist interpretation, 272-275,
    279-282
predictions, 351-355
Domestic audiences, 62, 276
Domestic factor, 10
Dreadnought, 49
Dreyfus, Alfred, 41
DRV (*see* Democratic Republic of
    Vietnam)
Dubcek, Alexander, 268
Dulles, John Foster, 218, 219, 225, 228, 233

East Germany (*see* German Democratic
    Republic)
Ecology and world politics, 351-355
Economic conditions (*see also* Political
    economy):
as environmental factor, 135, 272-275
and foreign policy, 113, 138-140,
    279-282, 292
and military expenditures, 140
predictions, 351-355
and world politics, 120, 138-140, 189,
    301

Eden, Anthony, 230
Edward VII, 43, 46
Egypt, 23, 230, 286 (*see also* Middle East; Nasser; Sadat)
   relations with Israel, 16, 24, 268–270, 299–300, 310
   relations with Soviet Union, 230–231, 251–256, 268–270, 298–299
   relations with United States, 230, 298–300, 310
Eisenhower, Dwight, 185, 218, 225, 247–248
Energy production, 130 (*see also* Oil)
Entente, 43 (*see also* Triple Entente)
Environmental factor, 10
Environment of system, 27–28, 134–136, 172, 237, 240, 287
Equilateral system, 130, 343–344
   five-state system, 170–172 (*see also* Balance of power system)
   three-state system, 132–134, 170
Escalation pattern, 23–25, 203, 268–269
Escape clause, in treaties, 42, 117
Eshkol, Levi, 269
Estonia, 86, 155, 177
Ethiopia, 35, 146–148, 309
European Economic Community, 217–218, 267, 302
Extrapolation, 336–338

Fait accompli, 95, 140, 159
Falk, Richard, 357–358
Falkland Island war, 331–334
Fashoda incident (1898), 38
Federal Republic of Germany, 206, 217, 258, 302
Feedback loop, 202, 316
Finland, 86
   war with Soviet Union, 155, 173–174
First strike, 70, 74, 95
   in nuclear war, 224–225, 293–294
"Five Principles," 231
Foch, Ferdinand, 76, 85
Force, 13 (*see also* Coercion)
Ford, Gerald, 305, 307
Foreign aid, 188–189, 222, 230, 276
Foreign policy, 14 (*see also* Policy making)
   as choice of options, 15
   as a compromise, 17, 63–64, 69, 71, 97–98, 199, 253, 258–260, 323–325
   consensus, 348–351
   contradictions in, 63–64
   of drift, 198–199, 253
   and economic conditions, 13, 113, 138–140, 279–282, 292
   and ideology, 122–130, 135–136, 143, 144, 183, 349–351
   and military balance, 237–238

   as organizational routines, 198
   as perceived by others, 64
   and public opinion, 244–250
Foreign policy lessons, 164–166, 349–351 (*see also* Lessons of history)
Forester, Jay, 353
Formosa (*see* Taiwan)
Fragile alliance, 345–347
France:
   Battle for (1940), 174–176
      repercussions, 177–178
   and decolonization, 191, 199–200, 219–220, 228–229
   diplomatic history:
      interwar years, 108–110, 111–112, 114–117, 139, 146–149, 152–154
      post-World War II, 199–200, 218–220, 230, 256, 267, 270
      pre-World War I, 41–42, 44–46, 68–69, 71
   and Indochina, 199–200, 219–220
   military plans, 76, 115, 145–146, 152, 174
   nuclear weapons, 10, 225, 256, 327
   relations with Czechoslovakia, 115, 146, 152, 161–162, 171
   relations with Germany:
      interwar years, 109–112, 114–117, 139, 148
      pre-World War I, 44–45, 68–69
   relations with Great Britain:
      interwar years, 109, 110, 112, 147–148, 152–153, 160
      post-World War II, 190, 200, 220, 222, 230, 267
      pre-World War I, 38, 43–45
   relations with Poland, 110, 114–115, 146
   relations with Russia, 39, 69
   relations with Soviet Union, 146, 147, 153
   relations with United States, 116–117, 198–200, 220, 230–231, 256
   in World War I, 74, 76–79, 84–86
   in World War II, 154–155, 174–176, 196
Franco, Francisco, 149, 177
Franco-Prussian War (1870–1871), 34, 39
Franz Ferdinand, 73

Gallipoli campaign (1915), 81
Gallucci, Robert, 15
Galtieri, Leopoldo, 333
Game theory, 19–20
   ending World War I, 98–103
   Falkland Islands crisis, 333–334
Gamson, William, 242
Gandhi, Indira, 257
Gandhi, Mahatma, 118

Gas warfare, 79, 156
Gender and world politics, 257–258
Geneva Protocol (1924), 113
Geography, 11–12, (*see also* Maps)
German Democratic Republic, 206, 233,
    256, 302
Germany (to 1949) (*see also* Federal
    Republic of Germany; German
    Democratic Republic; Hitler;
    William II):
  and Anglo-French Entente, 44–45
  systemic explanation, 59
  diplomatic history:
    interwar years, 108–112, 114–117,
      139, 145–149, 151–154, 158–163
    pre-World War I, 39–41, 44–47,
      50–51, 66–69, 71–74
  economy, 109–110, 111–113, 139
    depression, 138
  encirclement, 48, 95
  and League of Nations, 115, 146
  and league of states, 39, 40, 59, 67
  and military plans, 74–76, 97
  military tactics, 80–81, 175–176
  occupation of, 184–185, 190
  political collapse (1918), 82, 84–85
  post-war limitations, 86, 108–109,
    184–185
  rearmament, 115–116, 145–146
  relations with Austria, 139, 146, 151,
    158–159
  relations with Austria-Hungary, 34–35,
    52, 71, 73, 90, 94, 96–97
  relations with Czechoslovakia,
    151–152, 159–162
  relations with France, 44–45, 68–69,
    109, 114–117
  relations with Great Britain:
    interwar years, 114–115, 117, 147,
      154
    naval programs, 50–51, 67–68, 147
    pre-World War I, 39, 41, 44–45,
      67–68, 90
  relations with Italy, 43, 149, 154
  relations with Poland, 146, 153–154,
    163
  relations with Russia, 39, 46–47, 52,
    66–67, 73–74, 94–95
  relations with Soviet Union, 111,
    153–154, 171
  remilitarization of Rhineland, 148
  reparations, 108, 109–110, 111–113,
    117–118, 139
  Versailles Treaty, 85–86, 108
    circumvention, 109, 111, 114,
      146–148
    revision, 110, 112, 114, 139
  Weimar Republic, 85, 88
  in World War I, 74–76, 78, 81–85

  armistice, 82, 84–85
  in World War II, 154, 174–177,
    178–183, 207
    French campaign, 174–176
    Russian campaign, 178–181
Global 2000 Report, 351–352
Goals, in predictions, 341–343
Goals of policy makers (*see* Policy makers,
    goals)
Goering, Hermann, 151, 159, 176, 177
Goldmann, Kjell, 242
Gomulka, Wladyslaw, 226, 303
Great Britain:
  alliance, search for, 39–40, 42–44
  and decolonization, 118, 191, 228–229
  diplomatic history:
    interwar years, 108, 115, 117,
      146–149, 152–154
    post-World War II, 187, 188, 191,
      199–200, 218, 225, 230–231,
      267, 331
    pre-World War I, 38–41, 45–46,
      47–48, 50, 67–69, 71–72
  and Falkland Islands, 331–334
  and India, 118, 191
  military plans, 39, 45, 76, 154, 174
  naval policy, 50–51, 67–68, 108, 147
  nuclear weapons, 225, 241, 284, 327
  relations with Czechoslovakia, 152,
    161–162, 171
  relations with France:
    interwar years, 109–110, 112,
      147–148, 152–153, 160
    post-World War II, 190, 200, 220,
      222, 230, 267
    pre-World War I, 38, 43–45, 69
  relations with Germany:
    interwar years, 110–115, 117,
      147–148, 154, 163
    naval programs, 50–51, 67–68, 147
    pre-World War I, 39, 41, 67–68,
      71–72, 90
  relations with Japan, 42
  relations with Poland, 153–154, 163,
    184
  relations with Russia, 45–48, 51, 67
  relations with Soviet Union, 128, 153,
    184
    wartime diplomacy, 184–185
  relations with United States, 86, 88,
    108, 178, 182–185, 188, 190,
    230–231
  in World War I, 74, 76, 78–79, 81,
    83–86
  in World War II, 154, 174–183
    the Blitz, 177
Greece, 41, 70–71, 86, 118, 153, 178–179,
    187, 189, 267
Grey, Edward, 45, 71–72, 95

Gross national product war, 180
Guerrilla war, 262

Haig, Douglas, 79
Hammarskjold, Dag, 254–255, 256
Have-not game, 333–334
Hay, John, 44
Hermann, Charles, 18, 320
Hickenlooper Amendment, 273
Hirohito, 193, 195–196
Historical approach, 3–5, 30
  assumptions, 4, 30
  method, 3, 5, 30
  and scientific approaches, 14, 202, 317,
    330
Hitler, Adolf, 140, 142–143, 151–154, 183
  bargaining tactics, 158–161
  and Chamberlain, 156–157, 160–163
  coup attempt, 1923, 112
  and France, 143, 145, 174
  goals, 143–145, 151, 163, 176
  and Great Britain, 143, 151, 154,
    160–163, 176
  as military commander, 151, 175–176,
    179–180, 183
  and military officers, 148, 151, 154, 157
  peace overtures, 176–177, 181–182
  as perceived by others, 143–144, 161,
    162, 164–165
  perceptions, 143, 144, 151
  and Soviet Union, 153, 171, 177,
    178–179
Hoare, Samuel, 147–148
Ho Chi Minh, 191, 196, 198, 200, 220,
  222
Holsti, K. J., 6
Hoover, Herbert, 120, 133, 139, 188
Hughes, Charles E., 108
Hungary, 177, 181
  revolution, 226–227
Hunger, 351–353
Hussein, 298
Hypothesis:
  definition, 58
  testing, 120, 278–283

ICBM (Intercontinental Ballistic Missile),
  225, 258, 291, 294, 306, 307
Ideologue, 121, 271–272
Ideology, 121, 124
  and bargaining, 130
  definition, 121
  and diplomatic style, 124–125, 129
  as environmental factor, 135
  and foreign policy, 122–130, 135–136,
    143, 144, 183, 349–351
  and perception of conflict, 8, 129, 183
  as rationalization, 128–129
  and world politics, 121–122, 135–136

Images (*see* Perception)
Imperialism, 35, 37, 118, 141, 272–278 (*see*
  also Colonies; Neo-colonialism)
India, 118, 191, 267–268, 303
  as regional power, 235, 283, 326
  relations with People's Republic of
    China, 231, 257
Individual, role of, 245–246, 359 (*see also*
  Policy makers)
Indochina, 177, 196–201, 217, 219–222 (*see*
  also Vietnam)
Indonesia, 180, 191
Influence, of individuals, 15, 96–98 (*see also*
  Policy makers)
Information:
  and organizations, 196
  use in policy making, 97
Innovation, military, 80–81
Interaction approach, 18–25, 315 (*see also*
  Bargaining theory; Game theory;
  Pattern analysis)
  definition, 18
  Marxist interpretation, 274–276
  predictions, 333–334, 337, 345–347
  types (*table*), 25
Interdependence, 277–278, 345–347
International law, 107
International organizations, 5, 106 (*see also*
  League of Nations; United
  Nations)
International system (*see also* Bipolar
  system; Equilateral system;
  Ladder-like system; Monopolar
  system; Power distribution;
  Systems approach)
  boundary, 27–28, 58
  definition, 26
  environment, 27–28, 91–92, 134–136,
    171
  patterns of behavior, 26–28, 238
    identification of, 55–58, 208
  and power, 26, 53–55, 130, 207 (*see also*
    Power distribution)
  predictions for, 343–345
  and regional subsystems, 239–240,
    285–289
  rules, 26, 28–29, 60, 134–135, 170–
    171
    violation of, 171–172
  and security, 26–27
  stability, 134, 285
  structure (*see* International system, and
    power; Power distribution)
Iran, 35, 39, 48, 187, 220, 311
Irredenta, 70
Israel, 191, 288, 309
  relations with Arab states, 287–289,
    309–310
  relations with United States, 191,

230–231, 269–270, 298–300,
    309–310
and war, 23–24, 230, 268–270, 298–300
Issue arenas, decoupling, 115–116
Italy, 70, 118, 149, 218
    and Ethiopia, 146–147
    opposition to Hitler, 146–148
    relations with Germany, 43, 74, 149,
        154
    in World War I, 74, 83, 86
    in World War II, 176, 178, 181, 183
Izvolsky, Aleksandr, 47, 51

Japan:
    decision making for war, 64, 177–178,
        192–196
    diplomatic history, 38, 41, 61–65, 108,
        118–120, 140–142, 150–151,
        177–178
    impact on Asian colonies, 180, 191
    and Manchuria, 119–120, 140–142,
        150, 151
    military plans (1941), 193
    national character, 11
    navy, 188, 193
    occupation of, 205
    political instability, 120, 140–141
    as regional power, 235, 283, 326
    relations with China, 38, 118, 120,
        141–142, 150
        war of 1937–1945, 150–151
    relations with Great Britain, 42
    relations with Korea, 41, 61
    relations with Russia, 61–65
    relations with Soviet Union, 151, 178,
        186
    relations with United States, 8, 177–178
    relations with Vichy France, 177, 196
    in World War I, 83
    in World War II, 180–182, 185–186,
        192–196
John Paul II, 313
Johnson, Lyndon, 166, 220, 262–265
Joint Chiefs of Staff, 294, 318, 322–323
Jordan, 231, 269–270, 298

Kaplan, Morton, 26
Kellogg-Briand Peace Pact (1928),
    116–117, 133
Kennan, George, 7–8, 187–188
Kennedy, John, 17, 255–256, 259–260, 324
Khomeini, Ruhollah, 311
Khrushchev, Nikita, 218, 223, 225–227,
    233, 252–256, 258–260, 265
    foreign policy goals, 233, 254
    struggle for power, 223, 227, 253–254,
        265
Kiderlen, Alfred, 66–68

Kim Il-sung, 212
Kissinger, Henry, 291, 296, 297, 300, 302,
    307, 309
    as National Security Advisor, 319–324
    personal characteristics, 319
Klingberg, Frank, 337
Kondratieff, Nikolai, 353
Korea, 38, 42, 61–64, 212, 215, 218
Korean War, 164–165, 212–218, 239
    United States negotiating position,
        22–23, 216, 218
Kosygin, Alexi, 265
Kwangtung Army, 118, 120, 140–142, 150

Ladder-like system, 55, 58–60, 90–92,
    171–172, 344–345
    in Middle East, 286–289
    and war, 91–92, 172
Laird, Melvin, 295, 322–324
Laos, 220–222, 295, 308
Latvia, 86, 155, 177
Laval, Pierre, 147–148
Leader (*see* Policy maker)
Leadership, 62, 195
    and advisors, 96
League of Nations, 86, 88, 105, 113, 115,
    148
    disarmament, 115–116, 142, 145–146
    effectiveness, 106, 107, 133, 141, 148
    and Ethiopia, 146–148
    and Manchuria, 141
    powers, 105–106, 107
    systems explanation, 133, 171
League of states, 40, 47, 171
Lebanon, 231, 309
Lenin, V. I., 82, 125, 129, 135
    as ideologue, 121, 129
    on imperialism, 10–11, 272–273
    on opportunism, 129
    and Polish war, 126–127
    on revolution, 123, 126
    on World War I, 11, 123–124
Lessons of history, 80, 163–166, 186, 188,
    215, 349–351
    taught by Hitler, 163–166
Levering, Ralph, 245
Liberation movements, 25, 356
Libya, 43, 70
Limits to Growth, 351
Linkage, 291, 294–295, 306, 307, 312
Lin Piao, 1, 298
Lithuania, 86, 155, 177
Lloyd George, David, 109, 111, 118
Locarno Treaty (1925), 115, 133
Ludendorff, Erich, 81, 84–85, 112n
Lusitania, 84

MacArthur, Douglas, 182, 215–216

McCarthy, Joseph, 249
Mackinder, H. J., 11
McNamara, Robert, 17, 259, 324
Maginot Line, 115
Malenkov, Georgi, 218–219, 223
Manchukuo (*see* Manchuria)
Manchuria, 120, 140–142, 150, 151
    Russo-Japanese rivalry, 61–65
Mao Tse-tung, 190, 211–212, 232,
        265–266, 305
    and Nixon, 297–298
Maps:
    Asia, 181
    China, 119
    Europe in 1942, 175
    Europe in 1914, 75
    Europe in 1919, 87
    Indochina, 221
    Korea, 213
    Manchuria, 119
    Vietnam, 221
    World War I, 75
    World War II, 175, 181
Marne, Battle of (1914), 77
Marshall, George C., 189
Marshall Plan, 189
Marx, Karl, 121, 123, 341
Marxism, 121–123, 128, 138
    as an approach, 271–282
    and economic development, 128–129
    and predictions, 341–342
    on relations with capitalist states, 123,
        136, 183
    on relations with colonized, 126–128
Massive retaliation, 223, 225
Matsuoka Yosuke, 178
Meir, Golda, 257
Mendlovitz, Saul, 357
Middle East, 285 (*see also individual states*)
    Arab states in conflict, 23–24, 268
    peace negotiations, 16, 300, 309–310
    power distribution, 286, 288
    predictions for, 344, 355
    as regional subsystem, 285–289
    war, 23–24, 191, 230–231, 268–270,
        299
Military balance and foreign policy,
        237–238
Military plans:
    for World War I, 74–76
    for World War II, 174–175
Military power, 48
Military spending, 50–67, 139–140,
        214–215, 237, 247–248
    over time (*illus.*), 337
Military strategy, 15, 78–79, 182, 262
    attrition, 78–79, 102–103, 181–182
Military tactics, 74–75, 78–81, 175–176

MIRV (Multiple Independent Reentry
        Vehicle), 293–294
Moltke, Helmuth von, 76, 97–98
Monopolar system, 237–241, 283–285,
        328–329, 344
    and regional autonomy, 287–289
Monroe Doctrine, 36
Moroccan crises, 44–45, 68–69
Mozambique, 307–308
Mugabe, Robert, 308
Multinational corporation, 274
Munich conference (1938), 152, 162
Mussolini, Benito, 118, 146, 154, 183
MX missile, 350

Namibia, 256, 356
Narkomindel, 124
Nasser, Gamal, 230–231, 251–252,
        268–270, 298
National Liberation Front, 261–265
National security (*see* Security)
National security advisor, 318
National Security Council, 214, 324
    under Nixon, 321–322
Nation-state, 5, 357
NATO, 190, 217, 239, 302–303
Nazi party, 142–143
    ideology, 143–144
Negotiation (*see* Bargaining)
Negotiation for self-regulation, 345–347
Neo-colonialism, 273–274 (*see also*
        Imperialism)
Neurath, Constantin von, 148
Neutrality, 149, 191, 228, 326
    in wartime, 83–84
New Economic Policy (NEP), 128, 276
New York Times editorial, 33
Ngo Dinh Diem, 220–221, 261–262
Nguyen Van Thieu, 296
Nicaragua, 308–309
Nicholas II, 15, 74, 82, 94
    and Great Britain, 40, 46
    and William II, 39–46, 94–95
Nigerian civil war, 266–267
Nineteen Eighty Four, 340
Nixon, Richard, 1, 254, 270, 297,
        304–305, 319–325
    personal characteristics, 319
    and Vietnam, 265, 291, 295–296,
        322–325
Non-governmental actors, 6
North-South relations, 274, 276, 277
    predictions, 354–355
Norway, 174
NSC-68, 214–215
Nuclear deterrence, 223–225, 293–294
Nuclear proliferation, 223, 344, 354, 356
Nuclear warfare, 186, 223–224, 340

predictions, 344–345, 351, 354
Nuclear weapons (*see also* Nuclear warfare
    and individual states and weapons)
  and arms control (*see* Arms control;
      SALT):
  defense against, 21, 293
  delivery systems, 207
    missiles, 224–225, 258
  development, 185–187, 191, 222–224,
      258, 260, 293–294, 306–307, 356
  as measure of power, 207
  numbers of, 209, 236, 258, 284, 291,
      327
  proliferation (*see* Nuclear proliferation)
  role in world politics, 218, 220,
      223–225, 232, 240–241, 285
  sufficiency, 223, 294

Office of Strategic Services, 197, 198–199,
    200
Oil, 300–301
  depletion, 352
  embargo, 300
OPEC, 277, 300, 355
Open door policy, 44, 61, 62, 108
Organization of African Unity, 267
Organizations, 196–201, 318–325
  definition, 196
  innovations in, 80, 319–320
  interests, 15
  routines, 80, 196–197, 200–201
  shared jurisdiction, 198
Orwell, George, 340–341
"Our friends are enemies" problem, 232,
    287, 309

Pact of Paris (1928), 117
Paige, Glenn, 250
Pakistan, 191, 220, 267–268, 303
Palestine, 191
Palestinians, 268–270, 298, 309
Pattern analysis, 23–25, 201–206, 345–347
  alliance of necessity, 203–204
  arms race, 23, 203
  cold war, 202–206, 241–244, 337–338
  discovery pattern, 204–205
  escalation, 23–25, 203
  and historical approach, 202
  war, 203
Peaceful coexistence, 219, 226, 304
Pearl Harbor, 180, 193, 194, 195–196
Penetration by economic means, 61, 273
People's Republic of China (*see also* China):
  Cultural Revolution, 265
  diplomatic history, 1, 211, 215–216,
      218, 220, 231–233, 256–257,
      265–266, 297–298, 306, 312–313
  founding of state, 190, 211

internal politics, 232, 265, 298,
    305–306
  and Korean war, 215–216, 218
  nuclear weapons, 232–233, 327, 356
  political instability, 265, 305–306
  predictions for, 346
  as regional power, 235, 238, 326
  relations with Cambodia, 313
  relations with Democratic Republic of
      Vietnam, 265, 313
  relations with India, 231, 257
  relations with Soviet Union, 211, 218,
      231–233, 252, 256–257, 265–266
    summary (*table*), 346
  relations with United States, 215–216,
      218, 232
    rapprochement with United States,
        297–298, 306
    summary (*table*), 346
  and Third World, 231
Perception (*see also* Policy maker,
      perception):
  of conflict, 7, 9, 211
  definition, 95
  of Hitler's foreign policy, 164–165
  and ideology, 129, 136, 183
  of opportunity, 195
Perkins, Dexter, 244
Persia (*see* Iran)
Personality:
  and conflictual behavior, 93–94, 143
  definition, 93
Pétain, Philippe, 176, 177
Philippines, 38, 180, 182, 193, 220
Poincaré, Raymond, 114
Poland, 86, 184, 226
  and France, 110, 114–115
  and Germany, 153–154
    war, 154
  internal politics, 226, 303, 313
  and Soviet Union, 184, 226–227, 303,
      313
    war, 126–127
Policy maker (*see also specific individuals*):
  character, 319, 324
  characteristics of, 318–319, 324–325
  concept of, 14–15, 92–93, 317–325,
      348–349
  consensus, 348–351
  goals, 15–16
  influence, 15, 96–98, 195, 348–349
    definition, 96
    as function of presence, 98
  perception, 14, 95–96, 164, 215, 219,
      233, 349 (*see also* Perception;
      Lessons of history)
  personality, 93–95, 211
  and public opinion, 245–250

and rationality, 323, 348–349
style, 15, 319
worldview, 319, 324
Policy-maker and policy-making approach,
    14–18, 61–65, 317–325, 332–333
and power, 315
predictions, 347–351
Policy making:
    political model (*see* Political model of
        policy making)
    rational model (*see* Rational model of
        policy making)
    and weapons, 194–196
Policy-making process, 16–18, 317–325
Policy-making structures, 196–201,
    318–322, 324–325 (*see also*
    Organizations)
Polish Corridor, 153
Politburo, 225
Political (*concept*), 6
Political culture, 10–11
    of Japanese, 11
Political economy, 271–278 (*see also*
    Economic conditions)
Political model of decision making, 17,
    320, 348–351
    case studies:
        Germany, 1914, 96–98
        Japan, 1904, 64
        Russia, 1902–1903, 63
        Soviet Union, 1962, 253
        United States, 1970, 322–325
Political stability as measure of power,
    53–54, 207n
Political warfare, 82
Population as measure of power, 53–54
Port Arthur, 61, 64, 65, 185, 211
Portugal, 41, 307
    and decolonization, 191, 307
Power:
    calculation of, 53–55, 130, 207, 209n
    as capability, 13, 53, 187, 357
    colonies, 36, 59
    changing nature of, 301
    in classroom, 27
    as a concept, 314–315
    distribution of (*see* Power distribution)
    in domestic and environmental factor
        approach, 12–13
    hurt, hinder, help, 13
    limitations on, 48, 310–311
    military, 48, 102, 130
    nuclear, 207 (*see also* Nuclear weapons)
    projectable, 56, 65, 334
    in systems approach, 26, 53, 59, 135,
        237–239
Power approach, 12–13
Power distribution:

in Falkland Islands crisis, 334
in Far East, 1904, 65
in future, 343–345
in 1955, 235–236
in 1947, 208–209
in 1900, 55, 57
in 1975, 326–327
in 1965, 283–284
in 1910, 89–90
in 1930s, 166–169
in 1920, 130–131
World War II, 207
Prediction:
    of Hitler's behavior, 143–144
    methods of, 336–343
    outcomes, range of, 330–331
    probability, 330–331, 335
    by psychics, 338–339
    purpose of, 357
    quality of, 335–336
    self-fulfilling, 358
    types, 335–343
    uncertainty of, 194, 330–331
Presidium (*see* Politburo)
Prestige, 36
Prisoner's dilemma game, 99–100
Probability, of prediction, 330–331, 335
Probes of status quo, 69–70
    by SMP state, 239, 285, 287
Problem solving, 155–156, 357
Projectable power, 56, 65, 334
Proliferation (*see* Nuclear proliferation)
Protectorate, 35
Public opinion, 244–250, 264
    and foreign policy, 147–148, 264, 349
    and Korean war, 247–250
    and Vietnam, 264, 296–297
Punishment of aggressors, 215, 312

Railroads, means of penetration, 61
Rapallo Treaty (1922), 111
Rational model of policy making, 63–65,
    145, 253, 323, 348–351
    definition, 16
    methodology, 17n
Rationality:
    in bargaining theory, 156, 162
    in game theory, 19–20
    and policy makers, 323, 348–349
Reagan, Ronald, 305, 312, 329
Regional subsystem, 239–240
    autonomy, 286
    Middle East, 285–289
    socialist bloc, 239–240
Resolution 242, 270
Resource inequality and strategy, 102
Rhineland, 86, 117–118
Rhodesia (*see* Zimbabwe)

Richardson, Lewis, 23
Ridgway, Matthew, 22-23
Rogers, William, 295, 298, 319, 320,
    322-324
Romania, 71, 74, 83, 153, 177, 180-181,
    303
Rommel, Erwin, 178-179, 180, 181
Roosevelt, Franklin, 139, 177-178, 182
    on colonialism, 198
    and Soviet Union, 184-185, 201
    strategy, 182
    and United Nations, 184-185
Roosevelt, Theodore, 50, 65
Routines, organizational, 80, 196-197,
    200-201
Rules, of system, 26, 28-29 (*see also*
    International system, rules *and*
    specific system types)
Rusk, Dean, 166, 220, 318
Russia (to 1917) (*see also* Soviet Union):
    and Balkans, 41, 51-52, 70
    diplomatic history, 39, 41, 45-48,
        51-52, 66-67, 69, 70-71, 73
    and Far East, 61-63
    and Korea, 61-63
    in Manchuria, 38, 61-65
    policy making, 62-63
    relations with Austria-Hungary, 51-52
    relations with France, 39, 46-47, 69
    relations with Germany, 39, 46-47,
        66-67
        in 1914, 73, 94-95
    relations with Great Britain, 45, 47-48,
        51, 67
    relations with Japan, 61-65
        Russo-Japanese War, 64-65
    relations with Serbia, 51-52
    revolution of 1905, 48, 65
    revolution of 1917, 82
    in World War I, 74, 76, 77, 82, 83,
        124-125
Russo-Japanese War (1904-1905), 45-46,
    60-65

Sadat, Anwar, 298-299
    policy-making in 1977, 16, 310
SALT I, 293-295, 325
SALT II, 42, 306-307, 312, 325
Sarajevo, 73
Saudi Arabia, 286, 300, 310
Schlieffen plan, 74-76
Schuessler, Karl, 357
Schuman, Robert, 217-218
Schuschnigg, Kurt, 146, 158-159
Scientific approach, 4-5
    assumptions, 4
    and historical approach, 14, 317, 330
Scientific approaches:
    interconnections, 29, 314-317, 317-325

methods, 4, 31, 271-272
    subject of analysis, 29
SEATO, 222, 328
Second most powerful state, 238-240, 285,
    287, 329
Secretary of state, 318
Security, 48-50
    and armaments, 48-49
    and arms control, 50
    changing views, 104-105, 222-223
    and colonies, 36
    and economics, 109-110, 112, 137,
        140, 301
    relative strength, 48, 49
    in systems approach, 26-27, 134
Security calculations, 48-49
Selassie, Haile, 147, 309
Self-determination, 85, 86
Serbia, 41, 51-52, 70-71
    relations with Russia, 51-52, 71
Seyss-Inquart, Arthur, 159
Shah of Iran, downfall, 311
SLBM (Submarine Launched Ballistic
    Missile), 294, 306, 307
Small, Melvin, 244
SMP state (*see* Second most powerful state)
Socialism, 234-235
Socialist bloc, 239-240
Socialist states, relations among, 189,
    226-227, 231-233, 239-240,
    256-257, 265-266, 313
Socialization, 164, 277
Somalia, 309
Somme, Battle of (1916), 78
South Africa, Republic of, 256, 306, 356
Soviet Union (*see also* Russia *and* Brezhnev;
    Khrushchev; Malenkov; Stalin):
    and Afghanistan, 8, 230, 312, 315, 328
    allied intervention, 88
    coalitions, internal, 252-253, 292
    destalinization, 225-226
    diplomatic history:
        interwar years, 110-111, 117,
            124-129, 136, 146, 149, 151, 153
        1945-1962, 186-192, 202-206,
            210-212, 215, 217-220, 223-227,
            230-233, 251-260, 346
        1963-present, 265-270, 291-294,
            296, 298-299, 302-304, 306-313,
            329, 346
    diplomatic style, 124-125
    economy, 128-129, 135
    foreign aid, 230
    and foreign communist parties, 125,
        252
    foreign policy, 211, 253
    founding, 88
    Germany, occupation of, 184, 185, 190
    ideology and foreign policy, 121-130

internal politics, 218, 223, 225–227,
    252–254, 258–259, 265, 292
Kennan's analysis of, 8, 187, 188
and nuclear weapons, 186, 191,
    223–224, 233, 255, 258–260,
    284, 291–295, 306–309, 327
''our friends are enemies'' problem,
    232, 287, 309
and Pacific War, 184–185, 186
perceptions of United States, 218–219,
    253
perceptions of West, 126, 187–188
policy making, 124, 126–127, 253–254
predictions for, 337–338, 343–347, 354,
    356
purges, 149
relations with capitalist states, 123–126,
    126–127, 128–129
relations with colonial peoples, 127–128
relations with Cuba, 251, 258–260
relations with Czechoslovakia, 152, 268
relations with Egypt, 230–231,
    251–252, 268–270, 298–299
relations with Ethiopia, 309
relations with Finland, 154–155,
    173–174
relations with France, 146, 147, 153
relations with Germany
    interwar years, 110–111, 125,
        153–154
    non-aggression Pact, 153–154, 171
relations with Great Britain, 128, 153,
    184
relations with Hungary, 226–227
relations with Japan, 151, 178, 185–186
relations with Korea, 212
relations with Middle East, 287–289,
    298–300
relations with People's Republic of
    China, 211, 218, 231–233,
    256–257, 265–266
    summary (*table*), 346
relations with Poland, 184, 226, 313,
    328
    war of 1920, 126–127
relations with Somalia, 309
relations with United States, 8,
    186–191, 201–206, 254–256,
    258–261, 266, 270, 292–295,
    299, 302–307, 312, 328–329
    ''Basic Principles of Relations,''
        304, 325
    Cuban missile crisis, 258–260
    predictions, 346
    summary (*table*), 346
    in World War II, 184–186
and revolution, 126–128, 255
security policy, 223
and socialists, 125, 129

and Third World, 127–128, 230, 255
and United Nations, 211, 215, 254–255
World War I, 82, 123–124
in World War II, 154, 174–175, 177,
    179–183
Spain, civil war, 148–149
Sphere of influence, 35, 184, 188, 328
Stalin, Josef, 135, 185, 190, 210, 218
    and Chinese communists, 211
    distrust of West, 153, 183, 190,
        210–211
    goals, 184–187
    and Korean war, 212
    as a nationalist, 186–187
    perception:
        of Nazi Germany, 14
        of United States, 186–187
    and purges, 149
    and Third World, 191
    in World War II, 179, 180, 182
Stalingrad, Battle of (1942), 180–181
State, 5, 357
State capitalism, 276
State system, 357–358
Status quo, 238–239
Steel production as measure of power,
    53–54
Stimulus-response (*see* Pattern analysis)
Straits, 51, 81
Stresa Front, 147
Stresemann, Gustav, 112, 114, 117
Structure of international system (*see*
    International system, and power)
Style of policy maker, 15
Subject of analysis, 29
Submarine warfare, 81–82, 84
Subsystem (*see* Regional subsystem)
Sudetenland, 152, 160–162
Suez Canal, 38, 230, 269, 299–300
Sufficiency, of power, 48, 294
Superpower, 208, 238–241, 325–329
Syria, 286, 299–300, 309
    1967 war, 23–24, 268–270
System (*see* International system; Systems
    approach)
Systems approach, 25–29, 53–60, 315, 334
    classroom analogy, 27–28
    critique of, 240, 279
    definition, 25
    environment, 91
    Marxist interpretation, 276–278
    patterns, 26
    predictions, 343–345
    and specific events, 91

Taiwan, 38, 189–190, 193, 216, 232,
    297–298
Tanks, 79
Tannenberg, Battle of (1914), 77

Taylor, A. J. P., 69–70, 144
Technology, 12, 49, 79
Teng Hsiao-p'ing, 305
Thatcher, Margaret, 331
Third World, 230, 234
    and capitalist states, 271–282
    predictions for, 354–355
Tibet, 48, 231
Tito, 189
Total war, 91–92, 180, 215
    and neutrals, 83–84
Treaties, escape clauses, 42, 117
Trench warfare, 77–78, 79–81
Tripartite Pact, 177
Triple Alliance, 35, 42–43, 54, 60
    power, 90, 102
Triple Entente, 47–48, 54, 60
    power, 90, 102
Trotsky, Leon, 124, 126
Truman, Harry, 15, 186, 189–190, 199,
        217
    atomic bomb, 185–186, 206
    and Congress, 188–189
    image of Hitler-like state, 164–165, 215
    and Korean war, 164–165, 212–216,
        249–250
    and public opinion, 249–250
    and Soviet Union, 185, 188, 214–215
Truman Doctrine, 188
Trust in world politics, 100–103
Tsushima Straits, Battle of (1905), 65
Turkey, 41, 118, 153, 187, 220, 267
    Balkan Wars of 1912–1913, 70–71
    in World War I, 81, 85, 86
"Union busting," 277–278
United Nations in World War II, 182
United Nations organization, 184–185,
        211–212, 231, 239, 254–256,
        270, 298
United States:
    arms control, 350 (*see also* SALT)
        Washington Naval Conference, 108
    bargaining positions, 217, 219, 220,
        350
    and Berlin (*see* Berlin)
    and Cambodian invasion, 295, 318,
        322–325
    and communism, 200–201, 220, 231,
        234–235, 252
    containment, 201, 214, 217
    and decolonization, 198–201, 220, 228
    diplomatic history:
        interwar years, 108, 111–112,
            116–117, 139, 141
        1945–1962, 187–192, 198–201,
            202–206, 212–224, 228–235,
            254–260, 261–262, 346
        1963–present, 262–265, 269–270,
            291–313, 322–325, 329, 346

dissent, 264, 295
economy, domestic, 120, 137–138
    and economy of Europe, 112–113, 138,
        189
    and Europe, 37–38, 112–113, 138,
        189–190, 217, 302–303
    foreign aid, 222, 281
    foreign policy, 201–202
    foreign policy moods, 337–338
    Germany, occupation of, 184–185, 190,
        217
    and Indochina, 198–201, 217, 220–221
    Korean war, 212–216, 218
        League of Nations, 88
        public opinion and, 246–250
    and Middle East, 268–270, 287–289,
        298–300, 309–310
    and Nicaragua, 309
    and nuclear weapons, 185–187, 206,
        209, 218, 222–224, 258–260,
        284, 291–295, 303, 306–307,
        327, 350
    open door policy, 44, 61, 62, 108
    perceptions:
        of Ho Chi Minh, 200
        of Soviet Union, 8, 214, 256
    political instability, 304–305
    predictions for, 337–338, 343–347, 354,
        356
    relations with China, 189–190
    relations with Cuba, 201, 234–235,
        254, 256
    relations with Egypt, 230, 298–300, 310
    relations with France, 86, 88, 116–117
        post-World War II, 10, 198–200,
            220, 230–231
    relations with Germany, 178, 180, 217,
        258, 302
    relations with Great Britain, 86, 88,
        108, 188, 190, 230–231, 302
        in World War II, 178, 182–185
    relations with Israel, 191, 230–231,
        269–270, 298–300, 309–310
    relations with Japan, 8, 108, 177–178
    relations with Korea, 211, 212–216, 218
    relations with Latin America, 233–234
        Monroe Doctrine, 36
    relations with People's Republic of
        China, 191, 216, 232, 266
    rapprochement, 297–298, 326
    summary (*table*), 346
    relations with Soviet Union, 8,
        214–219, 222–226, 233, 242–244,
        254–256, 261, 266, 270,
        291–295, 299, 302–307, 312,
        328–329
    "Basic Principles of Relations,"
        304, 325
    cold war, early, 186–191, 201–206

Cuban missile crisis, 258–260
predictions (*table*), 346
summary (*table*), 346
in systemic terms, 238–239
during World War II, 184–186
relations with Vietnam, 222, 261–265,
291, 295–296, 308
and revolution, 233–235, 308–309
and Rhodesia, 308
security policy, 222–225
strategy, in Vietnam, 15, 262
and Third World, 228–235, 273,
279–282
and Vietnamese nationalism, 198–201
Vietnam peace talks, 264–265,
295–296, 322
and Vietnam War, 15, 261–265, 291,
295–296, 322–325
and World War I, 82, 83–88
in World War II, 180, 182–183, 185

Utopia, 341, 358
U-2 incident (1960), 254

Values, and world politics, 357–359
Verdun, Battle of (1916), 78
Versailles Treaty, 86–88, 107
circumvention, 109, 111, 114, 146,
148
and colonies, 118
enforcement, 109, 111–112, 146, 148,
151–152
Germany, restrictions on, 86, 108–109,
153
revision, 110, 114–115, 139, 146
Vichy France, 176, 196
Viet Minh, 196, 199–200
Vietnam, 199–201, 220–222, 261–265,
295–297, 308, 313 (*see also*
Democratic Republic of
Vietnam; Indochina)
Vietnam War, 15, 261–265, 295, 308
Vladivostock Agreement, 306

Wakatsuki Reijiro, 141, 142
Walesa, Lech, 313
Wallerstein, Immanual, 276
War:
and alliances, 42, 180
decisions for, as compromises, 64,
97–98
in equilateral system, 134
in ladder-like system, 91–93, 287
in *1984*, 340
as pattern of behavior, 25, 203
predicting outcomes, 65, 95, 193–194
predictions for, 353–354
renunciation of, 117
termination of, 98–103

total, 91–92, 180
weapons as cause, 192–196
War communism, 128
Warfare:
armored (*see* Armored warfare)
blitzkrieg (*see* Blitzkrieg)
conduct of, 74–75, 91–92, 180, 183
gas, 79, 156
guerrilla, 262
innovation in, 79–82
War option and polarization of
government, 64
War Powers Act, 305
Warsaw Treaty Organization, 217
War-weariness, 78, 84, 85, 88
Washington Naval Conference, 108
Watergate, 304–305
Weak states, influence over stronger, 52,
71, 227–228, 251–252
Weapons:
as bargaining chips, 50–51, 67–68, 258
machine gun, 49, 76
nuclear (*see* Nuclear weapons)
submarines, 81–82, 83–84
tanks, 79
and war decision, 192–196
and world politics, 12, 192–196, 259
Weigley, Russell, 180
Weimar Republic (*see* Germany, Weimar
Republic)
Weissberg, Robert, 245
West Germany (*see* Federal Republic of
Germany)
William II, 85, 93–94
and advisors, 44, 47, 68–69, 96–98
and Great Britain, 39, 46, 47, 67, 72,
95
league of states goal, 39–40, 67
mediation effort, 94–95
and Moroccan crises, 44–45, 68–69
and Nicholas II, 39–46, 94–95
in 1914 crisis, 94–98, 100
perception:
of war, 94–95
of world politics, 95–96
personality, 67, 93–95, 96
Wilson, Woodrow, 82, 84, 85, 86
and League of Nations, 86, 105
Versailles Treaty, 85–86
Women and world politics, 257–258
World Court, 107
World economy, 276–278
World government, 357–358
World-island, 11
World opinion, 157, 159
World Order Models Project, 358
World politics:
conflict, 6–10
cooperation, 6–10

definition, 5
and domestic politics, contrasted to, 6
and economic conditions, 120,
    138–140, 189, 301
and ideology, 121–122, 135–136
predictions for, 356
and weapons, 12, 192–196, 259
World War I:
    American entry, 82, 83–84
    armistice, 82, 84–85
    casualties, 85
    causes, 69–70, 73–74, 91, 96–98
    coalition nature, 83
    defense, power of, 78–80
    innovation, 79–82
    military operations, 77–85
    and neutrals, 83–84
    peace treaties, 86–88
    political warfare, 82
    stalemate, 77, 78
    strategy, 78–79, 81
    submarine warfare, 81–82, 83–84

as systemic event, 91
tactics, 79–81
    breakthrough, 78, 79, 80–81
World War II:
    Allied diplomacy, 182–186
    battle for the clock, 180
    in Europe, 154–155, 173–177, 178–183
    initiation, 154–155, 180, 192–196
    in North Africa, 178, 180, 181
    in Pacific, 180–182, 185–186
    second front, 180, 182–183
WTO (*see* Warsaw Treaty Organization)

Yalta Conference (1945), 184
Young Plan, 117
Yugoslavia, 86, 187, 189, 219
    in World War II, 177, 178

Zaire, 255, 256, 297
Zartman, I. William, 21
Zimbabwe, 308